Martin Murray

South Africa:
Time of Agony,
Time of Destiny

The Upsurge of Popular Protest

VERSO
The Imprint of New Left Books

**British Library
Cataloguing in Publication Data**

Murray, Martin
   South Africa: time of agony, time of
   destiny: the upsurge of popular protest.
   1. South Africa — Politics and government
   — 1978-
   I. Title
   968.06'3   DT779.952

   ISBN 0-86091-146-2
   ISBN 0-86091-857-2 Pbk.

OCLC 15663596

First published 1987
© Martin Murray 1987

Verso
6 Meard Street London W1

Typeset in Parliament by
Leaper & Gard Ltd, Bristol, England

Printed by The Thetford Press
Thetford, Norfolk

Contents

Preface

> The battle will simmer and spurt in an introverted way, pitting
> blacks against the emblems of what they see as their oppression
> while those deemed responsible for their plight withdraw behind
> a barricade of legislation and tightened security measures
> designed to co-opt, undermine, and neutralize the black majority
> but not to appease it.
>
> Alan Cowell. *New York Times,* 30 September 1984.

Enormous disparities in wealth, opportunity, and social rank do
not make South Africa unique. What distinguishes South Africa,
however, is that the sharp contrasts in every field of social life
seem to converge around the distinction between white privilege
and black frustration. The incongruous juxtaposition of sybaritic
white 'middle-class' suburbs and the bleak black townships typi-
fies the general pattern. Exclusive boutiques and luxuriant
shopping malls, hushed tree-lined streets, enclosed and well-
manicured gardens, and so forth, shape the environment of the
affluent white residential areas. The ubiquitous army of peripatetic day-labourers — maids, gardeners, 'nannies', cleaners,
and 'handy-men' of all sorts — ensures that white 'middle-class'
residents can avoid distasteful and distracting tasks if they so
desire. In the white Valhalla, 'leisure-time' and 'self-fulfillment'
depends in large measure on the availability of black 'casual'
labour. In contrast, it is difficult to imagine the monotony and
abject sparseness of the black townships and ghettos. Pockets of
relative affluence do exist, but these are the exception rather than

the rule. It is the persistent repetition of identical images — cheerless dusty streets, bare-footed and shabbily dressed children, endless queues of tired travellers, ribbons of exhausted workers trudging home, the sullen stares and probing glances — that creates an unforgettable collage of deprivation. In the townships, daily life is an endless grind, a seemingly ceaseless struggle for existence and survival. The exaggerated distances between home and work make travel both expensive and time-consuming. High rates of joblessness and even greater under-employment reinforce the cruel hoax that to have regular work is a privilege and a reward.

The townships, along with the factories and schools, have become the cauldrons of resistance to *apartheid* and the 'racial capitalism' that it sustains. Perhaps the most wrong-headed of mythologies about South Africa is that the country's rulers have admitted that *apartheid* is outmoded (as well as 'an affront to human dignity') and have embarked on a 'reform process' designed to dismantle all forms of racial discrimination through peaceful negotiation. In reality, the popular movement — the independent black trade unions and the community organizations — have over the past decade begun the arduous task of eliminating *apartheid* piece by piece and on their own initiative. Ironically, the National Party's 'reformist' programme reflects less the moderation of hard-line Afrikaner nationalist ideology than the solemn acknowledgement of the vital necessity of offering 'concessions' in order to preserve white power and privilege.

The subject matter of this study is the intersection of popular organizatons and political consciousness during the course of the 1984-6 rebellion. Unlocking this complex relationship is not a simple undertaking. The segmentation of the black working class, coupled with the social stratification of the townships, have always militated against the emergence of any single ideological current in the leadership of the popular movement. Similarly, not only the regional specificity of class and national struggles but also the implantation of distinctive localized 'political cultures' reinforced long-lasting attachments to various ideological traditions. Political consciousness thus reflects a fluid range of distinctive ideological hues that are sometimes combined in complicated hybrid mixtures.

In order to analyze this imbrication of different ideological strains with the mass popular movement in South Africa, I have combined an analytic assessment of the structural location of the principal social actors with a chronological and narrative approach to the unfolding drama itself. One great difficulty with writing a 'history' of a major event not only in the chronological order of its maturation but also before its outcome has been fixed is that one does not have the luxury of either hindsight or distanced reflection. Equally important, I felt very uneasy reconstructing events in which friends, acquaintances, and people otherwise known to me were intimately involved. They were making history and I was writing about it. I owe an enormous debt of gratitude to many people in South Africa who will remain anonymous for obvious reasons. Without the generosity and patience of those friends who provided me with comfortable quarters, companionship, advice, and encouragement, this project would never have been completed. With them, I share fond memories and a common desire for a better future. I know that everyone who reads these pages will have serious disagreements with some, and perhaps many, of my interpretations. I only hope that they conclude that the project as a whole was worth the effort.

I owe a debt of gratitude to Perry Anderson for first suggesting that I undertake this project. I certainly never anticipated that my original plan of evaluating the variant ideological currents within the broad 'liberation movement' would literally sweep me away along an uncharted course of investigation. Neil Belton at Verso/NLB provided insightful comments and invaluable suggestions at key junctures. I also would like to acknowledge the financial support of the National Science Foundation for underwriting my 1983 research visit to South Africa. The Foundation is, of course, not responsible for the ideas, or interpretations presented here. Rhonda Levine took care of the daily tasks that I seemed to overlook. Finally, I sincerely hope that Jeremy Robert (who thoroughly enjoyed tearing pages and eating footnotes) will appreciate that he did not always get my undivided attention because I was desperately trying to finish a project that assumed, at times, a monstrous life of its own.

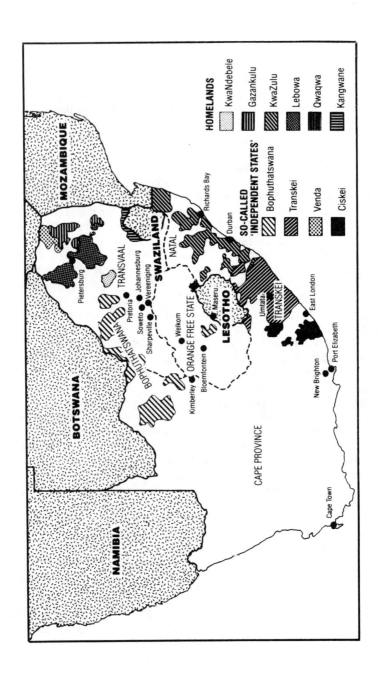

Glossary of Acronyms

(A)FCWU	(African) Food and Canning Workers' Union
ANC	African National Congress
ARMSCOR	Armaments Development and Production Corporation
AZACTU	Azanian Confederation of Trade Unions
AZANYU	Azanian National Youth Unity
AZAPO	Azanian People's Organization
BAWU	Black Allied Workers' Union
BOSS	Bureau of State Security
BPC	Black People's Convention
CAMU	Confederation of Associations and Mining Unions
CAYCO	Cape Youth Congress
CCAWUSA	Commercial Catering and Allied Workers' Union of South Africa
CMU	Council of Mining Unions
CNETU	Council of Non-European Trade Unions
COSATU	Congress of South African Trade Unions
CUSA	Council of Unions of South Africa
DPSC	Detainees' Parents Support Committee
FCI	Federated Chambers of Industry
FOSATU	Federation of South African Trade Unions
GAWU	General and Allied Workers' Union
GWU	General Workers' Union
HNP	Herstigte ('Purified') National Party

ISCOR	Iron and Steel Corporation
NAFCOC	National African Federated Chambers of Commerce and Industry
NCM	National Convention Movement
NIC	Natal Indian Congress
NUM	National Union of Mineworkers
NUSAS	National Union of South African Students
PAC	Pan-Africanist Congress
PFP	Progressive Federal Party
SAAWU	South African Allied Workers' Union
SACLA	South African Confederation of Labour
SACTU	South African Congress of Trade Unions
SADCC	Southern African Development Coordination Conference
SACP	South African Communist Party
SADF	South African Defense Force
SAIC	South African Indian Council
SANLAM	South African National Life Assurance Company
SATLC	South African Trades and Labour Council
SASO	South African Students' Organization
SSC	State Security Council
TUCSA	Trade Union Council of South Africa
UDF	United Democratic Front
UWO	United Women's Organization
ZCC	Zion Christian Church

Introduction

Demographic and Ecological Characteristics

South Africa is a land of stark contrasts and grim paradoxes. Over 31 million people inhabit a land mass of about 471,566 miles — roughly three times the size of California or almost as large as France, England, Italy, and the Federal Republic of Germany combined. South Africa covers about 4 per cent of the total land mass of Africa, making it the sixth largest political unit on the continent. In terms of population size, it is the third largest African nation.

In comparison to the rest of Africa, two features of South Africa's geography stand in bold relief. First, it contains perhaps the widest variety of landscapes anywhere in the continent. It possesses by far and away the longest coastline and it has a complex combination of mountainous zones, plains and plateaus, deserts, and watersheds. This peculiar combination of landscapes means that South Africa is endowed with a panoply of natural resources almost unmatched in the rest of Africa for their diversity. Second, in comparison with sub-Saharan Africa, South Africa contains a considerably larger proportion of arid land. About 12 per cent of South Africa's land is cultivatable and 2 per cent is forested. The remaining 86 per cent is comprised of a combination of deserts, uninhabitable waste lands, and urban space.[1] Ecological destruction, particularly soil erosion and advancing aridity, continues almost imperceptibly to alter the environmental physiognomy of the South African landscape.[2]

South Africa is a modern industrial giant that has spread its tentacles throughout the African sub-continent and beyond. Its principal exports include gold, diamonds, mineral products, iron and steel, coal, and agricultural goods. Its principal imports include machinery, vehicles and transportation equipment, chemical products, base metals, textiles, plastics, and oil. Its major industries are mining, automobiles, metal-working, machinery, textiles, iron and steel, chemicals, fertilizers, and fishing. Its main agricultural products include maize, wool, wheat, sugarcane, tobacco, citrus fruits, dairy products, and meats.[3] South Africa is one of the few mineral-rich nations in the world, comparable only to the Soviet Union.[4]

Roughly two million people are employed in the mining and manufacturing sectors alone. Commercial and 'service sector' employment has mushroomed, surpassing mining and manufacturing combined. Despite the fact that agricultural production has become increasingly mechanized, nearly two million wage-earners derive all or a significant portion of their income from farming or farm-related activities. Productivity in most sectors has increased steadily; and, correlatively, the demand for unskilled labour has declined dramatically. South Africa possesses nearly 45 per cent of the tractors in Africa and produces roughly one-third of the entire continent's maize. South African fishermen netted about 30 per cent of the total tonnage of fish for all of Africa.[5]

Under the *apartheid* system, the white minority regime has maintained the legal fiction that South Africa can be classified into four discrete 'population registration groups': the 4.5 million white descendants of European immigrants; the 2.5 million so-called coloured people, including both descendants of the original inhabitants of the areas where Europeans first settled and most people whose descent is traced from members of more than one 'population group'; the nearly 1 million Asians, consisting mainly of descendants of indentured workers brought from the Indian subcontinent in the nineteenth century; and the roughly 23 million African people who are again subdivided according to language, custom, and heritage. The oppressed people of colour have increasingly ignored these labels and instead prefer the generic self-designation 'black' to describe their common identity. Hence, any references to the 'racial' categories such as 'coloured', 'African', and 'Asian' is for purely descriptive convenience and in no way implies acceptance of this nomenclature as analytically serious.

The white minority regime has enforced strict territorial segregation. The 1913 Natives' Land Act set aside an estimated 87 per cent of the land for exclusive occupancy by the descendants of Europeans. The remaining 13 per cent consists of numerous fragments grouped into ten erstwhile units formerly referred to as Bantustans but now as Homelands. This legislative enactment has historically constituted the statutory bedrock for the core features of 'grand *apartheid*'. Under the terms of the 1950 Group Areas Act, the cities and towns in the 'prescribed (that is, white) areas' were divided into separate and segregated residential areas for each 'population group'.

In terms of the World Bank's comparative estimates, South Africa ranked 32nd of 117 non-Soviet bloc countries in Gross National Product per capita, but 47th in life expectancy at birth and 64th in infant-mortality rates. Whites have an infant mortality rate of 13 per 1000 live births. In contrast, the rate for Africans is seven times higher. It was estimated that some 50,000 black children die of hunger every year in South Africa, the richest country in sub-Saharan Africa.[6]

The Labour Market and the Black Working Class

Black urbanization is perhaps the most important socioeconomic phenomenon in South Africa during the post-1948 *apartheid* era. By the 1980s, more than 300 separate black townships were located in close proximity to white cities and towns. Urban black residents account for approximately 50 per cent of the total metropolitan population of South Africa. This figure is expected to increase to 65 per cent by the end of the century. According to the official 1980 census, 13.2 million people — or 53 per cent of the total South African population (excluding Transkei, Bophuthatswana, and Venda) — were urbanized. Using official population registration categories, more than 88 per cent of the estimated 4.5 million whites, 77 per cent of the approximately 2.8 million so-called coloureds, and 90 per cent of an estimated 800,000 persons of Indian origin lived in urban areas. Including the Transkei, Bophuthatswana, and Venda, only

33 per cent (or 6.5 million blacks) resided in urban areas.[7]

According to alternative demographic estimates, these official figures considerably underestimate the actual numbers of blacks residing in metropolitan areas.[8] In addition, the official figures exclude blacks living in informal settlements that ring the periphery of most white cities and towns and who earn their livelihood mainly in the urban areas. Excluding the TBVC areas (Transkei, Bophuthatswana, Venda, and Ciskei Homelands), an estimated two million people can accurately be included in this category. Apart from those who reside in informal settlements, approximately one million residents in rural enclaves in the Homelands have been 'functionally urbanized', that is, they are entirely dependent upon the earnings of migrant labourers for their subsistence.

According to official 1980 census figures, 5.3 million (or 82 per cent) of the 6.5 million urban blacks resided in so-called 'white South Africa'. The remaining 1.2 million resided in urban zones in the Homelands. The four major metropolitan regions (Cape Town; Port Elizabeth/Uitenhage; Durban/Pinetown; Pretoria/ Witwatersrand/Vereeniging) constitute about 4 per cent of the country's total land mass yet accommodate 4.4 million black people, or approximately two-thirds of the total urban black population.[9] With the exception of the Pretoria-Witwatersrand-Vereeniging area, the black urban population is settled chiefly on an ethnic basis.[10] On balance, only an estimated 17 per cent of blacks residing in the Homelands has been urbanized. An estimated 36 per cent of Ciskei residents and 22 per cent of KwaZulu residents are urbanized. These relatively high levels of urbanization can be attributed to the growth of Homeland towns on the peripheries of major metropolitan areas, which enable black workers to commute to the white areas on a daily basis. Without exception, the most populous towns in the Homelands are located in close proximity to large white urban concentrations (Umlazi near Durban, Garankuwa and Mapopane near Pretoria, Mdantsane near East London, Madadeni near Newcastle). The infrastructural development and business activities of these rapidly growing Homeland towns bear no relation to the number of inhabitants. In some instances, inhabitants of the towns spent less than one-third of their total consumption outlay there, engendering substantial 'leakages' of purchasing power to the adjacent white towns and cities.[11]

The black working class in South Africa is strikingly diverse. The so-called 'influx controls' regulating the flow of blacks from the rural areas to the cities have a long history in South Africa. During the 1950s and 1960s, the National Party systematically refined the existing statutory framework controlling the distribution and allocation of African labour. The centerpiece of this legislative onslaught was the blanket prohibition excluding Africans from the 'prescribed areas' for more than 72 hours unless they were exempted on specific grounds. These exemptions, generally referred to as Section 10 rights, were highly circumscribed and qualified 'privileges' contingent upon the ability of Africans to obtain lawful accommodation in a particular urban area. During the 1960s, the National Party embarked on a far-reaching programme to make the migrant labour system the essential foundation upon which the African work force would be employed in 'white South Africa'. Between 1960 and 1983, even official estimates acknowledged that over two million 'surplus' or non-productive black people were removed from the white urban areas, white farms, and so-called 'black spots' in white rural areas, and subsequently relocated in the Homelands.[12] Those removed included the aged, unfit, widows, and women with dependent children who did not qualify under Section 10 for residence in the prescribed areas, surplus black farm labourers, and credentialled black professionals whose services were not regarded as essential for blacks in the urban areas.[13]

The so-called 'pass laws' spun 'an Orwellian web of control, preventing the influx of people from the rural areas to the towns except in terms of rigidly defined procedures'.[14] They determined the position of black workers who were regarded as legal residents of the Homelands. Two categories of these workers — often called contract workers — can be distinguished: commuters and migrants. The 'frontier commuters' reside with their families in the Homelands and travel on a daily (or sometimes weekly) basis across what *apartheid* ideology depicts as national borders to their place of work in 'white South Africa'. The major flows of these 'frontier commuters' are from dormitory townships in Bophuthatswana to the Pretoria area and from parts of KwaZulu which adjoin the Durban/Pinetown region. In contrast, migrants usually enter into work contracts for a year. They are compelled by law to return annually to their assigned Homelands after the expiry of the labour contract in order to register at a local labour bureau for a new contract. This migrant labour system originated to serve the gold mines of the Witwatersrand but subsequently expanded in gradual steps. By the 1980s, an estimated 60 per cent of all economically active men in 'white areas' were officially designated as migrants. Migrants differ from commuters in that they are unable to have families with them near their place of work. The Witwatersrand remains the major focal point for the streams of migrants from the Homelands.[15]

All Homelands work-seekers are compelled to register for work at the nearest labour bureaux. Theoretically, they are not permitted to travel to the cities in search of work, but are required to remain in the Homelands until recruited. On initial registration, labour officers classify applicants into one of seventeen categories of employment. To obtain employment, work-seekers are requisitioned for labour or directly recruited by authorized agents who arrive at Homelands labour bureaux. Because they are seldom requisitioned by urban industrial employers, black women in the Homelands find it particularly difficult to obtain work in the urban areas. Unofficially, a very substantial proportion of men in the Homelands and an increasing proportion of women do not wait to be requisitioned for employment at their nearest Homelands labour bureau. Instead, they manage to 'shoot straight' as it is termed, travelling to the cities in search of work on their own accord. Those work-seekers who find employment then return to the Homelands labour bureaux to formally legitimate their newly-acquired status. The official labour recruiting, registering, and allocating agencies tolerate but do not sanction these costly and time-consuming practices.[16]

According to official estimates, over 4 million workers were employed in the so-called 'modern sector' in South Africa in 1981. An estimated 50 per cent of the black labour force possessed Section 10 rights. About 28 per cent of the black labour force were migrants and 22 per cent were commuters. Apart from the estimated three million urban black workers, almost one million black workers held regular employment in rural white areas.[17] These official figures, of course, grossly underestimated the actual size of the black working class.

For the most part, contract labourers (both migrants and commuters) form a distinct substratum of the black working class. In the main, the migrant labour system that evolved over decades has allowed a certain flexibility, permitting white employers — large and small — to adjust the composition of their labour force to the demands of the market. This migrant labour system has ensured that during periodic economic downturns employers were not saddled with labour surpluses. Since the early 1970s, the major emphasis of state policy-makers has centered on the construction of dormitory towns in the Homelands, from which commuters can travel to their place of work. This programme of creating peri-urban 'high density' living areas in the Homelands has coincided with the drastic curtailment of all new housing in black townships within commuting distance of the Homelands. In fact, the housing blacklog was conservatively estimated in 1982 to have reached 168,000 family dwelling-units in the prescribed areas.[18]

Homelands residents have experienced a steady deterioration in their ability to support themselves through farming activities, thereby contributing to the widening gulf between the number of work-seekers and available job opportunities. Simkins estimated that by 1970 the Homelands supported less than 20 per cent of their registered inhabitants. Between 1970 and 1976, the proportion of household income in the Homelands deriving from migrant and commuter wage remittances increased steeply from 55 per cent to 72 per cent.[19] The Homelands differed considerably, but in general, available agricultural land was overcrowded, infertile, and unproductive. The populations of the Homelands have more than doubled over the past 20 years, largely as a result of natural increase but also because of the forced removal of black South Africans from both urban and white-owned rural areas. Poverty is acute. It has been estimated that 80 per cent of the 8 to 10 million inhabitants of the Homelands live below the official poverty datum line. The proportion of households that could be considered absolutely destitute — who receive no income from any source and who own neither cattle nor land — increased from 5 per cent in 1960 to 13 per cent in 1980.[20] Yet in some relatively remote regions (particularly in the Transkei, Lebowa, and Gazankulu), the labour market has contracted to the extent that it is virtually nonexistent.[21]

Official unemployment amongst the black working class has climbed steadily from approximately 10 per cent in 1967 to nearly 25 per cent in 1986.[22] It is important to note that the labour-

market operated not as a single competitive mechanism governing the allocation of wage-labour but as a regulated hierarchy of
multi-determined privileges. One staggering fact is that since the
early 1970s considerably more than half of the first-time black
entrants onto the labour market have sought regular employment in vain.[23] It has been estimated that roughly one quarter to
one third of all economically active black people derive their
means of subsistence from 'informal sector' activities.[24]

Stratification of the labour market was further reinforced by
state-sponsored hierarchies of privilege and disadvantage. In
Greenberg and Giliomee's words, 'The black world includes
"legals" with access to the institutional labour market, larger
employers and manufacturers, and "illegals", who are in practice
restricted to the informal sector, seasonal and day labour, and
smaller, lower-paying firms. The black world also includes, on
the one hand, permanent (Section 10) urban dwellers with
opportunities for training and mobility, and on the other, legal
migrants with access to heavy and primary industry. It includes
furthermore the "commuters" who stand behind the permanent
urban residents in the labour queue, but ahead of the illegals and
those left behind in the more remote rural districts. It includes
those in the districts where labour markets are "open", and
those in areas inaccessible to the labour recruitment system. And
then there are also those who have taken their chances in the
illegal and legal urban labour-market, and those like rural
women and unskilled labourers, who in desperation must accept
very low-wage jobs on the farms, in municipalities and on road
construction. It is upon such distinction and such hierarchies of
"privilege" that the State has sought to construct a strategy of
control and collaboration.'[25]

Despite official claims that Homelands authorities have
steadily broadened their influence over labour matters, the opposite appears to have happened. Labour bureaux in the Homelands virtually disintegrated in the 1980s. Instead, South African
agencies, particularly the Administration Boards, have played an
expanding role in the regulation of the rural labour-market. In
collusion with local white magistrates, Administration Boards
appear to wield considerable discretion in conferring special
privileges on what is termed 'local labour'. By offering preferred
access to 'legal accommodation' and to more secure urban job
opportunities, the South African labour regulation agencies have

effectively driven a wedge between documented and undocumented work-seekers.[26]

Those rural migrants who fall beyond the pale of 'local labour' status are compelled to live illegally, without clearance certificates, in the black townships or in the emergent (or established) 'squatter' settlements. These 'illegals' operate outside the bureaucratic channels funnelling work-seekers to the larger firms that use the statutory employment mechanisms. For the most part, 'illegals' are confined to casual and low-wage sectors that are willing to risk employing them. In cities close to the Homelands, the entire bureaucratic system of restricting black entry into 'prescribed' areas has fallen into disuse. In fact, influx controls are virtually unenforceable. As a consequence, 'squatters' in many places have remained 'relatively free to find their niche on the margins of the legal labour market — in casual jobs in construction, domestic service, smaller firms, sections of commerce, and, for many, prolonged or intermittent unemployment'.[27] Yet as is often the case, those who eke out a meagre existence in the 'informal sector' operate outside the boundaries of the working class *per se*. For the petty traders, dress makers, hawkers, and others condemned to the 'limbo of the outcasts', as Rosa Luxembourg described it, the distinction between the provision of 'services' and outright criminality has been blurred.[28]

The Physiognomy of the Popular Uprising

The driving force that sustains the *apartheid* regime of accumulation is a decisive modification in the internal dynamics of capital accumulation. The mainsprings of South African economic growth have included: (1) the widening of the domestic economic base caused by rapid industrialization and the attendant expansion of regional commercial networks; (2) the deepening of internal economic structures by complementing the peripheral agro-mineral extractive sectors with 'autocentric' growth poles in manufacturing and commerce, thereby bringing South Africa's economic structure more in line with the metropolitan zones of the capitalist world economy; and (3) the institutionalization of rigid racial compartmentalization. The two most striking indices of the trajectory of economic expansion are the overall realignment of the capital accumulation process in

South Africa and the changing character of the black working class. On the eve of World War II, agricultural production and mining constituted the twin mainstays of capital accumulation, contributing more to national income than manufacturing and commerce combined. By 1975, the relationship had been reversed: manufacturing and commercial capital reached a point where they contributed almost half the national income and twice as much as mining and agriculture combined.[29] This economic transformation coincided with the accelerated growth of the increasingly settled urban black proletariat. Seen from another angle, the outflow of white wage-earners from semi-skilled and blue-collar occupations was matched by the dramatic growth of an increasingly variegated and stratified black working class.

Paradoxically, the secular expansion of the economy under the regime of accumulation identified with *apartheid* created its own inherent barriers. 'Hugely impoverished and oppressed, but at the same time concentrated in the huge workplaces of SA's factories, mines, etc.', Leggssick argued, 'the black working class has been the bedrock' around which the direct challenge to employers and the white minority regime has been concentrated over the period since 1973.[30] The Botha regime perpetrates the myth that the growth of black trade unionism is a product of the post-Wiehahn 'reforms' in industrial relations legislation. In reality, trade union rights were acquired through shop-floor battles, 'illegal' strikes, and so forth. The defense, consolidation, and advance of trade union rights has depended upon constant vigilance against state repression and victimization and harassment by employers.[31]

The key ingredient in the growth of black working-class militancy was the formation of black trade unions that focused their organization and struggle on the workplace. This maturation of shop-floor militancy was paralleled by the development of a huge mass movement in the townships and in the schools. Trade unionists, the unemployed and underemployed, and students have surged to the forefront of popular opposition to white minority rule. As Alan Cowell put it, 'After years of laying organizational groundwork and developing rank-and-file support, the black unions have attracted membership from nearly all sectors of the South African labour force. ... Far from being tamed, COSATU [the Congress of South African Trade

Unions] and other black labour groups have sought the political high ground in what unionists call "the struggle against white rule", desperately seeking to catch up with the protests of the youthful and violent black radicals in the townships. ... In a country that is Africa's most industrialized nation, the challenge now posed by the black unions is profound, holding out the possibility of a large scale withdrawal of labour from an economy that is increasingly dependent upon black skills.'[32] This massive upsurge in the townships, factories, and schools has exacerbated the economic and political crises. The white minority regime is thus confronted with the seemingly insoluble riddle of how both to contain the popular rebellion and to maintain the political unity of the dominant bloc of class forces. Trapped in this web of contradictions, the National Party has retreated into the shelter of the white *laager*, hoping to silence its domestic opposition through a combination of calculation, repression and indiscriminate terror, coupled with empty promises about 'the good life' just around the corner.

1.

South Africa and the Total Strategy Doctrine

In September 1978, P.W. Botha succeeded John Vorster as leader of the National Party and Prime Minister of South Africa. This pivotal event marked a decisive turning point in the political direction of the National Party and the white minority regime. Vorster's impending retirement had unleashed a bitter power struggle within the National Party over his successor, but revelations about the Information Department's secret influence-peddling scheme and widespread misappropriation of funds propitiously tipped the scale in favour of the then-Defense Minister, P.W. Botha. Botha's chief rival for the post of Prime Minister had been Cornelius ('Connie') Mulder, who headed the Information Department. Embarrassing disclosures that the Information Department had conspired in a worldwide scheme of propaganda, political manipulation, and assorted 'dirty tricks' further exacerbated the deep gulf that separated rival factions of the National Party.

The scandal, which came to be known as 'Muldergate', led to the disgraceful departure of leading figures from the National Party hierarchy, including John Vorster and 'Connie' Mulder, and eventually evolved into a wider political contest over the long-term policy objectives of the National Party. Prime Minister Botha adroitly manipulated the scandal to his advantage, discrediting opponents and consolidating the authority of the reformist wing of the National party.[1]

From the outset, the Botha regime sought to distance itself

from the 'Muldergate' debacle, engaging in a broad campaign to repair the tarnished image of the National Party and to restore the public credibility that had been so rudely undermined by charges of officially-sanctioned corruption.[2] More importantly, Botha took steps toward defining and implementing a series of interrelated counter-revolutionary measures, encapsulated under the all-encompassing rubric of the Total Strategy doctrine. 'We must adapt or we will die,' Botha declared.[3] This 'adapt-or-die' slogan subsequently evolved into a convenient shorthand symbolizing the National Party's determination to recast the parameters of white minority rule.

The origins of the Total Strategy doctrine can be traced to an influential White Paper issued by the Department of Defense in 1977. Following shortly the collapse of the Portuguese colonialist regimes in Angola and Mozambique and the unexpected ferocity of the Soweto uprising, the White Paper was premised on the observation that 'we [the Pretoria regime] are today involved in a war, whether we wish to accept it or not.' In order to meet this challenge of 'total war', it was imperative that national security not remain the sole responsibility of the Department of Defense. Instead, it was necessary to formulate and coordinate action under the guidelines of a 'total national strategy', that is, a 'comprehensive plan to utilize all the means available to a state according to an integrated pattern in order to achieve the national aims with the framework of the specified policies. A total strategy is, therefore, not confined to a particular sphere, but is applicable at all levels and to all functions of the state structure.'[4] According to General Magnus Malan, South Africa had become the target of a 'total onslaught' orchestrated by Moscow. This 'total onslaught', in his view, was 'an ideologically motivated struggle' whose aim was 'the implacable and unconditional imposition of the aggressor's will on the target state.'[5] Embellishing this thesis, Prime Minister Botha declared in the House of Assembly in February 1982: 'The onslaught is the result of the expansionist policy of Soviet Russia. ... The rationale lies in the strategic position and mineral wealth of the Republic of South Africa.'[6]

Key components of this Total Strategy initiative evolved relatively independently of each other. During his tenure as Defense Minister, P.W. Botha orchestrated a tremendous military expansion in response to the perceived 'total onslaught' directed against South Africa. With John Vorster at the helm, the National Party had timorously groped away from the maximalist Verwoerdian conception of *apartheid*. However, it was the growing assertiveness of broad layers of the urban black working class during the 1970s that weakened the capacity of the white minority regime to rule in the ways to which it had grown accustomed. The 1976-7 Soweto uprising signalled a significant turning point. These events were a dramatic radicalizing experience for the tens of thousands of participants. The new political generation born in the crucible of violent action was fundamentally intolerant of second-class citizenship.[7] Monopoly capitalist interests recognized that the National Party had temporarily lost its grip in 1976-7. Consequently, business associations not only increased their pressure on the white minority regime to make the alterations that would bring public policies in line with the changing requirements of capital accumulation but also actively intervened (through agencies such as the Urban Foundation) to promote the upgrading of deteriorating infrastructure in the urban townships.

The Total Strategy doctrine incorporated these independent initiatives into a coherent programme of adaption and containment. According to Frankel, 'Under Botha, a more conscious, concerted, and systematic effort [was] made to integrate the various mechanisms of white control to produce a counter-revolutionary package more rationalized and efficient than at any time before.'[8] The *sine qua non* underlying the Total Strategy doctrine was the historical convergence of the common material interests of South African capital, the leadership of the ruling National Party, and the upper echelons of the military establishment. As portrayed by the military strategists who first coined its usage, Total Strategy aims at protecting 'free enterprise' in South Africa from the 'Marxist threat' and the 'total onslaught'.[9] In the view of the military establishment, the maintenance of national security entails more than the defence of the frontier. It also requires healthy and robust economic growth and direct military participation in policy-making.

During the greater part of the 1950s and 1960s, South African capital experienced high levels of sustained economic growth and generous rates of profit. The corresponding 'widening' and 'deepening' of South African capital not only opened up new branches of industrial production and fields of profitable investment but also propelled South Africa along the path forged by its North American/European counterparts, that is, what has often been referred to as 'post-industrialism' or the 'service economy'. By the 1970s, South Africa began to exhibit some tangible features of the world capitalist crisis — increasing inflation and signs of balance of payments difficulties. During 1972-7, black workers took the initiative, touching off an unprecedented strike wave that swept through the manufacturing and mining sectors of South Africa's heartland. These spontaneous actions, pivoting on demands for higher wages to offset declining living standards, precipitated the growth of the independent black trade union movement. This growing challenge of black workers fueled a broader popular upsurge by all oppressed class forces that culminated in the countrywide 1976-7 Soweto uprising.

On a broader scale, the historical development and consolidation of capitalism in the African sub-continent has fashioned a distinctive regional sub-system in which the principal poles of capital accumulation were concentrated in South Africa. The corresponding centralization of wealth and political power is paralleled by the dispersal of poverty, stagnation, and marginality in ever-widening layers to the regional peripheries. One longstanding objective of South Africa's regional policy has been to ensure that the neighbouring territories were inserted into a social division of labour that served the interests of capital accumulation at the centre. These subordinated peripheries were thus transformed into labour reserves, supplying South Africa with an inexpensive workforce through periodic and regular migrations; into sources of cheap raw materials (minerals, agricultural products, and so forth) and suppliers of 'services' (principally transport); and, finally, into ready-made markets for South African-produced manufactured (or processed) commodities and outlets for surplus capital.[10]

Until the mid-1970s, the fundamental bedrock upon which the white minority regime based its regional objectives had been the existence of a number of compliant 'buffer states' surrounding South Africa. The abrupt collapse of the Portugese colonial regimes in Angola and Mozambique in 1974 and the subsequent acceleration of guerrilla insurgencies against unpopular settler regimes in Rhodesia and South West Africa/Namibia deprived Pretoria of its much-vaunted *cordon sanitaire* and left the National Party's regional policy in virtual shambles.[11] Equally important, the military triumph of FRELIMO in Mozambique and MPLA in Angola (despite a massive South African invasion) seemed to vindicate a political strategy of protracted guerrilla war aimed at the remaining bastions of white supremacy in the region.

By the late 1970s, the structural underpinnings of class domination in South Africa had begun to disintegrate. The economic, political, and ideological conditions that had sustained the regime of accumulation during the *apartheid*-era 'long boom' began to exhibit advanced signs of decay. The dominant classes were thus confronted with a hegemonic crisis of grave proportions. The combination of heightened popular struggle of an openly anti-capitalist character, the worsening economic recession, and growing regional instability indicated that the fusion of structural and conjunctural dimensions had produced an 'organic crisis'.[12]

The accumulation strategy associated with the period of 'grand' *apartheid* depended upon the maintenance of rigid controls over the allocation and mobility of black labour. By the 1970s, the predominance of inexpensive and unskilled black labour went hand-in-hand with a depressed consumer market for manufactured goods and periodic production bottlenecks caused by skilled labour shortages. The Vorster regime had tinkered with existing relationships, impelled by the confident belief that Verwoerdian *apartheid* policies were fundamentally sound and only required ad hoc adjustments to meet the challenge of changing circumstances. In contrast, the Botha regime recognized that the political response to the conjoined crises of accumulation and legitimacy had to extend beyond a mere defense of the status quo.

In broad terms, the Total Strategy doctrine marked a limited but real shift in the political direction of the dominant bloc of class forces. In its embryonic phase, it represented not a concise and deliberate blueprint but a flexible counter-strategy to the perceived 'total onslaught'. One of its chief architects, General Magnus Malan, described Total Strategy as 'a national reorientation aimed at survival while at the same time ensuring the continued advancement of the well-being of all South Africans.'[13] This 'national reorientation', however, did not emerge organically from an inherent logic of South African capitalism but instead was forged through bitter conflicts within the dominant bloc of class forces. The Total Strategy initiative represented a calculated response by the leadership of a new 'historical bloc' of class forces to the emergent 'organic crisis'. It did not symbolize a tactical retreat into the *laager* but a comprehensive and elastic counter-offensive designed to restore the reign of white capitalism in southern Africa. What lurked behind Malan's bland credo was a strategic arsenal that included 'a sophisticated matrix of economic and other "incentives" applied together with military and other "disincentives".'[14]

The Historical Origins of the Total Strategy Doctrine

The Class Realignment of the National Party

The white election in 1948 marked a dramatic watershed in South African political history. South Africa's entry into World War II on the side of the Allies provoked bitter political tensions at home yet sparked tremendous industrial expansion, above all in mining, steel, and textiles. 'Factories', in Davenport's words, 'turned to the manufacture of armoured cars, artillery pieces, munitions, boots and uniforms.'[15] Invigorated by this wartime boom, manufacturers displayed a seemingly insatiable appetite for wage-labour that exceeded the existing supply of white artisans, unskilled 'poor whites' and temporary black migrants. In order to meet production targets and avoid bottlenecks, employers increasingly relied upon unskilled black labour.

During the 1920s and 1930s, urban employers had depended upon a rigid migrant labour system as the principal mechanism regulating the townward flow of African work-seekers. A principal tenet of the 1930s Hertzog segregationist policy — itself a rather ad hoc cluster of legislative acts and regulations — had been to convert the so-called Native Reserves into subsistence enclaves that would serve as repositories for the floating component of the reserve army of labour. Nevertheless, the sheer magnitude of the labour shortages in South Africa's industrial heartlands and the disintegration of the 'carrying capacity' of the Native Reserves which were longer capable of sustaining the subsistence requirements of the growing mass of Africans who had become wage-dependent, together undermined the segregationist vision.[16]

On the political side of the equation, a concatenation of seemingly disparate developments signalled a growing ideological cohesion amongst the oppressed masses which threatened the political stability of the white minority regime. During the 1940s, black workers flocked to the principal urban industrial areas in search of work in the burgeoning war-related industries. Despite the complaints of mining and agricultural capital about labour shortages, 'shanty towns' seemed to germinate everywhere. A series of bitter disputes, pitting state authorities against 'squatters' who had established semi-permanent camps in the vicinity of Johannesburg, underscored the growing political consciousness of township residents. In addition, African trade unionism — nurtured in part through the herculean efforts of Communist Party organizers — expanded rapidly during the inter-war years. In 1941, the incorporation of a number of African trade unions into the Council of Non-European Trade Unions (CNETU) marked an independent path of political development for the organized black working class. Correlatively, the emergence of the Youth League of the African National Congress in 1943-4 and the formation of the Non-European Unity Movement in 1943 marked the infusion of radical ideological currents into the mass movements, and signalled an abrupt shift toward more confrontational tactics.[17]

The rising tide of political unrest culminated in the 1946 mine workers' strike. This massive work stoppage involving 70,000 black workers clearly demonstrated the emergence of a combined class and national consciousness which threatened to undermine the stability of bourgeois class rule. The ruthless suppression of the strike demonstrated the virtual futility of constitutional protests directed at an unresponsive state administration.[18] In 1946, the *Cape Town* editorialized: 'The race problem today in this country is worse than it has ever been throughout our history. ... Relations between European and non-European were never nearer the breaking-point.'[19]

The ruling United Party, in Bunting's words, served as 'the mouthpiece of the mining, financial, and industrial interests, mainly English and Jewish in composition, who stood to benefit from the industrial revolution through which the country was passing and were prepared to accept some of its [disruptive] social consequences.'[20] A sustained crisis of hegemony arose from growing political unrest and bitter conflicts within the white minority regime over how to meet the challenge of labour

demand and allocation, taxation, pricing and marketing legislation, food subsidies, migrant labour and the deteriorating
Reserves. The United Party leadership vacillated on a host of
questions, preferring to rely on the forces of economic development rather than active state intervention to determine the
course of events. At the time of the 1948 white Parliamentary
elections, the United Party stood on a platform emphasizing that
the advantages of industrial expansion — continued white
prosperity and economic security — outweighed the possible
disadvantages of an increased commingling of the different racial
groups. The United Party did not reject the prevailing segregationist ideals but instead called for adjustments and modifications that would more effectively manage what its leadership
insisted was an irreversible townward drift of Africans.

In contrast, the National Party was comprised of a coalition of
interests, including the Afrikaans-speaking petty bourgeoisie, a
handful of Afrikaner finance capitalists, and the Cape agricultural bourgeoisie. The National Party leadership, however,
broadened its ideological appeal to a wider spectrum of the white
electorate, who were persuaded that uniting around a common
Afrikaner nationalist alliance in opposition to any forms of racial
equality would correspond to their own immediate material self-
interests. The National Party's cryptic petty-bourgeois populist
themes captivated three broad-based constituencies within the
white electorate: white farmers (particularly in the Transvaal and
Orange Free State), Afrikaans-speaking white wage-earners, and
an emergent Afrikaner professional/small business stratum.[21]

The National Party's 1948 electoral campaign capitalized on
the paralysis and indecision of the United Party at a time of
heightened political turmoil. The National Party declared that
their liberal political opponents were 'soft' on communism, that
further interaction between the races would lead to a debase-
ment of the 'civilized standards' to which white South Africans
had grown accustomed, and that the Hertzog segregationist
policies should be strengthened rather than relaxed. In the end,
however, it was the failure of the United Party to assuage the
mounting fears of large sections of the white electorate that
tipped the scales in favour of the National Party.[22]

The National Party election platform concentrated on a mobilization of the Afrikaans-speaking segment of the white electorate through an intense manipulation of cultural symbols, and,

more importantly, an hysterical and racialist emphasis on the 'colour question' and the threatened erosion of white privilege.[23] The National Party's narrow electoral triumph passed political power into the hands of a dedicated group of South African (predominantly Afrikaans-speaking) whites with the most extreme commitment to perpetuating white supremacy and racial segregation. The National Party unveiled its *apartheid* manifesto, the strength of which, Davenport argued, 'lay in its simplicity, and in its appeal to the voters' desire for security in a world which seemed to be moving too fast in a liberal direction and turning its wrath against South Africa as it did so.'[24]

The National Party promised *apartheid* (or, literally, 'separate development'), a vaguely-defined notion that has undergone extensive revision and refinement in the course of National Party rule. Nevertheless, the National Party did advocate the vigorous enforcement of colour bar legislation to safeguard the segmented position of white wage-earners, a tightening of influx control to halt the townward drift of African work-seekers, the reinforcement of the migrant labour system to prevent the permanent settlement of Africans in European 'prescribed areas', and the continued non-recognition of black trade unions and collective bargaining rights.

Throughout the 1950s and 1960s, the National Party introduced wave after wave of legislation in a concerted effort to tighten its grip over the increasingly dissatisfied, restive, and militant black masses. On the one hand, the National Party responded to the growth of African nationalism and increased black working-class militancy by hastily enacting a collection of repressive statutes designed to silence all overt opposition and restrict greatly the freedoms of assembly, expression, association, and movement. The protracted popular unrest (1950-64) that spanned the period of the legalistic Defiance Campaign to the armed propaganda of the sabotage campaign eventually ran its course under the full weight of organized state repression. On the other hand, the National Party sought to institutionalize *apartheid* rule. In contrast to the 'race-mixing' ideologies of integration, the National Party portrayed *apartheid* as the culminating wisdom of South Africa's historical experience, designed to safeguard the racial identity of the white populace.[25] Residential and territorial segregation functioned as the capstone of *apartheid* ideology. Black people were permitted to reside in specially-demarcated locations (or townships) in the vicinity of every village, town, city, and industrial area of South Africa. Yet without political rights and with limited claims to permanent residence, African people could be forced to leave these locations in the European 'prescribed areas' as soon as they ceased, according to the 1921 Stallard formula, 'to minister to the needs' of the white population. The National Party extended statutory job reservation in key industries and occupations as a means of maintaining the historical privileges enjoyed by white wage-earners. Finally, the National Party took the first steps that would recast the Reserves into so-called Bantu Homelands dispersed throughout the remote areas of the countryside, where African 'citizens' would enjoy the political rights denied them in the areas reserved for exclusive 'white occupancy'. The rigid enforcement of influx controls was designed to maintain the migrant labour system.

One basic article of faith for South African liberalism from the 1950s onward was the proposition that economic growth (or industrialization) would in the long run undermine and eventually dissolve the racialist structures and rationale for *apartheid*. The centrepiece of *apartheid* ideology was contained in the phrase 'separate development', a vague notion — open to competing interpretations — projecting the long-term goals of administrative and territorial segregation of state-defined racial/national groups.[26] Nevertheless, certain economic developments, notably the geographical and occupational mobility of black job-seekers, have historically pointed in the opposite direction. In Johnstone's words, 'For the [South African] government is not in fact attempting literally to implement its official ideology of total separate development. The actual goal of *apartheid* policies is the pragmatic development of an economically powerful white supremacy. The whites want continued prosperity and continued supremacy, and the government is seeking to secure both of these goals together.'[27] The National Party historically invoked this official ideology not only to preserve the poly-class alliance of the imagined community of Afrikaner nationalism and the *herrenvolk*, but also to justify the denial of political rights (and the maintenance of servile status) for Africans in 'white South Africa' in the name of future rights and opportunities in the independent Homelands.

During the 1950s, the hegemonic project envisaged by the

National Party rested on the class alliance of emergent capitalist agriculture, non-monopoly capital (particularly in the industrial, commercial, and financial spheres), white labour, and the Afrikaner petty bourgeoisie. The maintenance of this class alliance depended upon the tremendous expansion of state activities. On the one hand, state investments in basic infra-structure served as an engine of capitalist economic growth. On the other hand, state regulation of the labour market not only sheltered nonpropertied white wage-earners but also ensured supplies of inexpensive and unskilled black labour at the points of production. By the beginning of the next decade, the National Party had abandoned the shrill tone of its 'anti-capitalist' and 'anti-monopolist' rhetoric. The National Party had weathered the storm of unprecedented popular struggle 'from below'. The introduction of an arsenal of draconian security measures coupled with savage police repression had effectively curtailed 'above ground' mass political campaigns and forced the leading oppositional popular organizations — the ANC and the Pan-Africanist Congress (PAC) — to go underground and/or into exile.

The Political Metamorphosis of the National Party Coalition

From 1948 to 1970, South Africa experienced the second highest growth rates (behind Japan) in the capitalist world. During the sustained economic boom lasting from 1963 to 1972, the rate of return on invested capital in South Africa was the highest in the world.[28] In the countryside, the combined enforcement of the 1937 Marketing Act and influx controls (including the tightening of pass laws and the implementation of state-sponsored labour bureaux) secured high prices for white farmers and greatly relieved the persistent labour shortage bottlenecks. The wide-spread introduction of mechanized production techniques in the 1950s and 1960s reinforced the growing social differentiation between a small stratum of wealthy farmers on the one hand, and a contingent of marginalized farmers on the other. Despite the relative prosperity of agriculture, the entire locus of capital accumulation had shifted. By the mid-1960s, the value contri-bution of manufacturing to South Africa's Gross Domestic Pro-duct exceeded that of agriculture and mining for the first time.

Between 1948 and 1975, Afrikaner control of private industry increased astronomically from 10 per cent to 21 per cent, and the Afrikaner share of control over industrial output — including that of state corporations — increased to 45 per cent. The state corporations that were established under the sponsorship of the National Party greatly enhanced Afrikaner participation in industrial undertakings, thus creating the conditions whereby Afrikaner businessmen could mount an effective challenge to the 'English-speaking' dominance of mining and manufacturing. To put it more precisely, a distinctive Afrikaner fraction of monopoly capital was the principal beneficiary of National Party rule. During this period, Afrikaner finance houses flourished. Formerly dependent upon appropriating the accumulated savings of agricultural capital, these financial undertakings — particularly the Cape-based SANLAM and Rembrandt groups — greatly extended their base of operations into manufacturing (and to a lesser degree into mining) during the 1950s, thereby lessening their reliance upon agriculture. By the late 1970s, three Afrikaner monopolies — SANLAM, the Rembrandt group, and Volkskas — were firmly implanted amongst the eight largest conglomerate groups that dominated South African capitalism. In 1981, SANLAM (the second largest conglomerate in South Africa behind the Anglo-American Corporation) controlled assets equivalent to two-thirds of total foreign investment in South Africa.[29] Other Afrikaner corporate groups — such as *Federale Volksbeleggings* (investments), Nedbank (banking), and the General Mining Corporation (the third largest mining finance house) — reflected this significant shift in the social composition of the dominant classes.[30] Correlatively, the proportion of Afrikaners in the professional strata of the petty bourgeoisie doubled between 1948 and 1975 and the proportion of Afrikaners in white collar occupational categories exanded from 28 per cent to 65 per cent of the total.[31]

Seen in bold strokes, the combination of the expanded breadth and depth of Afrikaner monopoly and non-monopoly capital and the implantation of an urbanized Afrikaner petty bourgeoisie (including the rapid growth of an Afrikaner 'new middle class' of salaried state employees, managers, supervisors, and the like), coupled with the relative decline of agriculture and the dwindling proportion of white labour in the working class, undermined the class alliance that had sustained Afrikaner

nationalism during the 1950s and 1960s. At the onset, the growing class cleavages within Afrikanerdom appeared in the guise of
regional conflicts in the National Party. During the premiership
of H.F. Verwoerd, the Cape wing of the National Party —
clustered around SANLAM, large-scale agrarian capitalist
interests, and the newspaper *Die Burger* — had explicitly advocated modifications in *apartheid* policies that would both deflect
international criticisms and adjust to the social realities of a
permanently-settled urban black working class. The assassination of H.F. Verwoerd in 1966 unleashed a lengthy period of
internal strife within the National Party. Bitter disagreements
over the direction and goals of the National Party took the form
of a conflict between the *verligte* ('enlightened') and the
verkrampte ('narrow') factions. The culmination of this power
struggle within the National Party was the dismissal of a number
of hardline right-wing *verkramptes* from the National Party
Cabinet and the subsequent formation of the right-wing splinter
grouping, the *Herstigte* [Restored] *Nasionale Party* in 1969. The
underlying class foundation for these ideological disputes
centred on the conflict between the conservative *verkrampte*
forces that wished to preserve the tenuous balance between the
propertied and nonpropertied white constituencies and the
verligte elements who 'sought to adapt the ideology and policies
of Afrikaner nationalism to the changing social composition of
the *volk.*'[32]

During the premiership of J.B. Vorster, the sustained high
rates of economic growth in tandem with relative political stability obscured the mounting political tensions within the white
minority regime and the National Party. A combination of the
incremental growth of popular protests (culminating in the
1976-7 Soweto uprising), growing economic uncertainty and
stagnation, and declining international business confidence converged in the mid-1970s. The debates over how most effectively to
invigorate economic growth and restore political stability not
only exacerbated the political conflicts dividing the white
minority regime but also reinforced the schism within the
National Party. On the one hand, the *verligte* faction had
coalesced around a reformist strategy that advocated market-
oriented economic growth, the relaxation of job reservation and
the provision of job training for black wage-earners, the provision of a broader range of social amenities for a permanently

settled urban 'black middle class', and, finally, the creation of opportunities for the formation of a black propertied class in both the townships and the Homelands. On the other hand, the *verkrampte* faction insisted on the maintenance of tight influx controls, continued restrictions on the employment of skilled African labour, non-recognition of black trade unions, and continued state controls over basic infrastructural undertakings.[33]

Despite the apparent dissimilarities, these two approaches shared a number of common characteristics. First, both *verligte* and *verkrampte* factions declared their allegiance to *apartheid* ideology. Second, both sides advocated piecemeal modifications in prevailing *apartheid* practices. In 1978, the appointment of P.W. Botha as Prime Minister not only confirmed the ascendancy of the Afrikaner bourgeoisie in the National Party but also marked the consolidation of a new political alliance between monopoly capital and the upper echelons of the military establishment. The Total Strategy doctrine represented a comprehensive political programme that aimed not only to restructure the dominant bloc of class forces but also to forge new forms of legitimation that relied more upon market forces than on formalized racial discrimination to secure bourgeois rule.

South Africa in the Capitalist World Economy

The Global Stake in South Africa

The wellspring of South Africa's economic prosperity has been its fortuitous endowment of natural riches, particularly gold and diamonds. South Africa is the largest single producer of gold in the world, contributing nearly 60 per cent of the non-Soviet bloc's output. South Africa's mineral riches also include chromium (of which it produced 34 per cent of the world's supply), manganese (23 per cent), uranium (23 per cent), the platinum group metals (44 per cent), diamonds (15 per cent), antinomy (14 per cent), and vanadium (30 per cent). Experts agree that chromium, the platinum group, manganese, and cobalt head the list of 'strategic metals'. An abrupt curtailment in the supply of these metals 'would shut down or throttle the steel, automotive, chemical, plastics, and petroleum industries. It would halt the production of optical fiber for the communications industry. It would severely hobble the production of food, computer components and weapons.' The platinum group metals, of which South Africa and the Soviet Union jointly contribute 93 per cent of the world's supply, 'are irreplaceable as catalysts in the manufacture of gasoline, fertilizers, plastics, and thousands of chemicals.'[34]

Seen in historical perspective, the late nineteenth-century mining boom in South Africa's interior sparked a flood of overseas trade, investment, and immigration. As early as 1896, American engineers — fresh from the California Gold Rush — operated roughly half of South Africa's mining facilities in the newly-opened gold fields. Virtually overnight, U.S. firms became the largest suppliers of machinery and equipment to the mines.[35] From this initial stake in mining ventures, U.S. companies gradually penetrated alternative branches of industry, including such key sectors as petrochemicals, metals, the motor industry, agricultural equipment, and other manufactured goods.[36]

The flow of overseas trade and investment played a pivotal role in South Africa's economic growth and diversification. For U.S. investors, access to cheap labour and readily available markets made possible exaggerated rates of return in comparison with other areas of overseas investments.[37] According to the U.S. Department of Commerce, U.S. direct investment in South Africa increased from $140.0 million in 1950 to $2.63 billion in 1982, a figure nearly triple the amount of U.S. direct investment a decade earlier.[38] This figure, it should be noted, was based on book value and not on market value or replacement cost, both of which were considerably higher. It represented 38 per cent of U.S. investment in Africa, 17 per cent of total overseas fixed investment in South Africa, and less than 3 per cent of total direct investment in South Africa.[39]

According to *Fortune* magazine, U.S. direct investments in South Africa amounted to $2.3 billion at the end of 1984 and a number of U.S. firms had either quietly reduced their holdings or divested altogether. The average annual after-tax return on investments for U.S. corporations had dwindled from 31 per cent in 1980 to only 7 per cent in 1983.[40] South Africa's profitability appeared to have lost a great deal of its previous attraction for investors.

According to a classified State Department document leaked to the Washington D.C. lobbying organization TransAfrica, these official estimates grossly understated the actual extent of U.S. holdings in South Africa. Entitled *U.S. Investment in South Africa: The Hidden Pieces*, this secret study acknowledged that U.S. Commerce Department figures included only those investments made directly by U.S. firms in their South African subsidiaries.[41] In a series of circuitous transactions, U.S. parent companies often made funds available to European (particularly British) affiliates that were directly earmarked for investment in South African subsidiaries. In addition, U.S. parent corporations indirectly enhanced their total investments in South Africa by permitting their European subsidiaries to retain earnings and transfer them to U.S. affiliates in South Africa in a referral of dividends. As a consequence of these intra-corporate transactions, 'informed experts estimate the real investment level to be at least $15 billion — six times the level publicized by the Reagan administration.' Official sources have estimated that only 1 per cent of total U.S. overseas investments were located in South Africa and that U.S. investments represented almost 20 per cent of total overseas investments in South Africa. In actuality, both figures were substantially higher.[42]

The full reach of U.S. financial entanglement in South Africa extended beyond direct investments by U.S. parent companies and their worldwide subsidiaries. According to the U.S. Federal Reserve Bank, U.S. bank loans to South African governmental agencies declined from $794 million in June 1978 to $285.5 million in December 1982, but loans to South Africa's private sector increased astronomically from $1.5 billion to $3.4 billion during that same period. About 60 per cent of these massive loans from U.S. financial institutions went to South African banks.[43] At the end of 1984, U.S. bank loans to South Africa had climbed to $4.7 billion (where loans to the South African private sector totalled $4.35 billion and those to the public sector amounted to $353 million). All in all, according to the Bank for International Settlements, South Africa's total borrowings from overseas banks had reached $15 billion, an increase of $4.5 billion from the end of 1982.[44] In addition, foreign shareholders accounted for at least 38 per cent of all mining capital in South Africa in 1982. U.S. investors alone were estimated to hold $8.1 billion worth of shares in South African mines, or about 25 per cent of total mining investments and more than half of all foreign holdings.[45]

Roughly 400 U.S. companies operated subsidiaries or affiliates in South Africa in 1984. This figure included half of the Fortune 500 corporations. More than 6,000 U.S. companies conducted business in South Africa through sales agents or licensing agreements. U.S. trade with South Africa grew steadily since the early 1960s. By the late 1970s, the United States established itself as South Africa's most active trading partner.[46]

The ties that bind the United Kingdom to South Africa have unique historical origins. In 1978, British assets in South Africa and holdings by British shareholders in South African companies were valued at $12 billion, with $5.1 billion in stock and $6.8 billion in direct investments.[47] By 1985, British investments had ballooned to an estimated $15.7 billion, of which $7.15 billion represented direct investments in plant and equipment with the remainder distributed mainly through individual and company stock holdings. Of course, the market or replacement cost of direct investments was considerably higher than these official estimates based on book value. According to official statistics, British overseas investments in South Africa ranked first, followed by the United States and West Germany. The British share amounted to slightly more than half the total foreign holdings in South Africa. West German investments accounted for about 10 per cent.

According to calculations of the London-based United Kingdom/South Africa Trade Association, Britain's overseas investments in South Africa accounted for approximately 7 to 10 per cent of total British investments abroad. With nearly $3.86 billion in annual trade with South Africa, Britain ranked third behind the United States and West Germany as South Africa's largest trading partners. Japan, France, Italy, Switzerland, and black African nations comprised the remainder of South Africa's leading eight trading partners. In reality, the U.S., West Germany, Japan, and Great Britain had far outdistanced their rivals and ranked more or less evenly in terms of trade with South Africa.[48]

Britain's earnings from commercial dealings with South Africa were substantial. Extrapolating from earlier figures, it is possible to estimate that Britain's earnings from exports to South Africa amounted to over $1.3 billion in the mid-1980s. Britain's income from visible earnings — investment income, insurance services, dividends, shipping costs — hovered around $2.0 billion. British firms earned over $500 million from re-export sales, that is, sales of commodities like diamonds imported from South Africa and later sold outside Britain. The United Kingdom's imports from South Africa exceeded $1.5 billion, much of which consisted of minerals and metals. In exchange, British firms exported miscellaneous inorganic chemicals, electrical power machinery and switching gear, and telecommunications equipment to South Africa.[49]

U.S. corporate involvement in South Africa has historically concentrated in key capital-intensive sectors (petrochemicals, computers, nuclear power, transportation equipment, etc.) that required sophisticated technology and/or access to raw materials not readily available in South Africa (including oil, chemicals, and electronics). U.S. oil companies have played a vital and strategic role in South Africa. Although South Africa has been generously endowed with mineral resources, it has lacked commercially exploitable quantities of liquid hydrocarbons. The South African government has declared petroleum to be a strategic commodity and figures revealing production, imports, and consumption have been tightly-guarded state secrets. Despite the paucity of information, it was estimated in 1983 that South Africa was dependent upon oil for roughly one-quarter of its energy production.[50] South Africa has large synthetic fuels facilities that produced oil from coal. Nevertheless, it must import practically all its crude requirements. In 1985, five major transnational corporations controlled about 85 per cent of the distribution and marketing of petroleum products in South Africa. Two U.S. corporate giants — Mobil Oil and Caltex — controlled an estimated 40 per cent of oil-refining capacity and captured an equivalent proportion of the local market for petroleum sales.[51] Mobil and Caltex service stations dot the South African landscape. Their combined assets in South Africa were estimated at over $500 million in 1985.[52]

U.S. transnational corporations are firmly installed in other strategic sectors besides the petroleum industry. Overseas companies dominate motor vehicle manufacturing in South Africa. The U.S. firms — Ford, General Motors, and Chrysler — have controlled about one-third of the market. General Motors was the only U.S. automaker that had a wholly-owned South African subsidiary. In 1984, General Motors had sales of $310 million — about 9 per cent of the South African market. The market leader,

Toyota, accounted for 23 per cent of South African automobile sales.[53] British and U.S. corporations dominate the rapidly growing computer market. In 1985, IBM led the highly competitive field with an estimated 40 per cent of the installed computer base.[54] Finally, large U.S. corporations are intimately involved in the construction of oil-from-coal operations and the South African nuclear industry.[55]

In sum, South Africa has relied upon overseas trade and investment for the well-being of its manufacturing operations and other basic industries. South African business depends upon imported machine tools, plant and machinery, electronic equipment, computers, oil, and chemicals to maintain regular production lines and to pioneer industrial expansion into new fields. A U.S. State Department assessment of South Africa's dependence upon transnational corporations for sophisticated technology concluded that lack of access to foreign sources could potentially cripple South Africa.[56]

The U.S. Policy of 'Constructive Engagement'

The common thread that linked U.S. foreign policy toward South Africa from the onset of the Cold War to the Reagan administration was represented by linear shifts, along a continuum from quiet to vocal support for the white minority regime.[57] Despite occasional rhetorical flurries deploring racial discrimination in South Africa, U.S. policy-makers never strayed far from what amounted to a *laissez-faire* approach to South Africa's internal affairs. During the Nixon administration, U.S. policy on South Africa exhibited a discernible tilt in favour of the white minority regime. The broad contours of this U.S. *rapprochement* with South Africa were contained in Option Two of a 1969 secret study on policy options in southern Africa, prepared in National Security Study Memorandum 39 at the request of Secretary of State Henry Kissinger, and later leaked to the press. Option Two recommended that U.S. objectives should be to 'maintain public opposition to racial repression but relax political isolation and economic restrictions on the white states.'[58] This approach was premised upon the view that 'the whites are here to stay and the only way that constructive change can come about is through them. There is no hope for the blacks to gain the political rights they seek through violence, which will only lead to chaos and increased opportunities for the communists.'[59]

Option Two advocated 'selective relaxation of [the U.S.] stance toward the white regimes' in order to 'encourage some modification of their current racial and colonial policies', and 'more substantial economic assistance to the black states' in order to 'help draw the two groups together and exert some influence on both for peaceful change' in addition to offering 'the black states an alternative to the recognized risks of mounting communist influence.'[60]

During the 1970s, U.S. political support for South Africa became increasingly overt. In 1971, the U.S. Export-Import Bank altered its policy to allow long-term loans to South Africa. Violations of the United Nations arms embargo on South Africa became an 'open secret'. U.S. loans and military assistance to Portugal increased sharply. But it was in Angola where U.S. policy took a dramatic turn: 'The Nixon years witnessed a veritable explosion of U.S. capital into the territory. Most notably there was Cabinda Gulf Oil, with $209 million invested by 1972 in the rich Angolan oil-fields, expanding rapidly into other forms of mineral exploitation.'[61]

The 'investment invasion' of Angola consisted of a tripartite consortium of French, U.S., and South African capital. 'The Angolan economy', Johnson argued, 'symbolize[d] more perfectly than any other the rich complexity of the political and economic relationships entwining the southern African region.'[62]

At the outset, the Carter administration's emphasis on human rights irked Pretoria. Nevertheless, the shift from the Nixon to the Carter policies amounted more to a change of style than of substance. While the tenets of 'constructive engagement' policy have been attributed to the Reagan administration, Carter himself could have coined the phrase.[63] In 1977, Carter declared that 'economic development, investment commitment, and the use of economic leverage' were 'the only way to achieve racial justice' in South Africa.[64] Carter's rhetoric on the South African issue subsided as the practitioners of *realpolitik* gained the upper hand during the latter years of his administration.[65] U.S. trade and investments climbed steadily upward during the late 1970s. Ambassador Andrew Young consistently vetoed United Nations Security Council resolutions calling for economic sanctions against South Africa.[66]

The key ingredients of the Reagan administration's 'constructive engagement' policy were largely the brainchild of Chester A. Crocker, then Assistant Secretary of State for African Affairs-designate.[67] In a seminal essay published in *Foreign Affairs* shortly before the Reagan inauguration, Crocker divulged the elements of what was to become the centrepiece of the Reagan administration's South African policy. He contended that the previous U.S. policy of placing overt, public pressure for change on the South African regime had appeared to promise much more to black South Africans that it could reasonably deliver. 'As in other foreign policy agendas for the 1980s', Crocker wrote, 'the motto should be: underpromise and over-deliver — for a change.' The key to a successful relationship with South Africa hinged on dialogue and cooperation rather than confrontation and moralistic rebuke. In Crocker's view, Prime Minister P.W. Botha had accomplished a 'drawn-out *coup d'etat*' that had installed a group of 'modernizers' who were 'pragmatic, flexible, [and] determined' in positions of power.[68] In order to reinforce this promising process of 'white-led change', U.S. policy-makers should applaud P.W. Botha's programme of limited reforms, if only to safeguard U.S. interests in South Africa and the region. 'Constructive engagement' policy, as Crocker envisioned it, should 'steer between the twin dangers of abetting violence in the Republic and aligning ourselves with the cause of white rule.' U.S. policy-makers ought to jettison the mistaken preoccupation with 'the ultimate goal', i.e., 'power-sharing' and 'full political participation', and devote greater attention to 'the process of getting there'. 'We must avoid the trap', Crocker insisted, 'of an indiscriminate attack on all aspects of the [*apartheid*] system.' U.S. policy objectives ought to focus on improving relations with Pretoria, said Crocker, 'providing the process is open-ended and consistent with a non-racial order.'[69]

In a television interview early in his first term, President Reagan extolled South Africa as a 'friendly nation', inquiring 'can we abandon a country that has stood by us in every war we've ever fought — a country that is strategically essential to the free world in its production of minerals we all must have?'[70] In a 'Scope Paper' to brief then Secretary Alexander Haig for a May 1981 meeting with South African Foreign Minister Roelf F. ('Pik') Botha, Chester Crocker emphasized that 'the political relationship between the United States and South Africa has now arrived at a crossroads of perhaps historic significance.' He additionally urged Haig to inform the Foreign Minister that the Reagan administration was prepared to 'open a new chapter in relations with South Africa' and that the United States was willing to promote 'a more positive and reciprocal relationship between the two countries based upon shared strategic concerns in southern Africa.' The Crocker memorandum pledged that the U.S. was willing to advance 'toward a future in which South Africa returns to a place within the regional framework of Western security interests', concluding that 'we can ... work to end South Africa's polecat status in the world and seek to restore its place as a legitimate and important regional factor with whom we can cooperate pragmatically.'[71]

After the achievement of political independence in Zimbabwe in 1980, Washington's foremost regional priority shifted toward the consummation of an internationally acceptable settlement in Namibia. In his landmark outline for a new South Africa policy, Crocker had argued that he believed that a Namibian settlement would boost U.S. credibility throughout Africa (and especially southern Africa), provide the Botha regime with confidence to move faster with its domestic reform programme, and pave the way for the United States to improve political relations with South Africa.[72] The solution to the diplomatic and military conflict over Namibia depended upon persuading Pretoria to implement United Nations Security Council Resolution 435, a 1978 compromise plan that called for a cease-fire in the territory followed by general elections under United Nations supervision. South Africa had originally occupied this former German colony under a League of Nations mandate in 1920. After protracted legal battles, South Africa continued to rule Namibia in defiance of numerous United Nations resolutions.[73] In mid-1982, the Reagan administration introduced a spurious East/West clause into the Namibia settlement plan, insisting that Namibian independence was absolutely contingent upon prior Cuban troop withdrawal from Angola. Assistant Secretary of State Crocker blamed the Soviet Union and Cuba for the spread of regional instability in southern Africa and enjoined the United States 'to play [its] proper role in fostering the region's security and countering the expansion of Soviet influence.'[74] This linkage provided Pretoria with considerable leverage to stonewall the implementation of the Namibia settlement plan if not to scuttle the negotiation process altogether.

As a corollary of this collaboration in derailing the Namibian independence issue, the Reagan administration renewed military contracts and restored nuclear cooperation (including the sale of enriched uranium and the exchange of technical information) despite Pretoria's steadfast refusal to sign the Nuclear Non-Proliferation Treaty and to comply with the International Atomic Energy Agency with regard to safety standards and on-site inspections.[75] In addition, the Reagan administration greatly eased U.S. Commerce Department regulations that had severely limited U.S. trade with the South African security forces. This wholesale relaxation of previous restrictions on commercial transactions still did not permit the export of arms and related equipment to South Africa. Nevertheless, lax U.S. enforcement of the United Nations arms embargo has meant that numerous unpunished violations have occurred [76]

Total Strategy in the African Sub-Continent

Regional Objectives of the Total Strategy Doctrine

In 1963, the Verwoerd regime proposed the formation of a 'common market/commonwealth' in southern Africa. This plan envisaged the establishment of a free trade zone as the first step toward greater regional cooperation. Eventually, it was hoped, the careful nurturing of these economic linkages would herald the formation of a political union of sorts — a commonwealth described by *apartheid* ideologues at the time as an 'association of black and white states' with South Africa as the 'centralizing mother country.'[77] This commonwealth strategy failed to materialize. In the interim, Pretoria forged tighter links with the colonial settler regimes in the surrounding buffer states. Buoyed by these tangible gains, the Vorster regime launched a political offensive in the late 1960s in direct response to the rapid pace of African decolonization and the increasing international condemnation of *apartheid*. This 'dialogue initiative', as it was called, scored some initial diplomatic triumphs but eventually reached its zenith in the early 1970s.[78]

Despite Pretoria's manoeuvers, the balance of political forces in southern Africa had slowly yet inexorably shifted in favour of the liberation movements in territories still under colonial rule. The collapse of the beleaguered fascist regime in Portugal in April 1974 set the stage for political independence in Mozambique and Angola in the following year. Almost immediately, the Vorster regime countered with a renewed diplomatic/political exercise known as 'détente'. The objective of this hasty reformulation of regional policy was a rather nebulous vision of a 'constellation of completely independent states' in southern Africa which would form a 'power bloc' and 'present a united front against common enemies.'[79] These overtures lost their momentum, however, in the wake of South Africa's large-scale military invasion of Angola in 1975 and the gathering internal political crisis associated with the 1976/7 Soweto uprising.

After P.W. Botha took office in September 1978, the Total Strategy doctrine became the nucleus of official state policy, inspiring not only a substantial reorganization of the state apparatuses but also a thorough reformulation of regional policies. Under the Total Strategy doctrine, the vague notion of a 'constellation of states' was rescued from near-oblivion. The Botha regime 'elevated it to a major foreign policy priority and gave it a content previously lacking.'[80]

In an important 1979 policy statement, Foreign Minister 'Pik' Botha unveiled Pretoria's grand vision of seven to ten states, comprising 40 million people, south of the Kunene and Zambezi rivers, joined together in a 'constellation of states'. This ambitious scheme included the so-called independent Homelands. Pretoria reasoned that the consolidation of a formal association between neighbouring black states and former Bantustans would imply recognition of Homeland independence and confer legitimacy on 'separate development'.[81]

'South Africa is to become the king-pin of all of us', President Kenneth Kuanda of Zambia charged, 'and all of us ... are going to be satellite or puppet states of South Africa.'[82] Lesotho's foreign Minister echoed this condemnation: 'Through this stratagem South Africa hopes to win support and respectibility for her grand *apartheid*, which fragments southern Africa into weak satellites dominated by a strong white state.'[83] The growing public outcry forced South Africa to scale down the dimensions of this scheme.[84]

In Pretoria's view, the 'moderate states of Southern Africa' faced a 'common Marxist onslaught'. Unable to depend upon political support from Western capitalist powers, it was imperative that South Africa play the pivotal role in the construction of a 'regional alliance'. Pretoria acknowledged that blatantly racialist aspects of *apartheid* policies undermined South Africa's international credibility and hence inhibited the establishment of formalized alliances with neighbouring states. The Botha regime recognized the necessity of fabricating an effective 'counter-ideology' to 'Marxism' in the region. Thus, key officials privately sought to enlist the support of neighbouring states for a number of joint economic projects. Because of the region's dire economic straits, it was hoped that the lure of tangible gain would entice reluctant neighbours into a common covenant with Pretoria and eventually demonstrate the superiority of South African capitalism over 'socialist' alternatives. It was also recognized that the economic viability of these joint ventures depended upon the active participation of the private sector.[85] From the outset, Pretoria surmised that the effectiveness of this 'counter-ideology' depended upon coaxing regional states into bilateral Non-Aggression Pacts as an initial step to promoting 'the concept of mutual defence against a common enemy'.[86] Pretoria reasoned that the tightening web of mutual obligations in the economic and security fields would slowly deepen the ties between South Africa and the neighbouring states and create the objective basis for what Prime Minister Botha hailed as 'a form of confederation'.[87]

Policy Implementation and the Reorganized State Apparatuses

The style of decision-making during the Vorster years was characterized by departmental autonomy and political competition. The resulting jurisdictional disputes and narrow rivalries between various branches of the state apparatus reinforced the bureaucratic paralysis that epitomized the final stages of the Vorster administration. 'Vorster's rule', in Grundy's words, 'was an organizational and administrative nightmare.'[88]

To correct these glaring deficiencies, P.W. Botha's group simultaneously reorganized the Cabinet, established an interlocking system of Cabinet committees to devise policy and to coordinate its implementation, enlarged and extended the scope of the office of Prime Minister, and launched a President's Council charged with the task of reviewing alternative constitutional proposals. By revamping the structure of decision-making within the state bureaucracy, Botha not only eradicated the source of previous institutional conflicts but also introduced an organization-minded and managerial approach to policy-making. More importantly, this administrative reorganization included, first, a decisive centralization of power in the executive branch (particularly the concentration of decision-making prerogatives in the office of the Prime Minister) and a corresponding diminution in the role of the Cabinet and parliament (in conjunction with downgrading the influence of the National Party caucus and congresses), and, second, a striking militarization of overall planning and decision-making within the administrative structures of the state.[89]

According to the 1977 Defence Department White Paper, the Total Strategy doctrine demanded a 'comprehensive plan to utilize all the means available to the state according to an integrated pattern in order to achieve the national aims within the framework of specific policies.'[90] The implementation of Total Strategy depended upon streamlining the maze of overlapping and competing jurisdictions that characterized the state apparatuses. Under the *apartheid* system, the state administration had evolved into a bureaucratic conundrum that included, *inter alia*, over 2,000 statutory bodies serving various interest groups and constituencies. The state employed an estimated 40 per cent of economically active white South African males.[91]

As part of the phased overhaul of the decision-making structures, Botha established a special cabinet secretariat in the Office of the Prime Minister in August 1979. The twenty separate Cabinet Committees that had existed on an ad hoc basis during the Vorster regime were eventually reduced to four permanent bodies — National Security, Constitutional Affairs, Economic Affairs, and Social Affairs.[92] In the past, National Party members of Parliament filled the available Cabinet seats. The administrative structure had ensured that the spectrum of political views spanning the National Party were represented in at least an advisory capacity. Under P.W. Botha's leadership, the membership of these Cabinet Committees was no longer restricted to the customary Parliamentary pool. Consequently, Botha appointed military and business leaders from outside Parliament. These men generally shared his political views.[93] The revamped Cabinet Committees were transformed from advisory bodies to the Cabinet, as they had been during the Vorster regime, into integral components at the highest level of the decision-making machinery. The Prime Minister assumed the authority to nominate those Ministers (whose identities were wrapped in anonymity) who headed each of the four Committees. While the Cabinet as a whole experienced a drastic reduction in both authority and influence, the four Cabinet Committees assumed greater power to make policy decisions.[94]

The Committee for National Security, known as the State Security Council (SSC), became the key organization through which the 'security establishment' shaped and coordinated regional and domestic defence policies. Technically, the SSC functioned as only one of four pivotal Cabinet Committees. In fact, it was *primus inter pares*. The SSC originally came into existence in 1972 through an Act of Parliament. During the Vorster regime, the SSC functioned as a purely advisory body and assembled only occasionally. Now, the SSC has evolved into the primary decision-making body within the South African state apparatus. It was chaired by the Prime Minister (and now by the State President). It is rumoured that its secretariat (that is, the operational and administrative arm) is staffed by high-ranking South African Defence Force personnel. The SSC stands at the pinnacle of what has been termed the 'national security management system'.[95] Its statutory responsibility embraces virtually every arena of internal and external state activity. In practice, the SSC has become the principal forum for formulating the implementation of the Total Strategy doctrine. It coordinates and plans the 'utilization of all the means available' to state bureaucrats in order to achieve the specific policy objectives subsumed under the rubric of Total Strategy.[96]

During his first two years as Prime Minister, P.W. Botha retained the Ministry of Defence portfolio, a position that he had held for the previous fourteen years. In 1980, this critical post was offered to General Magnus Malan, one of Botha's closest aides.[97] In a related development, Botha reorganized and militarized South Africa's intelligence services. As a consequence, he undercut the debilitating rivalries that had plagued the military intelligence and civilian intelligence branches operating under the Bureau of State Security (BOSS). In addition to appointing ambitious military officers to staff the high command of BOSS, Botha gradually curtailed its overall functions. In the wholesale reorganization of the state repressive apparatuses, the National Party leader centralized and integrated all intelligence-gathering operations under the SSC.[98] Dominated by a staff of high-ranking military personnel, the SSC assumed full responsibility for co-ordinating fifteen interdepartmental committees that extended security planning into all aspects of South African life. In addition, the SSC was authorized to supervise a network of fifteen internal and external Joint Management Centres. The ten internal Centres served different geographical areas of South Africa, whose demarcation coincided with the ten Area Commands designated by the Defence Force. Another Centre included the Namibian port of Walvis Bay, a docking and trans-port complex that South Africa claimed as its own territory. The four remaining external Centres covered Namibia and unspeci-fied countries of southern Africa. In sum, these Joint Manage-ment Centres were designed to serve as principal agencies for the implementation of Total Strategy in a coordinated fashion throughout the whole of southern Africa.[99]

In 1980, even before the process of full consolidation of politi-cal authority had been completed, it was observed that 'in many ways [the SSC] is already an alternative Cabinet by virtue of the decisions it makes.'[100] The Prime Minister chaired the SSC and its secretariat was comprised of high-ranking military officers. The social composition of the personnel at its summit symbolized the growing collusion between the military establishment and National Party civilians at the highest levels of decision-making. In effect, the SSC had become the most powerful policy-making body in the increasingly centralized executive branch.[101]

The Total Strategy programme envisaged the wholesale mobilization of economic, political, and social-psychological resources, as well as the military. Consequently, state planners devoted considerable effort to exploring the manner in which economic linkages could be utilized to extend their strategic objectives in the region. In the terminology of Pretoria's strate-gists, these economic links could be used either as 'incentive levers' or 'techniques of persuasion', on the one hand, or 'disin-centive levers' or 'techniques of coercion', on the other. Pretoria hoped to purchase at least the acquiescence of its neighbours by

dangling the offer of economic aid and the promise of cooperation in joint infrastructural projects.[102]

At the historic Carlton Centre Conference, P.W. Botha
expounded the idea of a 'constellation of states' before an
audience of 250 leading South African businessmen. 'We, and
the other countries of southern Africa', be declared, 'are thus
confronted by the challenge and the opportunity to consolidate,
in an evolutionary way, the undeniable economic interdependence between us to each other's mutual advantage and
towards a logical economic grouping.'[103] At this formative stage,
state strategists had imagined that 'incentives' would be
funnelled through a soon-to-be-established Development Bank
of Southern Africa (DBSA). Because this financial instrument
experienced 'a protracted and difficult gestation', other agencies
— such as the South African Customs Union and existing bilateral agreements — were utilized to package various 'aid' programmes. Full DBSA operations did not begin until February
1984, assuming an International Monetary Fund (IMF)-style
paternalism in dispensing loans, primarily for industrial development projects in the Homelands.[104]

The Implementation of the Total Strategy

The 'Constellation of States' Proposal

The initial phase of the Total Strategy initiative lasted from the
end of 1978 until mid-1980. During this period, the Botha regime
unveiled the 'Constellation of States' venture. In Pretoria's view,
this initiative depended upon cultivating truly symbiotic
collaboration between the state agencies and the private sector,
with the former providing the basic economic infrastructure and
the latter acting as the catalyst for economic growth. At the time
what made the prospect appear promising from Pretoria's vantage point was the distinct likelihood that the British-
orchestrated 'internal settlement' in Rhodesia would produce a
moderate African-led regime under Abel Muzorewa, heavily
dependent upon its own propertied white settlers and on the
white minority regime to the South.[105] International recognition
of Zimbabwean independence of this character would dovetail
neatly with Pretoria's desire to establish a malleable clientist

relationship with the new regime. In Pretoria's calculations, if Zimbabwe's allegiance could be secured effectively, neighbouring states — like falling dominoes — would gradually be pressured into deepening their economic links to South Africa.[106]

The strong showing of Robert Mugabe's ZANU(PF) in the Lancaster House independence elections in Zimbabwe dashed Pretoria's hopes for the implementation of its regional project as it was originally conceived. Zimbabwe quickly joined the Front Line states alliance. But what effectively thwarted Pretoria's planning for the grand 'Constellation of States' was the formation of the Southern African Development Coordination Conference (SADCC).[107]

The Southern African Development Coordination Conference (SADCC)

Although the proposed alliance had been discussed at a meeting of the Front Line States in Arusha in July 1979, SADCC was not officially established until April 1980. The nine signatories included the six Front Line States (Tanzania, Mozambique, Zambia, Zimbabwe, Botswana, and Angola) in addition to Malawi, Swaziland, and Lesotho. In the Lusaka Declaration, the nine SADCC member-states pledged their mutual cooperation across a range of common fronts with the long-term objective of progressively reducing their inherited economic dependence upon South Africa. Each of the SADCC member-states agreed to mobilize local resources as part of an overall plan for regional economic development. In addition, the SADCC signatories endorsed a commitment to act in concert vis-a-vis international lending agencies in order to obtain desperately-needed financial assistance and technical aid.[108]

The pattern of colonial incorporation of southern Africa and the subsequent 'decolonization' process had left a legacy of balkanized states that inherited stronger economic links with South Africa and their respective former colonial powers in the 'metropolitan centre' than with each other.[109] SADCC recognized the political heterogeneity of its member-states and hence did not require harmonization of domestic policies. Instead, SADCC concentrated on the formulation of a multi-lateral development programme that would reverse the historical dependence upon

South Africa. The cornerstone of disengagement from South Africa was identified as a radical reorientation of the regional transport and communications networks away from reliance upon South Africa's modern ports and railroad facilities.[110] The development of alternative railroad routes linking the interior to seaports was regarded as indispensable for SADCC's long-term strategy of restructuring economic relations between member-states, in addition to providing food security.[111]

SADCC represented a significant defeat for South African strategy. SADCC succeeded in incorporating all nine independent states in the region, including the conservative regimes with historic ties to South Africa. Long-term SADCC strategy threatened to frustrate Pretoria's immediate aim of maintaining and eventually deepening economic linkages within the region. In particular, SADCC offered a concrete alternative to the 'Constellation of States' initiative. SADCC thus represented a setback for South African regional designs. Pretoria scaled down its grand scheme to include only the 'inner constellation', that is, 'white' South Africa and the independent Homelands.[112] As a consequence, the Small Business Development Corporation (created in November 1980), the Southern African Development Bank, and the Multilateral Development Council (both formed in 1982) confined their financial operations to this limited constellation.[113]

South Africa: The Economic Collosus of Southern Africa

At the time of SADCC's formation, its nine member-states had a joint Gross National Product of U.S. $20 billion, an area of over five million square kilometres, and a population estimated at 60 million. The region possessed significant natural resources, including oil deposits, uranium, coal, iron, copper, nickel, cobalt, chrome, and vast energy potential in both hydroelectric power and solar energy. Nevertheless, whatever potential existed for complementary economic development remained far from realized.

The central feature of the southern African region has been South Africa's dominance. South Africa has historically functioned within the imperialist chain as a sub-metropolitan outpost on the African continent. Within the southern African region, the peripheral zones have been linked to South Africa as suppliers of raw materials, consumers of manufactured goods, and labour reserves in the migrant labour system. In 1980, the Republic of South Africa (including its occupied territory of Namibia) had a Gross National Product that was more than double the combined figure for the nine SADCC states. More importantly, South Africa possessed a highly developed industrial base and basic infrastructure that far surpassed its economic competitors. South Africa produced 87 per cent of all steel in Africa and accounted for about 52 per cent of continental African steel consumption. South Africa produced an estimated 30 per cent of all continental African cement. Finally, South Africa contributed an estimated 40 per cent of total manufacturing production in Africa.[114] The relative economic strength of South Africa with respect to the southern Africa region is illustrated in the following table.

In terms of trade, the three so-called 'Rand States' (Botswana, Lesotho, and Swaziland — or BLS states) were firmly integrated into the economic orbit of South Africa. Their membership in a common Southern African Customs Union meant in practice that they were incorporated into a common currency area under the control of the South African Reserve Bank. For purposes of accounting, the whole Customs Union area was regarded as a single trading area and complicated formulae were used to determine each 'Rand State's' share of total tariffs on commodities imported into the customs area. In broad outline, Botswana obtained 88 per cent of its imports from South Africa while it shipped only 8 per cent of its exports to South Africa. Similarly, comparable figures for Lesotho were 95 per cent of exports and 90 per cent imports. Swaziland acquired 90 per cent of its imports from South Africa and sent 20 per cent of its exports to South Africa. The BLS countries represented extreme cases of dependency upon South Africa in the field of commodity trade.[115]

In stark contrast to the degree of commodity transactions with South Africa, intra-SADCC exchanges amounted to no more than 2-3 per cent of their total foreign trade. Nearly all SADCC foreign trade was conducted with South Africa, Europe, the United States, and Japan. From the South African viewpoint, trade with SADCC countries remained quite small. Less than 7 per cent of South Africa's total exports were directed to the rest of Africa.

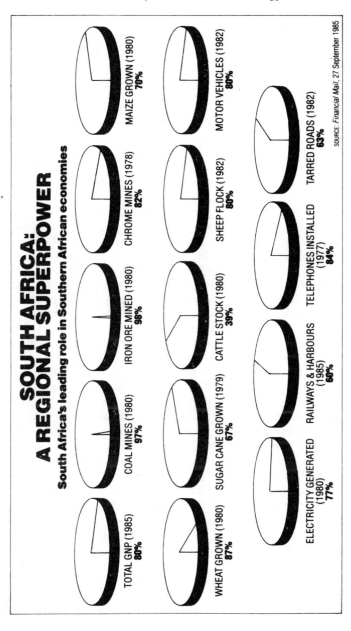

**SOUTH AFRICA:
A REGIONAL SUPERPOWER**

South Africa's leading role in Southern African economies

TOTAL GNP (1985)
80%

COAL MINES (1980)
97%

IRON ORE MINED (1980)
98%

CHROME MINES (1978)
82%

MAIZE GROWN (1980)
70%

WHEAT GROWN (1980)
87%

SUGAR CANE GROWN (1979)
67%

CATTLE STOCK (1980)
39%

SHEEP FLOCK (1982)
80%

MOTOR VEHICLES (1982)
80%

ELECTRICITY GENERATED
(1980)
77%

RAILWAYS & HARBOURS
(1985)
60%

TELEPHONES INSTALLED
(1977)
84%

TARRED ROADS (1982)
63%

SOURCE: *Financial Mail, 27 September 1985*

Imports to South Africa from the rest of Africa barely exceeded 4 per cent. Strictly in terms of South Africa's trade composition with Africa, precious metals accounted for 18 per cent, machinery and equipment for 16 per cent, chemical products for 13 per cent, and foodstuffs for 13 per cent. In contrast, exports from South Africa to the SADCC countries consisted in the main of foodstuffs and agricultural produce. In 1980, the nine SADCC members together imported 1.4 million tons of cereals (of which 700,000 tons was maize). Large quantities of these maize imports came directly or indirectly from the Republic of South Africa.[116]

During the entire post-World War II period, South Africa has been a net importer of investment capital on a large scale, particularly from Western European countries and the United States. This infusion of overseas capital has considerably strengthened South Africa's industrial base. In turn, South African companies have considerable and long-established investments in adjacent countries, particularly Zimbabwe (where South African capital in 1983 held in excess of 25 per cent of the total stock of foreign investment),[117] and have penetrated as far afield as Zaire and Mauritania. A considerable proportion of South African capital exports has been destined for mining operations in southern Africa: diamonds, copper, and nickel in Botswana; iron ore and coal in Swaziland; copper and cobalt in Zambia; gold, diamonds, iron ore, and oil in Angola.[118] Closely related to these mining investments, South African capital (from both private and parastatal corporations) has been engaged in the construction of basic infrastructure, such as railways and hydroelectric power plants. Railroad projects in Angola, Malawi, and Swaziland took place for the most part in connection with private investments in mining operations. South African capital also was involved in the Cabora Bassa (Mozambique) and Cunene (Angola) hydroelectric power plants.[119]

The United States and Great Britain have recently been the major magnets for South African direct overseas investments. By 1981, the Anglo-American Corporation ranked as the single largest foreign investor in the United States. The Rembrandt Group captured a large share of world tobacco markets through its Philip Morris subsidiary. Beginning in 1984, two other South African business groups, Barlow Rand and Liberty Life, each embarked on a major international diversification effort in Britain. Barlow Rand purchased the animal feed and industrial group, J. Bibby & Sons, for R550 million. This purchase was welcomed as a springboard for Barlow Rand's long-term goal of international expansion and growth. Similarly, Liberty Life purchased the seventh largest property development firm in Britain, Capital & Counties, for R800 million. This deal was described as 'a major step forward in the development of Liberty Life's international strategies that should be of considerable long-term benefit to the Group.' The acquisition of Capital & Counties was the main reason for the staggering 58 per cent increase in total assets reflected in the 1986 accounts of Liberty Life. In the words of Martin Nicol, '*Apartheid* is dead. It no longer provides Liberty Life and Barlow Rand with as good a return on capital as it used to. The companies show the extent of their commitment to a post-*apartheid* economic system in South Africa by making vast investments abroad. At the same time they are among the strongest critics of disinvestment. There is a contradiction, but no mystery. They want to have their cake overseas and eat someone else's here in South Africa.'[120] South African capital was also attracted to other European countries, Australia, Israel, and Latin America.[121]

Pretoria historically employed various types of financial and technical assistance in order to reinforce the reliance of its neighbours on South African capital. The Economic Cooperation Promotion Loan fund was established in 1968 as a means of extending loans on favourable terms for various infrastructure projects in the region. Lesotho and Malawi accepted this economic aid for railway and hydroelectric power projects, in addition to promoting aviation, broadcasting, tourism, and the recruitment of skilled personnel. In the main, financial assistance of this sort was linked to the purchase of commodities produced in South Africa. Railway projects initiated with South African sponsorship were linked to the South African railroad network. Similarly, hydroelectric power facilities were generally tied into the South African grid in order to supply South African consumers with electricity, of which the Republic has been in short supply.[122]

SADCC members have remained dependent in large measure upon the South African transport network not only for intra-regional trade but also for their trade links outside the African continent. This dependence is underscored by the fact that six of the nine (Botswana, Lesotho, Malawi, Swaziland, Zambia, and

Zimbabwe) are landlocked. Without ready access to harbours on the Indian or Atlantic coasts, they have been compelled to use the South African transport and harbour network for commodities in transit. The bulk of freight transport in the southern African region has been conducted *via* railway. An estimated 90,000 kilometers of railways crisscross the African continent. More than 25 per cent of this total is located in Namibia and South Africa. The length of the South African (and Namibian) railways far exceed the combined total for all nine SADCC countries. More importantly, South Africa maintains a marked superiority in terms of harbour capacity and handling efficiency at freight terminals.[123]

In varying degrees, South Africa's neighbours have been dependent upon the remittances of migrant labourers. The origins of large-scale labour migration can be traced historically to the late nineteenth-century diamond and gold discoveries in South Africa's interior. This enduring pattern of labour migration has been etched indelibly into the economic and social fabric of southern Africa. In 1978, an estimated 325,000 labourers from South Africa's neighbouring states were employed variously in the Republic's mining operations, manufacturing, and households. The largest single source, Lesotho, supplied approximately 155,000 labourers. About 50,000 originated in Mozambique, 35,000 from Botswana, and 39,000 from Malawi. The absolute number of migrant labourers declined precipitously in the latter half of the 1970s. In particular, mining companies have shifted their recruitment focus to South Africa itself. In 1975, foreign workers in the mines constituted about 75 per cent of the total labour force. In 1983, this proportion had been reduced to about 50 per cent,[124] but South Africa still recruited about 140,000 miners from the five principal labour-exporting SADCC states.[125]

Total Strategy and Regional Destabilization

Destabilization Tactics

Following the collapse of Portuguese colonial rule in southern Africa, Pretoria escalated both overt and covert efforts to undermine the political stability of the surrounding African states. This campaign of regional destabilization combined armed aggression with economic and political pressures to weaken the resolve of African regimes that dared to challenge Pretoria and to ensure the continued survival of South Africa's white minority regime.[126] From the outset, Angola and Mozambique — the Marxist successors to Portuguese colonialism — were singled out as the main targets of these destabilization efforts.

In Angola, Pretoria organized its destabilization exercise around a combination of the legacy of Angola's 1975-6 civil war and its own counterinsurgency project in Namibia.[127] South African incursions into Angola began in October 1975 during the height of the civil war. Two thousand South African troops were rushed into Angola in order to provide maintenance, logistics, reconnaissance, and combat support for UNITA and FNLA against the MPLA. In the offensive led by the SADF, the UNITA/FNLA forces were repulsed only after they had advanced to within sixty kilometres of Luanda, the capital city. In response to the South African military adventure, Angola requested the military assistance of Cuba.[128] By 1976, the MPLA had gained the upper hand and had established an internationally-recognized regime of broad national consensus in Luanda. Nevertheless, the rival UNITA movement had managed to retain the remnants of an organizational structure in addition to a base of political support among the Ovimbundu people in southern Angola. Pretoria quickly exploited this opportunity, coming to the assistance of the UNITA insurgents with military supplies, logistical support, and backing in the field from its own armed forces. The SADF initiated frequent military incursions into southern Angola, beginning in 1977, that gradually expanded in size and scope. By 1981, the SADF forays involved air strikes, sizeable commitments of ground forces, penetrations as deep as 200 miles into Angolan territory, and actual occupation of large stretches of southern Angola. Pretoria steadfastly defended these military actions as pre-emptive strikes directed at SWAPO military units that used Angolan sanctuaries for mounting operations within neighbouring Namibia. While Pretoria's determination to assault SWAPO base camps and staging areas was never in doubt, these actions were a convenient ploy that masked the SADF's direct military assistance to Jonas Savimbi's UNITA. The SADF's military actions were coordinated with UNITA, and towns and villages captured by SADF troops were subsequently transferred to UNITA administration.[129]

A report published in 1981 by a fact-finding mission of the European Economic Community estimated that the SADF had been implicated in nearly *two thousand* operations inside Angola. Between 1975 and 1980, South African attacks caused nearly $7 billion in damage and displaced 13,000 persons.[130] Pretoria's sponsorship of ethnic mercenaries in Angola was amply rewarded. UNITA concentrated on a campaign of economic sabotage. The destruction of key infrastructural installations — particularly the Benguela railway, which has been rendered virtually inoperable for over a decade — not only disrupted the flow of goods within Angola but also cut Zaire's and Zambia's vital lifeline to the sea. Zambia and Zaire depended upon the Benguela railway as the principal route for the shipment of copper, cobalt, and manganese exports.[131]

In Mozambique, South Africa conducted its destabilization efforts through its support, if not outright sponsorship and control, of the *Resistencia Nacional Mocambicana* (MNR). The MNR was composed originally of former African and European members of the Portuguese colonial army and secret police. It was later able to recruit defectors from FRELIMO's security agencies as well as take advantage of the growing political disaffection produced by Mozambique's economic disarray. By 1982, MNR had extended its military operations to seven of Mozambique's eleven provinces, and moved within the vicinity of the capital, Maputo, and the main port at Beira.[132] Available evidence indicated that a close liaison had developed between MNR and the South African military and intelligence services. Pretoria provided bases for MNR at Zvabostad in the Transvaal. The MNR radio station, *Voz da Africa livre*, began broadcasting into Mozambique in 1980 from a location in the northern Transvaal. South African military instructors inside Mozambique trained MNR cadres in weapons use, communications, and sabotage. South African forces supplied MNR guerrillas by sea and air.[133] The MNR guerrillas concentrated their destructive efforts on sabotaging rail and oil pipelines linking the port and harbour facilities at Beira to Umtali in Mozambique.[134]

From roughly mid-1980 to the end of 1981, Pretoria engaged in an apparently indiscriminate yet calculated campaign of economic and military destabilization against its neighbours. The persistent disruption of rail traffic, pipelines, and port facilities not only deprived Angola and Mozambique of vital foreign exchange earnings but also forced landlocked Zambia and Zimbabwe to divert their rail traffic through South Africa, thereby undermining SADCC's efforts to promote economic self-reliance.[135] In January 1981, an elite commando unit of the SADF assaulted ANC houses in the Matola suburb of Maputo, killing thirteen people and kidnapping three others. In October 1981, a South African SADF lieutenant was killed in an abortive effort to plant explosives on the rail line between Mozambique and Zimbabwe.[136] South African agents assassinated a number of key ANC operatives in neighbouring countries. A distinctive pattern had emerged. South African military strategists seemed to operate on the principle that any African state that actively supported the South African liberation movement was open to military reprisal.

Besides these acts of open aggression and sabotage, Pretoria also indulged in sanctions and other forms of subversion. South Africa's economic grip over SADCC member states gave Pretoria considerable economic leverage with which to wrest concessions from its recalcitrant neighbours. Zimbabwe in particular appeared to bear the brunt of these economic pressures, including the abrupt withdrawal of South African railroad locomotives at a time of record demand for transport services, mysterious delays and bottlenecks in the movement of vital commodities, and unpredictable price fluctuations.[137]

By 1982, Pretoria departed from its rather indeterminate destabilization campaign and instead embarked on a highly focused and selective course of action. This new strategy aimed at undermining its neighbours both economically and militarily. The principal mechanisms for realizing these refined strategic objectives were 'forward defense' and coercive economic leverage. South African military planners seem to have been motivated by two immediate goals. First, Pretoria energetically sought the cooperation of states in the region in containing ANC activities in their territories. In late 1983, Foreign Minister 'Pik' Botha emphatically underscored Pretoria's determination to establish new limits to what military strategists would tolerate: 'Out — they [the ANC] must get out. There is no compromise on this one.'[138] Second, Pretoria sought to ensure the maintenance of existing economic linkages and to frustrate the SADCC states' efforts to reduce their economic dependence upon South Africa. What distinguished this new phase of intensified destabilization from earlier campaigns was Pretoria's judicious mixture of economic incentives rewarding compliance and heavy-handed actions designed to punish those neighbouring states that refused to fall into line.

Swaziland became a principal target for Pretoria's largesse. Pretoria showered the conservative Swazi ruling caste with various economic 'incentives', including financial and technical assistance in building a railway line through Swazi territory linking the Eastern Transvaal with the port of Richards Bay (thereby bypassing Maputo), a huge cash settlement under the joint customs union agreement, and a controversial offer to cede the KaNgwane Homeland and part of KwaZulu to Swaziland. In exchange, the Swazi regime in February 1982 signed a secret Non-Aggression Pact with Pretoria, the terms of which were only acknowledged in public two years later. Both parties pledged in this agreement to individually and jointly combat and eliminate 'terrorism' and subversion in their respective territories. Almost immediately, the Swazi authorities complied with Pretoria's wishes, broadening restrictions on ANC activities there.[139]

The Swaziland case illustrated in a striking way how Pretoria was able to utilize economic incentives to strengthen reliance on South Africa. At the other extreme, Pretoria's destabilization programme assumed its most visible form in the accelerated campaign of military aggression that was justified under the rubric of 'forward defense'.

Throughout 1982 and 1983, Pretoria repeatedly launched high profile cross-border military assaults against Lesotho, Angola, and Mozambique on the grounds that these countries served as a 'springboard for terror against South Africa'.[140] Lesotho's dependence upon migrant labour earnings made it particularly vulnerable to pressure from Pretoria. In 1985, an estimated 150,000 Basuto nationals (including about 139,000 mine workers) were employed in South Africa. Their remittances — about 60 per cent of earnings — comprised over half the tiny mountainous kingdom's Gross National Product. In addition, the South African Customs Union contributed nearly 70 per cent of Lesotho's state revenues.[141] Erstwhile dissidents who called themselves the Lesotho Liberation Army escalated terrorist attacks, undermining the tourist trade and causing severe security problems. In December 1982, a South African Reconnaissance Commando conducted a large-scale night-time assault against suspected ANC offices and residences in which forty-three people were killed. General Viljoen, chief of staff of the SADF, described the raid as a 'pre-emptive strike aimed at forestalling attacks on South Africa during the festive season.'[142] In May 1983, South Africa unilaterally closed the border with Lesotho and threatened to repatriate Basuto migrant labourers working in South Africa. This pressure eventually took its toll. In August 1983, Prime Minister Leabua Jonathan announced that Lesotho would evacuate South African refugees through the appropriate United Nations Agencies.[143]

Despite repeated protestations of innocence, Pretoria was implicated in a bungled sabotage raid into southeastern Zimbabwe in 1982.[144] However, Angola and Mozambique were singled out for the harshest treatment. SADF conventional forces repeatedly invaded southern Angola, allegedly in 'hot pursuit' of SWAPO guerrillas. By the end of 1982, the SADF, in conjunction with its UNITA surrogates, had placed vast zones of southern Angola under virtual military occupation. South African regional goals and U.S. global policy converged around UNITA leader Jonas Savimbi. Despite his chameleonic ideological opportunism, Savimbi's staunch anti-communist rhetoric endeared him both to Pretoria and to Washington. The Reagan administration called him a 'freedom-fighter' and honoured him as a leader in its worldwide anti-Soviet crusade. Pretoria did not share Washington's high-sounding ideological pretensions. Savimbi was a convenient pawn in South Africa's long-term strategic objective of driving SWAPO guerrillas out of Namibian territory and establishing an internationally acceptable internal alternative to SWAPO. With the virtual collapse of the bogus internal settlement based on the Democratic Turnhalle Alliance in 1982, Pretoria once again stressed military options in its largely futile effort to destroy SWAPO influence and prestige. Simultaneously, Pretoria sought to punish Angola for the MPLA's principled support for the Namibian independence struggle. The programme of regular invasions and sabotage inflicted an estimated $10 billion in material damage between 1975 and 1982.[145]

In Mozambique, the escalation of MNR attacks that began at the end of 1981 resulted in an estimated $3.8 billion in damage over the next two years. Pretoria combined this covert war of economic sabotage with the crafty manipulation of economic 'disincentives', including a partial boycott of the Maputo port that reduced South African traffic in 1983 to only 16 per cent of the 1973 level. By undermining Mozambique's productive capacity and thoroughly disrupting FRELIMO development projects in the countryside, Pretoria reinforced its disingenuous propaganda offensive, alleging that Mozambique-style socialism was equivalent to economic chaos and material deprivation.[146]

By the end of 1983, Pretoria had established the precedent of employing military force and economic pressure to accomplish its political objectives. As Jenkins argued, this 'flexible and amoral application' of 'military and economic power' inflicted extensive material damage to Angola and Mozambique and aggravated the already tenuous political stability in the region. Pretoria had succeeded in 'throwing its weight' around the region but 'not yet ruling it'.[147] This reliance upon military aggression highlighted Pretoria's political incapacity to achieve its regional objectives through peaceful methods. The tendency to depend upon militaristic 'quick-fix' solutions produced immediate gains but threatened to undermine long-term strategic goals.[148]

On the international terrain, this chronic deployment of military force reinforced Pretoria's reputation for reckless adventurism. Under the doctrine of 'constructive engagement', the Reagan administration had encouraged Pretoria to temper its overtly aggressive posture and to seek *rapprochement* with its neighbours. At home, one visible expression of the deepening crisis was the expanding military budget. In 1960, South Africa's military expenditures had been estimated at $41 million. The 1983-4 South African budget provided for military expenditures of over $2.8 billion. In March 1983, Pretoria extended the call-up for all white males between seventeen and sixty-five. Under the new Defense Force Amendment Act, men were compelled to serve two years' active duty in the 'operational areas', after which they joined Citizen Force groups that were subject to one month of active duty per year for the next eight years.[149] The prolonged military occupation of Namibia with no apparent indications of a political solution created a seemingly permanent drain on the South African treasury.[150] The steadily rising casualty figures had begun to undermine the carefully-nurtured facade of patriotic duty and had engendered an inchoate domestic opposition to military conscription.

The Nkomati Accord: Pax Pretoriana?[151]

The combination of relentless South African destabilization efforts, a devastating drought followed by massive flooding, the world recession, and a certain degree of bureaucratic mis-management have left Mozambique economically crippled and politically vulnerable. In early 1984, Mozambique petitioned its creditors to renegotiate its debt, $4.5 billion of which was owed to Western lenders alone. In March 1984, President Samora Machel was compelled to capitulate to outside political pressure and to sue for peace. The Nkomati Accord on Non-Aggression and Good Neighbourliness, signed at a solemn border ceremony to a worldwide fanfare, formally bound South Africa and Mozambique in a mutual commitment to 'refrain from interfering in the internal affairs of the other.' In practice, however, this agreement meant that Mozambique pledged to restrict the activities of ANC members. In exchange, Pretoria promised to cease its covert support for MNR. Under the provisions of the Nkomati Accord, South Africa and Mozambique established a joint security commission with the aim of monitoring imple-mentation of the agreement. Mozambique judiciously upheld its side of the bargain by limiting the ANC presence to a small diplo-matic mission. In contrast, Pretoria took only minimal steps to check the activities of the MNR. In fact, the MNR escalated its reign of terror inside Mozambique in the post-Nkomati period.[152]

In December 1983, the SADF conducted yet another full-scale invasion of Angolan territory. What distinguished this 'Operation Askari' from previous incursions was that the high level of joint Angolan/SWAPO resistance and the large number of reported South African casualties shocked the white South African public. For the first time, the pro-regime Afrikaans press hesitatingly called for South African withdrawl from Namibia, arguing that the costs were becoming prohibitive.[153] In February 1984, Pretoria signed the Lusaka agreement with Angola through which both sides agreed to supervise the SADF departure from southern Angola.

Pretoria regarded this string of Non-Aggression Pacts — including the secret treaty concluded with Swaziland two years earlier — as unassailable confirmation of the success of the 'carrot-and-stick' approach to regional conflicts. The Nkomati Accord represented the capstone of Pretoria's regional destabilization efforts. The Botha regime had realized its ambition of binding into its prostrated neighbours agreements in which South Africa retained the upper hand. Pretoria christened this crude exercise in coercive diplomacy the 'peace process'.[154]

The Botha regime envisaged these Non-Aggression Pacts as not only enhancing South Africa's international prestige as a 'peace-maker' but also creating a window of opportunity to re-activate the dormant 'Constellation of States' initiative.[155] At the same time, Pretoria increased its pressure on Botswana and Lesotho in order to ensure their political acquiescence. Needless to say, the temporary suspension of the 'military option' and the ostensible thaw in regional political relations caused a consider-able stir among the outward-looking sectors of South African capital. In a conscious effort to gain their political support, P.W. Botha had invited a number of leading South African capitalists to the formal Nkomati ceremonies. In March 1984, the Chief Executive of the South African Associated Chambers of Com-merce (ASSOCOM) proclaimed optimistically: 'Most businessmen today — in the aftermath of the Nkomati Accord with Mozambique, new arrangements with Swaziland, conciliatory remarks by President Kaunda of Zambia, and peace moves in South West Africa [Namibia] — stand closer to the Prime Minister's goal [of a 'Constellation of States'] than ever before. Businessmen have an enormous stake in the success or other-wise of recent developments in southern Africa, especially in Mozambique.'[156] Similarly, the *Financial Mail* — the organ of large-scale business in South Africa — predicted that strengthened trade links between South Africa and Mozambique would result in the 'inevitable' dissipation of SADCC's 'fragile economic initiative'. 'For instance, Mozambique was to have played a key role in the coordination of transport in the SADCC region. It is a role that South Africa is much better placed to ful-fill more efficiently. Closer trade ties between South Africa and Mozambique must lead to recognition of that fact.'[157] The *Financial Mail* also explicitly advocated the creation of an enlarged South African-dominated rand monetary zone embracing all SADCC members except Angola and Tanzania in order to 'give these countries the access to capital markets that their poverty denies them'.[158]

The Nkomati Accord thus triggered renewed business optimism. In the first four years of its existence, SADCC had demonstrated modest yet steady progress toward achieving its long-term objectives. Mozambique was the weakest link in the SADCC chain. South African business leaders reasoned that if they could entice Mozambique to accept a 'trade-not-aid' formula under South African tutelage they could take a giant step toward their long-desired goal of gaining access to the potentially lucrative regional market.[159]

The Nkomati Accord was the crowning achievement of Pretoria's destabilization campaign. It served as a stepping-stone from which to mount a diplomatic and economic offensive against Botswana and Lesotho in order to pressure these countries to acknowledge South Africa's hegemony as the 'dominant power' on the subcontinent.[160] This pressure culminated in the SADF incursion into Botswana's capital, Gaborone, in June 1985, and the three-week economic blockade of Lesotho in January 1986.[161] The latter resulted in a military coup that deposed Prime Minister Leabua Jonathan and replaced him with a military council. Almost immediately, the military council ordered ANC supporters airlifted out of the country. Within a week of Jonathan's overthrow, P.W. Botha announced that South Africa and Lesotho had struck a deal that was similar in content — although not nearly so formal — as Pretoria's non-aggression pact with Mozambique.[162] The paradox was that while Pretoria had reached beyond its borders to deny sanctuary to ANC exiles (and to sever supply and infiltration routes), the popularity and influence of the ANC inside South Africa had grown tremendously.[163]

2.

The White Minority Regime and the Politics of Co-optation

The schism in 1982 South Africa's ruling National Party delivered a *coup de grace* to the legend of the Afrikaner monolith.[1] This conventional portrayal of white South African politics as a bitter contest between (modern, urban, liberal) English-speakers and (traditional, rural, conservative) Afrikaans-speakers did not collapse at once, but unravelled in stages. The split of the *Herstigte Nasionale* Party (the 'Reconstructed' or 'Purified' National Party — the HNP) in 1969 was the opening round in a sequence of events that eventually shattered the traditional image of ethnic mobilization as the basis for the white South African party system. The immediate provocation that led a dissident group of far-right-wing National Party Cabinet Ministers to establish the HNP was the relaxation of regulations governing racially segregated sports facilities. Although the National Party survived this rupture virtually unscathed, it was a prophetic warning of a deepening rift within the once solid edifice of Afrikanerdom. In 1978, the Information Department scandal helped to propel P.W. Botha into office. As we outlined in the previous chapter, under Botha's leadership, the National Party proposed 'reforms' aimed not only at broadening the Party's popular appeal but at bringing its policies more firmly into line with a 'free enterprise' ideology.

The Botha administration introduced a new social contract designed both to mask and to reinforce continued white minority rule. The centrepiece of this new dispensation was contained in the new constitutional proposals advocating the inclusion of Indians and 'coloured' people in a single Parliamentary body (albeit with separate voters' rolls and separate chambers for white, coloured, and Indian representation). The particularly acrimonious debate in regional National Party caucuses over the implementation of these constitutional arrangements precipitated a bitter split in the Party's ranks. Former Transvaal National Party leader, Andries Treurnicht, led the walkout that resulted in the formation of the Conservation Party (CP) later that same year.

In the face of this erosion of the legend of an impenetrable *volk*, most observers rejected the culturalist idiom of ethnic mobilization, substituting in its place an ideological emphasis on divergent world-views. In this new scheme, ruptures within Afrikanerdom could be attributed to differences in outlook between *verligte* ('enlightened') and *verkrampte* ('narrow') Afrikaners.[2] Both the culturalist and ideological motifs were useful hueristic devices for describing permutations within the framework of white South African politics. Nevertheless, they were unable to explain either the origins or the significance of National Party splits.[3]

The proximate cause for the 1982 split can be attributed to serious disagreements between the *verligte* and the *verkrampte* factions over the multiple crises confronting the white minority regime. The group around Botha proposed a remedy that included the twin strategies of containment and adaptation. This *verligte* formula was premised on two central propositions: first, the rigid application of *apartheid* practice and ideology had become outdated and outmoded; second, it was necessary to make substantial adjustments to restore business confidence and profitability, and to offer significant concessions to channel black political and economic aspirations in a manageable direction. In contrast, the *verkrampte* group reacted instinctively to the perceived threat to both the white monopoly over political power and the social order sheltering the privileged white minority. In the *verkrampte* view, any reformist political strategy that involved compromise and negotiation with the black majority would inevitably open a Pandora's Box of utopian dreams leading inexorably to a cycle of increased violence and repression.

The underlying cause for the shifting focus in white politics can be traced to the class transformation of South Africa and the class realignment of the white political parties. The National Party had evolved into a political vehicle that increasingly expressed the political vision of an emergent Afrikaner bourgeoisie. Gradually abandoning the specific alliance of class forces that supported its entry into political power in 1948, the National Party leadership sought a *modus vivendi* with English-speaking professional and propertied classes and tentatively sought the political allegiance of a carefully-nurtured black petty bourgeois stratum in the Homelands and urban townships.

This new constellation of class forces that came to dominate the National Party furnished a revitalized social formula designed to restore economic prosperity through market-propelled growth. The National Party's reformist strategy revolved around economic liberalization, the abrogation of certain racially discriminatory practices, and the introduction of experimental forms of political representation that fell considerably short of the popular demand for 'one-person, one-vote'. The Afrikaner bourgeoisie shared with its English-speaking counterparts a common interest in the efficient and rational exploitation of black labour. Yet the economic well-being of the Afrikaner bourgeoisie and its petty bourgeois political allies depended in large measure upon extensive state regulation, subsidies and patronage, thereby ruling out any wholesale elimination of the core structures of *apartheid* rule.[4]

The Propertied Classes and the Preservation of White Supremacy

The Dominant Classes and Party Realignment

The class alliance that propelled the National Party to its electoral triumph in 1948 gradually disintegrated. The political centre of gravity within the National Party shifted away from its original popular base amongst Afrikaans-speaking wage-earners and small farmers toward the propertied classes. The impulse behind this class realignment of the National Party was, in O'Meara's words, 'the emergence of a class of aggressive, self-confident Afrikaner capitalists, whose interests went beyond those of the narrow class alliance out of which they emerged.'[5] The accession of P.W. Botha to the office of Prime Minister in

1978 confirmed the ascendancy of the Afrikaner bourgeoisie at the summit of the National Party.[6]

A long-time Party bureaucrat from the Cape Province, P.W. Botha served as National Party MP from George, Deputy Minister of Interior (under H.F. Verwoerd), Minister of Community Development and of Coloured Affairs, Leader of the National Party in the Cape Province, and — for fourteen years — Minister of Defense. As Minister of Defense, Botha was instrumental in promoting South African self-sufficiency in arms production. This task was largely accomplished through the establishment of the Armaments Development Corporation (ARMSCOR) as a statutory body.[7] Botha personified South Africa's 'new men of power' — Afrikaner technocrats and academics who were not only *apartheid*'s social engineers but also the organic intellectuals of the emergent Afrikaner bourgeoisie.

The Botha regime inherited a political situation nearing the point of crisis. The severe repression that followed the 1976-7 Soweto rebellion had failed to dampen black political aspirations and had only succeeded in extinguishing the most overt forms of popular protest. Business efforts to unload the growing burden of sluggish growth rates — and the deepest recession in modern South African history — onto the increasingly restive black working class resulted in increased unemployment, higher inflation, and greater social misery.[8] The collapse of the colonial regimes in Angola and Mozambique in tandem with heightened guerrilla insurgency in Namibia and Rhodesia/Zimbabwe deprived South Africa of the friendly 'buffer states' that had insulated it from external military threat. The indiscriminate use of military force to quell popular opposition to the white minority regime had galvanized world public opinion against at least the most abhorrent and despicable symbols of *apartheid*. Waning global business confidence in the future political stability of the country discouraged overseas investments and promoted capital flight.

Confronted with what it defined as a 'total onslaught' both at home and abroad, the Botha regime countered with the Total Strategy doctrine to meet what was regarded as an unprecedented challenge to South Africa's survival. The National Party fashioned a comprehensive, integrated, and coordinated programme combining concessions designed to broaden popular support for the white minority regime with an aggressive military posture aimed at neutralizing opposition both at home and abroad. P.W. Botha's phrase 'adapt or die' evoked the survivalist mentality implicit in this approach.

The modified class complexion of the National Party trapped its leadership in a new web of contradictions. The National Party sought ways to cloak its narrow bourgeois class outlook within the broader framework of the 'general interest'. On the one hand, Afrikaans-speaking wage-earners remained the single largest constituency within the National Party's electoral bloc. The National Party sought to retain its carefully nurtured image as the penultimate Afrikaner ethnic party, the self-proclaimed defender of the *volk*. In order to prevent electoral slippage to the ultra-right-wing parties, the National Party maintained its traditional reliance on the manipulation of culturalist symbols interspersed with vague promises never to abandon the 'white community'. Without a broad popular appeal to the white electorate, the National Party feared that it would lose its parliamentary majority.

On the other hand, the overarching ideological themes that surfaced in the early years of the Botha regime coalesced around the pursuit of economic growth within the framework of a dynamic capitalism.[9] National Party ideologues increasingly extolled the virtues and advantages of free enterprise, proclaiming that the maintenance of white privilege was not incompatible with a less restricted labour market and expanded opportunities for black entrepreneurship. In Giliomee's words, 'In the Botha administration ... a strong tendency has developed ... to present the whites as a modernizing elite and to portray economic growth, training, job creation, food production, and above all political stability, which is seen as making all these things possible, as sufficient justification for National Party rule.'[10] Consequently, Party ideologues abruptly distanced themselves from overtly racialist themes. Instead of the Verwoerdian dicta — 'better poor and white than rich and mixed' — in vogue just a few years earlier, the National Party leadership substituted the idiom of technological rationality and market efficiency. In promoting these new technocratic and neo-liberal forms of legitimation for white minority rule, the National Party sought not only to synthesize and reconcile increasingly antagonistic interests within its own traditional historic bloc of class forces but also to broaden its appeal to the propertied and professionalized English-speaking electorate.

In 1979, the National Party unveiled its putatively reformist initiative, aimed at achieving the acquiescence of the oppressed black masses at home and support for the white minority regime abroad.[11] These prescriptions for economic recovery and political containment were deliberately ambiguous in order not to alienate its historic constituencies and to avoid commitments that could not be kept. The National Party leadership attempted to play both ends of the political spectrum against the middle. It is important to remember that the white electorate has never been a monolithic bloc. White voting blocs have been motivated, *inter alia*, by the desire for economic security and self-fulfillment. Prosperity depended in varying degrees upon the direct (and indirect) exploitation of black labour. The enormous power of South African monopoly capital has been buttressed by a field of propertied interests radiating in a series of concentric circles throughout the white electorate. The National Party sought to hold the political centre by projecting itself as the 'realist' alternative to the splinter far-right white supremacist parties, on the one hand, and the stalwart defender of minority rights (white privilege) against the 'accommodationist' and 'capitulationist' Progressive Federal Party, on the other.

For the National Party, the most significant policy modifications took place in the arena of labour and industrial relations. After the 1972-3 strike wave, monopoly capitalist business interests became increasingly vocal in their criticism of *apartheid* labour policies. In South Africa, the tightly-knit business associations traditionally have wielded considerable political influence. One by one, these powerful groups complained about existing impediments to economic growth, skilled labour shortages, labour 'unruliness', and so forth. As an alternative, they called for the relaxation of *apartheid* practices that restricted the cumulative spending power of black consumers and black skill 'upgrading'. Business leaders periodically made dire predictions that economic growth would continue to be severely hampered without drastic modifications in regulations restricting labour mobility and in the management of industrial relations.[12]

The National Party took tentative yet clear steps in the direction of satisfying employers' demands. Following recommendations presented in the 1979 Wiehahn Commission report, the Botha regime introduced legislation to relax statutory job reservation, to open apprenticeships to African workers, to offer large tax concessions to companies for 'in-service' occupational training for black workers, and to register independent black trade unions operating *de facto* outside the formal industrial conciliation mechanisms. At the same time, the National Party announced its intention to overhaul and streamline the pass laws. In particular, scrapping the pass laws depended upon the revision of the Natives (Urban Areas) Amendment Act of 1955, specifying that only Africans who had resided since birth in an urban area, or had worked continuously in the area for at least ten years, were legally permitted to remain there for longer than seventy-two hours. All other Africans required authorization to venture into urban townships, and were thus at the mercy of labour bureaux that controlled the so-called 'influx' of black labour to the cities. The 1979 Riekert Commission recommended that the legal right of a minority of Africans to reside in urban areas — the so-called Section 10 rights — ought to be retained and that influx control ought to be pegged specifically to availability of employment and accommodation.[13] The National Party voiced its approval of these proposals to loosen restrictions on labour mobility in the urban areas yet guarantee 'orderly urbanization'.

In essence, the Botha regime intended this reformist offensive to accomplish five separate objectives:

(1) To remove barriers to the social mobility of the emergent black petty bourgeoisie by offering new opportunities for entrepreneurship and educational attainment at the 'white' universities;

(2) To incorporate a layer of skilled black workers into a 'labour aristocracy' by offering a number of previously novel concessions, including permanent leasehold and home ownership schemes, relaxation of restrictions on occupational mobility and geographical mobility, and a modicum of self-governance in the urban townships;

(3) To mobilize resources to upgrade the socio-economic conditions of permanently settled urban black residents, while simultaneously tightening influx controls in order to seal off the urban townships and divert job-seekers into the burgeoning dormitory towns, located nominally in the Homelands but within commuting distance of employment in 'white South Africa';

(4) To entice a significant minority of so-called Coloureds and

Indians into central political apparatuses, albeit as junior partners;

(5) To eliminate those racially-discriminatory clauses in the existing *apartheid* legislation that attracted opprobrium abroad but made little or no difference with respect to ensuring white privilege.

Cultivating this novel image of enlightened reformers, the National Party hierarchy pranced and high-stepped through the motions of its crusade. In a purely symbolic gesture designed to offer the illusion of 'goodwill', P.W. Botha himself became the first South African Prime Minister to visit Soweto, where he conferred with selected black petty bourgeois dignitaries and 'influentials'. The white minority regime welcomed black entertainers and sports celebrities to perform in South Africa before racially-mixed audiences. In addition, the Botha regime announced with great fanfare that many public facilities would no longer be segregated and that many business establishments (for example, theatres, restaurants and shops) were 'free to choose' whether they wished to remain segregated or not. With evangelical zeal, the National Party announced its intention to scrap the infamous Immorality and Mixed Marriages Act — a litmus-test of far-right fanaticism. Knowledgeable observers rightly condemned these modifications in petty *apartheid* as superficial and cosmetic, a charade of smoke and mirrors designed to reinforce the core features of *apartheid* with a much-needed 'facelift'.[14]

From the point of view of the private sector, the rigid application of *apartheid* had always involved unnecessary state intervention in the form of restrictive labour legislation, job reservation covenants with white unions, pricing mechanisms that sheltered high-cost farmers from the vagaries of the market, and a bloated bureaucracy that drained the national treasury. The net result was that excessive state involvement stifled private initiative and unduly constrained production, profits, and access to an enormously expanding black market.[15] Leading Afrikaner businessmen originally endorsed the idea of a *modus vivendi* between the National Party and private enterprise. In 1977, Andreas Wassenaar, a pillar of the Afrikaner establishment and chairman of the Cape-based SANLAM conglomerate, scandalized the National Party hierarchy when he assailed what he regarded as an inexorable drift toward state capitalism. Wassenaar ridiculed National Party economic policies, attributing South

Africa's deepening 'national crisis' to government 'overspending' and denouncing the hypertrophic growth of the state bureaucracy. In his words, 'Economic history in the Republic of South Africa has produced an officialdom — including a bureaucracy which is extremely Afrikaner-oriented — which is extremely lukewarm if not antagonistic in its attitude towards private enterprise and certainly vehemently opposed to the profit motive to a degree which, in the long run, threatens the future of capitalism.'[16] Proclaiming that existing economic programmes were tantamount to a 'freeway to communism', Wassenaar instead advocated a coalition regime linking the National Party with private enterprise along the lines of the 'Brazilian model' where the military junta appointed cabinet members from the private sector and fostered joint state and private corporate ventures.[17]

The 1979 Carlton Centre Conference symbolized the high-water mark of the reformist offensive. Prime Minister Botha gathered together an estimated 150 leading English and Afrikaans-speaking businessmen — along with his entire cabinet entourage — for intense discussions covering a complex range of social and political issues. In his view, the aim of this new part-nership was to plan 'a national strategy for South Africa, voluntarily, as a team'.[18] The outcome of this unprecedented assembly was a broad consensus that impersonal market forces rather than racial legislation represented a firmer basis for the preservation of white privilege and wealth.

The *Financial Mail* referred to the Carlton Conference as P.W. Botha's 'most spectacular coup since reaching the premiership'.[19] Even Harry Oppenheimer, chair of Anglo-American Corporation and a political supporter of the Progressive Federal Party (PFP), cautiously championed this summit as opening a 'new era' in relations between business and the National Party.[20]

The National Party thus launched a pro-business crusade, espousing the values of the 'free market' with its confident fore-casts of wholesome economic growth and expanded prosperity. This wholehearted embrace of the ethos of free enterprise thus brought the National Party full circle from its inauspicious origins. It had abandoned the idiom of 'Hoggenheimer' — the capitalist caricature that symbolized the sworn enemy of Afrikanerdom — in favour of its newly-discovered capitalist creed.

P.W. Botha's reformist initiative met unexpectedly strong resistance within all the major Afrikaner organs of political power, including the civil service, the churches, and the Broederbond.[21] The farming, mining, and blue-collar constituencies — the 'little men' so often exalted in traditional Afrikaner lore and nationalist mythology — reacted to the National Party's ideological *volte face* by swinging their electoral support to the right. In the 1979 by-elections, the far-right-wing HNP scored impressive gains in traditional National Party farming and mining seats. In the 1981 general election, the National Party retained its huge parliamentary majority. However, the voting revealed a substantial reduction in National Party electoral support as its share of the vote slipped from 66 per cent in 1977 to 58 per cent. The HNP and other right-wing parties improved their share from 2 per cent to 15 per cent nationwide, gathering over 200,000 votes.

These voting results demonstrated that the ethnic alignments which dominated white South African electoral behavior in the post-1948 era had largely disintegrated. Class and status tensions had certainly cut deeply across the customary ethnic alliances. The National Party's timid steps toward reform — along with ambiguous hints of greater modifications in the future — produced a recognizable backlash from those electoral constituencies whose fragile prosperity depended upon the shelter of *apartheid*. The customary image of all Afikaners closing ranks behind the National Party evaporated. In 1981, an estimated 38 per cent of Afrikaner voters did not select the National Party. For the most part, the National Party retained its seats in the Natal countryside and in the large cities. However, the vote swung heavily toward the HNP in those districts with large concentrations of white farmers, dwindling ranks of blue-collar workers, and civil servants. Charney offered an explanation why these groups abandoned the National Party: 'A freer labour market and better black training would erode the inflated wages of the white labour aristocracy. Many wage-earning whites see real wages falling already as inflation sprints ahead and employers hold back on their increases to push up blacks' breadline wages. Over the period 1976-1979, real white wages fell on average by 9.7 per cent, while black wages rose 9.8 per cent (from a drastically lower base). Small farmers, threatened with being driven off the land, are worried about low maize price increases and government policies which increasingly favour big farmers. Farm incomes generally have not done too well in recent years, with the biggest losses sustained by the small farmers. All these groups are bound together by the rigid racism often found in those directly in the path of black advance.'[22]

Correlatively, electoral results also suggested that the political attitudes of well-to-do Afrikaans-speakers and English-speakers tended to converge. The number of Afrikaners working the land or in blue-collar occupations declined dramatically, from 71 per cent in 1946 to about 35 per cent in 1977.[23] Lower-ranking civil servants small farmers, and semi- and unskilled white wage-earners have depended in large measure on *apartheid* for their privileged socio-economic status. In contrast, the emergent Afrikaner middle class — whether self-employed or salaried — has been less dependent on artificial regulation of labour markets for its livelihood and continued well-being. Affluent Afrikaners have increasingly acquired a stake in the capitalist system. Consequently, they have tended to adopt more 'middle-class' outlooks, which led them to seek some sort of racial accommodation within the parameters of private property relations in order to forestall capitalism's violent overthrow.[24] On the other side of the political equation, the National Party increasingly relied on English-speaking voters, one-third of whom had consistently voted in its favour since 1977.

In 1982, the accumulation of tensions inside the National Party reached the boiling point. Twenty-three members of Parliament — led by the Transvaal Leader of the National Party Andries Treurnicht — staged a dramatic walkout from the party caucus. Within a month, this coterie of hard-line Afrikaner nationalists formed the Conservative Party. This split affected the National Party even more severely at lower levels. Taking their cue from higher ranking Party officials, fully one quarter of National Party district and branch committee members in the Transvaal hastily joined the Conservative Party.[25]

The electoral achievements of the HNP severely undercut its 'image as an oddball collection of ageing racists cranks'.[26] The HNP's new popularity reflected the growing disenchantment amongst blue-collar Afrikaners with the National Party's unwillingness to defend job reservation and its concession of trade union rights to African workers, as well as the economic discontent resulting from steadily rising inflation and a continued recession.[27] The National Party leadership, however, had greater reason to fear the electoral encroachment of the Conservative Party. The Conservative Party solicited support from those constituencies — small farmers, wage-earners, the civil service — that had historically constituted the mainspring of the National Party's appeal and the *raison d'etre* of Afrikaner nationalism.

Botha's decision to proceed with the new constitutional proposals providing a modicum of political representation for Indian and 'coloured' people triggered the National Party split. The original 1977 constitutional proposals had proposed an unwieldy formula of separate Parliaments for whites, coloureds, and Indians. In the 1982 National Party caucus, P.W. Botha unveiled an alternative plan, abandoning the earlier division of power between the 'races' and endorsing instead what was referred to as 'healthy power-sharing'. This new plan entailed the formation of a single Parliamentary body, albeit with separate chambers. Needless to say, the newly-formed Conservative Party and HNP balked at any remedy that even suggested a devolution of political power away from the white minority regime.

Party Realignment and the Changing Balance of Class Forces

Party realignment coalesced along regional lines. The 'Transvaal-versus-Cape' and 'town-versus-country' rivalries embedded within South African politics reflected deeper class divisions. Since the 1950s, the absolute numbers of white farmers have dwindled and the *platteland* has undergone a demographic shift as a disproportionate share of white rural dwellers have trekked to the cities and larger towns. South Africa's white farmers — mostly Afrikaners — tended historically to divide both by scale of enterprise (wealthy versus marginal operations) and market destination (domestic versus export).[28] The Botha regime implemented an agricultural policy that favoured large-scale agri-business over the traditional family farming operations, industrial undertakings over farming, and Cape and Natal exporters (for example, fruit, wine, and sugar) over the Transvaal and Orange Free State domestic producers (for example, grains and beef). In general, small and relatively marginal farming operations historically have depended upon labour-repressive policies in order to secure plentiful supplies of cheap black farm labour. Fearing relaxation of state labour policies and the abrogation of price supports, farmers — particularly in the Transvaal, northern Orange Free State, and northeast Cape — swung their political allegiance to the right-wing political parties. In contrast, the National Party retained the loyalty of the agricultural bourgeoisie and the export-oriented farmers of the Cape, Natal, and southern Orange Free State. The South African Agricultural Union (SAAU) — the voice of large-scale capitalist farming — remained staunchly pro-National Party. In particular, the western Cape wine growers received exceptionally favourable treatment under the Botha regime and sided with the *verligte* wing of the National Party. In 1983, twelve Cape National Party MPs were wine growers. Anton Rupert's Rembrandt group (South Africa's major spirits producer) historically has been the second strongest business influence — following the SANLAM group — on the Cape wing of the National Party.[29]

The Conservative Party attracted a growing political following from various categories of beleaguered white wage-earners in the civil service and the mining manufacturing sectors. Blue-collar residential communities, stretching from Boksburg to Krugersdorp along the Reef, suffered the effects of the economic recession. Many blamed the National Party, accusing its leadership of 'selling out the white race'. The notoriously die-hard Afrikaner nationalist Mine Workers Union (MWU) spearheaded the right-wing drive to unite all white wage-earners into a single white supremacist trade union.[30]

The ferment underlying this process of party realignment was a gradual shift in the social weight of class forces within Afrikanerdom. The expanding grip of the Afrikaner bourgeoisie within the National Party translated into an informal compact with large-scale capital but did not imply enhanced collaboration with the Progressive Federal Party (PFP). In the main, the PFP drew its political support largely from propertied, affluent, urban English-speaking constituencies in the Transvaal and the Cape. Despite its more than twenty Parliamentary seats (reflecting about 20 per cent of the white vote) and the status of official opposition, the PFP was hampered with a severely limited social base that was unlikely ever to expand beyond forty to fifty seats in Parliament.

The PFP underwent ideological metamorphosis over the course

of the 1960s and 1970s. Originally committed to the customary principles of South African liberalism (for example), a common voters' roll and gradual enfranchisement), the PFP gravitated toward a confederational and welfare-oriented 'social democracy' set firmly within the framework of monopoly capitalism.[31] Party leaders envisaged a decentralized structure of self-governing communities, in which membership would be strictly voluntary and hence not necessarily racially defined.[32] Despite the purposely vague nature of the Party's proposals, it was evident that the PFP endorsed a political and economic framework broad enough to accommodate some form of proportional representation and consensual, 'power-sharing' at the highest level of government, yet stopped far short of advocating straightforward majority rule in a unified South Africa by means of a common voters' roll.

In a nutshell, the paramount difference between the PFP project and the *verligte* Nationalist reform initiative centred on the question of formal political representation. The National Party insisted on retaining white dominance of all branches of the capitalist state apparatuses. The debate over the constitutional proposals reflected the divergent ideological positions. Despite the wider franchise incorporating the 'coloured' and Indian electorate, the National Party constitutional modifications gave the executive branch wide discretionary powers that were not subject to Parliamentary approval. The National Party's exclusion of the African majority from Parliamentary representation was integrally linked to its unwavering commitment to independent Homelands and to the white power of veto.

The philosophical premises that separated the PFP liberals from the *verligte* Nationalists were illustrated in the controversy over 'group rights' and 'individual rights'. While the lexicon denoting the conflict has varied, the National Party has always stressed that racial (or ethnic) groups were endowed with common rights expressing a more or less primordial 'group identity'. By substituting ethnic nomenclature for strictly racial categories, National Party ideologues tried rather clumsily to obscure their insistence on the use of ascriptive factors — rather than the meritocratic criteria generally employed by bourgeois-democratic regimes — in the determination of social policy.[33]

Ironically, the defection of influential *verkrampte* politicians from the National Party freed the *verligte* leadership to pursue economic policies more in line with the perceived interests of the propertied classes. The world view of the emergent Afrikaner bourgeoisie overlapped considerably with the class perspective of their English-speaking counterparts, particularly with regard to economic liberalization and modifications in petty *apartheid*. Leading *verligte* ideologue Jan Lombard declared: 'South Africa must "normalize" the character of its socio-economic regime in terms of the concepts used in the great debate between the forces of individual liberty, on the one hand, and communism, on the other hand. ... If ... the maintenance of order required discriminatory provisions in our legal system, these provisions must be defined in terms of other characteristics directly correlated to the maintenance of order. To declare or imply that racial differences as such are, in themselves, a threat to political order and socio-economic stability is simply no longer accepted.'[34]

The PFP proclaimed that the only way to avert a violent upheaval — and a potential 'race war' — was the incremental dismantling of *apartheid*. In this sense, the PFP fashioned itself as a pragmatic 'power broker' bisecting the ideological extremes of left and right. It has always been closely associated with large-scale business interests, particularly the Anglo-American Corporation. PFP leaders favoured the orderly transfer of political power to aspiring bourgeois sectors (regardless of racial group) and the incorporation of the popular masses into an elaborate federal system fitted with checks and balances to prevent a 'winner-take-all' outcome.

Despite deepening fissures in the historic Afrikaner alliance, the National Party remained a multi-class coalition expressing the political aspirations of widely divergent constituencies. What distinguished the party, however, was its preferential access to state-generated privileges. Afrikaner capital blossomed under the protective umbrella of state protectionism. Top-level Afrikaner managers of the parastatal corporations and high-ranking civil servants owed their influential positions to over thirty years of National Party rule. The swollen civil service — employing about half of South Africa's white wage-earners — had long been identified with Afrikaner nationalism because of its transformation after 1948 into a vast shelter for the employment of blue-collar Afrikaans-speakers. State employment had come to resemble a gigantic 'jobs trust' because of the *de facto* if not *de jure* 'colour bars' and job reservation mechanisms.[35] The

National Party thus commanded vast patronage powers, which the current party leadership manipulated to ensure the political loyalty of senior personnel in the state administration, the parastatal corporations, and the military.[36] In general, despite their rhetorical homage to free enterprise, Afrikaner business enterprises remained relatively dependent upon state subsidies and protection. Lastly, the agrarian bourgeoisie relied historically upon farm pricing, marketing, and credit policies. In short, despite proclamations of the National Party leadership that reform was 'an ongoing process', the dominant bloc set definite limits to both the character and the extent of modifications in the form of the capitalist state.[37] Even though the National Party did not enjoy unrivalled hegemony, it remained the principal arbiter within the white minority regime and the main political vehicle for ensuring white privilege. In Jan Lombard's words, 'the replacement of colour discrimination by classical norms of competition and democracy in the production and distribution of goods and services, both in the private and the public sector, does not automatically imply the subjugation of the sovereignty of the state to the whims of simple majorities in the total population. ... Under present circumstances, that would be tantamount to the destruction of all freedom in southern Africa.'[38] This manifesto expressed both the historic limits and potentialities of the National Party's reformist initiative.

The Evolution of Apartheid Ideology and Practice

Apartheid and Capitalism

Apartheid is a portmanteau concept that has been subjected to a bewildering variety of interpretations. The ideology of *apartheid* has often been seen as a precise and sinister blueprint for the complete separation in economic, political, and cultural spheres of distinctive racial groups. In particular, liberal critics have nurtured the wholly inadequate view that the abhorrent features of *apartheid* can be attributed solely to the triumph of the rigid, reactionary, and racialist ideals of a monolithic and intransigent Afrikanerdom over the modernizing and integrative effects of economic growth. In the liberal view, Afrikaners were at once tantalized by an atavistic vision of preserving the identity of an embattled 'white tribe' and motivated by misguided illusions of racial superiority.[39]

The liberal conventional wisdom thus placed *apartheid* within distinctive ideological parameters while simultaneously ignoring its deeper roots in South Africa's past and its symbiotic relationship with capitalism. Liberal orthodoxy laid considerable stress on racial discrimination, in turn viewed not only as an affront to 'human rights' but also as hindering a process of economic modernization capable of extending material benefits to all groups.[40] This liberal belief that the natural impulses of market-led 'progress' would eventually undermine the state's racial policies has been demonstrated to be utterly fallacious and need not detain us here.[41] Suffice it to say that the relationship between capital accumulation, state labour policies, and the core structure of white supremacy has been essentially collaborative and complementary. Political and ideological conflicts have emerged, yet these have been internal conflicts over the marginal distribution of class benefits and disagreements over the forms of domination through which bourgeois rule can be secured. In O'Meara's words, 'racial policy is an historical product ... designed primarily to facilitate rapid capital accumulation, and has been historically used by all classes with access to state power in South Africa. ... Racial policy is open to a sequence of somersaults, deviations, and permutations which endlessly confuse those who regard it as the product of a monolithic racial ideology.'[42]

The National Party in practice has exercised a great deal of pragmatism and flexibility in the implementation of *apartheid* policies. In short, *apartheid* ideology has never squared with *apartheid* reality, if by the former we mean the official racial policies of state functionaries and by the latter we refer to the racial policies actually pursued and implemented. The putative aim of *apartheid* ideology has focused on the increasing and eventual total segregation and separate development of South Africa's distinctive racial groups. However, 'the true rationale of *apartheid* policies', in Johnstone's words, 'is thus to maximize economic development both for the sake of white prosperity and for the material protection of white supremacy.'[43]

Contrary to certain received notions, the white minority regime has been comprised of quite diverse interests and constituencies. What cemented this multi-class alliance on the political terrain was its commitment to the preservation of white power and privilege at the expense of the black majority. Four interrelated and overlapping projects — the Bantustans/ independent Homelands, forced resettlement, influx controls, and industrial decentralization — constitute the main pillars that have sustained *apartheid* rule. These will be summarized in turn.

Historical Evolution of the Independent Homelands Policy

One central feature of *apartheid* strategy has been the implementation of regional and national spatial planning. *Apartheid* has entailed the artificial dissection of the Republic of South Africa into ten self-governing (or independent) Homelands. These territories were set aside as political entities where South Africa's African majority could fulfill their political aspirations and exercise the political rights denied them in 'white South Africa'.[44] The Homelands comprise about 13 per cent of the land mass of South Africa and in the main consist of scattered and noncontiguous strips of land varying considerably in size. For the most part, the Homelands fragments form a discontinous horseshoe pattern extending from the southeastern Cape Province to the northern Transvaal, including small sections of the Orange Free State and the northeastern zone of Natal. The geographical location of these Homelands reflect the historical legacy of European conquest and subsequent annexation during the eighteenth and nineteenth centuries.[45] The division of the African people into ten discreet 'tribal' groups in tandem with the spatial fragmentation of the Homeland territories themselves not only represented a blatant distortion of historical fact but was also an integral element in the strategy of divide and rule.[46]

Despite worldwide incredulity, the white minority regime persisted in the National Party's objective of transforming the ten Bantustans into independent Homelands. *Apartheid* ideologues proclaimed that the creation of these independent Homelands signified, in Geldenhuys's phrase, 'the highest stage of separate development'.[47] The flip-side of this putative 'nation-building' charade was that millions of Africans were stripped of whatever meagre birthright they enjoyed in 'white South Africa', along with any future claims to common citizenship in the Republic of South Africa.

In unilaterally proclaiming national independence for the Transkei (1976), Bophuthatswana (1977), Venda (1979), and Ciskei (1981), the white minority regime officially deprived nearly eight million Africans of their South African nationality.[48] Under the provisions of the 1970 Bantu Homelands Citizenship Act, Africans with genetic, cultural, linguistic, or residential links to a particular Bantustan were automatically deprived of South African citizenship on the day that specific entity was declared independent.[49] This 'denationalization' process applied not only to rural Africans who happened to live in areas designated as Homelands but also to urban Africans — whether or not they enjoyed Section 10 rights (allowing them permanent residence in an urban area) or had ever set foot in their supposed Homeland. The statutes were carefully worded in order to avoid withdrawing citizenship on ostensibly racial grounds. Nevertheless, whites, 'coloureds', and Asians have never been 'denationalized' under the Bantustan programme.[50] In a display of cynical demagoguery, the white minority regime insisted on observing the legal fiction that every African ethnic group (or 'tribal' entity) was not only entitled but was compelled to accept its own designated territory in order to 'develop separately'. In the official view, the Homelands were a formal recognition of (and a means to preserve) the ethnic and cultural identities of the separate African 'tribal' groups. While the state authorities proclaimed that *ethnic* criteria constituted an appropriate measure by which to divide the African people, all whites — including Portuguese, Polish emigrés, Greeks, white Rhodesians, Afrikaners, British descendants, and so forth — were judged by strictly racial criteria and constituted in the official parlance a single 'population registration group'.[51] In a revealing speech before Parliament, Minister of Bantu Administration and Development 'Connie' Mulder outlined the basic principles of the 'denationalization' programme: 'If our policy is taken to its full logical conclusion as far as the black people are concerned,' he emphasized, 'there will be not one black man with South African citizenship. ... Every black man in South Africa will eventually be accommodated in some independent new state in this honourable way and there will no longer be a moral obligation on this Parliament to accommodate these people politically.'[52] National Party ideologues have presented the independent Homelands as models that will eventually substantiate the efficacy of 'separate development'.

Instead, the Homelands have evolved into 'poverty-stricken fiefdoms, ruled by well-paid homeland politicians who have demonstrated little tolerance for opposition'.[53]

The National Party did not invent racial segregation or the Bantustan strategy. Nevertheless, Party leaders elevated the former into a full-fledged ideology and made the latter a crucial element in the implementation of this *apartheid* philosophy.[54] In order to trace the historical origins of the Bantustan strategy, it is necessary to recall key moments in the long drama of racial and political domination.

The great mineral discoveries at the end of the nineteenth century ushered in a period of tremendous industrial expansion that marked a decisive turning point in the class transformation of the African sub-continent. The specific pattern of combined and uneven capitalist development that emerged during this period thoroughly recast the relations between town and country. During the eighteenth and nineteenth centuries, the African people who had been dispossessed of their ancestral lands were crowded into Reserves or left to languish in scattered pockets where their survival depended on entering into grossly exploitative employment relations with local European farmers. From the outset, the Reserve strategy entailed resuscitating the shattered structures of tribal authority or creating such authority where it had not existed before. In their desire to attain military security in the rural areas, European overseers allowed malleable and renegade 'chiefs' to dispense their own forms of autocratic rule in the hopelessly fragmented Reserves. By the first decades of the twentieth century, the combination of capitalist industrialization and agrarian class transformation in the countryside had completely altered the role of the Reserves. Before the onset of industrial capitalism, the Reserves were subsistence redoubts where communal forms of production insulated large numbers of African agriculturalists from the market. With the expansion of capitalist relations, the Reserves were transformed into large pools of cheap labour. Consequently, African rural residents were increasingly compelled to seek temporary employment on European farms, mines, and factories for cash wages.

The 1913 Natives' Land Act codified the principle of territorial segregation. This statutory enactment signified the culmination of an extensive ruling-class debate over the 'agrarian question'. The persistent shortages of labour on European farms, in conjunction with the growing fear in some quarters that the gradual spread of African landownership threatened to stifle the initiative of marginal European farmers, prompted European politicians to endorse such drastic action. The Land Act demarcated approximately 87 per cent of the land surface of South Africa for exclusive European owner-occupancy (consisting exclusively of enterprising European farmers whose survival depended upon calculated investments in means of production and labour-power) and a mere 7.3 per cent (comprised almost entirely of the existing Reserves) for Africans. This European farming bourgeoisie firmly implanted itself as the dominant class in the countryside. The ensuing 'ruralization' of the *platteland* was stamped with a distinctly capitalist character.

By the early twentieth century, the Reserves provided a material foundation for the separation of the black working class into a permanently settled urban component and a considerably larger migrant element that retained access to means of subsistence in the rural areas. The migrant labour system was premised on the maintenance of agricultural subsistence activities capable both of subsidizing the pitifully low wages of the floating section of the reserve labour army and of accommodating the stagnant population. The flow of migrant labour intensified over time, but oscillated between town and country. The stringent implementation of influx controls prevented all but a tiny percentage of African households from establishing a permanent foothold in the urban townships. Equally important, by fabricating an African bureaucracy collaborating in the distribution of favours under the archaic rubric of 'tribalism', the ruling class inhibited the development of an emergent African national consciousness.[55]

By the 1920s, however, the Reserves began to exhibit signs of economic degeneration. Economically active adults were increasingly dependent upon long-term sojourns in the urban areas in search of work. Various European commissions chronicled the plight of poverty-stricken Africans in the Reserves. The 1932 Native Economic Commission, for example, proclaimed the 'desirability and necessity in the interest of the country, European and Native alike, of placing a well-planned scheme of improvement and development (of the Reserves) in the forefront of the national objectives'.[56] By the 1940s, the capacity of the Reserves to bear a portion of the real costs of labour force reproduction had deteriorated almost beyond recognition. The tangible evidence of overcrowding, soil erosion, declining productivity, rampant disease and malnutrition, and the dissolution of kinship obligations amply demonstrated that the Reserves were providing a diminishing proportion of the subsistence requirements of migrant worker households. The 1944 Witwatersrand Mine Natives' Wages Commission and the 1948 Native Laws (Fagan) Commission confirmed these observations. These Commissions not only charged that remunerative economic activities in the Reserves had come practically to a standstill but also placed the blame squarely on the migrant labour system which had almost completely denuded the Reserves of adult males in the prime of life.[57]

This structural underdevelopment of the Reserves undermined the material foundations of the migrant labour system. Despite a furious onslaught of influx control mechanisms, Africans flocked to the towns and cities to escape the rapidly deteriorating economic situation in the rural areas.[58] Rural-to-urban migration has always been the main alternative for people desperate to escape joblessness and grinding poverty. During the 1940s, the tremendous industrial expansion of the wartime economic boom seriously depleted available supplies of white labour. This combination of chronic labour shortages in industry and commerce and a rural exodus brought a flood of black work-seekers to the cities. Between 1921 and 1946, for example, the African urban population expanded from an estimated 587,000 to nearly 1.8 million (where males outnumbered females by a ratio of eight to one).[59]

The 1948 Native Laws (Fagan) Commission had reluctantly conceded that permanent African settlement in the towns — particularly the large industrial concentrations of the Witwatersrand, Cape Town, Port Elizabeth/East London, and Durban/Pinetown — was a 'natural and inevitable phenomenon'.[60] Fresh from their 1948 electoral triumph, the National Party rejected this assessment, seeking to stem the tide of African urbanization and 'detribalization'. The key element in the early *apartheid* strategy centred on revitalizing the Reserves as viable entities capable of sustaining the segregationist ideal encapsulated in the 1922 Transvaal Local Government (Stallard) Commission. The Stallard Commission recommended that 'it should be a recognized principle of government that natives — men, women, and children — should only be permitted within municipal areas in so far and for so long as their presence is demanded by the wants of the white population.'[61] This doctrine of Africans 'ministering to the needs of whites' was enshrined in the 1923 Native (Urban Areas) Act, the first of a long series of laws that sought quite unsuccessfully to regulate the drift of African work-seekers to the cities and to accommodate all urban Africans in racially segregated locations.

In the 1920s, Prime Minister Hertzog vowed that the Reserves would never achieve anything resembling self-government. However, in 1951, Minister of Native Affairs H.F. Verwoerd took a gigantic step in the opposite direction. The 1951 Bantu Authorities Act provided for the establishment of tribal, regional, and territorial authorities in the Reserves. While the 'tribal' authorities were initially given only advisory powers, Prime Minister D.F. Malan hinted obliquely that if these local chieftains demonstrated the requisite capabilities they might be entrusted with broader self-governing responsibilities. Nevertheless, Malan inserted the proviso that 'the Natives ... in their own areas will also stand under the guardianship and domination of the white man in South Africa. Call it *"baasskap"* or call it what you like.'[62]

In 1950, the National Party leadership appointed a special Commission under the chairmanship of F.R. Tomlinson to investigate the measures necessary to reverse the trend toward African urbanization and to achieve the desired goal of *aparte ontewikkeling* ('separate development'). The principal aim of this exhaustive four-year study was to develop 'a comprehensive scheme for the rehabilitation of the Native Areas with a view to developing within them a social structure in keeping with the culture of the Native and based on effective socio-economic planning'.[63] Couched in the racialist idiom prevalent at the time, the Tomlinson Commission both reaffirmed and refined the principle of territorial segregation: 'On the part of the European population there is an unshakable resolve to maintain their right of self-determination as a national and racial entity; while on the part of the Bantu, there is a growing conviction that they are entitled to, and there is an ever increasing demand for, the fruits of integration including an ever-greater share in the control of the country.'[64]

The Commission declared that 'there is no midway between the two poles of ultimate total integration and ultimate separate development of the two (i.e. European and Bantu) groups.'[65] In order to reconcile this dilemma, the Tomlinson Commission concluded that 'the only alternative is to promote the establishment of separate communities in their own, separate territories where each will have the fullest opportunity for self-expression and development.' One significant yet often ignored feature of the Tomlinson Commission report was the recommendation that the existing Reserves together with the three British High Commission Territories — Bechuanaland, Basutoland and Swaziland — should be consolidated into seven separate ethnic Homelands: Tswanaland, Vendaland, Pediland, Swaziland, Zululand, Zhosaland, and Sotholand.[66]

This precocious vision languished for the time-being on the drawingboard. In the interim, *apartheid* planners anguished over the upsurge of popular protest in the urban townships. Prime Minister J.G. Strijdom (1954-8) greeted the Commission's 'unequivocal rejections of the policy of integration and of any theories on a possible middle course' enthusiastically, praising the Commission for its 'justification ... of the policy of *Apartheid* (Separate Development).'[67] Nevertheless, the Strijdom regime was cautious and hesitant, refusing to make the 'speedy, definite and unambiguous decision' to implement the Tomlinson recommendations and declaring instead that total territorial separation — although it remained the ideal solution — was impracticable at the time.[68]

For the National Party, the Bantustan programme became the centrepiece of a broad strategy designed to contain the growing aspirations of the oppressed majority for formal political representation and full citizenship rights in a unitary South African state. *Apartheid* architects moved rapidly to reverse what they regarded as anathema — the drift toward the extension of (albeit circumscribed) bourgeois-democratic rights. However, National Party fears had little foundation in the actual historical record of authoritarian rule.

The 1910 Act of Union represented the capstone of British imperial efforts to ensure bourgeois hegemony over a politically unified South African state. This Act entrenched the exclusion of so-called 'non-whites' from Parliament and restricted the African and 'coloured' (qualified) franchise to the Cape Province alone. In 1936, Parliament enacted a compromise version of the Hertzog 'Native Bills' that further restricted the already exiguous forms of political representation. This legislation removed Africans to a separate voters' roll in the Cape, inaugurated the tragi-comic pantomime of indirect representation whereby qualified African voters selected white surrogates to represent their interests in Parliament, and introduced the (partly appointive and partly elective) Native Representative Council with largely *pro forma* advisory powers. During the 1930s and 1940s, the liberal bourgeoisie — through the United Party — conducted a largely defensive rearguard campaign to preserve some semblance of legitimacy. However, the National Party during the 1950s scrambled to dismantle even these token forms of political representation.

In 1950, the National Party passed the Population Registration Act, classifying all South African residents into discrete racial groups. The 1950 Group Areas Act sought to impose rigorous residential segregation in the 'white areas'. In the same year, the Suppression of Communism Act empowered the Minister of Justice with the license to ban organizations and individuals espousing broadly-defined 'statutory communism'.[69] In 1951, the National Party abolished the farcical and largely defunct Native Representative Council, erased the token enfranchisement of Indians, and reduced coloured representation to symbolic status through the elimination of the common voters' roll.[70] The 1959 Promotion of Bantu Self-Government Act completed the disenfranchisement of the African people. This Act removed the last remnant of indirect representation — the Parliamentary seats set aside for white 'Native Representatives' — and provided for the restructuring of the Bantu Authorities system by substituting eight separate Territorial Authorities.[71] Thus for the first time the principle of 'territorial segregation' was formally and consciously linked to ethnic separation.

The National Party's Bantustan strategy was premised upon the principle that 'no political rights could be granted to Africans within a common South African framework without inevitably provoking the demand for full political rights.'[72] Throughout the 1950s, the white minority regime sought to 'restore the [tribal] chiefdoms and to incorporate them firmly into the administrative grid'.[73] These efforts to revive modified forms of reactionary tribal authority prompted one member of Parliament to accuse the National Party of desiring 'to empower the Minister [of Native Affairs] to become the Big White Chief of South Africa and to appoint a number of underlings ... and puppets'.[74] The principal objective of these 're-tribalized' Bantu Authorities had been to cultivate the allegiance of 'indigenous chiefly elites as agents of political control', thereby creating a formidable bulwark against heightened African political consciousness.[75] The revived tribal authorities — in conjunction with an emergent caste of state bureaucrats, large landowners, and wealthy traders — became 'the camp commandants of the Bantustan labour camps. In this regard, the Bantustan strategy represented the streamlining of the labour bureau system and the closer control and direction of labour.'[76]

Under the guise of a devolution of political authority, the regime had gradually extended its jurisdiction over local affairs, revoking customary practices of decision-making and unilaterally appointing compliant chiefs to replace those who refused to act as auxiliaries of indirect rule. This gross meddling provoked widespread rural resentment. In the 1950s, undisguised popular rebellion erupted in widely dispersed areas, including the Marico district (northwestern Transvaal), Sekhukhuneland (eastern Transvaal), and Zululand. The climax of rural violence was reached in Pondoland — part of the premier 'showcase Bantustan', the Transkei — between 1957 and 1960.[77]

In 1961, Prime Minister Verwoerd acknowledged the possibility that the Bantu Territories might evolve toward political independence. In particular, he proposed the formation of a Commonwealth-type constellation of formally independent national sovereignties where 'political independence coupled with economic interdependence' would secure 'peace, prosperity, and justice for all'.[78] In 1963, Parliament conferred 'self-governing' status on the Transkei. Pretoria's surrogate, Chief Kaiser Matanzima, ruthlessly consolidated his authoritarian rule and declared his allegiance to *apartheid*.[79] The 1971 Black States Constitution Act streamlined the formerly cumbersome bureaucratic process of constitutional development of the Homelands, thereby bypassing the special legislation previously required by the South African Parliament and accelerating the movement toward self-governing status.[80] By the end of 1972, seven other Bantustans had joined the Transkei as self-governing entities: Ciskei, KwaZulu, Lebowa, Venda, Gazankulu, Bopthuthatswana, and QwaQwa. In 1981, KwaNdebele was given self-governing status. Finally, KaNgwane reached this supposed milestone in 1985. In 1986, the government announced that it was pressing ahead with plans to expand drastically the powers and autonomy of the self-governing states in addition to implementing the so-called 'second tier of government', including accommodating all 'racial groups' in Regional Service Councils.[81]

Industrial Decentralization

Since the 1930s, official commissions had recorded *ad nauseam* the economic deterioration of the Reserves and the desperate conditions of rural Africans. In the main, this litany of pleas fell on the deaf ears of state bureaucrats. So long as the Reserves continued to generate steady supplies of low-cost migrant labour, state officials were not tempted to tamper with their socio-economic structures. In 1954, the Tomlinson Commission injected such a shrill note of urgency that the white minority regime was compelled at least to address the previous policy of benign neglect.[82]

In previous decades, the migrant labour system had depended on the Reserves to subsidize the meager urban wages of temporary sojourners by accommodating their families on subsistence plots. The Tomlinson Commission inferred from their detailed investigations that the Reserves had collapsed beyond recognition and were no longer capable of sustaining the migrant labour system. What distinguished the Tomlinson Commission was that its prescribed remedy amounted to a reversal of existing policy. In particular, the Tomlinson Commission advocated that restrictions on individual landownership in the Reserves be lifted, that farmers be encouraged to seek improved marketing methods and be provided with better credit facilities, that industrial development be promoted in the vicinity of the Reserves in order to stem the flow of unauthorized African migration to the cities, and that prohibitions against investments of white venture capital be rescinded.[83]

The Verwoerd regime abstained from unqualified endorsement of the Tomlinson Commission proposals. Perhaps too committed to the doctrinaire interpretation of *apartheid* ideology, state administrators refused to tinker with customary land tenure arrangements and to abolish restrictions on white investments in the Reserves. However, the Verwoerd regime approved the

'Border Areas' industrial development suggestions, reasoning that investment projects would absorb significant numbers of unemployed languishing in the Reserves and thereby divert the uncontrolled exodus of impoverished job-seekers to the cities.

Some analysts have insisted that the Verwoerd regime retreated from endorsing the wholesale industrialization of the 'Border Areas' because the large-scale employment of low-paid black workers would have significantly displaced the *de facto* and *de jure* 'job colour bars', thereby undermining the privileged bargaining power of white wage-earners in the industrial heartlands.[84] Others have suggested that 'Tomlinson had grossly underestimated the amount of capital necessary for the decentralization of industries to areas which lacked any industrial infrastructure.'[85] For whatever reason, industrial decentralization proceeded at a glacial pace. By the end of 1966, less than 45,000 new jobs were created for Africans in the 'Border Areas' and in the Reserves — a slower rate of progress in a decade than the Tomlinson Commission had recommended for a single year.[86]

In the meantime, various *ad hoc* adjustments failed to prevent the massive influx of impoverished rural Africans to the cities. In 1958, the Viljoen Commission issued a dire warning: 'The urbanization of the population has led to the massing of large numbers of Natives, who have broken from tribal relations that gave their lives a content and a meaning, and have congregated in the industrial cities. The effect of the massing of large numbers of people, who are inadequately fed, whose family and social life are disintegrated, who are forced to travel long distances to and from their work and who consequently fall an easy prey to immorality and political subversion, represents the social cost of industrialization in this country.'[87] The *apartheid* architects were thus compelled to acknowledge reluctantly that an active effort would be necessary to revitalize the 'Bantu territories'.

The Bantustan strategy was thus a fusion of the need to preserve the migrant labour system and the desire to deflect Africans' aspirations for political representation in the central state apparatuses. During what has been termed the segregationist era (c. 1920-50), the Reserve strategy had depended upon the ruthless suppression of what — at the beginning of the twentieth century — had been a vibrant African agrarian petty bourgeoisie. In promoting the alternative Bantustan strategy, *apartheid* planners abandoned the 'class-leveling' aims of the Reserve strategy and instead moved tentatively toward fostering the growth of an African entrepreneurial class (albeit of a distinctive compradorial and bureaucratic type).[88]

In 1959, the white minority regime created the Bantu Investment Corporation (BIC) in order to underwrite the Bantustan scheme financially. The immediate aim of the BIC was to promote and encourage African private enterprise through financial, commercial, and technical assistance. At the time, the four major conurbations — the Pretoria/Witwatersrand/Vereeniging (PWV) region, Durban/Pinetown, the Western Cape, and Port Elizabeth/East London — accounted for nearly 80 per cent of total employment in the manufacturing sector. State-sponsored efforts to encourage capital investments in the Bantustans and restructure the spatial pattern of manufacturing operations dovetailed conveniently with the *apartheid* ideology of promoting the 'separate development' of the 'Bantu peoples'.[89] In 1965, the Bantu Homelands Development Corporations Act formed financial institutions for each of the Homelands with the objective of providing venture capital for African entrepreneurs. Despite the self-congratulatory fanfare accompanying this capitalization programme, the bulk of the available loans was extended to commercial and trading operations rather than manufacturing undertakings. For example, by 1974 the BIC had financed 1,300 undertakings throughout the Homelands. Eighty-six per cent were trading establishments (general dealers, cafes, butchers, and bottle stores), 13 per cent were service operations (mainly transport and garages), and only 2 per cent were light manufacturing operations.[90] Despite the marginal contribution of these projects to economic development and the relatively minuscule financing, these ventures played, in Southall's words, 'a decisive role in the creation of a small (but growing) stratum of African businessmen who are to a great extent a product of and dependent upon the structures of separate development within the homelands.'[91]

In addition, state 'industrial decentralization' planners hoped to lure urban entrepreneurs to the Border Areas through the stimulus of subsidized transportation rates, access to power and water sources, and generous allowances to offset the cost of

African housing.[92] In 1960, the Verwoerd regime established the Permanent Committee for the Location of Industry and the Development of the Border Areas. The principle aim of this statutory body was to oversee the complex of financial incentives such as tax concessions, low-interest loans for factory relocation and construction, exemptions from minimum wage determinations, and so forth. The most attractive sites to white investors were those Border Areas in close proximity to existing industrial concentrations. For example, Babedegi and Rosslyn — just northwest of Pretoria and straddling Bophuthatswana — offered the combined advantage of large supplies of readily available Homelands labour and easy access to the markets, skills, and management expertise in the nearby PWV region. Similarly, the Durban/Pinetown area (bordering on KwaZulu) and the East London area (bordering on Ciskei and its large dormitory township, Mdanstane) also attracted some outside investments. The combined impact of dispossession and expropriation in Homelands agriculture (due to increased capitalization and mechanization) and the 'industrial decentralization' strategy produced 'the confluence of people from the interior of the homelands to these border towns, in order to come into working distance of Pretoria, Durban and East London'.[93] As a consequence, massive urban slums sprouted overnight in some Homelands. By contrast, 'industrial decentralization' planners had great difficulty inducing white entrepreneurs to invest in the more remote Border Areas. Such potential 'growth points' as Pietersburg and Potgieteruus in the northern Transvaal (bordering on Lebowa), Rustenburg, Brits, Zeerust, and Mafeking (bordering on Bophuthatswana), Queenstown (bordering on Ciskei), and Ladysmith and Richards Bay (bordering on KwaZulu) failed to attract significant investments.[94]

Beginning in the late 1960s, the government took drastic steps to invigorate the 'industrial decentralization' policy which had so far failed to produce any significant results. The 1967 Physical Planning and Utilization of Resources Act empowered the Prime Minister and his Cabinet ministers to impose restrictions on the establishment or expansion of industries in what were termed 'controlled areas'. The principal aim of this legislation was to discourage businesses that already employed large numbers of black workers from expanding their operations in the overcrowded PWV region and the Port Elizabeth/Uitenhage area.

Likewise, the Vorster regime renewed the lucrative tax exemptions, favourable loan rates, road and rail tariff rebates, plus a panopoly of other concessions, hoping thereby to coax manufacturers to invest in labour-intensive undertakings in the outlying Border Areas.[95] In 1971, the Board for Decentralization of Industry was given expanded powers to coordinate 'decentralization' efforts. In addition, a special Growth Point Committee was authorized to clarify the principles for the selection of 'growth points' in the Border Areas.

The Vorster regime also gradually modified prohibitions against white entrepreneurship in the Homelands. Initially, white-owned firms were permitted to operate in the Homelands on an agency basis only. The BIC was entrusted to act as agent, holding legal title to purpose-built installations and to particular sites that could be leased to white entrepreneurs. By the mid-1970s, the Board for Decentralization of Industry had repealed the previous provisions of the agency agreement whereby white-owned businesses with operations in the Homelands were required to divest within fifteen years. In time, this Board became the principal conduit through which white-owned businesses seeking to invest in the Homelands acquired greater concessions than those available to entrepreneurs who wished to establish industrial undertakings in the Border Areas.[96]

In the field of industrial and labour relations, state officials sanctioned the payment of wages below the established minimum rates and ignored violations of health and safety standards in the Border Area 'growth points'. In 1970, the state authorities terminated all minimum wage legislation for black workers in the Homelands.[97] The attraction of these concessions and incentives produced some results. Between 1960 and 1972, an estimated 85,554 new jobs were created in the Border Areas and the Homelands. Nevertheless, this figure of less than 8,000 jobs per year fell considerably short of the 50,000-job target that the Tomlinson Commission had set as the minimum necessary to absorb the Homelands unemployed. By 1978, only 78,700 black workers were employed in industries in Border Areas and only 24,700 were employed in 'growth points' inside the Homelands.[98] Because of the economic recession, the rate of new job creation slowed to a snail's pace in the 1980s.

The Botha regime adopted a different tactic to stimulate the faltering 'industrial decentralization' policy. The Commission for

Cooperation and Development was formed in 1978 for the purpose of planning and implementing infrastructural development, initiating housing and township schemes, and overseeing the location of industrial sites in the Homelands. In a significant shift of ideological emphasis, the administration downplayed the commandist approach of the Vorster years and instead applauded the virtues of private enterprise, trumpeting the capacity of a robust capitalism to provide the Homelands and Border Areas with sustained economic growth. 'Decentralization' planners offered ridiculously generous concessions to investors and incorporated businessmen into the decision-making process, hoping to exploit the stimulus of market-propelled growth while preserving the essential features of *apartheid.*[99]

The 1982 *White Paper on the Promotion of Industrial Development* underscored the paradox of the revamped 'industrial decentralization' strategy. On the one hand, the National Party refused to budge on the inviolability of the ten independent Homelands. On the other hand, economic planners blithely ignored these 'national boundaries'. In the 1982 White Paper, South Africa — including both the 'self-governing' and the independent Homelands — was divided into eight separate regions, in turn differentiated by reference to three distinct criteria (rate of unemployment, *per capita* income, and development potential).[100] In this topography of economic interdependence, the Homelands were regarded as more or less irrelevant. On the basis of a complex calculus, the Board for Decentralization of Industry compiled handsome incentive packages to attract large-scale investments to 49 special Industrial Development Points and perhaps another 150 'growth centres'. For the Botha regime, the centrepiece of the rejuvenated 'industrial decentralization' programme was the Development Bank of South Africa (DBSA). The DBSA was a multilateral financial lending agency modelled on the World Bank. It replaced a host of smaller lending agencies with similar functions but burdened with overlapping or competing jurisdictions. The principal aim of the DBSA was not only to centralize the flow of capital to the Homelands and Border Areas but also to subsidize private enterprise indirectly by underwriting the costs of infrastructural development.

In addition, the newly-created Department of Constitutional Development and Planning dynamized the process of joint (as opposed to unilateral) decision-making. For the first time, businessmen were included as active participants in deliberations over 'industrial decentralization' policies. State functionaries and local entrepreneurs from the 'self-governing' and independent Homelands were also appointed to serve on those administrative boards, commissions, and agencies.[101] Leading corporate executives and bankers, played increasingly prominent roles in the decentralization policies. Proponents of these neo-liberal solutions were instrumental in convincing National Party leaders that the free play of market forces would eventually accomplish the goals of *apartheid* without the negative side-effects of brazen coercion. At the same time, Botha abandoned overly ambitious schemes, concentrating instead on encouraging capital dispersal to selected industrial development points rather than to remote Homelands.[102]

Forced Removals and Resettlement

Between the years 1962 and 1980, an estimated 3,522,900 people were subjected to some form of forced resettlement within South Africa. In 1985, nearly two million people were threatened with eventual relocation.[103] The sheer magnitude of these numbers attests to the ambitious scale of relocation projects. It is possible to identify clear patterns in a considerable number of these forced removals. Yet the irregular tempo, and the haphazard dynamics, of resettlement have made any strict classification of forced removals very difficult indeed.

The most authoritative account of the intricacies of population relocation in South Africa is the recently-published Surplus People Project. Aptly titled *Forced Removals in South Africa*, this six-volume set was produced entirely within South Africa and constitutes the most rigorous and thoroughly documented appraisal of population redistribution under *apartheid* rule. The Surplus People Project highlighted a hidden dimension of *apartheid* usually camouflaged behind the veneer of legality and official secrecy.[104]

At the risk of oversimplification, it is possible to distinguish two main types of resettlement — urban and rural — that have proceeded in tandem. It must be borne in mind that the immediate causes of specific forced removals have varied considerably in time and place. Local decisions to remove people forcibly have more often than not conformed to local and regional ambitions rather than to an overall design.

Rural Resettlement

English-speaking and Afrikaans-speaking South Africans have collaborated in the long historical process of dispossessing the indigenous peoples of their lands and transforming them into a propertyless and disenfranchised proletariat. At various critical junctures when the combined powers of persuasion and outright force were inadequate to generate sufficient numbers of wage-labourers, European employers turned elsewhere — notably to India in the mid-nineteenth century and to China in the early twentieth century — in their endless quest for inexpensive labour-power. Prohibitive legislation enacted after the 1910 Act of Union — the 1913 Natives' Land Act, the Natives (Urban Areas) Act of 1923, the Native Land and Trust Act of 1936, and so forth — laid the statutory groundwork for the country-wide system of territorial segregation in the opening decades of the twentieth century. The early achievements of the post-1948 National Party under the new rubric of *apartheid* merely syste-matized and extended the segregationist agenda. One notable difference, however, was that the early architects of *apartheid* made no effort to disguise their white supremacist motives. In introducing the 1950 Group Areas legislation, the Minister of the Interior, T.E. Donges, for example, argued that 'points of contact ['between the races'] inevitably produce friction and friction gen-erates heat which may lead to a conflagration. It is our duty therefore to reduce these points of contact to an absolute mini-mum.' He further explained that this Act was intended to ensure 'the paramountcy of the white man and Western civilization in South Africa ... in the interests of the material, cultural, and spiritual development of all races.'[105]

Perhaps the most ambitious type of 'forced resettlement' was that associated with the consolidation of the Bantustans. With the notable exception of the minuscule QuaQua, all the Home-lands were comprised initially of a conglomeration of non-contiguous fragments of land. In the extreme case, the KwaZulu Bantustan in the early 1970s consisted of no less than 48 large and 157 small sections of territory.[106] In 1975, the nine established Bantustans — excluding the so-called 'black spots' and small fragments — comprised 81 major pieces of land.[107] *Apartheid* planners pressed forward with their ultimate aim of eliminating this checkered mosaic of black communities and white farmlands. The consolidation of the Bantustans involved not only the purchase of white farms (at prices considerably above prevailing market rates) but also the transfer of former Reserve areas into white hands. Estimates of the exact numbers of Africans uprooted and deported under the consolidation schemes are sketchy.[108] But the simultaneous opposition of white farmers resisting incorporation into the Homelands (in lieu of selling their farmsteads) and black rural residents refusing to submit to enforced relocation has slowed but not deflected the process of population redistribution.

The forced removal of so-called 'black spots', that is, pockets of African freehold land lying outside the territorial boundaries demarcated by the 1913 Natives' Land Act and the 1936 Natives' Trust and Land Act has been one of the most consistent features of Bantustan consolidation. The celebrated case of the deportation of thousands of people from Magopa in the western Transvaal to Pachsdraai illustrated the chicanery of the Ministry of Co-Operation and Development toward rural communities. Literally hundreds of these small black communities — where land was purchased in common by syndicates — came into existence (particularly in the Transvaal) in the decade following the end of the Anglo-Boer war (1899-1902). The Surplus People Project estimated that 614,000 people had already undergone removal by 1983. It was estimated that another 1,153,000 people faced the threat of removal.[109]

The transformation of capitalist agriculture also generated a net outflow of farm labourers who were sent cascading from the countryside into the already overcrowded Bantustans. As late as the 1950s, white farmers in many agricultural districts were clamouring for farm labour, particularly during the peak periods of seasonal demand. White farmers welcomed the National Party's *apartheid* policies because they reckoned that the stringent application of influx controls would keep farm labour 'bottled up' on the farms. Beginning in the 1960s, the systematic introduction of mechanized production processes went hand-in-hand with the contraction of annual seasonal demand for hand labour.[110] As capitalist farmers found themselves overburdened with hands, they relentlessly pressured labourers to clear off their farmsteads. This class war of attrition — waged through layoffs, evictions, the clearance of 'squatter' communities, and a myriad of more covert means — precipitated the mass exodus of an estimated 1,129,000 farm labourers and their families during the 1960s and 1970s from the white farmsteads to the Bantustans.[111] Because of the influx control regulations, these 'surplus people' have had no alternative but to gravitate to the Bantustans, perhaps to one of the newly-established 'closer settlement' villages that are nothing more than dumping grounds for those of no further use to 'white South Africa'. The last loopholes preserving labour-tenant class relations (household-retained access to subsistence plots in exchange for labour) were finally closed in northern Natal in the late 1970s and early 1980s. The continued precarious access of labour-tenant households to land constituted, in the words of the president of the (white) Natal Agricultural Union, 'sanctuary' for hundreds of thousands of African farm labourers 'not really needed by the agricultural industry'.[112]

In defending the 'forced removals' policy against Conservative Party criticisms that its impact was inconsequential, a spokesman for the Ministry of Co-Operation and Development boldly exposed National Party tactics: 'The Honourable Member knows that we had to change our methods. Circumstances forced us to change our methods. Therefore it is not correct to allege now that the government is no longer prepared to move people. I have just proved that we caused 360,000 people to move [to the resettlement camps of Onverwacht in the Free State and KwaNdebele in the eastern Transvaal]. We caused them to move. ... They moved of their own volition. If this is not an achievement, I don't know what is.'[113]

Since the abolition of labour-tenancy and the introduction of quotas for black farm labourers on white farmlands, 'tens of thousands of black families have become vulnerable to eviction and prosecution for trespass. The result is widespread removals that don't look like removals — thousands of people desperately (voluntarily!) seeking homes and sustenance wherever they might hope to find it. ... Their numbers expanded by the thousands of people who no longer qualify to live in the scores of "locations" throughout the country which are "abolished", "deproclaimed" or "disestablished".'[114] The example of the maize industry — crippled by three consecutive years of drought — dramatically illustrated how thousands of black farmhands and their families were uprooted with 'no choice ... but to move to the "Homelands" where there would even be less food and no work'. 'Farmers can no longer afford to allow their farms to be used as slums', the chief manager of the all-white, Afrikaner-dominated National Maize Producers' Organization, Pieter Grous, proclaimed. 'The government has for long enough depended upon our patriotism to keep blacks to our disadvantage. Our prime duty is to produce maize at a profit.'[115] He continued: 'It is a socio-political problem which the farmers cannot be expected to solve. We cannot continue to provide welfare to relatives of black farm hands.'[116]

Urban Displacement

After the 1910 Act of Union, the state administration designed urban townships — where home ownership rights and the provision of social amenities rested with the local white authorities — to accommodate a number of 'semi-permanent' black workers sufficient to meet local labour requirements. During the 1920s and 1930s, the proliferation of congested ghetto areas (boasting of a vibrant and robust 'slumyard' culture) scattered in and around the predominantly white city centres undermined state efforts to prevent the formation of a permanently settled black proletariat.[117] Between 1936 and 1946, the number of urban Africans increased by 652,570 or 57 per cent.[118] In 1937, one exasperated segregationist anxiously proclaimed: 'The towns constitute the front trenches of our position in South Africa. It is in the towns that seige is being made against our civilized standards.'[119] The Prime Minister, General Smuts, proclaimed in 1942 with an obvious hint of resignation: 'A revolutionary change is taking place among the Native peoples ... — the movement from the old reserves in the Native areas to the big European centres of population. Segregation tried to stop it. It has, however, not stopped it in the least. The process has been accelerated. You might as well try to sweep back the ocean with a broom.'[120]

The location riots in Vereeniging in 1937, Pretoria in 1942, and Johannesburg in 1944 — along with police shootings in

Sophiatown (western Johannesburg) in 1942, the numerous bus boycotts in Alexandra township (Johannesburg) in the early 1940s, and the Orlando (Soweto) commonage 'squatter' movements of 1944-7 — merely highlighted the exponential growth of black political consciousness and militancy.[121] A number of incidental factors — the gradual encroachment of high-rise city centres, soaring crime rates, dilapidated buildings and tremendous overcrowding, and large numbers of casually-employed or unemployed residents — combined with the ideological commitment of *apartheid* planners to enforce a rigid urban residential segregation plan. The 1950 Group Areas Act (with later amendments) was the main statutory mechanism for urban removals. Under the deceitful motto of urban renewal and slum clearance, municipalities energetically bulldozed countless African ghettos, shantytowns, and informal residential communities and replaced them with geometrically planned and architecturally monotonous urban locations separated by a *cordon sanitaire* from city centres. Johannesburg's South Western Native Township (Soweto), Nyanga outside of Cape Town, and New Brighton outside of Port Elizabeth illustrated this pattern.[122]

Twin recurrent themes associated with the application of the Group Areas Act have been (1) the displacement of Indians and so-called coloureds from prime real estate to make way for white-owned business operations, such as industrial development and commercial ventures; and (2) the expropriation of African freehold settlements as sites for Indian and 'coloured' zones, thereby deflecting the hostility and resentment of the former residents onto the newcomers rather than against white legislators and municipal authorities. The 1950 Group Areas Act had primarily been used against the economically vibrant Indian and coloured communities. The destruction of Cape Town's District Six and the eviction of Indian traders from the centre of Durban have been perhaps the most widely publicized examples of urban Group Areas removals.[123]

More recently, the white minority regime has utilized 'forced removals' to displace people from the urban areas and situate them within the territorial boundaries of the Homelands. In those parts of South Africa where the Homelands adjoin urban-industrial areas, *apartheid* planners have merely 'endorsed out' large numbers of township residents, relocating them not to distant Homelands but to sprawling commuter zones within

Bantustan territory from whence they travel daily to work in 'white South Africa'. These commuters have been officially designated as foreigners in the land of their birth. 'In this way', Hallett argued, 'South Africa is cleansed of some of its "urban black spots".'[124] Officially estimated at 290,000 in 1970, the numbers of Homelands commuters expanded to 718,900 in 1979 and subsequently increased even more steeply. Newly-created 'dormitory suburbs' in Bophuthatswana and KwaZulu were established to 'service' the labour demands of Pretoria and Durban-Pinetown, respectively.[125] In some instances, the state authorities merely redrew Bantustan borders to include town-ships that were formerly part of 'white South Africa'. Formally under the jurisdiction of the Ciskei, Mdanstane (recently enlarged and provided with upgraded social amenities) is located about twenty kilometers from East London and accommodated an official population in 1983 of 200,000 people — a figure that represented about one-third the total population of this Homeland.[126]

Forced removals on a large scale also ravaged small town African communities. Large numbers of settled African residents of such Transvaal towns as Pietersburg, Rustenburg, Potgieters-rus, Ellisras, Naboomspruit, Vaalwater, Louis Trichardt, and Nylstroom were expelled from townships in close proximity to city centres. Most were transported considerable distances away into Venda, Bophuthatswana, Lebowa, and Gazankulu, requiring long hours of travel back and forth to work. Small towns in the Cape Province and Natal had similar experiences.[127]

The Surplus People Project estimated that 834,000 people had been removed under the jurisdiction of the Group Areas Act, 730,000 by means of urban relocations, and another 172,000 had been uprooted from 'informal settlements' ('squatter' camps).[128] It is difficult if not impossible to gauge accurately the degree to which forced removals have affected the demographic balance of South Africa. Nevertheless, the following figures strongly suggest that the unrelenting pressure of forced resettlement stalled and even reversed the former pattern of black urbanization.

In the end, this statistical enumeration reveals only one aspect of the reality, glossing over the deplorable plight of countless thousands of black people whose daily efforts to survive at a bare subsistence level are filled with anxiety and despair. Certainly, the oppressed people of South Africa have endured forms

TABLE 1
Geographical Distribution of De Facto African Population (%)

Year	White Urban Area	White Rural Area	Bantustan Area
1960	29.1	31.4	39.5
1970	28.2	24.5	47.3
1980	25.4	20.6	54.0

Source: Surplus People Project, *Forced Removals in South Africa: The Surplus People Reports. Volume II: The Eastern Cape,* Cape Town 1983, p. 6.

of forced resettlement throughout their history. In 1916, for example, Solomon Plaatje's eloquent *Native Life in South Africa* recorded the plight of countless African rural producers (particularly sharecroppers in the Orange Free State) who were summarily ejected and uprooted from European farmsteads throughout the South African countryside.[129] The popular mobilizations that erupted throughout the rural districts established the bedrock upon which the South African Natives National Congress (later renamed the African National Congress) mounted its first mass campaign for redress of grievances.[130]

Similarly, the popular protests of the mid-1950s over the destruction of a string of black suburban settlements (Sophiatown, Martindale, Newclare) straddling the Main Reef road on Johannesburg's western outskirts were admirably portrayed in Trevor Huddleston's *Naught for Your Comfort.*[131] This literary tradition continued with the publication of Cosmas Desmond's *The Discarded People.*[132] This report vividly exposed the fate of thousands of African people who were unceremoniously dumped in a desolate and godforsaken patch of arid ground in Natal called Limehill. Finally, Jonathan Wack's 1982 film documentary, *Crossroads,* preserved the grim testimony of the 60,000 to 80,000 people who crowded onto a sandy stretch of land outside Cape Town and built a bustling 'informal' community complete with schools and garbage collection, simply to keep families intact and to stay close to employment opportunities — however meagre they might be.

Influx Controls and the Regulation of Black Labour

'There can be little doubt', David Welsh argued, 'that the black population of South Africa's common area, and in particular of the urban areas, must rank among the most highly controlled and bureaucratically regimented people in any modern industrial society. It is no exaggeration to claim that they are enmeshed in a series of legislative coils of unique severity and comprehensiveness.'[133] These administrative measures — generically labelled influx controls — were, as we have seen, originally promulgated during the segregationist era in order to regulate black access to the 'white areas' of South Africa, thereby securing inexpensive labour.[134] These controls were tightened, streamlined and refined, becoming the cornerstone of *apartheid* strategy not only because they disorganized black labour but also because they legitimated the pretense that African people were temporary urban residents and therefore had no need for full political rights within 'white South Africa'.[135]

According to reliable 1980 statistics, nearly ten million African people (3,416,971 in large metropolitan areas; 1,903,447 in the remaining urban areas; and 4,323,545 in the 'white' rural areas) were subject to these bureaucratic controls.[136] The staggering litany of official pronouncements, statutory enactments, and restrictions literally defies the imagination. The Native (Urban Areas) Consolidation Act (No. 25 of 1945) codified, rationalized, and extended the key provisions of the 1923 Native (Urban Areas) Act in order to adjust to the unprecedented flood of Africans attracted to the metropolitan areas by the wartime boom in employment opportunities. This revamped legislation laid the foundation for the key tenet of *apartheid*, namely, that urban black residents were regarded as 'temporary sojourners' and placed the onus on individuals for their right to remain. An important codicil (the Native Laws Amendment Act of 1952) extended influx controls to all urban areas, included women in its provisions, and empowered state authorities to remove people deemed undesirable.[137] According to the original 1945 Act, Africans were granted domicile only on condition that they satisfied certain minimum requirements contained in the infamous Section 10. In particular, Africans are allowed to remain in an urban area for longer than seventy-two hours only if they have resided there since birth; if they have worked continuously in that area for one employer for not less than ten years, or have lived there continuously for fifteen years with official permission; if they are wives or unmarried children (under the age of eighteen) of a qualified male resident; or, finally, if they have received permission to remain in the area from a labour bureau official.[138]

A thicket of other equally coercive measures complemented this core structure of influx controls, radiating outwards in an ever-expanding network of administrative regulations designed to ensnare the oppressed masses in a bureaucratic morass. The misnamed Bantu (Abolition of Passes and Co-Ordination of Documents) Act of 1952 stipulated that all Africans were required to carry a reference book or 'pass' containing a photo-graph, race identity card, registered number, ethnic classi-fication, and (where relevant) official authorization to reside in urban areas.[139]

Outfitted with this battery of draconian statutes, a succession of white supremacist administrations pursued, with their char-acteristic bluntness and vigour, the goal of rigid labour regu-lation. In the late nineteenth century, the great mining houses established barracks-like compounds in order to control labour. These early experiments prefigured the single-sex hostels for migrant workers that remain in operation in the 1980s. During the *apartheid* era, the National Party has approached the issue of cleansing the prescribed areas of unwanted 'superfluous and frivolous appendages' with missionary zeal. In 1956, Minister of Native Affairs, H.F. Verwoerd proclaimed: 'These people ... will be like the Italians who go to France to take up employment there. They remain Italians and they remain anchored in their homeland; that is where they seek their rights; they do not expect and ask for rights in the other place.'[140] In 1959, the Secre-tary for Native Affairs, W.W.M. Eiselen, announced: 'All the Bantu have their permanent homes in the reserves and their entry into other areas and into the urban centres is merely of a temporary nature and for economic reasons. In other words, they are admitted as "work-seekers", not as settlers.'[141]

Influx controls have been the key mechanisms enforcing the migrant labour system. In 1964, the Bantu Laws Amendment Act rescinded the partial shelter provided by Section 10. Henceforth, even those qualified under Section 10 to establish permanent urban residence could be deemed 'idle and undesirable' or 'a threat to the maintenance of peace and order', and therefore liable to be forcibly removed from the prescribed areas and transported to a Homeland.[142] In 1972, the Secretary for Bantu Administration and Development expressed the official aim of *apartheid* policy: 'It seems logical to expect that, as far as we can foresee, there will always be a large or a smaller number of Bantu working in South Africa. ... What is certain is that no individual person can claim the right to stay in the White country permanently. He is here exclusively on account of his labour, and not in a permanent capacity which can give him access to rights which Whites enjoy in labour, economic, political and other fields. He can achieve rights in his own fatherland. ... Families should live in the homelands and the heads of these families who are working in white areas, should travel to their homes every day or every weekend. It is the Department's eventual aim to transport Bantu workers daily as far as seventy miles (113 km.) between their work and their homes.'[143]

Despite their extensive powers to apprehend and prosecute offenders, the state authorities have been virtually powerless to prevent the inflow of 'illegals' from the rural areas. In addition to the regular South African police, inspectors employed by the various Administration Boards have wide discretionary authority to locate and arrest violators. According to reliable calculations, nearly six million pass law prosecutions took place between 1965 and 1975. It was also estimated that the state's annual costs for this immense operation amounted to 32 million rand (about $36 million) in 1979 alone.[144] Beginning in the late 1970s, official figures seemed to indicate that the absolute number of arrests for violations of influx control and related offences had slackened, but rather than reflecting a relaxation of controls, these figures most likely indicated that the nineteen Aid Centres (established in 1971 to relieve the overtaxed court system) had begun to function as parallel 'extra-legal' channelling mechanisms.[145]

The high incidence of illegal entry into proscribed areas shows that large numbers of landless, impoverished, and unemployed people in the Homelands are prepared to risk conviction, jail sentences, and summary ejection from the cities.[146] These risks are entirely rational. For example, one researcher calculated that individual black workers migrating from Lebowa to Johannesburg would improve their living standards by 225 per cent per year even if three months were spent in prison; by 170 per cent if six months were spent in prison, and by 85 per cent even if nine months were spent in prison.[147]

Influx control instruments were successful in harassing and slowing the movement of 'illegals' from the Homelands. However, the state authorities acknowledged that an even greater effort was required to stem the tide of migrants to the cities. They buttressed the existing statutory proscriptions with a host of other measures in order to freeze the number of permanently-domiciled urban black people. In 1968, the white minority regime abolished the 30-year leasehold right to occupancy of houses in the urban townships. Henceforth, Section 10 urban dwellers were only permitted to rent houses from local municipal authorities and those already in private ownership (nearly 10,000 in Soweto) could not be bequeathed to heirs.[148] Equally significant was the state authorities' decision to discontinue the provision of low-income housing and to curtail family accommodation in the townships. Consequently, the housing shortfall in black urban townships by 1980 was estimated to have reached 186,000 units.[149]

If migrant workers lost their jobs in the cities (because of temporary layoffs or for whatever other reason), they automatically forfeited their right to accommodation and were required by law to return to their designated Homelands to register at the local labour bureau as job-seekers.[150] Inevitably, the serious housing shortage resulted in tremendous over-crowding and illegal squatting. One recent survey of Soweto suggested that the average number of residents per house was nine or ten persons per standard housing unit. These buildings were designed for a household of five.[151] Other sources provided comparable figures.[152] By the mid-1970s, this under-employed mass spilled over into the large squatter settlements that proliferated in the vicinity of Cape Town, Pretoria and Durban. A large proportion of the adult males in these squatter camps qualified for Section 10 rights but were unable to obtain family-sized accommodation in the townships or had wives and families not eligible to join them.[153]

South African police and administration board officials in 1982 arrested 206,022 people for alleged violations of the pass laws, or, put in another way, one person every two and one-half minutes, day and night, throughout the year. According to Black Sash (a liberal women's organization that monitors influx control), 'skill in disobedience and in evasion of the forces of law and order' had become the only way for most black people to survive in urban areas. The fact that administration boards overseeing the implementation of influx control laws have always been the targets of bombings, arson, and stone-throwing is ample testimony that black people generally regard them as a symbol of their oppression. These boards were established in the early 1970s and earned their administrative expenses from pass law fines and profits on township liquor sales, operating, in other words, a more or less legalized extortion racket.[154]

The Botha regime employed a calculated mixture of direct and indirect coercion to prevent further black urbanization outside the Bantustans. The Department of Cooperation and Development introduced computerized central control of the reference (or 'pass') book system. In addition, the Department in 1967 ruled that access to approved accommodation was a prerequisite of official permission to remain in the urban areas, while simultaneously slowing the rate of new housing construction, allowing urban and peri-urban 'locations' to decay to the point of squalor, and demolishing squatter camps. Finally, the state administration intensified the disincentives for white employers by imposing stiffer penalties for hiring 'illegals'.[155]

Perhaps the most calculated effort to exorcise the spectre of permanent black urban areas was encapsulated in the 'Koornhof Bills', a trilogy of proposals named after the Minister of Cooperation and Development, Piet Koornhof. The centrepiece of this controversial package — the Orderly Movement and Settlement of Black Persons Bill — was unveiled in 1982 and scrapped the following year. While the other two bills dealt with the provision of social services and community council elections in the urban townships, the Orderly Movement and Settlement of Black Persons Bill aimed to tighten the loopholes governing qualification under Section 10 of the Natives (Urban Areas) Act. Designed to put black urban residents under a state of virtual martial law, this Bill proposed to restrict qualifications under Section 10 to children born in the proscribed urban areas only if both parents were classified as permanent urban residents. It would be difficult if not impossible to estimate accurately the number of children who would be deprived of their right to permanent urban residence under this proposal. Nevertheless, one indication of the drastic threat this legislation posed to

Section 10 rights was the fact that in Soweto, for example, approximately 60 per cent of births occurred out of wedlock. In addition, the Bill proposed to make qualification absolutely dependent upon approved accommodation. Countless thousands of people who qualified for Section 10 rights had been forced to erect temporary shelter in squatter camps or had become illegal 'backyard' lodgers in residences approved for others: all of them would have become liable to expulsion had Koornhof's proposals become law.[156]

The Homelands and the Divide-and-Rule Strategy

The 'ethnic Homelands' were never more than fraudulent ploys in Pretoria's grandiose scheme to secure an inexpensive and politically acquiescent reserve army of black workers. By extending independent status to these Homelands, the South African authorities claimed that they were merely fulfilling the primordial aspirations of millions of Africans to exercise citizenship rights in culturally-distinct Homelands. Despite the fictional character of the Homelands scheme, it was a carefully calibrated policy that to a certain degree successfully drove a wedge between sectors of the oppressed people.

The Homelands were economic backwaters where only regular remittances from black workers employed in 'white South Africa' alleviated rampant starvation and malnutrition. At any given time, fewer than 20 per cent of the Bantustan work force were employed in the Homelands themselves. While considerable variation existed, sizeable proportions of the *de jure* Homelands populations were in fact residents of 'white South Africa'.[157] According to a 1983 study released by the Department of Cooperation and Development and conducted by the Bureau of Economic Research (Benso), 3.9 million out of a total *de jure* population of 8.5 million of the four independent Homelands (Transkei, Ciskei, Venda, and Bopthuthatswana) lived permanently outside their borders.[158] The example of tiny QwaQwa provides the most ludicrous illustration of this situation. According to the Surplus People Project: 'The *de facto* population of QwaQwa has increased at least tenfold since 1970. Approximately a quarter of a million immigrants have poured into the already overcrowded and badly eroded territory, mainly from the

white urban and rural areas in the Orange Free State. ...
QwaQwa today is a rural slum, a dumping ground for South
Africa's relative surplus population in the Orange Free State:
there is absolutely no prospect that jobs will be created for the
people either locally or at a distance.'[159] Despite this massive
population relocation, perhaps less than one-sixth of the *de jure*
population of QwaQwa actually lived there.[160]

Over the past decade, leading industrialists and business
associations (particularly in the Western Cape) have become
increasingly vocal in their condemnation of influx controls, arguing that these measures undermine free enterprise by retarding
necessary adjustments in the labour market.[161] Nevertheless,
labour migration shows no sign of abating. Migrant labour from
the Homelands increased from half a million in 1951 to over one
million by 1980. Truly dramatic upturns were registered in the
four independent Homelands: the total number of migrant
workers increased from 58,000 in 1977 to 634,000 in 1981 (when
over half the total came from Transkei).[162]

Equally important, as Nattrass demonstrated in a case study
of migrants from KwaZulu, the trend was for workers to emi-
grate at an earlier age and to stay away for longer periods of
time.[163] Border area commuter employment also expanded substantially. From perhaps a few thousand in 1951, the number of
black workers residing in the Homelands and commuting daily
to their place of employment in 'white South Africa' exceeded
three-quarters of a million by 1985.[164]

Conversely, the creation of 'growth points' for decentralized
industrial expansion did not improve the socio-economic status
of Homelands residents. Instead, this strategy merely transferred
the problems associated with underemployment and unemployment to the Homelands. The case of Bophuthatswana illustrates
the general trend. Perhaps best known as the 'casino mini-state'
because of the 'fantasy island'-like atmosphere of Sun City,
Bophuthatswana had a *de facto* population in 1983 of approximately 1.2 million. At least another half million Tswana-speaking
people lived and worked on a continuous basis in 'white South
Africa'. Despite the trappings of statehood, such as a legislative
assembly, a coat of arms, a flag, and a national anthem,
Bophuthatswana was hopelessly dependent on South African
officials.

The combination of forced resettlement and gerrymandering

of Bophuthatswana's phantom 'international borders' sent its officially resident population soaring between 1976 and 1985. One of Bophuthatswana's disparate fragments jutted to within 20 kilometres of Pretoria's northern suburbs. It was just across this border that large 'closer settlement' housing schemes were built at Mapopane and Ga-Rankuwa to accommodate black workers who previously would have been housed in places like Atteridgeville and Mamelodi on the outskirts of Pretoria proper. The vast majority of those who lived in these new dormitory townships travelled daily to jobs around Pretoria. Perhaps as many as 200,000 'frontier commuters' made the monotonous and time-consuming regular trek to work in 'white South Africa', in addition to about 75,000 migrant workers lodging in single-sex hostels.

The flow of labour from Bophuthatswana to the Pretoria region was matched, although not in comparable magnitude, by the movement of capital to the border area and to locations within the Homeland. South African planners established Rosslyn at a site northwest of Pretoria in 1960 as the first border areas industrial scheme. By 1975, Rosslyn had attracted about 130 South African and transnational corporations with an investment of R110 million (including R33 million from the state-owned Industrial Development Corporation). The major 'growth point' within Bophuthatswana was located at Babelegi where more than R105 million was invested after 1970. These two industrial satellite zones have bolstered Pretoria's industrial/manufacturing base.

The attraction of employment lured thousands to those places where the prospects seemed greatest. As a result, spontaneous settlements literally enveloped the formal townships. It was estimated that by 1983 half a million squatters had flooded the Winterveld, Klippan, and Oskraal areas around Ga-Rankuwa, Mapopane, and Temba. This impoverished mass represented about two-fifths of the entire resident population of Bophuthatswana. At the other extreme, a small· yet aggressive entrepreneurial class, ranging from shopkeepers and 'service merchants' to proprietors of supermarkets and manufacturing operations, had established a tenuous foothold in the competitive *milieu* of business and finance.[165]

Transfers and grants-in-aid from Pretoria to the Homelands account for approximately 85 per cent of their total annual budgetary outlays. Besides keeping these 'outposts of reaction' afloat financially through external funding, Pretoria has also proceeded with what is called 'constitutional development'. The partly-elected and partly-appointed legislative bodies in the Homelands — renowned for their bitter quarrels and internecine intrigue — serve as window-dressing obscuring the reality of autocratic single-party rule.[166] The profusion of Homelands agencies, boards, commissions, and so on — in conjunction with ceremonial flag-raising, honorific titles, and other pompous displays — project a mirage of Homelands independence. Despite the occasional bombastic tirades of Bantustan leaders such as KwaZulu's Gatsha Buthelezi and Bophuthatswana's Chief Lucas Mangope against particular aspects of *apartheid*, Homelands leaders are tied to Pretoria's platforms and march to the tune of their white advisors.

Modifying the State and Forms of Representation

The Character of the Capitalist State

Recent efforts to specify the class form of the capitalist state in South Africa have been tantalizingly diverse. At one extreme, Simson announced that the South African state exhibited the characteristic features of classical fascism.[167] At the other extreme, Kaplan has argued that the capitalist state in South Africa can be classified as a bourgeois democracy, albeit of a racially-exclusive kind.[168] Both of these approaches have been criticized elsewhere and the intricacies of these arguments need not detain us here.[169] Suffice it to say that the characterization of the South African state as fascist in content if not in form is recurrent in the literature. While the South African state has always displayed certain repressive features that resemble fascist-type apparatuses its underlying morphology has been considerably different. Kaplan's portrait of the South African state as a racially-exclusive bourgeois democracy has provided useful clues to the nature of bourgeois rule in South Africa and the mechanisms through which the dominant classes have achieved hegemony on the political terrain. Kaplan argued: 'The fact that universal franchise does not exist in South Africa should not blind us to one important feature of the South African state apparatus, that is, representation of class interest has taken place within the framework of parliamentary democracy. While black people in South Africa have been excluded from representation within the state apparatuses, whites have enjoyed democratic representation.'[170] At another point, he maintained: 'The democratic form [of the South African state] has always been accepted. There has never been any serious movement from within the bourgeoisie to abolish the operations of this democracy or to substitute an alternative state form. ... Organizing the state in the form of a parliamentary democracy allows for the simultaneous representation of the general collective interests of the bourgeoisie as a class and the direct representation of particular of the different bourgeois fractions. In South Africa, Parliament similarly functioned as the arbiter amongst the different bourgeois fractions, providing a simultaneous bourgeois concensus and "organic" representation for the bourgeois fractions directly through their own party political representatives.'[171]

Kaplan's otherwise perceptive analysis is flawed by the inference that parliamentary democracy and the bourgeois democratic form of the capitalist state are more or less synonymous. Kaplan's tendency to conflate political representation with the franchise therefore ignored mechanisms other than electoral participation in a centralized parliamentary/legislative body through which the dominant classes secured hegemony over subordinate classes. The historical *differentia specifica* of South Africa's capitalist state has not been its hermetically-sealed 'racial-exclusivity' *per se* but its racially-differentiated forms of political representation.[172] What distinguishes the bourgeois-democratic form of the state is the way in which racial domination serves as the principal mode of social organization.

For the white electorate, consent has played a qualitatively greater role than coercion in maintaining the hegemony of the dominant classes. Yet various modes of legitimation and forms of unequal political representation have bisected the extremes of consent and coercion, performing an intermediate function in securing stable capitalist rule. The hallmark of the Botha regime has been the gradual substitution of achievement and market criteria for the ascriptive category of 'race', modernizing *apartheid* by replacing strictly 'racialist' forms of legitimation with hybrid mechanisms. The nurturing of a black middle class has entailed the extension of economic privileges and rewards —

home ownership schemes and 99-year leaseholds in the townships, training and educational opportunities, improved social amenities, the elimination of petty *apartheid*, and so forth — aimed at creating 'buffer strata' with a material stake in the capitalist system. In the Homelands, the regime has sponsored the growth of a parasitic and compradorial class whose allegiance to the *status quo* is ensured by its dependence on the central state apparatuses. The autocratic rule of these Homelands leaders — auxiliaries of the South African state machinery — ensures political acquiesence throughout the frontier.

Seen as a topological system, the state machinery extends outwards from its mobile and centralized core in a series of concentric circles. Demarcations within this complex system of representation have historically crystallized predominantly (but not exclusively) around racial classifications. The Botha regime has tried to restructure the attenuated forms of political representation; its key efforts were the new Constitution and the revamped Community Council system.

Origins of the New Constitution

In the midst of the 1976 Soweto disturbances, the *Financial Mail* wondered aloud: 'After Sharpeville the economy plunged into one of its dark periods. Is the same going to happen now?'[173] By the end of 1976, net capital outflow sharply increased and long-term credit declined.[174] In the political reassessment that followed the crushing of popular resistance, leading business associations set the pace in their insistence that the white minority regime 'deracialize' the mode of political domination by substituting market competition as the basis for legitimation. For example, the powerful Transvaal branch of the Federal Chambers of Industry (FCI) encouraged the white minority regime to foster a 'black middle class' in order to 'ensure a stable, contented urbanized black community in our metropolitan and industrialized area. ... Only by having this most responsible section of the urban Black on our side can the Whites of South Africa be assured of containing on a long-term basis the irresponsible economic and political ambitions of those blacks who are influenced against their own real interests from within and without our borders.'[175]

In 1977, the new Urban Foundation represented the business response to the growing political gulf between the dominant and dominated classes. Leading business executives sought a cross-class alliance that could lobby the National Party on pressing social issues. The Urban Foundation sought to promote a spirit of philanthropy amongst South Africa's corporate giants in order to bring a 'higher quality of life' in the townships. These endeavours complemented the rediscovered conscience of U.S. signatories to the so-called 'Sullivan Principles'. These paternalistic ideas assumed a revived importance as an antidote to popular revolution. Large corporations inveigled the loyalty of their permanent black employees through tactics such as offering low-interest home improvement loans, broadening educational opportunities, and downplaying overt forms of racial discrimination at the workplace.

On the whole, the corporate response to the crisis of hegemony has been to leave the main pillars of *apartheid* alone — the Homelands and economic development, political representation and political power, residential and cultural segregation, influx control mechanism, and so forth — and instead to focus on remedial actions compatible with expanded economic growth and increased profitability. In the main, business associations have urged the relaxation of 'job colour bars' in industry and commerce, proposed that job advancement be brought in line with performance and skill criteria, encouraged 'self-help' solutions (instead of 'welfare-state' subsidies), and advocated the wholesale 'adoption of free enterprise values by urban blacks'.[176]

The common thread that united the powerful business associations and the white minority regime was their shared conviction that South Africa was 'deeply pluralized' and that racial identities formed the basic building block for the political future.[177] In short, South Africa's racial cleavages vitiated the possibility of a Westminster-style parliamentary democracy. Despite unanimity on a fundamental refusal to accede to the formal principle of 'one person-one vote' in an electoral system based on single-member constituencies, the government remained deeply divided over constitutional modifications that would both preserve white power and 'deracialize' the political system.

The Vorster regime floated the original blueprint for constitutional change in 1977. This scheme envisaged separate parliaments for 'coloureds', Indians, and whites, each with its own prime minister and cabinet. Each parliament would have possessed full legislative authority over its 'own' group's affairs. A consultative council of cabinets would have operated under the auspices of an executive President in order to decide 'joint' matters.[178] These proposed changes were so cumbersome that they seemed hardly feasible. More importantly, reform advocates correctly contended that this scheme left political power in white hands. In contrast, the *verkrampte* wing of the National Party fiercely opposed even the vaguest hint of 'power-sharing'. Faced with this impasse, the National Party unloaded the issue onto the Schlebusch Commission, which pondered alternative formulations for two years before recommending the establishment of a President's Council to consider the problem in greater detail.

Following the abolition of the Senate, the President's Council was established in 1980 as an official multi-racial advisory body responsible for framing practicable constitutional proposals. In May 1982, Prime Minister Botha unveiled the broad outlines of the new constitution. In subsequent months, Botha and his closest advisors gave this skeletal structure tangible form. After a long gestation period, the Republic of South Africa Constitution Act was introduced during the 1983 session of Parliament. On 2 November 1983, the white South African electorate participated in a national referendum intended to gauge political support for what amounted to a *fait accompli* since parliament had enacted the Constitution Act earlier that same year. In a poll in which 76 per cent of the 2.7 million eligible white voters cast ballots, 66 per cent expressed their approval for this 'new dispensation'. For the reformist wing of the National Party, this turnout was a political triumph. While a small proportion purposefully boycotted these proceedings, the Conservative Party, the HNP, and the PFP had all engaged in a vigorous campaign urging the white electorate to reject — albeit for different reasons — the new constitution.[179]

For the National Party leadership, the establishment of the multi-racial President's Council and the decision to abandon the truncated Westminster-style parliamentary system was a calculated risk. The Botha regime took five years to prepare the National Party's diverse constituencies for this ideological *volte face*. The party had come a long way from its initial 1948 *apartheid* formula of a complete and unadulterated 'separation of powers' to the uncharted course of 'healthy power-sharing'. For die-hard Afrikaner nationalists, the Botha regime had crossed an inviolable threshold, abdicating its historic responsibility to protect the 'white race'. In the view of the Conservative Party and the HNP, 'the admission of people who were not white to a symbolic equality and into the highest governing circles was the thin end of a dangerous wedge that would lead ultimately to the similar admission of [African] blacks.'[180] These right-wing parties appealed to the most threatened sections of the white electorate, resurrecting the shibboleth of 'race-mixing' and issuing dire warnings about the dangers of capitulation. The *Afrikaner Volkswag* gave birth to such phantasms as the creation of a racially-separate 'white Homeland'. In the view of Carol Boshoff (chair of the *Afrikaner Volkswag*), white self-determination in a state where whites constituted the majority was a prerequisite for Afrikaner self-determination. The *Afrikaner Weerstandsbeweging* (Afrikaner Resistance Movement) bawled out the most vulgar and genuinely fascist themes. This paramilitary organization (under the leadership of Eugene Terre Blanche) even has a swastika-like emblem, adorned with three representations of the number seven.

In essence, the National Party sought — in the words of a prominent Afrikaner businessman — 'the secret of sharing power without losing control'.[181] The 'new dispensation' offered a bureaucratic and illusory formula that formally broadened political representation by encouraging Indian and 'coloured' participation in tricameral parliamentary elections, but actually diluted the overall influence of the legislative branch. The National Party never enjoyed the trust of, nor more than shallow popularity in, coloured and Indian communities. However, it maintained control through a sprinkling of patronage and widespread intimidation. Botha hoped that these symbolic gestures would secure at least temporarily the political acquiescence of the privileged strata among these 'population registration groups'. But this strategy depended on the ability of collaborating intermediaries to use their newly-acquired patronage powers to confuse, divide, and demoralize the Indian and coloured masses.

Forms of Political Representation for Coloured and Indian People

Botha's effort to entice coloured and Indian participation in the tricameral parliament must be measured against the dismal record of disenfranchisement and political treachery practised against these communities. The 1910 Act of Union recognized only the European male franchise in the Transvaal and Orange Free state, restricted elected office to persons of 'European descent', accepted the qualified franchise for a handful of 'non-European' males in the Cape and Natal, and eliminated any further registration of Indian and African males in Natal. In 1930, the extension of the franchise to white women and the abolition of the last vestiges of franchise qualifications for white adults even further undermined the precarious 'non-European' franchise. In 1936, the remaining Cape African voters were transferred to a separate voters' roll and a purely advisory Native Representatives Council (under the jurisdiction of the Secretary for Native Affairs) was established to monitor African opinion.[182] In 1943, the J.C. Smuts administration created the Coloured Affairs Department (CAD) and established the Coloured Advisory Council. In the ensuing political struggle, the nationwide anti-CAD organization was formed. Its political principle of non-collaboration was concretized through boycotts. The anti-CAD campaign resulted in the mass resignation of the few remaining CAC participants in 1950.[183]

In 1951, the National Party established a separate voters' roll for coloured voters in the Cape and Natal, hoping to divert political aspirations along sectarian lines and to channel political demands away from full democratic participation in a unified South Africa. In an effort to rekindle dwindling political support, the government formed the Coloured Persons' Representative Council (CPRC) in 1969. The highly circumscribed functions of the CPRC were restricted to finance, local government, education, and community development insofar as they affected the coloured population registration group.[184] The mass anti-collaborationist movement condemned the CPRC as a 'dummy institution', a 'toy telephone', and a 'circus', referring disdainfully to the Cape Town CPRC offices as 'Uncle Tom's Cabin'. The obscure political parties that participated in the CPRC farce were opportunist organizations, warmly embracing *apartheid* and hoping thereby to wrest a few meagre concessions from the National Party in exchange for their collaboration.[185] The Labour Party — the only avowedly anti-*apartheid* political entity that stood for CPRC elections — claimed that its participation in this segregated political institution was a viable means for advancing the struggle to dismantle *apartheid*. Under increasing pressure from the coloured community, the Labour Party sabotaged the CPRC, bringing its administrative operations to a virtual standstill.[186]

The National Party dissolved the CPRC in 1980. Despite its 'confrontationalist' rhetoric, the Labour Party always exhibited a trancelike fascination with bureaucratic intrigue and the 'closed door' politicking that characterized the CPRC. It gained control over the Management Committees in the coloured townships, using its patronage to dispense favours and build a power base. At the beginning of 1980, the National Party proposed the establishment of an anaesthetized Coloured Person's Council consisting of government-appointed members to serve as a temporary consultative entity before the new constitutional proposals were actually implemented. However, the rising political polarization in Cape Town at the time ensured that this scheme came to nothing.[187]

The Indian community experienced similar disenfranchisement and political marginalization. Immigrants from the Indian sub-continent had originally come to South Africa as indentured labourers on Natal's expanding sugar plantations in the 1860s. A virulent anti-Indian campaign in the 1890s sought to restrict the granting of trading licenses because of 'unfair competition' and to limit Indian political rights. After the 1910 Act of Union, further immigration of Indians was prohibited. For decades, the official policy concentrated on curtailing Indian trading licenses, prohibiting land purchases, and encouraging repatriation.[188]

Over the course of many years the South African Indian Congress — founded in the 1890s by Mohandas K. Ghandhi — spearheaded the struggle against racial discrimination and abuse. In the 1950s, the Indian Congress cemented an alliance with the African National Congress. In 1965, the Verwoerd regime created the South African Indian Council (SAIC). The Minister of Indian Affairs originally appointed all members of the SAIC. The SAIC's first order of business was to advance a petty bourgeois programme demanding the formation of an Indian Investment Corporation (eventually founded in 1977), underwriting diverse entrepreneurial ventures, granting financial assistance to Indian landowners through the Land and Agricultural Bank, creating 'industrial zones' for the exclusive use of Indian businesses, and promoting education and training for the embryonic Indian middle class.[189]

Whatever initial credibility the SAIC did enjoy gradually evaporated. The fact that SAIC members were appointed and that its powers were rigidly limited contributed to widespread apathy and indifference. In the face of this chilly reception, the Department of Indian Affairs transferred the administration of education and welfare for the Indian population to the SAIC and gradually expanded SAIC membership to include five new positions subject to popular vote. Throughout the 1970s, the SAIC was preoccupied with questions of expanding trading and commercial opportunities and of technical training for Indian youth. In order to demonstrate their unswerving willingness to cooperate with the white minority regime, the SAIC proposed the establishment of an Indian Special Service Battalion (under the command of the South African Navy). The Department of Indian Affairs rewarded these and other indications of loyalty by not only expanding SAIC membership but also permitting all positions to be filled by ballot. In 1978, the white minority regime announced the abrogation of resettlement plans for Indian traders in accordance with Group Areas Act provisions (except for those in certain rural towns in the Transvaal and in Ladysmith, Natal.)[190]

In 1979, a prominent entrepreneur and member of the SAIC, J.N. Reddy, addressed the Carleton Conference of business leaders. In his speech, he praised the efforts of Prime Minister Botha to 'harness the resources of the private sector' and called for the removal of all statutory and nonstatutory barriers that had impeded Indians, coloureds, and blacks from making 'their maximum contribution to the growth and mobility of our nation and our economy'. Further, he urged that business leaders and high-ranking state functionaries join together 'as a matter of priority [to] create within our land conditions conducive to the participation of all race groups in the free enterprise system'.[191] This was an unabashed testimonial to the *modus operandi* of the Botha regime: if provided with a sufficiently secure stake in the capitalist system, propertied segments of the oppressed majority might be prepared to defend it.[192]

In 1981, the SAIC elections saw an average voter turnout of 10 per cent, with the lowest polls recorded in working-class districts. This popular rejection of the SAIC did not, however, bring about its collapse. While acknowledging that the election results were a grave disappointment, the Minister of Internal Affairs, Chris Heunis, declared that 'From the Government's side, it will look upon the newly elected South African Indian Council and its executive committee, as the only representative body of the Indian community to serve as their mouthpiece for furthering their interests.'[193] From the point of view of the white minority regime, the SAIC had not exhausted its usefulness until another vehicle — the new tricameral Parliament — had been firmly implanted as a substitute.

The New South African Constitution

The much-heralded 'new dispensation' was finally unveiled in the form of the 1983 Constitution Act. This Act established an executive branch headed by the State President and a tricameral parliament (with separate chambers for whites, coloureds, and Indians). The African majority was totally excluded from formal political representation in Parliament. The basic principle of the Constitution was the partition between 'general affairs' and 'own affairs'. The former category referred to matters — particularly legislation — affecting all population registration groups (including Africans). The latter referred to matters affecting only one of the three population categories participating in the new administrative system. 'Own affairs' were defined literally as matters that particularly or differentially affected a single registration group in 'relation to the maintenance of its identity and the upholding and furtherance of its way of life, culture, traditions and customs'.[194]

The newly created office of State President joined the functions of President of the Republic and Chair of the Cabinet, abrogating the former separation of powers between the Prime Minister and State President. In Danaher's words, '[The State President] has veto power over legislation. He can pass laws by means of plebiscite, and has the power to dissolve parliament. The president is not elected directly by the people. Rather, he is chosen indirectly by an electoral college composed of fifty whites, twenty-five coloureds, and thirteen Indians'.[195] In the selection of cabinet ministers, the president was authorized to appoint members from outside the ranks of Parliament, thereby further insulating the executive branch from the modest yet nagging criticism of white opposition parties.

The new South African constitution retained the existing House of Assembly (with 178 white members), adding a House of Representatives (with 83 coloured members) and a House of Delegates (with forty-five Indian members). Most (but not all) members of each chamber of Parliament were elected separately on the basis of separate voter rolls in accordance with the different population registration groups. Each of the three chambers legislate separately on 'group affairs'. While the three chambers can collaborate on 'matters of common interest', the president has the power to determine whether any particular issue falls under this rubric or not. In the event of a deadlock on 'matters of common interest' (an unlikely possibility because of the predominance of white members in Parliament), the President's Council is authorized to deliver a final verdict. Like the Cabinet, the electoral college, and the Parliament, the President's Council has a majority of white members.[196]

The lynchpin of the new Constitution is the office of State President. The occupant of this position is effectively the nominee of the ruling party in the House of Assembly. The State President is to be elected for a five-year term of office by an electoral college consisting of delegates selected from each of the three Houses of Parliament. In line with the 4:2:1 formula, the electoral college contains fifty white, twenty-five coloured, and thirteen Indian delegates elected by majority vote.[197] While the State President does not possess legislative veto power, the Constitution gives him extensive authority to orchestrate and manipulate the legislative process. His appointive powers are so extensive that the system resembles an executive autocracy.

This 'new dispensation' at least formally broadened political representation, yet weakened the already restricted authority of the legislature. As one commentator noted: 'Parliament ... is an irrelevance for most of the population [and] is becoming of decreasing significance to the white group as well.'[198] In order to deflect overseas criticism, South African state officials portrayed the institutional reforms as a mere substitution of an executive presidential model (patterned after the United States) for the

British Westminster-style model of parliamentary democracy. However, under the terms of the new constitution, the National Party is able to exercise full power as long as it remains the largest single white party, even if it acquires just 34 per cent of the seats in the white chamber.[199]

The Community Council System

The 1976-7 Soweto uprising demonstrated that the weakest link in the state's battery of administrative constitutions was the 'inner perimeter' of townships and ghettos housing the urban black population. In 1977, the Vorster regime introduced the Community Councils Act as the first step in containing political dissatisfaction in the urban areas. This Act embodied the hitherto unrecognized principle that urban black residents were a permanent feature of the 'white' metropolitan environment. In substance, it offered a form of 'self-government' to the black urban areas that paralleled 'self-rule' in the Homelands. These community councils were in theory the black counterparts to the town councils in the white municipalities.

Administrative and bureaucratic structures in the black townships have been modified considerably over the years. Prior to 1971, white municipal governments — in conjunction with other local white authorities — assumed primary responsibility for the administration of African urban townships. In the early decades of the twentieth century, white municipal governments enjoyed wide-ranging discretionary powers, particularly in such areas as influx control and the determination of residential patterns along racial lines. Over time, however, white municipal governments became conduits for national policy directives and their previous room for maneouvre was whittled away.

The 1923 Urban Areas Act provided for the appointment of white-staffed Advisory Boards. In 1961, the Verwoerd regime began to replace these administrative bodies with Urban Bantu Councils chaired by African appointees. These powerless bodies failed to attract the attention let alone the loyalty of township residents with the exception of a thin upper crust of well-to-do Africans. Widely derided as 'devices designed to inveigle them into the implementation of *apartheid*',[200] township residents dubbed the Urban Bantu Councils 'Useless Boys Clubs'.[201]

In 1971, the Bantu Affairs Administration Boards Act created twenty-two Bantu Administration Boards (the number was later reduced) scattered across 'white South Africa'. This Act empowered the Minister of Bantu Administration and Development to appoint their (white) chairs and members. These Boards reported directly to Pretoria, bypassing local white municipal governments whose previous authorities were abrogated. The underlying objective of this Act was to streamline administrative control over the black townships by excluding intermediary bodies, thereby ensuring greater uniformity in the implementation of *apartheid* policies.

These Administration Boards were responsible for administering services in the black urban areas, particularly the allocation of housing and labour recruitment. From the outset, the Pretoria central administration expected these Administration Boards to become financially self-supporting. They raised revenues from a variety of disparate sources, including various administrative and permit fees; fines and levies; the sale of home-brewed beer and liquor; house rentals; admission fees for cinemas, recreational halls, and sports grounds; and levies payable by employers who accommodated their black employees in township hostels.[202] In its exhaustive survey of Board practices, the Riekert Commission provided figures indicating that for the years 1973-7 inclusive the Administration Boards spent over twice as much on the manufacture and sale of home-brewed beer and other liquor than for the provision of housing. Revenues from the sale of beer and liquor exceeded three-fold the income from housing rentals.[203]

The Administration Boards were integral extensions of centralized departmental machineries and, hence, not exclusive agencies like local municipal authorities. As such, they were not empowered to make their own regulations but merely to follow directives issued from above. Despite these restrictions, the Administration Boards acquired a well-deserved reputation for bureaucratic meddling in township affairs and for obstructiveness. 'It is reasonably clear', Welsh admitted, 'that the Boards and the Department of Cooperation and Development are entrenched bastions of [white] conservatism, still to a large extent steeped in the ideology of Verwoerd.'[204] The Riekert Commission ventured a few cautious criticisms of the Administration Boards, including the charge that they had failed to improve the allocation and canalization of labour.[205] The Commission of Inquiry into the Uprising in Soweto and Elsewhere revealed widespread popular hostility to the Boards. Black witnesses before the Commission testified that the Boards were hated for their enforcement of influx control because their staffs put bureaucratic hurdles in the paths of urban black people attempting to iron out discrepancies in their Section 10 status. Others complained bitterly that Board officials were arrogant, unsympathetic, discourteous, and racist. In an explicit disclosure of findings unprecedented in its stark honesty, the *Commission* concluded: 'The dissatisfaction with the administration boards was of such an extent that Black inhabitants were so activated that they could easily go over to uprising.'[206] Similarly, the annual report of Black Sash's Johannesburg Advice Office reported that '[Board] officials make their own laws and impose impossible requirements on people. They often act unlawfully and increasingly black people believe that they have to pay somebody for something if they are to achieve recognition of their rights or to obtain redress of wrongs done to them.'[207]

During the 1970s, the financial chaos of the costly Administration Board system turned into a political crisis. On the one hand, the Administration Boards collected rents and implemented the allocation of labour through the labour bureaux. On the other, they failed to match the expectations of township residents for the provision of social services and amenities. During the 1976-7 uprising, township residents singled out — as exemplary symbols of their oppression — Administration Board beerhalls, offices, vehicles, and so forth as targets for their collective rage. This critique of fire further exacerbated the fiscal crisis.

Growing radicalization of township residents in the mid-1970s brought the entire Administration Board system to a state of disintegration if not total collapse. In this atmosphere of increasing social discontent, the position of the Boards became more and more precarious. The primary objective of the 1977 Community Councils Act was to defuse the urban political crisis by injecting an intermediate buffer between the centralized state apparatuses and the township population.

The Botha regime welcomed the Community Council system as a 'just dispensation [for urban black residents] on the level of local government'.[208] The new system had a double purpose:

first, to control the collective means of consumption in the townships more efficiently; and second, to extend conditional political rights to a small segment of the African people.[209] The Minister of Cooperation and Development was empowered to replace the moribund Urban Bantu Councils with Community Councils whose membership would be determined by township elections. To qualify to vote or to stand for election to the Community Council, voters had to be, *inter alia*, citizens of South Africa, without a criminal record, registered occupiers of township accommodation, and listed on the franchise rolls.[210]

After consultation with the local Administration Board, the Minister of Cooperation and Development was empowered to determine both the composition of each council and the basis for elections. At the apex of the bureaucratic chain of command, the Minister was also authorized to allocate their functions and duties to the councils, including (1) the allocation and administration of rented accommodation, dwellings, buildings, and other structures; (2) the prevention of squatting on land and in buildings; (3) the approval of building plans for private dwellings and the removal or destruction of unauthorized or abandoned structures; (4) the promotion of sound community development and the moral and social welfare of the people; (5) the maintenance of services as determined by the Minister; (6) and the control and management of a 'community guard'.[211] This last provision had sinister implications, reflecting the state's desire to legalize the Makgotla vigilantes that arose in many black townships. These groups supposedly enforced law and order, but many township residents have decried their ferocious and indiscriminate methods of dispensing 'justice'.[212]

In mid-1980, the Department of Cooperation and Development reported that a total of 200 Community Councils in 238 black urban residential areas had been established. An average poll of 39 per cent of registered voters was achieved in 163 elections. In 66 of the 163 elected councils, all those standing for election were returned unopposed. In 1978, Community Council elections conducted in Soweto recorded a poll of only 6 per cent.[213]

The Community Council system modified the prevailing chain of command linking the central state apparatuses to the urban townships. The formal relationship between the Community Council and the Administration Boards was described as a principal/agent arrangement. Community Councils were designed to function as decision-making bodies and the Administration Boards were authorized to serve as their agents in executing these decisions. In practice, the relationship was reversed. Community Councils operated under the 'guidance' of the Administration Boards. The Community Councils were nominally in charge of the allocation of housing accommodation, but the Administration Boards supervised housing allocations, rental collections, tenant evictions, and so forth, 'on behalf of' — and at the 'behest of' — the Community Councils. The two non-negotiable functions that remained firmly entrenched within the jurisdiction of the Administration Boards (in collaboration with the police) were that of influx control and labour allocation (through the official labour bureaux). Since the 1979 Riekert Commission report, influx control has been linked to the availability of housing and employment.[214]

From the outset, the Community Councils assumed responsibility for devising township budgets. However, the Administration Boards maintained strict control over financing. The Minister of Cooperation and Development declared emphatically that the Community Councils could not expect external funding. Local communities must 'either trim their needs and cut their expenses, or they must supply the income to pay for what they want'.[215] The lack of decent housing (with the attendant social amenities such as sewerage, electricity, indoor plumbing, weatherization, and so forth) was the most acute example of the shortfall in essential services. Since the publication of the Riekert Commission Report, privately-sponsored corporate welfare organizations have provided some essential services in the townships, thereby removing the political onus from state agencies (responsible for providing the collective means of consumption) and onto individuals' 'ability-to-pay'. A handful of corporations became involved in the provision and upgrading of housing for their employees. Philanthropic bodies such as the Urban Foundation provided housing loans on a case-by-case basis.[216]

In late 1978, the Urban Councils Association of South Africa (UCASA) was established. Comprising approximately two-thirds of the then-elected community councillors, the UCASA was supposed to conduct direct negotiations with state agencies such as the Department of Cooperation and Development. The black councillors who served on the Community Councils were drawn mainly from the ranks of the traditional petty-bourgeoisie (traders, businessmen, self-employed professionals, and so on). The character of the demands raised by UCASA provided a ready index of the class interests that it represented. In the main, UCASA articulated grievances associated with security of tenure and trading rights for African businessmen.

Local civic organizations and umbrella groups such as AZAPO rejected participation in these Community Councils on the grounds that they were lifeless 'puppet bodies', rubber stamping rent and other service increases decided by the Administration Boards while not providing any improvements in living conditions.[217] The Department of Cooperation and Development had hoped to deflect widespread popular dissatisfaction by replacing the white functionaries and bureaucrats of the Administration Boards with elected black auxiliaries. This diversionary tactic only succeeded in attracting and co-opting the largely conservative and accommodationist groups of black businessmen.[218]

High-ranking officials emphasized time after time that the ultimate purpose of the new bodies was to create autonomous black municipalities with a variety of extraordinary powers and with direct access to the central state apparatuses.[219] The 1982 Black Local Authorities Act marked the highpoint of the 'new deal' initiative aimed at the incorporation of urban blacks. This Act was one of the 'Koornhoff Bills', originally tabled in 1980. In essence, the Black Local Authorities Act (BLA) was a sophisticated plan to co-opt township residents in the management of their own oppression. It reconstituted the Community Councils into town (or village) councils, transferring the bulk of the powers, duties, and functions previously conferred on the Administration Boards (now renamed Development Boards) to the new semi-autonomous Local Authorities. However, the power of Ministerial intervention was not diminished. The Minister of Cooperation and Development retained his veto over Local Authority decisions. In fact, the Minister was authorized to 'act on behalf of' Local Authorities should they for any reason fail to carry out their responsibilities.

To many critics, the ideal of semi-autonomous black municipalities with their own police forces, schools, hospitals, and administrative structures seemed a rather crude effort 'to defuse black claims to national political power through the substitution of power at the grassroots level'.[220] The underlying principle that governed this experiment in crisis management was, as one white official put it, 'the phasing out of the Administration Boards altogether ... creative withdrawal'. By transferring day-to-day responsibilities for administering townships to black Local Authorities, the white minority regime hoped to 'deracialize' township supervision. In Cornell's words, 'The "Africanization" of control in the townships may prove a source of confusion, but it may also, on the other hand, reveal more clearly the real basis of *apartheid* — class rule.'[221]

The Botha regime introduced this BLA system in stages, to coincide with the entry of so-called Indians and Coloureds into the tricameral Parliament. The ostensible intention was to provide powerless town councils with the status and autonomy of elected white municipalities, without deviating from the policy that black residents had to exercise their full-fledged political rights in the Homelands. Township residents were unimpressed by this unilateral, imposition of the BLA system and mounted highly successful election boycott campaigns. Nevertheless, the Botha regime established 38 separate BLAs, of which 22 had been elevated in 1984 to the status of 'fully fledged black local authorities'. Still, this number fell far short of the hundred-odd town councils that the white minority regime had predicted for the end of 1984.[222]

The black townships have always been enfeebled by their wretched infrastructure. By linking self-governance of the townships with the cynical proviso that they should be self-financing, the white minority regime disentangled itself from the politically explosive problem of overseeing local transportation services, housing, hospitals, schools, electrification, refuse collection, and so forth. Without an industrial or commercial base, the councils lacked a viable tax base from which to finance desperately-needed services. In 1984, more than a dozen town councils announced rent increases — the main source of revenue for the local authorities. Many town councils also attempted to impose higher service charges for electricity and water. In some areas, township residents were enraged when they discovered that 'councillors voted themselves large salaries, houses, cars and council chambers'.[223]

The Search for an Alternative Route

The white minority regime reached a political impasse in the immediate aftermath of the Soweto uprising. Blanket repression brought an end to street demonstrations and mass rallies and temporarily silenced popular opposition. Nevertheless, the indiscriminate campaign of military terror effectively undermined the thin veneer of legitimacy that the white minority regime had so painstakingly nurtured over the course of the previous decade.

For nearly thirty years, the National Party had dominated a framework within which exclusively white political institutions co-existed uneasily with a relatively dynamic capitalist economic system. But continued economic growth increasingly depended upon the incorporation of skilled black labour and the wholesale expansion of the black consumer market. The National Party's *ad hoc* tinkering with (racially-designated) separate political structures for the permanently settled black population only worsened the underlying contradictions. This 'growth model' that combined rapid industrial expansion with rigid constraints on black upward mobility and political participation had reached its outer limits. The Soweto rebellion only hastened its demise. Against this background, Botha embarked on his restructuring of the conditions of the dominant classes' hegemony.

'The system', in the words of a commentator, 'is going through a profound and often agonized reappraisal.'[224] For Botha's regime, the paradox has been that in order to preserve the kernel of *apartheid* it was necessary to shed distinctive layers of its outer shell, thereby provoking a right-wing backlash from the National Party's hitherto staunchest political supporters. The reformist initiative consisted of two separate yet interrelated projects. The first involved establishing a *modus vivendi* with leading corporate and business associations. Prominent business executives and National Party leaders eulogized the capacity of market forces to reverse the recessionary cycle and create economic opportunities for all racial groups. The second involved a radical departure from the *apartheid* principle of 'racial exclusivity' in the central state apparatuses: a bold plan to incorporate a segment of the coloured and Indian registration groups as junior partners in an enlarged power bloc. The Constitutional changes, as we have seen, actually concentrated political power in the executive branch and weakened the influence of the legislative. Thus, the Botha regime 'imprinted its strategy for the defense of South African capitalism upon the country's political system'.[225]

In order to lend credibility to these political gyrations, the National Party downplayed its fiery racialist rhetoric and substituted a newspeak of 'consociational democracy', 'plural relations', and 'orderly urbanization', and promoted the idea that South Africa was a land of ethnic minorities, none of which could claim numerical preponderance.[226] All sections of the white political establishment — including the PFP — hurried to defend this specious proposition, and to argue that 'one-person one-vote' might actually undermine minority rights.

For many Afrikaans-speaking whites who had professed undying loyalty to the National Party, this 'bastardization' of white politics was an unspeakable betrayal of their heritage. Amid irate accusations of selling out the *herrenvolk*, significant numbers of white wage-earners, white farmers, small businessmen, professionals and others fled to the ultra-rightwing HNP and the Conservative Party. The leader of the HNP, Jaap Marais, warned that National Party policies aimed at economic equality between blacks and whites would 'soon be followed by social equality and, ultimately by political equality. . . . The Government is selling us out', he proclaimed. 'They are only concerned about blacks and are doing nothing for whites.'[227]

Botha followed a middle route between the liberal and conservative wings of the white minority regime. His administration has consistently rejected the liberal option, that is, a closer alliance with the English-speaking capitalists and their political allies in the PFP. This route would have entailed the extension of political representation to the African majority, albeit in a highly circumscribed, federated structure of checks and balances. The National Party leadership depended on privileged petty bourgeois strata as well as propertyless white wage-earners for its mass electoral support. Consequently, it was 'obliged to maintain preferential access to the state for whites, with the corollary of unequal citizenship for Africans'.[228] It was therefore out of the question for the National Party to contemplate any restoration of the coloured common voters' roll. After all, Party hardliners had fought a ruthless campaign to abrogate these rights, in part because coloured voters had historically cast their ballots for anti-Nationalist parties and would undoubtedly do so again if offered the opportunity.[229]

The principal objective of the Botha regime was to drive a wedge 'between an elite of urban black "insiders" and the mass of rural black "outsiders"'.[230] The National Party had commandeered the liberal belief that a crucial ingredient in the maintenance of political stability was the creation of a durable black middle class committed to the ideals of free enterprise.[231] Of course, only the most affluent black merchants were in a position to take advantage of the 99-year leasehold system (with its hidden economic costs) and new opportunities for business enterprise. The Total Strategy doctrine — with its reformist rhetoric of a 'new deal' and a 'new dispensation' — may have had a few liberal side-effects, but its central purpose was 'to rationalise *apartheid* and convert what is in many ways an incoherent system of control into a smooth-running machine of domination'.[232] 'The fundamental aim of the [reformist initiative]', another commentator argued, 'is to strengthen white hegemony, not dilute it, or, even less, abandon it.'[233]

3.

The Independent Black Trade Union Movement

By the 1980s, the independent black trade union movement had become a permanent fixture of the South African political scene. It developed out of a series of spontaneous strikes for higher wages and improved working conditions that erupted in Durban and the neighbouring industrial centre of Pinetown in early 1973. From mid-January to the end of February 1973, an estimated 70,000 black workers at 150 plants in the Durban area staged numerous walkouts and work stoppages. The strike wave spread, culminating in the September walkout at Anglo-American's Western Deep Levels pit in Carletonville near Johannesburg in which eleven gold miners were killed.[1]

The small, nearly moribund black trade unions that remained from the previous wave of unionization of the late 1950s and early 1960s played no active role in initiating or directing the strikes. Black workers had been able through their own efforts to inflict significant disruptions of production and to force employers to grant unaccustomed concessions.[2] These mass strike actions engendered a resurgence of working-class organization and militancy, bolstering the confidence and expanding the class consciousness of black workers. Following the strikes, a number of fledgling trade unions came into existence with the expressed purpose of organizing black workers around the pressing issues that had ignited the wave of walkouts. Despite numerous setbacks and the agonizingly slow process of organizational consolidation, these independent black trade unions grew in strength and in numbers. By the 1980s, they had achieved significant successes in improving wages and working conditions for their members and had made recognizable gains in protecting workers from arbitrary management decisions. Over the course of four years of often exasperating trade union 'unity talks', the independent black trade unions coalesced around five distinct principles of unity that called for workers' control, internal democracy based on proportional representation, an industrial base, nonracialism, and disciplined unity. The formation of the Congress of South African Trade Unions (COSATU) in November 1985 representing an estimated 500,000 workers signified a dramatic breakthrough for the working class movement.

Monopoly Capital in South Africa

Ownership and control of the principal means of production in the South African mining, manufacturing, transport, trade, and finance sectors has been consolidated in the hands of a small number of locally-based corporate conglomerates, state corporations, and a few foreign-based transnational corporations. The agricultural sector remains the last remaining bastion of competitive relations and small-scale ownership. Nevertheless, corporate penetration over the past decade has engendered a decisive shift in the direction of agri-business, particularly in the fields of plantation sugar production in Natal, cattle-ranching in the Transvaal, and wine production in the Western Cape.

In 1977, a special commission of inquiry established the previous year to review monopolistic competition reported that there was 'an exceptionally high degree of concentration of economic power in the major divisions of the South African economy'.[3] In 1981, eight private conglomerates and the state corporations controlled over 70 per cent of the total assets of the largest 138 companies. The largest cartel, Anglo-American Corporation, alone controlled assets in 1981 worth more than the combined Gross Domestic Products (GDP) of the nine member countries of the Southern African Development Coordination Conference (SADCC). Three of the conglomerates — SANLAM, Volkskas, and Rembrandt — could be classified as Afrikaner capital, thus demonstrating the degree to which monopoly capital as a whole had become thoroughly integrated in the post-1948 *apartheid* era. Equally important, the degree of centralization and interpenetration of capital in South Africa extended beyond the eight conglomerates to include the tremendous growth of medium-sized conglomerates that had in turn followed aggressive policies of acquisition and consolidation in all sectors of economic activity.

According to the authoritative McGregor's *Investors' Handbook*, Anglo-American Corporation exercised 54.1 per cent control of all Johannesburg Stock Exchange companies, followed by SANLAM with 11.3 per cent, and South African Mutual with 10.9 per cent in 1986. In South Africa, takeovers flourish unabated and, unlike other industrialized countries, anti-monopoly regulations are virtually non-existent.[4] Anglo-American Corporation remains perched at the summit of economic affairs. By far and away the largest and most powerful South African conglomerate, Anglo-American owns an estimated 69 per cent of the total capital invested in the South African mining industry. It possesses vast industrial holdings in various fields, including agribusiness. It has also successfully penetrated the South African insurance, finance, property, press, and service sectors. It maintains extensive holdings in all SADCC countries. By 1981, Anglo-American was the single largest foreign investor in the United States, in addition to maintaining substantial investments in Europe and the Third World. The leading Afrikaner insurance and financial conglomerate, SANLAM, represents the second largest concentration of economic power in South Africa outside the state corporations. Functioning primarily as an investment house, SANLAM distributes its holdings over virtually every sector. The Barlow Rand Group is the largest industrial conglomerate, consisting of an estimated 300 separate companies organized into 14 broad divisions. These companies are concentrated in the heavy industry (particularly metallurgical operations), food products, and mining sectors.

Reorganized in 1982, the South African Transport Services (SATS) is the largest state corporation as well as the largest single employer in South Africa. At that time, it maintained nearly 275,000 employees and held a near monopoly on all large-scale transport in South Africa. A number of other state corporations (the so-called 'parastatals') dominate specific branches of industry. The Iron and Steel Corporation (ISCOR) controlled more than 75 per cent of South African iron and steel production in 1982. The giant state-owned oil-from-coal and chemical producing corporation, SASOL, plays a key role in the white minority regime's plan of thwarting the effects of worldwide oil sanctions. The Armaments Development and Production Corporation (ARMSCOR) was established in 1964 to circumvent the threatened arms boycott and has become largely responsible for supplying the South African military.

Capitalist interests are politically represented through a number of large business associations: the Associated Chambers of Commerce (ASSOCOM), the South African Federated Chamber of Industries (FCI), the Afrikaner Handelsinstitut (AHI), the National African Federated Chambers of Commerce and Industry (NAFCOC), and the South Africa Foundation (SAF), a nonelected umbrella body that has been instrumental in paving the way for business unity on a number of sensitive political issues. Along with the Chamber of Mines and the Steel and Engineering Industries Federation (SEIFSA), these organizations represent 80 percent of national employment.[5] Whether operating through these business assocations or independently, the large corporate groups have fashioned 'well-established lobby bases within government circles'.[6]

The Working Class in South Africa

The Specificity of the Black Working Class

The relatively recent and nearly exponential growth of the independent black trade union movement cannot be properly understood without first studying the course of working-class formation in South Africa. The evolution and structural transformation of the social division of labour which has accompanied the processs of capital accumulation and the reproduction of social classes in South Africa has entailed a relatively distinct dimension, namely, the use of a racial/national classification to assign particular agents to specific places in the social division of labour.

The rapid industrial expansion brought about by mineral discoveries on the Witwatersrand at the end of the nineteenth century resulted in an enormous growth of the proletariat. European immigrants, lured by false hopes of material gain, and 'poor whites', who were expropriated from increasingly capitalized landed property, combined to form what has been described as the 'white working class'.[7] Without substantively addressing the particular contours of the overall process of class formation, it can be said that propertied/nonpropertied class relations have inexorably polarized along racial/national lines. The historical specificity of class formation — the 'colour of class' — has entailed the elimination of all but a few distinctive proletarian places in the social division of labour occupied by white workers.

The distribution of these places has been far from even. White workers over the past several decades have been overwhelmingly concentrated in the lower levels of state employment, specialized trades and artisanal crafts (including mining), transport, and office/service personnel. On the whole, white wage-earners have relied to a considerable degree upon the conjoined practices of customary racial discrimination, employer bias, closed shop agreements with whites-only unions, and the inferior quality of 'Bantu education' — buttressed by state policies (e.g., 'civilized labour policy', 'job reservation,' etc.) — for their privileged and protected status in relation to black workers.

Put in broad terms, white wage-earners historically have been elevated and displaced from the working class *per se* and have increasingly filled places in the social division of labour that involve skill, mental labour, supervision and coordination, authority, service activities, and technical expertise. This historical disappearance of white wage-earners from the working class is absolutely critical to an understanding of contemporary South African politics and social life. It is indeed surprising that it has not come under considerable scrutiny.[8]

Correlatively, black wage-earners have increasingly filled skilled manual and nonsupervisory places in the social division of labour, and have even begun in some instances to invade previously restricted nonmanual and supervisory posts. The character of the black industrial and commercial labour force was transformed in the process of black wage-earners filling higher rungs on the job-skill ladder. From a homogeneous, largely migrant, and unskilled proletariat with little formal training or education, the black labour force became a heterogeneous entity with a hierarchy of its own, whose skills and training were essential to sustaining the capital accumulation process. This metamorphosis of the black working class took place over a lengthy period of time and in a more or less decentralized and unplanned fashion.

The extended reproduction of monopoly capitalist relations of production in South Africa historically involved the progressive deskilling and increasing subordination of manual labour on the one hand, and the creation of a minority of specialized supervisory and mental wage-earning places on the other.[9] What has been called the 'floating colour bar' denoted one aspect of this process. In the context of the overall trend toward deskilling and mechanization of skilled production tasks, managers of factories and other work places that experienced difficulties in filling job vacancies at the lowest rung of the job ladder reserved for whites often negotiated with the trade unions representing white wage-earners, offering wage increases and other concessions for the right to convert particular occupational categories into low-paid 'nonwhite' jobs. The 'rationalization' of occupational categories *via* 'productivity agreements' with white trade unions often took place in tandem with the 'fragmentation', 'dilution', and 'reclassification' of artisanal tasks previously performed exclusively by white wage-earners. Employers recruited low-paid black workers to perform newly mechanized manual functions in the labour process previously reserved for whites. Concomitantly, the previous white incumbents were 'upgraded' and reassigned to places 'higher up' in the occupational hierarchy.[10]

This *ad hoc* approach to modifications in the racial division of labour involved costly delays in production and monetary concessions to redundant white wage-earners. However, the prevailing conditions of expansion and increasing profitability during the 1960s and early 1970s permitted capitalist employers to absorb whatever losses were incurred. With the collapse of the distinctive *regime of accumulation* that sustained the 'long boom' of capitalist expansion and relative political stability, it became imperative for capital, in the struggle to maintain and restore profitability, to seek a wholesale modification in the racial division of labour and the removal of 'job colour bar' legislation. This process of restructuring accelerated in the post-Soweto era. In 1977, the Minister of Labour scrapped a number of statutory job reservations. In 1979, an agreement between the SEIFSA and

the white trade union bureaucracies abolished closed shop agreements barring African employees from certain grades of work.
Following the 1979 Wiehahn Commission recommendations, a
flurry of legislative acts repealed the remaining statutory job
reservation codes (with the exception of the mining industry)
and prohibited closed shop agreements which had restricted certain places in the division of labour to members of particular
racial groups.[11]

It is difficult if not impossible to classify accurately the various
segments of the black working class. By the 1980s if not before,
black workers presented a tableau of striking diversity and constant flux. In potential, the economically active black working
class numbered nearly 10 million persons. The official unemployment rate has been estimated variously between 10 and 20 per
cent. Nevertheless, this figure grossly underestimates the actual
number and glosses over enormous regional disparities. Measured
either in terms of sectors or of the whole, no accurate figures
exist for casual labourers who eked out a marginal existence
through part-time employment. For the economically active
black working class, approximately 20 per cent were employed in
agriculture or agriculture-related activities, 10 per cent in mining,
15 per cent in manufacturing, 10 per cent in construction/
transport, 10 per cent in commerce/finance, and 25 per cent in
'services'.[12]

Class Representation of the Working Class

By the 1980s, few if any serious observers of South African
politics regarded white wage-earners as such as potential allies
and supporters of a broad political programme that would
extend the same political rights and privileges that the white
electorate enjoyed within the framework of the bourgeois-
democratic form of the capitalist state to the black working class
and the black petty bourgeoisie. Both in terms of their objective
class interests and their present political positions, white wage-
earners have been for the most part polarized in the direction of
allied and supporting class fractions of the bourgeoisie as a
whole. This argument is not to suggest that 'race prejudice' alone
can account for this ideological/political stance within the
framework of the overall class struggle. It is certainly not difficult

to reconstruct the historical pattern whereby white wage-earners have demanded and received exclusive and/or privileged access to objective places in the social division of labour. Nevertheless, to refer to racial discrimination as the principal mode of social organization in South Africa without situating it within the framework of the structural determination of social classes comes dangerously close to replicating the conventional liberal stance of identifying the principal contradiction in contemporary South Africa as the polarization between inveterately racialist white wage-earners and Afrikaners on the one hand, and progressive 'reformist-minded' capitalists and black workers on the other. This particular brand of liberalism is most often associated with the Progressive Federal Party, transnational corporate executives, the Anglo-American Corporation, and the Urban Foundation. It has provided the ideological justification for a political pro-gramme of 'bourgeois reformism' under the command of monopoly capital.

Large-scale capitalist interests in South Africa have pursued a successive litany of accumulation strategies in the period both preceding and following the formation of a united and tightly structured capitalist state apparatus (1902-10). In order to unify particularistic (and hence competing and frequently antagonistic) interests and to remove specific obstacles to capital accumu-lation, the bourgeoisie has forged various hegemonic projects designed to amicably resolve differences and adjudicate between rival fractions as well as to win the political allegiance of non-propertied classes. After the wholesale military suppression of the 1922 Rand Revolt of white miners and the subsequent Pact regime (1924-32), the bourgeois-led hegemonic projects have always involved a basic antimony — on the one hand, non-propertied white wage-earners were incorporated into a broad multi-class alliance on the basis of material concessions and symbolic rewards as supporting and allied classes under the leadership — at different times and places — of various fractions of the bourgeoisie. On the other hand, the ideological cement that secured substantive unity between propertied and non-propertied classes within this multi-class alliance historically corresponded to what can be broadly termed white supremacy.

The class compromise between the bourgeois and white wage-earning strata that was formalized during the Pact regime (1924-32) marked a political watershed in South African history.

Class conflict (albeit frequently interspersed with racialist exclusivity) abruptly gave way to class collaboration. Without going into great detail, suffice it to say that only those registered in South Africa as 'white' enjoy the privileges of bourgeois-democratic rights associated with idealized depictions of Western capitalism. Those registered as 'Coloured' and 'Indian' have only highly circumscribed rights set within the framework of separate representation. Those registered as 'African' exist in a veritable limbo, caught between the nightmare of Homelands citizenship and the perpetual uncertainty of urban township life in 'white South Africa'. Perceived from any angle, the oppressed people of colour are burdened with a subject status without full-fledged rights of citizenship in the land of their birth.

Comparatively speaking, the condition of the so-called 'African' segment of the working class has remained precarious in the extreme. Pogrund described the situation in the following way: 'It is in South Africa alone that the division between "haves" and "have nots", whether in terms of economics or citizenship, is universally and automatically fixed by skin colour; and it is in South Africa alone that this division is supported and maintained by a complex web of law and customary practice that has been reinforced over the past 27 years [i.e., since 1948] as comprehensively and systematically as the ingenuity of legislators allows.'[13] African workers have experienced an intersecting double handicap. As registered Africans with citizenship rights limited to the Homelands, they have been subjected to racial discrimination in South Africa with limited juridical and administrative redress. As workers, they are also the victims of particular restrictions on their occupational mobility and market capacities. Legislative machinery such as the Native (Urban Areas) Act of 1923 — amended again and again — stipulated the constricted terms under which Africans were legally permitted to live in so-called 'prescribed areas' (i.e., the 'white' urban areas). The various mechanisms of influx control were designed to regulate the movement of black labour and to perpetuate its availability, docility, and inexpensiveness.

South African Trade Unions and the Industrial Relations System

Early Industrial Relations Framework

The Industrial Conciliation Amendment Act 94 of 1979 marked a significant departure from the existing legal framework governing employer-employee industrial relations in South Africa. This act reversed the longstanding dualistic approach in operation since 1924 of excluding African workers from the industrial relations and wage bargaining system formally reserved for white, coloured, and Asian workers. These modifications in past practices followed almost immediately the announced recommendations of the Wiehahn Commission, a consultative body appointed by Pretoria in 1977 to examine the efficacy of the extant industrial relations system. The introduction of the Wiehahn labour 'reforms' was a direct consequence of the inability of the existing industrial relations framework to contain workplace conflict, and in particular the growth of black trade unions operating independently of the official channels.

While the actual number of recognition agreements remained small, a few unregistered black trade unions successfully pressured some companies to acknowledge them as *de facto* bargaining agents outside the existing industrial relations framework. Before the implementation of the Wiehahn 'reforms', the industrial relations system consisted of two separate, and fundamentally unequal, spheres of operation. Its cornerstone was originally codified in the 1924 Industrial Conciliation Act. This legislation was enacted in the wake of at least a decade of bitter labour disputes culminating in the 1922 Rand Revolt, an armed confrontation pitting white mine workers against the police and army. According to the terms of the 1924 Industrial Conciliation Act, a 'trade union' was defined as consisting of 'employees' where the latter were described as any workers 'other than Bantu'.[14] The centerpiece of this post-1924 industrial relations machinery was the industrial councils, statutory bodies in which representatives from employer associations and registered trade unions negotiated minimum wages and working conditions in those sectors where these administrative mechanisms were formed. Agreements that the industrial councils reached were considered legally binding on all parties. Strikes and lockouts were prohibited until all dispute-settling procedures outlined in the Act were exhausted. Admission to the industrial councils was limited to officially recognized and formally registered trade unions, which, because they were not included within the category of 'employees', Africans were by definition barred from joining.[15] Even though African workers were permitted to form trade unions, they were unable to obtain official recognition for them. Thus, Africans were formally excluded from participation in whatever industry-wide negotiating sessions were sponsored under the rubric of industrial councils. Instead, they were expected to channel their class grievances through largely ineffectual plant-level committees that lacked the authority to negotiate legally binding agreements.[16] The 'civilized labour' policy that was hastily put into motion under the Pact regime (1924-32) promised white workers and their trade unions a range of guaranteed economic benefits based on racial privileges in exchange for labour peace. Where industrial councils existed, the statutory labour relations machinery compelled trade unions to participate in highly formal, bureaucratic, and centralized bargaining procedures that effectively undermined strikes as vehicles for redress of class grievances. While the process was varied and uneven, this institutionalized system of 'social partnership' between employers' associations and trade union functionaries evolved — particularly during the post-1948 *apartheid* era — into a mechanism of class collaboration. The industrial council system had effects on working-class consciousness, buttressing the loyalty of white trade unions to the white minority regime and offering material benefits to those 'coloured' and Asian trade unions that cooperated in the implementation and enforcement of collective bargaining agreements.

Despite their formal exclusion from collective bargaining procedures, African workers never refrained from organizing trade unions. Formed in 1918, the Industrial and Commercial Workers' Union (ICU) claimed more than 100,000 members in 1928. Operating more as a mass-based social movement than as an effective trade union, the ICU attracted a large following of rural wage-labourers before it disappeared with hardly a trace in the early 1930s.[17] The outstanding feature of South Africa's economic expansion during the 1930s and 1940s was the rapid growth of manufacturing industries. Aided by massive state investments in basic infrastructural projects, this accelerated industrialization corresponded to the large-scale expulsion of farm workers and the massive influx of these dispossessed people into the urban areas.[18] On the one hand, the state administration identified the process of industrialization and the accompanying proletarianization with the collapse of so-called 'tribal' social controls to which rural Africans had been subjected. On the other hand, the state administration recognized that the massive dislocation of the rural population threatened to spill over into increasingly militant agitation for labour and other reforms as well as increasingly 'undisciplined' urban unrest.[19] The European authorities feared that the 'unprecedented influx of natives [into the urban areas] ... brought in its train chaotic housing conditions, the deteriorization of social bonds, and all the evils attendant upon controlled population pressure [including] the creation of anti-social groups'.[20]

Rapid proletarianization was inevitably accompanied by the broadening of class conflict at the point of production and the renewed efforts of black workers to form trade unions. In 1942, the Council of Non-European Trade Unions (CNETU) was formed. By 1945, the CNETU claimed 119 affiliates with a total membership of 158,000 African workers, largely in the mining and textile industries. During this period, the dominated classes took the initiative — albeit in a largely unorganized and generally spontaneous way — in challenging both employers and the white minority regime over a range of economic, political, and economic issues.[21] The 1946 African mine workers strike symbolized the highpoint of this particularly turbulent conjuncture of labour agitation and political unrest. This massive strike involved over 80,000 black workers, temporarily paralyzing the gold mining industry. This walkout was quickly crushed through a massive display of state violence.[22]

From its collective experience in dealing with the staggering number of strikes and 'slow-downs' during the 1940s, large-scale industrial capital concluded that labour unrest at the point of production could only be thwarted through state certification and registration of emergent black trade unions, albeit in a highly circumscribed and emasculated way.[23] Having little faith in the repressive capacity of the state administration to deliver a quiescent working class and afraid that 'free-floating' black trade unions were vulnerable to 'irresponsible' political leadership, industrial capitalists in the main recommended the extension of the protective umbrella of the industrial conciliation machinery to include African trade unions, hoping that this manoeuvre would tend to bureaucratize these organizations and deflect black workers from spontaneous action.[24] Business associations insisted, however, that all African trade unions be debarred from any political affiliation and be prevented from joining together in any confederation.

In contrast, agrarian capital opposed any formal recognition of African trade unions, forecasting that any enhancement of the marketplace bargaining power of black workers would only accelerate the 'drift' of poorly-paid and miserably-treated farm labourers from the countryside to the urban areas. Similarly, the Chamber of Mines resisted any concessions to black trade unionism because of mining capital's reliance upon migrant labour. Finally, nonpropertied white wage-earners opposed the extension of African trade union rights because it threatened to undermine their privileged place in the social division of labour.

After its 1948 electoral triumph, the National Party appointed an Industrial Legislation Commission of Inquiry (known as the Botha Commission) to investigate the salience of the existing industrial relations machinery in light of the divergent opinions that divided the dominant bloc of class forces. In 1951, the Botha Commission recommended that African trade unions should be extended nominal statutory recognition under a separate industrial conciliation apparatus. The Commission further suggested that if these proposals were accepted all strikes of African workers should remain illegal, that union officials be elected under strict state supervision and approval, and that labour disputes should be channelled through compulsory arbitration overseen by mediation boards.[25]

In testimony before this Botha Commission, the Chamber of Mines and agricultural capital vehemently opposed trade union recognition of any kind. The National Party concurred, regarding even limited recognition as a manifestation of appeasement tantamount to a reversal of its commitment to *apartheid*. The Party embarked instead on an ambiguous drive to suppress the militant upsurge of the black working class and the emergent black trade unions. It enacted the 1953 Bantu Labour (Settlement of Disputes) Act, reaffirming the World War II statutory prohibition against strikes and making provision for white-dominated industrial conciliation mechanisms incorporating

African wage-earners. Formal consultation between employers and African workers consisted of a peculiarly cumbersome bureaucratic labyrinth where these wage-earners were represented solely by in-plant works committees that functioned under the watchful guidance of Bantu labour officers, regional Bantu labour committees, and a Central Bantu Labour Board — all controlled by white administrators.[26] The principal objective of these works committees was to atomize and isolate industrial conflict on a factory-by-factory basis.

During the 1950s, the rapid concentration and centralization of capital created an increased demand for technical, supervisory, and clerical labour. White wage-earners were promoted from semi-skilled manual positions to fill the new openings on the mental side of the social division of labour. Correlatively, the wholesale transformation of the capitalist labour process not only accelerated the deskilling of many occupational categories that had been historically filled by white craft workers but also created new semi-skilled (operative) positions that were increasingly occupied by agents drawn from among previously unskilled black workers. This entire process of capitalist rationalization undermined the structural position of the trade unions associated with the South African Trades and Labour Council (SATLC).[27] The existing trade union groups collapsed under the strain, reappearing in a recast format that closely resembled the organizational nexus that had remained more or less intact into the post-Wiehahn period.

The trade union regroupment took place largely in the context of the debate over the 1956 Industrial Conciliation Amendment Act. This Act symbolized an even more proleptic effort on the part of the National Party to encapsulate and hence weaken independent black trade union activity. It prohibited the future registration of 'racially-mixed' trade unions, facilitated the separation of existing trade unions into separate branches representing different 'racial groups', and empowered the Minister of Labour to reserve certain occupational categories exclusively for white wage-earners.[28]

Put broadly, this 1956 Industrial Conciliation Amendment Act (in conjunction with the 1957 Wages Act) constituted the principal post-*apartheid* statutory foundation for state intervention in industrial disputes between capital and labour. These acts determined the contours of participation in the collective bargaining mechanisms that governed consultation in the Industrial Councils between industry-wide employers' associations and registered trade unions over wages and conditions of labour. Both these Acts retained the key 1924 definition of employee, thereby debarring African workers from membership of trade unions registered under the terms of the 1924 Industrial Conciliation Act and, consequently, excluding them from formal representation in collective bargaining procedures.[29]

At one extreme, the South African Confederation of Labour (SACLA) in 1957 united 'Christian National' trade unions and other 'white exclusivist' unions under a broad pro-*apartheid* banner seeking to preserve the sectional interests of white wage-earners. In contrast, the Trade Union Council of South Africa (TUCSA) was established in 1955 in the midst of the political controversy associated with the racialist provisions of the 1953 Native Labour (Settlement of Disputes) Bill and the subsequent demise of the SATLC. TUCSA constituted a 'middle-of-the-road' federation of registered trade unions. From the outset, it opposed the National Party's effort to separate trade unions in accordance with racial criteria. In principle, it proclaimed its political support for the eventual recognition and registration of African trade unions. In the meantime, it accepted (out of sheer opportunism) the terms of the 1956 Industrial Conciliation Act, refusing to register trade unions with African members. Instead, TUCSA called for trade union unity around a consultative relationship that would link the existing registered unions with unregistered African ones through liaison committees. This 'parallel union' policy aimed to recruit African workers into separate subsidiary organizations of the 'parent' — or registered — trade unions.[30] In short, TUCSA sought to secure and improve the living standards of its members without challenging the differential framework of the industrial relations system.

The insistence on the part of the TUCSA leadership that these African trade unions be limited to a subordinate role within TUCSA was motivated out of a crass self-interest far removed from working-class solidarity. TUCSA reasoned that the wages and working conditions of skilled and semi-skilled white wage-earners were positively pegged to the poverty-stricken wages of African workers. Therefore, any increase in wage-rates and improvements in bargaining position for African workers axiomatically constituted upward pressure on income and working conditions for white wage-earners.[31] Of course, TUCSA's 'pattern bargaining' signified — consciously or unconsciously — a commitment to retain the wage differentials that separated the highest-paid and the lowest-paid workers.

At the other extreme, the CNETU and the leftwing unions of the SATLC that regarded TUCSA's objectives as at best vaguely reformist and at worst paternalistic regrouped to form the South African Congress of Trade Unions (SACTU) in 1955.[32] Almost immediately, SACTU became enmeshed in the political mobilization that erupted with particular ferocity during the 1950s. In 1955, it joined with the African National Congress, the South African Indian Congress, and Congress of Democrats, and the Coloured Persons' Congress to form the Congress Alliance and participated in endorsing the Freedom Charter. SACTU functioned less as a trade union organization than as a conduit mobilizing workers in support of Congress Alliance political campaigns.[33] Five African trade unions did not join SACTU, choosing instead to maintain an unofficial (yet functioning) relationship with TUCSA. In 1959, nine African trade unions who opposed SACTU's participation in the Congress Alliance formed the Federation of Free African Trade Unions of South Africa (FOFATUSA) with the expressed purpose of representing African workers on an 'all-African' basis, closely aligned with the Pan-Africanist Congress (PAC). While never formally banned, SACTU had virtually disintegrated by 1965 as an above-ground organization due to severe police harassment and general repression directed against the liberation movement.[34]

The 1970s Reawakening of Working-Class Militancy

Whatever enduring credibility that the 1950s industrial relations machinery might have enjoyed disintegrated rapidly during the course of the mass strikes of black workers that began in 1973 in the Durban/Pinetown area. The Natal strikes achieved a scale and intensity that far surpassed any comparable moment in South African labour history. This sustained labour combativity reached its zenith between January and March 1973, during which time black workers took part in walkouts on at least 160 separate occasions, affecting an estimated 146 enterprises, and involving over 61,000 wage-labourers.[35] The origins of most individual work stoppages seem to be shrouded in mystery. As far as can be reasonably hypothesized, no trade unions or other organized body of workers can be attributed with either public or secret calls for work stoppages to achieve particular goals. Black workers frequently held informal discussions at the factory-gates before their shifts, when the decision to strike was made spontaneously. In other instances, workers simply stopped work in one section of the plant over particular grievances, at which time the strike spread, eventually closing the entire factory. Regardless of the actual causes for particular strikes or the precise manner in which they unfolded, the strike wave gathered momentum, exploding throughout the Durban/Pinetown industrial complex.[36]

In nearly all cases, the workers themselves conducted impromptu mass meetings on (or nearby) the premises of their employers. These work stoppages frequently involved processions or long marches (sometimes joined by Indian workers) through the streets of Durban and neighbouring areas. In most instances, the workers collectively presented their demands without wishing to negotiate with management through existing committees, perhaps fearing that if they elected their own representatives these leaders would be victimized. While little or no formal picketing occurred, workers generally milled around the factory/plant work-site. Some of the lesser strikes actually resembled slow-downs. Workers frequently returned together to the factory each day, preferring to cluster in small discussion circles in the immediate vicinity rather than to remain isolated at home. The fact that workers generally remained close to their factories probably contributed to the spread of the strikes, since employees in neighbouring plants could easily understand what was happening and were undoubtedly encouraged to join in at the insistence of friends already on strike.[37]

Remarkably, while they were always lurking ominously nearby, the police displayed by ordinary South African standards an unusual degree of restraint. State officials initially blamed agitators for instigating the strikes and trouble-makers for intimidating their fellow-workers. Nevertheless, the security police were unable to uncover any evidence to support these predictable claims. The actions of workers and the reactions of management varied considerably from plant to plant. However, a general pattern did emerge, typically unfolding along the following lines: initially demanding wage increases that were some-times three times the current scales, workers weighed management's counter-offers and returned to work relatively quickly after accepting much less than they had originally demanded.[38]

State officials and employers alike were gripped with char-acteristic anxiety, fearing that these mass strikes might spread unchecked to other regions of the country, particularly to the industrial heartland of the Witwatersrand. These fears never fully materialized. However, the mass strikes did produce two significant results. First, the work stoppages demonstrated in a dramatic way that workers were both willing and capable of mounting a direct assault on the prerogatives of capital with little coordination and preparation. Fearing further confrontation and realizing the extent to which a renewed round of work stoppages or slow-downs would shrink profit margins, employers cal-culated that slight wage increases would placate black workers and hence bring a degree of labour peace.[39] Second, state authorities began to contemplate the necessity of modifying the existing outmoded statutory provisions that governed the politi-cal representation of black workers.

The strike momentum continued almost unabated for several years. From 1973 until 1976, the average yearly number of African workers who went on strike never declined below 30,000, whereas the number had never exceeded 10,000 in a single year during the 1960s.[40] Not unexpectedly, employers and state authorities reacted to the altered balance of class forces by seeking to defuse the growing industrial conflict by channelling it into a manageable bureaucratic maze. The embodiment of this new strategy can be found in the 1973 Bantu Labour Regulation Amendment Act. This legislation was intended to apply to all industrial disputes involving African workers.[41] Paradoxically, it constituted an implicit recognition of the legal status of collective bargaining between them and management. Previously, the a priori declaration that juridical relations between white employers and African employees were restricted to criminal procedures meant that African workers had only a highly trun-cated form of political representation at the level of the state apparatus. With the 1973 Act, the state administration adopted a more flexible strategy designed to steer the settlement of dis-putes onto a more manageable level through civil procedures.[42]

This 1973 Act attempted to breathe life into the 1953 in-plant works committee structures first introduced in 1953 by actively encouraging workers to select plant-level representatives. The Act also explicitly recognized that African workers in principle could legally go on strike, although they first had to exhaust the available avenues for resolution of grievances and inform management through the works committee representatives of their intentions. Finally, this 1973 legislation empowered the Minister of Labour to accept proposals regarding black wages or other conditions of employment from a 'sufficiently representative group or association of employers' and to order that such proposals would be legally binding upon both employers and workers alike in the designated trade or branch of industry.[43] This starkly corporatist measure gave wide authority to the Minister of Labour both to rescind the blind market determination of wages (historically kept low by Western standards due to the abnormally large surplus population maintained as a reserve labour force in the Homelands) and to influence the parameters of 'acceptable' capitalist behaviour at the level of the individual firm. With this legislation, state authorities not only acquired a great deal of flexibility to shape long-term economic policy but also to 'punish' and 'reward' particular firms or branches of industries. Seen in broader perspective, this 1973 legislation symbolized a general trend whereby an increasingly centralized state apparatus used a specific crisis situation to claim additional and extended authority in an ever-expanding arena.[44]

The Independent Black Trade Unions in the Post-Wiehahn Period

The Wiehahn and Riekert Commissions

The appointment of the Wiehahn and Riekert Commissions of Enquiry in 1977 can be seen in retrospect as the opening gambit in an overall ruling-class strategy both to rescue economic stability (through enhanced productivity and profitability) and to broaden popular legitimacy amongst the black dominated classes. The Commissions' recommendations were circulated in 1979. They envisaged modifications in previous regulations governing the twin arenas of labour relations and manpower utilization — a euphemism for regulations concerning the rights of employment, residence, and geographical mobility of African people.[45]

Put broadly, the aim of the Wiehahn and Riekert Commissions was to address a host of problems that were structural rather than cyclical in nature. The capital accumulation process that accompanied the postwar 'long boom' of industrialization engendered not only a shortage of semi-skilled labour but, more critically, the creation of a relative surplus population of unemployed and underemployed black proletarians. The Soweto uprising demonstrated beyond a doubt that a significant portion of Africans with urban residence rights under Section 10 had not been politically pacified by the values or opportunities of the free enterprise system.

The Wiehahn Commission recognized without hesitation that the existing machinery for handling labour disputes and for regulating wage rates and working conditions between white employers and black workers had deteriorated almost beyond repair. In searching for a viable alternative that would both restore and guarantee labour peace, the Commission proposed that the basic tenets of the original Industrial Conciliation Act be amended to allow African workers to form and join registered trade unions. This recommendation attracted the most attention both domestically and internationally. In proposing the dismantling of the core structure of the dual system of industrial relations, the Commission envisioned the formal registration of the African trade unions into the officially-sanctioned industrial conciliation machinery instead of their relegation to non-voting observer status. Nevertheless, the Wiehahn proposals did not require employers to recognize trade unions and it permitted them to continue utilizing in-plant liaison committees to communicate and negotiate with African employees.[46]

The Wiehahn's rationale for extending legal recognition to African trade unions was a mixture of acknowledging that these bodies could no longer be ignored and that as unregistered entities they posed a greater threat outside the industrial relations machinery than within. The Commission noted that 'there were some 27 black [African] trade unions in existence in May 1979 representing in all between 50,000 and 70,000 workers' and operating in several key branches of industry. The Commission concluded, 'unregistered trade unions for black workers are becoming a prominent and permanent feature of the industrial relations scene'. With considerable irony, the Commission acknowledged that these unregistered trade unions 'in fact enjoy much greater freedom than registered unions'.[47] Desiring to promote 'a more structured and orderly situation', the Wiehahn Commission reasoned that formal recognition of African trade unions would be a small price to pay for labour peace. If these unregistered unions could be lured into the existing labour relations machinery, they would be subject to its 'protective and stabilizing elements' and 'its essential discipline and control'. Formal collective bargaining procedures locked trade unions into a seamless web of bureaucratic regulations, including binding arbitration of labour disputes, and subjected trade union leaders to the pressures of compromise and negotiation as well as to the statutory prohibition against strikes except under highly circumscribed circumstances.

The Wiehahn Commission addressed the associated problems of labour bottlenecks, skill shortages, and inefficient utilization of labour resources that had plagued manufacturing capital and, to a lesser extent, mining capital since the mid-1960s. The combination of the deepening economic crisis and the Soweto rebellion had convinced prominent industry and trade associations that decisive steps had to be taken in order to improve the business climate. Leading businessmen clamoured for the relaxation of the 'job colour bars' in order to open skilled occupations to relatively cheaper black workers, to stabilize some sections of the black urban labour force, to eliminate racial discrimination at the workplace, and to ensure better control over an increasingly restive black proletariat. Businessmen were nearly unanimous in their praise for the Wiehahn Commission proposals, confident that their implementation would improve labour relations, reduce the number of wildcat strikes, and blunt foreign criticism of South Africa's labour practices.[48] Both in tone and substance, the Wiehahn proposals must be understood as a political response to the intensification of worldwide condemnation of *apartheid*. The Commission's recommendations were at least in part tailored to defuse and deflate various overseas campaigns urging transnational corporations with extensive investments in South Africa to adopt various Codes of Conduct prescribing guidelines for 'deracialized' employment and labour practices.[49]

The Riekert Commission proposals paralleled and complemented those of the Wiehahn Commission. The principal aim of
these conjoined urban and trade union recommendations was to
drive a wedge between those who were deemed qualified urban
residents and those who were condemned to migrant labour.
Rather than rescinding the odious influx controls, the Riekert
Commission sought to improve their efficiency by overhauling
and expanding the labour bureaux, pass laws, and aid centres 'in
the interests of effective functioning of the labour market and the
administration of black workers in the white area'.[50]

The Riekert Commission recommended that Africans who
qualified for Section 10 rights be granted the legal status of
permanent urban residents. In practice, this 'new dispensation'
meant that the emergent African middle class and a segment of
the black working class would be deemed qualified to seek
employment in an urban labour market no longer fettered by the
nagging controls of labour bureaux and to live with their families
in urban townships. In addition, the Riekert Commission
discussed ways and means that employers could be encouraged
to hire qualified African workers in preference to migrants and
suggested that the existing restrictions preventing the unim-
peded movement of such qualified workers between job-sites
and townships be relaxed. The Commission also proposed that
the obstacles hindering the secular growth of a black business
class be gradually removed and recommended that more and
better-quality family housing be constructed in the townships.[51]
These proposals remained not much more than a thinly veiled
palliative aimed at deflecting widespread complaints about
rampant overcrowding and dilapidated housing conditions in the
black ghettos.

The Riekert Commission launched a direct assault on the sub-
altern and marginalized sections of the black working class and
its reserve army of unemployed. It suggested that the 'control of
employment should, with residential control, ensure the regulation of migration'. By tightening influx controls, the urban
areas would be cleared of the 'idlers and undesirables', the
'illegals', and those without accommodation and employment.
The Commission proposed that influx control could be streamlined through a variety of measures, including the validation of
migrant worker contracts through rural labor bureaux, the introduction of stiff fines for employers who hired 'illegal' labour, and

the reduction of urban occupational opportunities for migrants through a policy of encouraging white employers to hire Africans selected from amongst qualified urban residents.[52]

The strategic objective of the Riekert proposals was to exacerbate the existing class cleavages that already divided the black townships. By offering a material (and hence ideological) stake in the existing social system, the Riekert proposals sought to detach the 'haves' from the 'have-nots', that is, those who 'qualified' under Section 10 to live and work in 'white South Africa' and those who were relegated to the status of temporary migrants.

The Diverse Political Alignments of the Organized Trade Union Movement

The emergence of the independent black trade unions during the mid-1970s signified a vital and unprecedented step forward in the working-class movement. What distinguished this upsurge of trade unionism in the 1970s-80s from the historical pattern in South Africa was the deliberate choice of the leadership not to succumb to the temptation to plunge willy-nilly into the maelstrom of popular struggles. Because of the peculiar inter-section of class exploitation and national oppression in the country, the gravitational pull of radical populist currents has historically inscribed black trade unionism with the character of social movements. In the main, the class-wide activities of the independent black trade unions from the mid-1970s onward focused on questions of union recognition and shop-floor repre-sentation, the resolution of workplace grievances, and improve-ment of wages and working conditions. However, this upsurge in working-class consciousness and combativity was not restricted to the narrow quest for purely economic security and material gain. The independent black trade union movement increasingly intervened in the broader struggle for political emancipation.

The combination of the priviledged position of white wage-earners in the social division of labour and the pronounced differentiation along skill/artisanal lines historically inhibited popular as well as working-class unity across racial lines. Two major federations of registered trade unions objectively collaborated within the dominant bloc of class forces. At the end of 1985, the conservative (and white supremacist) South African Confederation of Labour (SACLA) represented approximately 100,000 white wage-earners grouped into eleven unions.[53] In the late 1970s, SACLA had represented about 190,000 white wage-earners in twenty-five affiliated unions. The proposed Wiehahn legislation caused considerable ideological discord within the Confederation's ranks, resulting in numerous disaffiliations and defections to the political right that drained it both of members and prestige within white politics. A large portion of SACLA's membership was drawn from non-salaried state administrative personnel, employees of state corporations, and employees in the mining industry.[54] SACLA consistently supported 'job reservation' for white wage-earners and resisted the growth of independent black trade unions. The Mine Workers' Union (MWU), under the virulent racialist leadership of Arrie Paulus, maintained an ambivalent relationship within SACLA, serving as an organized tendency and a lightning rod attracting rightwing splinters into its orbit. Following the legislative enactments inspired by the Wiehahn recommendations, the MWU unsuccessfully assumed a vanguard role in organizing opposition to what it regarded as the Botha regime's sell-out of white labour. In 1981, it claimed an exclusively white membership of 18,000 mostly Afrikaans-speaking wage-earners.[55]

TUCSA historically operated as a model for non-political trade unionism. Its leadership espoused the virtues of the free enterprise system, propagating the view amongst its affiliates that the interests of employers and workers were not mutually exclusive and that patient negotiation was the sole means of resolving management/labour conflict. In the face of internal disagreements and National Party intimidation, TUCSA frequently vacillated between opposite extremes, at times upholding a perfunctory version of trade union unity and at times yielding to the lure and expediency of expected gain. In the late 1960s, TUCSA abandoned without even the pretext of principle its affiliated African trade unions. In a *volte face* that reeked of opportunism, TUCSA once again reopened its ranks in the 1970s to unregistered African trade unions. It advised its affiliates to establish so-called parallel unions for African workers in the same industries.[56] These parallel unions functioned as appendages of their parent bodies and ultimately owed their existence to moderate white 'custodians'. On the ideological plane, progressive organizations have uniformly deprecated the TUCSA leadership for its timid, reformist, and conservative-minded opinions. The independent black trade unions consistently dismissed its unions as accommodationist toward management and generally untrustworthy.

Paradoxically, TUCSA benefited from the 1970s-80s general upsurge of black working-class militancy. By 1982, its sixty-five affiliates claimed a combined membership of approximately 250,000 workers. These affiliates included an estimated 170,000 Coloured and Indian workers, and approximately 32,000 African workers in parallel unions. On balance, this increase in the numerical size of the TUCSA unions was illusory. On the one hand, several large affiliates relied heavily on closed shop agreements and 'sweetheart' contracts with employers where union membership was a condition of employment. On the other hand, several large (and virtually all-white) trade unions joined TUCSA, bolstering its overall membership figures and exaggerating its erratic yet consistently rightward political drift. For instance, the conservative-minded 'white' unions led the opposition to resolutions at the 1982 annual conference that called for the commemoration of 16 June as a national holiday, a code of conduct governing the treatment of detainees, and the demand that the security forces charge or release detainees. One final example exemplified TUCSA's centrist approach to trade unionism: Lucy Mvubelo, the principal figure in the Council's parallel clothing workers' union, the National Union of Clothing Workers (NUCW), consistently served as a leading advocate of worldwide campaigns to promote foreign investment in South Africa.[57]

The TUCSA leadership boasted that its affiliates were 'the home of workers who recognize the interdependence of South Africa's race groups, and seek to strive together to achieve justice, equal opportunity, fair wages and better working conditions for all South African workers'.[58] However it was TUCSA's failure in 1982 to condemn the death in detention of trade unionist Neil Aggett and to participate in the nationwide work stoppages for his funeral that compromised its integrity as a trade union in the eyes of many black workers. Following the 1983 annual conference, about nine trade unions disaffiliated from TUCSA. Its largest affiliate, the 60,000-member South African Boilermakers' Society (SABS) withdrew in 1983, adopting an autonomous political position that overlapped considerably with the independent black trade unions. In 1984, the 26,000-strong Engineering Industrial Workers' Union of South Africa (EIWU) disaffiliated because of the 'exclusivist attitudes' of a number of TUCSA affiliates that restricted their memberships to skilled, mainly white, wage-earners. In 1985, the Council still claimed a paid membership of 360,000 workers (and an overall membership of just under 500,000) in forty-three affiliates. Its president Robbie Botha boasted that TUCSA's greatest strength lay in 'its recognition by employer bodies and, more important, by government'. Yet a steady stream of disaffiliations (as well as rumours of pending defections) revealed the shallowness of this *soi-disant* bluster. By January 1986, a number of desertions, including the 55,000-strong Garment Industrial Workers' Union, reduced overall membership to an estimated 252,000 workers in forty-odd unions. In May 1986, one of the oldest affiliates, the 6,000-strong Durban Integrated Municipal Employees' Society (DIMES) left TUCSA and began 'to investigate the possibility of affiliating to COSATU'. DIMES' organizing secretary 'D.K.' Singh claimed that 'TUCSA no longer represented the views of the majority of workers and failed to identify with the aspirations of black people. ... It had failed to respond to the challenges facing the country and identified too closely with the State and establishment.'[59]

The Origins of the Independent Black Trade Union Movement

The origins of the independent black trade union movement can be traced to quite diverse sources. At the risk of oversimplification, it can be said that a number of relatively independent initiatives launched in the early 1970s around such focal points as workers' advice bureaux, newspapers, benefit funds, legal aid, and so forth, gradually coalesced first into nascent organs of collective self-defence and eventually into full-fledged trade unions. In Durban, the General Factory Benefit Workers' Fund was formed in mid-1972 as a stepping-stone toward trade unionism proper. It was instrumental in the establishment of the Metal and Allied Workers' Union (MAWU) with branches in Pietermaritzburg and Durban in 1973. The General Workers' Benefit Fund soon was transformed into the Trade Union Advisory and Coordinating Council (TUACC) with the aim of coordinating the activities of the small number of unregistered unions that emerged in Natal. From its inception, TUACC 'was committed to open unions, nationally organized according to industrial sectors, and based on strong factory floor organization'. Organizers wanted to establish a 'strong coordinating body comprised at each level of a majority of worker representatives which decided policy for the affiliates and controlled the resources they jointly pooled'.[60] In 1976, the Council for the Industrial Workers of the Witwatersrand (CIWW) was formed to provide a coordinating body for the joint activities of the Industrial Aid Society (IAS), a workers' education and advice project, and the Transvaal branch of MAWU. In 1979, the TUACC unions spearheaded the organizational drive to form the Federation of South African Trade Unions (FOSATU) from a handful of unaffiliated unions, including three ex-TUCSA motor unions in the Western and Eastern Cape that merged to form the National Automobile and Allied Workers' Union (NAAWU). From its somewhat inauspicious origins, FOSATU emphasized that trade union power depended upon the effectiveness of collective organization. The FOSATU affiliates fused a tight-knit organizational structure with workplace militancy. The Federation professed non-racialism and permitted the involvement of white intellectuals as full-time officials, organizers, and specialist-advisors.

In 1980, the Council of Unions of South Africa (CUSA) emerged laterally from the amalgamation of nine independent black unions which had operated under the broad umbrella of the Consultative Committee of Black Trade Unions that had been in existence since 1973. This group had received assistance, training, and the use of office facilities provided by the Urban Training Project (UTP). A former TUCSA official who had become disgruntled with the Council's ambivalent attitude toward organizing African workers founded the UTP in Johannesburg in 1971. Two white intellectuals (Loet Douwes Dekker and Eric Tyacke) became the driving force behind the UTP, establishing offices in the early 1970s in Johannesburg, Durban, Port Elizabeth, Springs, Benoni, and Pretoria. The UTP provided training, legal assistance, finances, and educationl services for black workers and trade unionists — publicizing the existing rights of African workers under the prevailing labour legislation — rather a performing than a coordinating function.[61] It refrained from transforming itself into an organization structurally accountable to the various trade unions that it serviced and advised. With the formal establishment of CUSA, the relatively autonomous separation between the trade union confederation — with its command over day-to-day activities and decision-making — and the UTP became even more pronounced.[62]

From the mid-1970s onwards, a few nearly moribund non-aligned unions were rekindled and an even larger number were formed in the wake of the generalized upsurge of working-class militancy. These independent black unions shared two common characteristics: first, each more or less embraced the organizational form of all-inclusive general workers' unions in contrast to individual industry-specific trade unions; and second, each was more or less confined to specific geographical areas in its organizing efforts and political impact.[63]

By the early 1980s, these unaffiliated independent black trade unions could be classified into two broad categories. The first type was characterized by trade unions such as the General Workers' Union (GWU) and the (African) Food and Canning Workers' Union (AFCWU/FCWU). They shared a common organizational commitment to a well-demarcated chain of command linking rank-and-file members to elected leadership, internal democracy, a solid industrial base, and a strong on-the-shop-floor presence. The GWU originated from the Western Province Workers' Advice Bureau (WPWAB). Established in 1973, the WPWAB aimed 'to provide advice to workers on wages, working conditions, and on their rights as workers; to assist workers in the formation of factory committees and provide for the establishment of benefit funds for the workers'.[64] In its initial stages, the GWU brought together a diverse grouping of employees comprised in the main of unskilled African migrants with a high rate of job turnover. In the early 1980s, the GWU decided to delimit its organizing activities, concentrating principally on stevedores in the main port-cities of Cape Town, Durban, East London, and Port Elizabeth, in addition to some transport workers.[65] The FCWU/AFCWU was formed in 1941. To use Luckhardt and Wall's words, it became 'a model of militant trade unionism throughout South Africa as well as provid[ing] experience and leadership within SACTU in the 1950s'.[66] After undergoing a long period of degeneration, the FCWU/AFCWU was reinvigorated under able leadership during the 1970s.

The 'regional-general' trade unions represented the second

discernible trend that emerged from within the unaffiliated group. Unions such as the South African Allied Workers' Union (SAAWU), Orange Vaal General Workers' Union (OVGWU), the General and Allied Workers' Union (GAWU), and the Motor Assembly and Components Workers' Union of South Africa (MACWUSA) — a breakaway from the FOSATU automobile-based affiliate — were distinguished by their regional base and their active involvement in popular campaigns in the townships. At times, these groups resembled broad-based social movements recruiting employed and unemployed alike more than they operated as trade unions *per se*. Union participation and even sponsorship of township campaigns (such as rent strikes and boycotts) served as a principal conduit for the recruitment of new members.

SAAWU perhaps best illustrated this kind of regional-general trade unionism. It was formally convened in 1979 as a consequence of a political split in the then almost defunct Black Allied Workers' Union (BAWU). SAAWU disengaged from its progenitor over the question of black exclusivism. In practice, its membership was furnished from seemingly every working-class occupational subdivision of East London and its environs. For the most part, SAAWU members lived in Mdantsane, a dormitory township considered part of the Ciskei but within commuting distance of the industrial complexes of East London. After a series of bitter confrontations, the Sebe regime in the Ciskei declared SAAWU its principal enemy and activated a virtual state of siege against the union and its popular campaigns.[67] SAAWU conducted many of its recruitment drives at mass meetings. Organizers encouraged workers in factories to elect committees that would then seek to enroll members and broaden the union's support within the factory. When the SAAWU branch could claim to represent 60 per cent of the factory workforce, it would demand recognition from the particular employer. If employers refused recognition the union would call a strike as its chief weapon to extract recognition agreements from recalcitrant management.[68] Between 1979 and 1981, the union expanded its number of such agreements from five to thirty-three.[69] Yet this method of organizing was not without its obvious deficiencies. Employers often simply 'locked out' SAAWU supporters, contributing to the already large number of retrenched workers who formally belonged to the union but were without work. In principle, SAAWU had contemplated re-constituting itself as an industrial federation by establishing regional and provincial committees that would function as intermediate structures between the branch executive committees and its national executive committee.[70] Yet it never did so. Besides suffering a few internal splits, its recognized leaders spent long spells in detention.[71]

The working-class upsurge in South Africa that began in the 1970s took place under state surveillance and harassment. Hence, the choice of ideological identities and political directions was a highly circumscribed process that in no way resembled or can be compared to the conventional Western-style varieties of openly-debated trade union strategies. Members of the independent black trade unions exhibited a complex range of political beliefs reflecting the many strata of wage-earners in different trades and industries, social and geographical settings, regional variations, and local histories. Consequently, the independent black trade union movement embraced a balanced diversity of opinions, a complexity of organizational forms, and a fluidity of popular expressions. The enduring character of employer and state hostility compelled the union movement to adopt a semi-clandestine existence at time, obstructing unfettered debates and exacerbating rivalries and suspicions.

By 1979-80, a distinctive pattern had emerged: the fledgling independent black trade union movement had not only survived the litmus test of combined employer and state antipathy but had also succeeded in attracting exponentially expanding individual memberships. The features that united the independent black trade union movement were the principled denunciation of white minority rule and the shared determination to operate outside the framework of the existing 'industrial relations' machinery.[72]

In organizational terms, the independent unions either clustered around the existing coalitions — FOSATU and CUSA — or remained non-aligned. Outward appearances aside, these rival clusterings did not adhere to monolithic or homogeneous ideological positions. Nevertheless, it is possible to sketch in abbreviated fashion the main currents of political agreement and collaboration that prevailed at the time.

FOSATU and the Struggle for Workers' Power on the Shop-Floor

A small group of intellectuals and experienced trade unionists spearheaded the drive to forge a handful of industrially-based unions into FOSATU.[73] In 1980, FOSATU consisted of eight separate unions with its organizing efforts concentrated in the metal, chemical, food processing, textiles, automobile, and pulp and paper industries.[74] From the beginning, the federation relied upon in-plant shop steward councils (inspired by the British labour movement but adopted in accordance with South African circumstances) not only to challenge management prerogatives 'within the factory gates' but also to instill a sense of working-class solidarity with the unions on a day-to-day basis. The Metal and Allied Workers' Union (MAWU) was perhaps the strongest independent black trade union in South Africa. MAWU organized nearly one-tenth the estimated 500,000 workers in the crucial metals, machine-parts and tool-and-dye industries. It weathered the initial storm of employer enmity, developing effective shop-floor branch committees in the East Rand, Pietermaritzburg, and Durban/Pinetown heartland of the metal industry). In 1983, this union initiated over sixty-five independent worker actions (for example, strikes, slowdowns, temporary shut-downs), more than half the total number of disputes of all FOSATU affiliates.[75]

FOSATU approached union organizing through a mixture of trial-and-error pragmatism and a principled commitment to winning the workers' trust and allegiance through specific workplace victories. The strategy of the FOSATU affiliates centered on the achievement of incremental gains that could be translated into advances for the whole working-class movement. Ironically, FOSATU's organizing successes provoked a mild backlash in independent trade union circles. In December 1979, FOSATU announced that some of its affiliates would opt for registration — albeit under certain conditions — in terms of the post-Wiehahn amended Industrial Conciliation Act. In FOSATU's sanguine assessment, registration did not imply a retreat from its principled commitment to non-racialism but was only a tactical maneuver. Many independent black trade unions regarded the 'registration controversy' as symbolic, symptomatic of FOSATU's willingness to make unwarranted compromises with employers and to commit serious breaches of principle.[76]

In turn, the FOSATU leadership saw negotiations with management not only as an agitational platform but also as an opportunity for making concrete gains. For FOSATU, workplace disputes gave trade unions the opportunity to defend working-class interests and secure particular aims, thereby expanding the workers' understanding and confidence in their own collective capacities. FOSATU reasoned that only a militant, informed, and powerful shop-stewards' movement (in conjunction with factory committee structures) could advance the workers' struggle. FOSATU affiliates insisted that all negotiations between union and management be conducted on factory grounds. This practice instilled a sense of loyalty, camaraderie, and trust between union leadership and the rank-and-file.

Within FOSATU, MAWU developed the most advanced forms of workplace democracy. It emphasized the role of shop stewards, especially their factory and branch executive committees. At the regional level, MAWU helped found local shop stewards' committees, drawing factory representatives together *horizontally* from amongst all FOSATU affiliates in a particular locality. In describing the structure of the shop-stewards' council in the Germiston [East Rand] area, Baskin contended that 'it encourages unity between workers across union lines. Although workers' problems may differ from factory to factory, and from industry to industry, in most respects (and especially at a local level) they face the same problems. ... Workers are encouraged to see beyond their own union to the struggles of the workers as a whole.'[77]

The Loose Coalition of CUSA-Affiliated Unions

CUSA differed from FOSATU in three major respects: (1) whereas FOSATU affiliates depended upon white intellectuals to fill top administrative posts, CUSA was committed to exclusive black leadership; (2) whereas FOSATU advocated 'disciplined unity' in the hope of developing working-class solidarity and as the ultimate goal of trade union coalition-building, CUSA prescribed 'non-binding' structures on its affiliates; and (3) whereas FOSATU built its reputation on the militancy of its workplace shop-stewards, CUSA had a less 'confrontationist' approach towards both negotiations with managements and trade union organizing. By the early 1980s, CUSA's twelve affiliates with a combined membership of more than 200,000, made it the second largest labour federation after TUCSA. While officially, CUSA adhered to Black Consciousness, its leadership (as well as rank-and-file interpretation of the practical meaning of Black Consciousness remained open. Despite its growth (in membership and industrial bases), CUSA's political ideology remained unclear. The leadership developed strong ties with Western European and United States labour organizations, particularly the International Confederation of Free Trade Unions (ICFTU) and the AFL-CIOs African-American Labor Center. It failed to take a principled stance on the urgent question of registration under the amended Industrial Conciliation Act, while the leadership retreated to the safety of providing an inventory of the relative merits and demerits of registration. In time, CUSA did encourage its affiliates to register on practical — rather than political — grounds.

The CUSA unions concentrated their organizing efforts in the Johannesburg and Pretoria areas over a wide range of industries. To a considerable extent, the CUSA affiliates paralleled and over-lapped with the industrial base of the FOSATU unions, but in the metal, textiles, automobile, and municipal sectors they were weaker than their FOSATU counterparts. In the food processing, construction, and, before the defection of the NUM, mining industries they were stronger.[78] While criticizing certain aspects of the existing relations machinery, the CUSA affiliates in large measure 'adopted a strategy of attempting to reform it from within'.[79]

The National Union of Mineworkers (NUM) was the fastest growing trade union in the CUSA camp — both in terms of membership and political influence. Claiming in late 1982 to represent upwards to 50,000 members (about one-tenth the mine labor force), the NUM began its organizing drive in the wake of the July 1982 labour riots that erupted at six mines, leaving ten workers dead and more than one thousand 'sacked' in the worst 'disturbances' in the industry since the mid-1970s.[80] Its rapid advance, however, came face-to-face with three intertwined obstacles. The first was the newly-established Confederation of Associations and Mining Unions (CAMU), a hastily constructed amalgamation of unions that represented exclusively white skilled and supervisory personnel. Historically, the unions of white wage-earners enjoyed sole collective bargaining privileges in the mining industry where nine out of ten wage-earners were black. The NUM saw CAMU as a 'white racist bargaining front', assembled with the covert aim of subverting the collective interests of black miners. This coalition, renamed the Council of Mining Unions (CMU), represented about 24,000 white wage-earners who were concentrated in the building trades, as well as repair, maintenance and other specialized fields, in addition to supervisory functions.[81] The second obstacle was the Chamber of Mines. The Chamber took a practical and what — in the opinion of NUM — was a realistic approach to independent black unionism. It both recognized the NUM as a bargaining agent for certain categories of black workers (even though the union was not registered under the amended Industrial Conciliation Act) and allowed union activists access to the closed compounds that housed the bulk of the black migrant labour force on mining company property.[82] The Chamber, nevertheless, colluded with white wage-earners in preserving their monopoly over skilled occupations and only recognized the NUM as legitimate bargaining agent for certain job categories, potentially creating divisions amongst black workers.[83] The Chamber had granted three of the five independent black trade unions access to compounds for union recruiting purposes, thereby even further threatening to create factions and divisions amongst black mine workers.[84] The third obstacle was the continued practice of statutory job reservation. In the words of Cyril Ramaphosa, the general secretary of the NUM: 'the complexity of this problem [of job reservation] deepens when one looks at government's insincerity in effecting changes. Government has gone on record that it will protect white miners' interests. It is obvious that when black workers' interests are at stake, the government sidesteps the issue and passes the buck to the bosses and the white unions.'[85]

CUSA agreed to affiliate to the UDF, though it failed to get involved in either decision-making or joint campaigns. Contrary to the UDF, CUSA retained its commitment to exclusive black leadership in both the liberation movement and the independent trade unions. It also sent official observers to the National Forum inaugural meeting at Hammanskraal and to annual meetings of AZAPO. CUSA leaders participated in the trade union unity discussions, albeit at a distance.[86] Within the independent trade union movement, CUSA was reproached for frequently working too closely with management.[87] In its policy statement issued in

July 1982, CUSA reaffirmed its belief in the 'rightful leadership' of black people, and its opposition to influx control, 'separate *Apartheid* institutions', the Group Areas Act, and the Bantustan policy. Yet simultaneously, it appeared to retreat into a somewhat liberal corporatist image of labour and industrial relations: 'CUSA believes in a free and just society, and *accounts the truism that labour cannot exist without management*. The Council therefore is willing to meet and discuss issues of *common interest* with employer organizations or individual employers, but believes that employers should not interfere in trade union activity. . . . CUSA believes that the role of the State is a *facilitating role* in industrial relations.'[88] The most serious drawback plaguing CUSA was its loosely-federated structure and its lack of political clarity. Unlike FOSATU, the CUSA unions did not develop the complex organizational machinery linking workers from different plants and different industries in regional consultative bodies.

At the end of 1982, FOSATU enjoyed an active presence in at least 511 factories with some form of recognition in about 150. CUSA was involved in as many or more plants, though with fewer overall recognition agreements. While it enjoyed a numerical membership that more or less equalled FOSATU, CUSA affiliates' experience of leadership qualities, shop-floor representation, internal union democracy, potential growth and visibility, varied considerably.[89] CUSA's Food and Beverage Workers' Union (FBWU) signed eighteen formal recognition agreements with employers, more than half the confederation's total.[90] Yet on the bleaker side, the CUSA-affiliated South African Chemical Workers' Union (SACWU) was seriously compromised as a result of accusations from rank-and-file members in 1982 that its leadership was 'toothless and strongly believ[ed] in the industrial council system', held secret discussions with management, and appropriated funds through unauthorized dues' collections.[91] The FOSATU affiliate in the automobile industry, NAAWU, had majority membership among black workers at all, except one, motor assembly companies. In contrast, the CUSA-affiliated United African Motor Workers Union (UAMWU), had hopes of recognition at the remaining factory (Nissan) at Rosslyn. One observer referred to its Steel, Engineering and Allied Workers' Union (SEAWU) as 'lacklustre' and its Transport and Allied Workers' Union (TAWU) as 'moribund'.[92]

If these organizational difficulties were not enough, the

FOSATU-affiliated textile union (spread widely throughout Natal and the eastern Cape) gradually displaced that of CUSA in a number of plants in the Transvaal.[93] In 1984, the Commercial Catering and Allied Workers' Union of South Africa (CCAWUSA) left the CUSA camp to pursue an independent course of action. This decision was a serious blow to CUSA. By 1985, CCAWUSA's paid-up membership approached 40,000 and branches were established throughout the country, with the bulk of its following in the Transvaal. The union concentrated primarily on the commercial distributive trade, and had gained recognition agreements with most major retail chainstore groups. Involved in at least five major strikes in Johannesburg in 1982 and a two-week 'sit-in' demonstration at OK Bazaars chainstores in Port Elizabeth in 1983, CCAWUSA had acquired a reputation with management for being strike-prone. The union fought tenaciously for recognition, the right of shop stewards to advance worker grievances on the shop-floor, access to workers, 'stop-order' facilities, and pay increases. Perhaps CCAWUSA's most notable achievement was negotiating maternity agreements for its predominently female membership. Expectant mothers were given unpaid leave and guaranteed re-employment.

According to labour consultants Andrew Levy and Associates, about 25 per cent of South Africa's economically active population at the end of 1984 was unionized. Yet the rate of growth was spectacular: union membership was doubling almost every two years during the 1980s. Black workers experienced a five times faster growth rate in unionization than white workers. With more than 400,000 members in 1984, TUCSA remained the largest single trade union federation. Yet in the previous year, it lost 100,000 members because of its failure to recognize the growing trend toward independent black trade unions.

In contrast to other areas, the independent black trade unions were relatively weak in the Western Cape. Historically, the TUCSA affiliates had established a strong presence, particularly amongst settled segments of the working class. With the exception of GWU and FCWU/AFCWU, the independent black trade unions had made only small inroads into this region. However, the UDF affiliates, Clothing Worker's Union (CLOWU) and the Retail and Allied Workers' Union (RAWU), became active in 1984, and CCAWUSA established a small presence. Finally, the FOSATU-affiliated National Union of Textile Workers (NUTW) had started organizing. The dual issues of plant-level bargaining and the closed shop were foremost.[94]

Trade Union Discussions and the Formation of COSATU

Frustrations and Deadlocks

During the 1970s, most of the independent black trade unions sought to cooperate amongst themselves in their day-to-day activities. After all, they did share a common heritage. The successes of the union movement both necessitated and obviated good working relations amongst the various organizations. Perhaps the most troublesome issue was the question of jurisdictional disputes between unions operating within the same industry or in the same area. On what basis could a new trade union start to agitate and organize? This question of 'poaching' proved to be particularly vexing for those unions that tended to polarize around 'organizing styles', namely, the mass-meeting and 'all-in' approach that in the main characterized the general workers' unions versus the shop-floor approach of the FOSATU affiliates.

Equally telling, the white minority regime's sponsorship of the 1979 amended Industrial Conciliation Act provoked discord in the ranks of the emerging independent union movement. This Act succeeded the Wiehahn and Rickert Commissions, both of which made recommendations about labour and industrial relations under the guise of reform. In abolishing the dual industrial relations machinery and recognizing the legal status of African workers who joined trade unions, the 1979 Act fixed three criteria: first, it only recognized African workers with Section 10 rights and regular employment, thereby excluding migrants, commuters, domestic servants, and farm labourers — an estimated three-quarters of the economically active black working class — from the legal right to belong to registered trade unions; second, it contrived an elaborate packet of controls over unions' finances, elections, and educational programmes; and third, it established a National Manpower Commission as a statutory body armed with the authority to allow for full registration of black trade unions on administrative discretion rather than legally specified criteria. Clearly shaken, the independent black trade unions were temporarily put on the defensive. While these initial criteria were either rescinded or modified, this direct frontal assault on the independent black trade unions previously unfettered course of action forced them to re-evaluate their strategies and tactics in the interest of unity.[95]

Nearly all the independent black trade unions participated in the four separate summit conferences that began in 1981. At the first, held in Langa (Cape Town) in August 1981, eleven unaffiliated unions and the FOSATU and CUSA federations took part in discussions designed principally to lay the groundwork for future meetings.[96] Specifically, the delegates resolved that their respective unions were subject to control only by their own members: they pledged mutual support in defiance of the present legal restrictions on providing aid to striking workers; they rejected the newly enacted Industrial Council legislation (that offered to recognize African trade unions if they complied with certain requirements and registered with the Department of Manpower) and agreed to support each other in resisting employer pressure to participate on the Industrial Councils. The unions were unanimous in their condemnation of the banning and detention of trade unionists in South Africa and the harassment of union organizers by the Sebe regime of the Ciskei. To give substance to these resolutions, the delegates at the summit agreed to organize *ad hoc* regional 'solidarity action committees' to test the strength of word in action.[97]

The point of contention dividing participants at this inaugural meeting was the issue of registration with the Department of Manpower Utilization. Some trade unions rejected registration in principle, arguing that it would inevitably entangle them in a bureaucratic web of rules and regulations favouring employers and the state. The penultimate political question lurking in the background was straightforward: those who rejected registration feared that subordination to 'state controls would lead to cooption and prevent the unions from serving the long term interests of workers'.[98] In the main, the FOSATU unions (several of which were already registered) argued that registration was tactically expedient. If the trade unions were able to build formidable and democratic shop-floor structures, they would be able to resist the extension of state controls.[99]

The second unity summit was held in Johannesburg in April 1982. Its purpose was to construct a common platform for a working alliance. The participants agreed to aim towards one unified body or federation of unions. The starting point for the discussion was FOSATU's proposal to form a tight federation based on 'disciplined unity' in which there would be common political purpose, binding policy on affiliates, and joint organizational machinery. Two Port Elizabeth-based unions — the Motor Assemblers' and Component Workers Union of South Africa (MACWUSA) and the General Workers Union of South Africa (GWUSA) — walked out of the meetings, arguing that they could not ally with unions that had registered under the Industrial Conciliation Act or were participants in Industrial Councils.[100] Union delegates agreed to pursue their search for unity through consultations in the 'Solidarity Action Committees'. This commitment was intended to provide rank-and-file members of diverse unions the opportunity to express their views on the unity question.[101]

The unions reconvened for the third summit in July 1982 in Port Elizabeth. The discussions reached an impasse, concluding in near total breakdown. All the unaffiliated unions and the two federations in attendance agreed *in abstracto* to the formation of a common federation. Nevertheless, the unions were seriously divided over two principal issues: first, whether the preconditions for unity should be narrowly or broadly defined; and second, the question of registration and participation in Industrial Councils. The so-called 'group of seven' — Black Municipal Workers Union (BMWU), South African Transport & Allied Workers Union (SATWU), General & Allied Workers Union (GAWU), OVGWU, SAAWU, MACWUSA, and GWUSA — advocated a tight federation with unity of purpose and policies binding on all affiliates, and proclaimed, *pari passu*, that they could not enter at this stage into any federation with registered unions, especially those who participated in Industrial Councils. These criticisms were aimed in a less than surreptitious way at the FOSATU and CUSA federations, most of whose affiliates had registered and some of whom took part in the Industrial Council system.[102] In specific, the 'group of seven' proposed that seven non-negotiable principles should form the basis of a new union federation, *viz.,* non-registration; shop-floor bargaining; federation policy binding on all affiliates; workers control; non-racialism; participation in community issues; and rejection of reactionary bodies nationally and internationally.[103] Even a rather loose interpretation of the meaning of these principles would have excluded most of the trade unions outside the 'group of seven'.

The Port Elizabeth meetings marked a turning-point in the trade union unity initiatives with respect to the influence of the group of seven. These 'regional-general' unions shared certain distinctive characteristics that distinguished them from the industrial unions. In the main, they had each cultivated a local membership restricted to at most a few townships in a particular area. They tended to organize through strikes, relying upon charismatic leadership and, frequently, on mass public rallies and gatherings in the townships. Consequently, they had fashioned strong shop-floor committees for only a relatively small proportion of plants where they had gained recognition agreements with management. With the exceptions of SAAWU and MACWUSA, these unions had not been able to grow. When they were able to form branches, these appeared as 'relatively autonomous outposts of the mother union, connected mainly at the level of union leadership rather than through factory-to-factory linkages'.[104]

During the early 1980s, the 'regional-general' unions acquired large followings in a short space of time. Yet they were often unable to match these gains in signed-up membership with consolidation on the shop-floor. In contrast, a number of the industrial unions — particularly those associated with FOSATU — had gradually acquired a national presence through a process both of expansion and merger. While all the independent trade unions suffered setbacks through retrenchments during the 1981-2 recession, the industrial unions proved to be more capable of regrouping and consolidating under adverse economic conditions than the 'regional-general' unions. As a consequence, political influence in the unity discussions shifted decidedly in favour of the industrial unions who wished to accelerate the process of amalgamation.[105]

The fourth summit was held at Athlone (near Cape Town) in April 1983. Twenty-nine independent trade unions (representing approximately 250,000 workers) participated. The outcome was the establishment of a steering committee to investigate the actual structure of a new federation and a decision to reconvene before the end of the year with the objective of reporting on advances accomplished in the interim on the local level. Fourteen unions present at Athlone — the FOSATU affiliates, the CUSA-affiliated CCAWUSA, and a handful of unaffiliated unions (SAAWU, GAWU, the Cape Town Municipal Workers' Association, and FCWU/AFCWU — joined the steering committee, thereby deciding in principle to take immediate steps to form a new federation. CUSA subsequently joined the steering committee. All other unions agreed in principle to the idea of a federation but wished either to take the proposals back to their respective memberships for a popular mandate or to postpone to a future time the determination of the actual structure of the new federation.[106]

This fourth summit was marked by the presence of large delegations of elected worker representatives from all the major industrial centers. Hindson commented on the changed political complexion of the discussions: 'The numerical preponderance and active participation of workers was decisive in ensuring that the discussions at the meeting were, for much of the time, practical and constructive and gave the meeting a determination to see that wider unity was achieved. This can be contrasted with the previous unity summit in Port Elizabeth, a small gathering mainly of union officials, which broke down in disagreement over abstract principles.'[107] The negotiations at Athlone centered primarily on the practical steps to establish the new federation. Two main positions emerged. The 'regional-general' unions favoured a return to local solidarity action committees through which unity could be built 'from the base upward'. These unions insisted that the basic task of the trade union movement was to organize the 'unorganized'. Without this broadening of the base, trade union unity would be imposed 'from above' and not evolve organically 'from below'. This 'united front unity' approach was the logical outcome of their methods of organization, structures, and relatively small size. The reactivation of the regionally-based 'solidarity action committees' remained attractive to the 'regional-general' unions because it offered them opportunities to extend their range of influence. For the smaller and 'regional-general' unions, entry into a broad federation would almost unequivocally entail their breakdown into industrial components that would be fused into the existing larger industrial unions, hastening the end of a unique featue and lively component of the independent black trade union movement.[108]

In contrast, FOSATU and its allies proposed the immediate formation of a new federation on the basis of 'disciplined unity'. It was argued that the mandate for proceeding briskly toward the establishment of the new federation had been secured from organized workers in the meetings to discuss unity that had been held prior to the summits. The industrial unions contended that the regional solidarity committees were too loosely constituted and insufficiently integrated into union structures to ensure effective unity action.[109]

Despite formal agreements to establish a new federation, one question that continued to haunt the participants in the unity talks was the practical mechanics of recasting existing organizational and administrative structures. The internal structures of both FOSATU and CUSA were forged through a process of bitter struggle and acquired a certain durability and momentum that could not be readily or easily abandoned. FOSATU agreed to disband, albeit with the proviso that the new federation would not be too loosely organized. Because of their semi-autonomous linkages, the CUSA affiliates would have conceivably approached the question of organizational dissolution with less trauma than their FOSATU counterparts. FOSATU was much more centralized and streamlined in operation than CUSA. It combined both a powerful central committee and strong shop-floor representation. While FOSATU's regional structures actually promoted strong working-class identification and solidarity across industry lines, these were an impediment to any realignment necessary to form a new federation. The regional structures of FOSATU brought together all unions in a wide area (for example, Pretoria and the Witwatersrand) at executive and congress meetings, fostering identification with the federation rather than the specific union. One delegate pointed out at the fourth summit that this regional structure gave FOSATU the character of a large general workers' union, thereby tending to displace power from the union branch level to the central command and, consequently, eroding the foundations of direct worker control.[110]

The Athlone summit authorized the establishment of a feasibility committee to elicit the practical steps necessary for the independent black trade unions to amalgamate into a single federation. The next two meetings of the steering committee — one at Athlone in June 1983 and the second in Johannesburg in October 1983 — failed to produce any concrete results. There was acrimonious discussion over demarcation and the 'poaching' of members. The polarization between the 'regional-general' unions on one side and FOSATU and the large unaffiliated unions on the other became more pronounced. CUSA took an impartial stance. After two years and six meetings, the unity talks appeared deadlocked.[111]

Three Terrains of Discord

Put in broad perspective, three serious obstacles plagued the formation of a unified independent trade union federation. At the time, these differences could not be reduced to simply matters of opinion or of tactical nuance that could be resolved through reasoned and perhaps sustained debate. On the contrary, the disputes that divided the trade union movement invariably embodied fundamental principles concerning, *inter alia*, the relationship between leadership and rank-and-file membership, political aims, and strategies for advancement. Ultimately, these differences were only resolved in political practice. The main points of disagreement can be classified broadly into three areas: (1) registration and formal participation in Industrial Councils; (2) internal structures, democratic decision-making, and leadership accountability; and, finally, (3) the relationship to popular struggles, community-based politics, and multi-class alliances. Each of these will be reviewed in turn.

Formal Registration.

The question of whether to seek registration under the terms of the amended Industrial Conciliation Act 1979 and to participate formally in the Industrial Council system provoked a sustained and contentious debate amongst the trade unions themselves.[112] Three separate tendencies surfaced within the independent black trade union movement. One current advocated a straightforward refusal to apply for registration. This stance was most closely associated with the unaffiliated unions, although there was no unanimity on this matter. Some commentators had perjoratively referred to this position as 'boycottist', evoking images of intransigent purists with syndicalist leanings. For example, Government Zini, organizing secretary for MACWUSA, argued that his trade union would refuse to register 'as long as pass laws, the Group Areas Act, the Separate Amenities Act and influx control remained on the South African statute book'.[113] A second current was most closely associated with CUSA affiliates. This position was the most ambiguous and untheorized. In a published policy statement CUSA stated that it 'believes that the present registration procedure imposed on independent Black trade unions is an attempt to control them. The CUSA unions opted for registration under protest in the post-Wiehahn legislative changes as an indication of their *bona fides* [i.e., good faith] to assist in the creation of sound industrial relations in the country.'[114] In practice, some CUSA affiliates decided to register while others did not. Nevertheless, both the tenor and tone of official CUSA statements attested to a mildly critical, almost agnostic approach to registration that underscored the widely-held opinion that CUSA represented a potentially reformist and accommodationist tendency within the independent black trade union movement. The third current could be attributed to the FOSATU unions. Put simply, FOSATU rejected registration as an end in itself but accepted it as a tactical means of fortifying the workers' movement. It recommended the registration in part to deny any proximate advantage to the docile TUCSA 'parallel' unions. The amended Industrial Reconciliation Act required unions wishing to register to demonstrate their 'representativeness' as a condition for formal recognition. Consequently, TUCSA awaited the registration of their captive African affiliates, believing that these affiliates could 'steal the march' on the independent trade unions by quickly amassing recognition agreements with employers. FOSATU suspected that class conscious employers would encourage the registration of these TUCSA 'parallel' unions in order to fix virtual 'closed shop' arrangements *via* 'sweetheart' contracts, thereby squeezing out the independent trade unions.[115]

FOSATU's initial conception of registration as a pragmatic and tactical expedient gradually gave way to a more refined and sophisticated understanding. Through the collective experience of its membership, the federation correctly surmised that its affiliates with a strong shop-floor presence could use registration to not only contravene the terms of industrial relations legislation but also to outflank the state's efforts to divide the working class. Both because of their relatively small and scattered membership and because of their often weak shop-floor structures, most unaffiliated trade unions had forecast that registration would spell the 'death knell' for their independence of action. In practice, the FOSATU unions were able to circumvent the kinds of rigid controls that the unaffiliated unions predicted would follow inevitably from registration.

In 1981, the state unilaterally amended the Industrial Conciliation Act, making all but one of its requirements equally applicable to registered and unregistered unions alike, rendering more or less irrelevant most if not all trade union objections to registration.[116] The registration controversy faded gradually in significance. Yet it is important to point out that those unaffiliated unions that opposed registration did not universally adhere to the 'principled boycott' position of SAAWU, MACUSA, GAWUSA, GAWU, and other 'regional-general' unions. One major unaffiliated union — the FCWU/AFCWU — had always operated as a single integrated entity, despite the fact that its 'coloured' section was registered and its 'African' section was not. From its SACTU-affiliated days, this union enjoyed an exemplary record of ignoring and/or defying the stipulations of the 1956 Industrial Conciliation Act in its activities.[117] FCWU/AFCWU openly espoused non-racialism and declared its political opposition to registration. Perhaps most significantly, FOSATU affiliates demonstrated that it was possible to both accept registration and reject the terms that the state outlined for participation in the Industrial Council system.

The 1979 amended Industrial Conciliation Act (and clarifying clauses added later) extended registration privileges to the independent African trade unions, entrusting them with unmediated participation in Industrial Councils. Nevertheless, the relaxation of regulations prohibiting the direct participation of black trade unions in formal arbitration over terms and conditions of employment remained a two-edged sword. The composition of the Industrial Councils ensured that registered independent black trade unions could never win in those disputes resolved through formal vote-counting. 'Yellow unionism' abounded in South Africa. If that alone were not sufficient to ensure the 'swamping' of registered independent black trade unions, white wage-earners in every industry had at least one (and usually more) trade unions. Representatives from the white unions automatically sided with employers against black trade unions, hoping to change this collaboration for management favours. In the event of an impossible deadlock, capital-labour disputes were referred to the arbitration of an industrial court whose find-ings were legally binding. The independent black trade unions intuitively understood the Industrial Councils as pro-employer mechanisms aligned against the black working class. The most glaring feature of the councils was the manner in which they institutionalized class collaboration of white wage-earners and the bourgeoisie. In addition, those independent black trade unions who placed a premium on workplace democracy and the shop-stewards' movement recognized that the councils threat-ened to displace collective bargaining from the shop-floor, placing it instead in the hands of employers and union bureau-crats.[118]

The registered CUSA affiliates did not appear to have a defin-itive policy on participation in the Industrial Councils. The attitude of the unaffiliated unions was a corollary of their anti-registration stance. In the main, the unregistered status of most unaffiliated unions prevented their formal participation. Finally, FOSATU rejected the existing Industrial Councils because they 'were established and have been developed to serve the interests of employers and a minority of workers' and because 'most Industrial Councils are presently unrepresentative of the majority of workers and therefore undemocratic'.[119] In practice, FOSATU claimed that in those circumstances where trade unions were representative of workers in their industry 'industrial councils can be made to work to the workers' benefit'.[120] Two FOSATU-affiliated unions — MAWU and the National Automobile and Allied Workers Union (NAAWU) — participated on Industrial Councils with, by their own admission, mixed results.[121] But it was impossible to extrapolate from these experiences to con-clusions about Industrial Councils weakening the workers' movement and dividing the working class.[122]

Workers' Control and Democratic Decision-making.

In strictly organizational terms, the independent trade unions were polarized along a continuum. At one extreme, scores of workers' organizations eschewed the singular preoccupation with typical trade union activities (combining redress of shop-floor grievances with marketplace bargaining) and instead chose to forge their specific identities and particular roles within the larger mass movement. The decisive internal characteristic of these trade unions was their position in mass struggles and popular mobilization. In order to maintain the initiative and to implant themselves in the mass movement, these workers' organizations practiced what has been termed 'mass participatory democracy'. Generally speaking, those independent unions espousing 'mass participatory democracy' tended to rely upon full-time union staff and charismatic leadership styles in order to advance their cause. In the main, union programmes and decisions were 'put to the test' before mass meetings where proposals were ratified or rejected. This form of 'mass participatory democracy' contrasted sharply with variants of representative democracy where elected shop-floor representatives debated proposals that were passed back and forth between rank-and-file union members and the highest elected bodies.

Unregistered unions — such as SAAWU, GAWU and MACWUSA — were perhaps the chief proponents of this form of democracy. SAAWU's membership in the East London area alone had grown rapidly in the early 1980s, at one point exceeding 20,000 workers.[123] It enjoyed genuine and widespread support among working-class people in Mdsantsane and to a lesser extent in other townships where it had established branches. It had been able — through a series of lightning and whirlwind strikes — to achieve formal recognition agreements at a number of plants. SAAWU organizers were repeatedly detained and harassed. Through sheer tenacity and with remarkable endurance, this union succeeded in partially deflecting the assault of the aptly labelled 'triple alliance'. The combined forces of regional employers, Ciskei state authorities, and South African officialdom had embarked on a generalized offensive with the aim of weakening if not destroying the union. Partly as a direct consequence of being compelled to conduct largely defensive battles, SAAWU did not, in the words of Maree, 'adequately create the structures and practices with which to ensure workers' participation and control of the union'.[124]

The FOSATU affiliates represented the opposite end of the spectrum. According to its stated objectives, FOSATU saw itself as contributing to the formation and growth of a unified, non-racial movement based on nationwide industrial trade unions. In its effort to translate the principle of non-racial workers' unity into practice, the federation established structures that knit its affiliates together at national, regional, and local levels. The committees that shared resources and organized collective activities at these levels were worker-controlled. The cornerstone of FOSATU's emphasis on workers' control was its shop-floor structure. In its 1981 annual report, FOSATU remarked: 'One index of factory floor strength and democratic worker organization is the ability of shop stewards openly to represent their members in the factory. Major strides have been taken in this direction by all FOSATU unions over the past year. ... Over thirty comprehensive agreements have now been signed by FOSATU unions embodying shop stewards' rights (grievance handling, monthly meetings with management, time off for shop stewards' meetings in factory hours, mandate and report-back general meetings in factory hours, shop stewards' elections in factory hours), union rights (access, stop orders, negotiating rights, e.g., pay), dismissal, retrenchment, and arbitration procedures.'[125]

The general secretary, Joe Foster, outlined the federation's commitment to specific principles of internal organization, in terms of clearly-demarcated chains of command with accountability of elected leadership at every level. In his words, 'our organization is built up from the factory floor. As a result, the base of the organization was located where workers have most power and authority and that is where production takes place. This also had the effect of democratizing our structures since worker representatives always participate from a position of strength and authority in the organization. By stressing factory bargaining we involve our Shop Stewards in central activities and through this they gain experience as worker leadership.'[126]

The Relationship Between the Independent Trade Unions and Popular Struggles.

The participation of independent black trade unions in popular struggles became a major point of controversy. Under the conditions of state repression and surveillance, the trade unions generally refrained from public debate over how they understood their specific intervention and participation in the wider political struggle for national emancipation. Discussion of these volatile issues must be tempered by considerable caution and self-restraint. Yet even more importantly, the achievements and accomplishments that advanced the popular struggle were far more significant than the apparent sophistication of the ideas that were held. Over the course of the 1984 unrest, political ideas were often overshadowed by events.[127]

Broadly speaking, the political positions of the independent black trade unions bore a direct relationship to the 'various' ideological currents of the 'liberation movement'. It is thus possible to infer the diverse ideological commitments of the many independent black trade unions from their associations with popular organizations and from their participation in different political campaigns.[128] CUSA regarded South Africa 'as a country which is racialist, undemocratic and which exploits the larger Black community' where 'the present government is unrepresentative of the people' and 'legislation protects the White minority'.[129] It can be said that CUSA supported a form of 'worker populism'. Many unaffiliated unions (such as SAAWU, MACWUSA, GAWU, OVGWU, and others) gravitated toward the ideological stance of the 'progressive democrats' through their association and formal affiliation with the UDF.

The sharpest differences emerged between FOSATU and many unaffiliated unions over the precise relationship of the workplace to the community, the trade union to the community organization, and the working class to the popular struggle for 'national liberation'. At one extreme, SAAWU represented the tendency to submerge workplace grievances within generalized dissatisfaction with *apartheid* and to view trade union recruitment and organizing from this perspective. For example, Johann Maree interviewed a SAAWU spokesperson who argued: 'SAAWU is a trade union dealing with workers who are part and parcel of the community. Transport, rents to be paid, are also worker issues. I see SAAWU as a trade union. There's no doubt about it. The problems of the workplace go outside the workplace.'[130] None of the independent trade unions disputed the intimate and integral connection between the workplace and the community. From FOSATU's perspective, however, the community-based trade unions had too often avoided building a solid foundation at the point of production in favour of mobilizing a mass following in the townships on the basis of political intervention in popular struggles. Some of the smaller unaffiliated unions relied almost exclusively upon participation in such struggles in the largely working-class communities as a means of mobilizing and strengthening workers' consciousness. This *modus operandi* converged more often than not with the inclusive 'all-in' approach to union organizing.

Whether deserved or not, FOSATU acquired a reputation of being economistic in approach and non-political in orientation. In some quarters, it was derisively labelled 'syndicalist' and 'workerist'. For FOSATU, the immediate goal of the workers' movement was to build shop industrially-based, democratically-controlled, non-racial trade unions that could compete with management on a countrywide basis. While these aims did not in principle preclude participation in community struggles, FOSATU in practice retreated from direct involvement in the ongoing township battles. Nevertheless, on a number of occasions, FOSATU affiliates became involved in political disputes. In February 1982, the federation planned a funeral procession in downtown Johannesburg and the accompanying half-hour 100,000-strong work stoppages to protest the death in detention of Neil Aggett, a physician who hd served as Transvaal regional secretary for the FCWU. In early 1983, the Germiston shop-stewards' council — made up of worker representatives of FOSATU affiliates from different factories and different industries on the East Rand — spearheaded the political opposition to the decision of the East Rand Administration Board to demolish vast slum areas in Katlelong township. A considerable proportion of FOSATU's Transvaal membership was among migrant workers. Because they were denied legal access to township housing, these workers were compelled to seek makeshift accommodation in shack areas along both the East and the West Rand. MAWU, in particular, linked the problem of persistent housing shortages with the broader issue of influx controls, insisting that on this question employers join a common front against the white minority regime. In mid-1983, FOSATU initiated a broad-based trade union alliance that opposed the implementation of the new constitution and campaigned against the (Coloured) Labour Party's decision to participate in the tri-cameral Parliament elections.[131]

In a few dramatic instances, unaffiliated trade unions creatively incorporated consumer boycott tactics into their overall strategy of defending organizing workers. In 1979, the AFCWU seven-month strike at the Fatti's and Moni's pasta factory in Cape Town ended with the reinstatement of dismissed workers and pay increases. The union's success could in large measure be attributed to its mobilization of a broad-based community boycott of Fatti's and Moni's products.[132] Inspired by this example, the then-named Western Cape General Workers' Union organized a national 'red meat' boycott in 1980 in support of union workers dismissed from Table Bay Cold Storage Company. These two strikes dovetailed with the simultaneous outbreak of black student protests against inferior education in the Cape peninsula. SAAWU's appeal for a national boycott in 1981-2 of Wilson-Roundtree (candy) products over the issue of union recognition also represented this reliance of unaffiliated trade unions upon community mobilization to advance the workers' struggle.[133] Those unaffiliated trade unions that depended upon township support networks could not afford the luxury of being politically non-aligned when township residents requested their participation in popular campaigns.[134]

FOSATU's *Political Development*

Within the politically diverse independent black trade movement, FOSATU represented perhaps the clearest position on the question of class alliances, the methods of galvanizing the masses against the white minority regime, and a programmatic focus for ongoing political activities.[135] At its 1982 annual convention, the leadership endeavoured to reverse the federation's economistic image and to counter the accusation that it regarded community struggles as belonging in the realm of 'pure tactics'. For FOSATU, the existence of an independent working-class movement was necessary if the working class as a social force was to have any influence within the liberation movement.[136] In its 1982 statement, FOSATU applauded 'the very powerful tradition of popular or populist politics' that served during the 1950s as the ideological bedrock for the multi-class mass mobilizations under the leadership of the ANC and the Congress Alliance. The manner in which the relatively weak trade unions were incorporated into the popular movement at this time allowed capital 'to keep in the political background' and to 'hide behind the curtains of *apartheid* and racism'.[137] During the 1950s, the aim of popular mobilization had been to challenge the legitimacy of the white minority regime and its *apartheid* policies. In order to assemble the widest scope of popular discontent, the specific nature of the workers' struggle was submerged within a broader multi-class alliance. However, the class transformation of South Africa over the past thirty years has fundamentally altered the balance of political forces. The working class has 'experienced a birth of fire in South Africa' and it 'constitutes the major objective political force opposed to the State and capital. ... In the economy, capital and labour are the major forces yet politically the struggle is being fought elsewhere'.[138]

FOSATU objected to the particular 'political tradition of populism in South Africa' where 'all political activity, provided it is anti-State, is of equal status'. For working-class interests to be represented within the mass movement, 'it is, therefore, essential that workers must strive to build their own powerful and effective organization even whilst they are part of the wider popular struggle. This organization is necessary to protect and further worker interests and to ensure that the popular movement is not hijacked by elements who will in the end have no option but to turn against their worker supporters.'[139] FOSATU did not explicitly argue for a 'united front' approach to politics, but, it did point to the historical drawbacks of working-class organizations subsuming their interests under the broad banner of a 'popular front' strategy. Despite its growing social weight, the working class only possessed, in FOSATU's view, a 'potential power since as yet it has no definite social identity of itself as a working class'.[140] In order to achieve the goal of building 'a just and fair society controlled by workers',[141] it was not only necessary to build a disciplined, powerful, and democratic working-class movement but also to ensure working-class leadership of popular and ongoing community struggles. Without powerful organizational support, working-class participation in community struggles faced the possibility of being 'swamped by the powerful tradition of popular politics' that had dominated the liberation movement in South Africa.[141]

The Formation of COSATU

The Seventh Summit in March 1984

The meeting of the Feasibility Committee on 3-4 March 1984 in Johannesburg decided to create the new federation. The two existing trade union federations — FOSATU and CUSA — along with a number of allied unaffiliated unions (GWU, FCWU/AFCWU, CTMWA, and CCAWUSA) jointly announced that 'some unions taking part in the talks are not ready or able to join a federation'. These unions — SAAWU, GAWU, and the Municipal and General Workers' Union of South Africa (MGWUSA) — withdrew from the formal proceedings. One nagging problem was the question of intense rivalry that existed between independent unions operating within the same industry and, in several cases, within the same plant. The trade unions that remained committed to unity agreed to the principle of a 'federation of industrially demarcated unions, with the eventual aim of having one union for one industry. It follows that unions which are not demarcated along industrial lines or which have not yet formed industrial unions, are not ready to join a federation.'[142]

Representatives of twenty-four independent black trade unions with a total estimated membership of 300,000 workers met in Cape Town in August 1984 to finalize the draft constitution of the new federation and to fashion a declaration of principles.[143] In the meantime, CUSA experienced a serious ideological crisis as well as a partial organizational collapse. The NUM, CUSA's largest affiliate, had effectively broken its ties because of disagreements over a number of issues, including CUSA's affiliation to the International Confederation of Free Trade Unions (which the NUM denounced as a compromise of principles), the lack of worker control, and the resistance of CUSA affiliates to support wholeheartedly the new federation. It was reported that four out of CUSA's eleven affiliates did not bother to send representatives to the 1984 annual conference and that other affiliates were only represented by trade union officials.[144]

During 1984, labour conflict reached unprecedented levels. According to unofficial yet reliable estimates, unemployment for all racial groups exceeded three million. As the recession deepened, companies resorted to retrenchments to reduce labour costs and to technological innovation in order to maintain the competitive edge. The number of lay-offs that began as a trickle three years earlier became an avalanche in 1984. Labour consultant Andrew Levy reported (in what might have been a gross underestimation) that workers had been retrenched at a rate of more than 2,000 per week during the first four weeks of 1985, double the average for the previous year.[145] Many jobless workers faced 'the prospects of slow starvation in the "Home-lands"'.[146] In 1984, excluding the three political stayaways launched between September and November, an estimated 500,000 labour-days were lost due to strikes, more than in any previous year in South African history and nearly three times the number in 1982, the previous highwater mark. Workers took part in an estimated 469 separate strikes. While the number of work stoppages had not dramatically increased over the previous year, the number of striking workers doubled to over 180,000. Wage disputes triggered almost fifty per cent of the strikes. About half ended with either workers being dismissed or returning to work without making gains. This far higher incidence of strikes com-bined with the increased number of union defeats over the pre-vious year illustrated the increasing polarization between employers and workers on the shop floor. The economic recession reinforced this hardline approach by both sides.[147]

As the political unrest enveloped the eastern Cape, the UDF-affiliated Port Elizabeth Black Civic Organization (PEBCO) pioneered the drive for a March 1985 'Black Weekend' that included a three-day stayaway and a boycott of shops and buses. In large measure, this call for political action mirrored the highly successful November 1984 stayaway. At least two local trade unions — MACWUSA and the General Workers' Union of South Africa (GWUSA) supported the plan. But the bulk of the trade unions in Port Elizabeth — FOSATU, CUSA, GWU, FCWU/AFCWU, CCAWUSA, and the Domestic Workers Association — rejected this proposal, arguing that decisions of this sort required an explicit mandate from workers. Those trade unions that abstained from lending their formal support to the 'Black Weekend' argued that they had insufficient time to consult their members. This stance indicated a sharp division between the factory-based unions that regarded themselves as 'worker-controlled' and those that were led by political activists. This issue had been widely debated within the FOSATU-aligned trade union circles since November when they departed from previous policy and joined with com-munity organizations to support the Transvaal stayaway.[148]

These tactical differences within the independent trade union movement reflected a much more fundamental shift in political alignments. By late 1984 an estimated eighteen trade unions had gravitated into the orbit of the UDF 'as a means of attaining unity of workers throughout the country'. Without exception, these

unions fell into the 'regional-general' category. Excluding
SAAWU, GAWU, and MACWUSA, these organizations were
numerically weak and only recently established. Some of them,
like the Retail and Allied Workers Union (RAWU), were offshoots
of 'regional-general' parent bodies who had attempted to 'indus-
trialize' their progeny.[149] Equally important, a number of
'activist' unions affiliated to the UDF sponsored well-attended
meetings in Tembisa in March commemorating the 30th anniversary of the formation of SACTU. These activities amounted to
SACTU's first public rally in South Africa in decades, thereby supporting the widely-held belief that the UDF operated as a surrogate for the Congress Alliance politics of the 1950s.[150]

Following the 21 March police shootings at Langa, FOSATU
levelled serious charges against the UDF and its affiliate student
group, COSAS. These accusations paralleled FOSATU's political
reservations about the UDF-affiliated unions. The federation contended that the UDF and other organizations in the black townships had a dictatorial attitude toward workers, that some organizations deliberately ignored the 'reality that the liberation
struggle would be won by the working class', and that it was
'usually a few people in certain political organizations who
imposed their will on the majority after taking decisions alone'.[151]

Reconvening of Trade Union Unity Discussions

After a lengthy hiatus in progress toward cementing the new
federation, the leading trade unions convened once again in late
May 1985 in Germiston. The key aim of this informal meeting —
attended by representatives of over forty independent black
trade unions — was to conduct free-floating discussions particularly with those unions that had become 'marginalized' from
the mainstream 'unity' perspectives. Because many trade unions
with diverse ideological positions had been able to jointly
cooperate in successful May Day celebrations, insiders had
hoped that those points of contention that threatened to sabotage the broadest possible unity might begin to dwindle.[152]

The subterranean currents that guided the independent black
trade union movement had undergone a decided ideological shift
from the time when the 'unity talks' were first launched. The
political differences between the independent black trade unions

were certainly not rigidly fixed. Nevertheless, it is possible to identify a number of discrete political tendencies that had evolved in the discussions over the nature of trade union unity and the format of the 'super federation'. The so-called 'unity unions' represented the dominant ideological tendency. This grouping included the FOSATU affiliates, GWU, FCWU/AFCWU (that eventually fused into a single entity), CCAWUSA, CTMWA, and NUM. These trade unions maintained a commitment to disciplined unity, nonracialism, and an industrial foundation with an emphasis on shop-floor militancy and democracy. CUSA, while part of the original 'unity' perspective, remained inscrutable. This federation had always represented an organized alternative to FOSATU. Yet the CUSA leadership never seemed to advance beyond its original coordinating function and failed to develop a vision of a powerful national trade union grouping that could take the political steps necessary to challenge directly white minority rule. CUSA reached its organizational peak in 1983. CCAWUSA broke away first and moved into FOSATU's orbit. While the formal split with NUM did not occur until later, the *de facto* political rupture with CUSA had taken shape considerably earlier.

During the protracted period of political unrest, the 'regional-general' unions inclined in quite opposite directions. An estimated ten trade unions clustered around UDF. These included SAAWU, MACWUSA, GAWU, GWUSA, and OVGWU, all of which had been participants in the original 'unity talks' but had withdrawn in early 1984. Other trade unions in this ideological camp included the United Metal, Mining and Allied Workers of South Africa, Federal Council of Retail and Allied Workers, the (Port Elizabeth-based) Domestic Workers' Association of South Africa, and two groupings called the Retail and Allied Workers' Union (one based in Pretoria and the other in Cape Town).[153] To a certain extent, the trade unions that came under the political sway of the UDF had their base of operations in the volatile eastern Cape, the region where the ANC/Congress tradition had been the most deeply implanted. Despite its internal disarray and the split with its Natal branch, SAAWU found its roots and inspiration in Mdanstane outside East London. MACWUSA maintained a considerable following in the three Uitenhage townships.

Another grouping of unaffiliated unions established the Azanian Confederation of Trade Unions (AZACTU). The eight (or

nine) AZACTU affiliates represented a membership of an estimated 75,000 workers and adhered to a Black Consciousness perspective.[154] The most influential union in this alliance, the Black
Allied Mining and Construction Workers' Union (BAMCWU), had
organized workers in mining, construction, quarries, cement,
civil engineering, and related industries. Established in mid-1982,
BAMCWU was closely aligned with AZAPO both doctrinally and
organizationally. The Black Electronics and Electrical Workers'
Union concentrated on recruiting skilled employees. The
Insurance and Assurance Workers' Union of SA appealed to
white-collar workers from a range of financial and commercial
establishments. Finally, four AZACTU affiliates were 'general
workers' unions'. According to AZACTU's general secretary,
Pandelane Nefolovhodwe, the long-term objective of the Black
Consciousness alliance was to 'streamline' the 'general workers'
unions' into industrial unions when size of membership
warranted this.[155]

The largest and most representative gathering of independent
black trade unions convened in Soweto in June 1985. More than
200 delegates, representing an estimated forty-two different
unions, assembled in an eleventh-hour effort to broaden the base
of the proposed new federation. These discussions terminated on
an inconclusive note. In May, FOSATU had taken the initiative to
forward copies of the proposed draft constitution to 'all independent trade unions', including those that had only recently
disaffiliated from TUCSA — the South African Boilermakers
Society (SABS), the Engineering Industrial Workers' Union, and
the Motor Assembly Combined Workers' Union. One of the
oldest and largest unions in South Africa, the 50,000-member
SABS had increasingly steered an independent course from its
previously moderate alliances. With members drawn from the
gold, diamond, and coal-mining sectors (as well as industries
ranging from sugar to engineering), the SABS boasted of a membership of skilled blue-collar workers, 35 per cent of which was
white. As a union 'more responsive than most to the reality of
changing patterns of labour relationships', the SABS had frequently made tactical alliances with MAWU in confronting the
class power of SEIFSA.[156] On the one hand, the UDF-affiliated
unions balked at accepting as a fait accompli a draft constitution
that they had not helped formulate.[157] On the other hand, two
competing labour fronts — CUSA and AZACTU — alleged that the

'unity unions' had transformed the discussions into their 'own property'.[158]

Despite the ravages of retrenchment caused by the deepening recession, paid membership of FOSATU affiliates had increased by well over 50 per cent to 122,772 workers during 1984. By the end of that year, the eight affiliates had organized a total of 594 factories throughout the country and claimed more than 2,800 shop stewards on the shop-floor. MAWU displayed the most impressive growth. This union operated in one of the industrial centres worst hit by dismissals and cut backs and 12,000 members from its East Rand branch broke away after a period of severe internal tension to form the UDF-affiliated United Metal, Mining and Allied Workers of South Africa (UMMAWOSA). Despite these serious setbacks, MAWU expanded its membership in 1984 by about 75 per cent. It also inaugurated a drive to force all employers to engage in plant-level bargaining and to continue doing so independently of any Industrial Council negotiations. Over the past three years, MAWU had rejected all Industrial Council agreements covering the metal industry, charging that the council was employer-dominated and unrepresentative of black workers.[159] At the same time, the Paper, Wood and Allied Workers' Union and the Chemical Workers' Industrial Union both more than doubled in size.[160]

According to FOSATU's 1984 annual report, the November 1984 stayaway 'overshadowed many other developments in what was a tumultuous year'. Four leading FOSATU officials were included among a number of stayaway organizers who had been detained. 'Government actions and policies', the report noted, 'continue to draw FOSATU ever deeper into the political arena.' For the federation, the attainment of union recognition agreements as the official bargaining agent at individual plants no longer played the dominant role that it once had. A new dimension confounding trade union organizing drives was the growing battle with the older established TUCSA-affiliated unions which had altered 'closed shop' agreements with management so as to recruit 'unknowingly' black workers. FOSATU experienced its most serious difficulties with this TUCSA strategy in the clothing, textile, printing and packaging, motor components, and transport industries. In addition, TUCSA unions had successfully blocked FOSATU affiliates from joining a number of industrial councils. The report highlighted the near-total lack of legal pro-

TABLE 1
Paid-up Membership of FOSATU Affiliates

Affiliated	December 1983	December 1984
Chemical Workers' Industrial Union	6,260	13,752
Jewellers & Goldsmiths' Union	476	470
Metal & Allied Workers' Union	20,050	35,870
National Automobile & Allied Workers' Union	18,390	20,257
National Union of Textile Workers	13,150	21,408
Paper, Wood & Allied Workers' Union	5,030	11,430
Sweet, Food & Allied Workers' Union	10,150	12,255
Transport & General Workers' Union	6,335	7,330
Total	79,841	122,772

Source: Financial Mail, 19 July 1985.

tection for unions and their members in the Homelands. FOSATU condemned those transnational corporations which had established branch operations in these areas, accusing them of 'blatantly exploiting the separate development policies of *apartheid'*.[161]

The withdrawal of CUSA from the unity talks coincided with the decision of the NUM to disaffiliate due to 'lack of seriousness' demonstrated by other CUSA affiliates toward the unity drive. The NUM represented about half the total membership of CUSA unions. During the June unity discussions when it sided with AZACTU, CUSA had shown serious doubts over the question of white leadership. It argued that 'because of the present oppressive and exploitative system of *apartheid,* the black workers have reservations about participating in talks which do not enforce the principle of black leadership'.[162] The 'unity unions' — now including NUM — strongly acceded to the principle of nonracialism which remained a necessary condition for their participation in the new federation. CUSA responded that the non-negotiability of this principle illustrated the 'white policy of divide and rule'. The potential loss of CUSA's South African Chemical Workers' Union and the Transport and Allied Workers' Union — apart from NUM, CUSA's most influential affiliates — evoked obvious disappointment within trade union circles.

The 9 June unity talks were hindered by numerous conflicts, including the issue of nonracialism and white leadership, the attitude of the new federation toward the liberation struggle, and the federation's relationship to other political organizations. In July, GAWU, SAAWU, and GWUSA urged that the Feasibility Committee be expanded to include AZACTU, while other unions in the committee argued that this would only induce further ideological squabbles on seemingly irreconcilable issues and delay the formation of the 'super federation'. The unity talks reached a standstill. Three positions emerged. The pro-federation unions argued to move ahead with the plans. AZACTU and CUSA disagreed with the principles of the 'super federation' in their present form, while SAAWU, GAWU, the Municipal and General Workers' Union, and the National Union of Printing and Allied Workers took a neutral stand. Despite CUSA's withdrawal and the persistent hesitancy of the AZACTU and UDF-affiliated unions, twenty-five trade unions decided in August to proceed with plans to launch the much-awaited 'super federation' on 30 November [163]

The Formation of the 'Super-federation'

The formal establishment of COSATU took place in Durban on 30 November under the banner 'One Federation, One Country'. With thirty-four affiliates, a signed-up membership of over 500,000 workers, and 430,000 paid members, COSATU overtook TUCSA (with forty-three affiliates and 340,000 paid members) as South Africa's largest labour federation. The new 'super-federation' was comprised of the eight FOSATU affiliates, the NUM, CCAWUSA, FCWU, GWU, GTMWA, UNMAWSA, RAWU, and a number of unions affiliated to the UDF and the Natal-based National Federation of Workers. These trade unions agreed to five principles of unity: nonracialism, one union/one industry, worker control, representation on the basis of paid-up membership, and cooperation between affiliates at the national level. The federation's fundamental goal was to build a strong, industrially-based, centralized, democratic structure that would be able to both confront capital and to achieve and consolidate concrete gains for the working class. With the growing concentration and centralization of capital in South Africa, COSATU organizers wanted to establish a national trade union federation that would overcome the deficiencies of regional or local unions. Without a pooling of resources, capitalist management in South Africa retained the upper hand.[164]

To realize the principle of one union/one industry, several COSATU affiliates had already initiated merger discussions. In the automotive and metal sectors, discussions between MAWU, NAAWU, and UMMAWSA were well underway. A timetable had already been established for the merger between the Transport and General Workers' Union (TGWU) and GWU and between FCWU and the Sweet, Food and Allied Workers' Union. Another significant step involved the participation of the NUM in the formation of a Southern African Mineworkers' Federation. This federation was an ambitious attempt to forge subcontinental unity amongst trade unions who faced common employers.[165]

It was decided that the highest decision-making body of the new federation would be the national congress which would convene every two years. Consisting of the federation's president, vice-president, general-secretary, treasurer, and delegates from each union (where proportional representation would be based on paid membership), the national congress was authorized to adopt general and specific policies, to decide on constitutional amendments, and to conduct nominations and election of COSATU office bearers. The central committee was to manage the affairs of the federation between meetings of the national congress, establishing sub-committees, settling disputes between affiliates, administering funds, demarcating and establishing regions, and appointing officials and employees. Its membership was made up of the national officers, the chair of each region, and two representatives (one of whom must be a worker) from each affiliate. An executive committee of the national officers and four members elected from the central committee was to assist the general secretary and deal with specific issues delegated by the central committee.

The heart of the COSATU administrative structure was the regional congresses and shop stewards' councils (that is, shop stewards in a particular locality). Regional congresses were composed of representatives from three or more affiliates with branches in a demarcated geographical area. At the local level, shop stewards' councils also brought together representatives from different affiliates. The organs of popular control symbolized the wholesale effort to realize maximum unity through democracy. It was also mandated that the majority of national delegates would be workers. The formation of COSATU brought together 12,462 elected shop stewards from 1,443 shop steward councils. COSATU affiliates had organized 3,421 workplaces and negotiated 450 formal agreements with employers.

Despite the obvious sense of triumph at the inaugural congress, the decision of two federations — CUSA and AZACTU — not to join gave a sobering tone to the proceedings.

The reasons that underlay CUSA's decision to withdraw were unclear. In contrast, AZACTU had been excluded. In addition, two UDF-affiliated unions — MACWUSA and OVGWU — did not affiliate to COSATU.[166] CUSA's eleven affiliates and AZACTU's nine member trade unions were united by a commitment to black leadership that at the same time distinguished them from COSATU unions. The general secretary of CUSA, Piroshaw Camay, emphasized that the concept of black leadership did not exclude whites from leadership *per se.* It did, however, preclude whites from being imposed as leaders on black trade unions without working their way up through the ranks. Whites with 'working-class aspirations', he contended, were more than welcome to join black trade unions at the grassroots and the shop-floor level and to assume leadership positions if elected by fellow-members.[167] AZACTU coordinator Pandelane Nefolovhodwe maintained that trade unions (or a federation of trade unions) should be controlled by a leadership drawn from the most oppressed class, that is, black workers. While stressing the principle of black leadership, the CUSA-AZACTU alignment subscribed to the principle of anti-racism. The difference between anti-racism and the nonracialism espoused by COSATU was more than a quibble. It carried ideological overtones that dated back to the split in the late 1950s between the ANC and the PAC.[168] But more importantly, it symbolized divergent perspectives — particularly those that divided the UDF and National Forum — on the role of white intellectuals and organizational affiliations within the 'liberation struggle'.

The exhilaration and relief associated with the formation of COSATU overshadowed the accelerated pattern of labour unrest that had gripped South Africa. Labour consultant Andrew Levy and Associates had reported that more than 500,000 labour-days had been lost due to labour unrest in the first nine months of 1985. This figure had already surpassed by 30 per cent the total number of labour-days lost during the whole of 1984. Wage demands triggered almost half of these strikes. The strike-prone motor and mining industries led the field in the number of work stoppages. One feature that distinguished 1985 strikes from previous years was their coordinated character. Most strikes were industry-wide as rival unions joined together against employers.[169] One of the most dramatic tactical innovations took place in September at the Brits factory of the German-based multinational corporation, Robert Bosch. An estimated 300 workers who belonged to MAWU occupied the factory after negotiations over a longstanding wage dispute had collapsed. Almost immediately, Bosch acceded to MAWU's demands.[170]

Perhaps the most perplexing question that remained unanswered during the year-and-a-half political turmoil had been why most independent black trade unions decided to maintain a relatively low political profile compared with the popular organizations. This choice of political strategy was not accidental. The independent black trade union movement — unlike the role of SACTU in the 1950s — saw its political place within the liberation struggle as different from that of most popular organizations. In an authoritative position paper, FOSATU's education director, Alec Erwin, outlined in broad terms the political questions associated with the liberation struggle and economic transformation. He defined 'liberation politics' as the process concerned with the destruction of the legitimacy of an unjust regime so that it cannot govern successfully and must abdicate. For liberation politics to succeed, the popular opposition must be able to mobilize the greatest possible support, domestically and worldwide. The *apartheid* system, Erwin contended, has been so abhorrent to so many for so long that its very unacceptability has created a simple and powerful foundation for popular mobilization. However, the political problems confronting trade unions might be similar but are not identical to those of popular opposition to an unjust regime. South Africa's economic relations have produced structural imbalances requiring substantial transformation before the rural and urban working class can improve its material and social conditions. Trade unions faced political dilemma 'because the imperatives posed by opposition do not encourage political practices that address transformation'.[171] 'The challenge posed', Erwin argued, 'is whether political practices can be evolved that retain sufficient unity of purpose among a majority of the oppressed to undermine the legitimacy of the regime yet at the same time address the problems of transformation.'[172] He maintained that the FOSATU practice of building independent shop-floor unions, in which representatives were elected and accountable to their immediate constituencies, offered at least a partial answer to the political question of how to advance the 'liberation struggle'. Erwin castigated those political activists that deviated from this approach. 'At present', he contended, 'there is a tendency for activists to congregate around the honeypot of popular activity. From the perspective of transformation, this is not necessarily wise, in addition to its possible insidious threat to democracy.'[173] For FOSATU, the bottom line for unity in the struggle against *apartheid* was the acceptance of the centrality of working-class interests. A change in regime in South Africa — where the question of transformation had not been addressed directly — would leave intact structures and interests inimical to the working class.[174]

In his inaugural address that launched COSATU, NUM general secretary Cyril Ramaphosa set the political tone that was expected to guide the new federation. The principal concern of the trade unions was the struggle against management and their main area of activity was the workplace. Yet as the white minority regime had failed to find a solution to the severest economic and political crisis in South African history, the trade unions had increasingly broadened their political outlook to contribute to the popular struggle. 'P.W. Botha has failed to point a direction', Ramaphosa said, 'and it is time that the working class called on him to give up power so that the true leaders can take power.'[175] He pledged that COSATU would attempt to draw all people into a program to restructure South Africa's economic relations so that the wealth of the country would be 'democratically controlled and shared by all its people'. In what was tantamount to a socialist declaration of principles, Ramaphosa called for the elimination of unemployment and poverty and a redistribution of wealth.[176]

COSATU appeared to place political goals at the top of its agenda. In its first policy statement, the new federation endorsed the worldwide divestment campaign, nationalization of the mines, equal pay for equal work, the abolition of all discriminatory legislation (including the migrant labour system, influx controls, and the pass laws), the withdrawal of the SADF from the townships, and the unbanning of political organizations. In a spirited refrain, Elijah Barayi, the newly elected president of COSATU (and former vice-president of the NUM), issued an ultimatum to the white minority regime to abolish the pass laws within six months or face a trade union-sponsored civil disobedience campaign.[177] Jay Naidoo, COSATU's general secretary (and former general secretary of FOSATU's Sweet, Food and Allied Workers' Union), reiterated that the federation aimed to forge links only with organizations that represented the 'progressive sectors of the working class'.[178] He maintained that COSATU was committed to a position where the wealth of the nation was 'owned, shared and controlled by the people, and used to further the interests of those who produce it'.[179]

COSATU had three difficult tasks. First, it pledged to organize workers in the Homelands in defiance of legal restrictions on unions. The surrogate regimes in the Homelands had implemented restrictive labour codes that sometimes paralleled and overlapped South Africa's statutory provisions but that were everywhere a bureaucratic nightmare for employers and unions alike.[180] This commitment pitted COSATU against power-brokers who owed their allegiance to Pretoria and had not hesitated during the course of the 1984-6 political unrest to suppress their political opponents. Second, it set a deadline of six months for the reorganization (through mergers and dissolution) of its thirty-four affiliates into ten national industrial unions, and it planned to initiate organizing drives in the construction and agricultural sectors, though the actual number of sectors and their identification remained subject to further negotiation within COSATU. Third, COSATU confronted the sensitive issue of reconciling divergent ideological currents within its ranks. The federation's unity principles placed more emphasis on organizational codes than political tenets. In this sense, the CUSA affiliates seemed to have more in common with COSATU than some of the small, community-based, 'political' trade unions associated with the UDF. The amalgamation of the independent trade unions did not address directly the precise character of the relationship between the federation and the popular struggle against the minority regime.[181]

From the outset, COSATU outlined a complex agenda of commitments and demands. It resolved to struggle for a national minimum living wage, a 40-hour week at full pay, the abolition of overtime, and the formation of a national unemployed workers' council as a full-fledged affiliate. It was to oppose 'as a total fraud' the new national constitution and reaffirmed its belief in a unitary state with one-person and one-vote. It adopted a strong feminist platform, promising to fight 'against all unequal and discriminatory treatment of women at work, in society and in the federation'. This stand on women's rights represented 'the most outspoken position ever taken before in South Africa by a representative, and predominantly male body'.[182] The federation pledged its support for equal pay for all work of equal value and 'for the restructuring of employment so as to allow women and men the opportunity of qualifying for jobs of equal value'. It would struggle for childcare and family facilities 'to meet workers' needs and make it easier for workers to combine work and family responsibilities' and for full maternity rights 'including paid maternity and paternity leave'. It vowed to fight against sexual harassment 'in whatever form it occurs'.[183]

4.

The Popular Organizations and the Political Struggle

On 20-21 August 1983, an estimated 12,000 people crammed into an overcrowded ampitheatre at Mitchell's Plain (a sprawling black working-class suburb of greater Cape Town) for the largest single assembly of South African anti-government groups since the 1950s. Sensing the novelty of the event, the mood of the assembled crowd was jubilant — even defiant. This meeting launched the United Democratic Front (UDF), a broad-based alliance that eventually claimed a following of approximately 600 affiliates, including community-based civic associations, trade unions, Church and women's groups, youth and student organizations, sporting clubs, and professional bodies with a total membership estimated at over one million. The immediate goal of the more than 600 delegates from over 300 affiliates who gathered at the inaugural conference was a loosely-knit coalition of existing popular organizations to effectively unite and co-ordinate national resistance to the white minority regime's new constitutional proposals and to the so-called Koornhof Bills.[1]

Earlier in the year, Prime Minister P.W. Botha had unveiled the final draft of the constitution proposals, announcing that the National Party would spearhead the drive to gain the approval of the white electorate for this 'new dispensation'. P.W. Botha had set 2 November 1983 as the target date for the national referendum through which to gauge the degree of political support amongst eligible white voters for the proposals.[2] This national referendum provided an opportunity for disparate popular

195

organizations to unite in the broadest display of public opposition to the white minority regime in almost thirty years.

The formation of the UDF was indeed an historic occasion.
Despite official harassment and last-minute threats by local
apartheid authorities to ban the gathering, the UDF meeting began
on time. A national executive committee elected by popular
acclamation sketched the outlines of a political program.
Mobilized around the slogan '*Apartheid* Divides, UDF Unites', the
formation of the UDF signified a departure from the somewhat
erratic course that had typified popular opposition to *apartheid*
and to capitalism within South Africa since the failure of the
'over ground' Congress Alliance in the early 1960s.

A few months earlier, on 11-12 June 1983, the interim
National Forum Committee had convened an inaugural conference at Hammanskraal, near Johannesburg. Attended by
approximately 800 delegates representing 200-odd organizations,
this meeting tackled an exhaustive agenda, including the affirmation of a broad basis for political unity from which to mount
the public campaign against the Botha regime's 'new deal' — the
combination of the President's Council, the proposed constitutional reforms, and the so-called Koornhoff Bills. The sombre
tone of this assembly contrasted with the more festive air of the
UDF inaugural event.

The highlight of this conference was the adoption in principle
of the *Manifesto of the Azanian People*, an over-arching declaration
of objectives identifying 'racial capitalism' as the principal source
of oppression of the black masses and pledging political commitment to building an 'anti-racist, socialist Republic'. The
seventeen interim members of the National Forum Committee
represented a spectrum of black leadership from all spheres of
community life. There were delegates from political, religious,
student, youth, civic, and trade union organizations.[3]

Over the past decade, the structural underpinnings that have
supported and sustained white minority rule have suffered irreversible damage. The class struggle has shifted in the direction of
open and protracted conflict. The wellsprings of this explosive
growth of popular unrest have been the factory proletariat and
school-age youth. Largely through spontaneous workplace
militancy, the urbanized industrial working class has operated at
the forefront of the collective struggle to improve the material
well-being of the masses. This refusal of key sections of the black

working class to submit to the rule of capital posed a serious challenge to white employers. The class struggle to secure a living wage and decent working conditions was manifested through spontaneous strikes, walkouts, slowdowns, and a multitude of less organized and more obscure acts of defiance. The popular insurgency of school-age youth in the townships had broadened and extended the coordinates of class conflict. Acting principally as catalysts rather than as mass-based organizations, student and youth groups in the wake of the 1976-7 Soweto rebellion maintained unrelenting pressure on the white authorities and their black surrogates over a broad range of grievances (including inferior education, the poor quality township services, and the lack of direct political representation). Student and youth groups grew in tandem with neighborhood civic associations (the primary organs for the self-defense of material conditions of local communities).

The formation of the UDF and the National Forum marked a turning-point in the political complexion of the popular opposition. These popular organizations rode the crest of a groundswell of localized agitation. They represented a new correlation of social forces that had grown up in the townships. The inability or unwillingness of the white minority regime to fundamentally address the visible grievances that had sparked the Soweto uprising alienated and angered growing numbers of township residents.

Viewed through the narrow prism of their common antagonists, the UDF and the National Forum appear strikingly similar. Both seek to work within ongoing popular struggles and to synthesize rather than displace largely localized and spontaneous outbreaks of rebellion. Both have made appeals for organizational unity and disciplined political action. Both have appealed to the increasingly restive and radicalized black working-class residents of the urban townships, and used the National Party's 'new dispensation' — the transparent efforts to inject fresh vitality into the tarnished image of white minority rule — as a pretext for galvanizing popular support for broad national campaigns.

Over the past half century, the popular politics of mass mobilization in South Africa have swung between periods of frenzied public activity and demoralized quiescence. In South Africa since 1976, the tempo of popular protest had quickened considerably, animating a spirit of routinized and pervasive unease throughout the black townships. The battlelines separating the contestants had become so blurred and indefinite that a plethora of local grievances threatened to ignite at any moment a national conflagration that (as the highest-ranking state officials acknowledged) could only be extinguished through the massive use of force and violence.

It would be a mistake to believe that the recurrent outbreaks of popular protest always bore the mark of any single organization. The open defiance of ordinary people in South Africa has nearly always been impelled by a mixture of ideological sentiments that cannot be disentangled easily. While they do not derive from a single source or operate within a uniform frame of reference, they have historically engendered a sort of promiscuous populist blend that has inspired collective political action. The political slogan, 'One-Person One-Vote', indicates an underlying current of democratic radicalism that has been inscribed in the popular movement. The abstract universality of democratic citizenship and equally ambiguous notions of distributive social justice have figured prominently in popular political consciousness. These recurrent populist themes have invariably stemmed from the manner in which capitalist exploitation and racial/national oppression have been intertwined historically in South Africa.

The incongruous mixtures that make up popular political consciousness are perhaps best illustrated in the universally acclaimed national anthem of the liberation movement, *Nkosi Sikelel' i Afrika*. This song blends an obvious secular social meaning with a plea for spiritual salvation. On the whole, humanist sentiments have been innoculated with a deep religious tincture and have permeated popular consciousness, while specifically redemptive religious ideology has frequently fuelled the millenarian tendencies within the popular movement, translating latent class antagonisms into a moral contest between good and evil. After the 1960 Sharpeville massacre, the confident slogan of the Pan-Africanist Congress — 'liberation by 1963' — underscored this millenial fervour that frequently found expression in the liberation movements. Similarly, youthful township militants — unemployed, poorly educated, and politically inexperienced — who formed the nucleus of the street-fighting vanguard in 1984-6, and frequently operated on the fringes of the organized political movements in their communities, have also been captivated by apocalyptic visions of swift 'liberation'. The emergence of the UDF and the National Forum — both largely community-based formations with claims to a national presence — served to highlight long-standing political disputes that have recurred since the 1930s. While their mass constituencies have considerably overlapped and frequently converged, they represent divergent political currents. The dissimilar tone of their political programs stems in large measure from their separate historical origins.

The UDF traces its historical lineage to the ANC/Congress Alliance and the turbulent 1950s. For the UDF, the mass popular campaigns of that time denote a watershed in the breadth and depth of popular consciousness. Firmly ensconced within this tradition, the UDF emphasized that it does not consider its own organizational efforts to be a substitute for the 'accredited people's liberation movements'.[4] The architects of the UDF strategy subscribed to a multi-class coalition of progressive social forces. As a broad popular assembly of organizations the UDF resembles less a political party or even a political organization *per se* than an 'over-ground', legal vehicle for catalyzing and channelling popular discontent. UDF adherents have sought to achieve popular consensus in opposition to *apartheid* stating that the immediate task is to mobilize all opponents of white minority rule — whatever their class or racial/national composition — into a broad alliance of 'progressive national' and 'democratic' forces.

In contrast, the National Forum self-consciously approximates the central features of a federated body of affiliated organizations that retain their separate ideological identities and specific roles. National Forum affiliates coalesced around Black Consciousness, a highly nuanced and ambiguous ideological current that remained open to various interpretations. What distinguishes the National Forum from the UDF is that the former identifies 'racial capitalism' as the wellspring of national oppression in South Africa. This assessment of the South African situation denotes a series of delicate strategic implications. The National Forum remains adamant on three points: (1) the achievement of national liberation entails a struggle between oppressed and oppressors; (2) the black working class — both on the shop floor and in the townships — constitutes the principal vehicle for not only uniting the oppressed but also achieving the ultimate goal of national liberation; and (3) alliances — whether strategic or tactical — with organized members of the 'oppressor camp' pose a serious danger of impeding and derailing the struggle for national liberation.

In practical terms, the strategic differences separating the UDF from the National Forum centre on the character of political alliances with progressive white organizations. The UDF sees these alliances as the fulfilment of a non-racial vision of South Africa's future. In contrast, the National Forum has renounced coalitions with any organized white groups, proclaiming that the middle-class origins of their membership invariably generate reformist ideologies that could potentially 'hijack' the struggle against 'racial capitalism'.

The Topography of Popular Unrest, 1976-83

The 'Long Wave' of Popular Protest

The 1976 Soweto uprising marked the opening round of a 'long wave' of popular protest that has convulsed South Africa and kept the white minority regime off balance for almost a decade. What began on 16 June 1976 as a student demonstration against the official stipulation that Afrikaans be used as the principal medium of instruction became an outbreak of resistance to the *apartheid* system. Despite police shootings, beatings, tear-gassing, and massive arrests and detentions, the uprising spread and intensified, eventually involving an estimated two hundred black communities throughout the country. The popular rebellion subsided gradually by early 1977.

Nevertheless, the scale of the revolt was unprecedented in the history of mass struggle in South Africa. Tens of thousands of men, women and children, students, parents and workers in the black townships and ghettos actively participated in the uprising. They clashed regularly and ferociously with heavily-armed police. They used fire to damage or destroy government buildings and vehicles. They burned down beerhalls, liquor stores, and post offices. They boycotted schools, staged massive demonstrations and marches, and organized three stay-away strikes. They closed down state-affiliated structures such as the Soweto Urban Bantu Councils. They attacked the homes and property of black policemen and others considered to be collaborating with the white authorities. The pinnacle of the 'June Events' was reached in the September 1976 'stay-at-home'; an enormous countrywide work stoppage.[5]

Despite being caught nearly totally unprepared, the response of the state machinery was predictable: mass arrests, detentions without trial, and employment of overwhelming military force in the black townships. The white regime was forced to rely almost exclusively on repression to quell the disturbances. Through the use of their guns, tear-gas, armoured cars, helicopters, dogs, informers, the prohibition of gatherings, indiscriminate arrests, systematic house-to-house raids and road-block searches, the police imposed what the black people in the affected townships experienced as a reign of terror.[6] In October 1977, the security police banned (declared illegal) eighteen major black community, political, and religious organizations. Under provisions of the South African Internal Security Act, the police detained scores of church leaders, journalists, and community activists in a dragnet designed to decapitate the upper echelons of numerous organizations that had begun to sink roots into the embattled townships.

During the time of the Soweto rebellion and its extended aftermath, Black Consciousness emerged as the dominant ideological current, particularly amongst the militant youth who had played the pivotal role in igniting and animating the popular struggle. However, by 1980-81, there began to emerge a loose-knit alliance of civic associations, student bodies, and trade union organizations that rejected the Black Consciousness approach and coalesced instead around endorsement of the Freedom Charter. These groups also supported political connections with white radicals, at the time anathema to Black Consciousness adherents.[7]

In the meantime, the independent black trade union movement — particularly those trade unions clustered around FOSATU — had taken unprecedented steps towards rebuilding and reconstructing an organized working-class movement. In a few years, these unions had achieved significant gains for black workers, particularly with respect to wage increases and improved working conditions. Not unexpectedly, the rapid growth of trade unionism, both in numerical size and political strength, did not occur without controversy. For the most part, the independent black trade unions grew out of the political hiatus caused by the decline of progressive trade unionism in the 1960s. These independent unions developed in distinctive regional settings with their own peculiar political traditions. These factors alone were breeding-grounds for mutual distrust and suspicion, creating an unhealthy mix of rancour and factionalism that had prevented political unity.

Nevertheless, the differences within the independent trade union movement at this time paled in comparison to the internecine squabbles over political strategy separating the unions from the community-based civic, student, and cultural bodies. The community organizations — particularly those associated with the Chartist (that is, support for the Freedom Charter) camp — supported a popular democratic approach to mass political mobilization. The densely-populated townships became the battlegrounds where community organizers sought to unite black people across class lines (and in alliance with sympathetic white university-affiliated groups) around urgent issues of the day. This polyclass political approach was matched by an eclectic, barnstorming style. A host of tactics were used — free-wheeling petition drives contesting electricity billing procedures, mass meetings challenging rental or transport fare increases. These crusading mass campaigns, aimed at the redress of immediate grievances, were reminiscent in tone of the tactical approach of the ANC and its allies during its 'over-ground' heyday in the 1950s.

During the early 1980s, the independent trade unions — particularly those affiliated to FOSATU — emphasized an orthodox approach to trade union organizing. The FOSATU executive drew the ire of its political opponents by insisting that the massive industrialization over the past thirty years had created a strategically-located, yet unorganized, black industrial proletariat that called for an *autonomous* workers' political movement centered around strong factory-based organization.

The ideological clashes between the FOSATU wing of the trade union movement and the community-oriented organizations also reflected the dissimilarities in aims and backgrounds between what can be termed loosely the New Left of the 1970s and the Old Left of the 1950s. At the risk of over-simplification, it can be argued that white intellectuals who were influenced by pantisocratic New Left ideals played an important role in the resuscitation of the independent trade union movement. They were nurtured in an era in which the ANC and the South African Communist Party were in disarray and retreat within South Africa. Their political views were shaped by the worldwide revival of decidedly unorthodox Marxism, while the youthful black leadership of the independent black trade union movement gradually came to assert the view that the organized black working class constituted the principal vehicle for advancing the anti-*apartheid* struggle.

In contrast, the leadership of various community-oriented organizations was made up of 'old guard' figures schooled in the Congress-related movements of the 1950s. Younger activists operating within these were drawn from the post-1976 generation that matured against the backdrop of riots, strikes, school boycotts, and a rising tide of ANC guerrilla activities. During this period, the prestige of the ANC had risen sharply amongst the masses. Consequently, the younger leadership sought guidance from figures reared in the older Congress traditions.[8]

The Independent Black Trade Union Movement and the Wildcat Strike Wave

In 1980, the unregistered Black Municipal Workers' Union accomplished what had hitherto been unthinkable: it successfully organized thousands of migrant workers in Johannesburg and paralyzed municipal services in the city for nearly a week. All but 2,000 of 14,500 municipal workers in Johannesburg were migrants. In July 1980 the Johannesburg City Council dismissed 640 municipal workers who were seeking a higher minimum wage and equal pay for equal work. An estimated 10,000 workers went on strike under the leadership of the Black Municipal Workers' Union to protest these dismissals. It was the largest walkout ever faced by a single employer in South African history. The police successfully crushed the strike and deported more than 1,000 workers to the Homelands. Nevertheless, the militant defiance of these workers set the pace for independent strike actions during the following years.[9]

During 1981, the increasingly powerful independent black trade union movement took the political lead in the 'overground' resistance to apartheid. A series of wildcat strikes that spread across South Africa's industrial heartland during June and July were the prelude to a protracted outburst of working-class militancy. Just as this wave appeared to have subsided, a renewed round of work stoppages erupted, surpassing the initial wave in both intensity and duration. In mid-September, over 3,000 black workers at three separate metal works conducted well-orchestrated walkouts that successfully achieved the reinstatement of unfairly dismissed colleagues. The cafeteria boycott by all 7,000 workers of Volkswagen's Uitenhage plant-canteen received national attention. In the first week of October alone, over 10,000 workers were involved in at least thirty separate strikes in South Africa's three key industrial centres: Durban/Pinetown, the Eastern Cape, and the Vaal Triangle. One prominent grievance that surfaced during these strikes concerned the Preservation of Pensions Bill. The National Party intended this legislation to prevent workers from obtaining payouts of pension contributions until retirement age. The mass protests were so fierce that the National Party was forced to announce that it would indefinitely delay the implementation of this legislation. FOSATU affiliates joined with other independent black trade unions in proposing instead direct worker control over pension funds.

Other grievances that figured prominently during this strike wave were wage demands, union recognition agreements, and working conditions. In Natal, spontaneous walkouts at sugar mills owned by the gigantic Huletts conglomerate sparked strikes amongst stevedores in the port city of Durban and at least four branches of a major department store chain. In the Eastern Cape, a strike of all 2,600 black workers closed the plant of Mercedes Benz's South African subsidiary. Eleven major strike actions followed in rapid succession, slowing production in a number of manufacturing plants in the Port Elizabeth/East London area and disrupting the powerful automobile industry.

With over 20,000 workers involved in strikes in at least forty factories, the labour unrest during October marked the single largest spate of work stoppages since the historic strike wave of 1973. The apogee of working-class militancy was achieved on the East Rand. Despite its concentration of heavy industrial undertakings, this region had hitherto lagged behind the rest of the country with respect to independent black trade union organizing activities. Beginning in October, thousands of black workers in the East Rand engaged in an almost unbroken chain of strikes that buffetted the area's steel, paper, brewery, chemical, and services industries.[10]

In an orchestrated series of retaliatory measures, employers and the state authorities joined forces to shortcut the labour unrest and retard the growing confidence of the independent trade union movement. At the Triomf fertilizer plant where a work stoppage had crippled production, local farmers co-operated with the company's management to replace strikers with white scabs and white schoolboys on vacation. When a strike closed the giant Telephone Manufacturers of South Africa plant in Springs, the company summarily dismissed the entire black labour force.

As the strike wave spread with no apparent resolution in sight, companies responded by hastily recognizing compliant 'parallel unions' established by management or collaborationist white unions in a last-ditch effort to avert labour unrest. The state authorities intensified their harassment of trade union organizers. In Port Elizabeth, all union meetings were temporarily banned and eighteen members of the militant General Workers Union of South Africa were temporarily detained.[11] What distinguished this period of popular turbulence during the last four months of 1981 was the release of pent-up labour militancy and other forms of overt social protest, in combination with the upsurge of clandestine guerrilla activities.

South African Indian Council Elections

Student and community-based popular protests reached a high point in May 1981, coinciding with the Twentieth Anniversary Republic Day celebrations. Mass demonstrations were called around the slogan, 'White Republic, No! Peoples' Republic, Yes!' In October, protest meetings were held throughout the country to mark the fourth anniversary of the state's massive crackdown during which nineteen political organizations and two black newspapers had been banned. Proposed rent increases for black housing in the townships also sparked intermittent rioting and calls for rent boycotts.

One of the most significant protests of 1981 was the massive boycott by the Indian community of the orchestrated elections for the South African Indian Council (SAIC). Established in 1964, the SAIC had served as an ineffectual advisory board to the white Parliament. Except for a handful who took advantage of the opportunities afforded by their participation, most Indian people viewed the SAIC with skepticism if not outright disgust. The 1981 SAIC elections were symbolic because they represented the first official test of Botha's 'new dispensation'.[12] The Anti-SAIC Committee — headed by the Natal Indian Congress — came into existence in mid-1980 to galvanize public support for a total boycott of government-created bodies. The Committee called on the Indian people 'not to go along with the "stooges" and "sell-outs" who wanted to participate in an *apartheid*-oriented "Indian only"' election farce.[13]

In the months preceeding the scheduled SAIC elections, the Anti-SAIC forces gained an ever-widening endorsement for their boycott campaign.[14] The 1981 national Anti-SAIC conference held in October in Durban was not only a watershed for coalition-building politics but also prefigured the formation of the UDF. The 109 organizations represented pledged their 'non-participation in any constitutional arrangement that does not arise out of a national convention' and declared unswerving support for the principles contained in the Freedom Charter.[15] On the eve of election day, an estimated 3,000 people — 'believed to be the biggest ever at a political meeting in Lenasia', according to the *Rand Daily Mail* correspondent — dramatically underscored the national call for an election boycott.[16] Amid heavy security (prompting the Natal chief electoral officer to comment that there were more police than voters at the polling stations) and despite police intimidation, the boycott campaign was a massive success with the Natal Indian Congress estimating that over 90 per cent of the eligible electorate did not vote.[17]

Political Resurgence of the ANC

Over the past decade, the ANC — both as an overt political tendency and an organizationally separate underground wing — has experienced a rebirth, compared with the dark days of the 1960s. The ANC's guerrilla wing — Umkhonto we Sizwe — lapsed into virtual inaction in the years between the capture of almost all its active leadership at Rivonia in 1964 and the 1976 Soweto rebellion. The exodus of thousands of young militants during the repression following the Soweto uprising provided Umkhonto we Sizwe with 'a new army of highly motivated and well-educated (in contrast to the recruits of the early 1960s) saboteurs'.[18] One chronology of guerilla activity estimated that 112 attacks and explosions occurred between October 1976 and May 1981.[19] In March 1978, it was reported that one explosion per week had taken place since the previous November.[20] From the events that have been reported in the press or that have emerged from trial evidence, it is possible to discern the pattern of the guerrilla campaign. The initial phase of regroupment seemed to have been devoted primarily to establishing lines of communication and infiltration routes, to secreting arms caches, and to implanting a rudimentary cellular organizational structure in the principal urban areas.[21] Armed assaults on heavily-fortified police stations (particularly those in or near black townships) began to take place with increasing frequency. In addition, a number of suspected black security police were assassinated. Germiston, Daveyton, New Brighton, Chatsworth, Moroka, Soekmekaar, and Booysens police stations were all subjected to grenade, rocket, or bomb attacks between 1977 and 1980.[22]

In 1980-1, the Umkhonto guerrilla campaign entered a different and more dramatic phase. The aim of the accelerated sabotage campaign seems to have been to select targets of considerable strategic or economic importance, thereby creating the maximum popular resonance and inspiring confidence amongst the black masses rather than sowing terror in the white community. In July 1980, Umkhonto saboteurs inflicted heavy damge on the SASOL synthetic oil refinery installation at Sasolburg. This attack on South Africa's showcase energy project caused an estimated $4 million in damage. In July 1981, power stations were bombed in the eastern Transvaal. In apparent retaliation, south African agents assassinated former Robben Island prisoner, Joe Gqabi, in Harare, Zimbabwe, where he served as official ANC representative. In reprisal, Umkhonto saboteurs conducted a rocket attack in August 1981 on South Africa's largest military installation, the Voortrekkerhoogte barracks outside Pretoria, and exploded a bomb during working hours in the main shopping centre of Port Elizabeth.[23]

During 1981, Umkhonto engaged in more acts of sabotage and armed assaults than in any other year since the armed struggle campaign first began. According to figures provided by officially-sanctioned 'think tanks', incidents of sabotage trebled in the first six months of 1981 and then ballooned again in both scale and intensity before cresting and tailing off. Targets of armed attacks included police stations, fuel installations and power plants, rail lines, government offices, court buildings, and military installations. Unlike the sabotage campaign in previous years, this round of attacks appeared to be directed at inflicting maximum material damage on selected targets. Pretoria's chief of security police ruefully remarked that 'the drawn out, scattered, and fluid nature of the [guerrilla] conflict [is] especially aimed at overtaxing the country's security forces and at the same time its economic power base'.[24]

In 1982, an escalating wave of Umkhonto sabotage attacks began in late May and reached a peak in the following month coinciding with the anniversaries of the 16 June Soweto uprising and the adoption of the Freedom Charter on 26 June 1955. A succession of bomb explosions devastated a selection of targets widely scattered throughout South Africa. For example, a fuel depot and a power station were demolished in a small town near the Mozambican border. Bomb blasts seriously damaged several government buildings near Durban. A railroad line leading to the coal-exporting port of Richard's Bay was wrecked. Saboteurs inflicted considerable damage on the Cape Town building housing the President's Council. Explosions also downed power lines near Johannesburg.

In retaliation, the SADF intensified its campaign of assassination against ANC supporters both inside the country and abroad, indiscriminate arrests and torture of suspected ANC members and sympathizers, and military and economic pressures against neighbouring nations accused of harbouring ANC guerrillas. In January 1981, SADF commandos raided Matola on the outskirts of Maputo, Mozambique, ostensibly in search of ANC logistical support installations, training facilities, and 'safe houses' serving as final departure points for Umkhonto guerrillas infiltrating on sabotage missions into South Africa. In this raid, twelve ANC members were killed. On 4 June 1982, the deputy representative of the ANC in Swaziland, Petrus Nyaose, and his wife Jabu Nzima were killed when a bomb was detonated in their automobile. The use of torture against political detainees during interrogation greatly increased during 1981 and 1982. Two political prisoners — Dr Neil Aggett and Tshihiwa Muofhe — died in detention after undergoing extensive interrogation. These were the first such prison-related deaths since the 1977 murder of Steve Biko. Two others — Griffiths Mxenge and Moabi Dipale — died under suspicious circumstances. The mid-1982 report of the Rabie Commission — a panel originally established in 1979 in response to the public outcry over Biko's death in detention — endorsed further the widespread contention that the police security forces regularly employed various torture techniques in interrogation including physical assaults, psychological coercion, long periods of uninterrupted questioning, deprivation of food and sleep, and indefinite solitary confinement.

In July 1982, the ANC exile leadership announced that it was on the threshold of intensifying armed attacks inside South Africa and proclaimed that it intended to move beyond the present campaign of 'armed propaganda' by shifting the emphasis to bolder armed assaults in South African military installations as well as against properties of foreign corporate investors who defied international pressures to boycott the country. On August 5, 1982 three members of the outlawed ANC's military wing were sentenced to death after their conviction on charges of high treason and murder. The three — Simon Mogoerane, Harry Semano Mosololi, and Thabo Motaung — were found guilty of acts of sabotage against police stations and commuter rail lines in Soweto and against power plants in Pretoria. All three testified that they had been tortured during detention and interrogation. On August 17, Ruth First, ANC activist researcher and former wife of Joe Slovo, one of Umkhonto's commanders, was killed by a parcel bomb in Maputo, Mozambique.[25] In October, Barbara Hogan became the first South African ever to be found guilty of treason and sabotage without having been implicated in overt acts of violence. Hogan's ten-year prison sentence was an ominous sign because it broke the standard pattern of two- to five-year sentences for those convicted of ANC membership.[26]

In November, a leaked CIA report confirmed what journalists and opponents of *apartheid* had suspected for at least a year: that the Umkhonto guerrilla campaign had achieved notable political and military gains inside South Africa. Alarmed by this growing success, Pretoria had begun to suppress news of ANC attacks and was considering the imposition of even stricter limitations on press accounts of ANC actions. The report noted that Pretoria was concerned that widely publicized news accounts of successful ANC assaults on rail lines, police stations, military bases and government buildings would undermine the morale of the white minority. The CIA report disclosed that the number of 'major incidents' attributable to ANC underground saboteurs had dramatically increased from ten in 1980 to over forty in 1981. It was estimated that the ANC had 1,000 to 2,000 active members outside South Africa who had received military training and perhaps 2,000 to 3,000 others inside who recently belonged to the banned organization. However, government officials claimed that the ANC had provided guerrilla training for 10,000 to 15,000 fighters. Finally, the report acknowledged that the ANC's ability to conduct simultaneous bomb attacks in different parts of the country indicated an improved efficiency and co-ordination.[27]

By late 1982, the security forces expressed alarm that an estimated 43 per cent of the white farms on the Botswana border, 39 per cent on the Zimbabwe border, and 14 per cent on the Mozambique border were lying unoccupied and idle. According to a correspondent for the London *Sunday Times,* 'White farmers are abandoning the guerrilla-threatened northern areas of South Africa in such numbers that the ministers of Pieter Botha's government are considering whether to bring in a law compelling owners to keep at least one white person on every farm bordering Zimbabwe, Botswana, and Mozambique. The Government is also planning to spend money to attract more people and industries to towns in border areas, eventually integrating them in a defensive network with the farms.'[28] This shadowy clandestine war zigzagged forward with a certain *quid pro quo* regularity. On 8 December, a SADF raiding party launched a full-scale attack on Maseru, Lesotho, leaving twenty-nine alleged ANC members dead among the forty-two killed. This massacre appeared to have been staged in retaliation for the Congress's recent successes in sabotage against 'hard targets'.

In reprisal for the Lesotho massacre, Umkhonto undertook a sabotage attack on 18 and 19 December that hit South Africa's heavily-guarded Koeberg nuclear power station located 17 miles north of Cape Town. ANC saboteurs penetrated the supposedly impenetrable security that ringed the Koeberg reactor, rocking the facility with four explosions that occurred at staggered intervals over a twelve-hour period and reportedly causing extensive damage. The sequential pattern of the four explosions suggested that the bombing devices were Soviet-designed limpet mines capable of being timed days in advance. This attack was the ANC's most dramatic sabotage operation since the 1980 bombing of the SASOL oil-from-coal conversion plant near Johannesburg. Because the Koeberg plant was so tightly guarded, the success of the operation was viewed as a significant victory for Umkhonto we Sizwe and an embarrassing defeat for Pretoria.[29]

On 20 May 1983, Umkhonto saboteurs conducted the ANC's most audacious action in more than twenty years of guerrilla activity against the South African Air Force headquarters, the Directorate of Military Intelligence, and Navy offices in downtown Pretoria. This devastating car-bomb attack that was aimed primarily at military personnel killed at least eighteen people and wounded an estimated 190 persons. The car-bomb exploded in front of the Nedbank Plaza Building housing the military offices at about 4:28 pm during the height of the rush hour traffic.[30] The Pretoria blast marked a dramatic shift of tactics to include military personnel in its catalogue of targets. The fact that a number of innocent black bystanders were also killed in the explosion appeared to lend credibility to the proposition that the ANC had lifted its implicit ban on sparing civilian bystanders in its sabotage campaign. This attack in the heart of the white laager served as a reminder that the stakes in this low-key, shadowy civil war pitting security forces against guerrilla irregulars had been raised to new heights. Until the Pretoria bombing, it was possible to calculate, through an unofficial tabulation of acts of sabotage credited to the ANC in the heavily censored South African press, at least eighty-seven separate attacks since the beginning of 1981. These actions caused four deaths and injured about 114 persons.[31]

The expected retaliatory raid on neighbouring ANC facilities came almost immediately. On 23 May, South African Air Force jets rocketed and strafed suspected ANC facilities in a residential suburb of Maputo, Mozambique. In an official communiqué, South African military announced that these reprisal attacks were a 'clinical, finely planned operation directed against proven hiding places of the ANC'. Sources on the ground disputed this boastful claim, stating that the bombing appeared haphazard and indiscriminate. One aim of this military raid, a senior Mozambiquan official suggested, was to sow fear and uncertainty as a warning to Mozambique and other African nations harbouring South African exiles that retribution would be swift and unrestrained.[32]

Put in broad perspective, the ANC/Congress political tendency experienced a rebirth in the eight years that elapsed between the 1976 Soweto uprising and the formation of the UDF. This renaissance from virtual political obscurity took place in a series of stages more or less in tandem with the revival of clandestine guerrilla activities. One of the noteworthy features of the Soweto rebellion was the virtual absence of ANC/Congress themes in the political consciousness of the youthful militants. The exodus of thousands of young men and women during and after the popular uprising not only fueled Umkhonto we Sizwe with new recruits but also breathed much-needed new life into the exiled movement.

Umkhonto we Sizwe was able to capitalize on the resurgence of mass defiance precipitated by the Soweto events in mounting a persistent and occasionally spectacular campaign of sabotage and low-level guerrilla activities.[33] Knowledgeable observers have argued that the ANC's sabotage campaign has served three separate yet inter-related objectives in the political struggle: (1) to disrupt the economy and, consequently, undermine the confidence of foreign investors; (2) to undermine white morale and damage the ideological underpinnings of the *apartheid* regime; and (3) to catalyze black political consciousness in the direction of mobilizing various forms of resistance such as strikes, go-slows, mass demonstrations, and street protests.[34] While the scale and frequency of Umkhonto we Sizwe attacks definitely broadened after 1978-9, the degree to which the sabotage campaign has accomplished its intended results remains highly contentious.[35] Critics from within the liberation movement have claimed that there has been an historical tendency for Umkhonto we Sizwe to mount certain spectacular attacks designed primarily to achieve public recognition, gain international acclaim, and announce an ongoing guerrilla presence without substantively advancing the popular struggle. Other critics have argued that the sabotage campaign — initiated over twenty years ago — was never placed squarely within the framework of clearly-defined political goals, and that guerrilla activities have thus become ends in themselves where the only way out of a militaristic impasse is the almost inherent predisposition to randomly raise the stakes. An escalating spiral of violence, critics have maintained, has tended to limit the theater of popular challenge to the military field alone.[36]

The embodiment of ANC/Congress principles and aims is contained in the Freedom Charter. Consequently, declaring allegiance to the Charter's principles has come to indicate a broader adherence to the ANC/Congress movement. In 1980, the Soweto daily newspaper, *The Post*, engineered a 'Release Mandela' petition drive and referred with obvious admiration to the Freedom Charter. At about the same time, the newly-formed Congress of South African Students (COSAS) officially adopted the Freedom Charter as the centerpiece of its political platform. One significant and dramatic breakthrough came in 1981 when the Anti-SAIC Committee evoked the Freedom Charter as the 'people's alternative to *apartheid* and collaboration with it'.[37] In a related move, the Release Mandela Committee — with various branches throughout South Africa — used the occasion of the approaching twentieth anniversary of Nelson Mandela's arrest and subsequent incarceration to popularize the ideals of the Congress movement.

The legacy of the ANC/Congress evokes multiple images of popular struggle. At one extreme, ideological supporters fondly recall the 1950s as the apex of mass struggle — a period of heightened awareness, of widespread political participation, and of stubborn defiance to *apartheid* over-rule. At the other extreme, critics charge that the mass campaigns were largely blunted through the joint impact of inadequate organization and accelerated state repression. These detractors have claimed that the original sabotage campaign — improperly organized and easily infiltrated by security agents — represented a desperate and futile gesture of an unprepared leadership increasingly separated from its mass following.

Whatever the merits of these claims and counter-claims, the ANC/Congress ideological current has never strayed too far from the political centre of gravity within the South African liberation movement, enjoying widespread popular recognition and sentimental support within black townships. The launching of the UDF in 1983 symbolized the culmination of increasingly popular agitation within the ambit of Congress-style politics. At this historic conjuncture, the visible signs of the political revival abounded: speakers at rallies evoked the names of legendary ANC/Congress figures, hastily-drawn ANC slogans adorned building walls, songs and chants conducted at mass gatherings openly praised the armed struggle, funeral processions became the occasion for unfurling ANC banners, and so forth.

The UDF and Populist Politics

The initial call for a broad-based popular democratic front came in January 1983. In May 1983, thirty-two separate organizations met in Johannesburg to form the first regional UDF, rejecting 'in their totality and without qualification' the proposed constitutional modifications as a 'devious scheme to divide the people'. Membership in the Transvaal regional UDF included the South African Indian Congress, the revived Transvaal Indian Congress, Congress of Unions of South Africa (CUSA), South African Allied Workers' Union (SAAWU), the Catholic Bishops Conference, the Azanian Students' Organization, the National Union of South African Students (NUSAS), and the United Women's Organization. Similar local democratic fronts were formed in Durban and Cape Town during the months preceding the founding of the national UDF.

The UDF's initial strategy was to draw together as wide a range of opposition forces as possible under the general anti-*apartheid* banner with specific demands focusing primarily on rejection of the Botha regime's constitutional proposals. The Front also targeted the Koornhoff Bills, proposed legislation designed to tighten controls over permanent resident rights for urban black people, and pledged its willingness to contest rent hikes and to mobilize communities against forced removals. The UDF thus represented a decisive rupture from the prevailing forms of political action. First it took advantage of the contentious issue of the proposed constitutional reforms as a means to catalyze popular sentiment into a broad-based alliance cutting across lines of colour and class. Second, it channelled this newly-acquired organizational strength into a popular movement that openly advocated the building of a nonracial, democratic, and undivided South Africa. These declared aims might appear relatively bland. In the South African context, however, even meagre demands for the extension of bourgeois-democratic rights threaten to undermine capitalism itself. What distinguished this UDF appeal from efforts over the past two or three decades was the ability to conduct unified political action under the single banner of an 'over ground' coalition with a national presence and considerable popular support.

One of the principal speakers at the founding of the UDF, Dr Allan Boesak, a leading church minister and the president of the World Alliance of Reformed Churches, referred to the 'politics of refusal', arguing that civic associations, church groups, trade unions, student organizations, and sports bodies should pool their individual resources into one collective will in order to 'inform the people of the fraud that is about to be perpetrated in their name and expose those plans for what they are'.[38]

Rather than a single ideological tendency, the UDF represents a broad alliance of hundreds of local, regional, and national organizations of varying degrees of popularity, with different constituencies and disparate aims. The Front stresses potential involvement regardless of race or class origins, in a broad political assault against *apartheid*. Its leadership places considerable emphasis on political equality as being anterior to the resolution of economic problems.

One significant element of the UDF's platform involves unmistakable references to, and ideological links with, the banned ANC. Endorsement of the ANC is a criminal offense in South Africa. But the UDF has devised a number of clear signs to demonstrate that it represents the virtual re-emergence of Congress Alliance politics as an overt national organization inside the country. Most of the UDF's member organizations claim adherence to the 1955 Freedom Charter, a vaguely-worded document proclaiming democratic, multi-racial, and — arguably — socialist aims adopted at the 'Congress of the People' meeting at Kliptown, outside Johannesburg. The real importance of the Freedom Charter lay not in its general political philosophy but with its historic role of preserving and enlivening a political tradition. By openly subscribing to the principles embodied in the Freedom Charter (the *locus classicus* of the liberation movement), leading organizations in the UDF set the agenda for political action.

In a word, the UDF constitutes an organizational centre for those individuals and groups that refer to themselves as 'progressive democrats', 'Chartists, and/or 'progressive nationalists'. The Front reasons that all black people share a common interest in the dismantling of *apartheid* and that democratically-inclined whites who identify with popular struggle for national liberation can also be fully involved in this political movement. The UDF has declared that the black working-class is the largest single bloc amongst the millions who suffer from *apartheid*. Black workers constitute the principal engine for national liberation. Nevertheless, the UDF in practice clearly rejects distinct class mobilization and maintains instead that the issues of class should at this stage be largely subsumed under the broader umbrella of popular struggle against *apartheid*.

In schematic terms, the upper echelons and middle-range organizers of the UDF consist principally of three general types: (1) an older generation, veterans of the popular struggles initiated by the Congress Alliance in the 1950s and early 1960s; (2) a younger generation of radical/Marxist university-trained white intellectuals with little or no direct experience of earlier phases of struggle but firmly committed to the programmatic aims of the Freedom Charter; and (3) a youthful contingent of black people — the Soweto generation — impatient for radical change and seeking an organizational focus for their anti-*apartheid* energies. The older generation of veterans are readily identified with the Congress Alliance and the ANC. This group is ideologically wedded to the Freedom Charter as its principal pro-grammatic statement. The three elected presidents of the UDF are thoroughly embedded in the Congress *milieu*: Albertina Sisulu, a Soweto health-care worker and the wife of Walter Sisulu, the former general secretary of the ANC, who is currently serving a life sentence along with Nelson Mandela and other founders of the ANC's military wing, Umkhonto We Sizwe; Oscar Mpetha, one of the founders of the Food and Canning Workers' Union in Cape Town, a former official in the Congress-affiliated South African Congress of Trade Unions (SACTU), and recently brought to trial on terrorism charges at the age of 76; and Archie Gumede, a Durban lawyer whose father was president of the ANC more than a half century ago. The UDF has also appointed a number of patrons — not formally officials of the front because of legal restrictions — who symbolized the aims, ideological focus, and direction of the organization. These patrons are also drawn from the older generation veterans and a considerable number of imprisoned ANC members, especially Nelson Mandela, Govan Mbeki, Walter Sisulu, Ahmad Kathrada, and others, in addition to Helen Joseph (a septuagenarian former member of the Congress of Democrats, the white constituent organization of the 1950s Congress Alliance).

The whites who participate in the UDF are overwhelmingly recruited from English-speaking university backgrounds. They play little or no official role at the top but appear to have significant influence at the middle-level. With their access to funds, transport, printing facilities, and so forth, they serve a crucial support function for a range of the organization's activities. Both from design and the seemingly natural propensity of South Africans to divide along colour lines, whites tend to coalesce around distinct organizations. Three key examples suffice: the Johannesburg Democratic Action Committee (a pale replica of the Congress of Democrats), NUSAS, and the United Women's Organization (a nonracial women's group principally centered in Cape Town). Given their petty-bourgeois backgrounds and the continuing legacy of white supremacy, these whites too frequently assume an air of self-importance and occasional arrogance. In part, this attitude stems from an intellectual mastery of South African history coupled with the absence of any immediate experience of class oppression and racial discrimination. Younger whites add their special touch to public meetings of the UDF and the UWO where sometimes a carnival-like atmosphere prevails in the presence of balloons and streamers, and in the selection of topics for theatre presentations. Their enthusiasm reflects a definite anti-*apartheid* commitment but also a naivete about the true repressive character of the South African state.

The genuine leadership of the UDF appears to tolerate occasional frivolity in the hopes of broadening the ideological base of support for the anti-apartheid forces. No serious-minded political activist in South Africa would disagree with the proposition that a significant proportion of the nearly five million white people in the country would have to participate actively in the regime's downfall or at least acquiesce, in order for the black majority to seize the organs of state power. While it is never openly expressed in these terms, the UDF hopes to draw as many whites as possible into active participation in a broad multi-class assault on the *apartheid* regime where activities range from open defiance (draft resistance, for instance) to providing support (research, funding, and publicity) for ongoing popular struggles.

The overwhelming bulk of the rank-and-file membership of the affiliated organizations within the UDF coalition is drawn

from the oppressed black masses. In seeking redress of immediate grievances, these black members of the working class
strongly encourage political unity in order to join forces more
effectively in their struggle for freedom and justice. Without the
political dedication, resilience, and resolve of these people who
staff the 'middle-level' leadership positions and comprise the
rank-and-file militants of countless organizations, broad
coalitions like the UDF (and National Forum) would disintegrate.
The younger generation of black participants whose outlook was
fashioned through the unforgettable experience of the 1976
Soweto rebellion play a pivotal role in this respect. With a sense
of destiny, impatience, and pride, they stand poised on the
threshold of reinvigorated mass protest.

Organizationally, the UDF has adopted a rather cumbersome
form of representation. The national coordinating committee was
elected by a voice vote at the inaugural conference. Affiliated
organizations were divided into two types — leading and secondary — and given proportional representation on the National
Executive. Local level representation is even more complex. The
UDF is divided into six regions made up of its local affiliates. Each
region elects a general council and executive committee responsible for debating and defining policy. The National Executive
coordinates regional decisions. Cities are separated into districts
where the strongest UDF affiliate is given the official mandate to
draw all interested individuals into its organizational orbit. This
administrative procedure has produced the curious results, such
as one white suburb of Cape Town where university-trained
white males desiring to work with UDF were drawn under the
umbrella of the United Women's Organization as the 'mainline'
organization in the area. Charges that the UDF is top-heavy and
undemocratic (in the sense that there are no definite lines of
representation and representative decision-making) are not without foundation.

The ideological current that binds the affiliates of the UDF
together is captured in the generic slogan, 'Apartheid Divides,
UDF Unites!' At the last minute, the UDF half-heartedly joined
with the Progressive Federal Party — the loyal white opposition
— to urge the white electorate to cast a negative vote in the
national referendum of 2 November 1983 on the proposed constitutional changes. In December 1983 the UDF's national executive
failed to reach consensus on the issue of participation in possible

state-organized referenda designed to test the mood of the Indian and coloured communities with respect to the establishment of the separate Parliamentary councils. The Natal Indian Congress and the Transvaal Indian Congress — two strong affiliates of the UDF — reasoned that a resounding negative vote in a state-sponsored referendum for the Indian community would signify a definite setback for the *apartheid* strategist's proposals. Other UDF affiliates (for example, SAAWU) argued that participation would only give substance to the illusion of reform when, in fact, African people were excluded totally from the 'new dispensation'. These forces called instead for a boycott campaign. Tactical differences over these issues indicated that while UDF affiliates adhered to a common opposition to *apartheid* they did not possess a uniform political outlook with respect to mounting an effective challenge. The UDF leadership was thus confronted with the substantial task of forging a common program and a unified strategy without alienating significant blocs of its affiliated organizations

During 1984, the UDF embarked on a number of broad-based mass mobilizations: The Million Signatures Campaign (abandoned after mixed results), support for the November 'stayaway', campaigns against the implementation of the 1982 Black Local Authorities' Act, and the anti-election campaigns. The Front quickly expanded in both urban and countryside areas, claiming operational regional committees in the Southern Transvaal, Southern Cape (Oudtstioorn, George, Beaufort West), the Karoo, the Northern Cape (Voyburg, Kimberley, Bloemhof), and affiliates in the Orange Free State and Northern Transvaal.[39]

The National Forum: The United Front and Racial Capitalism

The Origins of the National Forum

At first glance, the casual observer is tempted to compare and contrast the UDF and the National Forum in accordance with identical criteria. Both emerged from a political vacuum and took advantage of the opportunity to rally opposition to the proposed constitutional 'reforms'. Both appeal to a largely identical mass base of urban (and peri-urban) constituencies. In addition, both aim to forge ideological unity from among a mixed assembly of community organizations, trade unions, cultural groups, and religious bodies that are themselves principally concerned with 'single-issue' politics, or local struggles. Finally, one factor that at least suggests the possibility of a *modus vivendi* is the overlapping memberships of organizations and individuals. Leading members of CUSA, Commercial and Catering Workers' Union (CCAWUSA), and the Soweto Civic Association — Phiroshaw Camay, Emma Mashinini, and Tom Manthata, respectively — serve as members of the National Forum Committee. Simultaneously, CUSA, CCAWUSA, and the Soweto Civic Association have at least nominal membership in the UDF.[40] But it would be an error to ignore ominous signs of deep rifts between these two ideological currents, at least at the leadership level. Two examples can usefully illustrate these differences. In a scathing verbal assault alluding to the National Forum conveners, Zinzi Mandela, daughter of imprisoned ANC leader Nelson Mandela, condemned those 'ideologically lost political bandits' who rejected the Freedom Charter and who 'diverted the struggle for liberation'.[41] On numerous occasions, those associated with Black Consciousness have suggested that the Freedom Charter was an outdated document that reinforced ethnicity and stopped short of condemning capitalism.[42]

Nevertheless, to attempt to contrast the UDF and the National Forum — point by point — along the same axis actually obscures the real significance of both. While the UDF formally emerged in the context of political opposition to the proposed constitutional changes and the Koornhof Bills, its core ideological current can be easily traced to its orgins in the Congress Alliance and the Freedom Charter. Despite occasional protestations to the contrary, the UDF leadership is solidly rooted within this *Chartist* heritage. For, the National Forum, it is difficult to identify a single heritage. It can be said that it has fused two distinct tendencies: (1) Black Consciousness; and (2) the 'non-collaborationist' and 'boycott' tradition of the Western Cape most closely associated with the Unity Movement perspective. Both the Unity Movement tradition dating from the 1940s and Black Consciousness had undergone tremendous ideological alteration before reaching tentative consensus under the umbrella of the National Forum in the 1980s.

The National Forum does not share the UDF's detailed concern with elaborate organizational structures. At the time of its formation, it remained a self-styled platform encouraging political debate and discussion amongst its 200-odd affiliated organizations. While it adopted a strongly-worded *Manifesto of the Azanian People*, it retained a federated structure in which all affiliates continue to operate without centralized coordination.

Both the UDF and National Forum stood against the President's Council and its proposed constitutional 'reforms'. The Botha regime had proposed town council elections in the African townships. The National Forum and UDF regarded these as 'dummy bodies' and treated black participants in any such councils as collaborators with *apartheid*. Both encouraged grassroots political organization in the schools, factories, and black communities.

The strategic differences between the two organizations center on the relationship between race and class.[43] The UDF argues for the building of a broad, multi-class, popular alliance against *apartheid*. In contrast, the cornerstone for the National Forum's analysis is the inseparability of *apartheid* and capitalism. 'The immediate goal of the national liberation movement now being waged in South Africa', argued Neville Alexander, a leading spokesman for the National Forum, 'is the destruction of the system of racial capitalism. *Apartheid* is simply a particular socio-political expression of this system. Our opposition to *apartheid* is therefore only a starting point for our struggle against the structures and interests which are the real basis of *apartheid*.'[44]

Nevertheless, it would be misleading simply to counterpose the UDF and the National Forum as respectively organizational incarnations of 'progressive democrat'/chartist versus Black Consciousness ideologies. Senior officials readily acknowledge that the UDF does not have ideological coherence across the spectrum of its affiliates. The identification of the National Forum with an undifferentiated Black Consciousness perspective would be equally disingenuous. Historically, Black Consciousness at times overshadowed alternative ideological currents, particularly in the Transvaal where AZAPO enjoyed ideological hegemony over National Forum affiliates. In the Western Cape, the Cape Action league (CAL), a National Forum affiliate with Unity Movement roots, did not situate itself wholeheartedly within the Black Consciousness camp. Youth and student groups, especially the Azanian Student Movement (AZASM), and independent black trade unions, particularly the Black Allied Mining and Construction Workers' Union (BAMCWU) — a leading member of the Azanian Federation of Trade Unions (AZACTU) — have endorsed an explicitly socialist solution to the 'national question' in South Africa and have argued that the trade unions should more actively shape the form and content of the National Forum.[45]

Diverse Origins of National Forum Ideology

The National Forum does not adhere exclusively to any single ideological current but has embraced a shaded spectrum of overlapping perspectives. One key ingredient is Black Consciousness ideology.[46] Its origins can be traced to the negative experience in the late 1960s of black university students within the predominantly white and English-speaking NUSAS. Inspired in large measure by the 'Black Power' movement in the United States, black university students formed their own separate organization — the South African Students Organization (SASO) — in 1969, espousing a commitment to Black Consciousness in its official manifesto. Black Consciousness ideology was perhaps most appropriately illustrated by the phrase, 'Black Consciousness is an attitude of mind, a way of life'. Steve Biko, undoubtedly its most articulate exponent in the early 1970s, provided the following definition: 'Black Consciousness is in essence the realisation by the black man of the need to rally together with his brothers around the cause of their oppression — the blackness of their skin — and to operate as a group in order to rid themselves of the shackles that bind them to perpetual servitude. It seeks to demonstrate the lie that black is an aberration from the "normal" which is white. ... [Black Consciousness] seeks to infuse the black community with a new-found pride in themselves, their efforts, their value systems, their culture, their religion and their outlook to life.'[47]

The imaginative and original contribution of Black Consciousness revolved around its steadfast refusal to accept the received notion that *apartheid* ideology and South African liberalism were somehow ideological opposites. The pioneering Black Consciousness visionaries doubted the willingness of white liberals to renounce the system that guaranteed their accumulated privileges. Black Consciousness adherents reasoned that liberalism as a doctrine was incapable either of unambiguously confronting the question of racial/national oppression or addressing the uniqueness of the South African black experience. From the outset, Black Consciousness repudiated the paternalism of white liberalism and embraced a distinctive cultural identity as an elemental feature of self-affirmation.

During the early 1970s, SASO served as the principal organizational vehicle popularizing the joint sentiments of self-awareness, group cohesion and solidarity, pride and dignity, and self-assurance. 'Black Consciousness', it was argued, 'derives a substantial degree of its strength precisely from the affirmation that all Black people are brothers ... united not only by common disabilities, but common tradition, common values, and a common outlook about life and society.'[48] One source of bitter resentment was the inferior quality of education. SASO ridiculed the entire segregated educational system as 'irrelevant to the pressing needs of the Black Community'. The resulting mass agitation demanding the abolition of 'Bantu education' crystallized in the shape of spontaneist organizational forms that came together under the common rubric of the Black Consciousness Movement (BCM). The formation of the Black People's Convention (BPC) as the post-student wing of the BCM provided committed activists with a relatively durable platform from which to launch prototype alternative educational ventures and health-care projects in selected black communities. These prefigurative programs were designed to offer — through what amounted to exemplary vanguardist action — a positive alternative to existing segregated *apartheid* institutions.[49]

Both SASO and BPC enriched their culturalist outlook with a concrete political analysis. In particular, Steve Biko heaped scorn on the 'Bantustans as the greatest single fraud ever invented by white politicians' and as 'tribal cocoons [that are] nothing else but sophisticated concentration camps'.[50] Black Consciousness adherents repudiated entirely the *apartheid* postulates of nationality as a cynical ploy designed to divide and rule.

It was the lengthy trial of the 'SASO Nine' — Black Consciousness activists from SASO and BPC charged under the Terrorism Act with fomenting public disorder at the 1974 FRELIMO support rallies — that overnight propelled the BCM into the national spotlight. Nevertheless, the political furor generated by this trial was overshadowed by the 1976 Soweto uprising. In the course of the ensuing countrywide political upheaval, Black Consciousness exerted a distinct ideological pull on the popular movement in search of an appropriate form of expression for its accumulated grievances.

The Soweto rebellion dramatically and abruptly transformed the terrain that had previously circumscribed the Black Consciousness debate. In their evaluation of the 1976-7 uprising, Black Consciousness activists reached two general conclusions. First, their inadequate diagnosis of the black predicament (coupled with the absence of a long-term strategy) had hampered their ability to provide any specific direction to the spontaneous outbreak of collective anger. Black Consciousness philosophy had emphasized the psychological, cultural, and economic liberation of the oppressed black masses but prescribed few if any precise guidelines for practical political action. During the 1976-7 unrest, the techniques of mass demonstrations, occasionally accompanied by stay-at-homes, had been used repeatedly despite their ineffectiveness against state repression once battle-weariness had taken its toll. Second, the limitations of the political consciousness and organizational capacities of school-age youth were manifested in the gulf that separated black students from the black working class. The Black Consciousness philosophy that stressed the fundamental unity of the black experience was never translated into a common programme effectively enlisting the support and participation of the black working class.

Seen in retrospect, the Soweto uprising signified a turning-point for the BCM. In 1977, most if not all Black Consciousness-affiliated organizations were banned. The youthful leadership underwent widespread state harassment, detention, and even death. The murder of Steve Biko in 1977 while in police detention underscored the perceived threat that Black Consciousness posed to the white authorities. In this context, adherents of Black Consciousness began to jettison the moral indignation implied in the assertion of the unity of black experience. They replaced what had been a largely symbolic reproach to 'white liberalism' with a focus on the social forces potentially capable of transforming South Africa. Adopting first the inchoate slogan, 'All blacks are workers' and eventually abandoning it, Black Consciousness thinkers have gradually adopted a class-analytic perspective that recognizes how discrete and often antagonistic political interests have arisen from the class differences amongst black people.

In South Africa, class divisions have always compounded political divisions amongst the black masses. Perhaps the most significant split is between 'town' and 'country' in the social division of labour. The roughly two million agrarian wage-labourers (and their dependents) live in isolated pockets under deplorable conditions with little or no access to basic amenities, skill-training and education. The urban townships and ghettos are also divided along class lines. While the overwhelming proportion of black urban residents are working-class, they are spread along a continuum of income and privilege where the gradations often overlap with ethnic differences. A few examples should be sufficient to illustrate the social meaning of these class gradations. Migrant workers — generally able-bodied young males who live in single-sex hostels and who are legally denied permanent urban status — wanted a steady job, perhaps saving a small portion of their cash-wages to send home, while workers with permanent urban status (under Section 10) wished to send their children to school (schooling beyond the primary level is not compulsory and in fact costly) and acquire luxury commodities. In sum, the social stratification of the black townships and ghettos was evident in an informal residential segregation by wealth and occupational differentiation, and by income and skill-levels.[51]

The black townships and ghettos were also differentiated between the working class and a petty bourgeoisie. A traditional layer of small-scale producers (artisans and/or small-scale family business) and small-scale owners (in the retail trade) gradually expanded. A growing sector of privileged black entrepreneurs invaded the 'informal sector' (taxi-transportation, shebeens and liquor trade, and various 'services'). With the gradual relaxation of restrictions on business, other entrepreneurs seized new opportunities to amass considerable wealth. While Ephraim Tshabalala was indeed an exception, this nattily-attired Soweto resident is worth mentioning. A millionaire and leading political figure in the tiny Mighty Sofasonke Party, he owned 'Tshabalala Motors, the Tshabalala Bazaar, in addition to a dry cleaners, a meat market, a cinema, a butcher shop and restaurant, eighty-one rental houses in one part of Soweto and twenty-two more in another part, on sale at the equivalent of around $43,000 each, and lots more'.[52]

In addition, a growing number of younger black urban residents had gradually entered the ranks of a new petty bourgeoisie of propertyless wage-earners. They were mental labourers — supervisors, teachers, civil servants, and salaried personnel in modern (multi-national and other) industry and commerce. The many new magazines presenting an affluent black middle-class life-style offer perhaps the clearest illustration of the growth of this petty bourgeois stratum.

In attempting to mold a Black Consciousness philosophy and mobilize the black communities around it, black activists were forced to confront the reality of class difference and, consequently, gradually adopted rudimentary class analysis. Black Consciousness supporters popularized twin slogans in the late 1970s: middle-class collaborationist elements were 'not black' and, conversely, 'all blacks are workers'. These propositions marked a phase in the development of a class analysis culminating in the proclamation of the *Manifesto of the Azanian People* adopted by the National Forum.

The Azanian People's Organization (AZAPO) inherited the ideological mantel of Black Consciousness. Formed in 1978, AZAPO attracted not only ex-SASO/BPC leaders but also a great number of former Robben Island prisoners. In 1984, the organization claimed to have ninety-six branches, divided between the regions of the Northern and Southern Transvaal, Natal, the Orange Free State, and the Eastern and Western Cape. It was strongest in the Transvaal and Eastern Cape. It proclaimed two principal organizational objectives: first, to consolidate its membership and administrative structures in its established branches; and second, to strengthen its local ties by working closely at the grassroots level with civic associations and youth groups. In large measure, the preoccupations of the AZAPO leadership paralleled those of the UDF: method and place of organization, the nature of links with civic associations and local-level bodies, and the character of tactical alliances sponsoring local or regional mass campaigns.

The second ideological current that contributed to the formation of the National Forum stems from the specifically Cape tradition of 'non-collaboration' with the oppressor and the principle of total boycotts of 'dummy institutions'. The Cape black intelligentsia have long been associated with a strident anti-capitalist perspective and an aversion to multi-class alliances, especially with petty bourgeois white liberals. This particular legacy can be traced to the All-African Convention (AAC) formed in 1936, the Non-European Unity Movement (NEUM) that came into existence in 1943, and the anti-CAD agitation (opposition to the proposed Coloured Affairs Council) during the 1950s. All too frequently, however, advocacy of the boycott strategy masked in recent years the reluctance of the organizational offshoots to become involved in mass-oriented forms of political activism, while the long-standing emphasis on education dovetailed conveniently with organizational inertia and abstentionism. Nevertheless, this ideological perspective has continued to hold considerable sway over the political behavior and understanding in the Western Cape.[54] Without delving into the detailed history of this local tradition, it can be stated that the four basic principles of the *Manifesto of the Azanian People* — anti-racism and anti-imperialism, non-collaboration with the oppressors and their political instruments, independent working-class organizations, and opposition to all alliances with ruling-class parties — bear its recognizable stamp.

The Cape Action League (CAL) represented its most clearly defined organized expression. The CAL evolved as the survivor of the Disorderly Bills Action Committee (DBAC), an *ad hoc* coalition of disparate groupings formed in Cape Town to coordinate political opposition to early versions of the proposed Koornhof legislation. The acrimonious debates over the question of tactical alliances that immobilized the DBAC represented in microcosm the political issues that separated the UDF from the National Forum. In 1984, CAL claimed 40 affiliates (civic associations, student and youth groups, sports bodies), of which twenty-five were active. Despite conflicting claims made by partisan organizers, 'some unaligned observers believe[d] that the CAL generates at least as much political activity and support in the Western Cape as UDF affiliates'.[55]

What distinguished the CAL was, in the words of its media officer, Armien Abrahams, 'a full commitment to the leadership of the working class, and the idea that only socialist solutions will bring about radical change in South Africa/Azania'.[56] Moreover, the CAL fundamentally rejected the strategy of mobilizing the popular masses solely on the basis of opposing racial discrimination. 'This is the argument of the two-stage position', Abrahams insisted, 'that once you've got an equal franchise all sorts of other things become possible. It is deceiving people to claim that mere mobilization against racial discrimination is going to bring about national conventions, negotiated agreements. It may be that some of this can happen, but it will be for the strengthening, rather than the erosion, of capitalism.'[57]

While no explicit draft proposals were formally discussed at its founding convention in 1983, the National Forum maintained a loose-knit structure akin to a federation of affiliated organizations, each with its own autonomy and separate membership. What distinguishes the Forum from the UDF is its avowedly class analysis and identification of the black working class as the *primum mobile* of genuine liberation. The *Manifesto of the Azanian People* states: 'Our struggle for national liberation is directed against the system of racial capitalism which holds the people of Azania in bondage for the benefit of the small minority of white capitalists and their allies, the white workers and the reactionary sections of the black middle class. The struggle against apartheid is no more than the point of departure for our liberation efforts. Apartheid will be eradicated with the system of racial capitalism. The black working class inspired by revolutionary consciousness is the driving force of our struggle. They alone can end the system as it stands today because they alone have nothing at all to lose. They have a world to gain in a democratic, anti-racist and socialist Azania. It is the historic task of the black working class and its organizations to mobilize the urban and rural poor together with the radical sections of the middle classes in order to put an end to the system of oppression and exploitation by the white ruling class.'[58] Despite the unambiguous commitment to building a socialist Azania, the National Forum remains a rather loose amalgamation of ideological currents from explicitly socialist to radical nationalist. Despite these differences, the Forum adopted an 'Away With All Collaborators' Campaign in 1985, focusing on crushing those 'institutions which are part of the state's incorporationist strategy directed at the black middle class'.[59]

The Differing Strategies of the UDF and National Forum

Both the UDF and National Forum have conceived of themselves as vehicles for advancing the liberation struggle in South Africa. yet they both approach the question of the necessary strategy and tactics from different angles. What is the nature of these differences? They can be grouped under three major headings.

(1) The Question of Class Alliances

Put loosely, the UDF resembles a multi-class popular front and the National Forum resembles a working-class dominated united front. Both boast of followings of working-class people who were incorporated through community-based civic associations, sport/cultural clubs, student and youth groups, and so forth. Nevertheless, neither has the wholehearted endorsement of the independent black trade unions. In its inaugural *Declaration*, the UDF focused specifically on the evils of *apartheid*, viewing the struggle as polarized between 'the freedom loving people of South Africa', on the one hand, and *apartheid* and white domination, on the other. The UDF advocated 'the creation of a true democracy in which all South Africans will participate in the government of the country', subscribed to a vision of 'a single non-racial, unfragmented South Africa ... free of Bantustans and Group Areas', and demanded the end of 'all forms of oppression and exploitation'. Further, the UDF proposed the unity of 'all community, worker, student, women, religious, sporting and other organizations under the banner of the United Democratic Front' to 'unite in action against the evils of *apartheid*'.[60] UDF publicity secretary, Patrick Lekota, put it bluntly: 'The UDF is not a class organization. It doesn't claim to work in the interests of the working class, the capitalist class or the peasantry. It is an alliance of these classes. All those who don't have political rights and who are willing to do battle, have a home in the Front. We have never claimed to be led by the working class.'[61]

In contrast, the National Forum views the fundamental political divide in South Africa in terms of the *oppressed* and the *oppressor* and called for the 'establishment of a democratic, anti-racist worker Republic in Azania where the interests of the workers shall be paramount through worker control of the

230

means of production, distribution, and exchange'.[62] The National Forum identifies radical capitalism as the source of exploitation and oppression 'where the working-class struggle against capitalist exploitation and the national struggle against racial oppression have become one struggle under the general control and direction of the Black working class'.[63]

While no formal position has been taken, the UDF has criticized the National Forum for 'acting alone'. Instead it proposed, in the words of Albertina Sisulu, that 'all must be united under the UDF because it will provide a forum for all. Any differences between people can be worked out in the UDF.'[64] In contrast, the National Forum has argued that the Front's 'all-in' conception of organization meant that the specific interests of the working class were swamped by those of the petty bourgeoisie. Specifically, the National Forum contended that, even though the working class constituted the mass base of the UDF, the petty bourgeoisie (*via* its financially stable and strategically-located organizations) maintained a stronger position to determine the political imprint of the UDF on the popular struggle.

In addition, the independent black trade unions have with few exceptions refused to officially join the UDF as active affiliates. FOSATU stated unambiguously that it believed that 'the unity of purpose created within worker controlled organizations whose class base and purpose are clear would be lost within an organization such as the UDF. The Front represents a variety of class interests with no clear constitutional structure within which the majority of citizens can control the organization.'[65] David Lewis, the general secretary of the 10,000 strong General Workers' Union (GWU) offered the most precise rationale for the reluctance of the independent black trade unions to uncritically flock to the UDF. He emphasized that the form and structure of organization of the independent unions differed considerably from most of the community-based groups associated with the Front. He contended that a large number of UDF-affiliated groups were 'activist organizations', that is, 'essentially a grouping of like-minded individuals who are brought together by a common political goal [where] their activity consists of propagating their lease amongst a constituency which they themselves define'.[66] In contrast, the independent trade unions were not organizations of activists *per se* but representatives of their rank-and-file membership. Their leaders did not appeal to 'the masses "out there"' but 'represent the workers inside [the] organization' through the popular mandate of the membership.[67]

Lewis also maintained that 'it has to be acknowledged that workers are a very special group in society. They are the class, unfashionable though that term might be, that produces the wealth of the country. As such, they are the most exploited and oppressed members of society.'[68] Identifying the UDF as a multi-class organization where skills and education had been dispro-portionately monopolized by the petty bourgeoisie, Lewis maintained that 'the UDF has to ask itself whether its style and tone, whether the language spoken, whether the pace at which it has developed, whether its programme, facilitate the fullest par-ticipation by working-class people. Our members simply do not feel that way.'[69] He emphasized this line of reasoning even more bluntly: '. . . workers must have a special status in multi-class organizations. Workers must have the opportunity to lead the pace and style and tone and language — in fact the whole dis-course — of the organization. The reason why it's important, and the reason why I think it's important to examine the questions raised with respect to the UDF, is that democracy in this country is inconceivable without the fullest participation in the national democratic struggle of the working class. This is not merely because the working class is the largest and most muscular group in society. Simply put, they are the only social grouping with a class interest in democracy. Other social classes or group-ings might have an interest in the relative or partial democra-tisation of society; other individuals might have a moral interest in a thorough-going democratisation of society. But the working class, which has every aspect of its life — its economic and political life, its working life and its leisure life — very rigidly controlled, is the one class in society that has an interest in a thorough-going democratisation of the economy and the polity.'[70] These views do not exhaust the political understanding toward the UDF of the independent trade unions, some of whom immediately affiliated with the Front. Nevertheless, FOSATU affiliates, GWU, and FCWU/AFCWU (in addition to practically all other industrial-based trade unions) retain a respectful yet criti-cal distance.

(2) The Place of the Radical Petty Bourgeoisie and the White Intelligentsia

The question of the role of the radical petty bourgeoisie and the white intelligentsia has always loomed as a highly controversial and gravely symbolic issue. Consequently, the particularly rancorous debate over this question has often assumed a veritable life of its own where sentiment and moralism frequently have substituted for lucid analysis. Ironically, the question of inclusion or exclusion of white groups became a touchstone in the broader debate about class alliance, or, specifically, the validity of the popular versus the united front. The acrimony that paralyzed the Cape Town-based DBAC — the precursor to both the UDF and National Forum — over the inclusion of NUSAS illustrated in microcosm the division at the level of national politics. Eventually, NUSAS affiliated with the UDF on the basis of its stated commitment to non-racialism, democracy, and anti-apartheid.

NUSAS was structured as a confederation of Student Representative Councils (SRCs) where affiliation had been decided through referenda on (white) University campuses. Historically, the SRCs affiliated to NUSAS were only located in the four English-speaking universities (University of Cape Town, the University of the Witwatersrand, Rhodes University, and University of Natal at Pietermaritzburg). Even at the English-speaking universities, affiliation to NUSAS has never been assured and has often passed back and forth across at least two campuses from year to year.[71] Describing itself as 'progressive' and 'democratic', NUSAS has been the home-base for the emergent white intelligentsia who were morally dissatisfied with the racialist configuration of South African life. Past NUSAS president, Kate Philip, expressed the ambivalent position of white university students: '... organizing on the white campuses is a particularly uphill battle because Apartheid is in fact very directly in the interests of our constituency and we have to mobilize and organize them to relinquish their interests as white South Africans benefiting from Apartheid and commit themselves instead to contributing to change as South African democrats. Unlike most democratic organizations we are actually organizing our members against their objective material interests at this level.'[72] NUSAS members played a minimal role in the decision-making executive bodies yet performed key organizational roles in the day-to-day functioning of numerous non-racial UDF-affiliated organizations. Post-university 'progressive' whites formed 'activist' groups such as the Johannesburg Democratic Action Committee (JODAC) with the express purpose of supporting the Freedom Charter, joining the UDF, and extending its influence.

Those organizations affiliated with National Forum were thoroughly opposed to what they regarded as the *organized presence* of the white petty bourgeoisie in their midst. For example, Temba Meyer-Fels, Secretary of the Western Cape Youth League (WCYL), argues that WYCL 'rejects forthrightly unprincipled alliances with the organisations of any section of the ruling class or their sons and daughters. By its continued relation with NUSAS and the UCT [University of Cape Town] "left" (without ever taking a stand to distinguish themselves on principle for these organisations), [any group] is clearly guilty of opportunism.'[73] Speakers at a South African Council of Sports (SACOS) rally denounced 'White liberals as "the most far-seeing agents of *apartheid* capitalism" who attempt to "infiltrate the organizations of the people and capture their leadership".'[74] Again, Lybon Mabasa, past President of AZAPO, contended that 'racial capitalism is maintained and sustained by the white middle class — petty bourgoisie who are themselves aspirant capitalists — and the "white working class" which is satisfied with the status quo and feel they have nothing in common with their counterparts, i.e., the Black working class. ... All these things point to one thing: that is, the unity of the oppressed.'[75] He warned further that 'the urgent nature of this crisis has tempted the oppressed in certain quarters to form dangerous and opportunist political alliances of the workers, petty bourgeois, liberals, and sheltered elements from the oppressor camp — in the hope of consolidating against the oppressors and exploiters. Such alliances seldom have a solid political content and at best they tend to blunt the anger and the militancy of the workers and are counter-revolutionary.'[76]

This highly contentious issue of what role whites should play in the South African freedom struggle has elicited the sharpest disagreements between UDF and National Forum participants. For the most part, Black Consciousness adherents rebuff 'progressive whites', fearing that they might be opportunists who could (wittingly or not) undermine and hijack the struggle of the oppressed. In a thinly camouflaged reference to the UDF and its inclusion of white liberal organizations such as NUSAS and Black Sash, Saths Cooper (former defendant in the SASO/BPC trial and principal convenor of the National Forum) condemned what he referred to as 'the marriage of convenience which would embrace elements of the ruling class and thus be a sell-out to bourgeois interests'.[77] The former President of AZASM, Kebalo Lengane, argued that 'progressive' whites — under the guise of 'multi-racialism' — joined popular organizations only on condition that they assumed positions of prominence, influence, and authority and not as rank-and-file members. Instead, he proposed that 'progressive' whites from petty bourgeois backgrounds should concentrate their political efforts on preparing white communities for the inevitable collapse of racial capitalism and white supremacy. 'The [Freedom] Charter', Langane argued, 'calls for national groups to be represented at a national convention. The national groups will be made up of minority groups based on ethnicity.' This emphasis on minority ethnic groups was a thoroughly specious formulation since it echoed the white minority regime's practice of divide and rule. 'In [Black Consciousness]', he contended, 'we recognize only two groups — the oppressed and the oppressors.'[78]

However, all organizations affiliated with the National Forum do not share homogeneous views on this question. After considerable debate, the Forum began to accept affiliated organizations with individual white members. Former political prisoner on South Africa's notorious Robben Island, Neville Alexander, argued that 'There are many among the whites who are committed to the ideal of liberation and who are prepared to make sacrifices. They must be allowed to play a part in the struggle — but the leadership of the struggle must remain with the black working class.'[79] Finally, in counterdistinction to the radical nationalist current in the National Forum, the CAL took an explicitly class line. In the words of Armien Abrahams: 'The fundamental point is that the constituency or social base of these organizations [NUSAS, Black Sash, etc.] is inherently bound by a capitalist perspective. They cannot go beyond a mere anti-*apartheid* stance. Individuals in these organizations, especially in leadership positions, are radicals, are people who are prepared to go beyond an anti-apartheid stance. We have no problems with working with such individuals. Our critique is not the same as the Black Consciousness one, which is against white participation.'[80] In short, CAL rejected the organized participation of groups like NUSAS, Black Sash and JODAC not because of their exclusive 'whiteness' but because of 'their social origins ... and the social matrix within which they operate'.[81]

(3) Race, Ethnicity and Nation

In South Africa, language as the expression of political sentiments has always assumed a pronounced and almost exaggerated importance. During the 1950s, the Congress Alliance operated under the ideological motif of 'multi-racialism' and 'multi-nationalism' in order to counter the prerogative connotations of the National Party's insistence on resuscitating 'Bantu tribalism'. One significant and enduring legacy of a Black Consciousness ideology has been adherence to the unity of oppressed people of colour. Thus, the 'multi-national' perspective of the Congress Alliance gradually lost much of its political resonance as the magnetism of Black Consciousness undercut the negative meaning attached to separate organizations of oppressed people.

After the 1976 Soweto uprising, the language of Black Consciousness — articulating 'nation-building' and the unity of the oppressed — gradually achieved paramountcy within popular political culture. It is within the context of this ideological shift that the recent rehabilitation of the Transvaal Indian Congress (TIC) — regarded, along with the Natal Indian Congress (NIC), as 'mainline' organizations in the UDF — has rekindled the political debate about the appropriateness of mass-based and multi-class ethnic organizations as *prime movers* within the liberation struggle.

Starting from the position that 'different "national" groupings amongst the black people experienced increased oppression differently', one defender of the organizational appropriateness of the TIC argued that 'a common national struggle with other oppressed groups could not be *assumed* but had to be *worked for* [because of] the continued problems of separation, prejudice, and suspicion' that divided 'the different "national" groups'.[82] The writer continued: 'Methods had to be adopted that would successfully mobilize the people within the Indian community and thus facilitate the *possibility* of then uniting in a common national struggle. ... The reality of political struggle is such that one cannot mobilize the people politically on the basis of some abstract notion of politics. Organization begins from where the people themselves are — from their perceptions of the *burning issues* of the movement, and proceeds from there. Organizations can only successfully mobilize the broad masses of people if they take these realities into account. The reality of South African racism is that it has succeeded in dividing the oppressed people "racially" — by imposing separation and a hierarchy of racial oppression.'[83] The author concluded on two notes: first, the TIC represented a multi-class alliance where 'progressives in the Indian community need to mobilise the broadest possible grouping of people under a progressive leadership and within a progressive direction', that is where the working class is the spearhead of the struggle. Second, the strategy of building a unitary, non-racial and democratic South Africa could not be guided by absolute principles but must be dictated by tactical consideration of the concrete historical circumstances.[84]

The independent black trade unions generally disagreed with this approach on three grounds: first, they regarded organizations like the TIC — despite its size — as activist-oriented movements that appealed to a self-defined community on the basis of popular mobilization, and hence were dissimilar in structure and function from the independent trade unions; second, they failed to see what methods have been employed to ensure that the specific interests of the working class could and would dominate these multi-class alliances; and third, because they themselves were engaged in recruiting black workers, they regarded any stance that *a priori* or in practice conceived of black workers in 'racial' categories as counterproductive and not conducive to working-class solidarity.

The National Forum's criticism of the UDF's conception of 'multi-national' and/or 'multi-ethnic' alliances is straightforward: to operate on the basis of four separate 'national' groups in South Africa is tantamount to accepting *apartheid* ideology and the terms in which the state has divided and ruled the oppressed people. Neville Alexander explained how the use of the terminology of 'national group' in South Africa was 'fraught with dangers ... because it fires expression to and thereby reinforces separatist and disruptive tendencies [in the liberation movement]': 'Those organizations and writers within the liberation movement who used to put forward the view that South Africa is a multi-racial country composed of four "races" ... have begun to speak more and more of building a *non-racial South Africa*. I am afraid to say that for most people who use this term "non-racial" it means exactly the same thing as multi-racial. They continue to conceive of South Africa's population as consisting of four so-called "races". It has become fashionable to intone the words a "non-racial democratic South Africa" as a kind of open sesame that permits one to enter into the hallowed portals of the progressive "democratic movement". ... The word "non-racial" can only be accepted by a racially oppressed people if it means that we reject the concept "race", that we deny the existence of "races" and thus oppose all actions, practices, beliefs, and politics based on the concept of "race". If in practice (and in theory) we continue to use the word non-racial as though we believe that South Africa is inhabited by four so-called "races", we are still trapped in multi-racialism and thus in racialism. Non-racialism, meaning the denial of the existence of races, leads on to anti-racism which goes beyond it because the term not only involves the denial of "race" but also opposition to the capitalist structure for the perpetuation of which the ideology and theory of "race" exist.'[85]

The verbal wrangling on occasion degenerates into hair-splitting. But these disputes are not simply reducible to sectarian battles over terminological abstractions. These controversies conceal the more fundamental political problem of the strategy and tactics defining the appropriate course of action for the liberation movement. The UDF acknowledges the historical reality of four separate 'national' groups and refers to itself as 'non-racial'. In turn, it criticizes the National Forum and other organizations for uncritically *assuming* unity when the historical experience of the oppressed has been one of racial divisions.[86] The Front actually refers to AZAPO and other Black Consciousness organizations as *racialist* because the latter — as the UDF sees it — denies a place for white organizations in the liberation struggle and promotes a separatist ideology of 'black awareness'. In contrast, the National Forum conceives of the UDF as 'multi-racial'. The Front is racist because this multi-racialism fan[s] the fires of ethnic politics ... and plays into the hands of the reactionary middle-class leadership'.[87] The National Forum refers to itself as 'anti-racist' and attributes the existence of 'population registration groups' to the ongoing strategy of the ruling class to divide and rule. In other words, 'races' have no distinct existence independent of the evolution of capitalism. They have been historically fashioned coterminously with the metamorphosis of capitalist relations. The National Forum argues that only the black working class can 'redefine the nation and abolish the reactionary definitions of the bourgeoisie and of the reactionary petty bourgeoisie. The nation has to be structured by and in the interests of the black working class.'[88]

5.

The Eruption of Popular Rebellion

On 20 July 1985 the white minority declared an indefinite state of emergency throughout vast areas of riot-torn South Africa in order to crack down on the wave of unrest that had swept the black townships for almost a year. The declaration was the first action of its kind since the emergency imposed in the wake of the Sharpeville massacre in 1960. It affected thirty-six magisterial districts concentrated in the eastern Cape region, industrial areas of the East Rand, and the Vaal River industrial region fifty miles south of Johannesburg, as well as Johannesburg itself. The state of emergency augmented South Africa's already formidable body of security legislation, providing the police and military with virtually unlimited powers in the designated areas to act against political opponents without fear of legal reprisals. Under the emergency measures, the security forces were granted broad powers to search and seize property without warrants, to detain without formal charges, and to hold individuals indefinitely without allowing them access to legal assistance if declared a threat to public safety. They were also permitted to seal off and censor all news from any of the designated areas and to impose curfews. Police and army personnel were indemnified against all legal claims arising from actions taken under the emergency powers. At the same time, South African newspapers were forbidden to identify those detained under the emergency, thereby, in effect, permitting the authorities to confront secretly their political opponents. Security forces were also empowered to assume jurisdiction over 'essential services', such as water and electricity, in urban areas.[1]

The imposition of the state of emergency symbolized the desperation of the white minority regime, hitherto unable to crush the popular rebellion in the townships. Residents in a large number of these segregated settlements expelled local governing bodies and the authorities could enter only by force of arms. The confrontation became a test of strength between the security forces fighting to re-establish control and black militants demanding political concessions that the authorities had refused to countenance. Between September 1984, when the latest unrest began and the state of emergency, about 500 people — overwhelmingly township residents — were killed in escalating violence. Army units were deployed alongside police in black townships where the indiscriminate use of fire-power (tear gas, rubber bullets, birdshot, and automatic weapons) became the sole method of quelling disturbances. In a desperate effort to stifle dissent, it also appeared that the authorities had resorted to the use of clandestine tactics, including assassinations by shadowy 'death squads' and the sowing of discord between rival groups.

The declaration of the state of emergency was an acknowledgement on the part of the Botha regime that the reform measures — including the constitutional changes offering junior status in Parliament to people of mixed and Indian racial descent — had failed to appease widespread black dissatisfaction. The security forces initially hoped to contain the unrest within isolated black townships, waiting for the daily protests to collapse through sheer exhaustion. However, township unrest from September 1984 to July 1985 become a daily chronicle of violent clashes in which black defiance crystallized into an increasingly radical call for political power.[2] Black activists hardened their demands, insisting that peace would only return once the white minority regime agreed to open a dialogue with black leaders such as the imprisoned Nelson Mandela, leader of the outlawed ANC. Regular attacks against community councillors, black police, and local informers — those deemed collaborators, 'stooges', and 'sell-outs' — threw the normal methods of township social control into disarray. Only five of the thirty-eight local community councils — designed by the white authorities to offer urban blacks a limited measure of local self-governance —

still functioned. For many town councillors, the situation deteriorated so completely that they required around-the-clock police protection. In some areas, councillors moved into guarded compounds in white areas and only ventured into the black townships under armed guard.

With the virtual collapse of black local government, incipient forms of dual power had begun to fill the void. Public gatherings in the townships — particularly funerals and memorial services — were increasingly marked by speeches and songs calling for an end to white minority rule. Perhaps the high point of this form of popular protest emerged at the 20 July graveside services for Mathew Goniwe, one of four community activists from the Cradock area killed after attending a political gathering in Port Elizabeth. The four men were buried to the strains of black protest songs lauding the ANC's armed wing, Umkhonto We Sizwe. As the coffins were taken to a dust-choked stadium, and later, as they were lowered into the ground, mourners unfurled the green, black, and gold banner of the ANC and the red banner of the South African Communist Party (emblazoned with a yellow hammer and sickle). The assertive and defiant mood of the crowd of 35,000 underscored the deepening rift that had lurched toward open civil war.[3]

The consumer boycott organized by township residents in mid-July against white-owned businesses in Port Elizabeth — the first fully-effective action of its kind — alarmed the white authorities. The Mayor of Port Elizabeth, Ivan Krige, proclaimed that the near-total suspension of trade with stores and supermarkets owned or managed by white shop keepers had created a 'desperately urgent' financial situation. Labour and community organizations together called on the consumer boycott — set to continue for two months — to press such demands as a freeze on the price of basic foodstuffs, the withdrawal of military personnel from black townships, and the dismantling of the town councils. The Port Elizabeth consumer boycott campaign overlapped with similar efforts in the Eastern Cape, particularly Grahamstown, Cradock, and Adelaide. In the latter, the trade boycott began in protest against white shop owners doing police reservist duty in the townships.

Youthful black militants were vigilant in enforcing these campaigns.[4] But the emergency powers were proclaimed only after the clashes had spilled over the previous week into Soweto,

Johannesburg's vast black satellite city (of nearly two million) close to the country's commercial and financial heartland. Brigadier Jan Coetzee, the police commander for the Soweto area, said violence had 'reached serious heights of intensity'. Soweto's earlier comparative calm had been ascribed variously to close police surveillance of political activists and to the relative affluence of some of its occupants. The white authorities were also motivated to declare the state of emergency because of fears that the violent clashes that had spilled into Johannesburg's white suburbs near Alexandra township and into downtown Vereeniging might engulf the commercial centres of white cities.[5]

The March 1960 state of emergency that followed the Sharpeville massacre lasted for 156 days, covered eighty-three of what were then 265 districts, and resulted in an estimated 11,503 arrests. In the first four days of the 1985 state of emergency, nearly a thousand people — priests, lawyers, students, labour organizers, community activists — were caught in the police dragnet.[6] The objective of this massive security manoeuvre had been to detain anyone capable of organizing and channelling black anger with the white minority regime into attacks on those labelled collaborators, as well as into labour strikes and consumer boycotts. With the emergency decree, the regime reverted to a near-total reliance upon compulsion, hoping that this customary reflex would offer some respite from the unrest that had by this time engulfed the broad 560-mile corridor reaching from the south coast near Port Elizabeth to the outskirts of Johannesburg. The minority regime hoped that with local leaders in detention the daily protests would soon abate from lack of coordination and direction.[7]

The Vaal Triangle Uprising

The Causes of Revolt in the Townships

The July 1985 state of emergency was the culmination of a nearly year-long frantic effort on the part of the security forces to quell the popular rebellion. In a strictly arithmetic calculation, the initial phase of the 1984-6 outbreak of violence resulted in fewer deaths than the 1976-7 Soweto uprising. In part, the lower death toll could be attributed to a refinement in police tactics and to the greater preparedness of the security apparatus for handling township rioting. In 1976, the South African police and army had resorted to indiscriminate automatic fire in a desperate effort to put down disturbances that had already erupted into large-scale rioting and looting.

During the early stages of the 1984 protests, the security forces employed new 'riot-control' methods, alternating between massive displays of force and highly mobile responses (with the generous use of tear gas and whips, rubber bullets, and bird-shot). These tactical manoeuvres were intended to contain localized disturbances. Yet as in 1976-7, crowds of youths — unarmed yet undaunted — were locked in fierce combat with police and army units in the dusty unpaved streets of the barren townships. The sheer magnitude of the firepower took a heavy and indiscriminate toll in lives in the daily unrest. Nonetheless, it is here that the similarities between the 1976-7 Soweto uprising and the 1984-6 rebellion collapse. In 1976-7, school children in Soweto hastily organized street marches to protest against the enforced use of Afrikaans as the principal medium of instruction. Hector Petersen's death on the morning of 16 June sparked the nationwide unrest that quickly broadened beyond the sphere of youth and student demands. The shift in the balance of political forces that occurred in the interim between 1976 and 1984 altered fundamentally the terrain of popular struggle. The nucleus of working-class militants, dèclassè intellectuals and community activists had constructed under conditions of semi-clandestinity an organizational apparatus of popular resistance that was designed to nurture and sustain a broad political movement in opposition to the white minority regime. The implantation of the community-based civic associations, student groups, and independent black trade unions was the cornerstone of these efforts, but, paradoxically, the organized opposition entered the 1984-6 fray to a large degree fragmented and disunited. Despite the bitter rivalries that divided the anti-*apartheid* left into at least three distinct ideological currents, the target of the popular revolt was fixed with much greater clarity upon the entire edifice of white minority rule. The great achievement of the popular organizations and the independent trade unions in the few years between the crushing of the Soweto rebellion and the 1984-6 strife hinged on a greater awareness of capitalism — and the inflexible exercise of state power to sustain it — as the foremost source of oppression.

Beginning in 1978, the Botha regime embarked on a strategy of containment that involved broadening the entrepreneurial opportunities of the black petty bourgeoisie and extending the parameters of the power bloc to include token formal representation of Indian and coloured people. The National Party thus steered a middle course between the atavistic reactionaries clustered around the Conservative Party and the HNP who refused to abandon the *apartheid* ideals, and liberals in the Progressive Federal Party who — from the National Party's viewpoint — would bargain away the birthright of the 'white tribe'. For the Botha regime, the greatest achievement of the 'new dispensation' was in the proposed Constitutional reforms. Yet it was the implementation of this new Constitution and the opening of the tricameral Parliament — offering a modest voice but no real power to people of Indian and mixed racial descent — that brought into relief the profound alienation of the excluded African majority. Many overseas commentators praised the new Constitution as a step in the direction of the gradual elimination of *apartheid*. However, its structure actually reinforced South Africa's racial compartmentalization by employing 'population registration groups' as a basis for political participation instead of extending a common voters' role.

The successful boycott campaigns opposed to polls for the separate coloured and Indian legislative assemblies were the main vehicles catalyzing anger against the new Constitutional measures. On 22 August 1984, only 18 per cent of the eligible voters participated in the staged elections for the coloured House of Assembly. In the Cape Town area, where half of the 2.7 million people of mixed-race were concentrated in a 50-mile ribbon of segregated townships, only 11 per cent of the registered voters (and 6 per cent of those eligible) cast votes. The country districts recorded considerably higher polls. White farmers, who held their labourers in virtual bonded servitude, helped to buoy the overall turnout in many instances by transporting their employees to polling stations. For the (coloured) Labour Party, the embarrassingly low turnout was a resounding defeat when measured against its boastful claims of widespread popular support and provided a weak mandate for its putative goal of undermining *apartheid* 'from within'. The Labour Party appeared on the verge of political collapse. Besides being shaken by unexpected defections of several key leaders, it had not managed to stage a major public meeting because of the threat of militant disruptions. In February, two Party leaders, Allan Hendrikse and David Curry, had to call for a police escort in order to be rescued in Stellenbosch from an angry crowd who denounced them as collaborators and 'sell-outs'. As one political analyst wryly put it, 'there appears to be a groundswell of anger against the Party'.[8]

On the eve of the August 1984 elections, Labour Party officials made a concerted effort to reconcile their low electoral expectations with the hopes of the Party faithful. Fred Peters, the national secretary, announced that the Party would regard a 15 per cent voter turnout as a popular mandate to join the new Parliament.[9] After the elections, it was widely speculated not only that ballot tampering had bolstered the final tallies but also that high-ranking Labour Party leaders had received large bribes from National Party officials for participating.

On 28 August 1984, only 13 per cent of the eligible Indian voters turned out to vote in the largely uncontested House of Delegates' elections. In the weeks preceding both elections, the manoeuvring of the white regime and the opposition reached fever pitch. The Minister of Law and Order, Louis Le Grange, had warned that efforts to disrupt the elections or intimidate voters would not be tolerated. An estimated 630,000 students boycotted classes in nationwide protests. On the eve of the first elections, Pretoria chose to crack down, authorizing predawn raids that netted key boycott leaders in Johannesburg, Durban, and Port Elizabeth. At least forty-one leaders of boycott organizations were detained under the Internal Security and Criminal Procedures Acts. At the polling stations on 28 August, the police frequently outnumbered both voters and campaign workers. Riot vans circled some polling sites. In Johannesburg and nearby Lenasia, the police repeatedly dispersed crowds of 'anti-election' demonstrators. As one correspondent exclaimed, 'Central Lenasia was transformed into the frontline of a battle zone last night. Hundreds of people were hurt, many seriously, when police fired teargas into homes, shops, crowds.'[10]

Throughout 1984, trouble sputtered in the black high schools near Pretoria and elsewhere throughout the industrialized, gold-enriched belt of the central Transvaal known as the Reef. Student unrest was so widespread in Atteridgeville, a black township west of Pretoria, that six high schools were closed for much of the year. 'Black education remains in a state of turmoil', as one commentator put it, 'and has become so politicized in the minds of young blacks that its ultimate solution lies only in the granting of meaningful political rights to blacks.'[11] By May, perhaps as many as 220,000 students were actively participating in school boycotts. At the centre of the controversy were the twin griev-ances of the low quality of education (resulting in declining achievement rates) and the exclusion of students from the decision-making process of educational policy. These grievances were reflected in student demands. COSAS spearheaded the student campaign, demanding the democratic selection of Student Representative Councils, the abolition of age limits for final high school examinations, an increase in the number of qualified teachers, the termination of politically-motivated suspensions and expulsions of both students and teachers, and the end to sexual harassment of female students.

The legacy of the harsher side of *apartheid* rule was perhaps nowhere more evident than in the educational system designed for black school children. In 1954, Hendrik Verwoerd, the main architect of *apartheid* who later became Prime Minister, pro-claimed that education for black people 'should have its roots entirely in the native areas and in the native environment and in the native community'. 'The Bantu must be guided to serve his own community in all respects,' he intoned. 'There is no place for him in the European community above the level of certain forms of labour.'[12] This was the attitude of the ruling National Party. After 1976, student boycotts and protests became ordinary features of the political landscape in the townships and ghettos. Student organizations remained permanent fixtures at the fore-front of political agitation. However, in the post-Soweto era, student politics underwent considerable alteration in their prin-cipal focus. During the 1976 uprising, students clustered around Student Representative Councils as the principal method for pressing demands and mobilizing rank-and-file support. In the political vacuum that prevailed at the time, these Representative Councils were often thrust willy-nilly into positions of promin-ence as catalysts of political opposition to the white minority regime. During the initial phase of the 1984 disturbances, student organizations continued to play a significant role in proselytizing and mobilizing black township residents against *apartheid*. But the organizations tended to come under the ideological ambit of the broad UDF and National Forum coalitions. The differing national political currents were reflected within their ranks. AZASM, for example, functioned as the student wing of AZAPO. In contrast, COSAS operated within the ideological parameters of the UDF. At the University of Cape Town where perhaps as much as 10 per cent of the student body was black, at least three separate black student organizations operated.

Nearly two million black students across the country came under the jurisdiction of various state agencies whose functions were to oversee what until the late 1970s had been labelled 'Bantu education'. An estimated 78 per cent of the 42,000 black teachers under the jurisdiction of the Ministry of Education were under-qualified. Although the eductional budget had increased five-fold since 1976, official statistics in 1984 indicated that Pretoria still spent six or seven times as much on the education of a white child as on that of a black. The pupil/teacher ratio in some black schools was as high as sixty-five to one, compared with the eighteen to one ratio in white schools.[13]

In the 1984 school boycotts, students linked their rejection of *apartheid* education with a broader condemnation of white minority rule. Large numbers of their leaders became embroiled in the wider confrontations with the white authorities. 'Student leaders apparently have come to view themselves', one commentator put it, 'as the cutting edge of community protest against the policies of racial compartmentalization called *apartheid*.'[14] In response to the boycotts, the authorities closed an estimated twenty-two schools and universities, following the refusal of students to return to classes until their demands were met.

Another immediate cause for the massive political explosion that rocked the Vaal Triangle in September was the imposition of across-the-board 15 per cent municipal rent increases on top of steadily-rising unemployment, higher food prices, deteriorating community services, greater bus and train fares, increased ground taxes and 'permit charges', and a 10 per cent jump in the general sales tax. Over the past few years, the Department of Cooperation, Development, and Education oversaw the shift of substantial local government powers to town (or community) councils in the segregated areas. Pretoria flaunted the Black Local

Authorities (BLA) as the nascent expression of formal black political participation in the urban areas. The 1982 Black Local Authorities Act mandated that these town councils finance their own operations. In addition, the councils gradually assumed sole responsibility for commuter services, health care facilities, road maintenance, sewage, rental collection, housing allocation, and a host of related 'services'. The white minority regime portrayed this process as a pioneering step in granting real political power to urban black people. Critics of the minority regime regarded this so-called 'new deal' as a cynical and manipulative effort 'to make blacks responsible for governing communities that are inherently unstable because of the legacy of *apartheid* laws that have ensured poverty in these areas.'[15]

In order to generate much-needed funds, the town councils in many areas had levied rental increases and imposed miscellaneous service charges. Animated by popular dissatisfaction and encouraged by energetic militants, the civic associations and tenants' groups mounted a far-reaching political challenge to the town councils (or their functional equivalents). Popular mobilization took the form of large rallies and protest meetings where various speakers exhorted the assembled to join in the refusal — in the words of a popular slogan — 'to pay for our oppression'. The civic associations served as embryonic organs of popular struggle. Left to their own devices, they appeared ideologically shapeless until they fell under the influence of a variety of political militants. The political mobilizations of the civic associations often meant brief skirmishes with police, occasional looting and burning of stores, injuries, and arrests. The intermittent flare-ups that erupted in Tumahole township in the Orange Free State in July 1984 were harbinger of the broader conflagration to come.

But what really triggered the eruption of rioting in the Vaal Triangle townships was the inaugural meeting of South Africa's tricameral Parliament. This occasion symbolized the exclusion of the African majority from even token representation in national politics. Widespread protests began on 30 August. In scenes reminiscent of the Soweto uprising, black township residents and the South African police were locked in pitched battles that echoed through the dusty unpaved streets. The popular rebellion almost immediately engulfed the townships of Tembisa, northeast of Johannesburg and Sharpeville, Sebokeng, Bophlelong, Boipatong, and Evaton — all clustered around the

Vaal industrial centres of Vereeniging and Vanderbijlpark. By the end of the first day, at least fourteen people had been killed. On 3 September thousands of residents of the Vaal townships stayed away from work and joined a planned procession to the Lekoa Town Council offices near Houtkop to protest proposed rent increases. Residents in the townships under the Council's jurisdiction purportedly paid the highest rent and service charges in South Africa. Police intercepted the marchers who, as early as 5 am, had thronged along the main roads leading to the council offices. Many were killed in the ensuing confrontation. As word of the carnage spread, roving crowds launched an all-out attack on the local *apartheid* administrative structures. Within the next few days, demonstrators had destroyed six black administration board offices, a teachers' training college, a block of quarters for single black policemen, forty-six shops, three liquor outlets, two beer halls, two bus depots, post offices, and sixteen houses (mostly belonging to community councillors and policemen). Most of these buildings were set on fire with homemade firebombs. Councillors and their families fled, taking refuge in the (white) Orange Vaal Development Board offices in Houtkop. In Sharpeville, the deputy mayor, Sam Dhlamini, was killed on his doorstep after shooting two demonstrators in a crowd that had gathered to protest rent increases. Three other members of town councils were killed.[16]

What distinguished this escalation of popular protests from the 1976 uprising was that the people not only combined a variety of forms of struggle, but had no illusions about appealing to the reasonableness of those black collaborators of the white minority regime. In the Vaal Triangle, all black schools were closed from 5-26 September. From a peak of 800,000 boycotting students during the 22 August elections for the coloured House of Assembly, the number of black pupils staying away from classes in support of a variety of demands fluctuated wildly. By October, nearly one million black students had taken part in school boycotts and other forms of mass action.

The response of the minority regime to the township uprising was frantic repression. Paramilitary police units — in their armoured personnel carriers derisively referred to as 'hippos' in township slang — raced down the main township thoroughfares, firing tear gas, rubber bullets, and birdshot in a vain effort to disperse and punish angry crowds. In the face of the escalating riots and street fighting, sweeping prohibitions on assemblies were issued, banning indefinitely all indoor meetings in twenty-one magisterial districts beginning on 11 September. Outdoor gatherings of a political nature had been outlawed in South Africa for many years.[17] The Minister of Law and Order, Louis Le Grange, described the extent of the ban, saying that it included 'all gatherings held where any government or any principle or any policy principle, or any actions of the government, or any statement, or the application or implementation of any act is approved, defended, attacked, criticized or discussed, or which is in protest against or support or in memoriam of anything'.[18] This comprehensive prohibition against both public and private political gatherings reflected Pretoria's inability to restore any semblance of law and order in the townships and amounted to a declaration of martial law.

Until this banning order, UDF-initiated demonstrations and mass rallies often opened and closed with readings from the Freedom Charter and the singing of the national anthem of the 'liberation movement', *Nkosi Sikheleli i'Afrika*. Virtually overnight, funerals — not subjected to the ban on outdoor gatherings — in commeroration of the victims of indiscriminate police shootings were transformed into militant rallies. Mourners often risked treason charges to sing freedom songs, carry ANC banners, and chant ANC slogans praising the guerrilla war.

In mid-September, the popular unrest spread to Soweto. On 12 September, day-long skirmishes between township residents and a massive contingent of paramilitary police resulted in the withdrawal of PUTCO bus service, stranding more than 100,000 workers on the outskirts of the sprawling township and preventing them returning home. In a massive display of defiance, thousands of youths openly challenged the official ban on public meetings. Pitched battles erupted when police attempted to halt a commemorative service for murdered Black Consciousness leader, Steve Biko. Tension continued to mount. On 13 September, six UDF and Natal Indian Congress leaders who had played major roles in the election boycott campaign took refuge in the British Consulate in Durban in anticipation of their impending arrests. Five of the six — UDF President Archie Gumede, Natal Indian Congress President George Sewpersadh, Mewa Ramgobin, Billy Nair, and M.J. Naidoo — had been released from detention following an unprecedented and successful supreme court appeal declaring their August detentions legally groundless. The Minister of Law and Order, Louis Le Grange, immediately issued new detention orders, yet not before the 'Durban Six' evaded the dragnet by going underground.

These events highlighted the massive wave of detentions that seemed to pass unnoticed amid the confident banter about reformist initiatives and a 'new deal' for urban black people. More individuals were detained in the first eight months of 1984 — in the period before the outbreak of popular rebellion — than in all of 1983.[19] The Durban Six also brought into sharp focus the Thatcher administration's claim that it, like the Reagan administration, maintained a 'constructive engagement' with Pretoria in order to influence the Botha regime toward an enlightened reformist path. During this crisis, Mrs Thatcher steadfastly refused to act as an intermediary between the UDF leaders and Pretoria, giving as her justification the need for 'proper diplomatic procedures'.[20]

Economic Recession and the Black Working Class

During the 1976 Soweto uprising, student activism overshadowed the independent initiative of the black working class. During 1984 and 1986, however, it was considerably more difficult to disentangle labour unrest from the broader popular disenchantment. South Africa's economic performance — measured by its gross national product — slipped 3 per cent in real terms in 1983. These economic difficulties can be traced to falling gold prices, severe drought that crippled agricultural production in certain areas, and poor markets for export commodities such as diamonds and coal. Large doses of expanded state spending, especially on education, national defense, and civil service salaries, widened the budget deficit and fuelled a consumer buying spree, thereby contributing to an inflationary spiral.

In August 1984, the Botha regime launched a comprehensive austerity programme designed to curb money-supply expansion and consumer spending. While businessmen and government economists agreed that these 'belt-tightening' measures were necessary to check spiralling inflation and avert a serious economic crisis, they also conceded these restraints would hit low-income black workers and the unemployed the hardest. By mid-1984, inflation had steadily risen to a 12 per cent annual rate. South African business liquidations averaged twelve firms per day, double the rate of 1982. Food prices surged: increases averaged 10 per cent for coffee, milk, tea, cooking oil, margarine, canned goods, soft drinks, and bread. Rents, utility rates, and fees of public services experienced a steep upward drift in most townships. According to official estimates more than half a million urban blacks — between 15 and 25 per cent of the total black labour force — were unemployed. Continuing factory lay-offs, lockouts, and plant closings only promised to exacerbate an already dire economic situation. The deteriorating living standards of black urban residents and the inability of the new black local authorities to provide real economic and political improvement contributed to the desperate mood of the Vaal riots. At the same time, the number of strikes dramatically increased. By October 1984, both the absolute number of strikes and the actual labour hours lost due to work stoppages had exceeded the comparable figures for the first three quarters of 1982, the country's most explosive strike year since the exceptional 1973 strike wave.[21]

During previous periods of political unrest, it seemed that sustained economic growth had cushioned the white minority regime. What distinguished this outbreak was the coincidence of a dramatic economic downturn with street rioting.

Labour conflict reached critical proportions in mid-September 1984 with the entry of black mine workers onto the political scene. The National Union of Mineworkers (NUM) had entered negotiations with the Chamber of Mines (representing the mining companies) by demanding an unprecedented 60 per cent wage increase. The purpose of this huge jump in wages was to close the gap between black miners and white foremen. When the talks deadlocked, the 90,000-strong NUM prepared to stage their first legal strike. A last-minute agreement raising the salaries of black miners 16.3 per cent failed to avert a series of wildcat strikes involving 45,000 miners that shut down a number of pits on 17 September. 'The settlement is a victory for collective bargaining and it sets the pattern for future negotiations,' announced a spokesman for Anglo-American Corporation, the giant conglomerate that owned seven of the mines where workers walked off the job. The settlement, however, was tarnished by the vicious efforts of employers to suppress the wildcat strikes. On the second day of this massive work stoppage, more than 8,000 miners clashed with paramilitary police in a six-hour meleé at the Western Areas mine site, causing extensive damage including the torching of employment and management offices and miners' records. This pitched battle was the most serious of the bitter confrontations pitting mine managements and their police reinforcements against angry and frustrated miners demanding higher wages and improved safety precautions. By the week's end, at least nine and possibly sixteen miners were dead and hundreds injured in the turmoil.[22]

The rebellion mushroomed as the labour unrest rocked the goldfields. On 7 October, the minority regime announced that the South African Defense Forces (SADF) would be used to bolster police efforts to quell the township unrest. Almost immediately, the SADF's 21st Battallion moved into Soweto. This deployment of regular army units signalled both an acknowledgement that greater muscle was required to cope with this broadening scale of revolt and the grim determination of the white authorities to stifle it through force. The standard paramilitary police procedures — tear gas, rubber bullets, shotguns, water hoses, 'sneeze machines', whips and dogs, widespread detentions, and so on — proved incapable of stemming the wave of popular mobilization. Increasingly militant confrontations between the security forces and groups of youths armed with petrol bombs and stones occurred. Pretoria revealed hastily-drawn plans to expand the civilian police force by 45 per cent, from 47,000 to 68,000 members. This decision reflected official recognition that the township unrest was unlikely to abate.[23]

On 23 October, a combined force of 7,000 army troops and heavily-armed police occupied first Sebokeng and then the neighbouring townships of Sharpeville and Boipatong. This unambiguous display of overwhelming military force was in part designed to assuage the mounting fears of the white electorate that the Botha regime was suffering from political paralysis. Sebokeng was a tawdry black township of approximately 20,000 matchbox houses that accommodated about 160,000 people, about thirty miles south of Johannesburg. Sharpeville and Boipatong had a combined black population of 55,000. Along with Evaton and a few smaller areas, these townships formed a cheap labour pool on the southern edge of the country's industrial centre. During September and October, the sustained character of the street-fighting forced the local auxiliaries of the white regime to retreat in disarray. The collapse of the detested township administrative machinery seemed to release deeper political resentments that dwarfed the original issue of municipal rent increases. A seemingly unending cycle of violence ensued: people killed in rioting were hailed as martyrs and the funerals provoked further clashes with more deaths.

Sebokeng had become, in the words of one police official, 'the most sensitive area' of the current wave of popular unrest. Paradoxically, Sebokeng 'was known as a model township with attractive and modern housing and a potential spending power of R 180 million a year ... a self-supporting community where private enterprise and development projects bloomed'. It was in Sebokeng that the Urban Foundation launched one of its initial township projects, 'spending vast sums of money to upgrade and redevelop housing'. Home ownership and home improvement were well-established with 'building society development corporations, major industries, and private construction firms acquiring stands [i.e., plots] and building houses'.[24] In the pre-dawn raid on 23 October, combined police and army units first cordoned off the entire operational zone before special squads searched dwellings suspected of harbouring 'troublemakers'. The white authorities defended their military crackdown in Sebokeng and neighbouring townships as a pre-emptive action designed to 'curb criminal and revolutionary elements' who had reduced the areas to a state of choas. AZAPO and the UDF condemned the SADF incursion, calling it an act of unwarranted aggression tantamount to a declaration of war.

By early afternoon, Sebokeng looked like an armed camp. As local residents watched impassively, white soldiers stood guard at fifteen-yard intervals along the main streets. The security forces detained about 400 people — only a few of whom were actually charged. Those not herded into police vans for further questioning were forced to wear orange armbands signifying that they had been through the interrogation and screening procedures. Security forces also used coloured ink to mark the hands of black people they had scrutinized. In a final insult, the SADF completed their clumsy counterinsurgency operation by distributing not only badges reading, 'I am your friend, trust me', and 'Cooperation for peace and Security', but also leaflets boasting of their fraternal relationship with township residents.[25] Residents of the occupied townships were required to wear these badges and have their hands stamped with identification marks before leaving for work.[26] Black anger was so fierce that just hours after the SADF completed its phased withdrawal from Sebokeng, Sharpeville, and Boitpatong, a crowd of about 2,000 squared off against the remaining police contingents in the debris-strewn streets of Sebokeng in a renewed round of street-fighting.[27]

From September to the end of October, combined SADF and paramilitary police actions left nearly one-hundred and fifty confirmed dead.[28] The struggle was largely confined to the sprawling townships of the Vaal Triangle. A regular pattern of official violence emerged. Paramilitary police fired rubber bullets, birdshot, and tear gas to disperse crowds of black youths who in turn hurled stones, looted small shops, and torched vehicles. In mid-October, there were clashes in the Eastern Cape in townships near Port Elizabeth and Grahamstown. The political unrest also engulfed the greater East Rand townships of Katlehong, Vosloorus, Tokoza (southeast of Johannesburg); Tsakane, KwaThema, Daveyton, Duduza (east of Johannesburg); and Tembisa (northeast of Johannesburg).[29] In late October, Kaiser Matanzima in the Transkei banned the UDF in what many observers recognized as a prelude to a nationwide clampdown on legal political activities.

In the desolate and barren townships, angry crowds improvised with whatever materials were at hand. Black youths often ambushed police foot patrols and government vehicles, armed with stones, bottles, and petrol bombs. They barracaded streets with burning tyres, crippled vehicles, and other debris, effectively blocking entry to the townships. The geometric design of the sprawling areas minimized the effectiveness of classic guerrilla hit-and-run tactics. In the typical case, townships were linked to local white towns by one or two modern highways and/or railroads, bisected by a single tarred road, and criss-crossed with dirt tributaries meandering off in various directions. Housing units — almost always single-storey and detached — were arranged in long monotonous rows, offering little concealment for protestors. These modest homes — called 'matchboxes' by the residents — were usually constructed of weathered red

brick or newer grey cinder blocks. With their line of fire unen-
cumbered by even sparse vegetation or rubble of any sort, the
security forces resorted to gratuitous acts of violence against
unarmed demonstrators. Reports that police officials unleashed
random and unprovoked assaults on bystanders were commonplace.

What distinguished the initial outbreak of popular unrest
(from September through early November) from the 1976-7
Soweto uprising was the convergence of numerous specific
grievances with many different forms of popular struggle. What
triggered the earlier unrest was a set of narrowly defined issues
articulated through the ideological prism of student activism. In
contrast, the township rebellion that erupted in August 1984 had
deeper roots in working-class dissatisfaction. Consequently, the
unrest almost immediately attracted the participation of broader
layers of the oppressed black masses with a wider spectrum of
ideological perspectives. The civic associations and trade unions
that had grown up in the townships since 1979-80 effectively
translated the immediate grievances of the residents into a broad
political assault on all oppression and injustice in South Africa.
Black rioters targeted town and village councillors, black policemen, and informers as the specific objects of their collective rage.
During the first few months of the riots, dozens of town councillors resigned their posts. For the most part, residents condemned the councillors and their allies as either wilful
accomplices or puppets of white minority rule, tending to ignore
and ostracize them. Angry crowds assaulted them and set fire to
their homes and shops in an effort to drive them out of the townships.[30] Increased rents and service charges were the catalysts
that sparked the rioting. The BLA system — the lynchpin of
Pretoria's plan for 'third-tier government' in the black townships
— became the principal target of the political unrest.[31]

The Transvaal Regional General Strike

The two-day Transvaal regional stayaway on 5-6 November was
the pivotal episode of the initial phase (August-November) of
the political unrest. This highly disciplined and successful strike
marked the first time since the nationwide work stoppage over
the 1982 death in detention of trade unionist Neil Aggett that so

many trade unions and civic organizations combined forces in protest.[32] This united action appreciably altered the political complexion of the ongoing township unrest. In the first place, the success of the Transvaal regional stayaway proved that the independent trade unions exercised considerable influence over the diverse and segmented layers of the black working class. Second, the linking of economic grievances with broader political issues in the list of strike demands indicated that the independent black unions and community-based organizations — often at loggerheads over strategic as well as tactical questions — were capable of mounting a joint campaign.

It was COSAS in late October which had first broached the idea of launching a two-day general strike in the riot-torn Transvaal region. Eventually, an estimated thirty-seven organizations — trade unions (including FOSATU, CUSA, the MACWUSA, the United Mining and Metal Workers' Union, and the Municipal and General Workers' Union), local UDF affiliates, the Release Mandela Committee, the Federation of South African Women, youth groups, civic associations, and church bodies — formed the nucleus of the Transvaal Regional Stayaway Committee. 'The object of the stayaway', according to Mark Swilling, a member of the *ad hoc* Labour Monitoring Group, 'was to articulate student, worker and civic grievances and to put pressure on the state to redress them.' A four-member coordinating committee made up of two union organizers, one unemployed worker from the Soweto Youth Congress (SOYCO), and a former detainee out on bail, was elected to handle practical preparations. Each participating organization was given specific tasks in the broad-based effort to mobilize non-unionized workers (particularly migrant hostel dwellers who had been generally ignored in the past) on the shop-floor. The Stayaway Committee distributed over 400,000 leaflets to popularize the two-day strike. The demands included withdrawal of the army and the police from the occupied townships; cessation of rent and busfare increases; resignation of all community councillors; unconditional release of all political prisoners and detainees; reinstatement of all recently dismissed workers; educational reform; and the termination of unfair taxation.[33] The security forces responded by issuing their own leaflets urging workers to defy the strike call. These were dropped by helicopter over the townships and distributed at roadblocks in the riot-torn East Rand area. The leaflets accused

258

anti-*apartheid* organizations of provoking the unrest and of causing unnecessary suffering amongst township residents.

The unprecedented scale of mass mobilization, coupled with the overlapping of working-class and popular demands, displayed the temporary cohesiveness and strength of the popular movement. 'The two-day protest stayaway', one reporter acknowledged, 'left industry in the East Rand and in the Vaal Triangle reeling. The widespread support for the stayaway call — made by union organizations, civic associations and student bodies — demonstrated effectively and for the first time the economic muscle wielded by organized black workers.' Employers grudgingly acknowledged that between 40 and 90 per cent of the approximately two million black workers in the industrial belt encircling Johannesburg had supported the stayaway. Vincent Brett, Manpower Secretary of the Association of Chambers of Commerce, observed that the strike action showed 'tremendous variation, by industry and by area', but was generally 'far more successful' than previous strike efforts. According to the Labour Monitoring Group's survey, 70 per cent of unionized factories reported a stayaway rate of over 80 per cent, with the strongest showing in the Vaal and the far East Rand, with the poorest participation amongst Homelands' commuters in the Pretoria area. The walkout completely shut down the labour-intensive steel, heavy engineering, and manufacturing companies on the East Rand. Unionized workers stayed away *en masse* and unorganized factories reported a five to ten per cent attendance rate — 'effectively bringing production lines to a grinding halt'.[34] An estimated 400,000 students supported the strike by boycotting classes.

The strike was the first time black workers joined student groups and civic organizations in a coordinated mass protest over political grievances. Political activists claimed the joint action as the most successful political work-stoppage since black people first made use of the stayaway as a protest tactic in 1950. On the morning of the first day, young demonstrators used a variety of innovative tactics to enforce the walkout. Crowds disrupted train and bus services. In Tembisa, youths stopped a commuter train by placing concrete blocks on the tracks. They then set train cars alight, preventing firefighters from extinguishing the blaze until police reinforcements drove them away. Buses were hastily withdrawn from six black townships — Soweto,

Tembisa, Atteridgeville, KwaThema, Natalspruit, and Vosloorus — after many were damaged and a number were hijacked. In Soweto, two branch bank offices were firebombed. Elsewhere, liquor stores and beerhalls were gutted by fire. In the townships, crowds erected make-shift barricades — of burning trucks or buses and whatever materials were readily available — to obstruct traffic and to hamper the mobility of armoured personnel carriers. Crowds attacked the homes of black police and of black local councillors, reflecting the disenchantment with Pretoria's efforts to install puppet administrations in the townships.

In a departure from standard policy, the white authorities resorted to a greater use of the SADF to contain the strike action. On the second day, army units put up roadblocks around the townships of Evaton and Sebokeng. Police in armed convoys moved into Tembisa to confront crowds attacking stores, trucks, and buses. The overwhelming success of the strike could be attributed to the support of the trade union movement. Nearly 100 per cent of the black labour force joined the walkout in the highly organized factories of the industrialized East Rand, barely eighteen miles from Johannesburg. The Rand's townships were the scene of the most intense street fighting, including stonings and arson matched by police counterattacks with tear gas and automatic weapons fire. In Tembisa, all streets were 'closed off after they were barricaded with stones, old cars and burning tyres'. SADF units were sent to both Tembisa and Tsakana on the East Rand to guard government buildings. 'Huge dustbins, old cars and boulders barricaded the streets of Daveyton, Katlehong, Vosloorus, and Tsakane, and youths milled around.'[35]

Police sources reported that sixteen people had been killed in the two days of rioting and arson in the townships encircling Johannesburg. The death toll within the first twenty-four-hour period was the highest since the protests had begun in early September. What was unprecedented about this two-day strike was its immediate and direct impact on the white community: 'filling stations ran out of gas, factories came to a virtual standstill, white managers were forced to staff supermarket checkout stations, maids did not turn up for work'.[36]

The chair of the Transvaal Region Stayaway Committee, Thami Mali, claimed that the protest action had proven to the Botha regime 'that we now have the power in our hands and can use it in any way we like. . . . Our duty is to create an ungovernable situation and actually force the state to declare some of the area as liberated zones.'[37] Committee members acknowledged that while the strike might not have been able to wrest concrete concessions from the white authorities, a number of long-term gains had been achieved: (1) unity had been accomplished among a substantial portion of township dwellers in South Africa's industrial heartland, including workers, and middle-class tradesmen and parents and students; (2) 'new ground had been broken in joint action by community groups and key trade union groupings, some of which have previously stood aloof'; (3) disciplined action had translated rhetoric into reality; and (4) 'vast numbers of people had shown they had seen for themselves the real face of the government . . . that it was a farce to say Pretoria was committed to change'.[38]

The 5-6 November strike was the most successful stayaway in thirty-five years.[39] The Botha regime retaliated in force. On 8 November, the security police raided the offices of the main supporting organizations, confiscating documents and arresting and detaining union leaders and activists under catch-all security laws. The principal targets for the security police raids in Johannesburg were the UDF, FOSATU, and COSAS. At the same time, the state-owned SASOL fired over 6,000 black workers at its oil-from-coal plant at Secunda, sixty miles to the east. This mass dismissal of workers who participated in the two-day general strike left SASOL with about 10 per cent of its black labour force. Nearly all those fired were migrant workers and they were compelled to return to their Homelands.[40]

The Ministry of Law and Order persisted in its charge that unidentified agitators, 'thugs' and 'hooligans' were responsible for the arson, looting, and stone-throwing in the townships. But this litany of well-worn clichés had lost its convincing ring. The cause of black dissatisfaction was the accumulation of economic deprivation and a profound sense of political alienation worsened by the new Constitution that ignored the African majority. In explaining the link between the 'strike demands', Chris Dhlamini, president of FOSATU, exposed the political meaning of the Transvaal general strike: 'It is crystal clear to us that our members and other workers are being sucked dry by blood-thirsty industrialists and the government. How can we be silent when the children of our members are killed like animals in the streets of the townships? How can we be silent when our children tell us they cannot take the educational inferiority any longer? How can we be silent when we are forced to pay high rents for houses that are mere sleeping dungeons? How can we be silent when we are denied basic human rights in the land of our birth? How much longer must we be silent when our very dignity as human beings is questioned?'[41] The two largest independent black trade union federations — FOSATU and CUSA — had in the past refrained from overt political activism, concentrating instead on their organizational presence on the shopfloor and pursuing economic objectives. The active intervention of independent trade unions marked a significant departure from their previous stance of consciously avoiding frontal collisions with the white minority regime.[42]

The Contagion of Popular Revolt

Signs that the popular uprising had spread to the Eastern Cape were frequent. At the beginning of November, school boycotts sparked 'a wave of rioting [that] swept through ... the Port Elizabeth, Uitenhage, and Grahamstown townships'. 'Township violence reached a bloody climax' as the Eastern Cape 'experienced its blackest week'.[43] After having been subjected to a three-week military occupation, township residents in Grahamstown staged a local general strike on 9 November, despite estimated 40 per cent unemployment in the area. On 15 November, police fired into a crowd of youths who had attacked the house of the mayor of the black township outside Graaf Reinet.

On 13 November, a combined SADF and police task force launched an invasion of Tembisa, a township of 250,000 residents fifteen miles northeast of Johannesburg near Jan Smuts Airport, in what the white authorities claimed was a 'crime prevention' operation. In this highly visible display of concentrated force, convoys of army and police vehicles cordoned off the area and, in house-to-house searches, detained about eighty people on various charges.[44] Police and army units also distributed pamphlets urging black high school students to abandon their school boycotts and ordering adults to return to work.[45]

On 14 and 15 November, SADF and paramilitary police

detained another 2,300 people in 'mopping-up operations', most of them netted in a lightning raid on hostels in Sebokeng. Bolstered by SADF reinforcements, the paramilitary stormed the squalid barracks that housed about 10,000 black migrants working locally on contract. These detainees were tried in three special courts for offenses ranging from trespassing and failure to produce work-permits to nonpayment of rent. In an effort to recoup lost revenues, local town councils attempted to force employers to dock rent from paychecks.[46] On 18 November, widespread rioting once again erupted in Vosloorus and Thokoza townships on the East Rand. Police retaliated by attacking crowds of black youths with rubber bullets, birdshot, and tear gas. In neighbouring Daveyton and Actonville, the SADF set up roadblocks and searched all traffic. They issued pamphlets stating that 'the police and army are in your areas to insure that the people can carry on with their normal activities: to go to work and to go to school'.[47] Within the next two weeks, SADF units, travelling in cavalcades of armoured vehicles, assisted the police in regular reconnaissance patrols in 'Sebokeng and Sharpeville, in the Vaal and most East Rand townships'. Police headquarters in Pretoria described these bolstered operations as 'normal routine crime prevention operations'. Township residents disputed this claim, expressing fears that the introduction of the SADF into police operations 'was in preparation for an army takeover of what were basic police duties'.[48]

The Political Impact of the Popular Rebellion

The popular rebellion that had begun in earnest in September had caused considerable physical damage to both state and private property in the townships. During the two-day general strike alone, PUTCO buses — longstanding symbols of the commuting imposed on local residents because of residential segregation and influx controls — sustained an estimated $550,000 in losses. In addition, local authorities suffered considerable loss of revenue because of the refusal of residents to pay rent and service charge increases and the destruction of income-generating beerhalls and liquor outlets.

Angry crowds attacked the homes and offices of literally

dozens of community councillors, mayors, and other local black officials, causing many of them to flee for their lives. One councillor from Kathehong was shot three times at close range as he left the Moshoeshoe supermarket in the township. It was reported that in the wake of the two-day general strike only four of the original town councils in the Transvaal still functioned.[49]

The political crisis exacerbated the growing rift within the minority regime over the proper course of action to restore stability, symbolized by the acrimonious exchange between South Africa's three major business associations and the Minister of Law and Order, Louis Le Grange. On 14 November, the *Afrikaanse Handelsinstituut* (AHI), the Federated Chamber of Industries (FCI), and the Association of South African Chambers of Commerce (ASSOCOM) issued a joint warning that the wave of detentions of trade union leaders could endanger 'labour peace' and had worsened a 'very delicate' labour situation. The statement also condemned security police actions as 'heavy-handed'.[50] The FCI labelled the detention of Chris Dhlamimi and Piroshaw Camay, leaders of FOSATU and CUSA respectively, as 'the single most serious threat to labour reform and collective bargaining in South Africa since the release of the Wehahn report'.[51] In response, Le Grange launched a vituperative attack on the three business associations for their public criticism of his handling of a 'security matter'.

It was subsequently disclosed that these associations had been engaged in delicate negotiations with the independent black trade unions to avert the possibility of another regional stayaway when the security police conducted their 'second wave' of detentions following the 5-6 November general strike. All in all, forty-one trade unionists had been detained since the beginning of 1984 (nineteen remained in detention under Section 29 of the Internal Security Act) in the most widespread police clampdown on unionists since 1981. Repressive action against trade unionists had undergone a sharp increase in the second half of 1984, coinciding with the increase in industrial strike action and the political unrest in the Transvaal.[52] For the FOSATU leadership, the mass victimization of over 6,000 SASOL workers — who had just recently been organized by the FOSATU-affiliated Chemical Workers' Industrial Union — had been a bitter pill to swallow. The federation's general secretary, Joe Foster, condemned this decision by SASOL's management to sack almost its entire work force as 'deliberately provocative'.[53]

In South African white politics, opinion had been split customarily between the more liberal whites of British descent and the more conservative whites of Afrikaans descent. Yet one of the business groups pressuring for liberalization, the AHI, a business lobby group, was made up of Afrikaans business executives and considered generally a dependable ally of the National Party and its *apartheid* policies. Along with the FCI and ASSOCOM, the AHI eventually reneged on its initial petition calling for the Minister of Law and Order to either release or charge detained trade unionists and instead pledged its full support for 'security police actions'. Nevertheless, the fissures within the once solid edifice of Afrikanerdom had widened.[54]

The November stayaway sent shockwaves through South Africa's ruling class. The ongoing political turbulence had graphically demonstrated the growing dependence of the country's business upon black people both as workers and as consumers. 'Seventy per cent of our sales are to blacks,' admitted Tony Bloom, chair of Premier Group Holdings, a food processing giant. 'There are no profits for business in disintegrating communities. Stability is terribly important for business.'[55] In December, the highly respected Johannesburg labour consultant firm, Andrew Levy and Associates, issued a detailed study forecasting that the independent black trade unions would in time become a 'major vehicle for black aspirations'. The steady growth in membership of these trade unions showed no signs of subsiding. 'Under present conditions', the Levy report concluded, employers could in the future be faced with losses caused by political grievances rather than just shop-floor issues. 'Failure to leaven the right blend of firmness with tact and sensitivity', Levy and Associates argued, 'will only accelerate what are already disturbing signs.' This stern warning underscored the apprehension of the leading business associations that unrelenting repression and strong-arm tactics had impeded a hasty resolution of the crisis and threatened to provoke further labour unrest, thereby reducing profits and undercutting efforts at economic recovery.[56]

FOSATU's call for a 'Black Christmas' seemed to confirm the worst fears of the associations. In announcing 'as a trade union movement we feel we have nothing to celebrate', FOSATU urged members of its affiliated unions to make only essential purchases over the Christmas holidays. The aim of this boycott was to protest the police detention of FOSATU president Chris Dhlamini, MAWU's Moses Mayekiso, and the mass dismissal of the SASOL workers.[57] Almost immediately, the UDF pledged its full support for the campaign. The president of the Front, Albertina Sisulu, proclaimed: 'Events in the Transvaal and other parts of the country have reached tragic proportions. More than 1,000 oppressed people have been killed by the brutal forces of *apartheid*. ... The full might of the SADF has been mobilised in order to intimidate and frighten residents into submission. The root cause of the suffering is the evil system of *apartheid* which our people have decided to challenge and destroy. In this context it becomes impossible for any South African of conscience to celebrate Christmas as a joyous occasion.'[58] All anti-*apartheid* organizations followed suit, endorsing this nationwide observance of 'Black Christmas' to honour those killed, injured, or detained during the long wave of popular unrest.

Repression and Counter-Revolution

In an end-of-year assessment, the Detainees' Parents Support Committee (DPSC) released figures showing that students and teachers formed the single largest group of security detainees, followed by community workers and political activists. Three major waves of detentions had taken place: (1) the crackdown on national leaders before the tricameral elections; (2) the response to protest against rents and the 'local authorities' system in the Vaal and elsewhere where the mass round-ups depleted the leadership ranks of the civic associations; and (3) the swoop on leaders of organizations associated with the November two-day stay-away.[59] Yet a considerable proportion of the arrests appeared to be purely arbitrary and random. It had been reported that police had toured hospitals, indiscriminately snatching unrest victims who had been admitted with gunshot wounds. Consequently, some of those injured were treated in makeshift 'backyard surgeries' rather than risk arrest in hospital. 'The backyard operations had become common in trouble-torn townships such as KwaThema', one report said, 'where boys have become "surgeons".'[60]

As the violent confrontations in the Vaal Triangle townships gradually subsided, the Southern African Roman Catholic Bishops' Conference exploded their own public relations bombshell. In a detailed denunciation of police conduct based on the sworn affidavits of unnamed victims, the bishops declared that police behavior resembled that of an occupying foreign army controlling enemy territory by force without regard for the civilian population and, it appeared, without legal restraint. These allegations from the Roman Catholic hierarchy — claiming a church membership of over 2.5 million of whom nearly two-thirds were black — represented a sweeping condemnation of police brutality. 'A kind of state of war is developing between the police and the people,' Archbishop Denis Hurley of Durban, the chair of the Southern African Catholic Bishops' Conference, maintained. 'The police', he said, 'seem to be in a mood which inspires them to say: "the people are our enemy, and we are out to impose our will upon them by any means that we find effective".' The report also alleged the indiscriminate use of firearms, including rubber bullets, birdshot, and conventional bullets. The police who engaged in assaults — the overwhelming majority of which appeared unprovoked — seemed to regard these actions as a 'kind of sport'.[61]

In December, the security forces took a giant step toward a crackdown on the leadership of the UDF. Six people — Mewa Ramgobin, George Sewpersadh, M.J. Naidoo, Essop Jassat, Aubrey Mokoena, and Curtis Nkondo — were charged with high treason and, alternatively, with furthering the aims of a banned organization — the ANC. In subsequent months, more names were added to the indictment, enlarging the original group to fourteen. The striking parallels tempted veteran anti-*apartheid* campaigners — gripped with a feeling of *déjà vu* — to compare the latest legal manoeuvre with the famous 1956-61 Treason Trial. Continuing for four long years, this political circus ended in acquittal for all 156 defendants who were accused of furthering the aims of the banned South African Communist Party.[62]

Friend or Foe?: The Kennedy Visit

Senator Edward Kennedy's whirlwind 'fact-finding' tour of South Africa in January 1985 evoked differing responses from the UDF and AZAPO/National Forum camps. Kennedy visited South

Africa at the invitation of Bishop Desmond Tutu, 1984 Nobel Peace Prize winner, and Allan Boesak, president of the World Alliance of Reformed Churches. Both were closely identified with the UDF. The Front's national executive also extended its tacit political approval for this visit, not only providing organizational support but publicly heaping praise on Kennedy for meeting with Winnie Mandela, the banned wife of imprisoned ANC leader Nelson Mandela, and for his critical observations condemning the seamy side of *apartheid*.

Meanwhile, AZAPO castigated Kennedy's eight-day barnstorming, labelling it a publicity stunt designed to secure a 'ticket to the Presidency' for the Massachusetts Democrat. Black Consciousness organizations that clustered around the National Forum used the Kennedy tour as an occasion to highlight their position on the question of class alliances and their anti-liberal stance. The Forum also took advantage of the opportunity to project themselves as more militant and anti-capitalist than their UDF rivals, despite the latter's reputation as a surrogate for the underground ANC. 'The Kennedy visit was a watershed because it illustrated the difference between the two organizations', Neville Alexander argued. 'The invitation to such a representative of capitalism is precisely the kind of compromise which we believe the UDF is inclined to make', he continued. 'It exposed the fact that they have placed middle-class leaders in charge of their organization.' National Forum affiliates hounded Kennedy throughout his tour, displaying 'Yankee Go Home' placards at every opportunity and reproaching him as an opportunistic capitalist spokesman and agent of U.S. imperialism. AZAPO charged that Kennedy was 'grandstanding' during his visit and cynically using black South Africans for his own political advancement. 'The manner in which he went around', confided Saths Cooper, an AZAPO leader who served time on Robben Island, 'like a great white god coming to offer hope and salvation, is just the kind of WASP arrogance that makes blacks here reject anything that smacks of Uncle Sam.'[63] The National Forum-affiliated Cape Action League transformed Kennedy's Cape Town stop into a political 'free-for-all' and others forced cancellation of his farewell speech in Soweto.[64] White right-wing political organizations, including the pro-*apartheid* Afrikaans-language newspaper *Beeld*, also denounced the Kennedy excursion as an unwelcome intrusion into South

African affairs. The UDF national executive used this coincidence to condemn AZAPO for siding with the Afrikaner far-right.[65]

Kennedy met with prominent business leaders in Johannesburg, reminding them that concern and involvement became more vital for business interests when the very nature or stability of a nation was at stake. He emphasized that free enterprise could flourish only in a 'free society'.[66] While Kennedy lamented that the 'winds of change' had more or less bypassed South Africa, six leading business associations — AHI, ASSOCOM, the Chamber of Mines, the National African Federation of Chambers of Commerce (NAFCOC), and the Steel and Engineering Industries Federation (SEIFSA) — upstaged his stinging criticisms of *apartheid* policies with their own 'manifesto'. In this memorandum, the associations repudiated the National Party's racial policies on the grounds that they were 'bad for business'. The business executives 'stole the thunder', as the *Wall Street Journal* exclaimed, from the Kennedy tour by condemning detention-without-trial, in addition to calling for black political rights, citizenship for all South Africans, free trade unions, the termination of forced removals, the end of statutory 'job reservation', and the right of anyone to own shops or conduct business anywhere in the country.[67]

South Africa's business leaders had cunningly taken advantage of this well-known liberal critic of the Botha regime, outflanking him to the left and painting themselves as anti-*apartheid* reformers. According to the *Financial Mail*, 'Not in modern times in this country have businessmen been so united in their condemnation of government and its social and economic policies. Nor has government itself been so dependent on the support and investment of the business community or needed it so much at the polls. ... Economically, businessmen are being taxed into revolt and swamped by a bloated public sector. ... *Business's United Front* [my emphasis — M.M.] ... told government that it must get down to real political and economic reform. ... These national employer organizations — ranging from the usually government-supporting AHI to the black NAFCOC — have never before combined forces.'[68] 'Businessmen are realizing more and more', emphasized Johan van Zyl, chair of the FCI, 'that it is up to them to defend the system of private enterprise.'[69]

The Deepening Political Crisis

The Government's Response

Two highly symbolic incidents seemed to confirm the wide-spread belief that the so-called reformist initiatives were nothing more than a clumsily-arranged charade designed to defuse international criticism. In the first instance, P.W. Botha had cultivated an image of reasonableness during January by offering to release long-term political prisoners on condition that they renounce violence as a legitimate means of achieving their goals. In early February, Chris Heunis, Minister of Constitutional Development, announced that his office planned to open forty-four unspecified commercial districts to merchants of all races, relaxing regulations that have segregated black and white traders for more than 300 years. This pronouncement was aimed squarely at convincing the critics of the white regime that the National Party was sincerely and ardently pressing ahead with its promise to dismantle *apartheid*. Opponents ridiculed these gestures, insisting that these measures ignored elementary forms of segregation, such as housing, education, and the common voters' roll.[70]

Yet it was the use of the judicial system to stifle peaceful dissent that exposed the duplicity of the Botha regime's double-edged approach to its international critics and its domestic adversaries. In predawn raids on 19 February 1985, South African security police conducted a nationwide crackdown on political opponents. At least thirteen UDF leaders were detained, seven of whom were charged with treason. These detainees joined the other UDF leaders who had been arrested in December and were held on similar charges. Those arrested for treason — a crime punishable under South African law by death — included Albertina Sisulu, a president of UDF and wife of imprisoned ANC leader Walter Sisulu; Cassim Saloojee, UDF treasurer; Reverend Frank Chikane, a UDF Transvaal regional Vice-president; and Samuel Kikine, Isaac Ngcobo, and Sisa Njikelana, all members of SAAWU.[71]

The South African authorities announced on 1 February 1985, that they were temporarily halting the relocation of black people living in so-called 'white areas'. This moratorium followed President Botha's major speech a week earlier in which he had promised modifications both in relocation policy and in the labyrinthine restrictions on black access to the urban areas. State authorities had been prompted to undertake an exhaustive review of relocation policies because of both growing foreign and domestic criticism and the refusal of most local communities to be uprooted. But in an accompanying news conference, Gerrit Viljoen, Minister of Cooperation and Development, qualified what had been hailed as a significant relaxation of the policy of forced removals. He admitted that if black communities agreed to their relocation, 'further removals can take place while the review is under way'. He further acknowledged that the review did not affect unlawful squatter communities, which were still liable to be dislodged.[72]

The chameleon-like posture of the Botha regime failed to reassure Crossroads residents. They believed that forced resettlement was imminent. In anticipation of impending demolition of their homes, they lined the roads encircling the encampment, erecting burning barricades and stoning any vehicles that ventured within range. The SAP retaliated with tear gas, rubber bullets, and birdshot. In the ensuing confrontation, at least eighteen people were killed and hundreds injured.

Crossroads was a sprawling squatter camp located on the southeastern outskirts of Cape Town. It consisted of makeshift shanties packed tightly together in a triangle of land between highways.[73] These corrugated metal shelters were patched with canvas, supported by tree limbs, and lined with pages from magazines. Crossroads residents had lived under the constant threat of imminent removal. Despite its cramped and incongruous appearance, Crossroads had gradually evolved from temporary sanctuaries into a thriving cluster of semi-permanent shanty-towns. In 1980, the white authorities had granted a reprieve to the area. Since that time, Crossroads had experienced a 'population explosion' of sorts, spawning a number of satellite squatter communities. The more than 100,000 people who made their homes in the overcrowded shacks were mainly black refugees, castoffs from the Transkei and Ciskei who were trapped in a poverty-induced diaspora and motivated by the hope of finding fixed employment in Cape Town. Their determined presence remained a testament to the complete failure of official policies under which the Western Cape had been reserved for people of mixed racial descent and whites to the exclusion of Africans. In an effort to control the mushrooming squatter colonies in the

Cape peninsula, the authorities built Khayelitsha (the name means 'our home'). This housing scheme was in the wind-swept sand dunes of the Cape Flats and was planned to eventually accommodate 250,000 black residents. Crossroads' squatters were profoundly suspicious of the options open to them, contending that the housing accommodation at Khayelitsha was too small and too costly and, furthermore, that the increased distance from Cape Town would create intolerable travelling expenses. Moreover, residents feared that the white authorities would take advantage of the move to Khayelitsha to banish 'illegals' once again to the impoverished Homelands.

As the clashes spread to nearby black townships and threatened to ignite a wider confrontation, the SAP staged a hasty tactical retreat. The Minister of Cooperation and Development, Gerrit Viljoen, proclaimed a truce promising that removals would not take place 'immediately'. Viljoen also offered official assurance that the Department of Cooperation and Development was no longer engaged in 'forced removals' but was now committed to 'urban renewal' projects and 'Homeland consolidation' schemes. However, these ambiguous promises of reform placated a shrinking circle of diehards. Despite the conciliatory tone, there was no indication that Pretoria had abandoned its ultimate goal of removing not only black people living in Crossroads but also those in the three authorized African townships around Cape Town. The removal plans raised the prospect of Africa's largest enforced population shift since Nigeria expelled hundreds of thousands of Ghanaians and other foreigners early in 1983.[74]

Within a week of the outbreak of fighting at Crossroads, Viljoen offered two ambiguous concessions designed to defuse a potentially explosive situation. In what was advertised as a significant reversal of longstanding policy, he announced that he was willing to extend ninety-nine-year leaseholds to qualified black residents of Nyanga, Langa, and Guguletu. However, critics claimed that proprietary rights would be confined to a relatively small privileged stratum because the number of blacks who could qualify was actually shrinking. In another modification of previously-stated official policy, Viljoen conceded that the white authorities were 'prepared to allow the upgrading and development of the areas on which the Crossroads and KTC squatter camps are situated', provided that black residents cooperated with the official blueprint.[75] This pledge unleashed a chain of intrigues that led directly to the factional violence that destroyed the 'Crossroads complex' in May-June 1986.

Political Unrest Spreads to the Countryside

Sporadic eruptions of political violence continued to take place in the urban townships of the Vaal and the East Rand from January through March of 1985. Civic associations in Katlehong (East Rand), Ratanda (East Rand), Alexandra (Johannesburg), and Sebokeng (Vaal Triangle) refused to pay rent or service charges unless the rates were reduced to an affordable level. Student boycotts continued in Mamelodi and Atteridgeville near Pretoria, the Vaal Triangle, the Orange Free State, and the Eastern Cape. Commuters boycotted buses at Empangeni and set up road-blocks to protest PUTCO's fare increase on the KwaNdebele-to-Pretoria route.[76]

For the white authorities, however, the most frightening and ominous sign that the political unrest had inched toward open civil war was the outbreak of violent confrontations in the small *platteland* towns of the Eastern Cape and the Orange Free State. Small-town South Africa has always been the bedrock of *apartheid* values where the segregation was a cherished way of life. In the sleepy *dorps* and *burgs* that were engraved in the land-scape every thirty or forty miles across the veldt, the social order was fixed against a backdrop of rigid racial compartmental-ization. 'City ghettos such as Soweto and Crossroads may burn with the anger of an oppressed race', Allister Sparks wrote, 'but here, for generations, the black folk have known their place, and the lowliest white man has been greeted deferentially as "baas" and "master".'[77]

Suddenly, this seemingly ingrained deference began to dis-integrate. Scores of unfamiliar names began to appear among the growing list of South Africa's trouble spots: Seeisoville and Phomolong (near Kroonstad), Oberholzer, Tzaneen, Ikageng, Thabong, Odendaalsrus, Clocolan, Virginia, Vryburg, Bothaville, Beaufort West, Paarl, Parys, Galeshewe, Vergenoeg, Mangaung (near Bloemfontein), Somerset East, Fort Beaufort, Newton, and Cradock. In the rural townships, familial bonds and attachments were more deeply rooted than in the sprawling urban townships.

Oppression was tangible and immediate. For black police-men, town councillors, and suspected informers, there was no easy escape into anonymity. Once the battlelines were drawn, the conflict assumed a peculiar viciousness that was quite distinct from the relatively impersonal quality of urban ghetto violence.

Cradock — a smallish, old fashioned rural town situated 120 miles north of Port Elizabeth in the heart of the sheep-farming plains of an arid central plateau called the Great Karroo — 'is hardly the place one would expect to find a flashpoint of the gathering South African racial conflict'.[78] Yet this Karroo village emerged as an emblem of determined resistance and commit-ment in the battle of South Africa's black people for human dignity and respect. 'It is a place of defiance', *New York Times* correspondent Alan Cowell said simply, 'the township with South Africa's most stubborn black resistance, in the restive eastern Cape.'[79] Militant schoolchildren had initiated a boycott of classes in February 1984 that was still in place at the end of March 1985. Black residents lived in the segregated area called Lingelihle two miles outside Cradock's 'white' boundaries. Eventually all school committees and the white-approved town council resigned after being subjected to relentless pressure from township residents.

The abdication of these puppet bodies — surrogates for white minority rule — left a political vacuum filled by the Cradock Residents' Association (commonly known as Cradora). Cradora had been formed in 1983 when the local authorities tried to impose rent hikes on state-owned housing in Lingelihle, an increase that many residents saw as an intolerable burden on their low incomes. In this sense, Cradora resembled literally scores of civic associations formed in the black townships throughout South Africa to struggle for redress of localized grievances. A bright young school teacher named Matthew Goniwe, the son of an illiterate domestic servant and an itinerant firewood merchant, was largely instrumental in Cradock's politi-cal awakening. He had returned to his birthplace after spending five years in Transkei's prisons for purportedly spreading Marxist propaganda. In order to stifle the growing influence of Cradora, the government authorities had transferred Goniwe to a school 100 miles away. When he refused to accept this transfer, he was fired. Outraged students organized the February 1984 school boycott in order to press their demand for his reinstatement.

A spiral of racial confrontation followed. Local authorities tried to decimate Cradora by detaining its leaders, banning its meetings, and terrorizing its supporters. Yet it 'still managed to organize itself by word of mouth and clandestine cells'.[80] The crackdown increased popular support for Cradora and hardened the resolve of the now cohesive black community of 15,000 to defy the white authorities. Clashes with police became more frequent and increasingly vicious. Angry crowds burned houses of town council members and other black residents associated with the local white administration. By January, all council members had resigned rather than take further punishment. In February, South Africa's official white opposition party, the Progressive Federal Party, sought a judicial inquiry to investigate widespread reports of unprovoked police violence and misconduct in Lingelihle, including the murder of a 15-year old boy.[81]

What was particularly troubling to the white authorities was that what started with a protest against rent increases gradually became a broad assault on white minority rule. 'The people have come to realize that they can defy the government', said Matthew Goniwe.[82] 'The people have been embittered and they react when the police attack them. They are not afraid anymore.'[83] The slogans that adorned the walls around what was referred to as 'the stadium' — a bare soccer field — proclaimed 'Viva Umkhonto we Sizwe' and 'Long Live the Spear of the Nation'. 'The authorities seem to acknowledge their impotence to "redeem" the township', Alan Cowell observed, 'for they come here only in armored trucks or in the person of security men with pistols tucked into their waistbands, without even the pretense of the usual white paternalism.'[84] Linelihle township achieved 'a kind of organized anarchy, beyond government control'.[85] In the panorama of South Africa's sustained wave of popular rebellion, Cradock symbolized a fledgling experiment in dual power, prefiguring the state of ungovernability that in the months ahead engulfed dozens of other black townships in the Eastern Cape and the Vaal Triangle.

Deepening Recession and Growing Fissures in the Power Bloc

In 1985, South Africa produced three-quarters of the non-communist world's gold. The 44 per cent tax revenue from its sale has historically enabled the state administration to pay extra costs associated with maintaining the *apartheid* order. When the world price of gold reached a record $820 a fine ounce in 1980, South Africa enjoyed the greatest economic boom in its history and the Botha regime faced no serious political challenges within the dominant bloc of class forces. This seemingly charmed economic existence quickly turned nightmarish. After 1980, the gold price plummeted, due mainly to the strengthening of the dollar. A standard rule of thumb used by financiers in Johannesburg was that for every $10 the gold price fell, the state administration lost $200 million in tax revenue averaged over a year. With the gold price stabilized at under $300 a fine ounce in 1985, South Africa suffered an annual revenue loss of more than $10 billion compared with 1980. In addition to its declining revenue, the state administration faced increased costs. The soaring dollar and South Africa's own depressed economy caused the rand to be devalued by more than 60 per cent in two years. The devaluation caused the price of imports to skyrocket. In February 1985, the price of gasoline increased 40 per cent. Public transport costs increased by 30 per cent. The price of basic commodities, such as bread and rice, increased by more than 21 per cent in a single year.[86]

Prominent business leaders have long maintained that economic growth was a precondition for political stability in South Africa. Many corporate executives criticized state regulations inhibiting supply-and-demand in the labour market and the barriers preventing black workers from acquiring usable skills. In March, the six leading business associations (representing the employers of 80 per cent of workers in South Africa's commerce, industry, and mining) issued a joint statement pressing P.W. Botha to give 'visible expression' to the vague promises of reform in order to counter the growing campaign in the United States and elsewhere calling for economic sanctions against the country. Within a week, the American Chamber of Commerce in South Africa pressed Botha for the first time to modify key elements of *apartheid* and to commit himself to serious negotiations with its political opponents. The Chamber — an unofficial private body — represented 350 companies, 300 of them American and the rest South African, employing 130,000 people. In its proposals, it urged the ending of influx controls, the opening of city center business districts to entrepreneurs of all racial groups, and the abrogation of the policy of consigning blacks to Homelands.[87] Leading figures in the administration responded to these criticisms with obvious irritation. Gerrit Viljoen cautioned South Africa's critics that the Botha regime had fashioned its own timetable. He emphasized that the implementation of the 'reform process' would take place in accordance with South African conditions and not because of external pressure.

In the meantime, new austerity plans were invented to cope with the worst recession in half a century. Acknowledging that the previous efforts at economic recovery had achieved only feeble results, Finance Minister Barend J. du Plessis announced tax increases affecting personal income, general sales, imported commodities such as automobiles and electronic equipment, as well as the country's lucrative gold, diamond, and other mining operations. The sales tax (which applied to all purchases except some protected basic foodstuffs) reached 12 per cent, or double the rate of January 1984. Economists worried that the entire austerity package which had been incrementally imposed over several months would push the inflation rate from the current 13.9 per cent to nearly 20 per cent by the end of 1985. Critics of the minority regime warned that any precipitous surge in the costs of living in the midst of deep recession and growing unemployment would fuel an already explosive situation in the black ghettos. At the other end of the political spectrum, the budget contributed to the prospect of backlash from white conservatives. The increase in income taxes meant that white South Africans, accustomed to one of the world's highest standards of living, ironically constituted one of the world's most heavily taxed groups. Those who earned more than $30,000 a year were taxed at a rate of 57 per cent.[88]

The Eastern Cape Uprising

A short respite temporarily separated the two regional outbreaks of popular rebellion. The upheaval that surged through the Eastern Cape did not displace the unrest of the Vaal Triangle but broadened it. Black anger in the Cape belied the superficial calm that had prevailed since September 1984. Collective rage did not reach a boiling point until February-March 1985. However, when the Eastern Cape townships exploded, the masses leapfrogged the early phases that had characterized the political unrest in the Transvaal, imprinting what would eventually become a country-wide rebellion with their own signature. The Cape's township residents had a relatively high level of political consciousness inherited from a rich legacy of resistance to autocratic over-rule.

Port Elizabeth has historically been the economic nerve centre of the Eastern Cape and the principal location of South Africa's motor industry. Its black townships — and those of Uitenhage — had acquired a well-deserved reputation for political activism as well as for uncompromising police countermeasures. During the 1940s and the 1950s, the townships around Port Elizabeth and further north in the vicinity of East London achieved a distinctive notoriety for unruliness and defiance of white authority. Many of the Xhosa-speaking people who inhabited the region regarded themselves as the premier standard-bearers of black resistance, identifying not only with the ANC but with Umkhonto we Sizwe. Many prominent ANC leaders traced their origins to the Eastern Cape. In 1980, South Africa's intelligence service — then named the Bureau of State Security — warned that the region would explode in political turmoil. The reasons for this assessment lay in years of 'official neglect that had left the region's black townships among the poorest in the country and the gap between black and white living standards among the widest'.[89] In March and April 1985, this premonition was fulfilled.

After a period of quiescence, the Port Elizabeth Black Peoples' Organization (PEBCO) had once again re-built its political reputation and had joined the UDF as a regional affiliate. Formed in 1979, PEBCO had experienced the kind of swings in political popularity typical of large numbers of civic associations. Its rise to prominence was matched by an equally swift plunge into internal disarray and inactivity. On 17 February, PEBCO called for a three-day stayaway beginning 16 March. It urged black residents of the townships encircling Port Elizabeth to stay away from work, to boycott shops in both the central business district and the outlying areas, and to refuse to use the bus service to protest gasoline price increases, the rising cost of living, increased bus and train fares, and mass unemployment.[90] Rival political organizations (notably AZAPO and major trade unions, including FOSATU, CUSA, CCAWUSA, AFCWU/FCWU, GWU, and the Domestic Workers' Union) refused to support this call for the three-day 'Black Weekend' stayaway on the grounds that working-class people had been inadequately consulted in its planning.

This disagreement over strategy, however, reflected divisions between community organizations and trade unions, between coloured and African workers, and (generally in Port Elizabeth) between employed and unemployed, which hindered the development of an organized working-class politics in the region. On the one side, PEBCO and MACWUSA embodied the 'populist' current, talking in terms of the national-democratic tradition and concentrating on building mass-based community organizations. On the other side, the National Automobile and Allied Workers' Union (NAAWU) — the most powerful FOSATU affiliate in the area — embraced an orthodox 'workerist' postion, concentrating on shop-floor grievances and refusing to enter into alliances with community organizations. The working class in the Port Elizabeth-Uitenhage region was almost equally divided between coloured and African. With unemployment estimated at 35 per cent coupled with high levels of poverty, militant youth congresses emerged, drawing support from the unemployed in particular. As Swilling argued: 'It is difficult to gain insight into the consciousness of these youths. They are unemployed, badly educated, and younger than the average activist. They come mainly from squatter areas, and generally have not been ade-quately educated within political organizations. As the com-munity organizations established dominance, the youth were drawn into political activity without substantially altering their positions on the fringes of legality ... they confront all forms of authority without always getting approval from community organizations.'[91] The combination of historic conflict between the trade unions and the community organizations, the mistrust of the radical populism of the unemployed youth, and the fact that the appeal for the 'Black Weekend' stayaway was only made in the racially-separate African residential areas lay behind the reluctance of the trade unions to support the action.

Despite these internecine quarrels, the strike was highly successful. Tony Gilson, chairman of the Port Elizabeth Chamber of Commerce, admitted that the work stoppage was 'pretty widespread. It did definitely have an impact on business.' 'The city centre resembled a ghost town' and impartial observers confirmed that the boycott of white shops was almost 100 per cent effective. A series of bloody confrontations between police and youth left at least twelve dead. Some were killed when police fired into crowds and the remainder died in clashes associated with arson attacks on the homes of town councillors.[92] Tear gas, rubber bullets, and birdshot were used to disperse gangs of youths who stoned and petrol-bombed government offices, police vehicles and patrols, and the shops and homes of those depicted as 'collaborators'. The effectiveness of these attacks across South Africa's riot-torn townships prompted the Commissioner of Police, General Johan Coetzee, to complain that members of the SAP had 'become the prime target of rioters in the recent unrest'. 'It has become evident', he contended,' that there was a well-organized attempt to kill, maim and injure policemen. ... Four policemen had already been killed and several others injured in recent attacks after members of the SA Police had been lured into ambush-type situations. ... The police were now victims of petrol and acid bombs and in some cases had been shot at.'[93]

Over seventy people were killed in the Eastern Cape region in the immediate aftermath of the 16-18 March 'Black Weekend' stayaway. Police violence reached an apogee on 21 March with the unprovoked killing of at least twenty unarmed black people at Langa township outside Uitenhage. Ironically, the Langa shootings occurred on the twenty-fifth anniversary of the 1960 Sharpeville massacre in which sixty-nine black people, gathered peacefully in an 'anti-pass' demonstration, were gunned down. In this latest tragedy, police opened fire with automatic weapons and shotguns, leaving a street beside a squatter camp littered with bodies and clothing. In the official version of events, Minister of Law and Order, Louis Le Grange, claimed that a nineteen-man police patrol had been first surrounded before they acted in self-defense, firing into a crowd of about 4,000 black rioters attacking them with stones, sticks, and firebombs. However, black people who witnessed the killings gave a radically different account. In sworn affidavits, numerous survivors of the incident claimed that an armoured personnel carrier at the crest of a slight incline had blocked the advance of a procession of 500 people on their way to nearby Kwanobuhle to attend a funeral. The killings began as a young boy riding a bicycle ahead of the marchers was shot without warning. In the fusillade that followed, police fired indiscriminately into the crowd from both front and rear, killing fleeing people who were trapped in the crossfire.[94]

The Langa massacre caused astonishment among many whites, prompting international outrage as well as disbelief from white liberal organizations at home. In order to deflect this growing concern, the authorities ordered a judicial inquiry under a Supreme Court judge, Donald Kannemeyer. In addition, a six-member 'fact-finding' team from the white opposition Progressive Federal Party conducted its own inquiry. The results of this independent investigation directly contradicted the official account. The independent report concluded that the police had fired without warning or provocation in a deliberate action that was 'punitive, not preventative' — as one white member of Parliament put it.[95] In subsequent weeks, the official version of the Langa incident gradually came unravelled. In sworn testimony before the official judicial inquiry, the police officer in charge during the incident offered an account at variance with Louis Le Grange's original pronouncement. This confirmed the widely-held suspicion that the police had fired without warning into a peaceful procession of funeral mourners.[96]

As word of the bloodbath spread, Langa and nearby Kwanobuhle exploded. For the next two days, 'Uitenhage was silent. ... The town's black workforce was conspicuous by its absence from the streets during the rush hour and no buses were seen in the township[s].' Langa was in 'a state of virtual seige ... as policemen in an assortment of vehicles, including armoured personnel carriers, mounted roadblocks at every entrance'.[97] Uitenhage was South Africa's automotive centre, just north of Port Elizabeth along the Indian Ocean coastline. The outlying townships of Langa and Kwanobuhle provide the bulk of the black labour for the automobile-related plants there. In reprisals for the Langa killings, crowds attacked town councillors and black policemen, seen as accomplices of the white minority regime. The security police banned all meetings in the Uitenhage townships, warning residents not to assemble in groups of more than four.[98] Despite this, Kwanobuhle was a scene of devastation. 'There's a veil of teargas over the town, houses are burning, helicopters are circling — it's a frightening atmosphere.' In the widespread 'revenge attacks' against those suspected of collaboration, eighteen houses were burned down in Tinus, another nearby township. In Kwanobuhle, youths destroyed the homes of at least eighteen policemen in petrol bomb attacks and looted shops that refused to support the hastily-organized stay-away. Angry mobs killed and burned at least seven blacks accused of being 'sell-outs', including T.B. Kinikini, the only remaining town councillor in Kwanobuhle. He had refused to resign. The owner of a funeral parlor, Kinikini had amassed a small fortune by township standards. His $30,000 home, a luxury mansion compared with the rudimentary dwellings of most township residents, was ransacked and burned.[99]

On 24 March, army and police units threw a cordon around Uitenhage as a crowd estimated at 35,000 from surrounding townships attended a funeral for the most recent black victims of the political unrest. Troops and police stood guard impassively along the route of the funeral procession and at strategic points — including the entrances to residential areas and factory gates — in and around Uitenhage. As the crowd converged on Kwanobuhle, government troops made no attempt to halt or disrupt it. In Kwanobuhle, the scene after three days of rioting resembled a war zone: streets were blackened by petrol bombs, barricades partially blocked main thoroughfares, and properties — homes, stores, and vehicles — owned by whites or suspected allies of the white minority regime smouldered under a grey winter sky.

Armed white civilians guarded the suburban residential zones next to the black townships. These individuals did not fit the stereotype of the affluent white middle class. Without private tennis courts or swimming pools (the badges of the sheltered segments of the white petty bourgeoisie) they owned only modest and unpretentious tin-roofed houses symbolizing their relative proximity on the economic ladder to the emergent black petty bourgeoisie.[100]

The Langa killings registered a decisive turning-point in the cycle of townships violence. After the Sharpeville massacre a quarter of a century earlier, the white authorities dealt with political turmoil in the all-too-familiar crackdowns on all forms of public dissent. In the 1980s, the authorities were as reliant as ever on force and violence. However, they seemed adrift ideologically, 'unable to provide any other answer to the questions

spawned by their own troubled racial history, reaching reflex-
ively for an iron fist to cope with a black anger whose readiness
for violence seems only to deepen in the face of official force'.[101]
The National Party abandoned the Verwoerdian formula
dictating that urban blacks did not qualify as permanent residents of 'white South Africa' and instead were relegated to
citizenship in the so-called 'tribal'' Homelands. But the Botha
regime was unable to find convincing alternatives to cope with
an urban black working class that had become an established
feature of South African economic life. Embattled and defensive,
Pretoria seemed determined not to abandon the official explanation that the blame for the long wave of political unrest could be
placed squarely on small groups of 'agitators' and 'intimidators'.
In shrill speeches, Botha declared repeatedly that the government would not tolerate violent dissent and that 'appropriate
steps' would be taken to restore calm.

The reality behind the rhetoric seemed to indicate an abrupt
change in police tactics. The recurrent failure of the security
forces to quell black unrest in the Eastern Cape produced a
ratchet-like escalation of repressive techniques. The Kennemeyer
Commission investigating the Langa shootings discovered that
the SAP had surreptitiously shifted from normal riot-control
procedures to lethal weapons and shoot-to-kill orders. It was
revealed that at least six weeks before the 21 March fatalities the
police counterinsurgency chiefs at national police headquarters
in Pretoria had extended permission to the Eastern Cape police
to switch from light birdshot to heavy buckshot in their anti-riot
shotguns, and were authorized to open fire with 9mm service
revolvers on 'selected and properly identified targets'. Two days
before the Langa incident, police headquarters in Pretoria issued
a general order to 'eliminate' anyone seen throwing acid or
petrol bombs. It was also disclosed that not only had police shot
those who had fallen to the ground but that seventeen of the
twenty confirmed dead had been shot in the back.[102]

'Bloody Thursday' at Langa sparked widespread rioting and
protest demonstrations throughout South Africa. In what had
become a regular occurrence, police headquarters ritualistically
recited the daily liturgy of clashes: Alexandra township,
northeast of Johannesburg, erupted in full-scale rioting; clashes
with police occurred in the Orange Free State at Parys, Welkom,
and Bloemfontein; and police were stoned at Galeshewe town-

ship near Kimberley, a diamond centre 300 miles southwest of Johannesburg. Serious confrontations between police and crowds were reported throughout the Eastern Cape.[103] Under heightened pressure, twenty-two councillors resigned from the Kayamnandi town council (overseeing New Brighton and Kwazekele townships outside Port Elizabeth). All in all, an estimated forty-six councillors in the Eastern Cape gave up their posts in the wake of the Langa massacre.[104]

The township violence that had gripped the country since August 1984 in an ever-widening confrontation with the white authorities had clearly moved beyond its initial causes, including rent increases, inferior education, and the tricameral Parliament election fraud. By late March 1985, it had become a broader challenge to the entire edifice of white minority rule. The defiant mood in the Eastern Cape townships clearly undermined and rendered anachronistic the official offer of vague and undefined political concessions for urban black residents. In most of these areas the visible symbols of *apartheid* — community councils, government offices and buildings, liquor outlets, the shops and properties of those deemed surrogates for white minority rule — lay in ruins, rapidly giving way to the reality of repressive force. In order to quell the political unrest that appeared endemic, on 22 March Pretoria issued a year-long banning on all indoor meetings dealing with school boycotts. On 29 March, the security forces ordered a blanket prohibition forbidding outdoor gatherings in eighteen magisterial districts in the Eastern Cape and parts of the Transvaal, prohibited indoor meetings aimed at organizing industrial action, and outlawed meetings of the UDF and twenty-eight other organizations for three months. The General Secretary of the South African Council of Churches, the Reverend Beyers Naude, condemned this clampdown as 'an act of desperation on the part of the Government to stem the tide of liberation'.[105] In Pretoria, Deputy Foreign Minister, Louis Nel, justified the actions by blaming the ANC for the unrest, linking both the ANC and the South African Communist Party to the UDF. 'There is incontrovertible evidence of an orchestrated attempt by forces from beyond our border, joined by radical elements inside the country', he argued, 'to make the country ungovernable and to bring about a revolutionary situation.'[106] This accusation marked the first time the outlawed ANC had been directly accused of provoking the wave of resistance.[107]

On 1 April, the Deputy Minister of Defence and of Law and Order confirmed that 'elements of the Defence Force have been deployed in support of the SA police in the Eastern Cape'.[108] Pretoria also disclosed that SADF units were 'assisting police in countering unrest in the East Rand, including the township of Tembisa'.[109] This display of military force represented an 'implicit acknowledgement that the Government's writ in such places runs only because the white authorities maintain massive superiority in firepower over a largely unarmed black population'.[110] At Zwide outside Port Elizabeth, an estimated 35,000 mourners gathered for what local organizers recalled as the largest funeral in memory. The coffins of unrest victims were draped with the distinctive black, green, and gold banners of the ANC. After the peaceful graveside ceremonies were over, clashes occurred between police and angry crowds. In nearby New Brighton, vicious confrontations took place as police used rubber bullets, teargas, and birdshot to disperse crowds. SADF and SAP roadblocks controlled all access to the townships in the Port Elizabeth and Uitenhage area. Heavily-armed police and the SADF mounted joint patrols in the townships.[111]

The stubbornness and determination of township residents in the Eastern Cape seemed to confirm the longstanding reputation of the region as the cradle of national resistance to white minority rule. A number of ingredients had contributed to the entrenchment of political resistance in the area. Some analysts contended that the white residents of the Eastern Cape were among those who embraced South Africa's crudest forms of racism. The Homelands policy had reached its highest stage of advancement there with the creation of not one, but two, Homelands for Xhosa-speakers — the Transkei and the Ciskei. Xhosa-speaking people — the most urbanized of South Africa's many ethnic groups — bristled at the blatantly 'tribalist' features of Chief Gatsha Buthelezi's Inkatha movement, the only political organization Buthelezi allowed in the fragmented KwaZulu Homeland, the supposed 'home' for six-million Zulu-speaking people largely confined to the Natal region. Most analysts claimed that the Inkatha movement — accommodationist in substance if not in tone — had been largely responsible for extinguishing the flames of unrest in Natal.[112]

In the seemingly endless cycle of violence that gripped the black townships, a discernible pattern took shape that caused anxiety within the higher circles of the Botha regime. Town councillors and black police increasingly became the main targets for political rage. When the unrest had begun, black activists had drawn distinctions between different categories of policemen. Those township residents who were recruited as body-guards protecting town councillors and their property were regarded as quislings because the community councils were seen as nothing more than fronts for white minority rule. In contrast, black members of the SAP — except for officers who had achieved notoriety for their brutality against fellow-blacks — were perceived as pitiful men who were merely doing a job, albeit in the pay of their white masters. Over the course of the six-month-long political turbulence, these finely-tuned distinctions collapsed. By official estimates, black police made up over 40 per cent of the 45,000-member SAP.[113] They played an increasingly wider role in the handling of the political disturbances. There was mounting circumstantial evidence that black security police had expanded their duties beyond the underworld of infiltration and surveillance to also include the roles of *agents-provocateurs*. In addition, it was beyond dispute that the SAP had used Zulu-speaking police to exploit rivalries between Zulu- and Xhosa-speakers. The deployment of Zulu-speaking police to Langa at the time of the massacre caused 'tremendous resentment' among local residents who referred to these 'outsiders' as 'Gatsha's impis'.[114]

'The deployment of the SADF in the eastern Cape', the *Cape Times* editorialized, 'confirms the unhappy trend in internal security policy which was evident in the Vaal Triangle last year.'[115] The SADF presence in the riot-torn townships 'is much greater than most people realize'. In Port Elizabeth's townships of New Brighton, Zwide, and Kwazakele and in Uitenhage's Kwanobuhle and Langa, soldiers 'were doing a great deal more than just playing "the supporting role" which the SADF claims'. Army units established temporary encampments at entrances to townships, policed and manned roadblocks, and performed guard-duty at government buildings. Armed police caravans escorted delivery vehicles into Port Elizabeth's townships. Meanwhile, some of the Eastern Cape's black areas had become virtually ungovernable. The Kwanobuhle town council in Uitenhage, the Llingelihle village council in Cradock, and the Kwanomzano community council in Humansdorp collapsed within a space of a few weeks. 'Mob executions by burning', it was reported, 'continue to be the standard form of "punishment" meted out to ['collaborators'].' Black policemen and their families were evacuated from Uitenhage's townships in the middle of the night after the 'Bloody Thursday' killings because 'rampaging mobs stoned and burned their homes'.[116]

On 13 April, an unprecedented gathering of between 60,000 and 80,000 mourners attended the largest funeral ever held in South Africa at Kwanobuhle for twenty-seven victims of the unrest. Fikile Kobese, president of the Motor Components and Allied Workers' Union, chaired the memorial service. The funeral ceremony 'mixed solemnity with politics, mourning with exhortation and clenched fists with the soft swell of African singing'.[117] As helicopters and light aircraft hovered over the area, speakers denounced the white minority regime as 'fascist' and praised the ANC. In a hitherto rare display of open defiance, the demonstrators who packed the soccer stadium unfurled an array of flags and banners. Laden with emotion, funerals had become vehicles for mass mobilization, offering a blend of religion and political proselytization, where the songs of various Christian denominations mixed with the anthems of black nationalism and slogans of the armed struggle.[118]

The number of funerals for unrest victims that took place in the following weeks seemed to mark a new phase of unrest. The rioting, burning, and looting spread to the coloured areas of Rosedale and Blikkiesdorp. 'Black communities in the eastern Cape', it was reported, 'are highly politicised and readily associate any state institutions with their hapless lot.'[119] Soldiers in the Port Elizabeth area were issued with live ammunition and patrolled the townships 'side-by-side with the police'. The SADF took 'a direct part in the frontline action, doing what police officers in charge require[d] them to do'.[120] According to the *Sunday Times* (U.K.): 'When a long convoy of armoured cars carrying troops and police moved two weeks ago into Kwanobuhle, they were confronting a township which had degenerated into lawlessness. Black radicals linked to the UDF claimed to have taken over power because the local black councillors had been driven out and the police could not keep control. The troops have set up a base in the centre of Kwanobuhle from which to send out armed patrols. ... Every single one of the 32 black policemen's houses in Kwanobuhle has been destroyed. A new block is being built where they will live together for greater protection. Troops from seven Cape regiments are involved in the present operation.'[121] Temporary police stations were also established in Zwide and at Tinus near Fort Beaufort because the local police had been forced to leave the areas. Further inland, 'there are still no-go areas where police venture only in force and anyone with a white face is risking his life'. One such place was Bontrug township near Kirkwood. In less than two months, it was transformed from a scenic holiday resort to what the *Eastern Province Herald* called a 'little Rhodesia', where farmers installed floodlights and wire fences and demanded nightly army patrols.[122] At the end of May, the Minister of Law and Order acknowledged that the popular unrest was no longer restricted to larger metropolitan areas and the Eastern Cape. Since January, the revolt had spread widely taking in small rural towns in all four provinces. In April alone, Pretoria reported more than 1,500 incidents of violence, a 30 per cent increase over the previous month.[123]

The Workplace Struggles of Black Miners

The mining industry was the centerpiece of South African economic prosperity for nearly a century. Despite its carefully-groomed image of beneficence and respectability, it remained, in the words of Cyril Ramaphosa, the leader of the NUM, 'the nub of racial discrimination'. In the course of its rapid rise to prominence within the labour movement, the NUM initially eschewed political demands but was eventually — along with the entire independent black trade union movement — forced to confront the political situation of its membership. The structure and organization of not only the mining industry but also each individual mine embodied the reality of *apartheid*. Black workers organized into underground work-teams experienced first-hand the fusion of economic exploitation and racial oppression through contact with white labour supervisors of the white supremacist Mine Workers' Union.

The black miners — about 40 per cent of whom were foreign migrants — were housed in single-sex barracks-like compounds (with upwards of twenty people in a single room), separated from outside influences, and forced to communicate in a specialized language (called *fanakalo*) used exclusively in the mines to ensure unquestioning obedience to management. They received an average wage of $175 per month, one-sixth the rate for white miners. Daily rations consisted in the main of corn porridge and beans, with meat three times per week.[124] These constraints were ample testimony to the fragility of capitalist rule on the mines where class warfare has always characterized relations between white management and black labour.

While the working conditions in the mining industry had remained unchanged for decades, the political circumstances were considerably different. Black miners scattered along the Reef and in the Orange Free State goldfields had coalesced around the NUM and membership soared. The NUM provided security for disenfranchised black workers who wanted to participate in the alleviation of their own misery. In order to ensure discipline and control over its increasingly restive membership, the union had built a tight-knit structure with recognizable lines of authority including regional and branch committees, and shop stewards' councils at each work-site.[125] It quickly became the principal means for collective organization and direct action in the mining industry, and equally important, emerged as part of the broad social vanguard of the country's black masses.

Township protests in the Eastern Cape proceeded in tandem with growing tensions on the gold mines. On 21 March, more than 42,000 black workers at Anglo-American's Vaal Reefs mining complex near Klerksdorp, 120 miles west of Johannesburg, went on strike, halting production at the world's largest gold mine. Anglo-American announced that this work stoppage was the largest ever recorded at a single mine in South Africa.[126] At least thirty-five miners were seriously injured the next day after police opened fire on a large crowd.[127]

In subsequent months, the growing insurgency amongst mine workers, particularly at Vaal Reefs and the nearby Anglo Vaal mine, took the form of deliberate slowdowns and intermittent walkouts where workers pressed for higher wages and improved working conditions. This anchor was contagious. The outbreak of what management deemed riotous behavior and labour unruliness had the cumulative effect of building confidence among the black mine workers. The NUM also initiated a host of localized boycott campaigns against liquor outlets, mine-owned concession stores, and taxi services on site. Mining companies reported numerous incidents of industrial sabotage of 'unknown origin'.[128]

Together, the Vaal Reefs and Anglo Vaal mining operations contributed one-sixth of South Africa's total gold production that in turn accounted for about one-half the country's export earnings. On 26-7 April, company officials dismissed 14,500 black miners at Vaal Reefs — more than a quarter of the black labour force and almost the entire assembly of underground workcrews — and 3,000 black workers at Anglo Vaal, claiming that those laid off had ignored authorized procedures for settling disputes. At Anglo Vaal, management called in police reinforcements who dispersed striking workers with rubber bullets, teargas, and shotguns. Thousands of dismissed employees were returned to the Homelands in a 'bus-lift' organized by the company.[129] Anglo-American Corporation claimed that the mass firings at both mining sites had been necessary in order to prevent anarchy. On 30 April, powerful bomb blasts ripped through two Anglo-American offices in the centre of Johannesburg. Umkhonto we Sizwe claimed responsibility, announcing that they 'signal our intention to intervene on the side of our workers in the battle against employers and the state, our intention to come to our workers' defense'.[130]

Behind these intermittent skirmishes pitting management against workers in the goldfields, a much broader confrontation between the powerful mining companies and the NUM loomed. South Africa's giant mining conglomerates produce 70 per cent of the gold mined in the west. Estimated at 662 tons in 1984, this output was more than double the total gold production of the Soviet Union. Even in a year of low gold prices, the metal accounted for half of South Africa's foreign earnings. In 1984, government taxes on the gold mining houses yielded one-tenth of official state revenues. Traditionally, the country's mining companies had relied upon a system of migrant labour to satisfy their huge demand for low-cost labour and reserved the cream of the occupational categories for well-paid white wage-earners. No more than 3 per cent of black mineworkers was permitted by law to live with their families near their workplace. The other 97 per cent must be migrants, living alone in overcrowded hostels. Conflict was inevitable. 'For more than two years', Alan Cowell asserted, 'the [mining] industry has been locked in increasing dispute, caught between its own traditions of paternalism and autocracy and the growing strength of a trade union whose demands far outstrip the companies' readiness or ability for compromise.'[131]

The NUM had reached formal agreements at fifteen of the country's forty-three gold mines. Eight of these settlements were signed with Anglo-American Corporation, a multinational giant that had nurtured a reputation for liberalized labour relations. The NUM claimed a membership of 110,000 — more than half of whom had paid their dues — and a total following of perhaps 200,000 out of South Africa's estimated 550,000 black mine workers.

During the first four months of 1985, more than 60,000 black miners had participated in strikes or work stoppages of some sort.[132] In May, the NUM launched its 'strategy of resistance' at the point of production, where strikes and boycotts were combined with 'work-to-rule' tactics that slowed production but purposefully did not contravene provisions of the Mines and Works Act. As Cyril Ramaphosa argued, 'We place more emphasis on worker organization at the workplace. ... If you start on other issues you are not able to build a strong union, cohesive in nature and strong enough to tackle issues outside the workplace. Workers don't have to be told that they are exploited as a class by the capitalist system. Our union's task is to arouse working-class consciousness among the miners.'[133]

The mining industry was the last bastion of statutory job reservation in the private sector. Longstanding regulations prescribed that only white wage-earners could hold what were called 'blasting certificates', necessary not only for handling and charging explosives but vital for promotion. For the NUM, the workplace struggle to abolish job reservation assumed the character of a secular crusade. The union claimed that the use of black miners to do 'white jobs' at lower wages was an open secret: mine managements contravened the terms of the Mines and Works Act, the statute that reserved certain jobs for 'scheduled persons' (that is, white miners). The union also targeted racist practices at the workplace, including physical assaults by white supervisors, promising that its members would retaliate in self-defense.[134]

The simmering disputes in the mines widened the breach between the powerful Chamber of Mines and politically conscious black miners. Some mining companies wanted to provoke the NUM into a showdown in order to cripple the union's growing influence. Hardliners speculated that the high rate of unemployment in South Africa — coupled with the fact that the average annual income for black mine workers was three to four times higher than that of work-seekers in neighbouring countries — would dissuade the NUM from strike actions of indefinite duration. In the contract negotiations that began in earnest in May, the NUM aimed for across-the-board wage increases of 40 per cent, extra money for dangerous work at the most hazardous mines, and the abolition of job reservation. Despite consistent gains that had narrowed the gap between white and black earnings in the industry, the ratio between different wage rates still stood at six to one.[135]

The Drift Toward Undeclared Civil War

The Botha Regime and the Search for Moderate Allies

On 1 May 1985, coordinated May Day rallies were held throughout South Africa, denouncing both economic hardship and the lack of political rights under white minority rule. The Joint May Day Coordinating Committee — representing thirty-one black trade unions — organized a series of actions. In Uitenhage and Port Elizabeth, more than 3,000 workers attended May Day events despite massive police and army parades in armoured personnel carriers through the nearby townships the previous day. In the Cape peninsula, students staged a one-day boycott of classes in solidarity with the student protests in the Eastern Cape where the Department of Education had closed all high schools in an effort to weaken participation. In Natal, May Day events were marked by rallies in the major industrial areas of Durban and Pietermaritzburg. More than 5,000 workers attended the Durban event sponsored by FOSATU and FCWU. In the Vaal Triangle, shops and businesses closed for five hours on May Day and high school students staged a massive boycott. Meetings were held in Soweto, Lenasia, and Alexandra. In Johannesburg itself, police used tear gas to disperse crowds of workers who had congregated for a rally at the headquarters of the South African Council of Churches. In the northern Transvaal, at the University of the North in Pietersburg, thousands of students and township residents clashed with the Lebowa police who attempted to disperse a rally.[136]

In the meantime, Pretoria took significant steps — combining reform and repression — to contain the mounting political challenge from below. In a highly-orchestrated media event, President P.W. Botha received a rare display of uncritical black support at the 75th anniversary Easter weekend celebrations organized by the Zion Christian Church (ZCC). With an estimated membership of 4 to 5 million well-disciplined followers, the ZCC was the largest of South Africa's black separatist churches. The young leader of the religious section, Bishop Barnabas Lekganyane, delivered the following injunction to the worshippers who had gathered on a remote farm in the northern Transvaal for the annual pilgrimage and convocation: 'Love and peace. The key to them is obedience to the laws of the headmen, the homeland governments, and the government of the Republic of South Africa.' This tactical alliance between the National Party and the ZCC was nothing new. For decades, the Church had functioned as a *de facto* buffer buttressing the white regime against subversion. 'At the very least', Patrick Lawrence suggested, 'ZCC support for the government guarantees the neutrality of the ZCC faithful in the townships where blacks, especially the young and unemployed, are increasingly defiant of authority. In some situations, it may facilitate, with official connivance or encouragement, the emergence of black vigilantes in favor of upholding "law and order" against the threat of anarchy.'[137]

In another well-timed media event, the minority regime announced its intention to repeal two longstanding laws forbidding sex and marriage between races. The Conservative Party and the HNP denounced the repeal as further evidence that the Botha regime had abandoned South Africa's whites to the vagaries of international opinion. Nevertheless, white liberals welcomed the decision as a breach in the fabric of *apartheid*, indicating a move towards a more flexible approach to race relations.[138] In addition, the Department of Cooperation, Development, and Education announced a reprieve for an estimated 700,000 black people living in fifty-two townships once threatened by forced removals to the Homelands. Yet this moratorium did not include a cancellation of plans to uproot forcibly the remaining areas of black freehold title surrounded by white-owned farm lands.[139]

Behind this reformist facade, Pretoria increasingly turned to the military option in order to quell township protests. The 90,000 men in South Africa's full-time military establishment included a 20,000-man Permanent Fighting Force made up of about one-quarter black soldiers, plus 55,000 national servicemen, almost all white conscripts. An additional Citizen Force numbered about 15,000. Finally, the Active Reserve totalled more than 130,000 part-timers available for immediate call-up. Almost one-third of South Africa's military preparedness programme was devoted to urban warfare training, indicating the preoccupation of the military command with the threat of internal subversion and domestic turmoil.[140] The increased use of both the SAP and SADF to blockade troubled townships in order to 'normalize living conditions'[141] prompted the PFP's van Zyl Slabbert to warn that the army was becoming 'politicised' and had lost its 'image of neutrality'.[142]

In early May, the unexplained deaths in detention of at least four persons (including Andries Raditsela, a senior shop steward in the Chemical Workers' Union and an executive member of FOSATU; and Sipho Mutsi, a student activist affiliated to COSAS in Odendaalsrust in the Orange Free State) rekindled fears that the security police had once again reverted to physical torture as a means of exacting confessions and information from political detainees. On 14 May, nearly 30,000 mourners under heavy police and army surveillance attended Raditsela's funeral in Tsakane on the East Rand. In a significant demonstration of solidarity, both FOSATU and CUSA along with the UDF and AZAPO endorsed a nationwide two-hour work stoppage in which an estimated 70,000 workers participated to mark Raditsela's death.[143]

These deaths in detention highlighted the more than 10,000 arrests on charges relating to the unrest between September 1984 and 22 March 1985.[144] In May 1985, a record number of about fifty persons were facing treason charges. The key allegation in the treason indictment was that the accused 'gave succor to a "revolutionary alliance" comprising the SACP, the ANC, the SA Congress of Trade Unions (SACTU), the Congress Movement and the Congress Alliance'.[145] According to the prosecution, the main objective of this 'sinister web' of organizations was 'the downfall of the state' and the 'armed seizure of power'. The prosecution's motive in seeking indictments under common law seemed to suggest the desire to depoliticize the 'treason trials' and alternatively present the accused as common criminals.[146]

Factional Struggles Between Anti-Apartheid Organizations

The schism between the UDF and AZAPO/National Forum had ideological roots. As the descendant of Black Consciousness, AZAPO retained the view that white liberal beliefs were ultimately opposed to black ambitions for liberation. In contrast, the UDF advocated alliances with those who shared the same general anti-*apartheid* commitment to a 'one-person one-vote' formula.

Relations between the two organizations were marked by the kind of polemics and verbal jousting that typically erupt among rival political groups competing for support. Yet in 1985 the particularly acrimonious debate deteriorated into factional bloodletting. Members of the UDF and AZAPO became entangled in a cycle of retaliatory petrol bombings, stabbings, abductions, and other attacks that left scores of activists homeless and dead. A leading black journalist, Percy Qoboza, lamented that the rising crescendo of violent incidents. Pitting one radical group against another was leaving the mass of the people 'confused, bewildered, and directionless', and playing into Pretoria's hands.[147]

The animosity between the UDF and AZAPO/National Forum should not be overestimated. Nevertheless, significant political differences both in substance and in style made any working alliance between them fragile and tenuous. Tensions surfaced around the January 1985 Kennedy visit. The UDF national executive stood behind the trip as a means of rallying international support for the anti-*apartheid* struggle. AZAPO/National Forum argued that an uncritical support for the Kennedy tour only bolstered liberalism. In addition, they maintained a longstanding grievance that the UDF tended to exclude its rivals from various political forums, including funerals, and instead 'hijacked' them to serve their own organizational ends.

In April and May, the intensified conflict between the UDF and AZAPO erupted into 'violent clashes' in the Transvaal and the Eastern Cape. The Front blamed 'agents of *apartheid*' (who acted in the names of the two organizations) of distributing bogus pamphlets, physically assulting members, and petrol-bombing homes.[148] Similarly, AZAPO declared: 'We are not fooled into believing that these senseless acts of vandalism and political hooliganism are the work of any political organization. It is clearly the work of those who are committed to nurturing conflict in our community.'[149] In the midst of this sectarian imbroglio, state-sponsored *agents-provocateurs* almost certainly exploited the already inflamed situation between the organizations. The UDF and AZAPO believed that police agents masquerading as members of one or the other group had conducted many of the attacks, but admitted that members of both organizations had been involved in violence. This discord within the anti-*apartheid* ranks prompted the ANC to issue one of its rare public communiques from its Lusaka headquarters, emphasizing that 'the careful preservation of our unity' must be 'made a top priority'. 'Let us stop the enemy from exploiting the temporary problems between UDF and AZAPO', the communique urged. 'We should not give comfort to an increasingly uncomfortable and frightened regime.'[150]

In New Brighton township, the truce committee formed to resolve the continuing conflict between the UDF and AZAPO failed to prevent a further outbreak of violence.[151] Eventually, a church-sponsored peace mission led by Bishop Desmond Tutu was able to defuse the in-fighting. On 19 May, UDF and AZAPO speakers shared platforms in Soweto, KwaThema on the East Rand, the Vaal Triangle, and Mohlakeng, near Randfontein, as part of the 'peace initiative'.[152] Another symbolic reunion took place in Soweto at the annual 16 June commemoration of the 1976-7 uprising. In a jointly-sponsored event, speakers from both organizations 'stressed the need for unity'. This service came three days after South African commandos raided Gaborone, capital of Botswana, to strike at insurgent 'safe houses' and other installations there alleged to have formed a 'nerve centre' of the ANC.[153]

The sequence of events that led to the violent quarrels between the UDF and AZAPO was only disclosed ten months later when AZAPO formally expelled the self-styled 'Reverend' Mzwandile Maqina for breach of conduct. An ex-teacher, playwright, and former political detainee, Maqina 'shot into prominence' after he founded iBandla LikaNtu Church and a Port Elizabeth vigilante group, called 'Roots', in New Brighton. As a 'self-proclaimed AZAPO leader' who never formally held an official position in the organization, Maqina vehemently opposed Port Elizabeth's highly successful 16-18 March 'Black Weekend' stayaway and boycott organized by the UDF-affiliated PEBCO and COSAS. This action prompted UDF-AZAPO confrontations. Maqina 'led AZAPO members in their bloody clashes with UDF supporters in Port Elizabeth's townships ... in which more than a dozen people died — clashes which led to confrontations between the two organizations throughout the country'.[154]

The Undeclared State of Terror

Pretoria pronounced the March 1984 Nkomati Accord with Mozambique as the 'death blow' to the ANC's campaign of armed struggle. In 1984, reported ANC attacks did decline to forty-four in contrast to fifty-six in 1983. The latter figure represented the largest number of attacks in a single year since the twenty-four-year-old ANC guerrilla campaign resumed in earnest after the 1976-7 Soweto rebellion. General Constand Viljoen had justified the SADF's Gaborone raid by declaring that Botswana had replaced Mozambique as the ANC's principal infiltration route into South Africa. In the first half of 1985, guerrilla insurgents had staged thirty-four separate attacks.[155] The actions, timed to correspond to the annual 16 June commemorative services, seemed to indicate that the ANC underground was able to take advantage of the persistent conflict to establish a more or less permanent infrastructure in black townships.[156]

On the other side of the equation, a series of incidents indicated strongly that the joint military police command had revived a number of previously latent options in their efforts to crush the popular unrest in the townships. Unmistakable signs pointed to the conclusion that the security forces had taken irrevocable steps toward a 'Latin American-style' solution to the political crisis. According to the National Medical and Dental Association of South Africa (NAMSA), police were stationed at area hospitals in order to arrest any black admitted with gunshot wounds. Those arrested were charged with riotous assembly, and armed guards were posted at their bedsides. NAMSA — an organization that broke away from the officially recognized Medical Association of South Africa because of the latter's failure to act against the medical personnel who treated Steve Biko before he died in police custody in 1977 — also accused the medical authorities at the state-run hospitals of colluding with the police. As a consequence, many injured blacks were forced to seek medical treatment clandestinely or went without it.[157]

There were also signs that the security forces had come close to an orchestrated reign of terror. Widespread reports of mysterious firebombings of the homes of community and student leaders occurred with increasing regularity over the period of political unrest.[158] The white authorities blamed these attacks on internecine rivalries between UDF and AZAPO. However, anti-*apartheid* activists attributed them, and the numerous deaths and serious injuries which resulted, to gangs of vigilantes operating under the umbrella of the security forces outside official channels.[159]

As the political unrest spread and intensified, both the number of unexplained deaths in police custody and the number of disappearances increased sharply.[160] In May, three key PEBCO leaders — Qaqawuli Godolozi, Sipho Hashe, and Champion Galela — vanished.[161] These abductions heightened the sense that the white authorities were somehow responsible for earlier disappearances that had escaped public scrutiny. The disclosure in late May that at least fifty unidentified bodies had been buried secretly in unmarked graves at Zwide cemetery near Port Elizabeth fuelled speculation that the security forces had systematically attempted to conceal the number of deaths attributable to the rebellion. The disclaimer that the corpses were those of 'paupers' who had died in Port Elizabeth Hospital undermined further the credibility of all official explanations concerning any aspect of the political situation.[162]

The strife in the townships moved into a new phase. The initial wave of political unrest had placed town councillors, black policemen, and other recognized collaborators on the defensive. Weakened by these early defeats and unable to obtain the necessary protection from the SADF and the SAP, the local puppets tried to regain lost ground. In a dramatic yet certainly not isolated illustration of this, town councillors and black businessmen in Thabong location (near Welkom in the Orange Free State) formed vigilante bands of migrant labourers who operated with impunity in disrupting gatherings of 'arsonists' and 'potential stonethrowers'. Gangs of men ruled the township, armed with an assortment of sjamboks, pangas, knives and even firearms. Nicknamed the 'Phakathis' or 'The A-Team', these vigilantes patrolled at night, 'arresting' and assaulting members of civic and political organizations in both the UDF and Black Consciousness camps. Those abducted were often taken to the town council offices and tortured. The town clerk of Thabong, James Ngake, admitted that the town council recruited its own law enforcement unit of forty-three members, some of whom had been trained by white police units at Bloemfontein. The remainder had been hired as private security guards to protect town councillors and their property.[163] In a related incident, UDF activists announced that they had proof that a group of right-wing whites had formed a thirty-member hit-squad to murder well-known opponents of the white minority regime.[164]

A crescendo of violence gripped the East Rand townships, particularly Duduza, KwaThema, Tsakane, and Tembisa. In May and June 1985, these areas once again became the focal point of confrontations where a loose coalition of civic associations and student groups competed with local black officials and their hired thugs for control over the townships. Hand grenade attacks mainly against town councillors and black policemen increased. The addition of this new weaponry to the arsenal of protest marked a significant step toward broadening the armed struggle in the townships. A low-intensity civil war had erupted and those deemed 'collaborators', or surrogates for white minority rule, were vulnerable.

Duduza symbolized the deep roots of South African violence. Its residents had their own particular memories of pain, betrayal, and broken promises. Their tale began in 1962, when the people of a township called Charterston, near Nigel, were told that they were to be moved into a new place, thirty miles east of Johannesburg called Duduza (meaning 'comfort'). Some residents had been in favour of the plan because the government had pledged that the new place would have tarred roads, electric lighting, and proper sewerage instead of night-soil buckets. What happened surprised even those who had been distrustful of the intentions of the white officials. When the black residents left Charterston, they lost their freehold rights. The white authorities demolished their old community and rebuilt it as a 'model' town for people of mixed race. In Duduza, electricity remained a privilege of the few. The bucket system of night-soil removal continued. In 1985, some residents still shared communal water taps. The authorities introduced a black community council. When the cycle of unrest began, pressure from community activists caused town councillors to quit. Residents took their night-soil buckets and emptied them outside the offices of the white Administration Board responsible for township development. The rents were increased in March 1985, provoking school boycotts and intermittent clashes with police. As one correspondent put it, 'the pattern — of a community grievance articulated by older people and then translated into a wider onslaught by their children — seems widespread in black townships'.[165]

The battlelines hardened. Both sides were drawn into a cycle of bolder and more ruthless actions. From April to June, crowds attacked homes of policemen and the shops and houses of town councillors. It was in this cheerless township where the masses managed to tip the delicate scales in the East Rand beyond the frontiers of governability. The 120-member local black police force had been chased from the township and evacuated to nearby Dunnotar where it was temporarily housed in tents in an SAP compound.[166] In late May, heavily-armed police, aided by SADF units, invaded Duduza at night-time in support of the local black authorities. Scores of youths between the ages of 10 and 20 were arrested in house-to-house searches for 'troublemakers'. Residents claimed that they were woken at midnight by groups of youngsters who warned all boys over ten years of age to go into hiding. It was also reported that some young boys dressed as girls in a bid to escape the police.[167]

The first reported outbreak of visible vigilante terror along the East Rand took shape in Duduza. Sometime in May, vigilante bands were formed to avenge the burning of houses (of businessmen, council members, policemen, and suspected informers) and shops in the township. The vigilantes had a 'hit list' of known activists from COSAS, the Duduza Youth Congress, and the Duduza Civic Association.[168] In a number of hand grenade explosions in the early morning hours of 26 June in Tsakane, Duduza, and KwaThema, at least eight people were killed and seven were seriously injured. The three killed in Duduza were founder members of the local affiliate of COSAS and 'had been living in fear because they believed they were on a "hit list" drawn up by "pro-government people"'.[168] Anti-*apartheid* activists charged that police agents had deceived a group of unsuspecting students into joining a conspiracy to drive police out of the East Rand townships. The provocateurs gave the youths booby-trapped grenades that exploded prematurely in their hands.[170]

The funerals for these grenade victims sparked a renewed round of attacks on the homes of policemen and suspected informers. The SAP retaliated with indiscriminate shootings. In one incident, dozens of people attending an all-night vigil for the grenade victims at KwaThema's Gugulethu Cinema were driven from the premises by volleys of tear gas. As they emerged, police opened fire, killing six. 'This was not police work', a local doctor lamented, 'it was butchery.'[171] In another development heralding the overt operation of death squads, a band of men wearing ski masks and carrying AK-47 rifles entered Duduza at dusk. Singing ANC freedom songs, they lured black youths into the streets. As the youngsters clustered around, the armed intruders shot some and beat or kidnapped others. It was reported that this had also happened in other townships.[172]

Perhaps the most visible sign of the advent of officially sanctioned political assassinations was the murder of four Eastern Cape activists in late June. Mathew Goniwe, Fort Calata, and Sparrow Mkhonto — all executive members of Cradora in Lingelihle township outside Cradock — and Sicelo Mhlawuli, a civic leader in riot-torn Oudshoorn, disappeared after leaving a UDF regional meeting in Port Elizabeth. The discovery of their mutilated and burnt bodies a few days later highlighted the disappearances of known political activists. In Lingelihle township, Cradora had led the popular resistance that had become an emblem of organized defiance of Pretoria. Mathew Goniwe was praised as 'virtually the embodiment of the community struggle in Cradock'. Fort Calata was the grandson of Canon Calata, the first general secretary of the ANC.[173] A catalogue of these acts of clandestine terror indicated that the kidnappings had occurred in areas where resistance to the white minority regime was strongest. In compiling a register of political assassinations and abductions, the UDF stated that twenty-seven people had disappeared in the Eastern Cape, the Transvaal and Orange Free State, that unknown assailants had carried out eleven political assassinations and that hit lists in Soweto and Duduza contained the names of at least twenty political activists.[174]

The State of Emergency

The Collapse of Township Rule

Before the declaration of the state of emergency, Pretoria had lost control over practically all the black townships in the broad arc from the Vaal Triangle, across the East Rand, to the Eastern Cape. The grievances that triggered the initial outbreak of rioting were almost immediately swept aside in a condemnation of 'the system'. The sprawling townships — with their overcrowded and squalid living conditions — were fertile ground for political dissent. In these areas of fading prospects and grim statistics, the civil unrest that erupted with unprecedented anger was a reminder of the inability of the white minority regime to crush the spirit of rebelliousness.

Stretches of the Eastern Cape resembled an operational area on the brink of open civil war. Describing SADF activities near Uitenhage, a newspaper correspondent reported that '... there was a predominance of military vehicles on the road. Armed police occupied the Casspirs while young white faces could be seen in the Buffels and other armoured carriers that travelled in and out of the black townships. Army tents have been pitched in the streets and the takeover of a sports stadium in Uitenhage for what appears to be a supply base was a chilling reminder of what I had seen in Ovambo [i.e., northern Namibia].'[175] Even the small townships in the outlying and arid Karroo did not escape. Bongolethu outside Oudtshoorn was an example. The estimated 10,000 residents of the ramshackle township were crammed into less than a square kilometer of iron shacks and mud-plastered houses without electricity and running water. A correspondent described the situation there: 'The situation in Bongolethu resembles nothing so much as that of people living under the heel of a foreign occupying army. Armoured vehicles rumble through its narrow lands day and night. Residents are dispersed with dogs, sjamboks, and shotguns. ... Political or community activity has a semi-underground atmosphere similar to war-time resistance movements. Key community figures jump over their back fences when cars stop in front of their houses. ... Six-year-old children carry stones and give black-power salutes. ... The administration board office has been reduced to a pile of rubble. Deserted houses formerly occupied by black policemen bear

further testimony to the bitter violence. ... Police maintain a
high level of activity in Oudtshoorn. Without the umbrella of
constant press attention, they also act with impunity. People
active in community affairs are under constant surveillance. ...
They say people support the UDF in large numbers, but insist
that acts of unrest are spontaneous and are not being
organized.'[176] The situation in Bongolethu resembled that of
numerous other townships.

The 21 July declaration of the state of emergency reflected the
desperation of the Botha regime. The SAP — along with their
SADF reinforcements — had been stretched to breaking point,
compelled to move from one flashpoint to another. The SAP
gradually limited its activities to riding through the streets of
black townships, taunting crowds from the protection of
armoured personnel carriers and firing bullets and tear-gas can-
nisters from private cars, the tops of covered pickups, and mini-
buses, a reminder that the white authorities only entered the
townships under armed protection. In dozens of areas, burned
vehicles and the charred remains of the homes of councillors and
local police dotted the landscape.

The Disintegration of the Town Council System

The system of black local authorities, cornerstone of the Botha
regime's strategy to contain black aspirations short of full political rights in racially undivided South Africa, had all but
collapsed. Often overlooked amid the daily reports of rioting and
death, the disintegration of the town council system had far-
reaching consequences. The councils were widely condemned for
serving as a protective shield for white minority rule. They were
subjected to a state of siege. In a significant departure from the
type of boycott politics that had characterized popular opposition
to the 'dummy institutions' in the past, 'political forces in the
townships', in the words of a correspondent, 'have effectively
countered the government's co-optive strategy. They have gone
beyond the traditional methods of *non-collaboration* and *boycott*:
they have resorted to direct and drastic measures against the collaborators.'[177]

In numerous townships, residents stormed council chambers,
disrupting proceedings and accusing the councillors of being

hirelings of the white regime. Under this political pressure, some councillors, such as Lucas Mosuma (a member of the Atteridge-ville town council near Pretoria), abandoned their colleagues: 'We are real puppets who do nothing except evict residents who do not qualify to stay or work in an urban area. ... We talk and do nothing.'[178] Between September 1984 and June 1985, 240 black officials, including twenty-seven mayors, resigned, the highest number in the Eastern Cape where the Lingelihle, Kwanobuhle, Nomzamo, Humansdorp/Alexandra, and Somerset East/Cookhouse community councils resigned *en masse*.[179] In July, it was reported that 'black radicals are now waging open war against black councillors and others they call collaborators'. An estimated 120 councillors had been attacked and at least five killed, including a mayor and two deputies. At least seventy-five had their homes burned down. Only two of the thirty-eight town councils with the greatest local autonomy continued to operate.[180] 'Township community councils have ceased to function', according to another correspondent, 'as councillors, afraid for their lives in the face of the unrest, disappear into hiding.'[181] In late May, the Department of Co-operation and Development reported an estimated 375 unfilled vacancies in town and community councils. In some instances, councillors had left their posts to join 'mass-based bodies as an alternative to the ill-fated councils'.[182] In a manoeuver to revive these puppet bodies, Parliament hastily considered draft legislation that would empower the Department of Co-operation and Development to fill the openings by nomination rather than popular vote. In subsequent months, the Minister of Consti-tutional Development, Chris Heunis, was forced to appoint white civil servants to manage township affairs and to lay the groundwork for new council elections.[183]

By mid-August, official sources acknowledged that over the past twelve months petrol bomb and hand grenade attacks left seven black policemen dead, 270 injured, and 300 homeless in 400 separate incidents. Most of these assaults took place in East Rand and Eastern Cape townships. It was also reported that about fifteen town councillors had lost their lives and well over one hundred had been assaulted in the township unrest. It was widely believed that these official tallies grossly under-represented the actual number of attacks because police 'situa-tion reports' released to the press were notoriously lacking in details about such incidents.[184]

The councils had no hopes of providing decent services for ghetto residents, in large measure because they were unable to squeeze more money from an already impoverished people. The white authorities created the councils as a way of contriving to have black elected officials bear visible responsibility for the overcrowding, inadequate roads and sewage, inferior health-care facilities and schools, and the generally poor living conditions that characterized the areas. The town councils not only 'further the means of our oppression', as black activists commonly put it, but also offered multiple opportunities for widespread abuse. The system that regulated where black people lived and worked was notoriously corrupt. Because most housing was state-owned and -operated and rents were paid to the councils, councillors were in a position to evict tenants and move applicants to the head of waiting lists, a situation that invited bribery.[185]

As the Black Local Authorities (BLAs) slipped further into debt, councillors searched for alternative sources of revenue. Some councils contemplated increasing business license fees, raising grave fees, and even increasing traffic fines for offenses committed within their jurisdiction. Parliament's decision to withdraw housing subsidies in a gradual seven-year phase-out meant that township residents were faced with the prospect of massive rent increases. The Chair of the West Rand Development Board, for example, contended that 'pensioners will now pay more in rent than what they will receive from the government in pensions'.[186] Deteriorating services and chronic overcrowding — it was estimated that there were roughly twenty people living in every four-room house in Soweto — contributed to the restive and angry mood of the residents.[187] '[We] are at present faced with enormous burdens — increased costs all round and large-scale unemployment', the Heideveld-Vanguard Civic Association announced. 'Clearly the poor are being made to pay for the facilities of the rich.'[188]

Councils were on the verge of bankruptcy. Councillors were confronted with the unenviable choice of announcing rent increases or drastically cutting back on services such as electricity, water, sewage disposal, refuse collection. In either case, residents countered with mass mobilizations (including marches and demonstrations), highly organized rent strikes and school boycotts, and short-term work stayaways. These actions were sometimes shortlived and mild affairs. In most instances, they represented successful tactics that involved a widening circle of township residents in mass struggle.

The tangled miscellany of black townships nestled in the industrial zone south of Johannesburg symbolized the polarization pitting those who collaborated with the system against those who refused to accept its legitimacy. The Lekoa Town Council administered eight separate areas (Sharpeville, Evaton, Sebokeng, Boipatong, Bophelong, Refengkgotso, Zamdela, and Residensia) with an estimated 325,000 residents crammed into about 30,500 authorized housing units. When the Council announced a rent increase on 3 September 1984, the residents refused to pay rents.[189] The Sharpeville Civic Association spearheaded the boycott that lasted for at least fifteen months. Despite the threat of evictions and the promise of home ownership, a substantial proportion of the residents refused to give in, and instead demanded a rent reduction of more than half. In Sebokeng, black councillors were forced to retreat to an encampment surrounded by an electrified fence with armed guards at the gate. Homes and offices within this enclosure were separated from the outer perimeter by a stretch of barren land, putting these buildings out of reach of thrown gasoline bombs.[190] These councillors were 'refugees from their own citizens' and referred to disparagingly as 'the government in exile'.[191]

The Botha regime hastily introduced new regulations empowering the white Administration Boards to resume control over areas where town councils no longer functioned. The campaign of making the townships ungovernable had succeeded in the Vaal Triangle and the Eastern Cape. 'Attacks on councillors are almost a daily occurrence', one correspondent concluded. 'Where black policemen still live in black townships they do so in a state of siege. Their houses are mini-fortresses.'[192] Emson Banda, a community activist in Langa township near Uitenhage, said that residents were establishing street and area committees to run local affairs, and barely noticed the demise of the council. 'The police don't like it; they've got no job now. But we've got our own government. That's the language we are using.'[193] These experiments in dual power had taken only nascent form in some townships. Yet they marked the forms of popular struggle of the coming months.

Under the emergency decree, police assumed absolute powers

to detain people, search homes, and seize property. These powers were bolstered by exemption from any legal action against them in performing their duties. On the day the emergency was announced, more than 25,000 black mourners gathered at Lingelihle for the funeral of the four black leaders murdered outside Port Elizabeth three weeks earlier. The mood at this event was symbolized by two huge red flags, announcing the presence of the outlawed South African Communist Party and the support of the Soviet Union for the popular struggle. Alongside the red flags was the banner of the outlawed ANC.[194] About 50,000 mourners gathered in KwaThema, a township of perhaps 150,000 residents east of Johannesburg sandwiched between the white towns of Brakpan and Springs and set amid the gold-mining dumps. The pleas of the clerics for nonviolence were rejected by young militants impatient for change. One unidentified speaker at the gathering proclaimed that 'armed struggle' was the only answer and called for the establishment of a 'communist-socialist state' in South Africa. In the songs and slogans, black activists called upon the leaders of the ANC to provide them with weapons and explosives.[195]

After failing to crush black revolt with treason trials and bullets, Pretoria hoped to undermine the opposition by detaining hundreds of grassroots activists. While the state of emergency appeared to restore calm in some areas, it highlighted the drifting of the Botha regime. Fredrik van Zyl Slabbert, leader of the Progressive Federal Party and a key spokesman for the liberal pro-capitalist opposition, responded to the emergency: 'What was supposed to be the beginning of an era of negotiation and consensus politics has seen us drift steadily into the present state of semi-siege. [The National Party had] neither the ability, the plans, nor the talent to cope with the demands of genuine reform.'[196]

6.

Broadening Popular Struggle and the July 1985 State of Emergency

It was the way in which the sustained popular insurgency not only spawned a radicalized mass movement, but also undermined the administrative structures of white minority rule in the townships, that provoked the Botha regime to declare the 21 July state of emergency. The emergency powers buttressed the already existing draconian legislation, enabling the security forces to operate under conditions resembling martial law in the thirty-six affected magisterial districts. This intensified repression of the mass organizations generated a shift in the co-ordinates of the popular struggle. The mass detentions, killings, and the numbers forced underground deprived many organizations of their leadership and severed the ties that had linked political groups in a loose but coherent organizational network. Township residents adjusted spontaneously to these modified conditions adopting new forms of flexible and decentralized struggle. The state of emergency did not crush the popular insurgency. Yet ominously, in the first month after its declaration, the number of deaths attributed to political violence tripled.[1]

Consumer boycotts of white-owned businesses emerged as the logical outcome of popular struggles in the Eastern Cape, predating and overlapping with the July state of emergency. Eventually, the spread of these localized boycott campaigns became focal points of political action where township residents, acting both as workers and consumers, joined in a common effort to press their economic and political demands. The outbreak of rioting and street fighting in the Durban townships and the Cape Town ghettos repeated the pattern of unrest that had gripped the Vaal Triangle and the Eastern Cape. Yet the youthful militants in the Durban and Cape Town areas left their own imprint on the nationwide rebellion, compressing into brief spasms of violence all the stages of the cycle of popular unrest that had taken months to develop elsewhere. The independent black trade union movement in the main had abstained from mass action over the previous year. The strike organized by the National Union of Mineworkers (NUM) in September was the most marked departure from the previous hesitancy of the independent black trade union movement to confront directly both large-scale employers and the state administration. Although the walkout fizzled, the experience confirmed that the mining magnates were uncompromising in their approach to shop-floor concessions despite their carefully-nurtured posture as enlightened advocates of political reform.

Consumer Boycotts

Historical Legacy of the Boycott Strategy

The tactic of consumer boycotts drew upon popular memories of resistance in South Africa. The 1957 Alexandra bus boycott was perhaps the most celebrated episode amongst many similar actions.[2] What distinguished the wave of consumer boycotts following the state of emergency in July 1985 was their ubiquitous character and the blanket choice of their targets. Unlike the bus boycotts where the targets were selective and the aim was to punish undividual companies, the consumer boycotts were directed against all local white-owned businesses catering primarily to a black clientele. The objective was simple: to squeeze the profit margins of retail outlets sufficiently to pressure white businessmen to intercede with the state authorities on behalf of township residents. Because consumer boycotts were one of the few remaining avenues for peaceful protest, they served tactically to refocus mass mobilization at a time when the security forces had sufficiently regrouped and increased their activities in the townships.

In the Eastern Cape, the consumer boycott campaigns (that

had gathered momentum by mid-July) fused with the violence and near-anarchy of the black townships. In Adelaide, where a boycott had been almost 100 per cent effective for over two months, the local businessmen's association and municipal officials met with the organizers in a vain bid to end it. The demands of the boycott committee varied from repairing roads to the removal of the police and army from the township. Over the following weeks, the campaign intensified rapidly, taking in many small towns and villages virtually overnight. Coalitions of local civic associations, student organizations, and religious bodies — for the most part local affiliates of the UDF — initiated boycotts in places like Cradock, Fort Beaufort, Grahamstown, Queenstown, Kirkwood, Port Alfred, Kenton-on-Sea, Colesburg, and many other settlements spread outward from the main conurbations of Port Elizabeth and East London.[3] In mid-July, a secret convocation in Grahamstown brought together representatives of the Chambers of Commerce of towns in the Eastern Cape and police, military, and other officials. The meeting expressed the mood of local white businessmen anxious to remain solvent.[4]

The consumer boycott campaign assumed a qualitatively different dimension after the declaration of the state of emergency. The boycott of white businesses launched in Port Elizabeth caused sales in the city's large retail outlets and supermarket chains to plunge. Duncan Village and Mdantsane residents began a boycott of East London's central business district. Local boycott organizers confronted white businessmen with a broad array of political demands, including the withdrawal of the police and army from the townships, the lifting of the state of emergency, the release of political detainees, the immediate resignation of community councillors, an official explanation for the disappearance of the three missing PEBCO leaders, an end to forced removals and the dismantling of the Homelands.[5]

The immediate and dramatic success of the consumer boycotts plainly traumatized white businessmen, exposing the dependence of their trade on the growing spending power of black South African consumers. It had been estimated that black peoples' share of total personal income had climbed from 26 to 40 per cent from 1976 to 1985. By 1984, black consumer spending accounted for nearly 50 per cent of the annual growth rate in the consumer goods market.[6]

In East London, white shopkeepers reported a decline in turn-over of between 80 and 100 per cent. Eleven out of the sixteen white-owned shops along Milner street, a main thoroughfare largely dependent upon the passing trade of black consumers, closed within the first week of the boycott. In Port Elizabeth, the prolonged boycott centering on the North End commercial spine forced at least two shops to close. Another thirty stores suffered between a 30 and 100 per cent slump in business.[7] The detention of boycott organizers, including Mkhuseli Jack (who allegedly supervised the boycott strategy from a rural hideout), had little demonstrable effect on the campaign. Taxis dropped youths in shopping areas where they spread out in all directions to 'remind' black shoppers to heed the protest. Police officials announced the formation of a special 'ghost squad' to combat large-scale intimidation of black consumers. Within a week, they had arrested over one hundred youths in white, coloured, and Indian shopping areas on charges of intimidation.[8] On occasion, youthful supporters policed the boycotts with harsher tactics. Groups roamed the fringes of isolated townships, taking action against black residents who bought from white-owned stores. They stopped bus commuters, demanding to inspect packages. Those who defied the economic boycott frequently found their purchases strewn on the street and trampled. In a few instances, zealots forced boycott violators to consume items such as cook-ing oil, resulting in their deaths.[9]

The campaigns spread wildly, to Pretoria, Johannesburg, the Western Cape, and Natal. The Pretoria Consumer Boycott Com-mittee announced a ban on local white business centres in early August to protest the state of emergency and the detentions of activists. The committee consisted of civic associations, youth organizations, and local branches of trade unions, including SAAWU and the National General Workers Union (NGWU).[10] The boycott of white businesses coincided with the call for a three-day stayaway. Youths barricaded all the main streets in Mamelodi and Soshanguve townships in order to prevent workers from leaving.[11]

Fourteen organizations spearheaded the boycott campaign in Cape Town.[12] In Natal, MAWU initiated a boycott of white traders in Howick to protest against the dismissal of 1,000 members at the BTR-Sarmcol rubber factory. MAWU had conducted a ten-year battle for union recognition and launched the boycott to force

Sarmcol to return to the negotiating table. A coalition of trade unions and community organizations extended the consumer boycott into nearby Pietermaritzburg to pressure the local white merchants into intervening in the labour dispute.[13] In Potchefstroom, the aim was the reinstatement of 440 workers dismissed from the Triomf fertilizer plant in April 1984 in a recognition dispute.[14]

In mid-August, the boycott campaign in the Reef opened dramatically in Soweto 'when groups of youth stopped cars and searched residents entering the township'.[15] More than 600,000 residents continued the campaign in Port Elizabeth and East London. Frank Wrightman, president of the Port Elizabeth Chamber of Commerce, admitted that the consumer boycott was still operating 'with 100 per cent success' in its third week, plunging the commercial sector of the affected areas into serious financial straits.[16] The UDF played a central organizing role in the ad hoc committees that blossomed in all urban industrial areas. But the independent black trade unions had been gradually drawn into the consumer boycotts. In the Transvaal, at least twenty-five trade unions committed themselves to intensifying the campaigns.[17]

Unnerved by declining sales and gloomy prospects for the future, eighty representatives of Chambers of Commerce (particularly the retail sector) from all parts of South Africa convened in Johannesburg in late August under the leadership of ASSOCOM to formulate a common strategy in the face of the mushrooming boycott campaigns and associated work stayaways. ASSOCOM emphasized communication and negotiation. In Port Elizabeth, the local Chamber of Commerce issued a highly critical declaration (by South African standards) urging P.W. Botha to remove legislation discriminating against black people, to include black people in decision-making bodies in the central state administration, and to restore common South African citizenship.

In settlements throughout the Eastern Cape, each of the local boycott campaigns achieved its distinctive notoriety. Despite the intransigent character of these campaigns, cautious contacts between boycott organizers and local businessmen more often than not took place. For example, in Kenton-on-Sea, where 400 whites lived in a small Indian Ocean resort town and more than 2,000 blacks occupied an 'emergency camp' that had existed for twenty-seven years, the three-week-old boycott of white-owned shops was lifted after the white Chamber of Commerce formed a joint committee with black residents to consider grievances such as the siting of the whites' garbage dump in the middle of the black township, the lack of water faucets, and overcrowded and dilapidated school buildings in the area.[18]

Yet the informal negotiations that evolved in a handful of small Eastern Cape towns — where dependencies and divisions were starker than in the large conurbations — were overshadowed by vicious counter-measures. In many instances, police detained the local black leaders with whom white businessmen had sought to negotiate. In other places, the boycott campaigns unleashed a white blacklash. In Colesberg, north of Port Elizabeth, white businessmen refused to sell anything to black people and threatened to sever water supplies to a local black township. 'They have reversed the boycott', residents proclaimed. 'They are starving us out.'[19] In Tembisa northeast of Johannesburg, the security forces invoked their emergency powers, detaining five black businessmen and closing their retail shops, a pre-emptive move designed to break the boycott by depriving black consumers of the opportunity of buying from black traders.[20]

The Impact of the Boycott Campaigns

Despite the apparent tactical similarities, the consumer boycott campaigns that developed in the wake of the state of emergency were dictated by quite heterogeneous strategic considerations. The broad aims were the same, that is, to cripple local retailers to the extent that they would pressure the Botha regime into lifting the emergency, withdrawing troops from the townships, and releasing political detainees. However, the actual trajectory and impact of the campaigns in the different regions of the country diverged considerably.

In those areas of the eastern Cape where the tactic was first introduced, campaign organizers seemed to acknowledge that boycotts were the last remaining avenue for peaceful protest under the state of siege. Particularly in the fringe townships that formed the periphery of the industrial areas around Port Elizabeth/East London, the boycott of white-owned shops grew out of community-based struggles. Similarly, in those townships

that accommodated a disparate, largely service-industry proletariat (and where unemployment was particularly high), the
boycotts became the sole vehicle for sustaining the mass movement. In contrast, the campaign initiated in the Western Cape
had been put into motion before large-scale street protests broke
out and before the state of emergency had been extended to the
region. Because the impulse for the campaign had been imported
from the outside, the boycott experienced a rather inauspicious
beginning.

One of the chief motives behind the whole campaign had
been to refresh the mass movement, to galvanize popular support around a coherent tactic, and to incorporate layers and
sectors of the popular masses that had been more or less pushed
aside in the ferocity of street-fighting. Paradoxically, the revolt in
the townships had developed so quickly and so spontaneously
that it left the organized political movement behind. The consumer boycott campaigns were one way in which various political organizations hoped to regain the political initiative and to
establish political direction in an often confused situation.[21]

Nevertheless, the success or failure of particular boycotts
depended more upon objective conditions than upon the enthusiasm of participants. The campaigns were largely successful
where white stores had only a few outlets in relatively isolated
townships. This was the situation in the Howick/Pietermaritz-
burg and East London areas. After nearly two months, sales in
white-owned stores in East London and Uitenhage had declined
an estimated 30 to 40 per cent. Similarly, by the end of
September, sixteen of the eighteen white shops in Port
Elizabeth's North End had shut their doors.[22] Dozens of retail
stores in the Eastern Cape were eventually forced to close.
FOSATU surveys among its members on the East Rand — a trade
union stronghold — indicated a 40 to 60 per cent decline in retail
business in the first few weeks of the boycott. However, the consumer boycott did not seem to have a lasting impact in the
sprawling townships in the Pretoria-Johannesburg area.[23]

For their part, the independent black trade unions used their
sponsorship of the boycott campaigns to intervene in the political struggle. In addition to the MAWU-initiated campaign in
Howick, the NUM sponsored boycotts in several Rand mining
towns (Boksburg, Orkney, Stilfontein, Klerksdorp, Springs,
Carletonville), some eastern Transvaal coal-mining towns

(Witbank), and in the Orange Free State goldfields (Welkom, Odendaalsrus, and Virginia) as an auxiliary tactic in their main battle against the mining companies. The results, however, were mixed.[24]

What distinguished the consumer boycott campaign in the Western Cape was the widely divergent views of the participant organizations. One consequence of this diversity was the precise choice of targets: not just white-owned shops but all business owned by 'collaborators' (including community councillors, members of management committees, and participants in the tricameral Parliament).[25] In late September, the flagging campaign was provided with 'some extra "muscle" and a new direction thanks to a list of suggestions volunteered by New Unity Movement affiliate, the South Peninsula Educational Fellowship (SPEF)'.[26] In a widely distributed pamphlet, SPEF emphasized that a successful boycott campaign depended upon reaching the broadest numbers of supporters. 'We cannot achieve unity if students or other groups have to be used to "police" the boycott.' SPEF further maintained that the struggle was not just against 'white' businesses but against 'the system'. 'A vague, ill-defined boycott', it concluded, 'can only spread confusion, demoralisation and division among the oppressed and exploited.'[27]

Nevertheless, the success of the consumer boycotts invited a backlash. In late September, FOSATU announced the cancellation of the boycott in Pietermaritzburg in order to avoid unnecessary bloodshed. The decision came in the wake of the (Inkatha-affiliated) Inyanda Chamber of Commerce's 'declaration of war' on the federation. The Chamber of Commerce had called on all KwaZulu citizens to cooperate in crushing the boycott, promising 'protection' for all consumers who wished to make purchases.[28] The most dramatic moment of the white rightwing's response was the bombing in late October of the Port Elizabeth home of Cheekie Watson, one of four white brothers who had publicly expressed their opposition to *apartheid*. The Watson brothers were well-known merchants with retail shops in Uitenhage and Port Elizabeth that catered primarily to a black clientele. The organizers had exempted the Watson Brothers' shops from the consumer boycott. In 1977, the four brothers had resigned from their whites-only rugby clubs in order to play for black teams in the nearby townships. The brothers were subsequently banned by the white rugby union for life and ostracized by many whites, who refused to patronize their shops. The brothers had earned genuine respect in the black townships of Zwide, Kwazakele, and New Brighton.[29]

The Spread of the Popular Rebellion to Natal

Popular unrest had been simmering in Natal's townships since August 1984. But the event that unleashed open defiance was the assassination on 1 August in Durban of Victoria Mxenge, a veteran civil rights lawyer and treasurer of the Natal branch of the UDF. She was the widow of Griffiths Mxenge, also a lawyer and former ANC political detainee who had been brutally slain in a similar fashion by unknown assailants in 1981. Victoria Mxenge was an important part of the legal defense team in the first of the many schedule 'treason trials'. The trial for these sixteen defendants began the Monday following her assassination.

The brutal murder of Victoria Mxenge raised once again the issue of quasi-official killings and abductions. The UDF and AZAPO contended that more than forty of their members had disappeared since this most recent phase of defiance toward *apartheid* had begun.[30] Mxenge's murder seemed to confirm the existence of the officially-sanctioned 'death squads' that were blamed for this growing number of unsolved murders. The UDF charged that 27 political activists had 'disappeared' and eleven political assassinations had occurred since 1977. According to an official statement of the Detainees' Parents Support Committee, 'Recent revelations of hired death squads with hit lists operating in at least two parts of the country have caused committees to fear for their leaders' safety. The existence of mysterious vigilante squads responsible for attacks on activists' houses, and repeated cases of whites being seen in these attacks, has led to a radically different picture from the official version. There is a growing belief that pro-*apartheid* forces are prepared to use any method to prevent legitimate opposition to the government from continuing.'[31] In addition, it was widely believed that the security police had since April intensified its disinformation campaign mainly aimed at sharpening the differences between the UDF and AZAPO. This propaganda war was accompanied by attacks on the homes and persons of UDF and AZAPO leaders. Consequently, an atmosphere of fear and suspicion prevailed. Police agents, it was alleged, had organized a number of these attacks, signing up unemployed men outside the labour bureaux, and outfitting them with T-shirts so they could fraudulently pose as members of rival anti-*apartheid* organizations before sending them on their 'path of destruction'.[32]

Victoria Mxenge's death came only days after Pretoria announced sweeping restrictions on funerals. Police banned outdoor services, ordered separate funerals for each victim of the unrest, and allowed only ordained clerics to speak, barring discussion of political issues. Funerals had become mass rallies addressed by dozens of speakers and attended by thousands of black activists carrying anti-*apartheid* banners and chanting the songs and slogans of dissent.

In the first test of wills following the funeral ban, the SADF used armoured personnel carriers, mounted troops, and foot soldiers to encircle a funeral in Daveyton outside Benoni on 6 August. It was at this funeral that Bishop Desmond Tutu negotiated a temporary truce with the security forces in front of international television cameras, averting what was potentially a major bloodbath. This full-scale SADF deployment represented the most extensive clampdown to date on funeral rallies in the townships, and signalled to residents that the white regime was prepared to employ still harsher measures against any visible signs of black defiance.[33]

In the first week of August, renewed rioting broke out in Soweto, in Bethal in the eastern Transvaal, in Mamelodi near Pretoria, and in New Brighton. This political unrest was quickly dwarfed by the outbreak of widespread rioting and looting in townships and ghettos north of Durban. A correspondent for *City Press* described the tense atmosphere: '"Get out of here — it's war", reporters were warned by one of the thousands of students who spent the week marching in protest at the murder of Durban civil rights' lawyer Victoria Mxenge. What began as a week of mourning for Mrs Mxenge turned into total chaos in almost all Durban townships.'[34] The home of Amichand Rajbansi, one of two 'non-white' members of Botha's Cabinet, was blasted with a hand grenade in Durban's suburb of Chatsworth, a wealthy Indian township. Police fought peripatetic street battles with groups of black youths who burned government office buildings in Umlazi and set fire to the homes of school heads refusing to observe the school boycott.

The port of Durban is the largest on the African continent in terms of the cargo handled. As a major seaport, Durban served the rich hinterland, including the Pretoria-Witwatersrand-Vereeniging industrial region. Since 1925, the Durban metropolitan region had experienced rapid growth in its manufacturing industries. By the 1980s, the area accounted for about 14 per cent of total employment in the manufacturing and construction industries in South Africa. In addition to a wide range of commercial and service industries in the area, Durban itself was the country's major tourist and vacation centre. With a population of slightly less than 2 million, the Durban metropolitan region was the second largest city in South Africa. Over the past thirty years, Indian people (who make up an estimated one-quarter the population of the city) have been subjected to considerable residential displacement, due mainly to the implementation of the Group Areas act (with its strict code of residential segregation) but also as a result of urban freeway schemes, railway development, and land-use zoning. African people (who make up nearly 60 per cent of the Durban metropolitan region population) moved to the surrounding townships after World War II in search of work in the expanding manufacturing industries. By 1950, nearly 50 per cent of greater Durban's African population was illegally housed in shacks rented from Indian landlords in an unhealthy and blighted slum called Cato Manor. In 1964, Cato Manor was demolished and the African inhabitants were relocated in two new townships (KwaMashu and Umlazi). While the South African authorities largely succeeded in clearing the informal shack settlements from within the Durban municipal region, these unauthorized 'squatter' communities mushroomed in outlying areas in which, by 1980, it was estimated that about one-third of the total African populace of the region lived. Shack communities were largely concentrated in two areas: (1) on the northern periphery, south of Pinetown and from Clermont stretching along the Umgeni River to the New Farm/Phoenix areas of the Inanda district north of KwaMashu; and (2) on the southern periphery, in the vicinity of Umlazi township.[35]

Many political observers attributed the relative tranquillity of Natal during the early part of the rebellion to the persuasiveness of Chief Mangosuthu Gatsha Buthelezi's Inkatha organization.

An estimated six million Zulu-speakers lived in Natal. About 800,000 owed allegiance to Inkatha yeNkululeko yeSizwe, a tribalist organization revived in 1975 that subsequently functioned as Buthelezi's political base in the KwaZulu Home-land. Inkatha's membership was largely drawn from rural KwaZulu but it did enjoy an appreciable degree of popularity in Natal's urban areas and even had numerous branches in Soweto. Appropriately described as Janus-faced, Inkatha's kaleidoscopic images evoked competing interpretations of its place within black politics. Despite its fiery rhetoric and self-definition as the authentic champion of the 'liberation struggle', Inkatha exhibited a decided bent toward compromise with the white minority regime and conciliatory cooperation with South African capital.[36]

The weekend after Victoria Mxenge's death, youth groups began blocking entrances to townships, apparently in preparation for a wider boycott and stayaway. Yet almost from the outlet, the violence that spread through the townships outside Durban displayed a distinctly ethnic character largely absent elsewhere. Durban, home to the vast majority of South Africa's estimated 800,000 persons of Indian descent, has a tortured legacy of tension between Zulu-speakers and Indians. Zulu-speakers have been unevenly distributed within the most marginalized and menial occupations. In contrast, Indians dominate a consider-able portion of the city's retail trade. In the patchwork pattern of the city's economic geography, middle-class Indian suburbs incongruously abut the ramshackle, slum-like townships reserved for Zulu-speakers. Thus, ethnic/cultural differences were overlaid by class antagonisms.

The class relationship was perhaps nowhere more evident than in Inanda, a shack-settlement of 250,000 people thirty kilometers north of Durban. Indian property owners doubled as shopkeepers and landlords. 'Blacks live on the land as tenants of Indian shack owners to whom they pay rent. It is lucrative busi-ness, because the shacks are clustered close together and as many as forty families live on one plot of land. Indians also monopolize the shops and trading and have been accused of sell-ing essentials at inflated prices. ... Tension rose with the eco-nomic recession as the shack-town harboured increasing numbers of unemployed frustrated and hungry people, many coming to Inanda from depressed rural areas. To the average black shack dweller, the substantial brick and tile homes of

Indians appeared as mansions and accentuated the perceived disparities.'[37] In the settlement, 45 per cent of the economically active tenants were without regular work. The accumulated rage of these destitute people — confronted with high unemployment, squalid living conditions, and artificially high prices for essentials — erupted with a peculiar vengeance.[38]

In the most concentrated bloodletting since the disturbances began eleven months earlier, the rioting in the Durban townships took a turn toward wanton destructiveness and senseless killings. Inanda shack-dwellers — many of them tenants of the shop-owners — looted local stores, 'running food and supplies into their houses'. Shops and supermarkets 'were targets for thousands of unemployed who have been unable to buy food for themselves and families'. 'We are starving and there is so much unemployment that we are prepared to die to get food', an Inanda shack-dweller explained. Hooligans also exploited a tense situation, undertaking random burning and looting. Indian families evacuated their homes and shops, salvaging what they could and leaving their properties 'to the mercy of looters and arsonists'.[39] At least 1,500 Indians took refuge in a community hall in nearby Phoenix, close to where Mohandas K. Gandhi once lived. 'Shacklords' who financed their own private armies controlled great stretches of Inanda's slumyards. The efforts of these thugs to regain command over their 'turf' contributed to much of the violence in the shack settlements.[40] Gangs terrorized and threatened 'African and Indian people alike'.[41]

In nearby KwaMashu, Indian merchants retreated to the roof-tops of their shops, firing pistols and shotguns into crowds of looters below. In Umlazi, rioters looted and burned Indian shops. Discovering an opportunity to exploit the discord, well-armed police kept clear of the rioting, eventually cordoning off the worst-hit areas with armoured personnel carriers.[42]

On the evening of 7 August, in what came to be known as the Umlazi Cinema Massacre, a large contingent of 'stone-throwing, knobkerrie-bearing assailants' broke up a memorial vigil for Victoria Mxenge, trapping the mourners who were like 'sitting ducks'. The service broke into fierce fighting between the two camps and the casualty rate soared, as at least twelve people were killed and many seriously injured. It was widely believed that these marauding 'impis' were Inkatha supporters and that the police had escorted them to the battle scene.[43] The injured were transported to King Edward VIII hospital; and the hospital reception area came to resemble 'a wartime casualty station'.[44] The police and SADF 'appeared barely able to control or contain the violence in the Durban area. Few patrols were seen as black crowds burned Indian homes and businessmen and set fire to crops in outlying areas so that an Indian ocean breeze might fan the flames toward Indian homes.'[45] As some Indians tentatively ventured back to recover whatever possessions might have been overlooked by looters, they were once again ambushed by mobs who 'had lain in wait'.[46] As in the Eastern Cape, 'Mafia-style protection rackets' grew up in the black townships surrounding Durban in the wake of the violence. In KwaMashu and Inanda, groups of unemployed youths stopped cars, buses, and taxis, demanding payments from drivers and passengers before allowing the vehicles out of townships.[47] On 13 August, the SAP announced that the official death toll from the unrest had reached sixty-seven, thirty-seven of these the result of 'police action'.[48]

At first glance, it might appear that the nightmarish violence and looting in the Durban townships quickly lost all political meaning. Yet in order to understand the peculiar causes of the chaos, it is necessary to outline the political currents that distinguished the Durban region from other parts of South Africa. In the atmosphere of increasing social discontent that swept across the country during 1984-5, no single political organization in Natal was able to claim unchallenged hegemony over the popular classes. The intense factionalism split the oppressed masses into two warring 'camps' — those that welcomed the KwaZulu Homeland as a steppingstone to formal political rights for Africans and those that regarded this approach as 'collaborationist' — and, paradoxically, created a political vacuum suspended between the extremes. Sectarian in-fighting created fertile ground for an implosion of violent factionalism where the assaults on property and privilege coalesced with 'anti-Indian' chauvinism.

Inkatha had staked out the black townships — particularly Inanda and KwaMashu north of Durban, together with Umlazi — as the exclusive fiefdom of Chief Gatsha Buthelezi. Clashes between Inkatha supporters, on the one hand, and the UDF and AZAPO, on the other, had become regular occurrences over the past year. In July, a spate of physical assaults and firebombings pitted UDF supporters against Inkatha members in a cycle of attacks and reprisals in Lamontville, a township south of Durban.[49] Gatsha Buthelezi fuelled the rapidly spreading violence by declaring that the trouble had been caused by his political opponents, especially the UDF and ANC: 'Chief Buthelezi last night warned "misguided children and their thugs" to beware of the anger of the people. The Chief said it grieved him that members of certain political organizations and the activities of the external mission of the African National Congress are promoting this black on black confrontation as well as promoting a programme of self-laceration in having blacks burning down their own facilities. Chief Buthelezi said he hoped the police would "take adequate steps to contain this unrest so that peace and stability can be maintained in our region".'[50] Buthelezi further alleged that the UDF had infiltrated activists from Lamontville — a township that had refused to be partitioned and ceded to KwaZulu — into the townships that were located in KwaZulu, particularly Umlazi and KwaMashu.[51]

The rivalry between inkatha and its political opponents seemed unbridgeable. At one time Gatsha Buthelezi enjoyed at least a thin veneer of respectability within the liberation movement. However, by the early 1980s he condemned international sanctions against the *apartheid* regime, enthusiastically favoured expanded foreign investment and trade, and offered to compromise on the 'one-person one-vote' political formula. In his own words, 'The free enterprise system and enlightened capitalism, leading to a massive development of the SA economy, are things that black SA simply has to accept. In our circumstances, the free enterprise system is the most potent force of development available to us. . . . Black SA has cherished the ideal of a one-man one-vote system in a unitary state for generations. I argue, I plead and I cajole with black South Africans, that if we are to avoid destroying the foundations of the future, we must commit ourselves to the politics of negotiation and we must be prepared to compromise.'[52] These political views, coupled with his willingness to accept the official post as Chief Minister of KwaZulu within the Republic of South Africa, steered Buthelezi onto a collision course with his political opponents. The UDF even accused Inkatha of complicity in Victoria Mxenge's murder.

The Durban riots provided Inkatha with the pretext it required to not only launch a crusade against the UDF but also to display its paramilitary muscle. In KwaMashu, Zulu-speakers were mobilized under the aegis of Inkatha and gathered together as self-styled battalions — or 'impis' — armed with knives, clubs, machetes, and short stabbing spears. Mobile brigades of two hundred or more surged through the riot-torn streets to restore their own version of peace and order. The police implicitly approved the formation of Inkatha battalions and did nothing to prevent joint Inkatha-Indian patrols from roaming freely (in numbers that sometimes reached a thousand or more) in KwaMashu. The security forces did not prevent these Indian vigilantes from openly displaying pistols and shotguns. A clear illustration that vandals and thugs had gained the upper hand in KwaMashu, Inanda, and Umlazi was the arson attack on the Phoenix settlement and the looting of the former home of Mohandas K. Gandhi and the buildings, schools, and clinics next to it. Mewa Ramgobin, one of the sixteen UDF leaders facing treason charges in Pietermaritzburg, served as the executive director of Phoenix House.[53] By turning a blind eye to attacks and subsequent reprisals, the police succeeded in sowing discord and hatred between Africans and Indians. This factional violence seriously undermined the loose-knit coalition (forged through the UDF) of Indians and Zulu-speakers — an emblem of multi-racial co-operation. The tacit and unofficial approval of Inkatha's political thuggery in turn prompted its political rivals to turn toward retaliations, thereby effectively institutionalizing intra-working class violence in the Durban area.

The political alliances forged in the heat of the Durban battle-ground signified locally the shifting constellation of class forces on a national scale. On the one side, the UDF joined with the Natal Indian Congress (NIC) as well as welfare, community, church, and student bodies to form a Crisis Committee in an eleventh-hour bid to defuse communal tensions in Umlazi, Inanda, Phoenix, Newlands East, and KwaMashu. The sectarian violence had escalated so wildly that it threatened to shatter the political unity that had been painstakingly nurtured amongst the popular masses. On 11 August, the NIC placed a full-page politi-cal advertisement in the Sunday Tribune under the broad banner: 'We Want Peace and Friendship. Indians, Africans & Coloureds Unite! Stay Calm. Don't Let Them Divide Us!' The NIC appealed for political unity 'with our African brothers in the UDF'.[54] On the other side, Inkatha coalesced with the (Indian) Reform Party, blaming the violence on 'outside agitators' and criminal elements. On 11 August, Inkatha's secretary-general, Oscar Dhlomo, and numerous other Inkatha luminaries, shared the speakers' platform at a 10,000-strong Inkatha-sponsored rally in Inanda with Amichand Rajbansi, leader of the Reform Party, chair of the Ministers' Council in the (Indian) House of Delegates, and member of P.W. Botha's Cabinet. Both Inkatha and the Reform Party represented developing bourgeois interests that had mounted political campaigns to acquire a share of political authority commensurate with their class aspirations. In his address to the crowd, Dhlomo declared that 'all branches of Inkatha have been fully mobilized and are to patrol the streets of KwaMashu and Umlazi to put an end to the violence and protect properties, public buildings, and businesses in the townships near Durban'.[55]

During the following week, the SADF occupied the riot-torn townships in their 'round-the-clock' military exercise called 'Operation Clean-Up'. The military intervention coincided with the full mobilization of Inkatha irregulars. 'Hundreds of chanting and armed impis' patrolled the streets, '"clearing them of trouble-makers and enforcing peace"'.[56] These Inkatha gangs consisted in the main of hostel inmates from Glebelands and KwaMashu single-sex barracks. In subsequent weeks, anonymous pamphlets attacking the UDF appeared in great quantities on the streets. These efforts at undermining the Front's credibility as the vanguard of multiracialism were buttressed by increasingly audacious assaults on UDF supporters. Many homes of UDF members 'were petrol-bombed or set alight, and owners and sympathetic neighbours who tried to put out the fires were shot at'.[57] 'Unknown assassins' murdered Nunu Kheswa, a founder member of the Natal affiliate of COSAS. Harassment and intimidation — including death threats — of political activists spread.[58]

The funeral conducted for Victoria Mxenge at Rayi, a village situated in the Ciskei just north of King William's Town, marked a watershed. Because funerals had represented one of few quasi-lawful outlets for black political expression, they served as an available barometer through which to evaluate black political thought. The fiery messages delivered before a throng of 30,000 mourners at Mxenge's memorial service signalled a decisive broadening of the parameters of political struggle. The ANC had

enjoyed widespread popular support in the towns and countryside of the Eastern Cape. At the funeral, women sentinels in
green and black uniforms led the procession under the ANC
banner. The style and the tone of the event reflected a hardening
in black political ranks. Songs and chants celebrated the arrival
of guerrillas who had come to 'liberate' South Africa. In a significant and radical departure, many orators abandoned the subdued innuendo that had characterized most speeches at public
gatherings and instead demanded forthrightly an escalation of
armed struggle. Steven Tshwete, acting head of the Eastern Cape
UDF and former political prisoner, exclaimed: 'If we have to liberate ourselves with the barrel of a gun, then this is the moment.'
In a kind of talk rarely heard at previous gatherings, Tshwete
referred to the Botha regime as 'surrogates of Yankee
imperialism, which is responsible for our misery and subjugation'.[59] 'No international world will give us our freedom',
Sister Bernard Mkube, a Roman Catholic nun from the Com-
panions of St Angela in Johannesburg, declared: 'We are going to
struggle to bring them down.' This attitude appeared to suggest
that some clerics, at least, were ready to shed the philosophy of
nonviolent resistance advocated by leading religious figures such
as the Reverend Allan Boesäk and Bishop Desmond Tutu and
had moved towards offering a theological justification for armed
self-defense.[60]

The Political Intervention of the Independent Black Trade Unions

The Political Struggle of the Black Working Class

Throughout the course of the year-long ferment, working-class
people actively participated in the upheaval as residents of strife-
torn townships and as members of popular organizations. The
desire for direct action and the feverish pitch with which the
masses plunged into the popular revolt left efforts at concerted
organization far behind. Leaders of the popular organizations —
themselves firmly rooted in township political culture and social
life — scrambled to keep a pace with the mass movement. For
the independent black trade unions, the complex problem of how
to effectively bridge the distance between their own workplace

battles and the wider popular revolt assumed critical political importance. The unions were themselves divided ideologically and organizationally. Leading unions, particularly FOSATU and its staunchest allies, spearheaded an ambitious drive to form a super-federation despite the objections of other unionists. For the most part, however, the independent labour movement was not organizationally prepared to assume effective leadership of the mass movement.

The highly successful November 1984 Transvaal Stayaway indicated a significant break from the prevailing pattern of trade union hesitancy to actively participate in the mass struggle. The open and democratic manner in which this stayaway was organized contrasted sharply with the spontaneous calls in 1976 for mass strikes. The key feature of the November stayaway, in which half-a-million workers took part, was the participation of organized labour and migrant workers, and the effective linking of community, student, and worker organizations.[61] Throughout the entire year, the trade unions were engaged in a number of bitterly contested industrial disputes. For the most part, these workplace confrontations were conducted within the collective bargaining machinery of existing legal rights. Industrial disputes involving slow-downs, walkouts, and mass dismissals continued over the course of the year. But the workers' movement gradually gained strength and confidence in its own capacity for independent political initiatives. This gathering momentum culminated in the NUM-organized miners' strike of early September 1985.

In retrospect, two seemingly isolated episodes prefigured the broadened workers' offensive. On 20 May, more than 1,500 black workers at five Corobrik plants initiated a legal strike in the Western Cape and Natal in the largest work stoppage ever organized by the General Workers' Union (GWU). The strike occurred after eight weeks of fruitless negotiation between management and the union conducted through the Industrial Conciliation Board.[62] At around the same time, the Metal and Allied Workers' Union (MAWU) launched a boycott of shops in Howick, Natal, to put pressure on local business to persuade BTR Sarmcol, a British-owned transnational corporation, to reach a negotiated agreement with the union. The company had dismissed more than 900 striking workers the preceding month. In an effort at solidarity, about 2,000 workers at Dunlop SA in

Durban threatened to strike if BTR persisted in their refusal to conclude a union recognition agreement with MAWU.[63] On 29 June, MAWU organized a protest involving about ten busloads of striking BTR Sarmcol workers who brought traffic to a standstill in the middle of Pietermaritzburg.[64] MAWU elected to call a national strike if its local affiliates were frustated in plant-level bargaining with individual employers. Four unions — MAWU, the Steel, Engineering, and Allied Workers (SEAWU), the South African Boilermakers' Society (SABS), and the Engineering Industrial Workers' Union (EIWU) — had agreed to bargain collectively under the banner of the International Metalworkers' Federation (IMF). The IMF unions refused to sign the annual industrial council agreement with the employers' association, the Steel and Engineering Industries Federation (SEIFSA). The IMF had steadfastly refused to accept SEIFSA's principal demand that all collective bargaining on wages take place at industrial council and not at individual plant level.[65] While the other unions eventually signed the annual wage agreements 'under protest', MAWU refused to capitulate. Instead, MAWU extended its struggle. In July, 50 striking workers 'invaded the Anglican synod in Maritzburg and urged the church to involve itself in settling their dispute with BTR Sarmcol'.[66] On 16 July, ten MAWU strikers were charged with murdering three strikebreaking BTR Sarmcol workers and a further 20 members were charged with intimidation and assaults on 'scabs'. Rioting broke out as striking workers blocked 'scab' labour from leaving the BTR Sarmcol factory at Howick at lunchtime.[67] During the following week, MAWU organized a massive stayaway in the greater Pietermaritzburg area in support of the BTR Sarmcol workers. 'Thousands of workers heeded a call from MAWU to stay away from work', one correspondent announced. 'Yesterday morning the streets of Pietermaritzburg and surrounding townships had more policemen than residents or workers. Many buses and taxis were not running.'[68]

MAWU estimated that 70 per cent of the total workforce in the area stayed away from work and that all Indian-owned businesses in the greater Pietermaritzburg area and all schools were closed. 'Howick has died. It's dead', a supermarket owner acknowledged. Despite the unrelenting pressure of the boycott, the Pietermaritzburg Chamber of Industries, the Pietermaritzburg Chamber of Commerce, and Afrikaanse Sakekamer refused to intervene in the strike.[69] In August, MAWU extended the boycott of white-owned shops to Pietermaritzburg under the umbrella of an *ad hoc* coalition that included the FOSATU executive and local civic associations.[70]

While the BTR Sarmcol industrial dispute received most of the media attention, FOSATU was gradually drawn into using strikes as a method of pressing political demands. On 11 August, 3,000 workers belonging to the National and Allied Automobile Workers' Union (NAAWU) downed tools at Volkswagen's Uitenhage factory to protest against management's offer to lend microbuses for the Springbok and New Zealand All Blacks rugby tour. The strike ended when the tour was cancelled. Industrial relations consultant Brian Allen of Andrew Levy and Associates acknowledged that this work stoppage was unusual for a FOSATU-affiliated union 'because these unions have often been wary of direct involvement in politics'. Despite the fact that NAAWU was located principally in the highly-politicized Port Elizabeth area, this union 'appeared to have kept itself fairly insulated from politicization in the past'. 'Of all the FOSATU unions', Brian Allen remarked, 'NAAWU in that area is the most likely to become involved in these broader issues because of its highly politicized membership. This demonstrated that a union grouping was compelled to a large degree to follow the ebb and flow of the aspirations of its membership.'[71]

Following the July state of emergency, the Transvaal regional executive committee of FOSATU announced that it was calling for workers 'to take a day off for every trade union member killed in the unrest'.[72] In early August, six unions — FOSATU, CCAWUSA, NUM, the Cape Town Municipal Workers' Association, the GWU, and the Food and Canning Workers' Union — proclaimed a co-ordinated national programme of action 'to protest against the state of emergency' and the 'repression of political rights' in South Africa. These unions blamed the '*apartheid* state' for the growing political crisis and condemned the use of repressive measures to suppress political opposition.[73] In late August, the shop stewards' council of Johannesburg-based affiliates of FOSATU agreed to intensify their campaign against the state of emergency. This regional council pledged its support for the escalating consumer boycotts and condemned both police raids on trade union offices and the detention of an estimated twenty-six trade unionists since the emergency powers were invoked.[74]

In the meantime, six independent black trade unions representing a combined membership of between 30,000 and 40,000 workers in the Vaal region, formed the Vaal Trade Union Co-ordinating Committee to intervene in the eleven-month rent strike in the sprawling townships south of Johannesburg.[75]

This accumulation of episodes marked a gradual shift toward political confrontation with the white minority regime. Yet these tentative steps were overshadowed by the giant strides of black mine workers clustered around the NUM. The Director of Manpower, Piet van der Merwe, reported that in the first quarter of 1985 an estimated 68,000 workers in all sectors were involved in eighty-seven strikes compared to less than half that number in the same period the year before. An estimated 52,000 workers had been involved in mine stoppages alone.[76] According to statistics compiled by labour consultant Andrew Levy, more labour-days were lost due to strike activities in the first six months of 1985 than in any full year in recent South African history. In this six-month period, nearly 500,000 working days were lost in more than 100 separate strikes, compared with the previous year's record total of 450,000 days lost. Levy confirmed that the single greatest factor accounting for the upsurge of labour action was the growing level of organization in the mining industry, which accounted for 75 per cent of the labour unrest. The NUM was the single largest contributor to strikes, followed by the FOSATU affiliates NAAWU and MAWU. 'It's difficult to quantify', Andrew Levy reported, 'but I would say political issues are making labour issues more sensitive and solutions more difficult to find.'[77] 'The black working class', the *Sowetan* editorialized, 'is angry, militant, and is resisting any form of oppression or exploitation and is prepared to fight *apartheid* on the shop-floor.' The fact that 30 per cent of strikes took place to protest 'unfair dismissals', retrenchments, and disciplinary actions underscored the growing politicization of workers' collective action.[78]

The Mining Industry

Trouble had been growing in the mining industry for quite some time. At the mid-1985 prices of about $340 per ounce, South Africa's annual gold production exceeded a value of $7.14 billion. In 1984, gold accounted for $8.1 billion — or about 45 per cent —

of South Africa's total export earnings of $17.7 billion. On this basis, a month's work stoppage could mean a total loss of nearly $600 million to the large mining houses. The decline in the local currency meant that the mining companies earned more rand for their overseas sales. The NUM used these expected windfall profits as leverage, pressing its claim for a 22 per cent across-the-board wage increase.[79] At the same time, and in sharp contrast to longstanding NUM demands, Arrie Paulus, president of the pro-*apartheid* Mineworker's Union, stood firm on the question of statutory job reservation denying blasting certificates to qualified black workers, arguing that its abolition would result in a 60 per cent decline in his 12,000-member union.

In June, the Chamber of Mines proudly announced ambitious plans for expanding gold mining operations. By opening new mines and deepening existing ones, industry experts estimated that South African gold output would exceed 720 tons in 1990, compared with 683 tons in 1984. The mining houses were able to finance these huge capital outlays for two principal reasons: first the rand price of gold — the crucial issue for the mining mag-nates — stood at a record annual average because of the depreciation in the rand from over $1 two years earlier to less than half that figure by mid-1985; second, the mining industry was able to manipulate a host of generous tax concessions — including total write-offs of all capital expenditure against future profits and exceedingly low interest rates — to its long-term advantage.[80]

One paradox of this tangled skein of overlapping and com-peting interests was that the mining magnates seemed to acknowledge — with varying degrees of confidence — that cen-tralized unions were necessary both to ensure labour peace and to achieve stability in the industry. Despite the fact that the inde-pendent black trade unions had cast themselves as the vanguard in the struggle against capitalist exploitation and *apartheid*, the mining companies had encouraged the growth of black union-ization, hoping to use it as a bargaining chip to reduce the entrenched position of highly-paid white wage-earners repre-sented by the white supremacist Mineworker's Union.

Because of the hazardous nature of mining, the NUM had made occupational health and safety a special priority in its con-tract negotiations. Official statistics revealed that between 1974 and 1983, more than 8,500 miners had died in work-related accidents. As part of their package of demands, the NUM proposed a Miners' Bill of Rights that included the recognition of safety shop stewards, the right to refuse to work in 'unsafe' conditions, the right to attend and participate in official inquiries on mining accidents, and the inclusion of work safety clauses in union recognition agreements.[81]

In early August, the NUM held a 10,000-strong meeting in Thabong township outside Welkom (in the center of the Orange Free State goldfields and the stronghold of the union) to debate the proposed strike action. 'The emotion-charged meeting', it was reported, 'was marked by the chanting of freedom songs, dancing and power-packed speeches made by officials of the NUM.' Speaker after speaker 'made scathing attacks on the government's *apartheid* laws and the Chamber of Mines for refusing to pay workers a "living wage"'.[82]

The Collapse of the Miners' Strike

On 28 August, the NUM scheduled a strike to begin on 1 September involving 62,000 of its estimated 150,000 members in gold and coal mines. This strike call also included a threat to widen the work stoppage if the mining houses and the white authorities attempted to break it. After months of stormy negotiations over annual pay increases and other matters, the two sides appeared hopelessly deadlocked.

South Africa's mining giants traditionally bargained as a tight-knit unit through the Chamber of Mines, a business association that fixed standardized pay rates and controlled labour recruitment for its associated members. Yet for the first time in its 100-year history, mining companies broke ranks with the Chamber of Mines, scrambling to make separate deals with the NUM. The NUM recommended strike action at mines owned by three companies — Gold Fields, Gencor, and Anglo Vaal — that had refused to improve upon the Chamber of Mines' initial offer of between 14 and 19 per cent wage increases for various categories of mineworkers. In contrast, the NUM had reached tentative agreement with Anglo-American, South Africa's largest mining corporation. Anglo-American agreed to fatten the Chamber of Mines' initial offer by proposing pay increases of between 17 and 22 per cent, in addition to increased leave allowances. Two smaller mining houses — Rand Mines and Johannesburg Consolidated Investments — followed suit, matching Anglo-American's offer.

Ironically, this split in the united front of mining capital posed a serious tactical problem for the NUM. The union claimed 150,000 registered members among the estimated 550,000 black miners working for the Chamber-affiliated companies. The union was recognized by employers at eighteen of South Africa's forty-four gold mines and eleven of the fifty-five collieries. It had also made inroads at diamond mines owned by DeBeers. The NUM was strongest in the largest of the companies, Anglo-American, where it had between 80 and 86 per cent of its membership. It was weakest at Gencor and the other two companies that had refused to budge on the issue of wage increases. Gencor was a predominantly Afrikaner-owned company with close links to the National Party. This discrepant wage offer left the NUM confronting a serious dilemma. If the union limited the strike to those mines where its following was the weakest, its members could face mass dismissals and other stringent countermeasures. The mining companies (including Anglo-American which was considered the most enlightened of the mining houses) always reverted to mass dismissals as a method of resolving industrial disputes.[83] The proposed walkout affected five of the forty-four gold mines and two of its fifty-six collieries. The NUM warned it would extend the strike to the twenty-two gold and coal mines where tentative agreements had been reached if the recalcitrant companies employed strike-breaking reprisals against the union. Labour specialists speculated that this industrial dispute contained all the ingredients to spark a general strike of organized black workers. Apart from the wage issue, the NUM demanded a reduction in the standard six-day work-week from fifty-one to forty-eight hours. It also included in its package of demands the lifting of the state of emergency and the abolition of job reservation excluding black workers from supervisory positions. These demands transcended purely economic issues in an open political challenge to the white minority regime.

On 1 September, the strike faltered almost from the moment it began. By the second day, only an estimated 28,000 workers remained out — 6,000 at mines where the strike had been officially declared and the rest at those where union members stopped work in support of the others. In all, some eleven gold mines and collieries were hit by the strike action. But the planned walkout at the largest mines — Gold Fields' Kloof and West and East Driefontein, along with Anglo-Vaal's Hartebeesfontein — did not materialize. The mining magnates had used all the means at their disposal to crush the strike. 'The intensity of intimidation was a lot higher than we expected', Cyril Ramaphosa admitted. The mine operators had gone 'through activities similar to an army preparing for total warfare'.[84] At the affected mines, employers put up fences around the single-sex hostels. Some mine owners threatened to shut off water supplies and refused to feed the strikers. Mine managements distributed leaflets threatening that workers who went on strike would be dismissed and repatriated to the Homelands. Security personnel used armoured trucks to patrol the hostels, firing tear gas, rubber bullets, and, in a few reported incidents, live ammunition, to scatter crowds of workers and to force them back to work. An estimated eighty-three shaft stewards and strike committee members were arrested at Kloof, Beatrix, Stilfontein, and Deelkraal mines. Hundreds of workers were injured by rubber bullets, sjamboking, and teargas in clashes with mine security personnel. At a number of mines, managements began mass dismissal proceedings.[85]

On the third day, the Executive Committee of the NUM suspended the strike in order to protect striking workers from dismissal and forcible deportation. Viewed in isolation, the unsuccessful strike appeared to be a definite setback for the workers' movement as a whole, and a crushing defeat for the union. In the context of the wider political struggle it represented a tactical retreat. For the union leadership, the most important lesson of the strike was the absolute necessity for serious preparation and organization.[86]

The Repressive Counter-Offensive

Massive Displays of Force

The events of the Durban townships seemed to overshadow the cycle of political unrest that endured in the Eastern Cape and the Vaal Triangle. While fierce clashes between street demonstrators and the security forces generally subsided, the popular struggle assumed a variegated shape. Though it differed sharply from region to region, a correspondent for the *Wall Street Journal* captured its essential character in mid-1985: 'The violence is so widespread that it is difficult for ordinary blacks not to become involved. Nearly every black community is in the midst of some sort of boycott. Soweto school children started boycotting classes last week. Mineworkers are boycotting white stores in mining towns until the state of emergency is lifted. The black consumer boycott that has gripped Port Elizabeth's ailing white retailers has spread to the industrial town of East London. Residents of Sebokeng, where the government sent 10,000 troops [in September 1984], haven't paid rent since then.'[87] Indeed, the popular challenge was a molecular process where the sheer number of defiant acts — multiplied again and again — invigorated a broad mass movement that refused to submit to the superior force.

During the popular unrest, the security forces suffered numerous setbacks in their attempts to limit if not destroy the challenge to continued white minority rule. The state of emergency in July marked a shift in strategic focus. In extending the frontier of repression, the security forces prescribed a hybrid antidote to the resistance, combining counter-insurgency methods with conventional warfare techniques. Pretoria clearly prepared itself for a protracted war of attrition.

'Driving landmine-proof armored vehicles and armed with semiautomatic rifles, shotguns, tear gas and rubber bullets', one correspondent reported, 'South African police and soldiers swept through the country's black townships like an invading army.'[88] In the first week of August, the police 'slapped the harshest restrictions so far under emergency rule on Graaf Reinet in an effort to break the cycle of violence and end a school and trade boycott'.[89] Perhaps 30,000 black residents inhabited Graaf Reinet, a dreary Eastern Cape town located in the Karroo. After detaining about seventy local activists, the police obtained lists of absent pupils from school principals and then proceeded to seize them from their homes and take them to schools in SADF Casspirs and police vans. The authorities barred children from leaving their schools or houses from 8 am to 2 pm without special permission from the police. They also decreed that only students could approach schools, that only residents could enter the township, that locals could possess petrol only in their cars, and that any shop suspected of promoting the boycotts could be closed.[90] On 12 August, a combined contingent of SAP and SADF units invaded KwaThema, outside Springs on the East Rand, cordoning off large sections of the town with road blocks and conducting house-to-house searches for boycotting school children. In the following weeks, the security forces repeatedly conducted these 'harassment and interdiction' raids. The description of one such operation in Soweto illustrates the pattern: 'The army and police yesterday conducted house to house raids in Diepkloof Zone 1, Soweto, urging pupils to go to school or face arrest in what the police described as a "crime prevention operation" in Soweto. Zone 1 was virtually under a siege, with the armed police and soldiers also asking for reference books from people found in the houses. A roadblock was manned on the Bara main road, where all vehicles passing, passengers and those on foot were thoroughly searched. Pupils and youths of school-going age had their arms stamped when allowed to go through the road-blocks.'[91] These 'crime prevention operations' — sometimes undertaken in the middle of the night — coincided with arrests of black store-owners in the effort to break the consumer boycotts of white-owned shops.

Police assaults on school-age children escalated. On 22-3 August, armed police and SADF troops entered Soweto, rounding up at least 800 school-age children. They pushed them into police vans and drove them to Moroka police station in a major drive to force the youngsters to abandon school boycotts. About half of those detained were under thirteen years of age, some of them only eight years old.[92] During the following week, officials in Pretoria announced that they had decided to outlaw COSAS, the country's largest organization of black high-school students. For the security police, COSAS had become an 'undesirable organization' serving as a major focus of the popular resistance. Many of those detained since the emergency decree had been issued were leaders or members of COSAS.[93]

The crackdown on COSAS highlighted the youthfulness of the most dedicated participants in the revolt. It was estimated that two-thirds of the more than 2,000 people arrested between the declaration of emergency and late August were children under the age of eighteen. It was also alleged that many of the children detained were held in solitary confinement for long stretches of time without charge. Security officers often interrogated children in the absence of lawyers or sympathetic adults in order to obtain information and exact 'confessions'. Many children complained of torture, including beatings, sleep deprivation, and suffocation with wet nylon bags. Many youngsters were also sexually assaulted by adult prison inmates. 'The children speak of poor food, no beds, lice-ridden blankets', one commentator reported, 'and a bucket-latrine shared among several inmates and emptied only at irregular intervals.'[94]

From reports of former detainees, it was possible to piece together a pattern in the *method* of the security forces. Under the emergency powers, all members of the security forces — regular police officers, soldiers, railway police personnel, and prison guards — were exempt from legal action for anything they did in enforcing the decree. One strand of official policy was to break the grip of student and youth groups in the townships. The white authorities suspected that militant high-school pupils, particularly those associated with COSAS, were largely responsible for taking the lead in township protests. Another element in official strategy was to dissuade members of activist groups from continuing their activities, seeking instead to force them to become informers. A third intention was to gather intelligence about township activism, including links with the ANC. Compared with the 1960 state of emergency, the number of detainees was relatively low. Political activists inferred from the lower figures that the security forces had a more comprehensive knowledge of their opponents drawn from a broad network of informers. A common thread in the reports of former detainees was that officials used physical torture and intimidation. In persuading prisoners to become informers, interrogators threatened to infiltrate activist organizations in order to spread false rumours about spies. Security police also made thinly disguised references to death squads, reminding prisoners of what was known in Soweto as the 'sophisticated death', which meant that a person might be found murdered, ostensibly by thieves who would leave the body on open ground as a reminder of their impunity.[95]

The state of emergency yielded few and ambiguous results for the authorities in the first two months. Since the decree took effect in thirty-six magisterial districts around Johannesburg and the Eastern Cape, the police reported higher weekly death tolls than before. Moreover, the agitation spilled beyond the areas covered by this virtual declaration of martial law.

The Escalation of Vigilante Assaults

In July, an independent investigative team loosely connected to the PFP uncovered what they regarded as convincing yet unsubstantiated evidence that a 'third force' had been responsible for a spate of unsolved political assassinations in the Eastern Cape. PFP members Peter Gastrow and Molly Blackburn sifted through widely-circulated rumours and allegations that 'some township terrorists are masquerading as members of AZAPO and have links with the authorities'. Political activists in the area discounted the police version that placed the blame on political rivalries between UDF and AZAPO, suggesting instead that the savage method of killing had been employed in order to 'cover the tracks of the real killers', perhaps a 'death squad in the South American mould, possibly composed of off-duty members of the security forces'.[96]

At the height of the August unrest, Inkatha formed free-lance vigilante groups to impose its will in the townships. The Inkatha leadership nominated Winnington Sabelo, a KwaZulu legislative assembly member from Umlazi, to take charge of these groups. Sabelo immediately issued a warning that all UDF sympathizers should leave Umlazi or face the consequences. The number of attacks quickly escalated. Armed mobs went on a rampage, burning homes and causing many residents to flee for their lives: 'An unprecendented wave of terror is sweeping the Durban black townships of Umlazi and KwaMashu', one correspondent proclaimed, 'where hordes of armed warriors are "purging" the townships of United Democratic Front (UDF) sympathizers.'[97] At least three prominent UDF activists were abducted from their homes and brutally killed 'by the "impis" who roam the streets at night, forcing males to join them on their murder and destruction spree'.[98] Political activists openly speculated that a hit list of Inkatha's opponents had been constructed.[99] In KwaMashu, armed mobs attacked protesting students and burnt to the ground homes of UDF supporters. Police who observed the assaults and beatings of school-age children refused to intervene. Busloads of armed impis travelled through the streets, entering houses and dragging pupils into the road where they were beaten.[100]

In related incidents, armed Inkatha members intercepted a busload of sixty AZAPO members in Maritzburg, causing serious injuries. AZAPO members in Imbali township outside Maritzburg and Mpumalanga township near Hammarsdale were living in fear.[101] In the meantime, Gatsha Buthelezi announced before a Durban meeting of the joint committee of the Metropolitan Chamber of Commerce, the Natal Chamber of Industries, and the Durban Sugar Association that Inkatha could not single-handedly 'hold revolutionary forces at bay'. 'I am asking big business to strengthen the resolve of white Natalians', he intoned, 'to make bold steps forward [in support of] the politics of reconciliation.'[102] In Pietermaritzburg, Inkatha joined with the local affiliate of NAFCOC in a concerted bid to crush the ongoing boycott of white businesses.[103]

At the end of September, Chief Gatsha Buthelezi launched a blistering verbal assault on the ANC before a crowd of 7,000 supporters at a King Shaka Day commemoration rally at Umlazi township. Clearly defining the battlelines between Inkatha and the ANC, he insisted that black people must choose between the ANC's 'dismal 20-year record of armed violence' that 'would only lead to a bloodbath' and Inkatha's route of peaceful negotiation. The KwaZulu monarch, King Goodwill Zwelethini, also issued an ominous warning to the ANC: Zulu-speakers would rise in the thousands to drive out its exiled leaders if they tried to set foot in South Africa. Zwelethini also claimed that 'the people know the names and addresses of those who worked for the UDF's aim of destroying their unity. The people will rise as one to reject the alien forces who are bent on our destruction.' Buthelezi exanded his attacks, contending that the ANC had ordered his execution and were subverting the children. He warned that Inkatha would 'clean out hornet's nests' and 'banish from our midst the agents of death and destruction who want black to kill black'. He scoffed at the ANC's exile leadership as men 'who drank whiskey in safe places', proclaiming that 'you must stop dancing to the tune of those who finance the ANC mission in exile'.[104]

The scale and intensity of township violence in the Durban area escalated immediately. On the morning of the King Shaka Day commemoration rally, a contingent of Inkatha 'impis' armed with sticks, assegais, and spears stormed into Lamontville township where they were confronted near the entrance by youths who stoned them. At midday, senior Inkatha member and deputy chief whip in the KwaZulu legislative Assembly, Prince Gideon Zulu, left Umlazi stadium during Buthelezi's speech with three busloads of armed supporters and travelled to neighbouring Lamontville where they began to terrorize residents. Counter-attacking youths caught one Inkatha supporter, killed him and placed a burning tire on his body in the main road. All in all, at least ten people were killed in the clashes. The security forces used these events as a pretext to move into Lamontville and establish a semi-permanent military camp. The Lamontville Co-Ordinating Committee, representing various civic associations and popular organizations, accused the security forces of operating in collusion with Inkatha 'impis' in order to divert local grievances against high rents, incompetent administration, and unrepresentative councillors into black-on-black conflict.[105]

Chief Gatsha Buthelezi not only presided over the administration of KwaZulu, the fragmented 'self-governing' Homeland for Zulu-speakers established by Pretoria, but also dominated Inkatha. For about a decade, Western business leaders and the international media had fondly paid tribute to Buthelezi, praising him as a welcome pragmatic and moderate voice in a highly fractured political arena that appeared to deny the possibility of a middle ground. Buthelezi's refusal to accept Pretoria's version of political independence for KwaZulu reinforced his carefully nurtured mien as a maverick unwilling to bow to Pretoria's wishes. If KwaZulu accepted independent status, the six million Zulu-speakers dispersed in the main throughout Natal and the Transvaal would automatically relinquish their South African citizenship and Buthelezi would thus forfeit any claim to a political voice beyond the twenty-nine noncontiguous chunks of land that formed the Zulu Homeland. By rejecting this charade, Buthelezi thwarted the grand design of *apartheid* and enhanced his own image as a recognized power-broker.[106]

Its active participation in attacking rival popular organizations in the Natal region townships unmasked Inkatha as a para-military force that opted to co-operate with the state security apparatus. In addition to this political role, Buthelezi progressively endeared himself to the pro-capitalist social forces. 'I think many black people are influenced to think that the best way to establish an El Dorado here is through a socialist future', he argued. 'I have myself come to the conclusion that despite its faults the free enterprise capitalist system is the best economic system which man has ever devised.' Nevertheless, according to a survey conducted by sociologist Mark Orkin and the Institute of Black Research, Buthelezi commanded only 34 per cent political support among a representative sample of black urban residents in the Natal/KwaZulu area. Orkin's appraisal did not take into account rural Zulu-speakers who almost certainly inclined strongly towards Buthelezi and Inkatha. His findings also suggested that political support for Buthelezi and Inkatha among urban Zulu-speakers outside of Natal/KwaZulu was markedly less. In the crucial Pretoria-Witwatersrand-Vereeniging area, Buthelezi enjoyed the support of 11 per cent of the respondents against 29 per cent for the ANC, 13 per cent for Desmond Tutu, and 13 per cent for the UDF and Black Consciousness radicals. Zulu-speakers living outside the core Natal/KwaZulu area were a numerically significant sector of the estimated six million Zulu-speakers. The majority of Soweto residents were Zulu-speakers. These findings undermined the credibility of Gatsha Buthelezi and Inkatha as a viable political alternative in the event of a negotiated internal settlement.[107]

Detention and Torture

The scattered reports of police brutality before the state of emergency became a torrential outpouring during August and September 1985. Township residents, particularly from the Eastern Cape and Vaal Triangle areas, alleged in dozens of sworn affidavits that the security forces routinely engaged in indiscriminate shootings and unprovoked assaults on bystanders. In mid-September, researchers at the University of Cape Town issued a detailed report alleging that 83 per cent of people detained suffered some form of torture while in police custody. This report suggested 'that the severity of torture differs regionally, being most severe particularly regarding physical forms in the Eastern Cape and border areas, while least harsh in the Western Cape'.[108] In signed affidavits, numerous former detainees in the Port Elizabeth region complained that security police regularly tortured prisoners during interrogation at the newly-opened Louis Le Grange police headquarters — 'an imposing multi-storied building atop the highest point in the area, hidden behind a five-metre brick wall'. Unrestrained police behaviour included forcing detainees to run a gauntlet of baton-wielding policemen and compelling elderly clerics to stand naked outside on a winter night.[109]

Even by South African standards, the charge of police brutality during September was 'shocking in its scale and indiscriminate character'.[110] In a dramatic and unprecedented legal decision, a South African judge issued a court order restraining the police from assaulting detainees at two prisons in Port Elizabeth and Uitenhage. The most telling testimony in this official inquiry into alleged incidents of systematic torture of political detainees in the Eastern Cape region came from Dr Wendy Orr, officially appointed district surgeon for Port Elizabeth. 'What disturbs me most', she stated in papers presented to the court, 'is that detainees are being taken out of my care for the purpose of interrogation and, during the course of their interrogation, are brutally assaulted.' She contended further that complaints of police brutality had been registered 'on a vast scale'. The police, who enjoyed immunity from prosecution under the emergency-powers legislation, were 'quite unrestrained' in their treatment of detainees.[111]

The scale of detentions under South Africa's catchall security legislation took its toll on the popular organizations in the months following the emergency decree. In late September, the Detainees' Parents Support Committee (DPSC) stated that almost five thousand activists had been detained at one time or another under the emergency provisions and that another 1,168 people had been arrested since January 1985 under separate security regulations allowing for indefinite detention without formal charges. The Committee reported that, while different regulations applied in the emergency and non-emergency areas, township residents experienced little difference in the severity of repression. Army and police units conducted heavily-armed patrols and even stationed permanent occupation forces in some areas. In emergency areas, classroom curfews prevented students from leaving their classrooms during school hours. Night-time curfews were strictly enforced. Shops, supermarkets, and nightclubs closed early. At least forty-seven of the eighty UDF office-holders were detained, put on trial, or murdered, thirty-four of them detained since the emergency was declared, the majority arrested in *non-emergency areas.* The DPSC suggested that the security forces had constructed special camps for the growing numbers of political prisoners.[112]

Popular Rebellion in the Western Cape

The Pollsmoor March

The Western Cape townships had been largely immune from the spread of revolt. In mid-July, fleeting skirmishes between the police and mourners attending commemorative services for the four Cradock martyrs — coupled with the firebombing of Development Board offices and a councillor's home in Worcester — signalled the opening round of a prolonged period of civil strife in the Western Cape.[113] In the wake of the state of emergency, student boycotts intensified under the umbrella of the Western Cape Schools Action Committee (WECSAC), at its peak representing about 80 schools and colleges.[114] In Guguletu, a daring grenade attack injured seven police officers, including Western Cape police divisional commissioner Major Dolf Odendaal, during a funeral service for a victim of police gunfire.[115] All in all, between June and the end of August, there were at least sixteen reported petrol and grenade attacks on the homes of councillors, policemen, and others believed to be working within 'the system'.[116]

In Cape Town, the first major outbreak of rioting occurred on 27 August when thousands of protestors defied a ban against public rallies by staging a series of marches to demand the release of jailed ANC leader Nelson Mandela. In the words of Moira Levy, 'the city that for long was known as being bigger on theory than on practice, that for months remained virtually untouched by the violence sweeping the country, suddenly came into its own'.[117] The clergymen who sponsored the event planned for marchers to converge on Pollsmoor Prison outside Cape Town (where Nelson Mandela was held) from numerous starting-points scattered throughout Cape Town and its suburbs. The police attempted to thwart this effort by breaking up the separate processions with whips, tear gas, and rubber bullets. At Athlone, a mixed-race suburb outside Cape Town, police detained clerics who had gathered at a sports stadium where one of the feeder marches to Pollsmoor Prison was to begin. At the predominantly white University of Cape Town, police fired tear gas after a crowd demanding Mandela's release threw stones at an advancing police line. At the University of the Western Cape, which under South African law is set aside for mixed-race students, police with riot sticks charged students assembled for the march.[118] Police later laid siege to nearby Hewat Teacher Training College where many demonstrators had taken refuge.[119]

The security forces detained twenty-seven leading opposition figures (for the most part members or supporters of the UDF) the day after Allan Boesak, president of the World Alliance of Reformed Churches, announced plans for the Pollsmoor march. Yet at this stage, arrests of prominent leaders no longer seemed to have any impact in dampening the popular defiance. Township residents had outdistanced the efforts of the popular organizations to direct the protests. These organizations enjoyed widespread grassroots support, but youthful militants began to operate on their own initiative outside the established organizational frameworks.

The wave of arson, looting, and stone-throwing erupted first in Cape Town's largest black township, Guguletu, located near D.F. Malan Airport. The police used harsh and provocative methods against crowds in Guguletu gathered for the march to Pollsmoor Prison, setting off a day and night of fierce clashes that left at least eleven dead. The unrest spread quickly to Nyanga and to Manenberg, a mixed-race district adjoining the township. Police dispersed those congregated there with tear gas and rubber bullets and sealed off the area with roadblocks after residents disrupted traffic along major highways leading to D.F. Malan airport and to Muizenberg. Angry crowds began a night-long spree of arson and stonings that continued throughout the next day and spread throughout the working-class districts east of Cape Town city centre. In the next few days, the unrest spread to five major mixed-race districts in the surrounding area. By nightfall of the second day, a ring of fire enveloped the black and mixed-race townships east and south of Cape Town's central business district. The fighting left office blocks and dozens of stores in ruins. The fire department and ambulance services refused to enter the areas of Bellville, Athlone, Swartklip, and elsewhere because of inadequate police protection.[120]

Well-armed yet ill-prepared and outmaneuvered, police and

soldiers, 'firing shotguns, rubber bullets, and tear gas at roving bands of residents who pelted them with rocks, bottles and homemade gasoline bombs' failed to put down the unrest. Fleet-footed crowds erected hundreds of makeshift barricades of burning tires, mattresses, and refuse to block police access to the rubble-strewn streets. Columns of thick black smoke mingled with acrid clouds of tear gas over a vast and irregular combat zone. In Mitchell's Plain, a residential settlement amid the sand dunes of the Cape Flats, police and young militants traded barrages of tear gas and stones throughout the day. Crowds broke windows and burned and looted stores in a nearby shopping centre. Police responded with shotgun fire and tear gas. They invaded school grounds, turning them into battle-fields.

The South African authorities had built Mitchell's Plain as a model residential area for people of mixed racial descent. It was a relatively affluent area, consisting of modest yet well-kept houses and modern shops spanned by broad four-lane highways. Many of its residents were forcibly removed under the Group Areas Act from older established communities like District Six, near to Cape Town's business district, in order to make way for high-rise apartment complexes and the white 'yuppie' invasion.

A typical pattern of struggle emerged in the sprawling townships around Cape Town. Youthful protestors gathered at intersections, putting up barricades of blazing tires and whatever debris was at hand. The police arrived. The protestors responded either by fleeing or throwing stones. The police then opened fire with tear gas, rubber bullets, or birdshot. On many occasions, they resorted to live ammunition with little or no provocation. The security forces travelled in caravans of armoured personnel carriers called Casspirs, firing from above the rim of the vehicles. In the densely-packed suburbs of Athlone and Retreat, street battles created extensive no-go areas. In Guguletu, almost invisible strands of barbed wire were strung between trees at a height seemingly selected to decapitate police officers.[121] It was reported that at least nineteen policemen had been injured in the unrest.[122] In Mitchell's Plain, the barricades of blazing tires and discarded mattresses slowed motorists to a virtual crawl. Drivers who returned a clenched-fist salute to the young people guarding the barricades were allowed to pass. Motorists who did not share this symbol of defiance were forced to run a gauntlet of stones, bricks, and bottles.

Rioting in the White Suburbs

In early September, political unrest spilled over into white neighbourhoods in Cape Town. Police and white homeowners armed with shotguns and pistols repulsed crowds of youths who threw stones and gasoline bombs at homes in Kraaifontein, where the boundaries of white and mixed-race residential areas meet.[123] This confrontation (along with another reported incident in East London's white suburb of Amalinda) was the first significant outbreak of violence in the white residential areas since the crisis began. It came a day after police officers with whips clashed with demonstrators in the commercial centre of Cape Town. In a manoeuvre designed to pre-empt further political unrest, the white authorities announced the closing of 454 schools and colleges in the Cape Town area, locking out an estimated 360,000 students. Allan Hendrikse, one of the two 'non-white' members of the Botha Cabinet and a leader of the mixed-race chamber of South Africa's segregated Parliament, approved the measure, contending that the schools 'have now become the meeting place for organizing protests and, more than protests, arson and promoting violence'.[124]

Throughout the year-long unrest, it is possible to discern a pattern in which township residents were enticed into a cycle of increasingly vicious confrontations with the security forces. In the Vaal Triangle and the Eastern Cape, the security forces resorted to extreme emergency powers to crush the popular movement. In the Durban townships, intersecting ethnic and class conflicts pushed the unrest along an alternative axis where it degenerated into thuggery. In Cape Town, the masses traversed the familiar route, yet with the significant difference that the battlelines took shape suddenly and hardened virtually overnight. This telescoped process catapulted the popular movement in Cape Town onto new territory where it required a distinctive inventiveness to sustain its momentum.

In the midst of the rapidly escalating revolt in Cape Town, police shot dead several people in a series of clashes between residents and security forces in Duncan Village — a slum of dilapidated shacks nestled close to East London. In late August, a crowd estimated at over 70,000 converged on East London for a massive funeral service — the largest of its kind since September 1984. During this event, two white construction workers were stabbed and burned to death after the driver plowed his automobile through a large procession of mourners, injuring twelve. Speakers at the funeral rally invoked the message of armed struggle.[125]

Over the year, the funeral speeches reflected the differences of emphasis within the popular movement, oscillating from pleas for a dialogue with those in power 'before it is too late' to fiery condemnations of the white minority regime. The 7 September funeral in Guguletu for eleven victims of police shootings attracted an estimated 20,000 mourners. A wide variety of political organizations was represented on the speakers' platform, including the UDF, the United Women's Organization, South African Council on Sport (SACOS), AZAPO, National Forum, the New Unity Movement, as well as prominent trade unions.[126] Judging from the mood of the rally, the uneasy ideological truce that linked the moral appeal of nonviolence with uninterrupted mass mobilizations was dead. The popular message invoked at the funeral put the theme of armed struggle centre-stage.

Protestors draped the banner of the ANC over the assembled coffins in a ceremonial ritual. Youthful militants chanted a distinctive argot inspired by visions of armed insurrection. In dance and rhythmic singing, children called the names of imprisoned or exiled leaders, enshrining them as living symbols in an almost liturgical litany of the liberation struggle. Banners and slogans openly implored the ANC to supply weapons to the townships. 'Tambo, we are ready', one banner said. 'Give us AKs.' The initials referred to the Soviet AK-47 rifles that were a symbol of the desire to avenge indiscriminate killings of unarmed protestors and to retaliate against 'the system'.

The security forces were ruthless in suppressing the street demonstrations that followed the funeral services. Police and army units cordoned off Guguletu and Nyanga before moving into the battle zone. Young street-fighters 'seemingly well-organized, constructed barricades of debris on narrow streets'.[127] Groups of between 200 and 500 were 'attacking police in the townships'.[128] Two military helicopters hovered over the streets littered with blazing barricades, directing the security forces to new trouble spots. As one reporter described it, 'The armored personnel carriers, nicknamed Hippos, reappeared and policemen clutching weapons leaped from them, some breaking up the barricades, others taking up firing positions around the vehicles. ... As the police fired, crowds on the street scattered, only to regroup once the police and army, sometimes traveling in convoys of three armored vehicles, left.'[129]

Cape Town and the 'Trojan Horse' Incident

Rioting had ebbed and flowed over the course of many weeks throughout Cape Town's widely-dispersed ghettos and townships. The secondary school boycott that began on 29 July 1985 served as a springboard from which a number of community struggles were launched. By *apartheid* standards, what made Cape Town unique of all South Africa's major cities was the almost random and nonconformist residential patterns. In the older settled areas, white suburbs abutted coloured ghettos. Nearly all the main thoroughfares connecting the Central Business District with the outlying suburbs — and including D.F. Malan Airport — cut through a jumbled maze of townships, ghettos, and shantytowns. The security forces had great difficulty in policing this patchwork of residential areas.

The masses offered stubborn resistance to blanket police encroachment into their territory. The tense political situation deteriorated. The security forces trucked in Zulu-speaking police to serve on riot-duty, but they acted like 'groups of marauding hooligans in police uniforms': 'Outsiders are being brought in to protect local policemen from reprisals. ... The result is that very ordinary communities of very ordinary middle-class people are being completely radicalised and alienated from the police. If they want to drive people into the arms of the Marxists they are going about it in an excellent way. If no action is taken in view of the massive amount of evidence available they will drive the western Cape into a state of anarchy.'[130] The PFP's Unrest Monitoring Committee reported that 'There is random beating and random shooting without any plan or objective.'[131] During early October, the police reinforced their patrols on the major thoroughfares radiating outward from downtown Cape Town because of the increase in apparently random stonings and fire bombings of passing automobiles. On 14 October, a white shopping centre in Wynburg, a suburb close to the heart of Cape Town, was attacked. The police became increasingly impatient in their efforts to quell daily street demonstrations and rioting in the older settled working-class communities in close proximity to City Centre. The narrow streets, convenient alleyways, and densely-packed built environment provided well-organized groups of street militants with a relative advantage in their war of manoeuvre with the police. Youth militants had fleetingly experimented with novel organizational forms in order to protect their anonymity. They improvised street-fighting tactics designed to maximize the confusion amongst the security forces and to minimize their own casualties. On 15 October, the 'Trojan Horse' incident occurred. The security forces commandeered a South African Transport Services (Railways) truck and cruised repeatedly along Athlone's Thornton Road. The slow-moving vehicle attracted throngs of youthful stonethrowers. Suddenly, mayhem broke loose. Heavily-armed police, hidden in wooden crates piled on the back of the truck, appeared, opening fire with pump-action shotguns in every direction.[132]

'It was like a war out here', one witness proclaimed. 'The firing kept up. Homes were peppered with shotgun blasts.' When the shooting subsided, three people were dead and at least ten seriously injured. As the outrage with the Athlone ambush turned to collective anger, battles with police raged in the streets of Cape Town and neighbouring townships. Crowds once again constructed makeshift barricades of blazing debris and youths angrily entered the city's white middle-class residential areas. Minor skirmishes erupted in at least ten separate places.

In Athlone, the pitched battles between police and demonstrators infringed upon an unwritten boundary that had informally governed these encounters over fourteen months of unrest. For the first time, the police acknowledged that security officers were subjected to sustained small arms fire on at least six separate occasions. In one incident, police surrounded St Athens Mosque where more than 2,000 Moslems had taken refuge. Youthful Moslem militants from the estimated 150,000-strong Moslem community in Cape Town — 'some with their faces covered in the checkered Arab scarves made familiar by years of ethnic warfare in the Lebanon' — had increasingly called for Jihad or Holy War against *apartheid*. In the exchange of gunfire, both sides sustained casualties..The near-continuous police actions in Athlone — of which approximately half the population was Moslem — and nearby working-class suburbs had deeply angered and radicalized residents of these older settled communities. This use of firearms introduced a new and potentially explosive element in the civil strife that perhaps anticipated the evolution of tactical warfare in the future. The masses had broken the exclusive monopoly of violence that the state security forces had enjoyed. In response to this transgression, the South African authorities ordered hundreds of armed troops into Athlone. Police made little effort to prevent young protestors from setting fire to countless barricades. However, the security forces discharged foot patrols into Athlone's narrow streets. Troops armed with automatic rifles, took up positions at 10-yard intervals along main thoroughfares, stopping traffic and conducting house-to-house searches.[133]

In late October, Moslem funeral processions and burial ceremonies seemed to add a new dimension of Islamic religious fervor into South Africa's political turmoil. Funeral events for these most recent victims of the political unrest not only engendered a rare crossover of religious lines as white-robed Islamic clergymen mingled with Christian churchmen but also evinced considerable anger amongst middle-aged churchgoing and struggling lower middle-class sectors which had previously remained distanced from the political unrest.[134]

In the meantime, the execution of Benjamin Moloise — the fifth ANC member to be hanged in South Africa — set off rioting in downtown Johannesburg. This spontaneous conflagration in central Johannesburg marked the first time during the political unrest that angry crowds roamed virtually unchecked throughout the city's white areas.[135] In KwaZakele township near Port Elizabeth, a white soldier was stabbed to death, reportedly the first combat-related loss of life in a combined SAP/SADF operation during the unrest. In Atteridgeville, widespread rioting erupted in the wake of an emotion-laden funeral ceremony. More than 15,000 mourners had gathered to protest the murder of a thirteen-year-old school child on his way to Zion Christian Church choir practice. Four white policemen had beaten the young boy to death.[136]

However, the most prominent theatre of political unrest remained the Cape Town region. In the aftermath of the

Thornton Road slaughter, small close-knit groups of young militants — with apparent unity of purpose and with an eye to well-organized preparation — began to systematically cut the main thoroughfares connecting the Central Business District with the outlying suburbs. To the east of downtown Cape Town, crowds passed through the black townships and working-class ghettos. Youthful ambushers heaving stones and gasoline bombs at white motorists completely disrupted traffic on the main roads that skirted a number of the most downtrodden black residential areas. Officials undoubtedly regarded these actions as a dress rehearsal for armed insurrection. In a twenty-four hour period, police reported 150 arson attacks, many involving gasoline bombs on automobiles and the homes of black policemen. In one incident, youth set fire to an automobile on a hillside and sent it rolling down the steep slope less than half a mile from the centre of Cape Town. This type of militant protest gradually inched toward the city centre. Youngsters entered a quaint shopping arcade in Cape Town's white suburb of Kraaifontein twice in one week, destroying two stores with firebombs and causing an estimated $380,000 in damage.

In Parliament, a member of the PFP's Unrest Monitoring Committee accused the security forces of terror tactics, including indiscriminate shootings and random beatings, in their futile efforts to quell the political unrest that had gripped the Cape Town area for weeks. Amid the widespread allegations that the white authorities employed excessive force and brutality to curb Cape Town's unrest, the police announced that they would not hesitate to deploy their newly-acquired riot-control equipment (including a water cannon shooting purple dye, a combat helicopter, and a rapid-fire gun) to combat the persistent rioting. Almost immediately, the police, as one resident in Mitchell's Plain wryly put it, 'tried out their new toy', a rapid-fire rubber-bullet gun mounted on the rear of an armoured truck.[137]

On 24 October, Cape Town's protests reached the heart of the city's downtown commercial district. Small groups of protestors gathered in the main fashionable shopping quarter, mixing with hundreds of city workers and lunchtime shoppers. When the surging crowds refused to disperse, the police produced a mobile water cannon that was moved along congested Adderley Street, spraying water that had been treated with purple dye on the fleeing throngs, including protestors and passersby alike. The treated water — youths nicknamed it 'purple rain' — was used to indelibly mark demonstrators so that they could be identified and arrested. Incensed protestors overturned cars and smashed windows. The turmoil lasted nearly three hours. The police used whips and police dogs to eventually clear the streets.[138]

The following day, President P.W. Botha extended the state of emergency decree to eight districts in the cape Town area and the Boland, which is the lower half of the peninsula on which Cape Town is situated. At the same time, the security forces detained at least sixty-nine anti-*apartheid* activists in the Western Cape, including virtually all the executive members of the UDF. Political commentators announced that these detentions marked the largest crackdown by security forces on political opponents of the white minority regime in the Cape Town area in recent memory. The community newspaper, *Grassroots*, reported that religious clerics, academics, students, trade unionists, community activists, and staff members of the newspaper itself had been arrested in predawn police raids.

These arrests followed two months of unrest in which more than sixty-five persons in the Western Cape area had died in anti-*apartheid* protests. In the preceding twelve days, at least thirty protestors had lost their lives in Cape Town and its environs alone.[139] Within a week, the white authorities announced that virtually every organization affiliated to the UDF and the National Forum — all in all, more than one hundred groups — were banned from holding meetings in Cape Town and surrounding areas.[140] Despite the partial lifting of the state of emergency in six small towns, the thirty-eight districts covered under the decree included an estimated 9.2 million people, or nearly one-third South Africa's population.

On 2 November, Pretoria imposed broad restrictions on news coverage of the protracted disturbances in South Africa's embattled townships in the 38 districts covered under the state of emergency, barring television crews, photographers, and radio reporters from areas of unrest. These measures also limited newspaper and magazine reporting of disturbances since they required correspondents to seek police approval and escorts for their presence in places deemed to be 'unrest areas'. In this penultimate *coup de grace* to informed press coverage, the security forces assumed power to curb at their whim access of reporters to areas deemed to be controversial.[141]

Despite these concerted efforts to contain political unrest, irreconcilable divisions continued to beset the country. Although Queenstown had been the site of earlier incidents, renewed concentrated rioting that erupted in this depressed farming centre appeared to signal the spread of South Africa's civil strife into yet another region. In one of the worst weeks of violence since the emergency was decreed, police reported forty-two deaths during a single seven-day period in mid-November. The Queenstown riots — accounting for nearly half the reported killings — were ignited when police swept through the local township in an apparent search for the leaders of the local popular organizations.[142]

The political turmoil continued to fester for weeks in the Western Cape after the proclamation of the state of emergency. Former Namibian war correspondent Tony Weaver exclaimed: 'In the Western Cape, civil war has broken out. There seems to be little justification in continuing to call it "unrest". ... No major route which goes anywhere near a township is "safe" for whites and delivery vehicles. Even Eastern Boulevard, the highway that floats above the city on the slopes of Table Mountain, is no longer "safe" at night, with petrol bombs and rocks being thrown at motorists from the footbridges.'[143] Athlone — a well-to-do middle-class suburb — became a local symbol of popular resistance. When militant action first broke out there, 'both sides were pretty raw and ragged'. By November, Athlone had become a 'seasoned war zone': 'It had come of age in the battle for Cape Town. When the police and army move in, there is wall-to-wall troops and police. Every block, every school has its "action squad", coordinating action, providing direction, helping build petrol bombs and seeking materials for barricades. ... The police no longer go in at night because now the people shoot back. As soon as someone is wounded, a private car arrives, the wounded person is smuggled out and taken to a sympathetic doctor.'[144] In Guguletu, every house 'has become a command centre. When the action starts, an ambulance immediately starts cruising the streets, picking up the wounded and ferrying them to safe clinics and doctors for treatment.' Elaborate networks evolved, hiding and escorting activists sought by the security forces. In Mitchell's Plain, youthful lookouts with binoculars perched on rooftops. From these vantage points, they kept watch over the main roads, providing ample warning against approaching Casspirs (called 'ghostbusters'), yellow landrovers (called 'mellow-yellows'), and Buffels 'hellbent on nailing as many barricade-erectors and stonethrowers as possible'.[145] In the descriptive parlance of the Western Cape, Mitchell's Plain was *'n ander soort plek* [a different kind of place]. The *hang-gat skollies* [unemployed and quasi-lumpenized youth] ruled the streets. The townships of Cape Town became for a time the frontline in a war of attrition with the SAP and SADF. Political activists no longer slept at home. Children feared to venture into the streets. Casspirs and Buffels patrolled the townships, arresting anyone who remotely resembled a 'trouble-maker'. The emergency powers were used to 'systematically destroy the mass-based organizations which have made massive gains and won widespread support since the institution of the tricameral parliament'.[146] Those who regarded themselves as irregular guerrillas in the struggle against white minority rule coined the slogan, 'The Western Cape will liberate South Africa'.[147]

In late November, an estimated 1,000 troops and police were involved in a combined security forces operation in Guguletu as a result of persistent unrest. Police diverted thousands of youths on trains who planned to stage a mid-day demonstration in City Centre.[148] In Crossroads there was a series of gun-battles in which a number of police were shot. The SADF conducted a major security blitz in the area. In early December, the township was completely 'sealed off as hundreds of soldiers and police lined the ramshackle squatter camp streets'.[149] Even though they lagged behind South Africa's other major urban centres, Cape Town's oppressed majority was finally baptized by fire.

7.

South Africa's Political Impasse

Economic Dimensions of the Crisis

Economic Recession and the Decomposition of the National Party's Class Alliance

For at least three decades, the dominant classes of South Africa have depended upon sustained economic growth and widening prosperity in order to deflect mounting challenges to their rule. Yet the combination of the worldwide economic downturn and the unravelling of the specific features that had sustained the country's particular 'growth model' produced all the visible signs of generalized crisis. For the white minority regime, the worsening economic situation only exacerbated the political disorder. A combination of factors contributed in South Africa to an unprecedented recessionary cycle and economic downturn. Gold production had for a century served as the barometer of well-being for the propertied classes. After experiencing an exaggerated boom in demand during 1979-80, the world price of gold declined drastically. Persistently high rates of inflation coupled with the decline of the relative value of the rand caused the price of imported commodities, mainly machinery, technology, and semi-manufactured goods, to double during the early 1980s. By mid-1985, the rate of corporate bankruptcies reached the level of ten insolvencies per day.[1] All in all, business liquidations averaged eight per day during 1985, more than doubling the rate of the previous year.[2] The abrupt reduction of state subsidies pushed food, electricity, and postal rates skyward. In the first quarter of 1985, retail sales declined 2.5 per cent over the previous year, new automobile sales plummetted by a hefty 50 per cent, and manufacturing slipped by 5 per cent. [3] In April 1985, petroleum prices experienced a quantum leap of 40 per cent.[4] The economic downswing reached a low point in the third quarter of 1985, but showed few signs of substantial improvement in subsequent months. In February 1986, sales by wholesalers in real terms had declined nearly 10 per cent from the previous year and reached their worst level since mid-1983. The manufacturing sector experienced in 1986 its worst February for physical volume of output since 1979.[5]

Economic planners at the commanding heights of the state administration reacted to this economic situation with their own peculiar versions of economic neo-liberalism and supply-side solutions. A rash of budgetary projections warned that across-the-board cuts would most certainly reduce spending on social programmes. In May 1985, the Central Bank increased interest rates to 25 per cent in order to combat the 16 per cent inflation. 'We will squeeze inflation out of the system Reagan-style, Thatcher-style', Gerhard de Kock, the chief of the Central Bank, confidently announced.[6] Despite these ambitious forecasts, the inflation rate reached a 65-year record of 20.7 per cent in January 1986 and in subsequent months only declined slightly.[7]

According to the South African Labour Research Development Unit (SALDRU), real wages suffered their sharpest decline in a decade during 1985.[8] The sluggish level of economic activity was reflected, according to figures supplied by the Central Statistics Services, in an increase of only 1.1 per cent in real Gross Domestic Product (GDP) between 1981 and 1985.[9] By mid-1985, officially registered unemployment was increasing at 'an alarming rate' — about 10,000 per month.[10] The actual unemployment rate probably doubled the official figure. In fact, by mid-1985, unemployment for the black labour force approached 35 per cent.[11] In Port Elizabeth/Uitenhage, the automobile industry — 'an industry in agony' reported the Financial Mail — retrenched at least 33,000 workers from early 1984 to September 1985. Unemployment in the townships in the vicinity of Port Elizabeth reached a catastrophic 56 per cent.[12] The large automobile manufacturers — Ford, General Motors, and Volkswagen

— slowed production to half capacity. The housing market collapsed. After the announcement of the emergency decree, housing prices nosedived with registered declines of almost 50 per cent in some elegant white suburbs.[13] It was reported that redundant farm labourers and their families in drought-striken white agricultural zones had been expelled in large numbers from white farms. These destitute ex-farm labourers assembled in squalid squatter villages where some literally starved to death.[14]

By January 1986, the officially registered white, Indian, and coloured unemployment reached 80,000 persons — more than double the figure of the previous year. African unemployment officially hovered near two million. In the engineering and metal industries alone, an estimated 24,000 workers had been retrenched during 1985.[15] Since the last quarter of 1984, job opportunities in so-called formal sector employment had evaporated at a rate of 8,000 per month. South Africa required an average growth rate of 5 per cent to absorb newcomers into the labour pool. Economists estimated that the growth rate would not reach 3 per cent during 1986.[16] By mid-1986, it was estimated that 'Black matriculants alone are coming into the [labour] market at a rate of 40,000 a year. Only about 5,000 of these are finding employment.' It was also reported that about 80 per cent of black people in South Africa between the ages of 18 and 26 were unemployed.[17] At the same time, increased taxes burdened those least able to afford them. According to official forecasts, it was estimated that the total tax revenues collected in individual income tax and the general sales tax between 1981 and the end of 1986 would have increased a staggering 538 per cent.[18] All economic indicators seemed to point to the fact that the persistent economic stagnation had inexorably approached the limits of social and political tolerance.

Ironically, some businesses have boomed in the midst of this economic downturn. The propitious circumstances of the decline in the rand's exchange rate has created enormous opportunities for South Africa's exporters who suddenly found that some commodities had become more competitive in overseas markets. The falling rand made South African coal the cheapest in the world. Sales of most minerals and metal accelerated. South African companies sold more platinum, manganese, and ferrochrome than ever before and at record prices. Exports of some foodstuffs and processed products also experienced a dramatic upswing.[19]

The National Party's austerity package included the gradual elimination of state subsidies to the agro-industrial complex. For over half a century, white farmers have reaped the financial benefits of state protectionist and pump-priming policies. In May 1985, the National Party snapped one more link of the chain that historically bound it to the white farming vote with its announcement that the Maize Board would be reconstituted. This action effectively broke the grip of the National Maize Producers' Association over the Maize Board, thereby advancing one step closer to the National Party's stated aim of driving agriculture towards the free market.[20] White farmers reacted angrily. On 3 May, an estimated 3,000 farmers gathered in Klerksdorp, a conservative gold-mining town 100 miles west of Johannesburg. These farmers vowed to withold corn crops from authorized state buyers for one week in order to press their demands for higher official prices. This price war locked the increasingly urbanized reformist-minded National Party leadership into bitter conflict with inferior maize farmers — twenty-five years ago the symbolic bedrock of National Party political support. The battle also underscored the fragility of the unstable alliance that the Botha regime had forged in order to embark on the uncharted path of putatively reforming and modernizing *apartheid*.

Small-town conservative whites have experienced economic uncertainty and occasional hardship for the first time in decades. Similarly, 'poor whites' in the urban areas have depended in increasing numbers on bread lines and hand-outs to feed their children. Consequently, many hard-pressed white voters shifted their political allegiances to the rightwing parties, finding solace in the promises of restoring genuine *apartheid*. This breach in the once monolithic bloc of Afrikaner unity represented a serious political challenge to the Botha regime that worsened as the political unrest persisted. In South Africa's splintered white politics, the Conservative Party successfully absorbed followers from amongst white farmers and blue-collar wage-earners who were previously firmly entrenched in the National Party camp. Yet the Conservative Party was even outflanked by other parties and organizations still further to the right.[21] While the *Herstigte Nasionale Party* (HNP) and the Volkswag seem to have crested, the neo-fascist *Afrikaner Weerstandsbeweging* (AWB) has experienced a substantial revival. The AWB's Eugene Terre'Blanche has assumed the role of generalissimo of the loose-knit ultra-rightist coalition. The AWB Programme of Principles rejects parliamentary democracy as a 'British-Jewish' system that weakens the Afrikaner *volk* by promoting divisions. The AWB programme of resurrecting the nineteenth-century Boer Republics as a modern Afrikaner *volkstaat* promises to reunite Afrikaners and to free them from 'spiritual and economic enslavement by Anglo-Jewish money'.[22]

In the yawning shuffle of political allegiances, the Botha regime contributed to the growing uncertainty and insecurity of National Party loyalists by recanting some longstanding rules implanted in the *apartheid* canon. National Party ideologues continued to stress the theme that '*apartheid* is dead' in order to convince South Africa's major trading partners, creditors, and foreign investors that the business climate remained robust. Yet at home the Botha regime frequently made recidivist gestures to the growing rightwing, pledging that the National Party would never capitulate to the 'one-person one-vote' formula in a unitary South Africa.

By mid-1986, the agricultural sector 'was faced with the most serious crisis in its history'. Despite large sums being pumped into agriculture by various state agencies, thousands of white farmers were in desperate straits.[23] According to the Land and Agricultural Bank, the accumulated debt of the white farming sector soared 374 per cent between 1975 and 1984. Over this ten-year period, the increase in farmers' debt averaged 18.4 per cent each year, in contrast to an average inflation rate of 15.6 per cent every year.[24] Between 1984 and 1986, the costs of farming increased an average of 36 per cent while prices for farm products remained at a standstll. Because of inflation, farmers were 50 per cent worse off in 1986 than a decade earlier. Farmers had an average debt burden of 190,000 rand per farmer.[25]

South Africa's Deepening Monetary Crisis

In June 1984, U.S. banks claimed an estimated $4.5 billion in total loans in South Africa. Most of these loans had been extended to banks, with the bulk of the rest offered to large private corporations.[26] These figures obscured the underlying countervailing trend. In 1983 alone, the flow of cash reserves out of South Africa amounted to $711 million. During 1984, lenders withdrew $2.1 billion. By mid-1985, this groundswell became a torrential flood. In late July, the Chase Manhattan Bank announced that it would no longer extend or renew maturing short-term loans to the South African private sector. Chase Manhattan quit making loans to the South African government eight years earlier.

Chase's loans to South Africa were relatively small (purportedly less than $500 million). Some U.S. banks downplayed Chase's decision. Citicorp, the largest banking enterprise in the United States, declared that it would continue lending to private borrowers in South Africa. 'We believe that our continued presence along with United States companies provides a positive force for opposition to *apartheid* and for substantial assistance to black South Africans', proclaimed Wilfred Koplowitz, director of international public affairs for Citicorp.[27]

Nevertheless, this tired litany of *clichés* did not inspire the usual nods of approval. Chase Manhattan's prestige in international banking circles (as the third largest U.S. bank) put pressure on other U.S. banks to follow a similar course of action. Chase Manhattan's decision to discontinue new loans to private borrowers in South Africa and to suspend the renewal of extant loans catalyzed a chain reaction, precipitating what resembled a classical bank run, as a noted international banker put it. The resulting frenzied panic drained the stockpile of foreign reserves and caused the rand to plunge 35 per cent in value in thirteen days.

Following Chase Manhattan's precedent, other U.S. banks also refused to renew, or roll-over, short-term loans as they came due. The gathering momentum of these actions alarmed the usually placid European banks and they also began to call for repayment of short-term loans as they matured. Barclays Bank of London, for instance, went a step further, announcing that it planned to reduce its share in its South African subsidiary — the largest bank in South Africa — from 55 to 40.4 per cent. In a related action, Barclays also disclosed that it was dropping its logo and its name from its South African subsidiary, which in 1984 accounted for 32 per cent of the parent company's overseas profits.

This gradual erosion in business confidence in South Africa evolved in a highly uneven fashion that was obscured in the aggregate data on capital flows. In 1976, many large overseas banks adopted policies prohibiting new loans to South African state agencies and corporations. Between 1982 and mid-1985, U.S. bank loans to the public sector declined by more than half. At the same time, overseas lending to the private sector soared. The tight monetary policy at home encouraged South African companies to borrow overseas where interest rates were considerably lower. In particular, South African banks dramatically increased their overseas borrowing, skyrocketing from less than $500 million in 1979 to $3.5 billion as of September 1984. The borrowings of South African commercial banks consisted in the main of short-term loans that had to be repaid in a few months. But these banks used the proceeds for making longer-term loans to South African companies. In global banking circles, such practices were considered a classical error. The apogee of overseas bank lending to South Africa was achieved in September 1984. From that date onward, all categories of loans have experienced a sharp decline.[28]

The Political Response to the Liquidity Crisis

The economic repercussions of South Africa's deepening political crisis caused the country's already skidding rand to fall about 10 per cent on a single day where, on 27 August 1985, it plummetted to a record low of 36.65 U.S.cents. In 1980, the value of the rand stood comfortably at $1.34. Finance Minister Barend du Plessis immediately suspended trading on the foreign exchange market and closed the Johannesburg stock exchange until 2 September. Commercial banks welcomed this drastic step, arguing that it was inevitable because of the unprecedented pressure exerted by foreign banks demanding the repayment of short-term loans.[29] Other prominent business leaders displayed considerably less optimism. The national commercial association, known by its acronym ASSOCOM, expressed fears that these actions might be a prelude to a reimposition of the exchange controls relaxed two years earlier.[30] For the second time in two weeks, the country's only financial daily, *Business Day*, called for the resignation of State President P.W. Botha.[31]

In late August, the governor of South Africa's Reserve Bank, Gerhard de Kock, flew first to Europe and then to the U.S. in a desperate bid to ease the deepening monetary crisis. He wished to negotiate with leading lending banks over a proposed re-scheduling of loan repayments. For their part, prominent bankers envinced a waning confidence in South Africa's financial stability. This caution stemmed for the most part from the prescient acknowledgement that international economic sanctions were about to be imposed on the country. Banking experts correctly expected de Kock to negotiate standby credit packages with European banks and suggested that he might also attempt to arrange a gold swap involving some of South Africa's gold reserves, at the time worth an estimated $2.2 billion.

At this time, South Africa's total net foreign debts stood at $16.5 billion. Most significantly, a disproportionate 67 per cent of these debts were scheduled for expiry within twelve months. It was the fear that the growing number of pullouts would drain South Africa of its foreign exchange reserves that caused the banking panic. The fact that South Africa's readily available reserves, in addition to the year's expected foreign trade surplus, amounted to less than $5 billion graphically illustrated the severity of the credit squeeze. Not wishing to risk further debt exposure, overseas lenders simply followed the old banking adage: 'Don't panic, but if you do, be the first.' If all banks demanded repayment, not everyone would be paid. Conse-quently, de Kock found himself in a position to do nothing other than warn South Africa's creditors that unless loans were extended South Africa would be compelled to declare a mora-torium on payments of foreign debt.[32]

On 29 August, four leading business associations — the Asso-ciation of Chambers of Commerce, Federated Chamber of Industries, National African Chamber of Commerce, and a business-financed organization called the Urban Foundation — issued a joint statement urging the white minority regime to take giant strides toward making 'structural changes to uphold the political, social, and economic values of our major trading partners', warning that if these actions were not initiated, 'investors and traders will increasingly shy away from South Africa without any formal laws forcing them to do so'.[33] These business organizations urged Pretoria to lift the state of emer-gency and to open negotiations with accepted black leaders, including those in detention. In the statement, business leaders called for 'a new political system of genuine power sharing'.

Nevertheless, while organized business came out in favour of major reforms, it stopped short of demanding a political system of one-person one-vote, fearing that such a condition would invariably lead to major political upheaval.

Anton Rupert, chairman of the Rembrandt group of companies (in addition to being a wealthy industrialist and perhaps the most powerful Afrikaner businessman in South Africa), joined this chorus of increasingly harmonized voices. 'Time has run out', Rupert said in a strongly-worded attack on the P.W. Botha regime. 'This is the Government's final opportunity to correct past wrongs and introduce the sort of reforms the country is strongly signalling its needs so urgently.' He blamed the astronomical growth of unemployment — it had increased 100 per cent over the past year — as the main cause of South Africa's current problems.[34]

South Africa's credit squeeze threatened to reduce the amount of capital available, thereby jeopardizing what appeared to be signs heralding a slight economic revival from what amounted to three years of the worst recession in 50 years in South Africa. Capital flight, if foreign loans were repaid on schedule, would depress the currency, making imported commodities more expensive. Some economists predicted that South Africa would impose restrictions on capital outflows. Banking insiders suggested that 'more stringent measures, such as a debt moratorium, might imperil South Africa's credit rating for years and substantially reduce the flow of foreign capital that would help the economy grow'.[35] Banking experts shared a concern that South Africa would declare a moratorium on payments of principal on the debt of its borrowers. For three years, major banks had grappled with Latin American debtors. Consequently, they developed little appetite for another round of debt rescheduling. Central and commcercial banks in Europe and the United States were thus trapped in a dilemma. 'If they do nothing', one commentator surmised, 'they risk a debt moratorium and international financial crisis. But they are reluctant to put private or public money into South Africa to ease the crisis, both because of doubts about the country's credit worthiness and alarm at the political consequences of being perceived as rescuing South Africa's Government.'[36]

On 1 September, Finance Minister Barend du Plessis announced a four-month freeze on repayments of principal on

South Africa's foreign debt. In a related development, the white minority regime imposed exchange control measures, including the reintroduction of a two-tier exchange rate for the rand that had previously been in place until it had been lifted in 1984. This two-tiered currency system entailed the creation of the legal fiction of 'financial rands'. Signifying the proceeds of sales of foreign-held assets, these financial rands were placed in restricted non-transferable accounts, thereby effectively blocking the drain of foreign currency reserves.[37] International economists reacted to these drastic developments, warning that they represented the precipitous slide toward a siege economy. Banking experts predicted that the debt moratorium and the exchange controls were bound to harm South Africa's credit rating and discourage new lending in the near future. 'Anybody is going to work like a bandit to get out of this situation', an economist at a major U.S. bank predicted.[38]

These dramatic steps designed to stem the flow of currency from South Africa followed months of accelerated capital flight that had been precipitated by the growing uncertainty about South Africa's immediate economic future. The rand rebounded from its all-time record low but soon plunged downward again. By halting repayments until 31 December, the P.W. Botha regime hoped to establish a breathing space to confront the imminent liquidity crisis.

The negotiations between Pretoria and South Africa's major creditor banks dragged on intermittently with little signs of progress toward a formal agreement regarding debt rescheduling. Fritz Leutwiler, former head of Switzerland's central bank, was appointed mediator in September 1985 after South Africa, facing a drain of funds and creditors' demands, stopped making repayments on $14 billion of its $24 billion in foreign debt. In December 1985, the country's Finance Minister, Barend du Plessis, proposed a freeze on repayment of all principal owed until 1990 and asked that all debt maturities be shifted forward by five years thereafter. Creditor banks resoundingly rejected these proposals.[39] In mid-February, Leutwiler persuaded the two sides to accept a short-term accord in which South Africa agreed to make some penalty payments on the frozen debt while the thirty major creditor banks agreed to roll over existing loans maturing within the period of the interim pact. In exchange for the extension of loans, South Africa's Finance Minister lifted the six-month moratorium on the repayment of the $14 billion of short-term debt and agreed to repay 5 per cent of the loans over the next twelve months.[40] In late March, Barend du Plessis announced that 'the major creditor banks have now agreed to maintain their exposure to South African borrowers at not less than 95 per cent of the present level until the end of June 1987, and South Africa will lift the repayment restrictions on 5 per cent of the "affected debt" that has already reached maturity or that will mature up to 30 June 1987.'[41] In April, when the 5 per cent of the previously blocked foreign loans was repaid, about half of the $420 million was re-lent to South Africa. It was technical considerations rather than any improvement in South Africa's credit rating that played the major role in the bankers' decisions to roll over these loans. In the meantime, between February and July, the value of the financial rand, the restricted form of the currency used for exporting capital, had fallen more than 35 per cent. From January 1985, about fifty-five U.S. companies with employees in South Africa decided to pull up the stakes.[42]

Political Dimensions of the Crisis

Limited Options

Two parallel leitmotifs, alternating and competing, have found expression in the programmatic focus of the National Party under P.W. Botha's tutelage. On the one hand, the National Party leadership has championed the drive for economic growth and modernization within the framework of free enterprise disciplined by market competition. This confident prescription for economic prosperity registered a marked departure from the state-centered policies of the post-1948 succession of National Party regimes. The preceding regimes seemed to be locked within the straightjacket dictated by the almost spiritual mandate to preserve the *apartheid* vision at all costs, including the risk of international opprobrium and the retardation of economic efficiency. Under the leadership of P.W. Botha, the official discourse of the National Party assumed a decidedly technocratic and market-inspired character. During the interregnum (1978-83), corporate business leaders both at home and abroad cautiously welcomed the National Party's proposed reforms as tentative yet meaningful steps toward dismantling discriminatory (and disdainful) aspects of *apartheid* policy. These vaguely-defined promises dovetailed nicely with free-market economic principles. In this overblown vision, the National Party appeared to inherit the prized mantle of a true modernizing oligarchy, an enlightened caste which confidently accepted the challenge of uplifting the black masses. Stripped of its evangelical fervor, this 'paradigm switch' — as Joseph Lelyveld referred to the reformist initiatives — symbolized a fashionable contemporary version of the colonialist 'white man's burden'.[43]

On the other hand, the National Party under P.W. Botha has clung to its unequivocal and uncompromising commitment to a racial caste system. Despite political appeals to broaden its popular support within the white electorate, the National Party steadfastly upholds Afrikaner nationalism as the consoling myth ensuring polyclass consensus in time of peril. With a seductive ring, this *laager mentality* has always served the unspoken purpose of rallying the *herrenvolk* to confront common enemies, real or imagined.

From the outset, the Botha regime envisioned an incremental process of controlled and gradual modifications of selective *apartheid* regulations. National Party leaders hoped that expanded economic privileges for the permanently urbanized black township residents (in tandem with broadened opportunities for political participation in local affairs) would placate the growing aspirations, particularly of the emergent black petty bourgeoisie, without diluting or contaminating the sacrosanct pillars of white prosperity and power. In its feverish effort to conceal their actual intentions, the National Party ideologues developed a unique vocabulary, coining such idiomorphic phrases as 'limited consociation', 'consociational democracy', and 'segmental autonomy'.

The escalating township unrest that rocked the white minority regime served as an effective veto undermining this two-pronged strategy. P.W. Botha's most trusted advisors seemed particularly unnerved by what officials depicted as anarchy in many black townships and by the rising crescendo of calls for worldwise economic boycotts that reinforced the disconcerting image of South Africa as an international pariah. The underlying cause of the violent upheaval was the persistent frustration of black people with *apartheid* policies that consigned them to virtual servitude and officially decreed inferiority. Despite the immediate effect of the state of emergency of dampening public displays of disenchantment, a growing conviction took hold within ruling-class circles that this impromptu emergency decree offered only a temporary respite in the ongoing civil strife. This conviction was linked with the widely-shared perception that the only way to escape the current political impasse lay along the treacherous path of delicate negotiations with what were termed 'responsible' black leaders. However, considerable disagreement existed within the white minority regime as to which black figures occupying positions of authority both possessed the requisite charisma and credibility and were dependably malleable.

In the weeks following the state of emergency in July 1985, high-ranking officials in the National Party made all sorts of oblique promises of continuing the 'reformist dialogue', as they put it. They hinted that housing ownership schemes would be extended, that trading restrictions in white areas might be lifted, that equal, but separate, educational opportunities for all population registration groups were contemplated and a thorough overhaul of the hated influx control regulations (restricting where black people could live, work, and travel) was on the legislative agenda. In a highly symbolic gesture, the white authorities permitted Tom Boya, mayor of the black township of Daveyton on the East Rand and a man widely condemned as an Uncle Tom because of his cooperation with the white minority regime, to appear on national television a few days after the imposition of the emergency decree. Boya welcomed the emergency as an interim measure to ensure the restoration of law and order. Yet he defined the bottom line for black people in terms that appeared well beyond the reach of the ruling national party. Boya declared that it would be virtually impossible to contemplate long-term peace unless imprisoned ANC leader Nelson Mandela were released to participate in formal discussions and unless black people were offered political representation at the national and not merely local level. Pretoria was caught on the horns of a dilemma. On the one hand, P.W. Botha and his high-ranking associates intuitively acknowledged that the persistent and intransigent reliance upon repression could not alone provide a lasting solution to what was an elemental political question. On the other hand, the Botha regime risked the wrath of right-wing hardliners who would certainly interpret any enlarged efforts at political accommodation as a sign of vacillation and political weakness. Correlatively, the white minority regime feared that black radicals would interpret even the vaguest hint of concessions as vindication of their confrontational politics. Robert Rothberg aptly described this quandary in his assessment of the emergency decree: 'The declaration was a desperate act. The government already possessed virtually all the powers it established by promulgating the emergency. Most have been employed throughout the past year of intensifying violence. Now, to demonstrate its toughness, and possibly to avoid a few legal complications, the government has chosen martial law, has arrested several hundred black leaders, thrown rings of police and soldiers around particularly violatile black cities, and introduced curfews. Instead of strength, the establishing of an emergency displays an underlying weakness of the state; unwilling to negotiate with blacks over the future of their country, and unable to provide or sanction non-violent channels of protest, the government has been driven to a Draconian choice. Most of all, a state of emergency acknowledges how broad and deep is the chasm between white attempts to reform and black aspirations.'[44] Business executives and politicians alike anxiously awaited P.W. Botha's 16 August formal address before the Natal provincial congress of the governing National Party. Semi-secret disclosures leaked in advance seemed to indicate that President P.W. Botha would unveil bold new pledges offering significant concessions to the black majority, including at least a preliminary blueprint for dismantling *apartheid*. In this rarified and intoxicating atmosphere of almost giddy optimism, P.W. Botha's carefully-crafted pronouncement amounted to nothing less than a disappointing betrayal of the high expectation and unsubstantiated speculation that preceded it.

The Rubicon Speech at the National Party Conclave

In what came to be known as the 'Rubicon Speech', P.W. Botha's defiant, uncompromising, and intransigent defence of the National Party's course of action — coupled with only the vaguest hints of undefined modifications in existing racial policies — thoroughly dismayed even his most zealous political allies. P.W. Botha seemed to retreat into the *laager*, evoking the emotional sentimentalities of the embattled Afrikaner *volk*, besieged by African hordes unready for civilization and abandoned by the nescient and effete West. 'I am not prepared to lead white South Africans and other minority groups on a road to abdication and suicide', P.W. Botha warned. 'Destroy white South Africa and our influence and this country will drift into factions, strife, chaos, and poverty.'[45] This apocalyptical vision seemed to rejuvenate the atavistic mythology of the 'native rising' or 'black peril'.

Both the tenor and the tone of P.W. Botha's announcement reaffirmed the suspicion that the National Party had not deviated from the elementary ideological canons of *apartheid*. Botha insisted that South Africa remained 'a land of minority groups' reflecting 'a diversity of peoples' where all groups should enjoy the rights of 'managing their own affairs and maintaining their own life styles, free of inteference by others'.[46] The vague and undefined promises about future 'power-sharing', 'co-responsibility and participation', and so forth, could not be interpreted as heretical ruptures with the past. Instead they were cleverly camouflaged window-dressing concealing highly circumscribed options within a limited spectrum of historical possibilities. The Botha regime steadfastly refused to budge from one principal tenet of *apartheid*, namely, that South Africa, in Alan Cowell's words, 'is a land of minorities and a patchwork of ethnic and racial nations, separate and competing'.[47] Under the guardianship of P.W. Botha, the National Party had embellished its official discourse with a new set of code words that did not alter the basic meaning of *apartheid* policies but merely filtered these through a neutral-sounding phraseology.

Political Inflexibility

The National Party sought to rebound from the political debacle of the 'Rubicon Speech'. Still reeling from the chilly international reception to his bellicose stance, President P.W. Botha announced on 11 September before the Orange Free State congress of the National Party that his administration was prepared to discuss steps to restore citizenship to the nearly 10 million black South Africans who had been stripped of these rights when their designated tribal Homelands were granted formal political independence from Pretoria. The following day, the President's Council, an appointed advisory body functioning more or less as an upper house of Parliament, recommended the abolition of influx control laws that curbed black access to the segregated townships on the fringes of white cities.[48]

If past practices served as any indication of current realities, all pronouncements of the white minority regime should be greeted with a heavy dose of scepticism. Reluctant to offer anything but the most cosmetic modifications of *apartheid* policies, the National Party seemed eager to reshape its language instead. Lexicographers for the white minority regime have perfected the craft of wordsmithing. For a brief time in the late 1970s, Pretoria concocted the pleasant-sounding phrase 'plural relations' to replace *apartheid*. Even though this new phrase fell into disuse, the word *apartheid* fell into disuse. Henceforth, it was scarely if ever uttered by those officials who held responsibility for enforcing its administration. Similarly, the fluctuating vocabulary of the white minority regime underwent even further metamorphosis. The quaint-sounding term, 'Homelands', was substituted for the outmoded 'Bantustans'. Similarly, the terminology of 'communities' and 'minorities' replaced the officially-decreed population registration groupings.[49]

In the midst of the political crisis, the P.W. Botha regime seemed poised once again to coin a number of new phrases to mask old practices. For the social engineers who fabricated the original *apartheid* design of racial compartmentalization, the prospects of contemplating even minor modifications would have signalled a heretical breach of Afrikaner loyalty tantamount to treason. In the sleight-of-hand word-games characteristic of contemporary media-conscious *apartheid* planners, all pronouncements heralding dramatic changes of heart were couched in obscure and vague caveats and provisos. The nuanced language of *apartheid* has purposefully engendered mixed messages. In the divided perceptions of the white electorate, those on the liberal end of the political spectrum chose to interpret cautious hints of reform as harbingers of real transformations. In contrast, those on the opposite end of the political spectrum condemned even the glacial pace of 'reform' as the opening wedge of black majority rule in a one-party socialist state. Consequently, this disparate admixture of wishful thinking and abject fear emerged as a mass psychological response to an increasingly volatile political situation where no one appeared in control.

With a distinctive rhetorical inventiveness, the white minority regime fully embraced the quasi-surrealist simulacrum that South Africa was a land of multiple minorities and a heterogeneous patchwork of ethnic and racial communities and national entities. In the coded and nuanced messages of white supremacy, the bottom line seemed to have evolved into a broad political commitment to assure that no assemblance of black ethnic 'minorities' should in the future be allowed to swamp and consequently take political power from the white minority of 4.5 million. The National Party's hints at 'power-sharing' and the restoration of citizenship did not contain provisions contemplating common voting rights in a unified and central political system. Despite liberal wishful thinking, the P.W. Botha regime appeared unwavering in its opposition to the establishment of a unified South Africa based on a single, central Parliament and universal adult suffrage for all its citizens, including the black majority. In April, P.W. Botha declared: 'I rule out totally a unitary state, whether it is a federation or not. ... We believe in the principle of one person, one vote as long as it is not in a unitary state.'[50]

Similarly, the recommendations of the special Presidential panel calling for the elimination of influx control did not imply the removal of all limits on black access to segregated urban townships any more than it connoted desegregation of residential and business areas. The President's Council suggested that the passbook (mandated by law to be carried by those of African descent) should be replaced by uniform identity documents for all South Africans and that it should no longer be an offence not to carry one at all times. The panel further urged that the vagaries of market discipline, not skin pigmentation, should dictate both the pace and the scale of urbanization. Some prominent business leaders and National Party chieftains have already renamed 'influx controls', substituting the less offensive argot of 'orderly urbanization' and 'labour facilitation'. As part of this legalistic charade, the Botha regime has increasingly utilized purely market criteria — proof of regular employment and the availability of housing accommodation — in conjunction with a vigorous enforcement of 'anti-vagrancy' legislation (concealed under the generic rubric of maintaining high hygienic standards) to rid the black townships of 'undesirable elements' in dilapidated slums, shantytowns, and informal settlements.

Growing Rifts in the Dominant Bloc of Class Forces

The Political Response of Monopoly Capital

The National Party remained transfixed in a desperate battle to adjudicate and arbitrate between competing constituencies in its broad polyclass alliance. Less constrained than the Botha regime by the political and ideological straitjacket of Afrikaner nationalism, leading representatives of large-scale monopoly capital put forward their class programme to break the political impasse.[51] On 13 September, prominent white South African business executives and newspaper editors held informal discussions in Zambia with exiled leaders of the outlawed ANC. This delegation of seven business executives was drawn for the most part from the ambit of Anglo-American Corporation, South Africa's largest mining company and a giant conglomerate that owned or controlled 70 per cent of the companies listed on the Johannesburg Stock Exchange. This meeting in the remote Luangwa Valley Game Park seemed to signify a clear rebuff of the Botha regime's cautious and limited programme of economic liberalization. Not unexpectedly, the Botha regime scorned these actions, branding them disloyal and a betrayal of trust. In the discussions, the ANC reaffirmed its long-standing commitment calling for the nationalization of some major corporations. 'They represent tremendous wealth in the midst of unspeakable poverty', Oliver Tambo said. 'Some move should be made towards bridging the gap and [promoting] a more equitable distribution of wealth.'[52]

On 27 September, 91 prominent South African businessmen — none of them from large-scale Afrikaner business circles — issued a strongly-worded declaration that urged the abolition of statutory racial discrimination; the granting of full South African citizenship 'to all our people'; and the 'restoring and entrenching of the rule of law'. Signatories included such prominent capitalist figures as Gavin Relly, Chair of Anglo-American Corporation; Harry Bloom, Chair of the Premier Group; Harry Oppenheimer of DeBeers Consolidated Mines; and the heads of the South

African subsidiaries of such transnational corporations as General Motors, Toyota, Hewlett-Packard, B.M.W., Kodak, Mobil Oil, Citibank, Colgate-Palmolive, Volkswagen, Coca-Cola, and General Electric.[53] The historic significance of this unprecedented declaration was two-fold: not only was it evident that a broad spectrum of prominent business leaders wished to distance themselves from what they regarded as the inept blundering of the National Party, but also these businessmen aimed to prod the white minority regime into opening formal negotiations toward a peaceful solution to the political unrest.

In the joint statement, they advocated 'equal opporunity, respect for the individual, freedom of enterprise, and freedom of movement'. Notably absent from the declaration was any reference to the popular demand for universal adult suffrage in an undivided South Africa. 'We believe in the development of the South African economy for the benefit of all its people', the businessmen said. 'We are, therefore, committed to pursue a role of corporate social responsibility and to play our part in transforming the structures and systems of the country toward fair participation for all.'[54] In the main, most prominent business leaders advocated limited political reforms. They endorsed the notion of common citizenship and an end to all racial discrimination. Yet they veered away from proposing a universal franchise in a unitary state and, instead, embraced a vague constitutional arrangement that *a priori* took into account the fact that South Africa 'is an extremely unhomogeneous society'.[55]

In the meantime, the Progressive Federal Party (PFP) took the initiative in a vigorous effort to revitalize the fractured centre of the broad spectrum of South African politics. Scores of political moderates gathered in Johannesburg in mid-September to shape a middle ground between the popular movement that has increasingly adopted a decidedly anti-capitalist stance and the obduracy of the ruling National Party that resolutely refused to present a blueprint for its putative goal of dismantling *apartheid*. Invited participants included corporate executives, white politicians from the PFP, white and black clergymen, black business leaders, Chief Mangosuthu Gatsha Buthelezi, and other reformist-minded liberals. All in all, representatives from an estimated one hundred organizations formed what they called the Convention Alliance with the principal aim of pressuring the Botha regime to establish a national constitutional convention that would fashion a negotiated framework for dismantling *apartheid*. Although this loosely-knit assembly did not formally adopt a strategic plan, it offered itself as a political third force between Pretoria and black militants. As if to convince the Botha regime that they were a political force with which to be reckoned, Frederik van Zyl Slabbert led a delegation of PFP members to Lusaka to meet with ANC leaders on 11 October. These highly visible discussions highlighted the quandry facing the Convention Alliance. Without at least tacit support from the ANC, it appeared unlikely that this third force would gain momentum as a political alternative to the growing polarization between the white minority regime and the popular masses.

By the end of the month, a group of Afrikaans-speaking university students and an interracial delegation of South African clerics announced similar plans to travel to Zambia to meet with ANC exile leaders. This flurry of planned pilgrimages reflected widespread despair among white South Africans who had grown weary of P.W. Botha's apparent inability to resolve the persistent social and political crises.[56] At the end of October, a hastily-formed group called the United States Corporate Council on South Africa, made up of prominent U.S. businesses with investments in the country issued a full-page newspaper advertisement echoing the call by 91 South African business leaders for an end to statutory race discrimination and other changes.[57]

In January 1986, the Federated chambers of Industry (FCI) released two documents, one a 'Charter of Social, Economic and Political Rights' and the other an 'Action Programme of South African Business'. The documents called for 'a realistic and visible programme both of political reform and of economic reconstruction'. The FCI defended this initiative on the grounds that South Africa faced 'growing economic and political isolationism and a drift into a repressive seige society'. Besides urging the removal of statutory discrimination and the strengthening of the trade union movement, the FCI listed as possible preconditions for negotiations between the National Party and black leaders such actions as the release of detainees, lifting the state of emergency, the abolition of influx control and the Group Areas Act, and 'power sharing at central level in a single institution'. Sceptics pointed out not only that the major business associations did not join in this declaration but also that these proposals were not particularly novel.[58]

At the end of January, P.W. Botha opened Parliament with the pronouncement that 'we have outgrown the outdated colonial system of paternalism as well as the outdated concept of *apartheid*'.[59] Yet he reiterated the National Party's fundamental commitment to an 'essentially group-based system of representation in which the white group retains ultimate control while co-opting a moderate elite in other groups in a supportive, symbolic role in government'.[60] Almost immediately, the leader of the Official Opposition, van Zyl Slabbert shocked members of Parliament by resigning both his Parliamentary seat and his central post in the PFP. In his farewell speech, Slabbert labelled Botha's vague promises of a 'new dispensation' the 'New *Apartheid*'.[61] Another PFP leader, Alex Boraine, also submitted his resignation from Parliament. These defections symbolized the growing frustration within liberal circles of negotiating and compromising in the Parliamentary system in order to legislate the end to *apartheid*.

The Metamorphosis of the Popular Movement

The Targets of Popular Revenge

The post-emergency spate of arrests and detentions depleted the popular organizations of their visible leaders and experienced cadres. The popular organizations — including local branches of countrywide groupings, affiliates of regional co-ordinating bodies, and local civic associations — were thus by necessity forced to alter not only their approach of mass mobilization and recruitment but also to experiment with new methods of semi-clandestine existence. The draconian security measures coupled with police spy networks effectively severed above-ground communications between national leadership bodies and local activist organizations. New leaders — generally younger, more radical in outlook, more militant in practice — emerged in the hiatus. The popular opposition to white minority rule evolved in a more decentralized direction. Consequently, the hydra-headed popular movement proved impossible to eliminate simply through detentions of key figures. Perhaps the most visible sign of the persistent spirit of rebelliousness were the nearly continuous school boycotts that endured despite the emergency decree. COSAS was the only popular organization banned outright during the state of emergency. It operated underground. 'Liberation before Education' became the slogan of the increasingly radicalized youth. The schools became symbols of the nationwide confrontation. In one incident, police detained an entire Soweto school of 775 children for two days. Fearful of the explosive potential of hundreds of thousands of youth on the streets of the black townships, the white minority regime imposed strict curfews on schoolchildren in a vain effort to force them back into the classrooms. In early November 1985, nearly 40 per cent of black schoolchildren in urban areas boycotted final examinations. In Soweto, only one in ten eligible students took the yearly examinations.[62]

The defiant refusal of the masses to submit to white minority rule cannot be easily classified into hermetically sealed categories of class and national consciousness. The challenge to minority rule that swelled from below fluctuated wildly between politically self-conscious behavior undertaken under the auspices and direction of the popular organizations and the more or less spontaneous agitation that kept both employers and the white minority regime off balance. The collective self-assertion of the masses during this historical conjuncture was motivated in the main not by conscious ideological predispositions but by a compendium of attitudes and commonsensical notions derived from day-to-day experience with class exploitation and national oppression.

Over the course of the current popular rebellion, the tactical focus on large-scale mass mobilizations (rallies, marches, street agitations, and so forth) gradually gave way to low-profile highly mobile hit-and-run actions. This assessment is, of course, not to suggest that these evolutionary tactics have taken place evenly or that they replaced the more visible expressions of popular politics. What can be argued, however, is that the cycle of mass mobilizations/police killings/public funerals reached a point of exhaustion in every community transfixed by the political upheaval. Small groups of self-conscious activists experimented with new organizational forms, modifying their tactics to correspond to the particular situation they faced.

Whatever ideological differences prevailed, the popular movement — the independent black trade unions, the political coalitions, and the like — instinctively coalesced around a common strategic campaign to prevent the white minority regime from ruling in the old ways and weakening its options for implanting new ways of ruling. The daily clashes between heavily-armed security forces and township residents gradually subsided but the underlying popular discontent remained. In dozens of places, police and soldiers in armoured personnel carriers continued to occupy riot-torn and ravaged black townships, guarding strategic roadblocks and conducting frequent military forays into the densely-packed interiors. Police stations in and around the strife-torn townships were transformed into heavily-fortified garrisons, resembling forlorn outposts, that were resupplied in men and material by armed convoys that ventured into hostile territory.

The targets of black anger were not limited to the distant white authorities but also embraced the local surrogates for white minority rule, that is, town councillors, black policemen, suspected informers and spies, and the coterie of other local officials perceived as collaborating with the white minority regime. On the eve of the state of emergency, Pretoria released casualty figures estimating that about 78 per cent of the nearly 500 people killed since September died in encounters with the security forces.[63] By mid-October, the assaults on those deemed puppets or stooges of white minority rule escalated and multiplied to the point where as many black people were dying at the hands of other blacks as were killed in clashes with the security forces.[64]

The assaults on those individuals who constituted the veritable 'eyes and ears' of the Botha regime in the strife-torn townships had become so frequent that a specialized vocabulary was invented to register the social meaning. 'A Kentucky' — an allusion to the brand of fried chicken of the same name — referred to the form of retribution in which those deemed to be collaborators were burned to death. Another form of summary execution by incineration, in which an old tire was placed around the victim's neck and then dosed with gasoline and ignited, came to be called a 'necklace'.[65] The SAP reported that fifty-four suspected police collaborators had been killed in this fashion in Port Elizabeth's townships between April and October.[66]

These acts of popular vengeance cannot be judged in isolation. Youthful militants were constantly barraged with the grim reminders of the intransigence of the white minority regime. The

seemingly senseless carnage and death conjoined with the endless round of funerals engendered a kind of numbing effect. A
subtle shift in political mood gradually overtook the townships,
propelling the masses toward a search for more radical solutions
that required increasingly harsh tactics. Over the course of
events, assaults on town councillors, black policemen, and other
local officials characterized as collaborators achieved a certain
popular legitimacy and resonance, replacing and superceding the
vague commitment to nonviolence that had historically deep
roots amongst the oppressed in South Africa.

The unarmed foot soldiers in what became an increasingly
underground civil war in the townships organized into small
semi-clandestine groups, trying to mold the unchannelled anger
of the residents into direct action. Groups of black youths frequently surrounded the homes of 'collaborators', attacking them
with a combination of petrol bombs, stones, knives, and
machetes.[67] Yet this flexible array of weapons was certainly not
an even match for those local officials who had hired armed
guards to protect them day and night in their hastily fortified
retreats.

Political Consciousness

The popular movement that formed and evolved in the black
townships did not adhere to a well-defined set of ideological pre-
cepts but blended a number of heterogeneous themes into a
rather complex yet flexible admixture. By way of self-definition,
youthful militants addressed each other as comrades, an all-
encompassing nomenclature that referred at once to friendship,
commitment, and shared outlook. The comrades distinguished
themselves from both their peers and their parents in their collective vow to reject any measure of compromise with the white
minority regime. For the young militants, their commitment to
social egalitarianism and democratic radicalism was matched by
their shared denunciation of 'the system', an almost infinitely
malleable term that was at once sneering epithet and a catchall
phrase referring to white authority and its many offshoots. After
touring the riot-torn black townships, one correspondent
described the popular movement in the following way: 'It is
highly disciplined, if diffuse, political action which is directed at

destruction of "the system", and which increasingly defines that "system" in radical Marxist terms as including any display of "bourgeois values". What is taking shape across the country, without any help from Moscow and very little from Lusaka, is a loosely organized, radical mass movement of youngsters who operate outside any law and without identifiable leaders. They see themselves as socialists and their enemy as white capitalism.'[68] This same correspondent also remarked that 'if the oratory at funeral rallies is anything to go by, the covert ideologues of the township struggle would steer it far to the left, with talk of class struggle and revolution'.[69] Despite the rhetorical edge, the increasingly radicalized language that animated and energized the popular movement could not be dismissed as hyperbolic expression or the effusive posturing of firebrands.

Township activism cast the ANC in a new role in the zones of contention, 'transforming the outlawed and exiled organization into more of a spiritual inspiration rallying point of protest than a director or controller of day-to-day events'.[70] Tom Lodge, who is widely regarded as South Africa's leading academic expert on the ANC, suggested that in the typical scenario localized grievances precipitated violent clashes between township residents and the security forces. 'But very quickly political movements come in and play a leading role,' Lodge argued. Those popular organizations, he said, had 'given a kind of purpose and a long-term agenda. In some ways, the unrest has taken the ANC by surprise, and they are certainly not in control of it or in any position to be able to control it. When the ANC calls for making the townships ungovernable, they are not leading the way, they are trying to associate themselves with what is happening.'[71]

It is indisputable that the enduring legacy of the ANC's long-standing opposition to white minority rule captured the imagination of young militants in the townships. The ANC achieved an almost folklore status, cloaked in near-romantic mystery and rooted in a mixture of fact and fantasy. At funeral rallies, youngsters raised their voices in support of the Umkhonto we Sizwe. 'Their chants provided a litany naming the Congress's imprisoned or exiled leadership', one correspondent observed. 'The dances, too, are choreographed to a theme of confrontation, mimicking guerrillas firing assault rifles from the hip, a charade of armed conflict in which only one side — the authorities — commands real firepower.'[72] The combination of ANC banners and flags displayed prominently at public gatherings, songs and dances, and the innuendo infused into fiery speeches proffered the distinct impression that the ANC was everywhere.

Paradoxically, these claims engendered the hint of disillusionment and a cynical backlash. The ANC promoted the slogan, 'Make the system unworkable and the townships ungovernable.' Yet with the virtual collapse of white authority in many townships and the ensuing state of siege, the ANC seemed incapable of actively participating on the side of partisans in the townships and of implanting a permanent base of operations in the months immediately following the emergency decree. On the ground, there was considerable evidence that the ANC became somewhat of a moral compass, influencing the direction of the mass movement. Yet there was little indication that it steered the course of events, and still less that is proved capable of providing weapons for its supporters.[73] The frustrated remark — 'We blacks are dying in the streets of Cape Town and the ANC is doing nothing except sitting back in Lusaka twiddling its thumbs' — represented perhaps an exaggerated opinion.[74] Yet available evidence appeared to indicate that the rising chorus of anonymous voices, pleading 'give us guns', went unrewarded.

The Emergence of Organized Vigilantes

In the propaganda war that complemented the conflicts in the black townships between the authorities and their adversaries, South African officials often complained that what was depicted as political protest could be largely attributed to a kind of desultory and monochromatic 'black-on-black violence'. The term seemed to be designed to 'absolve the white authorities of responsibility for some of the bloodshed and to support the notion that the national state of emergency [was] justified not as quelling dissent but as quelling random violence so as to permit political change.' The label, critics insisted, was quite misleading since 'in many instances the feuding among blacks in the townships reflects not so much the savagery implied by the official view, but the results of a bitter, often nocturnal war between those who style themselves anti-*apartheid* freedom fighters and those they see as stooges of a white authority delaying the struggle for majority rule'.[75]

During the latter half of 1985, a veritable smorgasbord of vigilantes, secret hit squads, and paid thugs surfaced in the riot-torn
townships and the Homelands. According to Nicolaus Haysom,
a civil rights lawyer, these extra-legal groups — generically
referred to as vigilantes (or Mabangalala) — shared three
common features: (1) they emerged more or less at the same time
'from regions as far afield as the Cape Peninsula and the
Northern Transvaal'; (2) they adopted a common objective,
namely, to neutralize or eliminate members or leaders of groups
associated with resistence to *apartheid* or Homeland rule; and (3)
the 'vigilantes operated brazenly, apparently believing that they
enjoyed police support, and indeed in some cases did allegedly
enjoy such support'.[76] Vigilante groups were able to implement
'a kind of terror that police are not capable of'. Police actions in
the townships tended to be unfocused and indiscriminate. In
contrast, vigilante activities in the main were directed at specific
targets. While there was only little evidence to support the contention that the security forces orchestrated widespread vigilante
activities from behind the scene, nevertheless it did appear that
the police 'were drawn in as a collaborating authority'.[77] In an
effort to provide a class analysis of the emergent vigilanteism,
Jeremy Seekings maintained that 'opposition to progessive township organization comes primarily from a growing group of
embryonic capitalists such as shop, shebeen, and taxi owners', in
addition to town councillors, local policemen, civil servants, and
others with perhaps a small stake in eradicating anti-*apartheid*
political activism. 'Their material interest in stability, a related
inclination toward conservatism and fear for their lives and
property', Seekings continued, 'form the basis for their violent
defense' of the *status quo ante.*[78]

Haysom distinguished two broad types of rightwing vigilante
groups that emerged in 1985. First, the Homelands' vigilantes
'appear to be litle more than paramilitary auxiliaries whose sole
function is to prevent the appearance of any organized resistance
to the Homeland authorities'.[79] These rightwing groups
resembled 'classical versions of fascist brownshirts' and did little
to obscure their political affiliation with authoritarian Homeland
leaders.[80] Second, township vigilantes were considerably more
heterogeneous than their Homeland counterparts. In the main,
the driving force behind the emergence of township vigilante
groups was the real fear of town councillors and local business-

men that the growth of the anti-*apartheid* activism would undermine their power-base and hence loosen their authority over
local residents. Yet it was also the case that the class and status
cleavages dividing the black townships exacerbated the latent
tensions, creating fertile ground for vigilante groups to 'manipulate or play on resentments or insecurities felt by sections of the
community'. The urban vigilantes thus generally exhibited a
specific dynamic peculiar to their own circumstances. The principal targets of these township vigilantes were youth groups and
civic associations which were 'perceived by the officially-
sanctioned municipal authorities as a threat to their status,
credibility, or security'.[81] Legal responses to vigilante activities
were 'generally not effective'. As a consequence, township residents were 'increasingly disillusioned' with seeking legal
remedies and, in some instances, the escalating cycle of violence
led to the emergence of armed 'counter-vigilantes'.[82]

Vigilante groups first came into existence in several Homelands from at least the early 1980s, operating either with the
passive connivance of Homeland authorities or under their direct
instruction and supervision. In Ciskei, Life President Lennox
Sebe's vigilantes acquired, over more than a decade, a reputation
for ruthlessness in confronting political opposition. In 1974, vigilantes operating under the shelter of the Homeland regime
became known as the 'Green berets' after they were called upon
to crush a bus boycott in Mdantsane — the largest town in the
Ciskei with an estimated population of 350,000 in 1985 — that
served as a dormitory suburb for black workers employed in and
around the port of East London. In 1977, this vigilante group was
deployed to quell disturbances after the death in detention of
Steve Biko. President Sebe once again regrouped the vigilantes
as a 'police reserve' to combat the 1983 Mdantsane bus boycott.[83]

By 1985, the Sebe clique had become so politically isolated
and so distrustful of intra-palace intrigue that loyalists tapped
the telephones of all senior civil servants with special equipment
provided by an Israeli security firm.[84] In October, President Sebe
authorized the formation of vigilante groups in all towns and
villages in the Ciskei. Promising that 'evil-doers' would be
'hunted like animals', he vowed that regular police would be
withdrawn from areas that did not form vigilante groups and
that men who did not join the vigilantes would be evicted from
their homes.[85] As the anti-*apartheid* protests spilled into the

Ciskei, vigilantes — operating more or less on their own initiative and without recognizable police supervision — came into existence in Zwelitsha township outside King William's Town in order to aid the security forces.[86] Residents reported that three state-owned white kombis patrolled the area at night, enforcing an undeclared curfew. On numerous occasions, these vigilantes — armed with sticks, sjamboks, and other weapons — indiscriminately assaulted, terrorized, and otherwise harassed township residents.[87] In time, the Sebe clique publicly distanced itself from the Zwelitsha group, yet not before some vigilantes had implicated high-ranking members of the Ciskei government in their activities.[88]

The formation of state-sponsored vigilantes in KwaNdebele — the smallest and one of the most impoverished of South Africa's Homelands — cannot be separated from Pretoria's longstanding commitment to establish tribal Homelands. Prior to 1975, KwaNdebele consisted of a miniscule 55,000 hectares. Since that time, Pretoria allocated large sections of neighbouring land to the original farmstead occupied by a small group of Ndebele.[89] KwaNdebele's population expanded dramatically as the result of forced resettlement and the influx of an estimated 50,000 residents of Bophuthatswana's Winterveld squatter camp who had been victimized because they were non-Tswana. As a consequence of these developments, KwaNdebele had grown to an estimated 350,000 hectares and the population to about 300,000 to 400,000 residents.[90] Despite official assertions to the contrary, knowledgeable critics have argued that 'only about 40 per cent of [KwaNdebele's] population are Ndebeles and that the area of shacks and barren ground was designed simply as a labour pool for Pretoria and elsewhere that would keep blacks away from white cities, but enable them to commute'.[91]

Despite widespread incredulity, Pretoria scheduled to annoint this tiny 'self-governing national state' with political independence in December 1986. In order to bolster both the size and the population of KwaNdebele, South African officials agreed to incorporate the district of Moutse — a fertile plot of 66,000 hectares nominally located in Lebowa — into KwaNdebele against the wishes of its 120,000 inhabitants and to annex the relatively modern township of Ekangala. Ekangala was a 'model' housing scheme comprised largely of urban people displaced from the East Rand and Pretoria townships because of the acute housing shortage in those areas. It was near Bronkhorstspruit, about sixty miles east of the main Pretoria-Witwatersrand axis. The people of Ekangala travelled between six and eight hours daily to their jobs on the Reef and in Pretoria. Few worked at the adjoining Ekindustria industrial zone because the wages there were exceptionally low and in only a few instances would be sufficient to pay the high rental charges.[92]

Vigilantes first emerged in Ekangala to eliminate any opposition to annexation. But it was at Moutse that gangs conducted an indiscriminate reign of terror. At midnight on 1 January 1986 — the morning that Mouste was formally ceded to KwaNdebele — truckloads of KwaNdebele vigilantes invaded Moutse, seemingly intent on enforcing the official edict and on establishing their new fiefdom.[93] In the scattered clashes over the next few days between Moutse residents and the self-styled 'Mbhokhoto' vigilantes (identified by white crosses painted on their foreheads), at least twenty people were killed. Armed vigilantes — in league with KwaNdebele state officials — abducted over 400 men who were transported to Siyabuswa, the capital of KwaNdebele, where they were beaten and flogged for hours before being released.[94]

In order to defuse a tense situation that had assumed a war-like character, South African officials offered those Moutse residents who did not wish to remain under KwaNdebele authority the option of resettling within Lebowa in transit camps at Immerpan and Saliesloot.[95] This solution was obviously a contortion of *apartheid*'s own logic. 'The inference from the offer', one correspondent who recognized the irony of the convoluted reasoning remarked, 'seemed to be that the so-called homelands, for the Moutse people at least, are interchangeable.'[96] In late January, Prime Minister Simon Skhosana — former truck driver and the most educated member of KwaNdebele's Cabinet in 1982 (despite the fact he had failed to attain standard six, the first year of high school) — officially launched the Mbhokhoto movement, creating in effect a private guard under his personal command.[97] Shop owners and local businessmen were the chief sponsors of the Mbhokhoto vigilantes. Popular resentment against the Skhosana regime, the Mbhokhoto reign of terror, and proposed 'independence' reached a climax in May and June. The combination of widespread rioting and a growing rift in the Ndzundza royal family threatened to topple the governing clique in KwaNdebele.[98]

The other Homelands were not immune from the actions of vigilantes operating outside the veneer of legality. In October 1985, former student leader and UDF activist, Bathwanda Ndondo, was executed in broad daylight in Transkei by an armed group suspected of being police officers.[99] In Lebowa, the president of the Student Representative Council at the Modjadji Training College near Tzaneen in the Northern Transvaal was beaten to death.[100]

In the Homelands, the sporadic incidents of vigilante terror gradually escalated into broader confrontations pitting Pretoria's client rulers — who turned to repression to maintain their tenuous grip — against an increasingly emboldened popular opposition. In March, Bophuthatswana's President Lucas Mangope publicly acknowledged that the growing unrest represented a challenge to his authority and leadership. Mangope warned Bophuthatswana residents that 'we are at war', urging 'every man' to 'stand up and fight back'. He singled out the UDF as being responsible for the unrest that spilled into Ga-Rankuwa, Mabopane, Winterveld, and the neighbouring Soshanguve commuter settlement near Pretoria. According to the *Financial Mail*, '[Mangope's] call for the people to stand up and fight seems to have been interpreted with gusto by the Bophuthatswana police and army. Scores of inhabitants — young and old, men and women — especially at Ga-Rankuwa, Mabopane and Winterveld have revealed appalling weals on their backs, claiming they have been brutally assaulted by police. The unrest appears to have reached crisis point in these areas. Inhabitants claim police brutality in the region is directed mainly at members of the Metal and Allied Workers' Union (MAWU), the Roman Catholic church, and schoolchildren.'[101]

On 26 March, Bophuthatswana police at Winterveld (a township of more than one million about sixty miles north of Pretoria) fired into a crowd of tens-of-thousands, killing at least eleven and taking about 2,500 into custody. The demonstration had been protesting housing conditions and the upsurge of arrests and indiscriminate beatings of children.[102]

In Lebowa, Chief Minister Cedric Phatudi convened a special session of the Homeland's various governing bodies to request that Pretoria provide soldiers and more police to aid the local authorities in eliminating 'subversive' organizations operating in villages and townships within the Homeland. In March, the security police detained AZAPO's national organizer and the entire northern Transvaal leadership. In April, the circumstances surrounding the deaths in detention of AZAPO member Lucky Kutumela and the UDF president of the Northern Transvaal, former Robben Island prisoner Peter Nchabeleng, highlighted the escalating repression. Nchabeleng's death came after two months of a state of civil war between the local armed forces and the people of the huge Sekhukhuneland region in the Groblersdal-Lydenburg-Pietersburg triangle. The unrest resulted in the declaration of no-go areas in the rural villages where the police feared to venture without massive reinforcements. By mid-April, Lebowa residents had lodged more than 440 assault claims against the security forces. There were also numerous allegations of police torture and direct police involvement in a spate of petrol-bomb and hand grenade attacks against known activists.[103]

In *Mabangalala*, Nicholas Haysom chronicled the rise of urban township vigilantes in considerable detail. Hence, there is no need to repeat his narrative here. A reign of terror gripped a number of townships. Gangs of vigilantes — some proudly named the 'A-Team' after the U.S. television series — struck back mainly at anti-*apartheid* activists who had gained the upper hand in many places. For the most part, community councillors sponsored the formation of such groups and, in many but not all instances, directly orchestrated their activities. In Haysom's words, 'Community councillors obviously have found themselves in a position where formal agencies of the state cannot guarantee popularity or continued position. The police, limited by law and by the publicity which inevitably follows extra-legal conduct, are unable to perform the function of terrorizing groups and coercing consent to the ambitions of the community councillors. The community councillors, now associated with vigilantes, have resorted to their private armies which they have either hoped or trusted would be sanctioned or tolerated by the authorities.'[104]

In some instances, vigilante groups simply press-ganged politically unsophisticated unemployed youth to join their ranks. In many instances, community councillors enticed so-called 'illegal residents' to take part in operations with the promise that their actions would be rewarded with official authorization to legally remain in the township. Armed with guns in some instances, vigilantes were most active in the townships of Fort Beaufort, Huhudi, and Zolani in the Cape Province; Chesterville, Umlazi, and KwaMashu near Durban; Thabong, Tumahole, Seeisoville, and Virginia in the Free State; and Atteridgeville, Ekangala, and Leandra in the Transvaal. At Thabong near the goldmining town of Welkom 250 kilometers south of Johannesburg in the heart of the Free State farm land, the 'A-Team' or the 'Phakathis' operated openly from Room 29 of the Phillip Smit Centre which belonged to the Southern Free State Development Board but was leased to the local township council. Floggings led to the deaths of at least three school-age children.[105]

At Huhudi near Vryburg in the arid northern Cape, vigilantes targeted the UDF-affiliated Huhudi Civic Association (HUCA) as the object of their wrath. In a memorandum addressed to the Northern Cape Attorney General, a lawyer wrote: 'Many members of HUCA have been subjected to a continuous pattern of harassment, intimidation, assaults and threats by members of vigilante groups and their henchmen in the township. The situation culminated in a number of particularly vicious and brutal attacks during the week 20 to 27 November 1985. As a result, people have been killed, houses gutted and many other people assaulted and/or their property damaged.'[106] In Fort Beaufort, in the Eastern Cape, community councillors formed vigilante groups that seemingly enjoyed the protection of the SAP.[107] Vigilantes who called themselves Amasolomzi emerged in Zolani township near Ashton. They operated in league with local police to enforce a 9 pm curfew and to violently oppose school boycotts.[108] In nearby Nkqububela township outside Robertson, residents were also subjected to a wave of vigilante attacks that resulted in numerous serious injuries and deaths. The collusion between the SAP and local community councils was revealed when a senior member of the Western Cape Development Board confirmed that the Board had supplied firearms and weapons-training courses to town councillors. On a broader scale, Chris Heunis, Minister of Constitutional Development and Planning, admitted that R388,000 had been spent arming community councillors in different parts of the country since 1984. He confirmed that out of the 1,227 councillors representing 194 councils, 245 councillors from 55 councils had been issued arms and ammunition 'on an on-going basis'.[109]

In Atteridgeville outside Pretoria, an unidentified group of thugs conducted a 'reign of terror' — combining arson attacks with physical assaults — against anti-*apartheid* activists that reached alarming proportions by November 1985.[110] In Leandra near Secunda in the Eastern Transvaal, the catalyst for the growth of rightwing vigilantes was the emergence of a popular and effective community organization, the Leandra Action Committee (LAC). Under the leadership of Abel Nkabinde and Chief Ampie Mayisa, the LAC successfully opposed forced removals and high rents. A series of bloody confrontations pitting the LAC against town councillors and local police transformed this hard-scrabble shantytown of about 18,000 residents into a battle-ground. Throughout November 1985, a wave of shootings, stoning, arson attacks, and assaults left a number of dead. In December, vigilante groups — who called themselves Inkatha — openly sided with the community council. The scale of violence quickly escalated, culminating in the murder of Ampie Mayisa, who was hacked to death and burned.[111] On the day of Mayisa's funeral, renewed fighting erupted between LAC supporters and pistol-wielding vigilantes. In the next few days, scores of Leandra residents were forced to flee their homes because of vigilante death threats. Some sought sanctuary in Roodepoort at the Wilgespruit Fellowship Centre and others found refuge in nearby KwaThema.[112] In late March, after spending more than two months 'in exile' at Wilgespruit Fellowship Centre on the West Rand, about fifty Leandra 'refugees' were attacked by 'car-loads of conservative vigilantes' during their abortive attempt to return to their homes. Two unidentified white men — 'acting in support of the vigilantes' — assaulted journalists who observed the ambush.[113]

During the August 1986 bloodletting in Durban's townships, Inkatha hastily sponsored the formation of 'warrior bands' called Amabutho to ostensibily prevent indiscriminate looting, combat hooliganism, and restore law and order. Large contingents of the Amabutho were made up of rural Zulu-speakers recruited in northern Natal, migrants, and hostel-dwellers. These armed mobs operated in Inanda, Umlazi, KwaMashu, Ntuzuma, and Lamontville. Inkatha itself either claimed that the Amabutho performed a useful social function or that they were provoked into violence by 'unruly elements'. In other cases, Inkatha leaders washed their hands of any responsibility, denying emphatically that these armed mobs had formal links to their organization.[114]

In Chesterville, a small well-established township northwest of Durban, a group of the 'A-Team' vigilantes were formed in late 1985, operating more or less as a paramilitary police unit that specialized in combatting the persistent school boycotts. This group consisted of paid ex-convicts and police informers and openly declared that its aim was to "eliminate" all troublemakers stirring up the unrest'.[115] Unlike Durban's other townships many of which are located within the nominal borders of KwaZulu, Inkatha did not have a strong presence in Chesterville. The area, which bordered the affluent white suburb of Westville, was quiet during the August 1985 unrest. In September, however, a local school boycott quickly escalated into petrol bombings, arson attacks, and street demonstrations. The 'A-Team' was formed to retaliate against suspected 'trouble-makers'. Township residents alleged that the security police had instigated the establishment of this vigilante group. The 'A-Team' targetted UDF members, trade unionists, and student activists. The spate of killings (where victims were often mutilated), assaults, and petrol bombings terrified residents. In January 1986, this conflict 'took a new turn with militant youths taking potshots at police and people alleged to be members of the "A-Team" vigilante groups'.[116]

White vigilante groups were also formed. In Cape Town, an anonymous group calling itself the Vigilante Act Group claimed responsibility for an arson attack in October 1985 that destroyed the offices of seven UDF-affiliated organizations. In November, this Vigilante Action Group — widely believed to be a white right-wing commando — also attempted to assassinate the publicity secretary for the South African Council on Sport (SACOS) in Port Elizabeth.[117] In early 1986, the Stallard Foundation, a newly-formed 'forum for conservative thinkers', launched a nationwide recruitment drive for white vigilantes with the stated aim of combatting crime in white urban areas. The Foundation's proposed system of 'neighbourhood watches' followed on the heels of the decision of the far-rightwing *Afrikaner Weerstandsbeweging* (AWB) to form a 'guard unit' in Krugersdorp after petrol-bomb attacks on a white suburb that abutted the black township of Munsieville.[118] White citizens of Krugersdorp, a conservative mining town west of Johannesburg, defended the decision to form a private security committee that would undertake sentry duties and mount night patrols on the grounds that 'the police and army have been too soft'.[119]

After two white policemen were stoned and stabbed to death during unrest at a nearby mining complex in January, a 'white right-wing vigilante group' wearing face-masks and overalls 'went on the rampage' for a week at the end of February in Kagiso township near Krugersdorp. These 'hooded vigilantes', wielding guns, pickaxe-handles, and whips, cruised the ghetto at night in an open van, driving without lights and attacking anyone they came across. 'The white people want to kill us all', one resident reported. 'They just shoot at us.' Many residents were seriously injured in these attacks and at least one youth was killed.[120]

Conflicts in the Townships

In the South African townships, the grinding poverty, high unemployment, and lack of opportunities for economic advancement created a fertile breeding ground for hopelessness and despair. The large numbers of unemployed ensured that thousands of able-bodied work-seekers drifted back and forth between casualized labour and criminal behaviour. Youth gangs found a niche in this festering miasma. These gangs were certainly not monolithic in social composition, character, motivation, or objectives. Yet reports began to trickle in from the embattled townships that bands of self-seeking bandits were exacting concessions and otherwise fleecing township residents under the pretext of advancing the popular struggle. In Mamelodi, gangsters indulged in the fanciful charade that they were 'comrades' engaged in 'the struggle' but instead they terrorized residents in the name of the UDF and the outlawed COSAS.[121] In Umlazi, parents of school-age children were forced to pay 'protection fees' to 'impis' who guarded schoolyards from circulating agitators.[122] In Cape Town, the Western Cape Civic Association hastily organized an impromptu meeting in October to defuse tensions that threatened to degenerate into violence between residents of Guguletu, Nyanga, and Langa, and contract workers living in men's hostels. Both sides reached an understanding that the repressive actions of the security forces had provoked a kind of undisciplined hooliganism.[123] As if on cue, gangs of youths on the following day rampaged through Langa and Guguletu townships, attacking sheebens because liquor sales were 'retarding the struggle'.[124]

In Soweto, several political organizations noted for their ideological diversity (AZAPO, AZASM, and the Soweto Civic Association) joined the Soweto Youth Congress (a UDF-affiliate) in a programme designed to rehibilitate thugs molesting residents and engaging in self-aggrandising banditry in the name of 'the struggle'. Gangs of youths masquerading as members of the banned COSAS had harassed township residents. In White City Jabavu (Soweto), thugs went 'on house-to-house raids demanding either "protection fees" or donations to cover "funeral costs" of fictitious students'. There were also widespread reports that undisciplined youth gangs deprived residents of their groceries — in some instances forcing boycott violators to drink cooking oil and detergent — since the commencement of the consumer boycotts. In perhaps the most brazen act of thuggery, one gang accosted two young women in their homes in Central Western Jabavu, robbed them of money, and sexually assaulted them in view of their parents.[125]

In Krugersdorp's Kagiso and Munsieville townships, the Kagiso Youth Congress and the Kagiso Consumer Committee joined together to impose a voluntary night-time curfew, to prevent vandalism, and to enforce a 'code of decent human behaviour'. Small groups of youths toured the townships at night, ordering loitering trouble-makers, drunks, and thieves off the streets. It was reported that, at least temporarily, serious crimes were almost totally eradicated.[126] In Soweto, the murder in early March of PUTCO bus driver, Jerry Mothibedi, highlighted the disturbing reality that 'bands of youths were committing acts of thuggery daily "in the name of the struggle"'. Members of major anti-*apartheid* organizations and trade unions, including COSATU, the UDF, and AZAPO, joined more than 5,000 mourners at Mothibedi's funeral in calling for 'black unity' and condemning 'black-on-black violence'. The Pretoria-Witswatersrand-Vaal Consumer Boycott Committee used the occasion of Mothibedi's death to assail the 'notorious "comrade robbers"', proclaiming that it 'was high time this type of thuggery was stamped out'. The Consumer Boycott Committee unveiled new tactics that revolved around the formation of sub-committees in the townships charged with monitoring the campaigns and combatting 'thugs masquerading as political activists'.[127] Despite these efforts to combat hooliganism, conflicts between political activists and criminal gangs surfaced with regularity. In late March, a renewed wave of violence erupted between comrades and gangsters in Diepkloof and Orlando in Soweto. At least six persons were killed in the fighting. The Makabasa gang vowed to slay fifty youths in retaliation for the necklace killings of two of their members. Residents of Jabavu, Zola, and Emdeni districts formed neighbourhood watch groups to expel unruly elements from their districts. In April, a gang leader, nicknamed 'Rambo', was necklaced with a burning tyre in Zone 6, Meadowlands (Soweto). He allegedly went on a rampage, killing a number of people, including schoolchildren, after his home was firebombed by 'comrades'.[128]

The People's Courts

In countless townships, community councillors, policemen, and other officials were either killed, forced to flee, or resigned. The resulting disintegration of the township administration left a vacuum that the popular organizations sought to fill. In many instances, 'people's courts' were formed to replace the collapsing police and court systems that had lost their legitimacy. In the words of one correspondent, 'Police and troops patrol these townships by day, but by night the Comrades rule. ... In several areas they are known to exact taxes and to have organized ... courts which, residents say, have dramatically reduced townships crime.'[129] Some partisan observers hailed the people's courts as a functional alternative to *apartheid* justice because of the emphasis on education and compensation (such as the return of stolen goods) rather than punishment and retribution.[130]

However, there was another side to these improvised tribunals. In some instances, the people's courts (modelled after the popular U.S. television charade of the same name) were transformed into 'kangaroo courts' where the style of 'frontier justice' and hasty verdicts often claimed victims who were the targets of private enmities or political animus. By October, the seemingly senseless and random killings were commonplace in the townships of the Eastern Cape. During the previous six months, at least eight-three people died in what the police termed 'the doorstep killings'. The death tally included women and children who were sometimes forcibly taken from their homes and murdered outside their front gates by death squads who called themselves comrades. According to township residents, clandestine people's courts were formed to 'punish' those alleged to have hindered 'the struggle', meting out primitive sentences on wrongdoers. For those condemned to death, a tire dowsed in petrol was draped as a 'necklace' around the head and shoulders of the accused and then set alight. In a propaganda blitz, the security forces claimed that political activists who controlled these apparatuses aimed to undermine established judicial procedures and replace them with a code of their own. They also alleged that in some areas those that operated the 'people's courts' funded their operations by collecting rents from intimidated households and by demanding protection money from shopowners. Finally, they suggested that this new trend was rooted in the struggle for regional supremacy between UDF and AZAPO.[131]

Both UDF and AZAPO vehemently denied that their organizations had authorized such random killings. In early October, UDF activist Stone Sizani briefly emerged from hiding to 'condemn the parading of people before these so-called kangaroo courts'. Other activists echoed the plea that UDF members should not allow themselves to become unwittingly trapped in these debilitating exercises — to be used by the security forces or by 'corrupt elements' in the townships.[132] There seemed to be widespread speculation that the large-scale detentions of trade union and community leaders had left the townships 'rudderless and open to takeover by extremists'.[133]

In late October, the uneasy truce between UDF and AZAPO ended with clashes in Kwazakele and Zwide townships outside Port Elizabeth. These sporadic outbursts of violence and recrimination for months 'had threatened to tear Port Elizabeth's black areas apart and people on both sides died horribly — many were victims of the "necklace"'. Despite the numerous and desperate efforts to end the fighting, AZAPO claimed that their members were 'being hunted down by anti-peace rebels among the UDF'. In one of the bloodiest encounters, a 1,000-strong group armed with rifles, shotguns, pistols, and an assortment of other weapons spilt into four and converged on homes of AZAPO members in a double pincer-type commando-style military assault. One member of the group allegedly carried a sign that read: 'SADF we are not fighting you — we are fighting AZAPO.'[134] A UDF executive member in Kwazakele denied that those who provoked the feud were UDF supporters. He insisted that they were a criminal element involved in the 'people's courts'.[135] This renewed feuding between AZAPO and youth groups claiming to be UDF supporters seemed to give substance to the widely-held speculation that gangster elements had somehow gained the upper hand and were attempting to assert control over the townships in the name of various political organizations.[136]

In a related development, the entry of a mysterious 'third force' in the midst of this factional violence seemed to provoke even greater bewilderment and surprise among both UDF and AZAPO leaders. This group, commonly known as Amaphantsula by township residents, was believed to have its headquarters in 'AZAPO territory'. Amaphantsula did not exhibit any distinct political character. Violence seemed to be the only bond uniting members, who adopted a 'breakdancer' style of dress with 'baggy pants and coloured tackies'.[137]

In a bold move that seemed to indicate the gravity of the situation, UDF executive members once again condemned the so-called 'people's courts' that were established 'under the guise of the peoples' organizations'. Front leaders disassociated themselves from those claiming allegiance to their organization who were responsible for instigating factional strife with AZAPO. Henry Fazzie, regional vice-president of UDF, acknowledged that certain elements 'used the UDF as a shield when carrying out their criminal acts and presiding at trials to mete out severe sentences on innocent people with different political convictions'.[138]

The 'people's courts' certainly signified a striking detour from the lofty ideals originally invoked by the organized opposition. Yet they also represented the malaise that befell the popular movement. Without the massive influx of weaponry to the townships, armed insurrection was completely out of the question. In fact, any direct confrontation with the security forces was tantamount to suicide. In some townships, the popular movement turned inward, in effect creating phantom adversaries and striking at available targets of opportunity. This undermined the movement, weakening the resolve of even the most ardent sup-

porters and strengthening the hand of local puppet administrations.

In January 1986, the president of AZAPO, Saths Cooper,
attempted to negotiate a truce between members of the Azanian
National Youth Unity (AZANYU) and the local UDF affiliate in
Mbekweni near Paarl in the Cape Peninsula. At least seven
deaths were attributed to clashes between these rival groups and
all local efforts to settle differences had failed.[139] In the Eastern
Cape regional leaders of the UDF and AZAPO managed to 'bury
the hatchet' but local splinter groups continued their in-fighting.
A month-long feud between two rival factions simmered in the
Jansenville township.[140] Similarly, in Soweto, a dilapidated
shantytown of 100,000 impoverished residents on the periphery
of Port Elizabeth, weeks of internecine conflicts climaxed in five
necklace deaths in mid-February. The previous year, a local
group called the Soweto Committee of Ten was formed as a
youth subsidiary of the UDF-affiliated PEBCO. However, the Committee soon fell out of favour with the UDF leadership because of
deviations from official policies. While continuing to proclaim
allegiance to the Front, this dissdent faction advocated the implementation of 'people's courts'. The UDF leadership maintained
that these practices of 'met[ing] out bush justice' by people who
claimed to be members 'were dragging the Front's name through
the mud'.[141]

In nearby Walmer township, several days of feuding — in
which guns were used — between AZANYU and the local UDF
affiliate left a number of people dead.[142] AZANYU had split away
from AZAPO and in the Eastern Cape townships came under the
influence of the Reverend Ebenezer Maqina. After his explusion
from the organization, Maqina claimed that AZAPO had betrayed
the Africanist cause by 'pleading for a non-racial solution to South
Africa's problems'. 'They might just as well join UDF now', he
stated.[143]

In early April, at least three people died in violent clashes
between 'terror gangs', said by observers to be those claiming
allegiance to the UDF, and residents of the unrest-torn
Motherwell transit camp near Port Elizabeth. A large contingent
of youths with a variety of weapons 'invaded' the squatter area
after residents failed to observe funeral services for eight victims
of police shootings at a bottle store. Residents and UDF supporters organized 'fortified bases' to counter attacks from the

'terror gangs', whom they believed were recruited from the Soweto shack area near Veeplaas.[144]

The Flexibility and Breadth of the Popular Struggle

Street and Area Committees

The virtual collapse of civil administration in the black townships under the jurisdiction of the Eastern Cape Development Board took place. The bureaucratic machinery for collecting rents disintegrated and rental and service charges were 12 million rand in arrears. Accumulated debt at the beginning of 1986 was estimated at nearly 20 million rand. Black staff were able to work indoors only because they were at risk from township residents. Revenues fom liquor sales — the principal source of funds for the township treasuries — declined dramatically.[145]

In large areas of the Eastern Cape, the Eastern Transvaal, and the Vaal Triangle, the system of black local authorities, 'advertized by the Government as a significant shift from its granite stand of denying blacks outside the Homelands a say in the running of their affairs', virtually collapsed. Administration Boards were hopelessly in debt because residents refused to pay rents. In an effort to retain a semblance of order in the Eastern Cape, the Minister of Constitutional Development and Planning, Chris Heunis, appointed the town clerks of white municipalities to administer the two most problematic communities — Lingelihle and KwaNobuhle. The townships of the Vaal Triangle, wellspring of the tide of political unrest, were also beyond governability. Elections to fill eleven council vacancies failed to attract any candidates. In the West Rand, town councillors were forced to abandon their posts or go into hiding. In those townships like Langa and KwaNobuhle, cauldrons of the Eastern Cape, and Duduza on the East Rand where the entire local police force had fled, the 'maqabane' —in Xhosa, loosely translated as 'comrades' — filled the void to maintain order.[146]

In the wake of the state of emergency, the popular organizations were forced to regroup in order to survive the intensified repression. It was in the embattled Eastern Cape townships that the formation of street and area committees first gained ground. The mass detentions of community leaders under the emergency powers depleted the mass-based student and youth groups and civic associations of their most visible leaders. At the height of the state of emergency, more leaders were detained in the Eastern Cape than in any other area of the country. According to Henry Fazzie, Vice President of the Eastern Cape UDF, the restrictions on public gatherings and the banning of all meetings of UDF affiliates disrupted the lines of communication that linked the civic associations, such as PEBCO, with township residents. The purpose of the street committees was to provide alternative channels both to assess popular sentiments and to coordinate local actions such as school and consumer boycotts. Another objective was to offer protection to those residents who were being terrorized by criminals and vandals. In a broader scheme, political activists hoped that these street and area committees would become an alternative administrative structure replacing the discredited town and community councils.[147]

It was community leader Matthew Goniwe who first introduced the idea of street and zone committees in Cradock. Before his assassination, he argued that 'democracy for the people in Lingelihle should not be a vision of the future or an abstract ideal. It should be something real, something to give ordinary people the power to bring about changes.' In Lingelihle, Cradora and the Cradock's Women's Organization survived the on-slaught of repression because of their roots in the township. Lingelihle, with about 17,000 residents, was divided into seven zones. About forty activists were assigned to these different areas and were responsible for holding meetings in each zone. Activists went from street to street and house to house explaining what Cradora represented and hoped to achieve. Meetings were held in each area to elect officials and each household could vote for their street representative. This process resulted in the resignation in November 1984 of all the Lingelihle town council members.[148]

The first public acknowledgement of these experiments in grassroots 'dual power' came at a December 1985 prayer meeting in Port Elizabeth, attended by more than 1,000 people, in which residents elected area committee members — all recognized church and civic leaders — from the ranks of the semi-clandestine street committees. The idea of the street committees had a historical precedent. Anticipating the banning of popular organizations in 1953, Nelson Mandela devised a scheme —

popularly known as the M-Plan — to organize the townships from individual households upwards in a multi-tiered system. The security police quickly suppressed these forms of grassroots democracy in most places, but in the Port Elizabeth townships they endured longer than elsewhere. In 1985, the street committees emerged as part of the groundswell of local resistance in Port Elizabeth townships as well as other Eastern Cape areas such as Cradock, Uitenhage, Queenstown, and East London. In Grahamstown, a slightly different model emerged: separate street committees were established for youths and adults. Their aim was to draw militant youths into political organizations in order to channel their actions in a more focused manner. As one activist argued, 'There are already semi-liberated areas which we think we are going to conquer forever. Our guys have learnt to devise combat tactics against the army.' He added that day-to-day affairs in these 'semi-liberated areas' would be transferred to people's committees.[149]

The spread of the idea of street committees to the Rand and elsewhere prompted Piet Muller, the assistant editor of the Afrikaans-language newspaper, *Bleed*, to make a candid admission: 'The crisis ruling in SA's black townships is no longer a law-and-order crisis. It is a crisis of legitimacy. The crisis is that in many townships the state has lost its ability to influence daily events positively. ... Today the state's authority does not go much further than its ability to order a Casspir with armed policemen to patrol township streets. But once the police turn their backs, the townships once again belong to the feuding groups fighting for political control. The townships then belong to left-wing radicals and right-wing "vigilantes". ... If one applies the classic theories of revolutionary warfare to SA, it becomes clear that "liberated zones" already exist in various townships, where the state's authority does not fully apply any more. ... In these "liberated zones" revolutionaries then start collecting "taxes" and rendering governmental services useless until eventually they gain control over the local administration of justice. ... This makes one wonder if the unrest in SA is not entering a dangerous new phase.'[150] Street committees took root in many townships, particularly in the Eastern Cape, and in February, in Alexandra, northeast of Johannesburg. If a committee member was detained, another was selected to fill the vacuum. Anonymity was strictly observed. In Alexandra, the committees were so well organized that first aid teams were established to deal with victims of police shootings. Committee members knew the people on their streets. The committees liaised with bereaved families and kept records of everyone killed, missing, injured, or detained.[151] In some instances, these street committees collected the rents and fees that the Administration Boards had proved incapable of doing and determined syllabuses for the schools the Government could not control.[152]

Escalation of Guerrilla Warfare

According to semi-official figures released by Pretoria University's Institute of Strategic Studies, the number of guerrilla attacks during 1985 soared by nearly 300 per cent over the previous year. The location and the nature of the 136 guerrilla attacks reported in 1985 suggested that small-scale actions directed at SADF personnel, state witnesses, police informers, and selected sabotage had replaced the previous emphasis on spectacular 'armed propaganda' exercises. According to Tom Lodge, the ANC demonstrated 'a qualitative advance in its ability to conduct guerrilla warfare'. It was probably the case that 'most guerrillas are based within South Africa and more attacks are being carried out by people who are trained here and have never left the country'.[153] The security forces reported the increasing use of small arms, including AK-47 assault rifles, and hand grenades in guerrilla assaults on 'collaborators' in the townships.[154]

The mass exodus of thousands of militants during the eighteen months of unrest swelled the ranks of Umkhonto we Sizwe. More people left South Africa from July 1984 to January 1986 than during the entire 1976-7 students' revolt and an estimated four out of every five joined the ANC. Security police estimated that 4,000 people left the country to undergo military training immediately after the 1976-7 rebellion. With three-quarters of them joining the ANC, it was reliably estimated that ANC military strength stood at 7,000 formally trained guerrillas in Umkhonto we Sizwe. Observers believed that this boost in personnel provided the ANC 'for the first time in its history ... a capacity to commit large numbers of guerrillas to battle and move for the development of what is called "people's war"'.[155]

Because there was certainly no lack of willing participants

yearning to acquire weapons in the townships, it would be impossible to detect which specific popular organizations were actually responsible for expanding and deepening the low-intensity guerrilla war. What is certain, however, is that the ANC dramatically increased its sabotage attacks in November and December 1985. In the Eastern Transvaal, ANC insurgents launched a 122-millimeter rocket assault on the SASOL II and SASOL III coal-processing installations at Secunda. In the northern Transvaal, a graduated series of land mine explosions near Messina along the isolated Zimbabwe border killed a number of civilians and injured at least four soldiers.[156] In Natal, grenade and limpet mine assaults — including the Christmas holidays bombing at the posh Amanzimtoti shopping arcade — seemed designed to inflict pain and suffering on white civilians by inflating the number of casualties.

In early January 1986, a landmine explosion killed two white farmers at Stockpoort, a small rural town straddling the Botswana border. These incidents appeared calculated to deflate the sense of security and to narrow the comfortable distance from which white civilians had been able to contemplate their country's political agonies. Well-placed observers strongly suggested that the Amanzimtoti bombing was conducted by an Umkhonto we Sizwe 'quick response unit' operating without sanction or direction from the exile leadership.[157] Others speculated that the attack was carried out in retaliation for the SADF raid on Lesotho a few days earlier in which nine people, including six ANC members, were killed at a private Christmas party in a hail of gunfire from weapons equipped with silencers.[158] In any case, it seemed that the ANC's 'unwritten rule' distinguishing between 'hard' and 'soft' targets was blurred. In the wake of the Natal bombings, the police tightened their security net, uncovering at least six arm caches in the Durban area alone and detaining thirteen suspected 'terrorists'.[159]

The landmine offensive — particularly the attacks in the Messina area — appeared to be part of a coordinated strategy of 'wrest[ing] control in crucial geographical locations from the South African authorities'.[160] These border incidents highlighted the growing fears amongst the white farming community that rural guerrilla war was imminent. Since 1980, the border area was subjected to a large-scale military build-up. Heavily-armed soldiers were stationed on most farmsteads which themselves came to resemble mini-fortresses. Farm houses were surrounded by security fences and were linked via radio communication to local military headquarters. The SADF even assumed responsibility for transporting white farm children to and from school.[161] It was also discovered that in order to reverse the dwindling white school population in the Northern Transvaal the local education authorities secretly subsidized the costs of schooling for hundreds of white pupils who had recently emigrated from Zimbabwe and Botswana.[162]

In February, a shoot-out between 'suspected terrorists' and SADF units and the subsequent detonation of another landmine brought farming operations virtually to a standstill in the northern and northwestern Transvaal. Troops poured into the area, combing farm and district roads with mine-sweeping equipment. Routine checks of driveways and essential roads for landmines become a way of life.[163] In the Eastern Transvaal, a string of attacks on elderly farm couples prompted angry farmers to demand that the SADF establish a cordon of military fortifications that would ring the neighbouring Homeland of Lebowa. White farmers also used this occasion to condemn the Botha regime's plans to scrap the pass laws and permit systems that regulated the flow of black farm labourers in the area. In the following months, farmers in the Steelpoort area complained that 'communist agitators' infiltrated from Lebowa, burnt farm vehicles, stole cattle and crops, tried to enforce higher wages for farm labourers by 'necklacing' workers who agreed to work for less than R5 per day, and threatened to attack farmers on their own farms. These farmers demanded the installation of an electric fence along the Lebowa border to repel these 'agitators and thieves'.[164]

The eight separate landmine explosions that took place along South Africa's northern borders were dwarfed in comparison with the political impact of the detonation of a single landmine that wrecked a police Casspir on a dirt road on the outskirts of Mamelodi near Pretoria.[165] The townships are all criss-crossed with unpaved roads. These all have to be patrolled in crisis situations and, more ominously, all are vulnerable to landmine attacks. The Mamelodi landmine explosion merely underscored the growing fusion between activities of externally-trained guerrillas and internally-based dissidents. On a number of occasions, particularly at Crossroads and Gugulethu outside Cape

Town and Alexandra on the northern edge of Johannesburg, police confirmed that they came under AK-47 fire.[166]

In March, the police claimed to have killed seven heavily-armed ANC guerillas in a shoot-out in Gugulethu. This event once again rivetted attention on the dramatic development of guerrilla activities. The use of grenades, landmines, and assault weapons steeply increased while the use of pure explosives had declined over the past several years. Unanswered questions continued to fuel controversy over the Gugulethu incident. Witnesses claimed that police ambushed the group as they disembarked from a mini-bus and had shot the wounded rather than take prisoners.[167] During the same week, saboteurs slipped a limpet mine through the supposedly airtight security at divisional police headquarters at John Vorster Square in downtown Johannesburg. The blast injured two policemen and caused intense embarrassment. A few days later, another limpet mine shattered the women's toilet at the Hillbrow (Johannesburg) police station.[168] In mid-April, the police confirmed that 'new tactics' were emerging in the Western Cape townships. During 1986, there were 'five or six' gun battles between residents of the Gugulethu-Crossroads-KTC complex. 'In the past they fired at us during the night so that we could not see who was doing the shooting or establish which direction it was coming from', reported Lieutenant Attie Laubscher. 'Nowadays they open fire on us during the day. They are not scared to shoot anymore.' The warrens of ramshackle and densely-packed shanties in the squatter settlements offered ample protection for the residents who took up arms against SAP patrols. The overcrowded camps with their narrow lanes and winding pathways became virtual no-go areas for the police.[169]

Rent Strikes and Consumer Boycotts

It would be impossible to chronicle accurately the ebb and flow of rent strikes and consumer boycotts that swept the townships from mid-1985 onward. At the risk of oversimplification it can be said that numerous outlying townships that escaped the cycles of earlier unrest were in large measure engulfed in these localized actions as the frontiers of protest advanced into the countryside. In early 1986, an explosive situation threatened to plunge the

Eastern Transvaal bushveld into near-anarchy. A dramatic upsurge of violent confrontations that were practically all linked to the ongoing popular opposition to rent increases spilt the townships into warring factions. In July 1985, the Eastern Transvaal Development Board announced rental and service charge increases in townships at Waterval Boven, Barberton, Carolina, Breyton, Piet Retief, Nelspruit, Amsterdam, Belfast, Ermelo, and elsewhere. Residents refused to pay the increases. The acute housing shortage in eMgwenya township near Waterval Boven illustrated the pattern in the Eastern Transvaal townships. Sprawling shanty-areas of what were called 'zozos' and single rooms of corrugated iron and tin bore witness to the overcrowding.[170] In the rioting that erupted there, homes of councillors, Development Board offices, and the local beerhall were stoned and burnt. At least five people were fatally shot during rent protests in Piet Retief's e Thandukukhanya township and KwaZanele near Breyton. In January 1986, all KwaZanele's councillors fled after youths attacked and burnt their homes.[171]

The rent strikes also hit the Witwatersrand. Residents at the Chiawelo flats in Soweto refused to pay 'exorbitent rents'. The huge Chiawelo Extension 3 complex consisted of fifteen four-story block overcrowded apartments.[172] In mid-1985, Alexandra residents initiated a rent strike. In March 1986, neighbouring areas joined this ongoing strike, refusing to pay water and electricity and service charges in addition to rental fees.[173] In order to break the back of the rent strike in Katlehong, the mayor, Thami Siluma, warned that all residents with rental payments in arrears would have their water and electricity supplies suspended.[174]

In Sibongile outside Dundee in the heart of KwaZulu, the cry 'Ayithelwe' ('we won't pay') became a popular slogan for residents who continued a rent strike that had lasted almost a year. Residents complained that their homes were unfit for human habitation: the toilet bucket system was still in use, communal water taps on each street were shared by more than twenty families apiece, and so forth. Because of their gritty determination, Sibongile residents acquired the reputation for their township as 'the liberated zone of the north'.[175]

In the Western Cape, over 30 per cent of Khayelitsha residents had kept alive a rent strike that began in November 1985. The core housing units — of two rooms plus a lavatory — frequently had as many as thirteen people living in a single room.[176] The rent strike spread to the older, settled townships of Gugulethu, Langa, and Nyanga, in addition to Crossroads, KTC, and other surrounding shanty areas.[177] Demands included reductions (because of high unemployment and low wages in the area), cancellation of rent arrears, and improvement of housing units.[178] In April, the strike took a new turn when almost 1,000 women marched on the offices of Western Cape Development Board, demanding redress of grievances.[179] In order to counter the spread of rent strikes, legislation was introduced in Parliament in April amending the 1982 Black Local Authorities Act that would allow town councillors to recover rent and service charges by forcing employers to deduct them from employees' wages.[180]

In April, Tom Boya, deputy president of the Urban Council's Association of South Africa (UCASA), claimed that thirty-two community councils and three town councils — mostly in the Eastern Cape — had completely collapsed. He emphasized that rent debts — accumulated mainly in Katlehong on the East Rand, the Vaal and Mamelodi in Pretoria — exceeded 60 million rand. In his view, rent strikes made some townships 'ungovernable and caused the collapse of several others'. UCASA listed Lingelihle, KwaNobuhle, and Nonezwakazi in the Eastern Cape as the town councils that had collapsed. The community councils that disintegrated were Taskane and Duduza on the East Rand; Parys and Vredefort in the Free State; Maritzburg in Natal; Aberdeen, Adelaide, Alexandra, Beaufort West, Colesburg, Hanover, Humansdorp, Jansenville, Queenstown, Kirkwood, Naauwpoort, Richmond, Somerset East, Steytlerville, Victoria West, Paterson, Waterval Boven, Steynsberg, and Sterkstroom.[181]

Consumer boycotts gained a certain momentum during the later half of 1985 but only achieved mixed results. The UDF obliquely acknowledged that the boycott tactic occasionally backfired, causing hardship and resentment in the townships. The National Forum publicly condemned the enforcing of boycotts 'in an undemocratic manner'. Instead, the Forum committed itself to consumer boycott campaigns 'only after proper consultation and full and free discussion with members of the community had taken place, thereby eliminating the emergence of faceless committees who have no mandate from the community'.[182]

In truth, the boycotts experienced a somewhat 'on-again, off-again' existence. By early 1986, they were lifted in some northeastern Cape towns. Nevertheless, they remained in force in most townships in the region. In small towns such as Aliwal North, Molteno, Burgersdorp, Dordrecht, Cathcart, Stutterheim, and Queenstown local white businesses that catered principally to black consumers struggled to stay afloat.[183] The four-month East London boycott remained almost 100 per cent effective until its suspension in late November 1985. On 3 March, 1986, civic associations decided to resume it because the demands raised the previous year had not been adequately addressed. The boycott committee dissolved itself in order to 'protect its members' and responsibility for the new boycott appeal was borne by all popular organizations collectively.[184] In Port Elizabeth, the Consumer Boycott Committee threatened for months to reinstate its highly-successful campaign. Much to the chagrin of the local Chamber of Commerce, the security police banned the two most influential boycott leaders in the Eastern Cape, Mkhuseli Jack and Henry Fazzie.[185] The fact that the courts almost immediately overturned these banning orders reflected the deep divisions within the white minority regime. In early April, the Port Elizabeth Consumer Boycott Committee launched its much-anticipated action against white shops in the area.[186]

School Boycotts

Throughout the course of a long wave of unrest, school-age children played a central role in catalyzing the popular struggle. The classrooms themselves became meeting-places where issues were debated and strategies planned. Even in the historical strongholds of political agitation, student organizations tended to outstep large sections of the politically conscious mass movement. The grossly inferior educational system came to symbolize for militant black activists their status under *apartheid*. The slogan 'No Education Before Liberation' became a rallying point for many student boycott campaigns that swept the black townships. Radical student leaders vowed to extend their boycotts of classrooms into 1986, the tenth anniversary of the Soweto uprising that began over educational grievances.

Within the broad popular movement, there was a feeling that student activism had perhaps lost its vision. On 28 December

1985, a national conference attended by about 700 delegates from 200 national and regional organizations brought together black parents, students, and teachers. The conference resolved to urge radical black high school students to lift the boycotts and to return to their classrooms. In an unprecedented manoeuvre, the Soweto Parents' Crisis Committee (SPCC), a group formed in October to defuse the national eductional crisis and the sponsor for the meeting, declared that it had conferred with ANC representatives in Harare, Zimbabwe, in order to reach consensus on the education issue. The UDF lent its political support for the return to classes, albeit under various conditions.[187] This step seemed to indicate that the school boycott campaigns were out of control and had outlived their initial impact. 'If [the students] do not go back they will fail to organize themselves and will not be able to work as a coherent force', argued Curtis Nkondo, president of the National Educational Union of South Africa and a Release Mandela Committee member. 'If they are not together they will be easily manipulated and divided by the system.'[188]

In January 1986, the Port Elizabeth Crisis in Education Committee organized a huge rally attended by an estimated 30,000 parents and pupils where it was decided to suspend the year-old school boycott in the Eastern Cape.[189] In the Western Cape, scores of popular organizations endorsed the formal return to classes and pledged instead to 'work toward maximum unity of all students, teachers and parents on a single, national programme of action that will be carried out by all of us, no matter in which ghetto we live or what language we speak'.[190] Despite the fact that more than 100 organizations (including the UDF, AZAPO, trade unions, and community and educational groups) supported the return of students to their classrooms, some militant student groups were determined to continue the boycott. In Sowteo, continued efforts to prevent schools reopening prompted the SPCC to assert that 'only agents provocateurs and political megalomaniacs can embark on such dangerous gimmicks. ... No amount of opportunism and adventurism should be allowed to derail the student movement. Students must be vigilant against this pseudo-radicalism based on empty rhetoric and crass opportunism.'[191]

By mid-February, the 'return-to-school' began to crumble in the face of an upsurge of shootings and detentions.[192] In late March, more than 1,500 representatives of pupils, parents, and teachers countrywide convened under the auspices of the National Education Crisis Conference (NECC) to discuss the situation. At the time of the conference, an estimated 80,000 students in more than 100 schools across the country were involved in boycotts, stayaways, and suspensions of classes. The aim of the conference was to forge tighter links between parents, teachers and the school children. In a marathon meeting conducted amid the tension of an Inkatha attack, the NECC resolved to suspend the boycotts, encouraging students to return to school 'so that they could devise new and creative techniques to oppose the State'.[193] Conference decisions, however, were marred by a degree of controversy. National Forum delegates withdrew their participation at the last moment, alleging that the NECC was constituted by an 'extremely sectarian, undemocratic and manipulative process',[194] and 500 delegates from the pupil's organizations complained that decisions reached at the conference were not fully and adequately discussed.[195]

Alexandra and Crossroads

The outbreak of street-fighting in such distant areas as Alexandra township near Johannesburg and Crossroads outside Cape Town symbolized the degree to which South Africa appeared on the verge of open civil war. Founded in 1913 on land purchased from a white farmer, Alexandra was a teeming township of more than 100,000 people located on an incline on the northeast outskirts of Johannesburg. It was a squalid, ramshackle maze of steep dirt roads, dilapidated buildings, congested houses, and giant hostels for migrant workers. In the course of time, Alexandra became enveloped by white residental areas. For this reason, Prime Minister Verwoerd condemned it as a 'black spot' in 1962. Nestled 'cheek by jowl' beside Johannesburg's most affluent and 'elegant mink and manure white [northern] suburbs', Alexandra residents repeatedly resisted efforts to demolish the township and remove the entire community.[196]

The fatal stabbing of Mukukeng Kumuka, chair of the local branch of AZAPO, sparked the widespread rioting that erupted in Alexandra in late February 1985. 'The township's teenagers went to war' as the streets were transformed into battle zones, barricades were built, and police vehicles were petrol-bombed and stoned.[197] Troops armed with automatic weapons and gas masks 'lined perimeter roads', protecting Sandton, the country's richest white residential area.[198] Residents claimed that the death toll reached forty-six over nearly a week of clashes, a casualty figure nearly double the official one.[199] On 5 March, more than 40,000 people 'crammed into the township's dusty soccer stadium' to attend an emotion-laden funeral for seventeen unrest victims. Flags of the ANC, the UDF, AZAPO, and the South African Communist Party — potent expressions of defiance — 'waved to the rhythm of freedom songs'.[200] In the following weeks, local councillors began, one by one, to resign their posts.[201] Large stretches of the township became virtual no-go areas as policemen and their families were evacuated because 'their lives were at risk'.[202]

In late April, 'mobs of balaclava-clad men went on a witch-hunt' in the area. It was widely believed that off-duty policemen who 'disguised themselves as activists and used liberation rhetoric' were responsible for this four-hour rampage that left eight political activists dead, scores injured, sixty homes fire-bombed, and ten razed to the ground. This attack — conducted with an assortment of weapons, including 'guns, pangas, axes, and knob-kieries' — ironically came hours after the resignation of the controversial mayor, the Reverend Sam Buti, and only two days after the launching of a rent strike and a consumer boycott of white-owned shops. The Alexandra Boycott Committee announced that these actions were initiated to protest the continued presence of the SADF troops in the township and the disappearance of bodies of people shot by the security forces during the February rioting. In sworn affidavits, residents alleged that white policemen with blackened faces also took part in some of these armed assaults and that police vehicles escorted the attackers or appeared on the scene shortly after the attacks started and did nothing to halt them.[203] Alexandra Action Committee chair (and MAWU official), Moses Mayekiso, claimed that the police had 'formed vigilante groups of up to 200 to patrol the township on foot in a bid to eliminate activists'.[204] The following day, a confrontation between a crowd of 10,000 angry residents and police erupted into gunfire as 'youths — some armed with AK-47 rufles — fired volley after volley' at the police.[205] At a massive rally held in the local stadium, 45,000 residents resolved to form 'self-defence units to protect ourselves fom the agents of the system'.[206] Residents built what they called 'tank traps' on several of the main dirt roads. 'They are digging holes in the road and camouflaging them with tarpaulins in the hope some of the armoured police vehicles will drive into them', one witness said. 'It's not just teenagers doing it. Everyone seems to be involved as if it were some kind of community project.'[207]

Direct police participation in violent attacks on political activists was certainly not a new phenomena. But this involvement seemed to be more brazen and coordinated than in the past. Dave Dalling, PFP Member of Parliament from Sandton proclaimed that the 'police had erected roadblocks at entrances to Alexandra on Tuesday 22 April at about 5:30 pm and sealed it off. At about 7:30 pm three separate teams of men, supported in some cases by Hippo personnel carriers, attacked certain targets. Some had been dressed in plain clothes, others wore police shirts and trousers.'[208] In response to a new round of killings of political activists by 'unknown assailants', the Alexandra Action Committee announced that its members were forming 'street defence units' and that residents continued to dig 'tank trenches' at strategic points in roads 'to obstruct the passage of "vigilante" vehicles'. All black police were forced out of the township and, in early May, militants proclaimed that 'they were in complete control of the area'. On 10 May, a combined police and army force of 1,670 surrounded the square-mile township at midnight, putting up roadblocks and preparing for a daylong sweep that included house-to-house searches. This show of force came two days after a series of petrol-bomb attacks in neighbouring white surburbs.[209] It was also reported that police directly participated in attacks in Carletonville, Kurgersdorp, Bophelong in the Vaal Triangle, Welkom in the Free State, and Diepkloof in Soweto.[210] In Soweto, at least six houses of political activists were firebombed in a single week in April. The most serious outrage occurred at an all-night funeral vigil in Diepkloof. A gang of about forty set fire to the tents before turning on the mourners. In the ensuing fracas, the attackers killed six people, wounded thirteen, and abducted others. Diepkloof had been a no-go area for more than two months, with young activists 'running the township'. In the following weeks, West Rand Administration Board police escalated their assaults, including a midnight ambush in which four students were shot dead.[211] As a consequence of these and other attacks, the Soweto Civic Association announced plans to form self-defence units to protect residents from unprovoked attacks. 'The police, the SADF, councillors and their henchmen have been seen at scenes of petrol-bombings and other savage acts of brutality', the statement read. 'We can no longer stand idly by while our wives, children, and property are being attacked. We have no option but to defend ourselves.'[212]

In the midst of these visible manifestations of officially-sanctioned terror, the popular organizations painstakingly erected clandestine alternative political structures to replace the disintegrating town councils. Two examples can be used to illustrate the general trends in the most politically conscious townships. In Mamelodi outside Pretoria, the undeclared state of emergency during 1985 made it impossible for residents to hold public meetings or to organize large gatherings. Over the course of the year, hooligans had 'hijacked' political causes, extorting money from businessmen in the name of COSAS. In response, the Mamelodi Youth Congress (MAYO) launched 'Operation Clean-Up', a campaign to weed out criminals and opportunists using 'the political struggle for their own ends'. After the 21 November unprovoked shootings outside the Mamelodi administration offices, residents initiated house-to-house canvassing to persuade the people to isolate the police and the local council by not paying rent or laying any charges at the police station. This campaign resulted in the formation of 'people's courts' to handle petty crime and local disputes. On occasion, individuals took advantage of these impromtu forums (as they were called) in order to settled personal vendettas. To counteract this misuse of these novel organs of popular power, street committees were formed to oversee neighbourhood relations. The committees effectively 'decentralized' the mass-based civic associations, opening avenues for grassroots decision-making. The executives of street committees formed the local section committees. In turn, section committees and five delegates of all other progressive organizations operating in the township together formed an area committee. The area committee then formed a civic association.[213]

In Port Alfred, the Port Alfred Residents' Civic Organization (PARCO) 'has taken over all the administrative functions of the community' following the collapse of the community council in May 1985. 'We're the first community to introduce people's education', Gugile Nkwinti proudly exclaimed. Various street committees, area committees, the Port Alfred Youth Congress, Nonzamo Student Guardians' Association, Port Alfred Workers' Union, Port Alfred Pensioners' Association, Port Alfred Progressive Teachers' Association, and the Port Alfred Women's Organization were all formed as affiliates to PARCO. Not only was the township 'self-governing', 10,000 residents at an early May mass meeting decided to   re-name the township after Nelson Mandela. 'The residents have given up hope that the authorities will ever upgrade the area', Nkwinti said. 'They are now pinning all their hopes on Mandela.'[214]

The conflicts that divided residents at Crossroads can be traced principally to struggles over scarce land and resources and the continuous threat of forced eviction. The Crossroads complex itself was in reality a collection of discrete hamlets joined loosely together. These were created as 'squatters' in ever-expanding numbers poured into the informal settlement area over the course of more than a decade. As newer settlements mushroomed on its periphery, the orginal site became known as Old Crossroads and its satellites assumed their own separate identities with their own distinctive leadership groups. Struggles for control of the Crossroads complex took place in tandem with state strategies to both divide and co-opt the emergent leadership. In August 1978, Johnson Nqxobongwana was elected 'chairman' of Crossroads. Nqxobongwana came to realize along with other influential men in the community that 'political control of Crossroads meant control of the community's economic resources and the resources promised by outside organizations' (including state agencies and moralistic liberal philanthropists). In the formative years when Crossroads was transformed from a provisional settlement into a community with roots, women played a significant ideological as well as organizational role. The 'rot' in Crossroads began to set in when women relinquished control over the settlement to a male-dominated system of headmen. 'Outsiders' either 'consciously or unconsciously' reinforced this process. Nqxobongwana's Crossroads central committee blended traditionalist values with the mind-set of an aspirant petty bourgeoisie. As Josette Cole had argued, 'it soon became apparent that there was little room for dissent. Those who dared to challenge the new authority found themselves faced with repression, in the shape of the homeguard system.' The 'home-guards' were gradually formed into a 'semi-police unit' under the direction of Sam Ndima, a Nqxobongwana loyalist. In the early 1980s, there were frequent allegations that Nqxobongwana was a 'sell-out' willing to negotiate with state officials without a mandate from the Crossroads constituencies. In the midst of deepening power struggles inside Crossroads, Nqxobongwana became involved with the embryonic progressive movement in the Cape Peninsula which eventually solidified into the UDF. What further complicated this overlapping power struggle was that since 1982 Nqxobongwana served as president of the Western Cape Civics Association, an important UDF affiliate.[215]

When Gerrit Viljoen, the Minister of the then-Department of Co-operation and Development, announced in October 1984 that all 'squatters' — legal and illegal — would be moved to Khayelitsha, all the 'squatter' communities banded together to refuse to leave. The political deadlock was shattered during the February 1985 confrontation over forced removals when eighteen residents were killed and 230 seriously wounded in battles with the police. In order to defuse the tense situation, Viljoen offered Old Crossroads a long-awaited upgrade scheme. However, the feasibility of these promised improvements was hindered by congestion and overcrowding. By using the offer of eighteen-month permits, Tino Bezuidenhoud, the chief of the Western Cape Development Board, was able to persuade a number of 'squatter' leaders to move their followers to the newly prepared Site C at Khayelitsha. By May 1985, more than 35,000 people were moved there. Many residents remained adamant in their refusal to move to Khayelitsha unless they were extended full legal rights to stay and work in Cape Town.

By the time Nqxobongwana was released from detention in April 1985, the 'squatter' communities were polarized and the fragile alliance between the UDF and the Nqxobongwana clique collapsed. On the one side, Nqxobongwana and his 'Old Cross-roads Committee' represented a more accomodationist tendency that came to be called 'amododa' ('men') or simply 'the fathers'. On the other side, 'progessive community organizations' such as the Cape Youth Congress (CAYCO), the United Women's Organization (UWO), along with other UDF-affiliated groups not only acquired a popular following in the satellite squatter areas but also condemned Nqxobongwana as corrupt.[216] This power struggle reached boiling point in late 1985 and early 1986. In four days of bloody clashes that left four dead, the 'fathers' had patrolled the streets of New Crossroads and KTC searching for '*maqabanes*' — the township name for militant youths — and members of UDF-affiliated organizations. In the fighting, there were widespread allegations that the police had 'turned a blind-eye to the activities of the "fathers"'.[217] The source of the conflict was rooted in complex longstanding factional disputes over political control of the Crossroads complex. One proximate cause, however, for this violent outburst hinged on growing dissatisfaction of Crossroads residents with the haphazard and arbitrary manner the '*maqabane*' enforced boycott campaigns and with the formation of contoversial 'kangaroo courts' in Nyanga East, KTC, and Site C. What seemed to really exacerbate the intergenerational conflict was resentment over the severity of the wanton punishments meted out to adults after the politically unaffiliated Nyanga Youth Brigade assumed control over the 'people's court' in Nyanga East and the formation of 'Omo Squads' during the 1985 consumer boycott when suspected boycott-violators were forcibly made to drink Omo detergent.[218] In mid-January, 'younger "comrades" and adults from KTC and Nyanga' formed 24-hour armed patrol around the perimeter of the enbattled KTC squatter camp after repulsing an attack by conservative 'fathers' from Site C.[219] The ongoing conflict between the 'comrades' and the old-guard 'fathers' intensified in February when Nqxobongwana, in an effort to reestablish his credibility and authority, called elections for a new community committee. Several members of the old committee refused to stand for reelection, declaring that the process was undemocratic. Residents widely condemned Nqxobongwana's stipulation that residents pay a R15 fee in order to vote — or else face expulsion from the community. In an election that was not independently monitored, Nqxobongwana claimed that 5,683 people voted out of a total population of 47,000.[220] In a letter to the Minister of Constitutional Development and Planning, the newly-elected committee pledged to act as 'a link between us as a community and [the] Urban Foundation and your Planning and Development Department'.[221]

The uneasy truce orchestrated by local religious leaders collapsed in late March in renewed fighting precipitated by disputes over alleged extortion and misuse of 'bail funds'. In the interim, Nqxobongwana established his own 'police force' called *witdoeke* — named for the white strips of cloth worn around their heads or as armbands to distinguish themselves from the comrades. It was widely believed that Nqxobongwana and his Old Crossroads executive committee forged links with the SAP and community councillors from the settled Langa-Gugulethu complex. A defector from the Nqxobongwana camp charged that Nqxobongwana 'had held a meeting with community councillors from his surrounding townships where plans were made to appoint him chief president of all the community councils in the Western Cape'.[222] In late April, the Old Crossroads committee forbade their political rivals to enter their 'territory'. Their decision to 'ban' a funeral service for a CAYCO member in Old Crossroads sparked a renewal of fighting between comrades and 'fathers'.[223] Over the next few weeks, scores of activists were forced to flee as Nqxobongwana's committee accelerated its campaign to purge the area of all progressive organizations.[224]

In mid-May, the accumulated tensions in the Crossroads complex exploded in a display of violence and wholesale destruction. In the week-long carnage and bloodletting, the *witdoeke* vigilantes — aided both by SAP indifference and by security force 'advisors' — succeeded in overrunning Nyanga Bush, Nyanga Extension, and the Portland Cement Works, three satellite camps adjacent to the main Old Crossroads settlement. These areas were strongholds for 'progressive' organizations opposed to the autocratic rule of the Old Crossroads leadership. In the violent clashes, it was estimated that at least forty-four people were killed with a larger number seriously injured, more than 30,000 routed from their homes, and nearly all the estimated 4,800 ranshackle shanties destroyed.[225]

What began to emerge from the chaos and devastation of these events was a coincidence of interests of three groups with much to gain from the eradication of the three satellite camps: the Old Crossroads elite, the South African authorities, and the SAP. More than half the new committee in Crossroads consisted of relatively affluent businessmen desperate to maintain an economic foothold, extend their political control over the area, and to upgrade Old Crossroads. This leadership of Old Crossroads was ' rich through "farming of people"'. Nqxobongwana was consistently accused of being a 'warlord' who relied upon dictatorial methods of leadership and, it was alleged, earned between R5,000 and R40,000 each month from rentals in his territorial fiefdom. Under the leadership of Nqxobongwana and his chief lieutenant, Sam Ndima (the acknowledged militarist in the camp), the residents of Old Crossroads were in a sense cajoled to join in the 'land greed' because they were promised that they would benefit from the 'upgrading' of the camp. Until the *witdoeke* razed the area, the land set aside for the improvement scheme (including the requested 'tennis courts', 'four-room houses', and 'police station') was occupied by other squatter groups.[226]

The result of the wave after wave of vigilante attacks on neighbouring camps was that in about a week the *witdoeke* of Old Crossroads were able to do what the South African authorities were unable to accomplish in years of dickering. 'What we have witnessed', one correspondent reported, was 'essentially a removal of a very special kind.' By using the vigilantes as surrogates, the South African authorities sought to achieve by force what could not be done by persuasion. The inevitable outcome of the vicious fighting enabled the white authorities to move the homeless refugees to Khayelitsha 'without the stigma of sending in bulldozers and front-end loaders to destroy the camps with all the attendant bad publicity'.[227]

Police and army units patrolling the densely-packed squatter areas failed to interfere during the fighting, but intervened on some occasions when it appeared that the comrades had gained the advantage. Over previous months, 'miltant "comrades" who had access to arms were able to operate more freely from the squatter camps than from the established townships because of the inaccessibility of the narrow tracks' and the close quarters.[228] The SAP was quite pleased to gain control over an area 'seen to be a security risk and hot-bed of radical resistance'.[229]

Sporadic clashes took place over the next few weeks. This brief lull was shattered on 9 June when the *witdoeke* vigilantes and the police mounted a carefully-planned military invasion of the KTC squatter area in the heart of Nyanga township, the last remaining territory under the waning control of the comrades. In an eyewitness account, Tony Weaver described police participation in the fighting: 'With police moving in front, the vigilantes first attacked the Zolani Centre, focal point of aid distribution to the estimated 33,000 refugees left homeless in three weeks of destruction in the Crossroads satellite camps.... I watched late in the day as police Casspirs moved ahead of vigilantes, firing teargas and birdshot at KTC residents trying to defend their homes against the vigilantes. I watched as the vigilantes milled around the Casspirs, and the police waved to them and cracked jokes.'[230] In three days of fighting, the KTC area was transformed into a *de facto* war zone. Both sides were armed with a wide assortment of weapons, including axes, pangas, iron bars, machetes, and a number of handguns and rifles. 'Gunfire', exclaimed Micheal Parks, 'a rarity until now in South Africa's civil conflict, was almost continuous, and police patrols repeatedly came under attack by gunmen.'[231] In the end, the small quantity of AK-47 assault rifles used by the comrades were no match for the police armoured personnel carriers and their withering firepower. On the second day, witnesses reported that the stalemated battle was turned 'when police laid down a carpet of tear gas and advanced into KTC, sending the comrades fleeing and permitting the vigilantes to overrun the place'. As the comrades withdrew, the vigilantes 'torched hundreds of flimsy shacks made of zinc and plastic sheeting'.[232] Relief workers estimated that the number of fatalities was probably twice the official figure of seventeen deaths in the first two days of this renewed round of fighting. As the vigilantes completed their conquest of KTC and extended their control from the centre of the original Crossroads shanty area to the outlying districts, they effectively denied the comrades a base in the camps. In the month-long fighting, nearly 80,000 people were left homeless and destitute and about one hundred were killed.[233]

The Expanding Political Role of the Independent Trade Union Movement

Upsurge in Worker Militancy

In the first month of 1986, South Africa experienced its most strike-bound January in a decade. According to labour relations consultant Andrew Levy, more than 385,000 labour days were lost due to industrial action. Mining and retail sectors were most affected, followed closely by food and chemicals. 'The patterns suggest a lot of grassroots activity with unions not fully in control of their members', Levy argued. 'Workers are increasingly striking over issues such as racial incidents, and in many cases refusing to negotiate. ...We're heading back into the jungle.'[234]

In the three month period from December through February, an estimated 90,000 mine workers at scores of gold, coal, and platinum mines went on strike. These included Gencor's Impala platinum mine in Bophuthatswana, Johannesburg Consolidated Investments' Western Areas and Randfontein Estates gold mines, as well as colleries such as Matla, Duvha, SA Coal Estates, Goedehoop, and Wolvekrans. In January, at least eighteen people, including two white policemen, were killed and dozens injured during clashes between angry black miners and mine security guards, operating in collusion with the SAP. At Foscor and Phalaborwa Mining Company in Phalaborwa, about 1,500 workers went on strike to protest the fact that they were forced to work under armed guard. The giant mining companies expressed grave concern that the persistent unrest, including strikes and slow-downs, was seriously reducing profits. The huge Randfontein mine, besieged by full-scale rioting, was expected to lose about R301 million in earnings from the resulting decline in underground production. The massive strike of 23,000 workers at Gencor's Impala mine in January disrupted production and slashed profits by R45 million.[235]

In February, about 19,000 workers went on strike at Anglo-American's Vaal Reefs gold mine near Klerksdorp. Enmity with the police and solidarity with ten fellow-workers arrested in connection with the deaths of four 'team leaders' the previous week figured prominently in the dispute. While the issues varied, the strike at Vaal Reefs was symptomatic of the growing trend that wage disputes were no longer the only motivating factor in 'walk-outs'.[236] The entire work force — more than 1,000 — of the Ekandustria complex northeast of Pretoria (and located in KwaNdebele) downed tools in protest against low wages.[237] By early March, tensions between black miners and white supervisors in the coal fields near Witbank in the Eastern Transvaal reached a point where white employees 'threatened to arm themselves for protection'. This situation followed weeks of black unrest protesting rising unemployment in the area, a successful week-long stayaway, and sporadic strikes by black miners.[238]

In March, the voluntary end of the three-week sit-in strike at Haggie Rand — the longest factory occupation in recent South African history — highlighted a shift in working-class tactics. The 40,000-member MAWU took the lead as metalworkers staged at least ten separate 'overnights' from January to mid-March. Workers adopted this tactic to counter the 'management weapon of firing strikers *en masse*, not allowing them back into the factory, and replacing them with fresh recruits'.[239] In January, striking workers at the Cheesborough Ponds plant in Wadeville, Germiston, occupied the factory for two days and three nights, bringing production to a complete standstill. Relatives of workers helped sustain the strike by providing 'food and clothing on a daily basis'. After negotiating with the Chemical Workers' Union (CWIU), management agreed to the demand that May Day be a paid holiday, to a one month annual bonus, to an increase in hourly wages, and to a reduction of working hours to forty-four per week.[240] In February, members of the Sweet, Food and Allied Workers' Unions (SFAWU) conducted a sit-in strike at Renown Pork Packers at Olifantsfontein.[241]

However, management embarked on a vicious counter-offensive. In March, Anglo-American closed four shafts as well as the gold and uranium plants and workshops on its east and west divisions at the Vaal Reefs mine, thereby locking out the estimated 15,500 workers who had conducted a five-day work slowdown. Rand Mines closed its Blyvooruitzicht gold mine near Carletonville, locking out the 11,000 workers who had participated in 'wildcat' strikes and literally starving out the remaining 1,200 miners who had engaged in a 36-hour underground sit-in.[242] At the Pan African shopfitter strike in Germiston, management used police reinforcements and dogs to forcibly drive 300 striking workers off company property. MAWU and PWAWU members had occupied the factory for more than two weeks in defiance of a court order to vacate the premises.[243] Despite these management measures, the sit-down strikes continued. MAWU conducted a two-day occupation of three BTR Dunlop plants. In April, the unaffiliated Orange-Vaal General Workers' Union staged such a strike at the Welkom Provincial Hospital in a dispute over wages and union recognition.[244]

'Politicized Trade Unionism'

Since the formation of COSATU, the independent black trade unions took a much more visible role in the ongoing political struggle. At its fourth annual congress attended by an estimated 10,000 members in February 1986, the NUM — claiming a membership of over 150,000 mineworkers — called for the eventual nationalization of South Africa's mines, proclaiming that 'the wealth of the country should be shared amongst those who work it.' In a highly symbolic gesture, the union elected Nelson Mandela as an honorary life president. In addition, it called for the abolition of job reservation and the unbanning of the ANC and the PAC.[245] At the same time, the COSATU leadership assumed a high profile in both sponsorship of political campaigns and policy pronouncements. At a rally marking its inauguration in the Western Cape, COSATU hardened its stand against the white minority regime, calling for the release of jailed trade unionist 76-year old Oscar Mpetha and threatening to initiate rent and tax boycotts.[246] The newly formed Witwatersrand region of COSATU warned that it would consider industrial and other action if the Botha regime did not act to resolve the black education crisis.[247] At a 'Free Mandela' rally organized by the Mitchell's Plain region of the UDF, the general secretary of COSATU, Jay Naidoo, proclaimed that the 'ruling class was floundering and increasingly direction-less'. The time for 'shouting socialist slogans is over', he said. 'The time for implementing socialist programmes is now.'[248]

The extent to which the political mood in the townships had permeated the labour scene was reflected in the annual wage negotiations in the metal industrial council, the country's largest collective bargaining forum. These yearly bargaining rites began in mid-April against the background of a recession that had deci-mated South Africa's foremost manufacturing industry. From a high of 450,000 workers employed by affiliates of Steel and Engineering Industries Federation of South Africa (SEIFSA) in 1982, only an estimated 300,000 workers were left in mid-1986. Yet this blight on employment did not lead to more acquiescence on the part of workers. The metal industry, second only to the mining sector, witnessed an extraordinary upsurge in worker militancy during 1986. In the country as a whole, the number of labour-days lost through strikes reached 550,000 in the first quarter of 1986, a figure that exceeded the total for the whole of 1984 and almost reached the number for all of 1985, which was itself a record year. According to labour relations consultant Andrew Levy, black trade union membership was increasing at an annual rate of 200 per cent. The record number of labour-days lost to industrial action was linked to a spillover of eighteen months of unrest in the townships. The pattern that emerged was that trade unions were unable to manage strikes or control the growing militancy of members on the shop-floor.[249]

In mid-April, more than 30,000 metal workers at plants throughout the country staged a coordinated one-hour stoppage to protest the slow progress in the annual industrial council wage negotiations. The council was responsible for establishing the pay and working conditions for the 300,000 black and white, unskilled and skilled, wage-earners in the metal industry. After three years of wage increases below the inflation rate, trade unions (particularly MAWU) were reluctant to accept another wage deal from SEIFSA that did not at least reach the inflation rate of 18 per cent.[250]

MAWU's mobilization of workers around the annual collective bargaining differed sharply in style from the factory-by-factory approach that characterized the FOSATU-affiliated unions in the early 1980s. MAWU held a series of mass meetings in the townships, drawing as many as 10,000 to a rally on the East Rand. As the single largest black union on the industrial council and by far the most militant, MAWU put forward a set of proposals in April that 'left more than a few employers aghast and wishing for the good old days when recognition agreements and more pay were the limit of worker demands'.[251] One of MAWU's key non-wage demands was that SEIFSA affiliates refuse to produce armaments and other equipment for the police and military.[252] This demand 'goes to the heart of the new politicized unionism ... and is probably an accurate indicator of the sentiments of black workers in the industry'.[253]

MAWU's demand for a paid holiday on May Day had been largely defused when SEIFSA agreed to a policy of 'no work, no pay' on 1 May. In a further step, SEIFSA acceded to MAWU's wishes when it announced that it would lobby the Botha regime to have 1 May be declared Labour Day to replace an existing paid public holiday. SEIFSA's attitude contrasted greatly with that of the Chamber of Mines, which attempted to block through the industrial courts the NUM's efforts to organize a general stay-away on the mines on May Day.[254]

The longstanding and explosive dispute between MAWU and SEIFSA over the forum for negotiating wages and working conditions remained unresolved. For a number of years, MAWU insisted that the industrial council should set one minimum for the entire industry, with plant-level bargaining setting wage rates over and above that minimum. In contrast, SEIFSA supported sectoral bargaining, as opposed to a single industrial council agreement.[255]

The COSATU Ideological battle with Inkatha

The formation of COSATU in November 1985 marked the end of the unofficial and uneasy truce between Inkatha and COSATU affiliates that had prevailed in Natal. At COSATU's inaugural conference, trade union officials scathingly attacked the Homelands system, including KwaZulu and Inkatha's willingness to participate in 'Pretoria's sham'. Gatsha Buthelezi quickly responded that Inkatha would meet COSATU's declaration of war'. In January 1986 Inkatha plunged into the labour field, pledging to form a trade union federation that would challenge COSATU's dominance. An organizing committee — the Co-ordinating Association of Trade Unions — was established to oversee the formation of the new federation loyal to Gatsha Buthelezi's Inkatha movement. A disaffected ex-official from the COSATU-affiliated Paper, Wood, and Allied Workers' Union was selected to spearhead these efforts. The two main planks of this proposed trade union federation were support for foreign investment in South Africa and alignment with the free enterprise system. The first step in the Inkatha initiative toward forming rival trade unions entailed the establishment of Inkatha committees in the factories. Once there were a number of these committees operating in the same sector they would form themselves into genuine industrial unions.[256]

Over the next several months, COSATU became increasingly embroiled in an ideological sideshow with Inkatha. In the war of words, both sides sniped at each other from public platforms. COSATU condemned this proposed federation as a 'tool of Inkatha' and as 'sweetheart' unionism. In response to Inkatha's supportive free enterprise stance, COSATU inquired rhetorically: 'Does Inkatha want us to support a system that has resulted in the enslavement and poverty of our people?' In turn, Inkatha denounced COSATU as 'another surrogate' for the ANC. The continued imprisonment of Nelson Mandela and the banning of the ANC, Buthelezi charged, generated sympathy that allowed the ANC's mission in exile 'to bask in the illusion of popularity'.[257]

On 1 May, the launch of Inkatha's United Workers Union of South Africa (UWUSA) in Durban drew from 60,000 to 75,000 people, the single largest May Day rally in the country. The event itself assumed a 'carnival atmosphere, buses and trains ferrying the [participants] to and from King's Park [in Durban]'. The main speaker, Gatsha Buthelezi, attacked COSATU and various church organizations for their support of sanctions and disinvestment. Representatives of only three small unions — the African Domestic Workers' Union, the Black Staff Association of SA Transport Service Employees, and the National Union of Brick and Allied Workers — addressed the crowd. All in all, while UWUSA organizers claimed to have organized three factories on the East Rand and a few in northern Natal, UWUSA had less than 10,000 workers. Its executive committee was also announced at the Durban launch. It included Simon Conco, the general secretary, Petrus Ndlovu, the president, Pepsi Msomi, the vice president, and Peter Davidson, the treasurer. Conco, the one-time chairman of Khulani Investments and a well-known Ulundi businessman, served as Chief Whip in the KwaZulu Legislative Assembly. He was also a founder and former president of the National African Chamber of Commerce. Conco declared that he was opposed to boycotts and strikes — 'except as a very last resort'. Ndlovu was employed in the personnel relations department at Tongaat Hullett in Natal. Finally, Msomi was township superintendent in Tembisa and Davidson was an Umlazi businessman.[258] UWUSA leaders openly praised the free enterprise system and condemned divestment, arguing that without 'a healthy economy there would be no jobs, no unions, and therefore no pressure for peaceful change'.[259]

The May Day General Strike and the June State of Emergency

The May Day General Strike

The 1986 May Day stayaway drew the support of over 1.5 million workers — making this action 'the largest national general strike in South African history'. According to the Labour Monitoring Group, the stayaway was most successful in the Port Elizabeth-Uitenhage area (99 to 100 per cent African workers and a significant proportion of coloured workers participated). African workers in eighteen of twenty-four small towns surveyed in the Eastern Cape observed a virtually 100 per cent stayaway. It was least successful in the Western Cape, where only 15 per cent stayed away — including an estimated 51 per cent of the African workforce, but only 8 per cent of coloured workers. In the Transvaal, more than 80 per cent (over one million) of the black workforce participated in the strike action. In Durban, 61 per cent of the workforce (including 68 per cent of the African workers and 31 per cent of the Indian workers) were involved in the stayaway. The Labour Monitoring Group also claimed that the stayaway on the mines exceeded 80 per cent in some places, involving some 210,000 workers. The NUM gave slightly higher figures, claiming that about 270,000 miners on forty-five mines — about half the black mining workforce — refused to work. The Chamber of Mines, however, disputed the accuracy of these estimations, maintaining the strike was 'only partially success-ful'. Anglo-American reported an 83 per cent stayaway on its gold mines, but other mines and collieries claimed that 'oper-ations were proceeding normally'. The Associated Chambers of Commerce (ASSOCOM), with 23,000 employer-members, acknowledged that between 70 and 100 per cent of its members' black workforce stayed away, except in the Free State and Natal, where 'absenteeism was claimed to be low'. ASSOCOM manpower secretary Vincent Brett claimed that virtually no transport was available on the Witwatersrand because of 100 per cent absentee-ism among PUTCO bus-drivers, disrupted railway services, and widespread support for the stayaway by black taxi-drivers. The SEIFSA said that its members experienced an almost total stay-away on the Reef, while only about 50 per cent stayed away in Natal.[260]

The COSATU meeting in Soweto attracted about 30,000 people, the biggest political rally ever held in Orlando Stadium.[261] About 30,000 attended a COSATU rally at Witbank and 20,000 people assembled at Wadley Stadium in Martizburg. An estimated 10,000 people attended the COSATU rally at Curries Foundation in Durban. But the size of this gathering was dwarfed by the esti-mated 70,000 Inkatha supporters who gathered at nearby King's Park in Durban to witness the launch of the Inkatha-inspired rival trade union federation, the United Workers Union of SA (UWUSA). All in all, security police banned six of the sixteen COSATU meetings. Troops and police disrupted four COSATU rallies in the Western Cape, injuring scores of people and arresting at least sixty-six.[262]

The significance of the nationwide May Day work stoppage cannot be simply reduced to an assessment of the numbers of workers who participated. One sympathetic reporter argued: 'Many [workers] stayed away because they were organized workers who identified with the day; but many others did because, as in other stayaways, they did not wish to incur the wrath of the"comrades". As in other mass actions, it is simply not possible to measure how many stayed away because they are organized and politicized, how many because they simply did not want to make waves.'[263] The May Day rallies brought into sharp focus the fact that the longstanding distinction within the popular movement between 'populism' and 'workerism' was blurred. In Friedman's words, 'the message of May Day, 1986, is . . . ambiguous. It tells us that both "workerism" and "populism" are alive, but it doesn't tell us which is dominating; at present, anti-*apartheid* resistance seems to be an uneasy mix between the two.' On the one hand, the May Day work stoppages signalled a stunning triumph for 'workerism': the observance of May Day has historical and worldwide significance for the working class. On the other hand, the rhetoric which accompanied the COSATU rallies often strayed from working-class concerns. COSATU President Elijah Barayi, 'managed to issue a May Day message without mentioning a single worker issue and many of the rallies held on that day were dominated by speeches which stressed "populist" issues only'.[264]

Preparation for 16 June

The interval between the May Day stayaway and the 12 June State of Emergency was filled with reports of widespread preparation for massive protests commemorating the tenth anniversary of the 16 June Soweto uprising. Both the Botha regime and the broad popular movement seemed determined to use this occasion as a test of strength and of wills. 'Each year the anniversary of the riot [sparking the 1976 rebellion]', one commentator remarked, 'has assumed a new significance as a day of protest rather than simply a day of commemoration.'[265]

As the showdown approached, the escalating political violence appeared to surpass yet another milestone in the almost two years of unrest. Clashes between rival groups were so endemic that many townships and ghettos were transformed into battle-fields. In the swirling confusion of attacks and counter-attacks, uninvolved bystanders were increasingly caught in the cross-fire. As the numbers of casualties mounted, the proportion of innocent victims of random violence escalated.

The mounting night raids on homes of political activists took a dramatic turn in late May when a captured unemployed youth confessed to receiving money in exchange for participating in vigilante attacks on the East Rand and directly implicated the police. Nineteen-year-old Abraham Zwane claimed that he began working for the police as a paid informer after he was arrested for smoking dagga. He said that he helped the police carry out a series of arson-attacks in which at least two people, including a three-month-old baby, were killed. Zwane was caught after he and thirteen other vigilantes, accompanied by two white and three black policemen, petrol-bombed the homes of seven activists in Thokoza and Katlehong townships.[266] Zwane's confession merely confirmed the widely-shared conviction that the police actively participated in planning and coordinating vigilante attacks under the convenient cover of 'black-on-black' violence.[267] A flood of allegations, including reliable eyewitness accounts, pointed to police support for vigilante activities.[268] In response to this cycle of vigilante attacks the popular organizations 'have now made it clear they will no longer be passive about the attacks — they state unequivocally that they will now meet force with force to repel any attackers'. In the words of former treason trialist and vice-president of the UDF, Reverend Frank Chikane: 'The attacks by the police, the SADF, masked people and so on have forced us to form defence committees.'[269]

The armed incursions of the conservative *witdoeke* into 'comrade' territory in the Crossroads squatter complex symbolized only the most sustained and brutal instance of vigilante bloodletting. This scenario, albeit on a smaller scale, was repeated elsewhere. 'Battles in the Durban area have left dozens dead in recent weeks', a *City Press* reporter proclaimed, 'and many activists have gone into hiding to escape the Amabutho — or Otheleweni, as they're also called, after their warcry.' The Lindelani shack settlement was transformed into the headquarters and the main operations area for the most notorious 'impi' vigilante combatants. In a published interview, Amabutho leader Emmanuel Khanyile boasted: 'I long for the day when there will be open war between the UDF and Inkatha — it will prove who is who in the political battle.' Inkatha Central Committee and KwaZulu MP, Thomas Shabalala, admitted that he had a small army of 208 'cops' under his personal command, each paid R130 a month. This 'salary' was raised from R3 monthly contributions from each household in the 9,000 shacks in the Lindelani camp. Shabalala confessed that it had been 'decided' that all councillors and Inkatha branches in the area should establish *abavikeli* (protectors) to 'stamp out UDF-created unrest'.[270]

Members of progressive organizations were increasingly subjected to murderous assaults. In late May, a hand-grenade attack on the home of MAWU organizer David Modimoeng killed his wife and seriously injured his two children. Modimoeng worked closely with the Brits Action Committee — a residents' organization resisting the resettlement of the Brits Location community to Lethlabile, 20 kilometers away.[271] This bombing was the fifth violent attack on a MAWU member or official over the previous six weeks.[272]

In the midst of the upsurge of vigilante activites, rival anti-*apartheid* popular organizations proved incapable of preventing violent feuding between factions amongst their affiliates. In Soweto, political violence between UDF-affiliated organizations and groups adhering to Black Consciousness escalated in April and May. It reached a climax in late May when more than nine activists died, scores were left homeless, and more than a dozen homes destroyed — mainly in Soweto and Mohlakeng on the West Rand. The source of the tension was traced to 'territorial disputes' between the UDF-affiliated Soweto Students Congress (SOSCO) and the Black Consciousness-oriented Azanian Students Movement (AZASM). In the midst of this fratricide, AZAPO supporters had to rescue their Transvaal vice-president, Dan Habedi, after he was kidnapped and beaten in Diepkloof by a group claiming allegiance to SOSCO. Nationally-recognized leaders on both sides condemned the allegations that these attacks and counter-attacks were sanctioned by top officials from each of the rival camps. Yet the bitter acrimony remained. AZAPO publicity secretary, Muntu Myeza, claimed that rival anti-*apartheid* organizations carried out attacks on thirty-six AZAPO members resulting in two deaths in Soweto alone between June and December 1985.[273] On the other side, Murphy Morobe, the UDF acting publicity secretary, announced that his organization 'had come to the realization that quiet diplomacy has now failed in dealing with these [trouble-making] organizations, especially AZASM'. As a result, the UDF and its affiliates decided 'that no progressive organization is now going to have any working relationship with them'.[274]

While the UDF accused AZASM of entering into an unholy alliance with the 'Kabasa gang' in Soweto, Henry Fazzie, vice-president of the UDF in the Eastern Cape, acknowledged that a '"small army of armed criminals' had infiltrated United Democratic Front ranks' for their 'own selfish ends'. He also condemned those who claimed to be members of '"Comrades" or "*Ambabuthu*" and stoned homes of members of AZAPO'.[275] In what appeared to be an almost unilateral acknowledgement that the township unrest was at least on occasion slipping out of control, the ANC, the PAC, AZAPO, and the UDF condemned (within the space of one week) the use of the 'necklace' to silence those believed to be informers and 'sell-outs'.[276]

The Battle for Control Over the Townships

The ANC increased the number of its guerrilla actions, maintaining a constant rhythm of land-mine attacks in rural areas, urban bombings, and assaults on township policemen and other officials. According to Wim Booyse of the Department of Strategic Studies at the University of Pretoria, the incidence of 'armed revolutionary violence' had increased by 800 per cent from mid-1984 to May 1986.[277] In mid-May, the SADF conducted simultaneous raids on three frontline state capitals: Harare, Lusaka, and Gaborone. While acknowledging that the motive behind these coordinated military ventures might be to 'ward off' the strong challenge to the National Party from the ultra-rightwing parties, perplexed observers rated these forays 'a dismal intelligence and military failure'.[278] In the last week of May, the SAP reported that police units came under fire several times in different areas of the country, including Katlehong, Nyanga in Cape Town (three separate incidents), and Gugulethu.[279]

Schools became fortresses of popular resistance. The Department of Education and Training (DET) was forced to relinquish a considerable degree of authority, particularly in Soweto and the Eastern Cape, where pupils dismissed their principals and appointed staff members of their choice to supervise their education. School-time was set aside every Wednesday and Friday for the implementation of alternative curricula. The aim of this 'people's education' was to 'promote a spirit of collectivism as opposed to the capitalist spirit of individualism'. A DET liaison officer confirmed that in the Eastern Cape townships of Port Alfred and East London teachers implemented an alternative educational format and that they were consequently no longer on the DET payroll.[280] In a courageous move, the Port Elizabeth Crisis in Education Committee announced that it planned to renovate the fifty-five schools damaged in the unrest and to implement a 'people's education' syllabus in all schools because the 'DET had abdicated its responsibility'.[281]

In late May and early June, a new wave of boycotts and localized work stayaways swept large parts of South Africa. A massive upsurge of violence engulfed strife-torn KwaNdebele. 'One of *apartheid's* most squalid fictions', KwaNdebele consisted of not much more than 'a few northeastern Transvaal farms turned into shanty slums' for 400,000 residents on the periphery of the Witwatersrand.[282] The uprising that erupted on 12 May claimed an average of fifteen deaths per week for over two months. The result of the temporary political alliance between comrades, civil servants, school teachers, and dissident members of the royal family was a reversal of the Skhosana regime's decision to accept Pretoria's offer of 'independence'.[283] The three-day work stayaway (including the entire 2,000-strong civil service) that began on 3 June coincided with the nearly continuous clashes between *Imbokotho* vigilantes and youthful comrades. Consumer boycotts hit major centres in the Transvaal, including Potchefstroom, Boksburg, Springs, and Nigel. In Port Elizabeth, about one hundred more white businesses closed by early June and another five hundred were threatened with bankruptcy because of the effectiveness of the boycott that resumed on 8 April. Residents in parts of the Vaal Triangle and the Eastern Cape were involved in rent strikes for almost two years.[284] In Cradock, the sheer enormity of outstanding rent and service changes indicated that, in the words of the Minister of Parliament from Johannesburg North, 'the situation was out of control. . . . There is no way this money can be collected. It is a total write-off.'[285] Suddenly, rent boycotts seemed to gain momentum all across the country. In Soweto, the Civic Association announced plans for a boycott that would not be ended until the white authorities acceded to a set of demands that included rent reductions, the regular collection of refuse, the resignation of town councillors, and the withdrawal of the SADF.[286] In the Dobsonville section, residents went a step further. The Civic Association defied the local town council and unilaterally staged occupations of some four hundred new council houses, allocating them to homeless families who in some instances had been ten years on 'waiting lists'. 'Only death will move me out of this house I have chosen', declared Mavis Mlotshwa, mother of four children, in a statement that accurately reflected the defiant resolve of the Dobsonville 'squatters'.[287] The Soweto rent boycott underscored the rising tension in the sprawling township. Loosely-associated youth groups — the comrades — pledged to close all West Rand Development Board (WRDB) liquor stores by 16 June. By the first week of June, six bottle stores were destroyed as a result of looting and burning. Another was demolished by a bulldozer. In one incident, police used grenades and small arms fire to dislodge a group of about one hundred who had seized a liquor outlet. One policeman was fatally wounded by shotgun fire. All in all, a liquor industry source acknowledged that all but four of the WRDB's estimated eighteen liquor outlets in Soweto were forcibly closed. Armed security guards were placed outside the remaining bottle stores.[288]

Over the next several months, rent boycotts, known to have emerged in twenty-eight townships in all four provinces, became 'the most organized form of sustained nationwide opposition to *apartheid*'. These were not the result of a co-ordinated national campaign but appeared to arise at different times, depending upon the level of organization and nature of grievances within each area. It also seemed that the rent strikes were most success-ful where organized resistance was the strongest.[289]

Political Struggle on the Labour Front

The spirit of resistance was not confined to the townships alone. In June, Project Free Enterprise released a comprehensive report sounding dire warnings about how covert industrial sabotage 'was taking place on a large scale in many, if not most, industrial plants in South Africa'. These 'modern-day Luddites' dropped objects into moving machinery, pilfered and destroyed company property, purposefully failed to report mechanical problems, and otherwise slowed the pace of work. Black workers were so antagonistic to the free enterprise system that industrial sabotage, the report concluded, 'is becoming a major cause of low economic productivity in South Africa'.[290]

After months of delicate negotiations, COSATU's 'one industry, one union' programme finally came to at least partial fruition. In late May, the Transport and General Workers' Union and the General Workers' Union merged to form the 26,000-strong Transport and General Workers' Union with a commitment to organize in the transport, cleaning and security, and building industries. Within a week, the new Food and Allied Workers' Union (FAWU) representing 62,000 workers in the food and beverage industry was formed from the merger of the Food and Canning Workers' Union; the Sweet, Food, and Allied Workers' Union; the Retail and Allied Workers' Union; and other food industry workers previously represented by COSATU-affiliated general workers' unions. FAWU had members in more than 340 food and beverage factories throughout South Africa.[291] This streamlining of COSATU's organizational structures paralleled the increasingly vocal calls by its principal leaders for socialism as an alternative to the free enterprise system.[292]

In the meantime, the battle between COSATU and UWUSA took a violent turn. Despite the massive May Day turnout to mark its launch, UWUSA only attracted three trade union affiliates and it was widely believed that employers secretly sponsored the formation of two of these.[293] Nevertheless, what UWUSA lacked in trade union support it compensated for in 'organized muscle'. In Madadeni township outside Newcastle in northern Natal, at least five homes belonging to UWUSA's progressive trade union rivals in COSATU and CUSA were razed to the ground in a spate of petrol-bomb attacks and counter-attacks in mid-May. 'Word is out', one correspondent noted, 'that there is a "hit list" of union members opposed to UWUSA who will either be killed or have their homes burnt by the end of the month.' This rumour prompted about twenty trade unionists to go into hiding.[294] In June, at least ten miners died and 115 were seriously injured in clashes between UWUSA supporters and NUM members at the ISCOR-owned Hlobane Colleries near Vryheid in northern Natal. The violence erupted after UWUSA supporters — many of whom were not employed at the coal mining complex — attempted to break a NUM-organized strike over higher wages and improved working conditions.[295]

The Imposition of the National State of Emergency

In a major television broadcast on 12 June, President P.W. Botha announced the imposition of a nationwide state of emergency. This pre-emptive manoeuvre was designed to undermine the mass mobilization commemorating the 16 June Soweto uprising a decade earlier. Opposition politicians decried this action as 'the most severe clampdown on civil liberty and the most far-reaching denial of freedom of speech and assembly in the history of South Africa'. Ken Andrew of the PFP declared that the 'wide-ranging, vague, and arbitrary' emergency regulations were 'a perfect recipe for a police state in which legal organizations are prevented from pursuing legitimate objectives'.[296] The emergency regulations incorporated sweeping new powers that included outlawing all illegal strikes, 'any boycott action', the participation in unlawful demonstrations and protests, in addition to banning vaguely-defined 'subversive statements' and imposing severe restrictions on all publications.[297] Far stronger than the decree that was lifted on 7 March, the 12 June emergency regulations covered the entire country and offered the authorities broad powers including an indemnity from prosecution and the right to arrest without a charge and to search without a warrant. The state of emergency was introduced after the National Party failed to push two comprehensive security Bills through the (Indian) House of Delegates and the (Coloured) House of Representatives. These two Bills would have given the security forces additional powers and enabled the Minister of Law and Order Louis le Grange to declare 'unrest areas'.[298]

Within days, the security police detained over one thousand people. The principal targets of the police dragnet appeared to be trade unionists, members of political and community organizations, students and members of educational organizations, clergy and church-workers, and the media. One notable feature of this emergency was the high number of shop stewards, rather than union officials, detained. COSATU and the UDF were the two chief organizations most affected by the detentions.[299] Despite these draconian measures, the 16 June national stayaway — while subdued — was highly successful. According to the Labour Monitoring Group, the number of workers involved in the massive work stoppage was at least equal to the 1.5 million who participated in the May Day strike. The greater Pretoria-Witwatersrand-Vereeniging area and the Eastern Cape were the most affected regions. In the Western Cape, the stayaway amounted to 78 per cent of African workers and 26 per cent of coloured workers, with an estimated overall total of 37 per cent. In contrast, regions such as the Free State, Northern Natal, and Natal South Coast showed a low incidence of absenteeism.[300] In subsequent days, these figures were subjected to revision upwards as more accurate surveys of work-attendance were obtained.[301]

On 19 June, the white authorities ordered night-time curfews in thirteen magisterial districts in the Eastern Cape. Shortly thereafter, the security police slapped major curfew restrictions on the movement of black residents in KwaNdebele. On 21 June, the police commissioner for the Western Cape banned 119 organizations from publishing material and from holding meetings in any of the six magisterial districts ringing Cape Town. Then, on 27 June, the authorities extended the curfew to eleven more magisterial districts in the Orange Free State, bringing to at least 600,000 the number of South African black people living under such formal restrictions.[302] The white authorities once again resorted to repressive measures in order to maintain their tenuous grip over a political situation that was beyond their capacity to control let alone comprehend. This 12 June state of emergency marked the end of one phase of the popular struggle in South Africa and the beginning of another.

8.

The 'Organic Crisis' and the Struggle for Political Power

Those who read about or see pictures about the army in town-ships and the police in action do not know the extent of the unrest that is in South Africa. We are afraid this may just be the tip of the iceberg. Very few people have a sense of the poverty and utter helpless frustration in many townships. We have seen townships in the East Rand that make Soweto look like an elite conurbation of elegance. We have seen the conditions in places like Duduza in the Far East Rand which are a scandal to a civilised society. Even nearer home, that is nearer Johannesburg, in a place like Katlehong — just the other side of Germiston — the conditions under which people live are extremely bad. Many of us know Alexandra township. Despite all the high talk from local autho-rities there, Alex is just a glorified slum. It is a ghetto of unbe-lievable filth and poverty where people share shacks in dirty yards; where houses are falling apart and some of the streets are death traps.... Now, people have been living under such burden-some conditions for years, with a stoicism that is amazing.

'Editorial', *Sowetan*, 26 April 1985.

The Political Stalemate

Disarray Within the Dominant Class Bloc

The magnitude and intensity of the 1984-6 popular rebellion that swept the black townships came as a profound shock to the

431

dominant classes. South Africa's privileged and possessing classes have always exhibited a unique blend of smugness and over-confidence that belies their precarious grip at the pinnacle of a steadily collapsing social order. This pretence of *noblesse oblige* stems from the abiding legacy of white supremacy. Having ignored the warning signs of the impending upheaval, the dominant classes paradoxically found themselves enmeshed in the throes of a generalized social crisis without a uniform diagnosis of how to extricate themselves from its disturbing consequences.

The avalanche of popular unrest revealed with particular sharpness that *ad hoc* tinkering and fine-tuning were no longer capable of sustaining economic growth and political stability. In mid-1985, Gavin Relly, Chairman of Anglo-American Corporation, warned President Botha that South Africa's unparalleled turmoil was 'far more serious' than any previous crises and that it had 'a long-term thrust'.[1] In other words, South Africa's generalized social crisis was not merely conjunctural but 'organic'.[2] It was certainly not difficult to trace over the past decade the faultlines indicating deep structural strains that were imbedded in the particular historical trajectory of capitalist accumulation and the specific form of white minority rule in South Africa. This inventory of observable symptoms — meagre growth rates, recession, bankruptcies, unemployment, and so forth — signified the physiogmony of the organic crisis. Yet a catalogue of social indicators cannot substitute for a rigorous analysis of the anatomical character of the crisis. Strictly speaking, the post-World War II *regime of accumulation* — defined by a distinctive 'engine of economic growth' and rigid *apartheid* controls over black labourers and consumers — did not collapse all at once but came unravelled in stages. Put another way, the organic crisis did not evolve in the form of straight linear development but was made up of many overlapping and intersecting structural contradictions that converged within a particular historical conjuncture of unspecified duration.

The exhaustion of the *regime of accumulation* that reigned supreme throughout the *apartheid* era was marked by a crisis of hegemony that in turn took the particular form of a graduated deterioration rather than an abrupt decomposition in the internal coherence of white minority rule. The principal reason for this particular dynamic was that the National Party was able to maintain a stranglehold over white politics and thus remained the principal arbiter within the dominant bloc of class forces. Nevertheless, the ferocity and depth of the 1984-6 rebellion shattered the spurious illusion that the National Party would be able to orchestrate 'from above' a smooth transition *via* incremental steps to a neo-*apartheid regime of accumulation* that would both ensure economic growth and restore political stability.

South Africa's 'unsettled circumstances' unleashed a cacophonous din of acrimonious voices across the spectrum of the white minority regime, each hawking a rival panacea promising to reverse the fortunes of those who had the most to lose in a revolutionary upheaval. Within the limited parameters of white politics, the National Party fought tenaciously to hold the 'middle ground', prophesizing monumental changes yet vowing never to submit to 'chaos' or to 'preside over white abdication'. The National Party under P.W. Botha remained firmly entrenched at the helm of white political affairs. Yet for the first time in nearly forty years, the party leadership confronted a simultaneous political challenge from both ends of the white political divide. Large-scale financial, industrial, and commercial business interests became increasingly shrill in their condemnation of the snail's pace of promised yet vaguely-defined 'reforms'. Large-scale capital joined with the Progressive Federal Party in cajoling the National Party for its ineffectual blundering in its futile efforts at crisis-management, advocating instead expunging those untenable features of *apartheid* that rested on legalized discrimination and that retarded economic growth.

The 1984-6 rebellion exposed the unbridgeable gulf between what even the most liberal and pragmatic wing of the white minority regime was prepared to concede in order to resolve the crisis and the minimum demands of the overwhelming majority of South Africa's people.[3] The sharp divide between the powerful and the powerless is no more evident than on the question of 'one-person one-vote' in a unitary South Africa. The National Party insists repeatedly that this formula is a non-negotiable issue. Both the liberal wing of the bourgeoisie and the PFP concur on this fundamental principle. Those who repudiate universal suffrage in an undivided South Africa justify their position on spurious grounds: South Africa is a plural society (racially, ethnically, culturally, and so forth), composed of a variety of constituencies where an authentic democracy would preserve and protect the rights of different groups.[4] P.W. Botha put it succinctly: 'We are a country of multi-cultural societies. Every one of these multi-cultural societies has certain rights — cultural rights, language rights, a way of life that should be protected. In South Africa, you do not have a white minority as against a black majority. That is quite a wrong way of looking at things in South Africa. We have a country of different minorities — a white minority and black minorities.'[5] The lynchpin of the liberal solution to the crisis was a mild dose of 'democratization' set within the confines of a vaguely-defined and regionally-based federalism, that is, a political system of checks-and-balances that would at once leave property relations intact and provide the white electorate with substantive veto-powers over the black majority on fundamental questions.

Whatever secretive plans that National Party leaders might entertain with respect to acquiescing to the increasing pressure from large-scale business interests and the PFP to broaden the ambiguous reformist initiative seemed to stall in the face of growing rightwing popularity. The National Party suffered electoral setbacks in the November 1985 by-elections for the (white) House of Assembly. Surprisingly, the ultra-rightist HNP captured its first seat in the Sasolburg district in a close but decisive white backlash electoral contest.[6] The HNP remained the fortress of *apartheid* orthodoxy. Its leader, Jaap Marais, ridiculed the National Party as the 'biggest *kaffir-boetie* [kaffir-loving] government in the world'.[7] Likewise, the Conservative Party registered electoral gains, particularly in the Transvaal, Free State, and Northern Cape. 'If an election were held tomorrow', a correspondent remarked in mid-1986, 'the Nats [Nationalist Party] would be in real trouble ... there is no longer a safe Nat seat in the whole of the country's "Deep South" — the racially benighted Transvaal *platteland*.'[8] The Conservative Party continued to heap abuse on the National Party's policy of *toenardering* [rapprochement] and appeasement, instead promising deliverance in a white Homeland if the necessity arose. Yet it was the neo-fascist *Afrikaner Weerstandsbeweging* (AWB) that appeared to have captured the imagination of rank-and-file Afrikaners. Portraying P.W. Botha as a *volksverrater* [betrayer of the *volk*], the fanatic fringe fondly evoked the spectre of the nineteenth-century Boer Republics as prototypes for a modern *volkstaat*.[9] The militant AWB assumed the role of what rightwing enthusiasts liked to call *dryfkrag*, or drive behind the whole ultra-right movement. In a series of widely publicized open confrontations, the paramilitary AWB successfully disrupted National Party meetings on four separate occasions. In a joint statement issued in late May, the Conservative Party and the AWB proudly predicted that the encounter at Pietersburg — the 'Pietersburg Putch' as it came to be called — was the National Party's Waterloo.[10]

The growing rightwing backlash coincided with the waning influence of South African liberalism. The abrupt resignations from Parliament of Progressive Federal party stalwarts Frederik van Zyl Slabbert and Alex Boraine stunned and angered their white colleagues in the House of Assembly. In van Zyl Slabbert's final speech, he assailed Parliament as 'the playground of politicians', chastizing its response to South Africa's crisis as 'a grotesque ritual of irrelevance ... a macabre ballad by a bunch of sinecured cowards too scared to raise their heads above their trenches'.[11] This diatribe seemed to reflect the fission of liberal opinion, increasingly cast adrift from recognizable ideological moorings and without unity of purpose.

The stillborn National Convention Movement (NCM) — the brainchild of van Zyl Slabbert and co-convened with Gatsha Buthelezi — epitomized the malaise of South African liberalism. The 1910 Act of Union — the result of the successful effort of British imperialists to forge a negotiated compromise with defeated Boer ex-Generals in the aftermath of the Anglo-Boer War — represented the historical precedent for round-table discussions amongst former battle-tested adversaries. The idea of a National Convention seemed always to reappear during South Africa's periodic conjunctural crises. It signified the apotheosis of liberalism: a last-ditch manoeuvre of moderate pro-capitalist forces to convene power-brokers, self-appointed leaders, and other notables, out of the glaring spotlight of public opinion, to negotiate a compromise solution to the general crisis that would avert a revolutionary alternative. Lamenting the passing of this lost opportunity, Slabbert blamed the UDF and the ANC for 'blow[ing] [the NCM] out of the water' because of their rivalry with Buthelezi's Inkatha.[12]

The growing political rifts within the social fabric of white minority rule exposed the internal contradictions inhibiting the dominant bloc of class forces from closing ranks behind a

mutually acceptable political programme. The National Party —
the historical vehicle for reconciliation and compromise within
the power bloc since its 1948 electoral victory — appeared unable
within the narrow social boundaries of its class base to unilaterally engineer the type of far-reaching modifications of
apartheid that would ensure at least a modest respite from economic stagnation and political turmoil. The extended minuet
between the National Party leadership and prominent business
leaders, on the one hand, and the ultra-rightwing parties, on the
other, failed to reduce the acrimony. The route that the National
Party chose to handle the political crisis rendered public
discussion in general and Parliamentary debate in particular
increasingly irrelevant. As one observer put it, 'Decisions are
increasingly taken, not by parliament or even by the cabinet, but
by the State Security Council and, at the local level, by police
commissioners vested with vast powers. Parliament's role
increasingly is merely to approve decisions formally, *ex post
facto*.'[13] The National Party was thus trapped in a dilemma. Party
leaders acknowledged that any concessions offered in the midst
of political unrest would be interpreted as compromises that
would in turn encourage black militancy and strengthen the
hand of the ultra-rightwing. The National Party thus appeared to
be trapped on an escalator of repression.

The Popular Masses and Organized Resistance to White Minority Rule

The 1984-6 countrywide rebellion marked an unmistakable
watershed in what in retrospect can be acknowledged as an
almost unbroken chain of events that originated in the 1972-3
mass strikes, reached a highpoint during the 1976-7 Soweto
rebellion, erupted in the Western Cape in 1980-1, and returned
with even greater fury during the mid-1980s. At each of these
decisive intervals, the white minority regime progressively lost
ground in the ongoing battle to limit the aspirations of the
exploited and oppressed majority. Each distinctive episode in
this long wave of popular unrest also reinforced the growing
polarization along class and racial lines.

What distinguished the 1984-6 popular upsurge was not only
the duration and intensity of open confrontations but also the

unprecedented degree to which broad layers and sectors of the subordinate classes actively participated in pushing the townships beyond the frontiers of governability and rendering 'the system' unworkable. Provoked by the enduring and deadening indignities associated with *apartheid* and the economic prerogatives that it buttressed, the masses demonstrated repeatedly their collective refusal to submit to their own oppression. Often with only the vaguest idea of the specific programmes of the organized political movements, angry township residents took the initiative and resolutely stood their ground against the firepower of the army and police. The cumulative effect of these countless confrontations was that the battle-lines were constantly in flux without recognizable fronts or fixed positions. Civic associations, student groupings, youth congresses, and trade unions — the most rudimentary organs of popular defence — displayed inordinate degrees of endurance and tactical flexibility in the face of a relentless enemy. Operating sometimes with limited organizational links beyond a single township and often with tenuous ideological attachments with the broad urban-based political coalitions, hastily-formed groups in dispersed and peripheral areas demonstrated quite conclusively that the white minority regime and its local surrogates had decisively lost its grip in quite unexpected places. This abrupt awakening of political consciousness in areas of the country (both urban and rural) with little or no previous record of visible protest took the organized political movements by surprise. Without a real organizational network and a concrete perspective to sustain them, these localized groups tended to lose momentum, to wither, and to fall into a state of suspended hibernation. Nevertheless, the experience of revolt remained etched on the collective memory of the township residents.

In an address to Parliament, P.W. Botha claimed that from September 1984 through April 1986 an estimated '508 people, mostly moderate blacks, were brutally murdered by radical blacks'. In addition, he affirmed that 'no less than 1,417 black-owned businesses, 4,435 private homes — including 814 homes of black policemen — 28 churches, 54 community centres, several hundred schools and a number of clinics, all serving the black community, were either totally destroyed or badly damaged by petrol bombs or other forms of arson'.[14] These figures suggest that the administrative mechanisms of township governance were severely disrupted if not destroyed. The bureaucratic tangle of government agencies, boards, and town councils imposed on the townships were the weakest link of white minority rule. The local 'collaborators' who staffed these outposts along the outer perimeter of *apartheid* became the frequent targets of the collective wrath of local residents. The town council system — along with its coterie of local black policemen and assorted henchmen — constituted an essential pillar of the Botha regime's scheme to entrench white minority rule while cleansing it of visible signs of racial demarcation. Severing these invisible threats linking the black townships to the centralized state apparatuses left the Botha regime no other recourse but to revert to increased repression and its superior firepower to regain the upper hand.

Both in terms of personal misery and social cost, the price that township residents paid was enormous. Ongoing rent and service charge strikes meant that amenities were reduced to the barest minimum. Indiscriminate killings, arbitrary arrests, detentions-without-trial, torture and abuse of prisoners contributed to the climate of fear and uncertainty, which was heightened by suspicions about *agents-provocateurs*, spies, and informers. The proliferation of vigilantes and death squads further exacerbated the pervasive state of terror. On an even more menacing side, the May–June events at Crossroads seemed to indicate that armed vigilantes supported by police detachments were used as a surrogate exercise in counter-insurgency.[15]

While the mass movement shared a basic consensus in its anti-*apartheid* analysis, the popular organizations did not possess a common strategic perspective guiding the implementation of their goals. This diversity, however, was double-edged: on the one side, the various trends of opinion enriched and dynamized the mass movement, sparking ideological debate and growth; on the other side, rival organizations offered sharply divergent remedies for action, often provoking discord and division within the movement. Keeping in mind the regional specifics of 'political cultures' and longstanding local traditions in South Africa, it can be said that the mass movement generally adhered to radical–populist themes (one-person one-vote, equality of opportunity, abolition of racial discrimination, and so forth) as the basic framework determining political consciousness. During the course of the 1984-6 rebellion, the movement was impelled by the lived experience of ordinary people with their common exploitation and oppression. Yet there was a marked shift on the ideological terrain. The radical–populist currents began to shade almost imperceptibly into explicitly anti-capitalist sentiments. Increasingly, the independent trade unions and the popular organizations embraced socialist ideas. One sure indicator that 'dangerous dogma' began to resonate throughout the mass movement was the sudden preoccupation of South African pro-business lobbies with offering a defence of business freedoms and exalting the virtues of free enterprise for black advancement. Socialist rhetoric on occasion seemed to serve more as a point of reference — an identifiable antithesis to 'the system' — than as a detailed ideological alternative. Nevertheless, while socialist ideas did not occupy centre-stage within political consciousness, this ideological current was not just the ritualized vision of the radicalized intelligentsia but a concrete signpost guiding the formulation of a socio-economic alternative. 'There might be tactical differences [within the mass movement] but the goals of all sections of the community are the same', Jay Naidoo, secretary general of COSATU argued. 'What we say is that we reject the present economic system because it has denied people fundamental human rights. We believe that the wealth should be democratically controlled.'[16]

Social violence has become so routinized and endemic in the townships that it appears to have evolved into the 'normal' state of affairs. At discrete times and places, both sides were catapulted over the threshold of rocks and petrol-bombs incongruously matched against tear gas, rubber bullets, and shotguns, coming close to civil war. 'If South Africa is not in fact in a state of incipient or low-level war', one analyst argued, 'then there can be no doubt that what now prevails is a state of permanent civil disobedience, in which acts of resistance against the state and those who are seen to collaborate with it are commonplace and increasingly violent.'[17] The possibility of open civil war across a range of fluid fronts receded almost as quickly as it appeared. Yet the profound experience of pitched and bloody confrontations between increasingly polarized antagonists seems to have convinced growing numbers on both sides that a military test of strength and wills is both an unavoidable and inevitable outcome of the continuing political unrest.

Notes

Introduction

1. Kevin Danaher, *In Whose Interest? A Guide to U.S.–South African Relations*, Washington, D.C. 1984, pp. 111-12.
2. *Financial Mail*, 8 April 1977.
3. *Ibid.*
4. *The Economist*, 22 June 1985.
5. Robin Hallet, 'South Africa in an African Setting', in Nikolaas van der Merve and M.E. West (eds.), *Perspectives on South Africa's Future*, Cape Town 1979, pp. 4-5.
6. *The Economist*, 2 June 1984, 'The Poverty of *Apartheid*'.
7. Philip Smit, 'The Process of Black Urbanization', in Hermann Giliomee and Lawrence Schlemmer (eds.), *Up Against the Fences: Poverty, Passes, and Privilege in South Africa*, New York 1985, p. 117.
8. Charles Simkins, *The Distribution of the African Population of South Africa by Age, Sex, and Region-Type: 1960, 1970, and 1980*, Cape Town 1981.
9. Smit, 'Process of Black Urbanization', p. 118.
10. Philip Smit and J.J. Booysen, *Urbanization in the Homelands: A New Dimension in the Urbanization Process of the Black Population of South Africa*, Pretoria 1977.
11. Smit, 'Process of Black Urbanization', p. 118.
12. Hermann Gilimoee and Lawrence Schlemmer, 'Introduction: The Influx Control Fence', *Up Against the Fences*, pp. 3-4.
13. *Ibid.*, pp. 3-4.
14. *Ibid.*, p. 4.
15. David Smith, 'Urbanization and Social Change Under *Apartheid*:

442

Some Recent Developments', in David Smith (ed.), *Living Under Apartheid*, London 1982, p. 28.

16. *Ibid.*, pp. 4-5.

17. *Ibid.*, p. 5.

18. Committee to Investigate Private Sector Involvement in Resolving the Housing Backlog in Soweto, *Report of the Committee to Investigate Private Sector Involvement in Resolving the Housing Backlog in Soweto*, Pretoria 1982.

19. Charles Simkins, 'Agricultural Production in the African Reserves of South Africa, 1969-1981', *Journal of Southern African Studies* 7, 1981, pp. 256-83.

20. *The Economist*, 2 June 1984, 'The Poverty of *Apartheid*'. See Jill Nattrass, 'The Dynamics of Black Rural Poverty in South Africa', *Up Against the Fences*, p. 20.

21. Stanley Greenberg and Hermann Giliomee, 'Managing Influx Control from the Rural End: The Black Homelands and the Underbelly of Privilege', *Up Against the Fences*, pp. 69-71.

22. See Trevor Bell and Vishru Radayachee, 'Unemployment in South Africa: Trends, Causes, and Cures'. Paper presented at the Second Carnegie Inquiry into Poverty and Development in Southern Africa. Cape Town, April 1984.

23. See Greenberg and Giliomee, 'Managing Influx Control from the Rural End', p. 73.

24. A. Roukens De Lange, *The Informal Sector and Unemployment: Present Realities and Future Prospects*, Stellenbosch 1984.

25. Greenberg and Giliomee, 'Managing Influx Control from the Rural End', p. 78.

26. *Ibid.*, pp. 76-81.

27. *Ibid.*, p. 81.

28. See Lawrence Schlemmer, 'Squatter Communities: Safety Valves in the Rural–Urban Nexus', *Up Against the Fences*, pp. 167-91.

29. Hermann Giliomee, *The Parting of the Ways*, Cape Town 1982, pp. 48-9.

30. Martin Legassick, 'South Africa in Crisis: What Route to Democracy?' *African Affairs* 84 (337), 1985, p. 593.

31. *Ibid.*

32. Alan Cowell, 'The Struggle: Power and Politics in South Africa's Black Trade Unions', *New York Times Magazine*, 15 June 1985, p. 16.

Chapter 1

1. Richard Leonard, *South Africa at War: White Power and the Crisis in Southern Africa*, Westport 1983, pp. 13, 161-7; Alex Callinicos, *Southern Africa After Zimbabwe*, London 1981, pp. 97-9.

2. Philip Frankel, 'Race and Counter-Revolution: South Africa's *Total Strategy'*, *Journal of Commonwealth and Comparative Politics* 18(3), 1980, pp. 272-3.
3. *Star* (Johannesburg), 7 August 1979.
4. Republic of South Africa, Department of Defence, *White Paper on Defence*, 1977. Supplement to *Paratus* (South Africa), May 1977, p. ii.
5. General Magnus Malan, 3 September 1980. Cited in Deon Geldenhuys, *Some Foreign Policy Implications of South Africa's Total National Strategy; with Particular Reference to the '12-point Plan'*, Johannesburg 1981, p. 3.
6. South African Institute of Race Relations, *Annual Survey of Race Relations in South Africa 1982*, Johannesburg 1983, p. 351.
7. Frankel, 'Race and Counter-Revolution', pp. 272-3.
8. *Ibid.*, p. 273.
9. Robert Davies and Dan O'Meara, 'The State of Analysis of the Southern African Region: Issues Raised by South African Strategy', *Review of African Political Economy* 29, 1984, p. 69.
10. Robert Davies and Dan O'Meara, 'Total Strategy in Southern Africa: An Analysis of South African Regional Policy Since 1978', *Journal of Southern African Studies* 11(2), 1985, p. 186.
11. *Ibid.*
12. See John Saul and Stephen Gilb, *The Crisis in South Africa: Class Defense, Class Revolution*, New York 1981.
13. *Rand Daily Mail*, 20 September 1979.
14. Davies and O'Meara, 'Total Strategy in Southern Africa', p. 183.
15. T.R.H. Davenport, *South Africa: A Modern History*, London 1977, p. 239.
16. Martin Legassick, 'Legislation, Ideology and Economy in Post-1948 South Africa', *Journal of Southern African Studies* 1(1), 1974, pp. 5-35.
17. Tom Lodge, *Black Politics in South Africa Since 1945*, Johannesburg 1983.
18. Dan O'Meara, 'The 1946 African Mine Workers' Strike and the Political Economy of South Africa', *Journal of Commonwealth and Comparative Politics* 13(2), 1975, pp. 146-73.
19. *Cape Times*, 17 October 1946.
20. Brian Bunting, *The Rise of the South African Reich*, Harmondsworth 1967, p. 127.
21. Dan O'Meara, *Volkskapitalisme: Class, Capital, and Ideology in the Development of Afrikaner Nationalism, 1934-1948*, Cambridge 1983, pp. 225-48.
22. Davenport, *South Africa*, pp. 252-3.
23. Martin Murray, 'Monopoly Capitalism in the *Apartheid* Era, 1948-1980', in Martin Murray (ed.) *South African Capitalism and Black Poli-*

444

tical Opposition, Cambridge, Massachusetts 1980, pp. 398-9.

24. Davenport, South Africa, p. 253.
25. Peter Walshe, The Rise of African Nationalism, Berkeley 1971, p. 286.
26. Frederick Johnstone, 'White Prosperity and White Supremacy in South Africa Today', African Affairs 69 (275), 1970, pp. 126-9.
27. Johnstone, 'White Prosperity and White Supremacy', p. 126.
28. O'Meara, Volkskapitalisme, p. 247.
29. Davies and O'Meara, 'The State of Analysis of the South African Region', p. 68; Hermann Giliomee and Herbert Adam, Ethnic Power Mobilized: Can South Africa Change?, New Haven 1979, pp. 169-71; and O'Meara, Volkskapitalisme, pp. 247-50.
30. Callinicos, Southern Africa After Zimbabwe, p. 95.
31. Giliomee and Adam, Ethnic Power Mobilized, pp. 169-71.
32. O'Meara, Volkskapitalisme, p. 251.
33. Ibid., p. 252.
34. The Economist, 22 June 1985; The Economist, 10 August 1985; New York Times, 15 July 1986, 'Fearing Instability, West Seeks to Replace Minerals from Africa'.
35. See Myra Goldstein, The Genesis of Modern American Relations with South Africa, 1895-1914. Unpublished Ph.D dissertation, State University of New York at Buffalo, 1972; and Thomas Noer, Briton, Boer, and Yankee: The United States and Africa, 1870-1914, Kent (Ohio) 1978.
36. Kevin Danaher, In Whose Interests?, Washington, D.C. 1984, p. 47.
37. Jennifer Davis, James Cason, and Gail Hovey, 'Economic Disengagement and South Africa: The Effectiveness and Feasibility of Implementing Sanctions and Divestment', Law & Policy in International Business 15(3), 1983, p. 545.
38. 'Investing in Apartheid', TransAfrica Forum Issue Brief 2(12), 1984; Washington Post, 8 August 1982; New York Times, 3 November 1982, 'New Interest in South Africa'.
39. John Chettle, 'The Law and Policy of Divestment of South African Stock', Law & Policy in International Business 15(2), 1983, pp. 461-2.
40. Fortune, 30 September 1985, 'Time to Quit South Africa'.
41. See James Cason and Michael Fleshman, 'Dollars for Apartheid', Multinational Monitor 4 (November 1983), pp. 8-9.
42. 'Investing in Apartheid', TransAfrica Forum Issue Brief 2(12), 1984.
43. Ibid. See also Carole Collins, 'Sharp Rise in U.S. Lending to South Africa', Africa News, 9 May 1983, p. 5.
44. Anne Newman, 'The U.S. Corporate Stake in South Africa', Africa News 24(10), 20 May 1985, pp. 6, 19.
45. 'Investing in Apartheid', TransAfrica Forum Issue Brief 2(12), 1984; Washington Post, 30 July 1983, Jack Anderson, 'United States Understates Business Stake in South Africa'.

46. Glenn Goldberg, *IRRC Directory of U.S. Corporations in South Africa*, Washington, D.C. 1982.
47. Chettle, 'The Law and Policy of Divestment', pp. 445-528.
48. *Press and Sun Bulletin* (Binghamton, New York), 3 November 1985; *Christian Science Monitor*, 12 June 1985, William Proxmire, 'South Africa's No. 1 Trading Partner'; *Fortune*, 30 September 1985, 'Time to Quit South Africa'; *Wall Street Journal*, 20 June 1986.
49. Desaix Myers, *Business and Labor in South Africa*, Washington, D.C. 1979, pp. 119-21.
50. See Jennifer Davis, et al., 'Economic Disengagement', pp. 547-8.
51. *Ibid.* See also *Fortune*, 30 September 1985, 'Time to Quit South Africa'.
52. Anne Newman, 'The U.S. Corporate Stake', p. 4.
53. *Fortune*, 30 September 1985, 'Time to Quit South Africa'.
54. Anne Newman, 'The U.S. Corporate Stake', p. 5.
55. See Ronald Walters, 'The United States and South Africa: Nuclear Collaboration under the Reagan Administration', *TransAfrica Forum* 2(2), 1983, pp. 17-30.
56. Jennifer Davis, et al., 'Economic Disengagement', p. 556.
57. Elizabeth Schmidt, '"Marching to Pretoria": Reagan's South Africa Policy on the Move', *TransAfrica Forum* 2(2), 1983, p. 3
58. Barry Cohen and Mohammed El-Kawas (eds.) *The Kissinger Study of Southern Africa*, Nottingham 1975, p. 44.
59. *Ibid.*, p. 66.
60. *Ibid.*, pp. 66, 69.
61. R.W. Johnson, *How Long Will South Africa Survive?*, New York 1977, p. 59.
62. *Ibid.*, p. 60.
63. Schmidt, '"Marching to Pretoria"', pp. 4-5.
64. Thomas Karis, 'United States Policy Toward South Africa', in Gwendolen Carter and Patrick O'Meara (eds.), *Southern Africa: The Continuing Crisis*, Bloomington 1979, p. 348.
65. Sanford Ungar and Peter Vale, 'South Africa: Why Constructive Engagement Failed', *Foreign Affairs* (Winter 1985/1986), p. 244.
66. Schmidt, '"Marching to Pretoria"', p. 5.
67. *Ibid.*, p. 6.
68. Chester A. Crocker, 'South Africa: Strategy for Change', *Foreign Affairs* (Winter 1980/1981), pp. 323-51.
69. *Ibid.*, pp. 323-51.
70. 'U.S. Attitude Toward South Africa', Document 32, *The United States and South Africa: U.S. Public Statements and Related Documents, 1977-1985*, Washington, D.C. Department of State 1985, p. 85.
71. Chester Crocker, 'Scope Paper'. Reprinted in *TransAfrica News Report*, vol. 1, no. 10 (Special Edition), August 1981.

72. Michael Clough, 'Beyond Constructive Engagement', *Foreign Policy*, 61, 1985/1986, p. 4.
73. Leonard, *South Africa at War*, pp. 61-5.
74. Chester Crocker, 'Regional Strategy for Southern Africa'. Address before the American Legion in Honolulu, Hawaii, 29 August 1981. United States Department of State, Bureau of Public Affairs, Washington, D.C.: Current Policy No. 308, p. 3.
75. Schmidt, '"Marching to Pretoria"', pp. 10-12.
76. Leonard, *South Africa at War*, pp. 131-60; Michael Klare, 'Evading the Embargo: Illicit U.S. Arms Transfers to South Africa', *Journal of International Affairs* 35(1), 1981, pp. 15-30.
77. Davies and O'Meara, 'Total Strategy in Southern Africa', p. 188.
78. See Sam Nolutshungu, *South Africa in Africa*, Manchester 1975.
79. Deon Geldenhuys and T.D. Venter, 'Regional Cooperation in Southern Africa: A Constellation of States?', *South African Institute of International Affairs Bulletin* (Johannesburg) 3(3), 1979, p. 49.
80. Deon Geldenhuys, *South Africa's Black Homelands: Past Objectives, Present Realities and Future Development*, Johannesburg 1981, p. 21.
81. Quoted in D. Geldenhuys, *South Africa's Black Homelands*, p. 23.
82. *Rand Daily Mail*, 26 November 1979.
83. Quoted in D. Geldenhuys, *South Africa's Black Homelands*, p. 23.
84. Deon Geldenhuys, *The Constellation of Southern African States and the Southern African Development Co-ordination Council: Towards a New Regional Stalemate?*, Johannesburg 1981.
85. Deon Geldenhuys and Venters, 'Regional Co-operation in Southern Africa', pp. 50-4.
86. *Ibid.*, p. 52.
87. Republic of South Africa, House of Assembly, *House of Assembly Debates*, Pretoria 1980, 6 February 1980, col. 249.
88. Kenneth Grundy, 'South Africa's Domestic Strategy', *Current History* (March, 1983), p. 111.
89. Davies and O'Meara, 'Total Strategy in Southern Africa', pp. 191-2; Grundy, 'South Africa's Domestic Strategy', pp. 110-11.
90. Department of Defence, *White Paper*, p. 5.
91. *The Star* (Johannesburg), 11 August 1979.
92. Davies and O'Meara, 'Total Strategy in Southern Africa', p. 192.
93. Kevin Danaher, 'Government Initiated Reform in South Africa and Its Implications for U.S. Foreign Policy', *Politics & Society* 13(2), 1984, p. 193.
94. Robert Davies and Dan O'Meara, 'Total Strategy in Southern Africa', p. 192.
95. *Ibid.*, p. 193. See also Grundy, 'South Africa's Domestic Strategy', p. 112.
96. Robert Davies and Dan O'Meara, 'Total Strategy in Southern Africa,' p. 193.

97. Robert Jaster, *South Africa's Narrowing Security Options*, London 1980, p. 29.
98. Kenneth Grundy, 'South Africa's Domestic Strategy', pp. 111-14, 132-3; *Washington Post*, 30 May 1980; and *The Times* (London), 1 September 1980.
99. Davies and O'Meara, 'Total Strategy in Southern Africa', p. 194.
100. *Washington Post*, 30 May 1980.
101. Dan O'Meara, 'Muldergate and the Politics of Afrikaner Nationalism', *Work in Progress* 22, 1982, Supplement, p. 17.
102. Davies and O'Meara, 'Total Strategy in Southern Africa', p. 195.
103. Republic of South Africa, Department of Information, *Towards a Constellation of States in Southern Africa*, Pretoria n.d.
104. Davies and O'Meara, 'Total Strategy in Southern Africa', p. 195; Alan Hirsch, '"Banking on Discipline": The Development Bank of Southern Africa', in South African Research, *South African Review III*, Johannesburg 1986, pp. 372-80.
105. Robert Price, 'Pretoria's Southern African Strategy', *African Affairs* 83(330), 1984, 15.
106. Davies and O'Meara, 'Total Strategy in Southern Africa', pp. 196-7.
107. *Ibid.*, p. 197.
108. Roger Leys and Arne Tostensen, 'Regional Co-operation in Southern Africa: the Southern African Development Co-ordination Conference', *Review of African Political Economy* 23, 1982, pp. 52-3.
109. Arne Tostensen, *Dependence and Collective Self-Reliance in Southern Africa: The Case of the Southern African Development Coordination Conference (SADCC)*, Research Report Number 62, Scandinavian Institute of African Studies, Uppsala 1982.
110. See Amon J. Nsekela (ed.) *Southern Africa: Toward Economic Liberation*, London 1984.
111. Davies and O'Meara, 'Total Strategy in Southern Africa', pp. 196-7.
112. Deon Geldenhuys, 'South Africa's Regional Policy', in Michael Clough (ed.), *Changing Realities in Southern Africa*, Berkeley 1982, p. 152.
113. Robert Price, 'Pretoria's Southern African Strategy', p. 16.
114. Roger Leys and Arne Tostensen, 'Regional Co-operation in Southern Africa', p. 58.
115. *Ibid.*, pp. 58-9.
116. *Ibid.*, p. 59.
117. David Kaplan, 'The Internationalization of South African Capital: South African Direct Foreign Investment in the Contemporary Period', *African Affairs* 82(329), 1983, p. 475. See also Ann Seidman and Neva Seidman Makgetla, *Outposts of Monopoly*

Capitalism: Southern Africa in the Changing Global Economy, Wesport (Connecticut) 1980.

118. Roger Leys and Arne Tostensen, 'Regional Co-operation in Southern Africa', p. 60.

119. *Ibid.*

120. *Weekly Mail*, 18 April 1986, Martin Nicol, 'What About the South Africans Who "Divest"?' See also Kaplan, 'The Internationalization of South African Capital', p. 465.

121. Kaplan, 'The Internationalization of South African Capital', p. 475. For Latin America, see David Fig, 'South Africa's Interests in Latin America', in South African Research Service, *South African Review II*, Johannesburg 1984, pp. 239-55.

122. Leys and Tostensen, 'Regional Co-operation in Southern Africa', pp. 60-1.

123. *Ibid.*, pp. 60-1. See also *New York Times*, 20 May 1986, 'Beyond South Africa's Borders: The Three Neighbours'.

124. *Ibid.*, pp. 63-4.

125. Douglas Anglin, 'SADCC After Nkomati', *African Affairs* 84(335), 1985, p. 169.

126. Michael Fleshman, 'In Defense of Apartheid: South Africa and Its Neighbours', *Socialist Review* 85, 1986, pp. 99-118.

127. Walton R. Johnson, 'Destabilization in Southern Africa', *Trans-Africa Forum* 2(2), 1983, p. 67.

128. Price, 'Pretoria's Southern African Strategy', p. 18.

129. *Washington Post* 29 May 1983; *Christian Science Monitor*, 1 June 1983; Simon Jenkins, 'Destabilization in Southern Africa', *Economist*, 16 July 1983, pp. 20-1; Price, 'Pretoria's Southern African Strategy', pp. 18-19.

130. *Cape Times*, 20 January 1983; Johnson, 'Destabilization in Southern Africa', p. 67.

131. Robert Davies and Dan O'Meara, 'Total Strategy in Southern Africa', p. 198; Roger Leys and Arne Tostensen, 'Regional Co-operation in Southern Africa', pp. 61-2.

132. Jenkins, 'Destabilization in Southern Africa', p. 26.

133. 'Mozambique I: Havoc in the Bush', *Africa Confidential*, 21 July 1982, pp. 1-8; 'Mozambique II: Havoc in the Bush', *Africa Confidential*, 4 August 1982, pp. 5-7.

134. Roger Leys and Arne Tostensen, 'Regional Co-operation in Southern Africa', p. 65.

135. Anglin, 'SADCC after Nkomati', pp. 170-1.

136. *Africa Confidential*, 21 July 1982.

137. Davies and O'Meara, 'Total Strategy in Southern Africa', p. 198.

138. Cited in Davies and O'Meara, 'Destabilization in Southern Africa', p. 199.

139. Davies and O'Meara, 'Total Strategy in Southern Africa', pp. 200-1.

140. Schmidt, '"Marching to Pretoria"', p. 13.
141. *Financial Mail*, 3 January 1986.
142. *Morning Star* (UK), 5 March 1983.
143. Davies and O'Meara, 'Total Strategy in Southern Africa', p. 201.
144. Walton Johnson, 'Destabilization in Southern Africa', p. 68.
145. Davies and O'Meara, 'Total Strategy in Southern Africa', p. 202.
146. *Ibid.*, p. 203.
147. Jenkins, 'Destablization in Southern Africa', p. 26.
148. Davies and O'Meara, 'Total Strategy in Southern Africa', pp. 204-5.
149. Walton Johnson, 'Destabilization in Southern Africa', p. 74.
150. Leonard, *South Africa at War*, pp. 59-97.
151. Davies and O'Meara, 'Total Strategy in Southern Africa', p. 207.
152. Anglin, 'SADCC after Nkomati', p. 163; Davies and O'Meara, 'Total Strategy in Southern Africa', pp. 207-8.
153. Davies and O'Meara, 'Total Strategy in Southern Africa', p. 206.
154. Anglin, 'SADCC after Nkomati', p. 163.
155. Davies and O'Meara, 'Total Strategy in Southern Africa', p. 207.
156. *The Star* (Johannesburg), 23 March 1984.
157. *Financial Mail*, 27 April 1984, pp. 31-4.
158. *Ibid.*
159. *The Star* (Johannesburg), 24 April 1984.
160. Anglin, 'SADCC after Nkomati', p. 163.
161. *Morning Star* (UK) 15 June 1985; *The Star* (Johannesburg), 14 June 1985.
162. *New York Times*, 24 January 1986; *Ibid.*, 26 January 1986.
163. *Ibid.*

Chapter 2

1. Craig Charney, 'Class Conflict and the National Party Split', *Journal of Southern African Studies* 10(1), 1984, p. 269.
2. See Hermann Giliomee and Herbert Adam, *Ethnic Power Mobilized: Can South Africa Change?*, New Haven 1979.
3. Charney, 'Class Conflict and the National Party Split', p. 269.
4. *Ibid.*, pp. 269-70.
5. Dan O'Meara, 'Muldergate and the Politics of Afrikaner Nationalism', *Work in Progress* (Johannesburg) 22, (1982), Supplement, p. 10.
6. Charney, 'Class Conflict', pp. 269-72; and O'Meara, 'Muldergate', pp. 7-11.
7. Shelagh Gastrow, *Who's Who in South African Politics*, Johannesburg 1985, pp. 46-51.

8. See *Cape Times*, 13 November 1982, 'Three Million Jobless in SA'.
9. Charney, 'Class Conflict', p. 271.
10. Hermann Giliomee, *The Parting of the Ways: South African Politics, 1976-1982*, Cape Town 1982, p. 150.
11. Craig Charney, 'Towards Rupture or Statis? An Analysis of the 1981 South African General Election', *African Affairs* 81(325), 1982, p. 527.
12. *Sunday Tribune*, 12 April 1981, 'Businessmen Recommend Wide Labour and Race Reforms'; and *The Star* (Johannesburg), 10 February 1981, 'Why SA has a Manpower Crisis'.
13. Republic of South Africa, Commission of Inquiry into Legislation affecting the Utilisation of Manpower, *Report of the Commission of Inquiry into Legislation affecting Manpower*, RP32/1979, Pretoria 1979, p. 168.
14. Judy Seidman, *Facelift Apartheid*, London 1979.
15. Philip Frankel, 'Race and Counter-Revolution: South Africa's Total Strategy', *Journal of Commonwealth and Comparative Politics* 18(3), 1980, p. 278.
16. Andreas D. Wassenaar, *Assault on Private Enterprise*, Cape Town 1977, pp. 86, 119, 148-50, 153.
17. *Ibid.*, pp. 148-50.
18. P.W. Botha, 'Opening Address', *Carlton Conference*, Pretoria 1979, p. 12.
19. *Financial Mail*, 30 November 1979.
20. *Rand Daily Mail*, 23 November 1979.
21. Charney, 'Towards Rupture or Statis?', p. 528.
22. *Ibid.*, p. 535.
23. Giliomee and Adam, *Ethnic Power Mobilized*, p. 169.
24. Charney, 'Towards Rupture or Statis?', p. 535.
25. Tom Lodge, 'Introduction', in Shelagh Gastrow, *Who's Who in South African Politics*, pp. 5-6.
26. Charney, 'Towards Rupture or Statis?', p. 530.
27. Lodge, 'Introduction', p. 6.
28. O'Meara, *Volkskapitalisme*, pp. 22-38.
29. Charney, 'Class Conflict', pp. 278-9. See also *Rand Daily Mail*, 26 March 1983.
30. Charney, 'Class Conflict', p. 279.
31. See, for example *Cape Times*, 9 December 1982, Alex Borraine, 'A Seven Point Plan to Come to Grips with Unemployment'.
32. Lodge, 'Introduction', p. 8.
33. Charney, 'Class Conflict', p. 280.
34. Jan Lombard, 'The Economic Aspects of National Security', in M.H.H. Louw (ed.), *National Security: A Modern Approach*, Pretoria 1978, p. 86.
35. *Washington Post*, 3 March 1985, 'Austerity Pay Cut Angers South

Africa's Government Employees'.

36. Lodge, 'Introduction', p. 6.
37. See Sam Nolutshungu, *Changing South Africa: Political Considerations*, Manchester 1982.
38. Lombard, 'The Economic Aspects of National Security', pp. 92-3.
39. David Harrison, *The White Tribe of Africa*, Berkeley 1981.
40. David Smith, 'Urbanization and Social Change Under *Apartheid*: Some Recent Developments', in David Smith (ed.), *Living Under Apartheid*, London 1982, p. 25.
41. See *inter alia*, Frederick Johnstone, 'White Prosperity and White Supremacy in South Africa Today', *African Affairs* 69(275), 1970, pp. 124-40; M.L. Morris, 'The Development of Capitalism in South Africa', *Journal of Development Studies* 12(3), 1976, pp. 280-92; and Martin Murray, 'Theoretical Controversies and Methodological Approaches', in Martin J. Murray (ed.), *South African Capitalism and Black Political Opposition*, Cambridge 1980, pp. 1-16.
42. Dan O'Meara, 'The 1946 Mine Workers' Strike', *Journal of Commonwealth and Comparative Politics* 13(1), 1975, p. 147. For a defence of non-racial capitalism, see Merle Lipton, *Capitalism and Apartheid*, New Jersey 1985.
43. F.A. Johnstone, 'White Prosperity and White Supremacy in South Africa Today', pp. 125-6.
44. Smith, 'Urbanization and Social Change', p. 25.
45. Robert Schrire, 'The Homelands: Political Perspectives', in Robert Schrire (ed.), *South Africa: Public Policy Perspectives*, Cape Town 1982, p. 114.
46. Smith, 'Urbanization and Social Change', p. 25.
47. Deon Geldenhuys, *South Africa's Black Homelands: Past Objectives, Present Realities and Future Development*, Braamfontein 1981, p. 2.
48. John Dugard, 'Denationalization: *Apartheid*'s Ultimate Aim', *Africa Report* (July–August, 1983), p. 43.
49. Kevin Danaher, 'Government-Initiated Reform in South Africa and its Implications for U.S. Foreign Policy', *Politics & Society* 13(2), 1984, p. 195.
50. Dugard, 'Denationalization', p. 45.
51. Danaher, 'Government-Initiated Reforms in South Africa', pp. 194-5.
52. Cited in Dugard, 'Denationalisation', p. 44.
53. Miriam Lacob, 'Homelands: The New Locus of Repression', *Africa Report* (January–February, 1984), p. 44.
54. Gavin Maasdorp, 'Industrial Decentralization and the Economic Development of the Homelands', in Schrire (ed.), *South Africa: Public Policy Perspectives*, p. 235.
55. Frank Molteno, 'The Historical Significance of the Bantustan Strategy', *Social Dynamics* (Cape Town) 3(2), 1977, pp. 20-2.

56. Union of South Africa, Native Economic Commission, 1930-2, *Report of the Native Economic Commission, 1930-1932*, U.G. 22-1932, Pretoria 1932, p. 48.

57. Union of South Africa, Witwatersrand Mine Natives' Wages Commission, *Report of the Witwatersrand Mine Natives' Wages Commission*, U.G. 21-1944, Pretoria 1944, pp. 1-10.

58. Roger Southall, *South Africa's Transkei: The Political Economy of an 'Independent' Bantustan*, London 1982, p. 26.

59. Union of South Africa, Native Laws Commission, 1946-8 [Fagan Commission], *Report of the Native Laws Commission, 1946-1948*, U.G. 28-1948, Pretoria 1948, paragraphs 7, 13.

60. *Ibid.*, p. 18.

61. Transvaal Local Government Commission, *Report of the Transvaal Local Government Commission*, T.P. 1-1922, Pretoria 1922, para. 167.

62. Union of South Africa, Parliament, House of Assembly, *House of Assembly Debates*, Pretoria 1951. D.F. Malan, 16 May 1951, columns 6820 and 6821.

63. Union of South Africa, Commission for the Socio-Economic Development of the Bantu Areas within the Union of South Africa, *Summary of the Report of the Commission for the Socio-Economic Development of the Bantu Areas within the Union of South Africa*, U.G. 61-1955, Pretoria 1955, p. 3.

64. *Ibid.*, p. 105.

65. *Ibid.*, p. 194.

66. *Ibid.*, pp. 105-6, 206-7.

67. Union of South Africa, *Memorandum: Government Decisions on the Recommendations of the Commission for the Socio-Economic Development of the Bantu Areas Within the Union of South Africa*, W.P.F.-1956, Pretoria 1956, p. 3.

68. *Summary of the Report of the Commission* [Tomlinson], p. 194.

69. 'Statutory communism' was defined as any doctrine or scheme 'which aims at bringing about any political, industrial, social or economic change within the Union by the promotion of disturbances of disorder, by unlawful acts or omissions or by the threat of such acts or omissions or by means which include the promotion or disturbances or disorder, or such acts or omissions or threats'. Peter Walshe, *The Rise of African Nationalism in South Africa*, Berkeley 1971, p. 287.

70. See Leo Kuper, 'African Nationalism', in Leonard Thompson and Monica Wilson (eds.), *The Oxford History of South Africa, Volume II*, London 1971, pp. 460-1.

71. T.R.H. Davenport, *South Africa: A Modern History*, London 1977, p. 282.

72. Molteno, 'The Historical Significance', p. 22.

73. Southall, *South Africa's Transkei*, p. 104.

74. Union of South Africa, Parliament, House of Assembly, *Debates of the House of Assembly*, Pretoria 1951. Sam Kahn, 18 June 1951, column 9886.
75. Southall, *South Africa's Transkei*, p. 103.
76. Molteno, 'The Historical Significance', p. 24.
77. Govan Mbeki, *South Africa: The Peasants' Revolt*, Baltimore 1964.
78. Republic of South Africa, *South Africa 1980/1981: Official Yearbook*, Johannesburg 1981, p. 182.
79. Mbeki, *South Africa*, pp. 135-48.
80. Deon Geldenhuys, *South Africa's Black Homelands*, p. 6.
81. *Business Day*, 25 April 1986; *Sunday Times*, 14 September 1985.
82. Trevor Bell, *Industrial Decentralization in South Africa*, London 1973, pp. 3-4.
83. See Davenport, *South Africa*, pp. 270-1. See also *Summary of the Report of the Commission* [Tomlinson], pp. 3, 105.
84. Martin Legassick, 'Legislation, Ideology and Economy in Post-1948 South Africa', *Journal of Southern African Studies* 1(1), 1974, pp. 5-35.
85. William Beinart, 'The Policy of Industrial Decentralization in South Africa', in Study Project on External Investment in South Africa and Namibia (S.W. Africa), *The Condition of the Black Worker*, Uppsala (Sweden) 1975, p. 92.
86. Davenport, *South Africa*, p. 296.
87. Union of South Africa, Commission of Inquiry into Policy Relating to the Promotion of Industries, *Report of the Commission of Inquiry into Policy Relating to the Promotion of Industries*, U.G. 36-1958, Pretoria 1958, p. 7.
88. Molteno, 'The Historical Significance', pp. 23-5.
89. Christian Rogerson, '*Apartheid*, Decentralization, and Spatial Industrial Change', in David Smith (ed.), *Living Under Apartheid*, pp. 53-4.
90. Southall, *South Africa's Transkei*, p. 38.
91. *Ibid.*
92. Davenport, *South Africa*, p. 295.
93. William Beinart, 'The Policy of Industrial Decentralization', pp. 85-125. See also Jan Lombard, 'Background to Planning the Development of Bantu Homelands in South Africa', in John Barratt, Simon Brand, David Collier, and Kurt Glaser (eds.), *Accelerated Development in South Africa*, New York 1974, pp. 464-6.
94. Lombard, 'Background to Planning', p. 465.
95. Davenport, *South Africa*, p. 298. See also Alan Hirsch, 'The Study of Industrial Decentralization in South Africa — Some Comments', in Martin Fransman, Adrian Graves, and Nomthetho Simelane (eds.), *Southern African Studies: Retrospect and Prospect*, Edinburgh 1983, pp. 131-60.

96. Hirsch, 'The Study of Industrial Decentralization in South Africa', pp. 138-42.
97. Christian Rogerson, 'Decentralization and Industrial Change', p. 57. See also K. Gottschalk, 'Industrial Decentralization, Jobs, and Wages', *South African Labour Bulletin* 3(5), 1977, pp. 50-8.
98. Maasdorp, 'Industrial Decentralization and the Economic Development of the Homelands', pp. 242-3.
99. R. Tomlinson and J. Hyslop, 'Industrial Decentralization, Bantustan Policy, and the Control of Labour in South Africa'. Paper presented at African Studies Institute, University of the Witwatersrand, 1984.
100. See Republic of South Africa, Department of Foreign Affairs and Information, *White Paper on the Promotion of Industrial Development: An Element of Co-ordinated Regional Development Strategy for Southern Africa*, Pretoria 1982.
101. R. Tomlinson and J. Hyslop, 'Industrial Decentralization'.
102. Helen Zille, 'Deciphering Decentralization: An Analysis of the Government's Industrial Decentralization Strategy', in Linda Cooper and David Kaplan (eds.), *Reform and Response: Selected Research Papers on Aspects of Contemporary South Africa*, Cape Town 1983, pp. 175-6. See also William Cobbett, et al., 'South Africa's Regional Political Economy: A Critical Analysis of Reform Strategy in the 1980s', in South African Research Service, *South African Review III*, Johannesburg 1985, pp. 137-68.
103. Surplus People Project, *Forced Removals in South Africa: The Surplus People Project Reports. Volume 1: General Overview*, Cape Town 1983, pp. 6-7.
104. For a shortened version, see Laureen Platzky and Cherryl Walker, *The Surplus People: Forced Removals in South Africa*, Johannesburg 1985.
105. Union of South Africa, Parliament, House of Assembly, *House of Assembly Debates*, Pretoria 1950. T.E. Donges, 29 May 1950, column 7453.
106. Robin Hallett, 'Desolation on the Veld: Forced Removals in South Africa', *African Affairs* 83(332), 1984, p. 315.
107. Robert Schrire, 'The Homelands: Political Perspectives', in Schrire (ed.), *South Africa: Public Policy Perspectives*, p. 117.
108. Barbara Rogers, *Divide and Rule: South Africa's Bantustans*, London 1976, p. 25.
109. These figures are cited in Hallett, 'Desolation on the Veld', p. 315.
110. Michael de Klerk, 'Seasons that will Never Return: The Impact of Farm Mechanization on Employment, Incomes, and Population Distribution in the Western Transvaal', *Journal of Southern African Studies* 11(1) 1984, pp. 84-105.
111. Hallett, 'Desolation on the Veld', p. 315.

112. Cited in Bill Freund, 'Forced Resettlement and the Political Economy of South Africa', *Review of African Political Economy* 29, 1984, p. 51.
113. *Sunday Express*, 17 February 1985.
114. *Ibid.*
115. *Rand Daily Mail*, 10 October 1984.
116. *Ibid.*, 5 October 1984.
117. Eddie Koch, '"Without Visible Means of Subsistence": Slumyard Culture in Johannesburg, 1918-1940', in Belinda Bozzoli (ed.), *Town and Countryside in the Transvaal*, Johannesburg 1983, pp. 151-75; and Tom Lodge, 'The Destruction of Sophiatown', in Bozzoli, *Town and Countryside*, pp. 337-64.
118. David Welsh, 'The Growth of Towns', in Monica Wilson and Leonard Thompson (eds.), *The Oxford History of South Africa, Volume II*, pp. 190-1.
119. Union of South Africa, Parliament, House of Assembly, *House of Assembly Debates*, Pretoria 1937. G. Heaton Nicholls, column 6100.
120. Jan Christian Smuts, 'Address (1942)'. 556 Box J, no. 147. Jean van der Poel (ed.), *Selections from the Smuts Papers, Volume VI*, Cambridge 1973, p. 336.
121. Eddie Koch, '"Without Visible Means of Subsistence"', pp. 170-1; Alf Stadler, 'Birds in the Cornfields: Squatter Movements in Johannesburg', in Belinda Bozzoli (ed.), *Labour, Townships and Protest Studies in the Social History of the Witwatersrand*, Johannesburg 1979, pp. 19-48.
122. Davenport, *South Africa*, pp. 340-1.
123. Hallett, 'Desolation on the Veld', pp. 308-9.
124. *Ibid.*, p. 316.
125. Freund, 'Forced Resettlement', p. 52.
126. Surplus People Project, *Volume II: The Eastern Cape*, pp. 177-96.
127. Freund, 'Forced Resettlement', p. 52.
128. Cited in Hallett, 'Desolation on the Veld', p. 316.
129. Solomon Plaatje, *Native Life in South Africa: Before and Since the European War and the Boer Rebellion*, London 1916.
130. See Peter Walshe, *The Rise of African Nationalism in South Africa*, pp. 38-52.
131. Trevor Huddleston, *Naught for Your Comfort*, London 1956.
132. Cosmas Desmond, *The Discarded People*, Braamfontein 1970.
133. David Welsh, 'The Policies of Control: Blacks in the Common Areas', in *South Africa: Public Policy Perspectives*, p. 87.
134. Southall, *South Africa's Transkei*, p. 43.
135. Martin West, 'The "Apex of Subordination": The Urban African Population of South Africa', in R.M. Price and C.G. Rosberg (eds.), *The Apartheid Regime: Political Power and Racial Domination*, Berkeley 1980, pp. 128-31.

136. Charles Simkins, *The Distribution of the African Population of South Africa by Age, Sex, and Region-Type 1960, 1970, and 1980*, Cape Town 1981, pp. 21, 37.
137. Martin West, 'From Pass Courts to Deportation: Changing Patterns of Influx Control in Cape Town', *African Affairs* 81(325), 1982, p. 465.
138. Southall, *South Africa's Transkei*, p. 43.
139. *Ibid.*
140. A.N. Pelzer (ed.), *Verwoerd Speaks: Speeches, 1948-1966*, Johannesburg 1966, pp. 120-1.
141. W.W.M. Eiselen, 'Harmonious Multi-Community Development', *Optima* 9(1), 1959, p. 3.
142. Murriel Horrell, *Laws Affecting Race Relations in South Africa, 1948-1976*, Johannesburg 1978, p. 40.
143. I.P. van Onselen, 'Bantu Outside Their Homelands', in South African Bureau of Racial Affairs (SABRA), *Bantu Outside Their Homelands*, Pretoria 1972, pp. 28, 31.
144. South African Institute of Race Relations, *Annual Survey of Race Relations in South Africa 1979*, Johannesburg 1980, pp. 390-1.
145. Welsh, 'The Policies of Control', pp. 95-7; West, 'From Past Courts to Deportation', pp. 466-7.
146. Welsh, 'The Policies of Control', p. 97.
147. Cited in *Ibid.*, p. 97.
148. Pauline Morris and Sheila van der Horst, 'Urban Housing', in Sheila van der Horst and Jane Reid (eds.), *Race Discrimination in South Africa*, Cape Town 1981, p. 94.
149. South African Institute of Race Relations, *Annual Survey of Race Relations in South Africa 1980*, Johannesburg 1981, p. 310.
150. *Natal Mercury* (Durban), 27 January 1983, 'Board Creating Problems for Blacks' Claim'.
151. Pauline Morris, *Soweto*, Johannesburg 1980, p. 43.
152. Stephen Hlophe, 'The Crisis of Urban Living under Apartheid Conditions: A Socio-Economic Analysis of Soweto', *Journal of Southern African Affairs* 2(3), 1977, pp. 343-54.
153. Welsh, 'The Policies of Control', p. 97.
154. *Cape Herald*, 5 March 1983; and *The Star* (Johannesburg), 14 March 1983.
155. *The Star* (Johannesburg), 14 January 1983; *Sunday Express*, 17 February 1985.
156. *Rand Daily Mail* (Johannesburg), 21 September 1982; *Sowetan*, 17 January 1983; and *Rand Daily Mail* (Johannesburg), 5 March 1983.
157. Schrire, 'The Homelands: Political Perspectives', pp. 119-20.
158. *Rand Daily Mail*, 24 January 1983.
159. Surplus People Project, *Volume III: The Western and Northern Cape and Orange Free State*, p. 164.

160. See Maasdorp, 'Economic Decentralization', p. 245.
161. *Cape Times*, 29 March 1983.
162. *Daily Dispatch* (East London), 13 January 1983.
163. Jill Nattrass, *Migrant Labour and Underdevelopment: The Case of KwaZulu*, Durban 1977, p. 4.
164. Schrire, 'The Homelands: Political Perspectives', p. 120; *Rand Daily Mail*, 24 January 1983.
165. David Smith, 'Urbanization and Social Change', pp. 38-41.
166. Schrire, 'The Homelands: Political Perspectives', p. 120.
167. Howard Simson, 'Is the Apartheid State a Fascist State? A Framework for Analysis', Fransman, et al., *Southern African Studies*, pp. 75-98.
168. David Kaplan, 'The South African State: The Origins of a Racially Exclusive Democracy', *Insurgent Sociologist* 10(2), 1980, pp. 85-96.
169. Harold Wolpe, 'Towards an Analysis of the South African State', *International Journal of the Sociology of Law* 7(4), 1980, pp. 399-421; Harold Wolpe, 'The Analysis of the Forms of the South African State', in Fransman, et al., *Southern African Studies*, pp. 49-71.
170. Kaplan, 'The South African State', p. 85.
171. *Ibid.*, pp. 87, 88.
172. Special thanks to M.G. for these insights.
173. *Financial Mail*, 25 June 1976, 'The Coming Crunch', p. 111.
174. William Raiford, 'International Credit and South Africa', *U.S. Corporate Interests in Africa: Report to the Committee on Foreign Relations, U.S. Senate*, Washington, D.C. 1978, pp. 69-76.
175. Transvaal Chamber of Industries, 'Memorandum to the Honourable B.J. Vorster, Prime Minister', 29 July 1976, p. 2. [Cited in Stanley Greenberg, *Race and State in Capitalist Development: Comparative Perspectives*, New Haven and London 1980, pp. 205-6.]
176. *Rand Daily Mail*, 1 December 1976. See also *Financial Mail*, 19 November 1976, 'The Quality of Life', p. 697 and *Ibid.*, 3 December 1976, 'Singing in the Streets', pp. 889, 891.
177. Frankel, 'Race and Counter-Revolution', p. 279.
178. Craig Charney, 'The Politics of Changing Partners — Control and Co-option in the New South African Constitution', *Review of African Political Economy* 29 (1984), pp. 122-4.
179. David Welsh, 'Constitutional Changes in South Africa', *African Affairs* 83(332), 1984, pp. 147-56.
180. *Ibid.*, p. 156.
181. Quoted in Hermann Giliomee, 'The Botha Quest: Sharing Power Without Losing Control', *Leadership S.A.*, 2 (1983), p. 27.
182. Frank Molteno, 'The Coloured Persons' Representative Council: Its Place in the Evolving Strategy of South Africa's Rulers: An Overview', in Martin J. Murray (ed.), *South African Capitalism and Black Political Opposition*, pp. 623-33.

458

183. Trevor Abrahams, '"Coloured Politics" in South Africa: The Quislings' Trek into the Abyss', *Review of African Political Economy* 29, 1984, p. 133.
184. Molteno, 'The Coloured Persons' Representative Council', pp. 623-33.
185. *Ibid.*
186. Abrahams, '"Coloured Politics" in South Africa', p. 134.
187. Wolfgang Thomas, 'The Coloured People and the Limits of Separation', in Robert Schrire (ed.), *South Africa: Public Policy Perspectives*, 1982, p. 157.
188. T.R.H. Davenport, *South Africa*, pp. 76, 92-3.
189. Cindy Postlethwayt, 'What if they Gave a Puppet Show and Nobody Came? The South African Indian Council, 1964-1982', in Linda Cooper and David Kaplan (eds.), *Reform and Response*, pp. 57-8.
190. *Ibid.*, pp. 60-70.
191. Cited in *Ibid.*, p. 72.
192. *Ibid.*, pp. 72-3.
193. *Transvaal Leader*, 26 February 1982, 'Heunis Edict Flayed'.
194. Welsh, 'Constitutional Changes in South Africa', p. 150.
195. Kevin Danaher, 'Government-Initiated Reform in South Africa and Its Implications for U.S. Foreign Policy', *Politics & Society* 13(2) 1984, p. 187.
196. *Ibid.*, p. 188.
197. Welsh, 'Constitutional Changes in South Africa', pp. 152-3.
198. Christopher Hill, *Change in South Africa: Blind Alleys or New Directions?*, London 1983, p. 144.
199. Craig Charney, 'The Politics of Changing Partners', p. 125.
200. David Welsh, 'The Policies of Control: Blacks in the Common Areas', in Robert Schrire (ed.), *South Africa*, p. 102.
201. *Ibid.*
202. *Ibid.*, pp. 98-9.
203. Republic of South Africa, Commission of Inquiry into Legislation Affecting the Utilisation of Manpower (excluding the Legislation Administered by the Depts of Labour and Mines), *Report of the Commission of Inquiry into Legislation Affecting the Utilisation of Manpower (excluding the Legislation Administered by the Depts of Labour and Mines)*, RP 32/1979, Pretoria 1979, pp. 69-70. [Hereafter cited as *Riekert Commission Report*.]
204. Welsh, 'The Policies of Control', p. 100.
205. *Riekert Commission Report*, pp. 200-1.
206. Cited in Welsh, 'The Policies of Control', p. 101.
207. *Cape Argus*, 25 March 1983, 'Officials Working '"Outside the Law"'.
208. *The Star* (Johannesburg), 25 April 1979.

209. Vaun Cornell, 'Community Councils: Puppets, Magicians, or Fledgling Local Authorities?', in Linda Cooper and David Kaplan (eds.), *Reform and Response*, p. 5.
210. *Ibid.*, pp. 4-6.
211. Welsh, 'The Policies of Control', p. 102.
212. *Ibid.*
213. *Ibid.*, pp. 102-3.
214. Cornell, 'Community Councils', pp. 9-10.
215. *Ibid.*, p. 10.
216. *Ibid.*, pp. 11-13.
217. *Ibid.*, pp. 13-15.
218. R. Bloch, 'Community Councils — Control and Co-option', *Work in Progress*, October 1980, pp. 5-21.
219. *The Star* (Johannesburg), 9 June 1979; *Rand Daily Mail*, 21 April 1979.
220. Frankel, 'Race and Counter-Revolution', p. 282.
221. Cornell, 'Community Councils', pp. 35-41.
222. *Sunday Star* (Johannesburg), 21 July 1985; *Weekly Mail*, 28 November 1985.
223. *Sunday Star* (Johannesburg), 21 July 1985.
224. *World Business Weekly*, 6 July 1981, 'At the Crossroads', pp. 29-38.
225. Charney, 'The Politics of Changing Partners', p. 122.
226. Welsh, 'Constitutional Changes in South Africa', p. 149.
227. *The Times* (UK), 17 March 1981, 'Can Mr. Botha Fight Off the Hardest of Hardliners?'
228. Charney, 'The Politics of Changing Partners', p. 125.
229. Welsh, 'Constitutional Changes', p. 148.
230. *Rand Daily Mail*, 5 July 1979.
231. Frankel, 'Race and Counter-Revolution', p. 283.
232. *Ibid.*, p. 284.
233. Quoted in Barry Streek, 'The Myth of Reform', *Africa Report* (July-August, 1983), p. 55.

Chapter 3

1. David Hauck, *Black Trade Unions in South Africa*, Washington, D.C. 1982, p. 1; and Sam Mhlongo, 'Black Workers' Strikes in Southern Africa', *New Left Review* 83, 1973, pp. 41-9.
2. Sam Mhlongo, 'Black Workers' Strikes', p. 49.
3. Commission of Inquiry into the Regulation of the Monopolistic Conditions Act, 1955; *Report of the Commission of Inquiry into the Regulation of the Monopolistic Conditions Act, 1955*, Pretoria 1977, p. 1.

4. *Business Day*, 24 March 1986, 'Call for Anti-Takeover Laws'; *Weekly Mail*, 13 March 1986, 'Who Owns South Africa'.

5. See Rob Davies, Dan O'Meara, and Sipho Dlamini, *The Struggle for South Africa, Volume 1*, London 1984, pp. 51-130, 96-105. See also Duncan Innes, 'Monopoly Capitalism in South Africa', in South African Research Service (ed.) *South African Review 1*, Johannesburg 1983, pp. 171-83.

6. *Business Day*, 24 March 1986, 'Call for Anti-Takeover Laws'.

7. See Robert Davies, *Capital, State, and White Labour in South Africa*, London 1977; Robert Davies, 'The White Working Class of South Africa', *New Left Review* 82, 1973, pp. 40-59; and Charles van Onselen, *Studies in the Social and Economic History of the Witwatersrand, 1886-1914. Volume I, The New Babylon*, London 1982.

8. There are, of course, notable exceptions. See Robert Davies, *Capital, State, and White Labour in South Africa*.

9. Robert Davies, 'Capital Restructuring and the Modification of the Racial Division of Labour in South Africa', *Journal of Southern African Studies* 5(2), 1979, p. 182.

10. *Ibid.*, p. 185.

11. *Ibid.*, pp. 181-98.

12. See Johann Maree, 'Current Labour Utilization and Underemployment in South Africa', *Foreign Investment in South Africa, The Conditions of the Black Worker*, Uppsala, Sweden 1975, pp. 85-126; Charles Simkins and D. Clarke, *Structural Unemployment in South Africa*, Durban 1978.

13. Benjamin Pogrund, 'Constraints on Black Workers and White Employers in South Africa', *The Conditions of the Black Worker*, p. 129. See also Darcey Du Toit, *Capital and Labour in South Africa: Class Struggles in the 1970s*, Boston and London 1981, pp. 216-18; and Robert Davies, Dan O'Meara, and Sipho Dlamini, *The Struggle for South Africa, Volume II*, London 1984.

14. Pogrund, 'Constraints on Black Workers', *The Conditions of the Black Worker*, pp. 161-202.

15. Hauck, *Black Trade Unions in South Africa*, p. 5.

16. Nicolas Haysom, 'The Industrial Court: Institutionalising Industrial Conflict', in South African Research Service (eds.), *South African Review II*, Johannesburg 1984, pp. 108-9; and Hauck, *Black Trade Unions in South Africa*, p. 4.

17. Peter Wickens, *The Industrial and Commercial Workers' Union*, Cape Town 1978.

18. See Rodney Davenport, 'African Townsmen? South African Natives (Urban Areas) Legislation Through the Years', *African Affairs* 68(271), April 1969, pp. 95-109. For a broad survey, see Francine de Clercq, 'The Organized Labour Movement and State Legislation: Unity or Fragmentation?', *South African Labour Bulletin*

5(6-7), 1980, pp. 18-43.

19. See M.L. Morris, 'The Development of Capitalism in South African Agriculture: Class Struggle in the Countryside', *Economy & Society* 5(3), 1976, pp. 292-343.

20. City of Johannesburg, Annual Report, Manager of the Native Affairs Department, July 1949 — June 1950, paragraphs 199-200. [Cited in David Lewis, 'African Trade Unions and the South African State, 1947-1953'. Unpublished manuscript, University of Cape Town, 1977, pp. 8-9.]

21. See Jon Lewis, 'The New Unionism: Industrialization and Industrial Unions in South Africa, 1925-1930', in Eddie Webster (ed.), *Essays in Southern African Labour History*, Johannesburg 1983, pp. 121-42.

22. See Dan O'Meara, 'The 1946 Mine Workers' Strike and the Political Economy of South Africa', *Journal of Commonwealth and Comparative Politics* 13 (2), 1975, pp. 146-73.

23. Martin Legassick, 'Legislation, Ideology, and Economy in post-1948 South Africa', *Journal of Southern African Studies* 1(1), 1975, pp. 5-35.

24. Lodge, *Black Politics in South Africa Since 1945*, pp. 188-9.

25. Rob Lambert, 'SACTU and the Industrial Conciliation Act', *South African Labour Bulletin* 8(6), 1983, p. 27; Francine de Clercq, '*Apartheid* and the Organized Labour Movement', *Review of African Political Economy* 14, 1979, pp. 69-77.

26. Ken Luckhardt and Brenda Wall, *Working for Freedom: Black Trade Union Development in South Africa Throughout the 1970s*, Geneva 1981, p. 7; Lodge, *Black Politics in South Africa*, pp. 189-90.

27. Eddie Webster, *Cast in a Racial Mold: Labour Process and Trade Unionism in the Foundries*, Johannesburg 1985.

28. de Clercq, '*Apartheid* and the Organized Labour Movement', p. 72.

29. See Pogrund, 'Constraints on Black Workers', *The Conditions of the Black Worker*, pp. 161-202.

30. See Davies, *The Struggle for South Africa*, Volume II, pp. 241-80.

31. John Lewsen, 'The Role of Registered Trade Unions in the Black Trade Union Movement', *South African Labour Bulletin* 3(4), 1977, pp. 46-8; David Lewis, 'African Trade Unions and the South African State: 1947-1953'. Unpublished manuscript, Cape Town 1977, pp. 12-15; Linda Ensor, 'TUCSA's Relationship with African Trade Unions: An Attempt at Control, 1954-1962', *South African Labour Bulletin* 3(4), 1977, pp. 33-5; Clive Emdon, 'TUCSA Congress: No Debate', *South African Labour Bulletin* 3(4), 1977, pp. 14-18.

32. Ken Luckhardt and Brenda Wall, *Organize or Starve! The History of the South African Congress of Trade Unions*, London 1980; and de Clercq, 'Apartheid and Organized Labour', p. 72.

33. See Luckhardt and Wall, *Organize or Starve!*, pp. 259-443, for greater details. See also David Hemson, 'Trade Unions and the Struggle for Liberation in South Africa', *Capital & Class* 6, 1978, pp. 1-41.

34. While it contains useful information, Edward Feit's book, *Workers Without Weapons: The South African Congress of Trade Unions and the African Working Class*, Hamden, Connecticut 1975, maliciously distorts the historical record in order to demonstrate that SACTU was a 'failure' and that trade unions ought to disengage themselves in political struggles for state power.

35. Institute for Industrial Education, *The Durban Strikes, 1973*, Durban/Johannesburg 1976, pp. 9-22.

36. *Ibid.*, pp. 38-40.

37. *Ibid.*, p. 40.

38. *Ibid.*, p. 42.

39. This observation cannot be construed to suggest that the higher wage awards brought the general level of paid wages to a level above the Poverty Datum Line, let alone closed the significant gulf between white and black earnings.

40. de Clercq, '*Apartheid* and the Organized Labour Movement', p. 73.

41. Pogrund, 'Constraints on Black Workers', *The Conditions of the Black Worker*, p. 149.

42. See Colin Bundy, 'The Abolition of the Masters and Servants Act', *South African Labour Bulletin* 2(1), 1975, pp. 37-46. See also Robert Davies and David Lewis, 'Industrial Relations Legislation: One of Capital's Defenses', *Review of African Political Economy* 7, 1976, pp. 56-68; and Dudley Horner (ed.), *Labour Organization and the African Worker*, Johannesburg 1975.

43. Pogrund, 'Constraints on Black Workers', *The Conditions of the Black Worker*, pp. 153-5.

44. *Ibid.*, pp. 155-60. See Hemson, 'Trade Unions', pp. 21-2.

45. Luckhardt and Wall, *Working for Freedom*, p. 41.

46. Hauck, *Black Trade Unions*, p. 10; and Luckhardt and Wall, *Working for Freedom*, pp. 41-2.

47. Hauck, *Black Trade Unions*, p. 10.

48. *Ibid.*, pp. 13, 15.

49. de Clercq, '*Apartheid* and the Organized Labour Movement', p. 75.

50. Luckhardt and Wall, *Working for Freedom*, p. 62.

51. Lodge, *Black Politics in South Africa*, p. 337; de Clercq, '*Apartheid* and the Organized Labour Movement', p. 74; and Luckhardt and Wall, *Organize or Starve*, pp. 460-1.

52. Lodge, *Black Politics in South Africa*, p. 337; and Luckhardt and Wall, *Working for Freedom*, pp. 56-77.

53. *City Press*, 17 November 1985.

54. Davies, et al., *The Struggle for South Africa, Volume II*, pp. 255-7.

55. *Ibid.*, pp. 258-61.
56. *Cape Argus*, 9 November 1983; *Financial Mail*, 10 October 1982; *Big Deal*, August 1982; *Cape Argus*, 26 October 1982; and Tom Lodge, *Black Politics in South Africa Since 1945*, Johannesburg 1984, p. 346.
57. Rob Davies, et al., *The Struggle for South Africa, Volume II*, pp. 250-5.
58. *The Star* (Johannesburg), 8 November 1984.
59. *City Press*, 17 November 1985; Eddie Webster, 'New Force on the Shop Floor', in South African Research Service, *South African Review II*, Johannesburg 1984, pp. 84-5; *Financial Mail*, 7 December 1984; *Rand Daily Mail*, 8 July 1984; *Business Day*, 2 June 1986, 'TUCSA is Anchored in Troubled Waters'; *Post*, 3 May 1986, 'DIMES Pulls Out of TUCSA'; *City Press*, 4 May 1986.
60. Luckhardt and Wall, *Working for Freedom*, p. 27.
61. Lewsen, 'The Role of Registered Trade Unions in the Black Trade Union Movement', pp. 51-2.
62. See Johann Maree, 'Democracy and Oligarchy in the Independent Trade Unions in the Transvaal and the Western Province General Workers' Union in the 1970s', African Studies Institute, University of Witwatersrand, Seminar Paper, 19 August 1983. See also *CUSA News* 1(1), 1983.
63. Lodge, *Black Politics*, pp. 344-6.
64. Luckhardt and Wall, *Working for Freedom*, p. 28.
65. Maree, 'Democracy and Oligarchy in the Independent Trade Unions', pp. 14-15.
66. Luckhardt and Wall, *Organize or Starve!*, p. 63.
67. Nicolaus Haysom, *Ruling with the Whip: A Report on the Violation of Human Rights in the Ciskei*, Johannesburg 1983.
68. Lodge, *Black Politics in South Africa*, pp. 348-9.
69. Johann Maree, 'SAAWU in the East London Area: 1979-1981', *South African Labour Bulletin* 7(4-5), 1982, pp. 34-49.
70. Hindson, 'Union Unity', SALB, pp. 11, 14.
71. See Maree, 'SAAWU in the East London Area', pp. 38-41.
72. Rose Innes Phaale, 'Prospects for Trade Union Unity', *Azanian Worker* 1 (1), 1983, p. 5.
73. Maree, 'Democracy and Oligarchy in the Independent Trade Unions', pp. 13-14.
74. Craig Charney, 'Trade Union Unity Moves', *Work in Progress* 27, June 1983, pp. 4-7.
75. Jeremy Baskin, 'The 1981 East Rand Strike Wave', *South African Labour Bulletin*, 7(8), 1982, pp. 21-41; Eddie Webster, 'MAWU and the Industrial Council: A Comment', *South African Labour Bulletin* 8(8), and 9(1), 1983, pp. 1-3.
76. See, for example, Mike Morris, 'Capital's Responses to African Trade Unions post Wiehahn', *South African Labour Bulletin* 7(1-2),

464

1981, pp. 69-85; and General Workers' Union, 'Reply to Fine, de Clerq, and Innes', *South African Labour Bulletin* 7(3), 1981, pp. 16-25.

77. Baskin, 'Growth of a New Worker Organ: The Germiston Shop Stewards' Council', pp. 47-8.

78. Charney, 'Trade Union Unity Moves', pp. 4-7.

79. Hauck, *Black Trade Unions*, p. 19. See also Lodge, *Black Politics*, pp. 344-6; and Luckhardt and Wall, *Working for Freedom*, p. 27.

80. *The Star* (Johannesburg), 8 October 1982; *Cape Times*, 5 November 1982; *Sowetan*, 8 December 1982; *The Star* (Johannesburg), 12 December 1982.

81. *Financial Mail*, 28 February 1983; *Rand Daily Mail*, 23 November 1982; *Sunday Tribune*, 18 May 1986; *Business Day*, 22 May 1986.

82. *The Star* (Johannesburg), 10 December 1982; *Financial Week*, 16 March 1983, John Kane-Berman, 'Black Miners Advance'.

83. *Financial Mail*, 21 January 1983; *Ibid.*, 28 February 1983.

84. *The Star* (Johannesburg), 10 December 1982.

85. *Financial Mail*, 28 February 1983.

86. Cape Town Correspondent, 'Unions and the UDF', *South African Labour Bulletin* 8(8), and 9(1), 1983, pp. 3-6.

87. Personal interviews with trade union organizers. See also *Sowetan*, 27 October 1982.

88. 'CUSA: Union Future', *Big Deal*, August 1982. •

89. *Sowetan*, 9 March 1983; Craig Charney, 'The Race to Organize Black Workers', *Management*, April 1983.

90. *Rand Daily Mail*, 2 March 1983.

91. *Cape Argus*, 7 February 1983; *Sowetan*, 10 February 1983.

92. Craig Charney, 'Trade Union Unity Moves', pp. 4-7; *Financial Mail*, 12 April 1985. Supplement 'Manpower and Industrial Relations'.

93. *Rand Daily Mail*, 19 April 1983.

94. 'Shop Floor Bargains', *SASPU Focus*, December 1982; *Rand Daily Mail*, 1 November 1982; *The Star* (Johannesburg), 30 November 1982; *Cape Herald*, 1 March 1983; *Financial Mail*, 12 October 1984.

95. de Clercq, '*Apartheid* and the Organized Labour Movement', pp. 75-6.

96. Phaale, 'Prospects for Trade Union Unity', p. 5.

97. Jeremy Baskin, 'Briefings: No Unity Yet', *South African Labour Bulletin* 8(4), 1983, pp. 11-15; Doug Hindson, 'Union Unity', South African Research Service, *South African Review II*, p. 90.

98. Hindson, 'Union Unity', p. 91.

99. *Ibid.*

100. Baskin, 'No Unity Yet', p. 12.

101. Phaale, 'Prospects of Trade Union Unity', p. 5.

102. Baskin, 'No Unity Yet', pp. 13-14.

103. *Ibid.*, p. 14. See also General Workers' Union, 'Union Unity',

South African Labour Bulletin 8(4), 1983, pp. 74-6.

104. Doug Hindson, 'Union Unity', *South African Labour Bulletin,* (*SALB*) 8(6), 1983, p. 13.
105. Hindson, 'Union Unity', *South African Review II,* p. 94.
106. Hindson, 'Union Unity', *SALB,* p. 9; Phaale, 'Prospects for Trade Union Unity', p. 5.
107. Hindson, 'Union Unity', *SALB,* p. 9.
108. *Ibid.,* pp. 13-14.
109. Hindson, 'Union Unity', *South African Review II,* p. 95.
110. Hindson, 'Union Unity', *SALB,* pp. 12-13.
111. Hindson, 'Union Unity', *South African Review II,* pp. 96-7.
112. See Rose Innes Phaale, 'Prospects for Trade Union Unity', pp. 6-7.
113. See, for example, Bob Fine, Francine de Clercq, and Duncan Innes, 'Trade Unions and the State: The Question of Legality', *South African Labour Bulletin* 7(1-2), 1981, pp. 39-68; General Workers' Union, 'Reply to Fine, de Clercq, and Innes', *South African Labour Bulletin* 7(3), 1981, pp. 16-25; Fink Haysom, 'In Search of Concessions: Reply to Fine, et al.', *South African Labour Bulletin* 7(3), 1981, pp. 26-41; Alan Hirsch and Martin Nicol, 'Trade Unions and the State: A Response', *South African Labour Bulletin* 7(3), 1981, pp. 42-50; and *Eastern Province Herald,* 11 April 1983, '8000 Workers Back Union Unity Move'.
114. 'CUSA Policy Document', *South African Labour Bulletin* 8(3), 1982, p. 69.
115. Rose Innes Phaale, 'Prospects for Trade Union Unity', p. 7.
116. *Ibid.,* p. 7.
117. Rob Lambert, 'SACTU and the Industrial Conciliation Act', pp. 41-3.
118. Rose Innes Phaale, 'Prospects for Trade Union Unity', p. 8. See also Johann Maree, 'Current Labour Utilization and Underemployment in South Africa', in *The Conditions of the Black Worker,* pp. 85-126.
119. FOSATU, 'Principles of Collective Bargaining', *South African Labour Bulletin* 8(1), 1982, p. 82.
120. *FOSATU Worker News,* August 1981. Reproduced in 'Briefings', *South African Labour Bulletin,* 7(4-5), 1982, pp. 104-16.
121. FOSATU, 'Report', p. 110; John Copelyn, 'Problems in Collective Bargaining', *South African Labour Bulletin* 8(1), 1982, pp. 59-80; Eddie Webster, 'MAWU and the Industrial Council: A Comment', *South African Labour Bulletin* 8(5), 1983, pp. 14-19.
122. See MAWU, 'MAWU and the Industrial Council', *South African Labour Bulletin* 8(5), 1983, pp. 48-50.
123. Johann Maree, 'SAAWU in the East London Area: 1979-1981', *South African Labour Bulletin* 7(4-5), 1982, pp. 34-49.
124. *Ibid.,* p. 48.

125. FOSATU, 'Report', p. 107.
126. Joe Foster, 'The Workers' Struggle: Where Does FOSATU Stand?' *South African Labour Bulletin* 7(8), 1982, p. 79.
127. See, for example, Goran Therborn, 'Why Some Classes are More Successful than Others', *New Left Review* 138, 1983, pp. 37-56.
128. Rose Innes Phaale, 'Prospects for Trade Union Unity', p. 9.
129. 'CUSA Policy Document', *South African Labour Bulletin* 8(3), 1982, pp. 68-72.
130. Johann Maree, 'SAAWU in the East London Area', p. 40.
131. *Rand Daily Mail*, 2 March 1983; *Ibid.*, 14 March 1983; Edward Webster, 'New Force on the Shop Floor', *Management*, September 1983; *Rand Daily Mail*, 1 July 1983.
132. Liz McGregor, 'The Fatti's and Moni's Strikes', *South African Labour Bulletin* 5(6-7), 1980, pp. 122-31.
133. Mike Morris, 'Wilson–Roundtree: History of SAAWU's Organization', *South African Labour Bulletin* 7(4-5), 1982, pp. 18-27.
134. Western Province General Workers' Union, 'The Cape Meat Strike', *South African Labour Bulletin* 6(5), 1980, pp. 68-9; Lodge, *Black Politics in South Africa*, pp. 348-9.
135. See Martin Nichol, 'Legislation, Registration, Emasculation', *South African Labour Bulletin* 5(6-7), 1980, pp. 44-56.
136. See A.M., 'Black Workers Confront the State', *Southern Africa* 15(6), 1982, pp. 7-9. See also 'FOSATU Decides not to Join UDF', *FOSATU Worker News*, November/December 1983.
137. 'The Workers' Struggle — Where Does FOSATU Stand', pp. 70-2.
138. *Ibid.*, p. 74.
139. *Ibid.*, p. 76, 77.
140. *Ibid.*, p. 70.
141. *Ibid.*, p. 68.
142. Hindson, 'Union Unity', *South African Review II*, p. 105.
143. *Rand Daily Mail*, 20 August 1984.
144. *Ibid.*, 30 October 1984.
145. *Sunday Tribune*, 24 February 1985.
146. *Sowetan*, 17 December 1984.
147. *Financial Mail*, 21 December 1984; *Sunday Times*, 9 December 1984; *Sunday Tribune*, 24 February 1985; *Rand Daily Mail*, 8 March 1985.
148. *Rand Daily Mail*, 18 March 1984.
149. *Sowetan*, 15 January 1985; *The Star* (Johannesburg), 14 January 1985.
150. *Rand Daily Mail*, 18 March 1985.
151. *The Star* (Johannesburg), 18 April 1985.
152. *Sowetan*, 21 May 1985.
153. *Financial Mail*, 14 June 1985.
154. *Business Day*, 3 July 1985.
155. *Financial Mail*, 12 April 1985, Supplement 'Manpower and Indus-

trial Relations'; *Ibid.*, 22 April 1983.

156. *The Star* (Johannesburg), 17 April 1985.
157. *Financial Mail*, 24 May 1985.
158. *Business Day*, 3 July 1985.
159. *Weekly Mail*, 30 August 1985; *Financial Mail*, 20 July 1984.
160. *Financial Mail*, 19 July 1985.
161. *Ibid.*
162. *Ibid.*, 9 August 1985.
163. *City Press* (Johannesburg), 25 August 1985.
164. *Weekly Mail*, 19 November 1985, Jon Lewis and Estelle Randall, 'Super Union Finds its Wings'.
165. *Cape Times*, 21 November 1985.
166. *Financial Mail*, 8 November 1985.
167. 'COSATU', *Azania Frontline* (London) 12, January 1986.
168. *Weekly Mail*, 19 November 1985, Jon Lewis and Estelle Randall, 'Super Union Finds its Wings'.
169. *Sunday Tribune*, 20 October 1985.
170. *FOSATU Worker News*, September 1985.
171. *Financial Mail*, 18 October 1985.
172. *Ibid.*
173. *Ibid.*
174. *Ibid.*
175. *Sunday Tribune*, 1 December 1985.
176. *Cape Times*, 2 December 1985.
177. *Wall Street Journal*, 5 December 1985; *New York Times*, 2 December 1985.
178. *Business Day*, 3 December 1985.
179. *City Press*, 8 December 1985.
180. Carole Cooper, 'Bantustan Attitudes to Trade Unions', in *South African Review II*, pp. 165-84.
181. *Weekly Mail*, 29 November 1985; 'COSATU', *Azania Frontline* (London) 12, January 1986.
182. *Cape Times*, 3 December 1985.
183. *Ibid.*

Chapter 4

1. *New York Times*, 9 October 1983.
2. Howard Barrell, 'The United Democratic Front and the National Forum: Their Emergence, Composition, and Trends', South African Research Service (ed.), *South African Review II*, Johannesburg 1984, pp. 6-20.
3. *Rand Daily Mail*, 18 June 1983.

4. Barrell, 'The United Democratic Front and the National Forum', p. 13.
5. For a fuller elaboration of the causes and effects of the 1976 Soweto rebellion, see John Kane-Berman, *Soweto: Black Revolt, White Reaction*, Johannesburg 1978; Baruch Hirson, *Year of Fire, Year of Ash: The Soweto Revolt*, London 1978; and South African Institute of Race Relations, *South Africa in Travail: The Disturbances of 1976/77*, Johannesburg 1978.
6. Frank Molteno, 'The Uprising of the 16th June: A Review of the Literature on Events in South Africa 1976', *Social Dynamics* 5 (1), 1979, p. 54.
7. *Frontline* (South Africa), July 1983, Craig Charney, 'Leaking Solidarity'.
8. *Ibid.*
9. *New York Times*, 2 August 1980.
10. Anstides Sitas, *African Worker Responses on the East Rand to Changes in the Metal Industry, 1960-1980*. Unpublished Ph.D. dissertation, University of the Witwatersrand, Johannesburg 1983.
11. *Guardian* (New York), 18 November 1981, 'Black Unions Shake South Africa'.
12. *Rand Daily Mail*, 8 June 1981, 'Big Campaign for Indian Poll Stayaway'.
13. *The Star* (Johannesburg), 17 March 1980; *Financial Mail*, 19 October 1979.
14. *The Star* (Johannesburg), 20 August 1981.
15. *Transvaal Leader*, 23 October 1981; *Ibid.*, 16 October 1981; *Cape Herald*, 24 October 1981.
16. *Rand Daily Mail*, 2 November 1981.
17. *Daily News*, 5 November 1981; *Rand Daily Mail*, 5 November 1981.
18. Tom Lodge, *Black Politics in South Africa Since 1945*, Johannesburg 1981, p. 339.
19. *Work in Progress*, 18 (1981), pp. 22-6.
20. *Rand Daily Mail*, 10 March 1978.
21. South African Institute of Race Relations, *Annual Survey of Race Relations, 1980*, Johannesburg 1981, p. 61.
22. Lodge, *Black Politics in South Africa*, p. 340.
23. *Ibid.*, p. 341.
24. *Guardian* (New York), 25 November 1981, 'Resistance on the Rise'.
25. *New York Times*, 18 August 1982.
26. *Ibid.*, 22 October 1982.
27. *Washington Post*, 3 November 1982; *New York Times*, 1 August 1982.
28. *London (Sunday) Times*, 7 November 1982, 'White Farms Hit by Border Exodus'.
29. *New York Times*, 20 December 1982; *Ibid.*, 26 December 1982.

30. *Ibid.*, 25 May 1983; *Cape Times*, 21 May 1983; and *The Star* (Johannesburg), 23 May 1983.
31. *New York Times*, 23 May 1983; *Ibid.*, 22 May 1983; see also *Cape Argus*, 21 May 1983; and *Rand Daily Mail*, 3 August 1983.
32. *New York Times*, 25 May 1983; *Ibid.*, 24 May 1983.
33 Lodge, *Black Politics in South Africa*, pp. 339-40. See also *The Star* (Johannesburg), 17 December 1983; *New York Times*, 12 October 1983; *The Star* (Johannesburg), 13 December 1983; and *Cape Argus*, 16 December 1983.
34. Paul Rich, 'Insurgency, Terrorism and the *Apartheid* System in South Africa', *Political Studies* 32, 1984, pp. 68-85.
35. *New York Times*, 12 October 1983.
36. Rich, 'Insurgency, Terrorism and the *Apartheid* System', pp. 68-85.
37. *Ukusa* (South Africa), 23 October 1981, 'Spirit of Non-Racialism is Thriving'.
38. *SASPU National* 4, 3 September 1983.
39. *New African* [London], May 1984, 'Opposition from Within', pp. 22-3; Tom Lodge, 'Introduction', in Shelagh Gastrow, *Who's Who in South African Politics*, Johannesburg 1986, pp. 14-17; and Jo-Anne Collinge, 'The United Democratic Front', in South African Research Service, *South African Review III*, Johannesburg 1986, pp. 248-66.
40. *Rand Daily Mail*, 16 June 1983, 'The National Forum — A First Step Towards Unity'.
41. *The Star* (Johannesburg), 25 June 1983; *Cape Herald*, 28 June 1983; and *Rand Daily Mail*, 6 July 1983.
42. *Transvaal Leader*, 20 May 1983; *Transvaal Leader*, 21 May 1983.
43. *Boston Globe*, 19 June 1983.
44. Neville Alexander, 'Nation and Ethnicity in South Africa', *National Forum*, Johannesburg 1983, p. 19.
45. 'UDF and AZAPO: Evaluation and Expectations', *Work in Progress* 35, 1985, p. 12; Na-iem Dollie, 'The National Forum', in *South African Review III*, pp. 267-77.
46. See Gail Gerhart, *Black Power in South Africa*, Berkeley and Los Angeles 1978, for a detailed investigation of early 'Black Consciousness' views. For a more recent view, see Thomas Ranuga, *Marxism and Black Nationalism in South Africa (Azania): A Comparative and Critical Analysis of the Ideological Conflict and Consensus Between Marxism and Nationalism in the ANC, the PAC, and BCM, 1920-1980*. Unpublished Ph.D. Dissertation, Brandeis University 1982, pp. 247-300.
47. Steve Biko, *I Write What I Like*, London 1978, p. 49.
48. 'Black Allied Staff Association (University of the North)', in Gessler Nkondo (ed.), *The Dilemma of a Black University in South*

Africa, Johannesburg 1976, p. 86.

49. See, for example, J.G.E. Wolfson (ed.), *Turmoil at Turfloop*, Johannesburg 1976.

50. Biko, *I Write What I Like*, pp. 83, 86.

51. See, for example, Stephen Hlophe, 'The Crises of Urban Living Under Apartheid Conditions: A Socio-Economic Analysis of Soweto', *Journal of Southern African Affairs* 2, 3, 1977, pp. 343-54.

52. *New York Times*, 2 December 1982.

53. 'UDF and AZAPO: Evaluation and Expectations', pp. 15-18.

54. Tom Lodge, *Black Politics in South Africa*, pp. 11, 39, 86-7.

55. 'UDF and AZAPO: Evaluation and Expectations', p. 12. For a similar assessment, see Tom Lodge, 'Introduction', in Gastrow, *Who's Who in South African Politics*, pp. 18-19.

56. 'Challenging the Cliches?' *Work in Progress* 35, 1985, p. 21.

57. *Ibid.*, p. 22.

58. 'Manifesto of the Azanian People', *National Forum*, p. 68.

59. 'Seeking Socialism', *Work in Progress* 35, 1985, p. 26.

60. See *Grassroots*, 20 August 1983, 'National Launch of UDF'.

61. 'Solidarity Interviews', *Azania Frontline* 8, 1984.

62. 'Manifesto of the Azanian People', *National Forum*, p. 88.

63. *Ibid.*, p. 69.

64. 'Sisulu's View of the UDF', *SASPU National*, 4, 3, September 1983.

65. 'Critical Responses to the UDF', *Azania Frontline* 4, February 1984, p. 4.

66. 'General Workers' Union and the UDF', *Work in Progress* 29, October 1983, p. 12.

67. *Ibid.* See also *Financial Mail*, 16 December 1983, 'Workers and Politics'.

68. 'General Workers' Union and the UDF', p. 14.

69. *Ibid.*, p. 15.

70. *Ibid.*, p. 16.

71. 'NUSAS Scores Right at PMB', *SASPU National* 4, 3, 1983.

72. 'NUSAS Confirms the Right Wing', *SASPU National* 4, 3 1983.

73. Temba Meyer-fels, 'The Role of Youth', *National Forum*, p. 35.

74. *New York Times*, 21 August 1983.

75. Lybon Mabasa, 'In Search of National Unity', *National Forum*, p. 58.

76. *Ibid.*, p. 59.

77. Saths Cooper, 'Forward', *National Forum*, pp. 5-6.

78. *The Star* (Johannesburg), 12 December 1983, 'Freedom Charter Can't Work'.

79. *Rand Daily Mail*, 16 June 1983, 'The National Forum — A First Step Towards Unity'.

80. 'Challenging the Cliches?', p. 18.

81. *Ibid.*, pp. 18-19.

82. 'The Transvaal Indian Congress', *Work in Progress* 28, August 1983, p. 18.
83. *Ibid.*, pp. 18-19.
84. *Ibid.*, p. 19.
85. Alexander, 'Nation and Ethnicity in South Africa', pp. 22-4. See also Neville Alexander, 'An Approach to the National Question in South Africa', *Azania Worker* 2, 2, 1985, pp. 3-14.
86. 'The Transvaal Indian Congress', pp. 19-20.
87. Alexander, 'Nation and Ethnicity in South Africa', p. 25.
88. *Ibid.*, p. 28.

Chapter 5

1. *New York Times*, 12 July 1985, 'State of Emergency Called in 36 Cities in South Africa'; *Ibid.*, 22 July 1985, 'South Africa Says Police Detain 113'; *Ibid.*, 2 July 1985, 'Scores Arrested in Night Raids in South Africa'; *Washington Post*, 21 July 1985, 'Emergency Rule Begins in S. Africa'.
2. *Washington Post*, 21 July 1985, 'Emergency Rule Begins in S. Africa'.
3. *New York Times*, 22 July 1985, 'South Africa Says Police Detain 113'.
4. *Ibid.*, 19 July 1985, 'South African Blacks Boycotting Whites' Stores'; *Ibid.*, 21 July 1985, 'South Africa's Emergency becomes Official'.
5. *Washington Post*, 22 July 1985, 'South Africa Crackdown'; *New York Times*, 18 July 1985, 'Widespread Unrest Reported in Soweto'.
6. *New York Times*, 24 July 1985, '441 Are Detained by South Africans'; *Ibid.*, 26 July 1985, 'South African Strife'.
7. *Ibid.*, 23 July 1985, 'Scores Arrested in Night Raids in South Africa'.
8. *The Economist*, 1 September 1984; *Washington Post*, 8 February 1983, 'Minority Split in S. Africa'; *Cape Argus*, 23 August 1984.
9. *New York Times*, 22 August 1984, 'South Africa Arrests 17 Non-whites'.
10. *The Star* (Johannesburg), 29 August 1984; *Sunday Tribune*, 26 August 1984.
11. *Christian Science Monitor* 28 November 1984, 'A Superficial Calm'.
12. Union of South Africa, Senate, *Debates of the Senate*, Pretoria, 1954. 16 June 1954.
13. *New York Times*, 21 October 1984, 'Education Troubles Haunt South Africa'.
14. *Ibid.*
15. *Christian Science Monitor*, 30 October 1984, 'South Africans Debate

How to Control Future Unrest'.

16. *Newsweek*, 17 September 1984, 'Bloody Return to Sharpeville'; *Sowetan*, 23 August 1985; *Guardian* (UK), 5 September 1984.

17. *New York Times*, 13 September 1984, 'Protestors Battle Police in South Africa'.

18. *Guardian* (New York), 3 October 1984, 'Make South Africa Ungovernable!'

19. *New York Times*, 14 September 1985, '6 South African Fugitives Enter British Consulate'.

20. *Guardian* (UK), 19 October 1984; *Financial Times* (UK), 20 October 1984; and *Guardian* (UK), 17 November 1984.

21. *Wall Street Journal*, 14 September 1984, 'South African Leaders Conceal Austerity'; *Los Angeles Times*, 30 September 1984, 'South African Blacks' Discontent Increasing'; *Rand Daily Mail*, 25 August 1984.

22. *Wall Street Journal*, 19 September 1984, 'Black Miners' Union in South Africa Wins Modest Concessions'; *New York Times*, 20 September 1984, 'Mine Toll in South Africa is 7'.

23. *New York Times*, 8 October 1984, 'Pretoria will use Army to End Riots'.

24. *Sunday Times*, 7 October 1984.

25. *New York Times*, 24 October 1984, 'Pretoria's Troops Raid a Township'; *Sunday Express*, 28 October 1984.

26. *New York Times*, 28 October 1984, 'South Africa Sends in Army'.

27. *Sunday Times*, 28 October 1984.

28. *Sunday Star* (Johannesburg), 28 October 1984.

29. *Rand Daily Mail*, 30 October 1985; *Sunday Times*, 28 October 1984.

30. *Financial Mail*, 12 October 1985; *The Sowetan*, 11 October 1984.

31. *Christian Science Monitor*, 28 November 1984, 'A Superficial Calm'.

32. *Daily News*, 1 November 1984; *Rand Daily Mail*, 1 November 1984.

33. *Rand Daily Mail*, 1 November 1984; Mark Swilling, 'Stayaways, Urban Protest and the State', in South African Research Services (SARS), *South African Review III*, Johannesburg 1986, pp. 27-9.

34. *Daily News*, 7 November 1984; Swilling, 'Stayaways, Urban Protest and the State', pp. 29-31.

35. *Rand Daily Mail*, 7 November 1984.

36. *New York Times*, 9 December 1984, 'South Africa Gets a Hint of Black Power'; *Ibid.*, 6 November 1984, '10 South Africans Killed in Protests'; *Ibid.*, 7 November 1984, 'Toll Rises to 16 in South Africa's Rioting'; *Evening Press*, 6 November 1984, '6 Blacks Killed'; *Ibid.*, 7 November 1984, 'Thousands of Blacks Strike in Transvaal'.

37. *Rand Daily Mail*, 7 November 1984.

38. *The Star* (Johannesburg), 7 November 1984.

39. *Rand Daily Mail*, 8 November 1984.

40. *New York Times*, 9 November 1984, 'South African Protesters' Offices Raided'; *Evening Press*, 8 November 1984, '6,000 South African Strikers Fired'.
41. *Guardian* (New York), 21 November 1984, Heinz Klug, ' "Bigger than Soweto" '.
42. *Rand Daily Mail*, 9 November 1984.
43. *Sunday Times*, 4 November 1984.
44. *Rand Daily Mail*, 15 November 1984; *Daily News*, 14 November 1984.
45. *New York Times*, 14 November 1984, '50 South African Blacks Held'; *Ibid.*, 15 November 1984, 'South Africa Arrests First Whites in Recent Unrest'.
46. *Sowetan*, 16 November 1984.
47. *Guardian* (New York), 28 November 1984; *Boston Sunday Globe*, 18 November 1984, '23 Injured in South Africa'.
48. *Rand Daily Mail*, 23 November 1984; *The Star* (Johannesburg), 26 November 1984.
49. *Guardian* (New York), 28 November 1984.
50. *Rand Daily Mail*, 15 November 1984.
51. *The Star* (Johannesburg), 15 November 1984.
52. *Ibid.*
53. *Sowetan*, 9 November 1984.
54. *The Star* (Johannesburg), 30 November 1984.
55. *Wall Street Journal*, 18 January 1985, 'Why South Africa's White Businessmen Oppose *Apartheid*'.
56. *New York Times*, 9 December 1984, 'South Africa Gets a Hint of Black Power'.
57. *The Star* (Johannesburg), 10 November 1984.
58. *Sunday Times*, 11 November 1984.
59. *The Star* (Johannesburg), 15 November 1984.
60. *Rand Daily Mail*, 26 November 1984.
61. *The Times* (UK), 7 December 1984.
62. *Rand Daily Mail*, 22 December 1984.
63. *Washington Post*, 21 January 1985, 'S. Africa's Anti-U.S. Radicals'.
64. *The Star* (Johannesburg), 14 January 1985.
65. *New York Times*, 6 January 1985, 'Kennedy is Jeered in Johannesburg'.
66. *Sowetan*, 9 January 1985.
67. *Wall Street Journal*, 18 January 1985, 'Why South Africa's White Businessmen Oppose *Apartheid*'; *Financial Mail*, 11 January 1985; *The Star* (Johannesburg), 8 January 1985.
68. *Financial Mail*, 18 January 1985.
69. *Ibid.*
70. *Washington Sun*, 9 February 1985, 'S. Africa Opens Business Districts'.

71. *Christian Science Monitor*, 20 February 1985, 'Police Crack Down'.
72. *New York Times*, 2 February 1985, 'South Africa Temporarily Halts the Relocation of Black Settlements'.
73. *Sunday Times*, 30 December 1984.
74. *New York Times*, 19 February 1985, '5 Killed as Blacks Near Cape Town Battle Police'; *Christian Science Monitor*, 20 February 1985, 'S. African "Squatters" Dig in Heels'; *Rand Daily Mail*, 19 February 1985.
75. *Christian Science Monitor*, 25 February 1985, 'Cape Town's *Apartheid* Dream Fades'. See also *Washington Post*, 27 February 1985, 'South Africa Says it May Spare Squatter Camp'.
76. *Sowetan*, 17 January 1985; *The Star* (Johannesburg), 24 January 1985; *Sowetan*, 14 January 1985; *Ibid.*, 22 January 1985; and *The Citizen*, 2 February 1985.
77. *Washington Post*, 11 March 1985, 'S. African Unrest Spreads to Country'.
78. Alan Cowell, 'Defiance in South Africa', *New York Times Magazine*, 14 April 1985, pp. 30, 32.
79. *Ibid.*, p. 30.
80. *Ibid.*, p. 32.
81. *New York Times*, 12 February 1985, 'Inquiry is Sought in South Africa'.
82. Alan Cowell, 'Defiance in South Africa', p. 32.
83. *Washington Post*, 11 March 1985, 'S. African Unrest Spreads to Country'.
84. Alan Cowell, 'Defiance in South Africa', p. 32.
85. *Ibid.*
86. *Washington Post*, 7 March 1985, 'Austerity Pay Cut Angers South Africa's Government Employees'.
87. *Ibid.*, 15 March 1985, 'Business Leaders Press South Africa for Race Reforms'; *New York Times*, 20 March 1985, 'U.S. Group in South Africa urges Changes'.
88. *Washington Post*, 19 March 1985, 'South Africa Raises Income, Sales Taxes'.
89. *New York Times*, 7 April 1985, 'South Africa's Caldron of Resistance'.
90. *Cape Argus* (Cape Town), 15 March 1985.
91. Swilling, 'Stayaways, Urban Protests and the State', pp. 20-50.
92. *Cape Argus* (Cape Town), 19 March 1985; *New York Times*, 19 March 1985, 'Pretoria Plans to Cut Arms Spending'; *Cape Argus*, 19 March 1985.
93. *The Citizen*, 21 March 1985.
94. *New York Times*, 22 March 1985, '17 Blacks Slain in South Africa'; *Ibid.*, 23 March 1985, 'South Africa Orders Investigation'; *Ibid.*, 29 March 1985, 'Officer Testifies in South Africa'; *The Star* (Johannesburg), 22 March 1985.

95. *New African*, May 1985, 'Spectre of Sharpeville'.

96. *Washington Post*, 7 April 1985, 'S. African Police Altered Riot Tactics'.

97. *The Star* (Johannesburg), 22 March 1985.

98. *Ibid.*, 23 March 1985.

99. *Observer* (UK), 24 March 1985.

100. *New York Times*, 25 March 1985, 'Soldiers Protect a White Town'; *Washington Post*, 25 March 1985, '35,000 Show for Funeral in S. Africa'; *New York Times*, 24 March 1985, '7 Die as Unrest Flares up Anew', *Ibid.*, 22 March 1985, '17 Blacks Slain in South Africa by Police Fire'; *The Argus* (Cape Town), 25 March 1985.

101. *New York Times*, 27 March 1985, 'South Africa's New Mood'.

102. *Boston Globe*, 7 April 1985, 'Probe Reveals S. African Police were Issued Shoot-to-kill Orders'; *Daily News*, 3 April 1985; *The Star* (Johannesburg), 12 April 1985; *Observer* (UK), 21 April 1985.

103. *Rand Daily Mail*, 25 March 1985; *Sowetan*, 26 March 1985; *The Star* (Johannesburg), 27 March 1985.

104. *Rand Daily Mail*, 3 April 1985.

105. *Financial Times* (UK), 30 March 1985; *New York Times* 30 March 1985, South Africa Bars 29 Groups'; *Rand Daily Mail*, 23 March 1985.

106. *BBC Monitoring Report* (Johannesburg), 29 March 1985.

107. *New York Times*, 29 March 1985, 'Officer Testifies in South Africa'.

108. *Cape Argus*, 1 April 1985.

109. *Rand Daily Mail*, 3 April 1985.

110. *New York Times*, 27 March 1985, 'South Africa's New Mood'.

111. *Rand Daily Mail*, 1 April 1985; *Financial Times* (UK), 1 April 1985.

112. *New York Times*, 7 April 1985, 'South Africa's Caldron of Resistance Boils Again'.

113. *Ibid.*, 2 April 1985, 'Black Policemen in South Africa: Targets of Increasing Black Rage'.

114. *Sowetan*, 25 April 1985.

115. *Cape Times*, 3 April 1985.

116. *The Star* (Johannesburg), 12 April 1985.

117. *New York Times*, 14 April 1985, '60,000 Blacks at South African Funeral'; *The Times* (UK), 15 April 1985.

118. *New York Times*, 28 April 1985, '23 Victims of Unrest are Buried'.

119. *The Star* (Johannesburg), 20 April 1985.

120. *Rand Daily Mail*, 22 April 1985.

121. *Sunday Times* (UK), 19 May 1985.

122. *Ibid.*

123. *BBC Monitoring Report* (Johannesburg), 24 May 1985.

124. Dunbar Moody, 'Mine Culture and Miners' Identity on the South African Gold Mines', in Belinda Bozzoli (ed.), *Town and Countryside in the Transvaal*, Johannesburg 1983, pp. 176-97. See also

476

Sunday Tribune, 4 August 1985. See also *The Star* (Johannesburg), 14 December 1984.

125. *Cape Argus,* 4 May 1985.
126. *Rand Daily Mail,* 22 March 1985.
127. *The Star* (Johannesburg), 23 March 1985.
128. *Cape Argus,* 4 May 1985.
129. *New York Times,* 28 April 1985, '23 Victims of Unrest are Buried'; *Ibid.,* 30 April 1985, 'South African Gold Mines Fire 15,000 Blacks'.
130. *The Star* (Johannesburg), 30 May 1985; *Guardian* (New York), 22 May 1985.
131. *New York Times,* 14 May 1985, 'South African Union Storms *Apartheid*'s Bastions'.
132. *Sowetan,* 24 May 1985.
133. *The Star* (Johannesburg), 25 May 1985.
134. *Cape Argus,* 4 May 1985; *Sowetan,* 24 May 1985.
135. *New York Times,* 14 May 1985, 'South African Union Storms *Apartheid*'s Bastions'; *The Economist,* 4 May 1985, 'The Battlelines are Drawn'.
136. *Guardian* (New York), 22 May 1985.
137. *Christian Science Monitor,* 12 April 1985, 'Botha Bolstered by Black Support?'; *New York Times,* 8 April 1985, 'Botha ... Warns of Evil from Abroad'.
138. *New York Times,* 21 April 1985, 'South Africa Drops a Barrier to Relations Between Races'; *Christian Science Monitor,* 17 April 1985, 'Loss of Two Race Laws'.
139. *New York Times,* 10 May 1985, 'Pretoria Cancels Settlement Plan'.
140. *Wall Street Journal,* 9 May 1985, 'South African Army Gets Role Curbing Unrest'.
141. *Daily Telegraph* (UK), 6 May 1985.
142. *The Star* (Johannesburg), 30 May 1985.
143. *Financial Mail,* 24 May 1985; *The Star* (Johannesburg), 11 May 1985; *Business Day,* 14 May 1985; *The Star* (Johannesburg), 18 May 1985; *Business Day,* 15 May 1985.
144. *Citizen,* 30 April 1985.
145. *Sunday Times,* 12 May 1985.
146. *Christian Science Monitor,* 15 April 1985; 'South African Treason Trials'. *Ibid.,* 20 May 1985, 'Treason Trial Opens in South Africa'.
147. *Guardian* (UK), 13 May 1985, 'When Black Turns Against Black'.
148. *Cape Argus,* 7 May 1985.
149. *Ibid.,* 6 May 1985.
150. *Guardian* (UK), 13 May 1985, 'When Black Turns Against Black'.
151. *The Star* (Johannesburg), 14 May 1985.
152. *Sowetan,* 13 May 1985; *The Star* (Johannesburg), 20 May 1985.
153. *New York Times,* 20 May 1985, 'Tutu Urges Black Unity'; *Ibid.,* 17 June 1985, 'New Soweto Clash Mars Observance'.

154. *City Press,* 19 January 1986.
155. *Washington Post,* 13 June 1985, '2 Mixed-Race Legislators Attacked'; *Christian Science Monitor,* 17 June 1985, 'South African Raid into Botswana'.
156. *Guardian* (UK), 24 June 1985.
157. *Washington Post,* 5 June 1985, 'Wounded S. African Blacks Facing Arrests'.
158. *Sunday Times* (UK), 19 May 1985; *Sowetan,* 29 May 1985.
159. *Financial Mail,* 12 July 1985.
160. *The Star* (Johannesburg), 6 June 1985, 'Detainees' Parents Support Committee Report'.
161. *Sunday Tribune* (Johannesburg), 19 May 1985.
162. *City Press* (Johannesburg), 26 May 1985.
163. *Sowetan,* 3 June 1985; *The Star* (Johannesburg), 31 May 1985; *Sowetan,* 3 June 1985, 'Editorial'; *Ibid.,* 29 May 1985; *Sunday Star* (Johannesburg), 9 June 1985.
164. *Sowetan,* 13 June 1985.
165. *New York Times,* 5 August 1985, 'A Reporter's Notebook'.
166. *Ibid.,* 3 August 1985, 'Differing Loyalties, Similar Fates'.
167. *Sowetan,* 23 May 1985.
168. *Ibid.,* 21 June 1985.
169. *Weekly Mail,* 28 June 1985; *Business Day,* 27 June 1985.
170. *Los Angeles Times,* 11 July 1985, 'Bishop Tutu Defies a Black Mob'; *Sowetan,* 10 July 1985.
171. *The Star* (Johannesburg), 10 July 1985; *Los Angeles Times,* 10 July 1985, 'South African Cops Kill 7 More Blacks'.
172. *Newsweek,* 22 July 1985, 'A Test for Bishop Tutu'; *Ibid.,* 5 August 1985, 'A Second Tier of Leaders'.
173. *The Star* (Johannesburg), 2 July 1985.
174. *Sunday Star* (Johannesburg), 30 June 1985; *Cape Times,* 1 July 1985; *Sowetan,* 5 July 1985; *New York Times,* 5 July 1985, 'Opposition Says Death Squads Roam South Africa'.
175. *Cape Times,* 4 July 1985, 'Eastern Cape "Like a War Zone"'.
176. *Ibid.,* 28 June 1985.
177. *Rand Daily Mail,* 24 April 1985.
178. *Sowetan,* 20 May 1985.
179. *Sunday Star* (Johannesburg), 21 July 1985; *Daily News,* 14 June 1985; *Rand Daily Mail,* 22 April 1985.
180. *Sunday Times,* 21 April 1985; *The Economist* (UK), 27 July 1985, 'Very Vicious Circle'.
181. *Sunday Star* (Johannesburg), 21 July 1985.
182. *Sowetan,* 27 May 1985.
183. *City Press,* 26 May 1985; *Guardian* (UK), 31 May 1985; *Weekly Mail,* 22/8 November 1985.
184. *Sowetan,* 12 August 1985.

185. *New York Times*, 29 March 1985, 'Officer Testifies in South Africa'; *Boston Globe*, 7 April 1985, 'Black-against-Black Violence'.
186. *Sowetan*, 22 June 1985.
187. *The Star* (Johannesburg), 4 July 1985.
188. *Cape Times*, 18 June 1985.
189. *Sunday Times*, 14 July 1985; *Sowetan*, 26 September 1985; *The Star* (Johannesburg), 2 October 1985.
190. *New York Times*, 4 September 1985, 'Sharpeville: Symbolism Burns Anew'.
191. *Observer* (UK), 12 May 1985.
192. *Christian Science Monitor*, 19 July 1985, 'Violence in South Africa causing Collapse of Black township Governments'.
193. *Sun-Bulletin* (Binghamton), 15 July 1985, 'Black Local Governments Fall'.
194. *Christian Science Monitor*, 22 July 1985, 'S. Africa Tries to Put a Lid on Unrest'.
195. *New York Times*, 24 July 1985, '444 are Detained by South Africans'.
196. *Christian Science Monitor*, 22 July 1985, 'S. Africa Tries to Put a Lid on Unrest'.

Chapter 6

1. *Sowetan*, 12 August 1985.
2. See, for example, G.H. Pirie, 'Urban Bus Boycott in Alexandra Township, 1957', *African Studies* (Johannesburg) 42(1), 1983, pp. 67-77; Alf Stadler, 'A Long Way to Walk: Bus Boycotts in Alexandra, 1940-1945', in Philip Bonner (ed.), *Working Papers in South African Studies, Volume II*, Johannesburg 1981, pp. 228-57; and Tom Lodge, '"We Are Being Punished Because We Are Poor"', in Philip Bonner, *Working Papers in South African Studies, Volume II*, pp. 258-305.
3. *The Star* (Johannesburg), 12 July 1985; *Business Day*, 15 July 1985.
4. *The Star* (Johannesburg), 19 July 1985.
5. *City Press*, 4 August 1985; *Business Day*, 18 July 1985; *Financial Mail*, 16 August 1985.
6. *Christian Science Monitor*, 11 September 1985, 'S. Africa's Black Boycott Takes Hold'.
7. *Financial Mail*, 9 August 1985; *Weekly Mail* (Johannesburg), 15 August 1985.
8. *Sunday Times*, 28 July 1985; *Ibid.*, 4 August 1985.
9. *New York Times*, 4 October 1985, 'South African Boycotts Bring Cautious Contacts'; *Newsweek*, 29 July 1985, 'Pretoria's "Mailed Fist"'.

10. *Sowetan,* 7 August 1985.
11. *The Star* (Johannesburg), 12 August 1985.
12. *Cape Times,* 12 August 1985.
13. *Sunday Times,* 28 August 1985.
14. *City Press,* 11 August 1985; *Sowetan,* 15 August 1985.
15. *City Press,* 18 August 1985.
16. *Sunday Times,* 11 August 1985.
17. *The Star* (Johannesburg), 19 August 1985.
18. *New York Times,* 4 October 1985, 'South African Boycotts Bring Cautious Contacts'.
19. *Cape Times,* 18 August 1985.
20. *Christian Science Monitor,* 11 September 1985, 'S. Africa's Black Boycott Takes Hold'; *City Press,* 1 September 1985.
21. *The Star* (Johannesburg), 25 August 1985.
22. *Business Day,* 1 September 1985; *City Press,* 22 September 1985.
23. *Financial Mail,* 11 October 1985.
24. *Sunday Times,* 11 August 1985.
25. *Financial Mail,* 16 August 1985.
26. *The Herald,* 28 September 1985.
27. *Ibid.*
28. *Daily News,* 26 September 1985; *Financial Mail,* 11 October 1985.
29. *New York Times,* 21 October 1985, '4 Killed Around Cape Town'.
30. *Sowetan,* 5 August 1985; *Sunday Tribune,* 4 August 1985.
31. *The Star* (Johannesburg), 22 July 1985.
32. *City Press,* 4 August 1985.
33. *The Star* (Johannesburg), 7 August 1985.
34. *City Press,* 11 August 1985.
35. Gavin Maasdrop, 'Informal Housing and Informal Employment: Case Studies in the Durban Metropolitan Region', in David Smith (ed.), *Living Under Apartheid,* London 1982, pp. 143-63.
36. See John D. Brewer, 'The Membership of Inkatha in KwaMashu', *African Affairs* 84 (334), 1984, pp. 111-35.
37. *Weekly Mail,* 16 August 1985.
38. *Ibid.,* 8 November 1985.
39. *Ibid.,* 16 August 1985; *Sunday Times,* 11 August 1986.
40. *Weekly Mail,* 8 November 1985.
41. *City Press,* 11 August 1985; *Weekly Mail,* 16 August 1985.
42. *Business Day,* 8 August 1985.
43. *Weekly Mail,* 16 August 1985; *The Star* (Johannesburg), 9 August 1985; *City Press,* 18 August 1985.
44. *Sowetan,* 9 August 1985.
45. *New York Times,* 10 August 1985, 'Violence Spreads in Durban Areas'.
46. *Sowetan,* 9 August 1985.
47. *Sunday Times,* 11 August 1985.

48. *Daily News*, 13 August 1985.
49. *City Press*, 21 July 1985; *Citizen*, 23 July 1985.
50. *Citizen*, 8 August 1985.
51. *New York Times*, 8 August 1985, '4 Die as South African Unrest Spreads'.
52. *Sunday Star* (Johannesburg), 11 August 1985. Statement, Chief Gatsha Buthelezi.
53. *New York Times*, 10 August 1985, 'Violence Spreads in Durban Area'.
54. *Sunday Tribune* (Durban), 11 August 1985.
55. *Daily News*, 12 August 1985.
56. *City Press*, 18 August 1985.
57. *Ibid.*; *New York Times*, 15 August 1985, 'Violence and *Apartheid*'.
58. *City Press*, 25 August 1985; *Sunday Tribune* (Durban), 18 August 1985.
59. *New York Times*, 12 August 1985, 'Violence Erupts at Black's Rites in a "Homeland"'; *Guardian* (UK), 19 August 1985.
60. *New York Times*, 21 August 1985, 'Violence Erupts at Black's Rites in a "Homeland"'.
61. *The Star* (Johannesburg), 13 March 1985.
62. *Business Day*, 21 May 1985.
63. *Sowetan*, 20 May 1985; *Daily News*, 7 June 1985.
64. *Sunday Times*, 30 June 1985.
65. *Weekly Mail*, 28 June 1985.
66. *Business Day*, 12 July 1985.
67. *Financial Times* (UK), 17 July 1985.
68. *Weekly Mail*, 25 July 1985.
69. *Sunday Tribune* (Durban), 21 July 1985; *Financial Mail*, 26 July 1985; *Weekly Mail*, 25 July 1985.
70. *Business Day*, 5 August 1985.
71. *Ibid.*, 12 July 1985.
72. *Weekly Mail*, 25 July 1985.
73. *Sowetan*, 6 August 1985.
74. *Ibid.*, 20 August 1985.
75. *Ibid.*, 21 August 1985.
76. *Business Day*, 5 June 1985.
77. *Ibid.*, 9 July 1985.
78. *Sowetan*, 23 July 1985.
79. *Washington Post*, 29 August 1985, 'Black Gold Miners Plan Strike Sunday'.
80. *The Economist* (UK), 8 June 1985, 'Rich Seams of Tax Breaks'.
81. *The Star* (Johannesburg), 27 June 1985; *Ibid.*, 4 July 1985.
82. *Sowetan*, 5 August 1985.
83. *Washington Post*, 29 August 1985, 'Black Gold Miners Plan Strike Sunday'; *New York Times*, 30 August 1985, 'South Africa's

Economy Faces 2 Urgent Threats'; *Ibid.,* 5 August 1985, 'Black Union Plans Walkout'.

84. *New York Times,* 2 September 1985, 'Union's Determined Leader'; *Ibid.,* 'Strike at 7 Mines'; *Ibid.,* 3 September, 'South African Mine Strike Falters'; *Weekly Mail,* 6 September 1985.
85. *Business Day,* 3 September 1985.
86. *New York Times,* 4 September 1985, 'Black Mine Union Calls Off Strike'; *The Economist,* 7 September 1985.
87. *Wall Street Journal,* 13 August 1985, 'Blacks in South Africa Shape a Strategy: Making *Apartheid* System Ungovernable'.
88. *Newsweek,* 5 August 1985, 'South Africa's State of Siege'.
89. *Financial Mail,* 9 August 1985.
90. *Sunday Times,* 4 August 1985; *Newsweek,* 12 August 1985, 'Politics of the Laager'.
91. *Sowetan,* 21 August 1985; *Ibid.,* 13 August 1985.
92. *New York Times,* 31 August 1985, 'Third Day of Unrest in Cape'; *Ibid.,* 26 August 1985, '4 Areas of Unrest in South Africa'; *Ibid.,* 27 August 1985, 'Tutu's Son Arrested in Soweto'.
93. *Weekly Mail,* 6 September 1985.
94. *New York Times,* 28 August 1985, 'How Are South Africa's Jailed Children Faring?'
95. *Ibid.,* 26 August 1985, 'Ex-Detainees in South Africa Say Police Methods Have Been Harsh'.
96. *Sunday Star* (Johannesburg), 26 July 1985.
97. *Weekly Mail,* 13 September 1985; *The Star* (Johannesburg), 12 September 1985.
98. *Weekly Mail,* 13 September 1985.
99. *City Press,* 8 September 1985.
100. *Cape Argus,* 12 September 1985.
101. *Ibid.*
102. *Sowetan,* 10 September 1985.
103. *The Star* (Johannesburg), 30 September 1985; *Daily News,* 26 September 1985; *City Press,* 29 September 1985.
104. *Daily News,* 30 September 1985; *Sunday Times,* 29 September 1985; and *Guardian* (UK), 30 September 1985.
105. *Weekly Mail,* 10 October 1985.
106. *New York Times,* 25 June 1985.
107. *Weekly Mail,* 11/17 October 1985.
108. *New York Times,* 4 August 1985, 'Black Mourners Defy South Africa'. See Don Foster and Diane Sandler, *A Study of Detention and Torture in South Africa,* Cape Town 1985.
109. *Sunday Tribune,* 29 September 1985.
110. *New York Times,* 23 September 1985, Anthony Lewis, 'South Africa Says No'.
111. *Ibid.,* 26 September 1985, 'Pretoria Ordered to Stop Beatings'.

112. *The Star* (Johannesburg), 23 September 1985; *Sowetan*, 31 July 1985.
113. *City Press*, 28 July 1985.
114. *Ibid.*, 11 August 1985.
115. *Ibid.*, 18 August 1985.
116. *Weekly Mail*, 26 December 1985.
117. *Ibid.*
118. *New York Times*, 29 August 1985, 'Cape Town Police Battle Thousands Trying to March'.
119. *Washington Post*, 29 August 1985, 'S. African Police Rout Protestors'.
120. *New York Times*, 30 August 1985, 'Fighting Spreads near Cape Town'; *Cape Times*, 30 August 1985.
121. *Washington Post*, 30 August 1985, '11 Are Killed in Clashes near Cape Town'.
122. *New York Times*, 30 August 1985, 'Fighting Spreads near Cape Town'.
123. *Sunday Tribune*, 1 September 1985.
124. *New York Times*, 7 September 1985, '454 Schools Shut for Mixed Races in Cape Town Area'.
125. *Ibid.*, 2 September 1985, 'Strike at 7 Mines'.
126. *Sunday Times*, 8 September 1985; *Weekly Mail*, 6 September 1985; *Cape Times*, 6 September 1985.
127. *New York Times*, 8 September 1985, 'Black Funeral Near Cape Town Ends in Violence'.
128. *Sunday Times*, 8 September 1985.
129. *New York Times*, 8 September 1985, 'Black Funeral Near Cape Town Ends in Violence'.
130. *Sunday Tribune*, 22 September 1985.
131. *Ibid.*; *City Press*, 29 September 1985.
132. *Weekly Mail*, 17/24 October 1985; *Business Day*, 17 October 1985.
133. *New York Times*, 19 October 1985; *Business Day*, 17 October 1985; *Financial Times* (UK), 19 October 1985.
134. *New York Times*, 20 October 1985.
135. *Guardian* (UK), 19 October 1985.
136. *Sowetan*, 15 October 1985.
137. *New York Times*, 22 October 1985.
138. *Ibid.*, 25 October 1985.
139. *Ibid.*, 26 October 1985.
140. *Ibid.*, 29 October 1985; *Cape Times*, 28 October 1985.
141. *New York Times*, 18 October 1985.
142. *Los Angeles Times*, 17 November 1985.
143. *Weekly Mail*, 14 November 1985, Tony Weaver, 'Cape Town'.
144. *Ibid.*
145. *Ibid.*

146. *Ibid.*
147. *Ibid.*
148. *Cape Argus,* 27 November 1985; *Cape Times,* 30 November 1985.
149. *Weekly Mail,* 6 December 1985.

Chapter 7

1. *Financial Mail,* 18 October 1985; *Business Day,* 18 October 1985; *Daily News* (Johannesburg), 30 May 1985.
2. *The Star* (Johannesburg), 4 March 1986; *Africa Confidential* 26 (22), 30 October 1985, 'South Africa : The State Unravels'.
3. *Christian Science Monitor,* 23 July 1985, 'South Africa's Economy Beset by Recession'.
4. *Wall Street Journal,* 30 April 1985, 'Economic Woes Shatter South Africans'.
5. *Cape Argus,* 22 April 1986.
6. *Daily News* (Johannesburg), 30 May 1985.
7. *Business Day,* 22 April 1986.
8. *Cape Argus,* 1 March 1986.
9. *Business Day,* 13 March 1986.
10. *Cape Times,* 22 September 1985.
11. *Financial Mail,* 18 October 1985; *Ibid.,* 23 August 1985.
12. *Ibid.,* 27 September 1985, 'Vehicle Manufacture: An Industry in Agony', pp. 44-5.
13. *Cape Argus,* 29 August 1985.
14. *Sunday Times,* 4 August 1985.
15. *Sunday Tribune,* 11 January 1986.
16. *Sunday Times,* 5 January 1986.
17. *Evening Post,* 22 May 1986, '80% of Young Blacks Jobless'.
18. *Cape Times,* 19 March 1986.
19. *Cape Argus,* 24 August 1985.
20. *Business Day,* 21 May 1985.
21. *New York Times,* 4 May 1985, 'South African Farmers'.
22. *Weekly Mail,* 12 June 1985, 'Top of the AWB Hate List: "Anglo–Jewish Money"'.
23. *Cape Argus,* 26 April 1986.
24. *Ibid.,* 25 March 1986.
25. *Ibid.,* 26 April 1986.
26. *New York Times,* 1 August 1985, 'Chase Ends Loans to South Africans'.
27. *Ibid.*
28. *Ibid.,* 5 August 1985, 'U.S. Banks Cut Loans Sharply'; *Ibid.,* 16 September 1985, 'South Africa's Credit Crisis: A Mix of Politics and Banking'.

29. *Washington Post*, 28 August 1985, 'South Africa Seizes *Apartheid* Opponent'.
30. *Ibid.*, 29 August 1985, 'Black Gold Miners Plan Strike Sunday'.
31. *Business Day*, 28 August 1985.
32. *Washington Post*, 29 August 1985, 'Police, Army Halt March to Prison'; *Ibid.*, 30 August 1985, 'Business Groups Urge Talks with Blacks'; *New York Times*, 31 August 1985, 'Pretoria's Chief Banker Brings Loan Plea to the U.S.'.
33. *Washington Post*, 30 August 1985, 'Business Groups Urge Talks with Blacks'.
34. *New York Times*, 31 August 1985, 'Afrikaner Executive Speaks Out'.
35. *Ibid.*, 29 August 1985, 'Loan Halt Tied to Credit Risks in South Africa'; *Ibid.*, 30 August 1985, 'South Africa's Economy Faces 2 Urgent Threats'.
36. *Ibid.*, 31 August 1985, 'Pretoria's Chief Banker Brings Loan Plea to U.S.'.
37. *Ibid.*, 2 September 1985, 'Curb on Currency'; *Ibid.*, 3 September 1985, 'As Exchanges Reopen, Rand Surges'.
38. *Ibid.*, 2 September 1985, 'Bankers Say Credit Rating Will Suffer'.
39. *Cape Times*, 30 January 1986; *Cape Argus*, 31 January 1986.
40. *Daily Dispatch*, 25 February 1986.
41. *Cape Times*, 25 March 1986.
42. *Business Day*, 18 April 1986; *New York Times*, 5 July 1986, 'South Africa is Pressed into Economic Isolation'.
43. Joseph Lelyveld, *Move Your Shadow: South Africa, Black and White* (New York: *New York Times* Books, 1985), pp. 67-9.
44. *Christian Science Monitor*, 24 July 1985, 'South Africa: Legitimate Demands'.
45. *New York Times*, 15 August 1985, 'Excerpts from Botha's Speech'.
46. *Ibid.*, 14 August 1985, 'South Africa Dampens Talk of Racial Change'.
47. *Ibid.*, 16 September 1985, 'Pretoria's Latest Hints'.
48. *Ibid.*, 12 September 1985, 'Citizenship Plan Offered by Botha'; *Ibid.*, 13 September 1985, 'End of Pass Laws'.
49. *Ibid.*, 28 September 1985, June Goodwin, '*Apartheid* in Other Words'.
50. *Christian Science Monitor*, 26 July 1985, 'Negotiation Seen as Only Way Out of S. African Impasse'.
51. Adelman, 'Recent Events in South Africa', *Capital & Class* 26, 1985, p. 28.
52. *New York Times*, 14 September 1985, 'South Africans Meet in Zambia with Guerrillas'.
53. *Ibid.*, 28 September 1985, 'South African Army Begins a "Human Aid" Drive'.

54. *Ibid.*, 30 September 1985, 'Business Leaders in Pretoria Urge an End to *Apartheid*'.
55. *Ibid.*, 18 November 1985, 'Gold, Turmoil and a Job Style'.
56. *Ibid.*, 23 October 1985, 'South African Clerics Planning to See Botha Foes in Zambia'.
57. *Ibid.*, 2 December 1985, 'New Group Voices Opposition'.
58. *Weekly Mail*, 26 January 1986.
59. *Cape Argus*, 1 February 1986.
60. *Cape Times*, 1 February 1986.
61. *Sunday Tribune*, 9 February 1986.
62. *Wall Street Journal*, 8 November 1985.
63. *Los Angeles Times*, 14 July 1985, 'South Africa Ignores the Lesson of Steve Biko'.
64. *New York Times*, 13 October 1985, 'White South Africans Meet with Rebels'.
65. *Ibid.*, 18 September 1985, 'Generation Gap Adds Tension Among South African Blacks'; *Newsweek*, 16 September 1985, 'The Young Lions'.
66. *Cape Times*, 9 October 1985.
67. *New York Times*, 10 September 1985, 'Mandela Kin Reported to Win Extra Prison Visit'.
68. *Ibid.*, 18 September 1985, 'Generation Gap Adds Tension Among South African Blacks'.
69. *Ibid.*
70. *New York Times*, 3 September 1985, 'One Year Later in South Africa'.
71. *Ibid.*
72. *New York Times*, 18 September 1985, 'Generation Gap Adds Tension Among South African Blacks'.
73. *Ibid.*
74. *Newsweek*, 16 September 1985, 'The Young Lions'.
75. *New York Times*, 29 June 1986, 'Fiery "Necklace" Becomes Emblem of Deepening South African Violence'.
76. Nicolas Haysom, *Mabangalala: The Rise of Right-Wing Vigilantes in South Africa*, Johannesburg 1986, p. 1.
77. *Cape Argus*, 14 April 1986.
78. *Weekly Mail*, 13 February 1986, 'Those Violent Men of Peace'; *New York Times*, 8 July 1986, 'Turf Fight in the Townships: Black Battles Black'.
79. Haysom, *Mabangalala*, p. 9.
80. *Cape Argus*, 14 April 1986.
81. Haysom, *Mabangalala*, p. 137.
82. *Cape Argus*, 14 April 1986.
83. Haysom, *Mabangalala*, p. 55; *Weekly Mail*, 8 November 1985.
84. *City Press*, 27 October 1985.
85. *Weekly Mail*, 8 November 1985.

86. *Cape Times*, 20 October 1985; *Ibid.*, 15 November 1985.
87. *Daily Dispatch*, 18 October 1985; *Cape Times*, 15 November 1985.
88. *Weekly Mail*, 22 November 1985; *Daily Dispatch*, 19 November 1985; *Ibid.*, 14 December 1985.
89. Haysom, *Mabangalala*, pp. 62-3.
90. *The Star* (Johannesburg), 18 September 1985; *New York Times*, 10 August 1985.
91. *New York Times*, 6 January 1986, 'South Africa: A Web of Dogma and Tribalism'.
92. *Weekly Mail*, 7 February 1986.
93. *New York Times*, 2 January 1986.
94. Haysom, *Mabangalala*, pp. 3, 76-9; *Weekly Mail*, 7 February 1986.
95. *Weekly Mail*, 16 February 1986.
96. *New York Times*, 6 January 1986, 'South Africa: A Web of Dogma and Tribalism'.
97. *Sowetan*, 20 January 1986; Haysom, *Mabangalala*, p. 66; Joseph Lelyveld, *Move Your Shadow*, p. 122.
98. *Weekly Mail*, 22 May 1986, 'Revolt May Topple Homeland Leaders'.
99. *Ibid.*, 18 October 1985.
100. *Cape Times*, 25 October 1985.
101. *Financial Mail*, 21 March 1986, 'The Homelands Burn'.
102. *Business Day*, 27 March 1986; *Sunday Tribune*, 30 March 1986.
103. *City Press*, 9 March 1986; *Business Day*, 15 April 1986; *Financial Mail*, 18 April 1986, 'Homeland Horror'.
104. Haysom, *Mabangalala*, pp. 17-18.
105. *Financial Mail*, 3 January 1986, 'Vigilantes Hit Back'; *Cape Times*, 4 December 1985.
106. *Financial Mail*, 3 January 1986, 'Vigilantes Hit Back'.
107. Haysom, *Mabangalala*, pp. 46-54; *Weekly Mail*, 10 January 1986; *Sunday Tribune*, 19 January 1986.
108. *Cape Argus*, 27 February 1986.
109. *Cape Times*, 10 March 1986; *BBC Monitoring Report*, 18 July 1986.
110. *City Press*, 10 November 1985.
111. *The Star* (Johannesburg), 18 December 1985; *Business Day*, 14 January 1986; *Cape Times*, 21 January 1986; *The Star* (Johannesburg), 13 January 1986.
112. *Cape Times*, 19 February 1986; *The Star* (Johannesburg), 14 February 1986.
113. *The Star* (Johannesburg), 29 March 1986.
114. *Sunday Tribune*, 23 March 1986.
115. *City Press*, 10 November 1985.
116. *Weekly Mail*, 10 January 1986; *City Press*, 12 January 1986.
117. *Cape Times*, 16 October 1985; *Ibid.*, 5 November 1985.
118. *Business Day*, 11 February 1986.

119. *Cape Times*, 31 January 1986.
120. *Ibid.*, 4 March 1986; *Ibid.*, 10 March 1986.
121. *City Press*, 22 September 1985.
122. *Ibid.*, 13 October 1985.
123. *Cape Times*, 22 October 1985.
124. *Ibid.*, 23 October 1985.
125. *Ibid.*, 25 October 1985; *Weekly Mail*, 1 November 1985; *Sowetan*, 31 December 1985.
126. *The Star* (Johannesburg), 30 December 1985; *Sowetan*, 14 January 1986.
127. *Sowetan*, 12 January 1986; *Cape Times*, 14 March 1986.
128. *Cape Times*, 20 March 1986; *City Press*, 6 April 1986; *Cape Argus*, 24 April 1986.
129. *Daily Telegraph* (UK), 17 March 1986.
130. *Cape Times*, 14 April 1986.
131. *Sunday Times*, 20 October 1985.
132. *Post*, 7 October 1985.
133. *Sunday Times*, 20 October 1985.
134. *Ibid.*, 3 November 1985.
135. *Eastern Province Herald*, 2 November 1985.
136. *Ibid*, 30 October 1985.
137. *Sunday Times*, 3 November 1985.
138. *City Press*, 13 November 1985.
139. *Cape Argus*, 9 January 1986.
140. *Eastern Province Herald*, 14 January 1986.
141. *Weekly Mail*, 14 February 1986; *Wall Street Journal*, 20 June 1986, 'A Life Apart'.
142. *Evening Post*, 11 February 1986.
143. *Cape Argus*, 15 February 1986.
144. *Cape Times*, 8 April 1986.
145. *Financial Mail*, 14 February 1986.
146. *Sunday Tribune*, 2 March 1986, 'Masses March to Their Own Drum'; *Ibid.*, 'Into the Vacuum . . .'
147. *Weekly Mail*, 10 January 1986, 'Meeting Told of "Street Committees"'; *Eastern Province Herald*, 9 January 1986.
148. *City Press*, 9 February 1986.
149. *Weekly Mail*, 10 January 1986, 'Meeting told of "Street Committees"'; *Ibid.*, 17 January 1986.
150. *City Press*, 6 April 1986.
151. *Sunday Tribune*, 2 March 1986, 'Into the Vacuum . . .'
152. *Cape Times*, 6 March 1986.
153. *Weekly Mail*, 20 December 1985; *Business Day*, 19 February 1986.
154. *Cape Times*, 18 December 1985.
155. *City Press*, 12 January 1986.
156. *Cape Times*, 16 December 1985.

157. *Weekly Mail,* 10 January 1986, Tom Lodge, 'Enter the Year of Land-mines and Grenades'.
158. *Ibid.,* Howard Barrell, 'A Militant Mood Reigns in Lusaka'.
159. *Cape Argus,* 11 January 1986.
160. *Weekly Mail,* 10 January 1986, Tom Lodge, 'Enter the Year of the Landmines and Grenades'.
161. *Ibid.; City Press,* 22 December 1985.
162. *Sunday Tribune,* 16 March 1986.
163. *Business Day,* 14 February 1986.
164. *Cape Argus,* 13 February 1986; *Cape Times,* 10 May 1986.
165. *Business Day,* 19 February 1986.
166. *Cape Times,* 4 February 1986; *Ibid.,* 5 February 1986; *Weekly Mail,* 28 February 1986.
167. *Cape Times,* 4 March 1986; *Sunday Tribune,* 9 March 1986; *Cape Times,* 20 March 1986.
168. *Cape Times,* 5 March 1986; *Ibid.,* 8 March 1986.
169. *Weekly Mail,* 10 April 1986.
170. *New Nation,* 27 February 1986, 'We Won't Pay Your Rents'.
171. *Financial Mail,* 14 February 1986; *Weekly Mail,* 23 January 1986.
172. *Sunday Times Extra,* February 1986.
173. *City Press,* 9 March 1986.
174. *Sowetan,* 20 February 1986.
175. *City Press,* 2 February 1986.
176. *Cape Times,* 27 February 1986.
177. *Ibid.,* 22 March 1986.
178. *Cape Argus,* 8 April 1986.
179. *Weekly Mail,* 18 April 1986.
180. *Cape Argus,* 23 April 1986.
181. *Cape Times,* 10 April 1986.
182. *Weekly Mail,* 11 April 1986.
183. *Daily Dispatch,* 21 February 1986.
184. *Weekly Mail,* 7 February 1986.
185. *Sunday Times,* 9 March 1986; *Cape Times,* 13 March 1986.
186. *Business Day,* 8 April 1986.
187. *New York Times,* 30 December 1985, 'Blacks Urge End to School Protest'.
188. *Natal Mercury,* 24 December 1985.
189. *Eastern Province Herald,* 7 January 1986.
190. *Cape Times,* 27 January 1986.
191. *Weekly Mail,* 31 January 1986; *Cape Times,* 28 January 1986.
192. *Cape Times,* 13 February 1986.
193. *Ibid.,* 31 March 1986; *Ibid.,* 21 March 1986; *Business Day,* 27 March 1986; *Cape Argus,* 26 March 1986.
194. *Weekly Mail,* 10 April 1986.
195. *Cape Times,* 31 March 1986.

196. *Weekly Mail,* 27 February 1986; *Cape Times,* 6 March 1986; *Sowetan,* 26 April 1985.
197. *Weekly Mail,* 27 February 1986, 'Five Mad Days in Alex'.
198. *Cape Times,* 11 February 1986; *Sunday Tribune,* 16 February 1986; *Business Day,* 19 February 1986.
199. *Sunday Tribune,* 2 March 1986, 'Into the Vacuum . . .'
200. *Cape Times,* 6 March 1986.
201. *The Star* (Johannesburg), 12 March 1986.
202. *Cape Times,* 9 April 1986.
203. *Ibid.,* 24 April 1986; *Cape Argus,* 24 April 1986; *The Star* (Johannesburg), 24 April 1986.
204. *Weekly Mail,* 2 May 1986.
205. *Cape Times,* 24 April 1986.
206. *The Star* (Johannesburg), 24 April 1986.
207. *Sunday Times,* 27 April 1986.
208. *The Star* (Johannesburg), 1 May 1986.
209. *Sunday Times* (Cape Town), 11 May 1986; *Cape Times,* 29 April 1986; *New York Times,* 11 May 1986.
210. *Weekly Mail,* 2 May 1986.
211. *Ibid.,* 22 May 1986.
212. *Ibid.,* 2 May 1986.
213. *Ibid.,* 15 May 1986, 'Street Committees: People's Power or Kangaroo Courts?'; *Ibid.,* 'Filling the Void'.
214. *City Press,* 11 May 1986.
215. Josette Cole, 'Crossroads: From Popular Resistance to Mini-Bantustan'. Paper presented at Centre for African Studies, 'Western Cape: Roots and Realities' Conference, University of Cape Town 1986; Mamphela Ramphele, 'The Male–Female Dynamic Between Migrant Workers in the Western Cape'. Paper presented at Centre for African Studies, 'Western Cape: Roots and Realities' Conference, University of Cape Town 1986; Waldorf, 'Life in Crossroads', *New Republic,* 25 August 1986.
216. *Cape Times,* 23 May 1986; Haysom, *Mabangalala,* pp. 104-16.
217. *Sunday Tribune,* 5 January 1986.
218. Haysom, *Mabangalala,* pp. 108-9; Lars Waldorf, 'Life in Cross-roads', pp. 17-19.
219. *Cape Times,* 16 January 1986.
220. *Weekly Mail,* 16 May 1986.
221. *Cape Times,* 23 May 1986.
222. *Weekly Mail,* 16 May 1986.
223. *Cape Times,* 22 April 1986.
224. *Weekly Mail,* 16 May 1986.
225. *Cape Times,* 31 May 1986; *Weekly Mail,* 29 May 1986, 'Tension High in War-Zone Crossroads'.
226. *Weekly Mail,* 29 May 1986, 'Crossroads War not a Faction Fight';

Cape Times, 12 June 1986.

227. *Cape Times,* 23 May 1986; *Ibid.,* 12 June 1986; *New York Times,* 26 May 1986.
228. *Cape Times,* 12 June 1986.
229. *Ibid.,* 23 May 1986.
230. *Weekly Mail,* 19 June 1986.
231. *Boston Globe,* 11 June 1986, 'Blacks Flee Clashes Near Cape Town'.
232. *New York Times,* 11 June 1986.
233. *Boston Globe,* 11 June 1986, 'Blacks Flee Clashes Near Cape Town'.
234. *Weekly Mail,* 20 February 1986.
235. *Ibid.,* 28 February 1986; *Cape Argus,* 18 February 1986; *Sowetan,* 4 February 1986.
236. *Weekly Mail,* 28 February 1986.
237. *Ibid.,* 21 February 1986.
238. *The Star* (Johannesburg), 18 February 1986; *Business Day,* 19 February 1986; *The Star* (Johannesburg), 5 March 1986.
239. *Weekly Mail,* 21 March 1986.
240. *Business Day,* 27 January 1986.
241. *Cape Times,* 19 February 1986.
242. *Financial Mail,* 14 March 1986; *Weekly Mail,* 14 March 1986; *Business Day,* 12 March 1986; *The Star* (Johannesburg), 13 March 1986.
243. *Weekly Mail,* 21 March 1986; *Cape Times,* 17 April 1986, 'Unions Now Much More Politicized'.
244. *Business Day,* 10 April 1986; *Natal Mercury,* 12 April 1986; *The Citizen,* 23 April 1986.
245. *Cape Times,* 11 February 1986.
246. *Cape Argus,* 24 March 1986.
247. *Cape Times,* 25 March 1986.
248. *Cape Argus,* 7 April 1986.
249. *Cape Times,* 17 April 1986, 'Unions Now Much More Politicized'; *Sunday Times,* 20 April 1986.
250. *Weekly Mail,* 18 April 1986.
251. *Cape Times,* 17 April 1986, 'Unions Now Much More Politicized'.
252. *Weekly Mail,* 18 April 1986.
253. *Cape Times,* 17 April 1986, 'Unions Now Much More Politicized'.
254. *Weekly Mail,* 18 April 1986.
255. *Cape Times,* 17 April 1986, 'Unions Now Much More Politicized'.
256. *Financial Mail,* 17 January 1986, 'Shaping Up for Battle'; *Ibid.,* 24 January 1986.
257. *Sunday Tribune,* 2 March 1986; *Weekly Mail,* 6 May 1986; *The Citizen,* 3 February 1986.
258. *Weekly Mail,* 8 May 1986; *Sunday Tribune,* 4 May 1986.
259. *Business Day,* 10 March 1986.
260. *Weekly Mail,* 8 May 1986, 'Over 1.5 Million in Biggest-Ever Strike'; *Business Day,* 2 May 1986, 'Millions Stay Away from Work'; *The*

Citizen, 2 May 1986, 'Huge Stayaway'; *Ibid.*, 'Mines Stayaway Only Partially Successful'.

261. *Sowetan*, 2 May 1986, 'Massive Stayaway'; *City Press*, 4 May 1986, 'Biggest May Day in SA History'.
262. *Business Day*, 2 May 1986 'COSATU Men Save Youth'; *Cape Times*, 2 May 1986, 'Millions Stay Away'.
263. *Weekly Mail*, 15 May 1986, Steve Friedman, 'The Real Signals from that May Day Stayaway'.
264. *Ibid.*
265. *Sunday Tribune*, 8 June 1986.
266. *Weekly Mail*, 5 June 1986, 'Confessions of a Captured Vigilante'; *Sunday Star* (Johannesburg), 1 June 1986.
267. *The Star* (Johannesburg), 3 May 1986.
268. *Business Day*, 29 May 1986.
269. *Sunday Star* (Johannesburg), 1 June 1986.
270. *Business Day*, 29 May 1986; *City Press*, 1 June 1986.
271. *Cape Times*, 29 May 1986.
272. *Weekly Mail*, 30 May 1986.
273. *Evening Post*, 23 May 1986.
274. *Weekly Mail*, 30 May 1986.
275. *Evening Post*, 21 May 1986.
276. *Business Day*, 13 June 1986.
277. *Sunday Star* (Johannesburg), 25 May 1986.
278. *City Press*, 25 May 1986.
279. *Sunday Star* (Johannesburg), 1 June 1986.
280. *Business Day*, 28 May 1986.
281. *City Press*, 18 May 1986.
282. *Weekly Mail*, 21 August 1986, 'Drawing the Curtains on Verwoerd's Dream'.
283. *Ibid.*, 'The Students Trickle Back to School'.
284. *Cape Argus*, 3 June 1986; *Weekly Mail*, 6 June 1986, 'PE Boycotters Present Six-Point Plan'.
285. *Eastern Province Herald*, 30 May 1986.
286. *Cape Argus*, 3 June 1986.
287. *Sowetan*, 3 June 1986.
288. *Sunday Times*, 8 June 1986; *Cape Argus*, 5 June 1986.
289. *Weekly Mail*, 24 July 1986.
290. *Cape Times*, 9 June 1986.
291. *The Star* (Johannesburg), 28 May 1986; *Cape Times*, 5 June 1986.
292. *The Star* (Johannesburg), 10 June 1986.
293. *Weekly Mail*, 15 May 1986, Steve Friedman, 'The Real Signals from that May Day Stayaway'.
294. *Sunday Tribune*, 18 May 1986.
295. *Business Day*, 9 June 1986; *Sunday Tribune*, 8 June 1986.
296. *Cape Times*, 18 June 1986.

297. *Ibid.*, 13 June 1986, 'SA May "Go It Alone"'; *Cape Times*, 13 June 1986, 'Crackdown on "Subversion"'; *New York Times*, 13 June 1986, 'State of Emergency'.
298. *Business Day*, 13 June 1986.
299. *Weekly Mail*, 29 June 1986; *New York Times*, 13 June 1986.
300. *The Star* (Johannesburg), 17 June 1986.
301. *New York Times*, 19 June 1986.
302. *Ibid.*, 28 June 1986; *Ibid.*, 22 June 1986; *Sunday Star* (Johannesburg), 22 June 1986; *Cape Times*, 26 June 1986.

Chapter 8

1. *Financial Times* (UK), 12 August 1985.
2. John Saul and Stephen Gelb, *The Crisis in South Africa*, New York 1981.
3. Martin Legassick, 'South Africa in Crisis: What Route to Democracy?' *African Affairs* 84 (337), 1985, p. 587.
4. *Ibid.*
5. *Financial Mail*, 31 May 1985.
6. *Time Magazine* (New York), 11 November 1985.
7. *The Times* (UK), 17 March 1981. 'Can Mr. Botha Fight Off the Hardest of the Hardliners?'.
8. *Weekly Mail*, 5 June 1986, 'The Arithmetic of a Far-Right Victory'.
9. *Ibid.*, 29 May 1986, 'Nats Shaken Up By AWB's "Dynamite"'.
10. *Sunday Star* (Johannesburg), 1 June 1986; *Cape Times*, 26 May 1986.
11. *Weekly Mail*, 20 February 1986, 'Swansong to the "Macabre Ballad"'.
12. *Ibid.*, 'Rivalry's Wrecked the Convention Movement'.
13. *Ibid.*, 'Swansong to the "Macabre Ballad"'.
14. *New York Times*, 8 July 1986, 'Turf fight in the Townships'.
15. *Ibid.*
16. *New York Times Magazine*, 15 June 1986, Alan Cowell, 'The Struggle: Power and Politics in South Africa's Black Trade Unions'.
17. Adelman, 'Recent Events in South Africa', *Capital & Class* 26, 1985, p. 28.

Index